MODERN PERSPECTIVES IN PSYCHIATRY
Edited by John G. Howells

6

MODERN PERSPECTIVES
IN
THE PSYCHIATRY OF OLD AGE

MODERN PERSPECTIVES IN PSYCHIATRY

Edited by John G. Howells

Modern Perspectives in the Psychiatry of Old Age

Edited by

JOHN G. HOWELLS

M.D., F.R.C.Psych., D.P.M.

Director, the Institute of Family Psychiatry
The Ipswich Hospital
England

BRUNNER / MAZEL, Publishers • New York

EDITOR'S PREFACE

The sixth volume of the Modern Perspectives in Psychiatry Series concentrates on the age group of increasing concern to clinicians and to planners of health services—old age. An expanding but aging population creates accumulating demands on the health services of most countries—and, not least, the psychiatric services.

Thus, distinguished contributors from many countries were asked to present an up-to-date account of the subjects in which they are the acknowledged masters. This is in keeping with the tradition of the Series, to bring before clinicians developments in international psychiatry. In this volume contributions come from authorities in Canada, Denmark, Finland, Japan, the United Kingdom, the United States of America, the Union of Soviet Socialist Republics and West Germany.

A textbook coverage is not attempted; each volume of the Series concentrates on the *growing points* of a subject. While a single volume is not a textbook, the Series has been planned as a whole and each succeeding volume is a step towards completing an international system in the theory and practice of psychiatry.

Material related to the theme of the psychiatry of old age may be found elsewhere in the Series. Indeed the psychiatry of old age falls naturally into two parts. Firstly the psychiatry which is basic to all age groups. This the reader will find in the whole of volume 2—*Modern Perspectives in World Psychiatry*. Secondly, the psychiatry which is particular to old age—the reader will find such material here.

The volume has full subject and author indices. The reader will also find it invaluable to consult the cumulative index of volume 5. Together they probably constitute the widest channel of entry into the literature of psychiatry. As with previous volumes the indices have been prepared with care and insight by my Editorial Assistant, Mrs. M. Livia Osborn, to whom I express my admiration and thanks.

Grateful acknowledgement is also made to the following publishers and editors of journals, and to the Authors concerned for kind permission

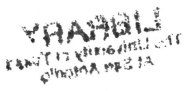

to reproduce the material mentioned: Dr. Jack Botwinick, for Fig. 1 of Ch. 6, which appeared in *Cognitive Processes in Maturity and Old Age* (Springer, 1967); Rosen et al. for the left panel of Fig. 3 of Ch. 6 from *Annals of Otology* (1962); Glorig and Nixon for the right panel of Fig. 3 of Ch. 6 from the Wisconsin State Fair (1964); Dr. Walter Spieth for Fig. 4 of Ch. 6, which appeared in Ch. 20 of *Behavior, Aging and the Nervous System,* edited by A. T. Welford and J. E. Birren (Springer, 1965); Dr. J. A. N. Corsellis for Fig. 1 of Ch. 7 from "Cerebral Degeneration and the Mental Disorders of Later Life" in *Psychiatric Disorders in the Aged,* report on the Symposium held by the World Psychiatric Association (London, 1965); Dr. M. Roth for Figs. 2 and 3 of Ch. 7 from Ch. 1 in *Recent Developments in Psychogeriatrics: A Symposium,* edited by D. W. K. Kay and A. Walk; Dr. Alex Comfort and George Weidenfeld and Nicolson Ltd., London, for permission to reproduce Figs. 1 and 2 from *The Process of Ageing* (1965) in Ch. 17; the following for permission to reproduce the plates in Ch. 28: The Louvre (Pl. 1); The Monastery of Montserrat (Pl. 2); The Museum of Capodimonte (Pl. 3); The National Gallery (Pls. 4 and 6); Uffizi, Florence (Pl. 5); Rijksmuseum Kröller-Müller (Pl. 7); The Tate Gallery (Pls. 8 and 10). Plate 9 is reproduced by gracious permission of Her Majesty The Queen.

Contents

vii

MODERN PERSPECTIVES IN PSYCHIATRY
Edited by John G. Howells

6

MODERN PERSPECTIVES
IN
THE PSYCHIATRY OF OLD AGE

1

GENETICS

EDITH ZERBIN-RUEDIN, P.D. DR. MED.

Max Planck Institut für Psychiatrie, Munich, Germany

INTRODUCTION

Gerontology is gaining increasing importance with the gradual extension of the human life span, since the growing percentage of old people gives rise to a variety of health problems as well as social problems.

In a Danish island population investigated by Strömgren (84) 38% of the population aged 65 years and over presented a psychiatric problem during the investigation period. By far the largest diagnostic group was that of the dementias with 56% (40% mild, 8% severe, 8% cerebrovascular). Ten percent suffered from psychoses and 34% from other mental disorders, neurosis, epilepsy, or alcoholism. Only 1% was hospitalized in a mental hospital; 91% managed to live in the community and 58% had never been seen by a psychiatrist. Among the hospitalized psychiatric patients the percentage of persons aged over 65 had risen from 29% in 1957 to 36% in 1962.

Essen-Möller (20, 21), in a Swedish field study, considered no more than 20 to 30% of the population over 50 years of age to be in perfect mental health. The standard mental illnesses (psychoses, mental deficiency, dementias) afflicted about 15% of the population; the remainder, though socially more or less adapted, were affected with neuroses and personality disorders of different kinds and grades. Essen-Möller is right when stating that the borderline between "healthy" and "sick" must be drawn differently depending on different points of view.

The useful classification of mental disorders in old age by Roth (69) has become widely known and provides the basis for the subdivision of this chapter: 1) affective psychoses; 2) senile dementia; 3) late para-

1

phrenia; 4) acute confusional states; 5) arteriosclerotic dementia. However, we don't consider the confusional states as a separate entity. On the other hand, we think the genetic aspects of "normal" old age should be included in this chapter, as there are considerable overlapping and a continuous range of variation in neuropathology, as well as in psychopathology, between persons diagnosed as suffering from some old age mental disorder and persons whose mental impairment is still considered to be a normal consequence of old age. Furthermore, there might be some relationship between senile dementia and the so-called presenile dementias—Alzheimer's disease and Pick's disease—which therefore will be discussed here too.

Genetic factors are operating in normal and pathological aging processes in several ways (39, 40, 41). 1) They provide the biological basis for a long life span. That the potentiality for a long life can be modified by adverse life conditions does not lessen the importance of the genetic elements. 2) They contribute to the general condition of body and mind before and during old age and they are in part responsible for the adjustive plasticity necessary to cope successfully, and without mental breakdown, with the manifold stresses involved in getting and being old. 3) They give rise to specific disturbances in the last sector of human life. The mechanisms operating in group 1 and 2 are likely to be the result of several or many genes (polygenes), whereas the disorders observed in the third group might result from one single major mutant gene.

"NORMAL" OLD AGE

Aging and death are necessary components of the biological systems which have developed on earth. Eternal youth and fertility together with an infinite life of the individual would result either in a terrible amassment of individuals culminating in a catastrophe, or in the drastic restriction of reproduction so that the population would be stagnant instead of being dynamic. No genetic recombination, no selection, no evolution could take place any more.

The theories about the basis and the essentials of the aging processes differ widely. Thus aging is considered to be the consequence of wearing out, of the accumulation of age pigment and other waste products, of an increased incorporation of calcium, of endocrinologic changes, of an increased amount and decreased quality of collagen, of blocking of cell metabolism by cross linking of big molecules such as proteins or nucleic acids. These theories don't necessarily exclude each other and all of them have in common the idea of morphological and physiological changes in the somatic cells. To be sure, the genetic material takes part in these changes. Thus the frequency of hypodiploid cells, i.e. cells that have lost a whole chromosome, seems to increase with age, especially in females (35, 62).

Perhaps more important, though less spectacular, are somatic cell mutations. The mutation theories have been reviewed by Curtis (17). Mutations or chromosome loss can damage the cell so heavily that it gets inactivated and/or dies. When the loss of cells surpasses some threshold, the individual dies too. The immunologic theory (89), however, supposes that the mutations do not kill the cells concerned, but interfere with their capacity of self-recognizing, whereby auto-immune reactions develop. The immunologic theory considers aging as an active auto-catalytic process in dividing cell populations which culminates in self-destruction of the organism.

It can be theorized that not only can correct genetic information be altered or switched off by somatic mutations, but also wrong information might be switched on by release of hitherto inhibited genes. Whereas the "switch-off theory" explains aging as the result of continuous repeated "hits" resulting more or less from exogenous factors, the "switch-on theory" considers aging as something intrinsic to the genetic code from the beginning.

The average life span varies greatly throughout the animal kingdom though it is specific for each species (10), e.g. 4 days for the house spider and 177 years for the Galapagos tortoise. A relationship between length of life on the one side and rate of metabolism, mutation rate and ratio of brain weight to body weight on the other side has been suggested, but not established as a general rule.

Besides the inter-species differences, there is some intra-species variation. The higher expectation of life for the females, observed in most animal species, seems to be a trend rather than a law. In the human the sex difference certainly is not due to the less stressful life of the more attractive sex! But to what else? To hormones? To the homozygosity for the X-chromosome? We don't know. If subpopulations living close together, e.g. Jews and non-Jews, show differences in mortality, in all probability genetic *and* environmental factors are responsible (27).

Individual differences in life span might be due to environmental events such as accidents, catastrophes, famines, etc., or to genetic factors, since they control the general state of health and may give rise to definite illnesses shortening life. Walford (89), from his experiments with mice, suspects that immunologic mechanisms are involved—homozygosity for the more important histocompatibility factors provides the potentiality for a long life.

That in the human, too, genetic factors influence the individual life span is strongly suggested by the family and twin data. Galton (26), as well as Pearson (63) and Darwin, considered the life span as a hereditary characteristic as early as late nineteenth century. The results of family studies differ somewhat but all of them show the same trend and demonstrate statistically significant parent-offspring and sib-sib correlations of the length of life (13, 47, 91).

Kallmann (39, 40, 41, 42, 43) and his research group have provided the most extensive and instructive findings in 1603 twins over age 60. The life spans were much more alike in the monozygotic twins (MZ) than in the dizygotic twins (DZ). And though the intra-pair life span differences decreased in all twin pairs as they progressed towards a lower and lower residual lifetime ceiling—which was to be expected—the differences related to zygosity, rather than being wiped out, persisted beyond the age of 80. On the other hand, however, the data show that natural death of one twin does not necessarily imply the death of the co-twin and that the life span even of one-egg twins does show some variability. A German series studied by von Verschuer (88) and Koch (49), and a Danish series studied by Hauge et al. (32), do not demonstrate the difference in life span similarity between MZ and DZ as clearly as Kallmann's data do. These series, however, are much smaller, the propositi were younger and in the German series the risk of violent death in war for middle-aged men was very high. The later series "proves mainly that disrupted political conditions make it as difficult for twins as for ordinary people to take full advantage of optimum longevity potentials" (41).

Thus, a human being lives long, if 1) on the ground of a fortunate combination of health-conferring genes he is able to maintain a physiological equilibrium and adaptability, and to compensate symptoms of wearing out and the increasing amount of exogenous small "hits" for a comparatively long time; 2) he is free from life shortening pathologic gene mutations and chromosomal aberrations; and 3) he does not suffer a violent death. With the decreasing importance of environmental factors such as famine and pestilence (unfortunately war and car accidents can't be mentioned here as examples!), the importance of the hereditary component increases.

Though the regular and absolute identity of life history, illnesses, time and cause of death in MZ twins is a fairy tale told by more or less serious journals, there is no doubt that MZ twin partners are much more alike in the rate and pattern of aging than DZ twin partners are. This pertains to somatic qualities such as getting bald, wrinkled or grey-haired as well as to EEG patterns (33) and psychological characters. Kallmann et al. (42) described aged MZ twin sisters, who, despite extremely different life histories, resembled each other "like two eggs" whereas a pair of DZ twin sisters who had always lived in very similar conditions looked very different.

A sample of 150 same-sexed pairs was chosen out of the twin series mentioned above and subjected to repeated psychological testing (8, 36). The intra-pair differences of the test scores were clearly higher in the DZ twins than in the MZ. This was true for the first examination as well as for the retests. The difference between the DZ and the MZ groups, however, was not demonstrated in all tests. From this it follows that psychological and intellectual functions as expressed in test scores are controlled by genetic factors to a different extent. Tests measuring vocabulary, digit symbols, block designs and taping showed the strongest genetic components, whereas tests measuring memory did not reveal any difference between MZs and DZs, thus indicating no or a low contribution of genetic factors. Not all intellectual functions declined similarly in the course of time. For instance, the vocabulary was relatively well preserved for many years, whereas the scores of two speeded performance tests requiring visual-motor coordination had declined rapidly. There was a positive correlation between test performance and life expectancy which could not be explained completely by the fact that younger persons not only have a higher life expectancy but also show better test performances.

Growth and aging are controlled by a multitude of genes, disturbed by single genes and influenced by the environment. The efficiency of genetic control even in oldest age is evident. However, the genetic elements cannot be expressed in Mendelian ratios and an exact gene analysis is not possible.

SENILE AND ARTERIOSCLEROTIC DEMENTIA

Though classical forms of these two illnesses can be distinguished quite well this, unfortunately, is not true for the majority of cases. Mixed types are frequent from a clinical as well as an anatomical point of view. Therefore both illnesses are treated together in most genetic studies and they shall be discussed together here.

Precise and complete information is difficult to obtain, indeed, as it is nearly impossible to perform clinical, anatomical and genetic studies on the same series of patients with the same thoroughness and success. When starting from hospital patients, findings from autopsies are not available in most cases, and when starting from dissected patients the clinical picture has to be reconstructed retrospectively from hospital records, which are sometimes scarce. Whatever starting point the geneticist chooses, precise clinical data on the similarly affected relatives are difficult to obtain, in part because of the late manifestation of the disease under study, and autoptic findings are practically always lacking, not to mention problems with phenotypically inconspicuous family members. This is a severe handicap for genetic research, since, as is well known, the anatomical and clinical picture is far from being strictly correlated, not only in the senile and presenile dementias (see also page 15) but throughout human medicine.

Frequency

The average frequency of senile and arteriosclerotic dementia cannot be stated in general terms, as it is influenced by many variables, the first of which is the age distribution in a given population. Larsson et al. (50) in Sweden found an average morbidity risk for senile dementia of 1.8% for males and 2.1% for females. When differentiating among age cohorts, the correlation between morbidity risk and age distribution shows up clearly. These percentages are true only for Sweden and for the point of time when the study was done. Nielsen (61, 62), however, in a Danish island population over age 65, reported a prevalence of 2.8% for males and 3.2% for females, which is in line with Larsson's risk figures. Åkesson (1), in a second Swedish series, found a lower prevalence in the population over age 60—for senile dementia $0.63\pm0.17\%$ for males and $0.85\pm0.02\%$ for females; for arteriosclerotic dementia $0.1\pm0.07\%$ for males and $0.33\pm0.12\%$ for females. The absolute number and the percentage of senile patients in mental hospitals increased during the past decades and this obviously results from the increased life expectancy rather than from an increased morbidity risk (84).

Empirical Risk Figures

The early studies on the genetics of senile and arteriosclerotic dementia comprise very heterogeneous cases (survey Zerbin-Rüdin (91). A thorough clinico-genetic study has been done by Larsson et al. (50). Forty out of 377 patients with senile dementia showed arteriosclerotic symptoms too;

in 55 cases an autopsy was performed, which in a few cases showed neither atrophy nor arteriosclerosis of the brain, which is in agreement with the experience of other authors. Details may be found in the original paper which contains an abundance of data, specifications, groupings and mathematic analyses. In short, it can be said that the morbidity risk for parents and sibs of senile demented patients was about 4.3 times higher than the general morbidity risk (see Table 1).

TABLE 1

Morbidity risk for senile dementia in the general population and in relatives of index cases with senile dementia (after Larsson, Sjögren, Jacobson (50))

Age up to	General population	Morbidity risk (%) for Siblings male	female	m + f	Siblings and parents
70 years	0.4	0.8	2.3	1.6	1.7
80 years	2.5	7.5	9.6	8.6	10.8
85 years	3.8	9.6	19.7	15.7	16.3

Constantinidis et al. (15) studied the families of 814 patients: 229 with senile dementia, 423 with arteriosclerotic dementia, 60 with mixed dementia, 97 with Alzheimer's disease and 5 with Pick's disease. Autopsy was performed in 155 cases. The secondary cases in all diagnostic groups were mostly of the same kind as the propositi, but other forms of old age dementias also occurred (see Tables 2 and 3).

TABLE 2

Morbidity risks for senile and presenile dementia in the relatives over age 50 of index cases with senile dementia (calculated from Tables 3 and 4 in Constantinidis, Garrone, de Ajuriaguerra (15))

Diagnosis of secondary cases	Parents	Morbidity risk (%) in Siblings	Offspring
Senile dementia	7.0±1.6	5.5±1.1	4.3±1.2
Alzheimer's disease	—	0.4±0.3	2.9±0.9
All kinds of senile and presenile dementia	9.3±1.8	8.3±1.3	9.8±2.2

TABLE 3

Morbidity risks for senile and presenile dementia in the relatives over age 50 of index cases with arteriosclerotic and "mixed" dementia (calculated from Table 3 and 4 in Constantinidis, Garrone, de Ajuriaguerra (15))

Diagnosis of secondary cases	Index cases arteriosclerotic dementia: Morbidity risk (%) in			Index cases mixed dementia: Morbidity risk (%) in		
	Parents	Offspring	Siblings	Parents	Offspring	Siblings
Mixed dementia	0.3±0.2	0.2±0.2	0.1±0.03	7.0±1.0	10.3±3.9	1.7±1.2
Arteriosclerotic dementia	3.8±0.7	3.9±0.9	2.3±0.5	1.4±1.4	5.2±2.9	0.9±0.8
All kinds of senile and presenile dementia	5.8±0.9	4.8±1.0	3.1±0.6	14.1±1.7	15.2±4.7	10.4±2.8

Åkesson (1), though having found a rather low general prevalence, stated the highest family risks (see Table 4). When comparing the results, however, it must be kept in mind that the authors calculated the risk figures in different ways. The most refined method of age correction is used by Larsson (50), whereas Åkesson (1) prefers the abridged Weinberg method, reasoning that complicated mathematical methods are useless as long as the series under examination is probably heterogeneous and the disease entity cannot be identified unambiguously by some specific biological substrate.

TABLE 4

Morbidity risk for old age dementia in the relatives of index cases
with senile and arteriosclerotic dementia
(after Åkesson (1))

Age	47 index cases with senile dementia: Morbidity risk (%) in		31 index cases with arteriosclerotic dementia: Morbidity risk (%) in	
	Parents	Siblings	Parents	Siblings
60-70 years	5.6±5.4	7.1±4.9	7.1±6.9	2.3±2.3
70-80 years	8.7±5.9	15.5±4.8	16.7±8.8	6.1±4.2
Over 60 years	15.0±4.0	18.4±3.5	9.6±4.1	5.6±2.4
Over 80 years	23.1±6.7	30.8±7.4	5.0±4.1	14.3±9.4

The twin data on senile dementia (38) and arteriosclerotic dementia (31) are scarce and inconclusive. Kallmann's (38) series, though heterogeneous, strongly suggests genetic elements, the concordance rates being 43% in the MZ and 8% in the DZ pairs.

Mode of Inheritance

The percentage of senile dementia with a family history is low and ranges from 7% (15) to 16% (78). The 27% in the early series of Meggendorfer (56) is to be taken with some reservation. This has made some students deny genetic factors as a whole. More reasonable seems the statement by Delay and Brion (19) that a hereditary influence does exist but cannot be recognized clearly at present. Larsson et al. (50), as well as Cresseri (16), plead for incomplete dominance, whereas Kallmann suggests a multifactorial etiology. He thinks that the search for a single mutant gene effect as the primary cause of psychotic phenomena in the involutional and senile period of life is unrealistic. Polygenes, increasing impairment of adaptability, psychological stress resulting from loss of relatives and friends, loneliness or fear of illness and invalidism, changes in the circulatory system and in the metabolism—all of these factors work together in producing old age mental disorders.

Heterogeneity is to be considered seriously. It necessarily follows from Kallmann's concept and is considered by most authors at least as an alternative. Of course there is the danger that the hypothesis of heterogeneity and that of polygenic systems, when applied in an uncritical way, explain everything and therefore nothing!

In arteriosclerotic dementia the empirical risk figures in the families are still lower than in senile dementia (see Tables 3 and 4). The genetic situation is widely unknown and Kallmann considers it to be at least as complicated as the genetics of diabetes. Assuming cerebrovascular disorders and arteriosclerotic dementia are special cases of general arteriosclerosis, the results obtained there can be applied here. For instance, obviously hypertonia and increased cholesterin blood level 1) contribute to the etiology of arteriosclerosis, and 2) are influenced by heredity and environment. But we don't know anything about why and when the arteriosclerosis is localized just in the brain and why and when the cerebral arteriosclerosis gives rise to dementia. General arteriosclerosis does not always include the brain, and cerebral arteriosclerosis is not inevitably followed by dementia. Constantinidis et al. (15) suggest dominant inheritance for a basic liability for disorders of the brain vessels with variable expressivity and 40% penetrance.

Nature and Nurture

Senile and arteriosclerotic dementias are rarer in Japan than in the Western countries, though the general age distribution is comparable (76). Japan, on the other hand, has one of the highest mortality rates with apoplexia in the world. The arteriosclerotic changes of the brain differ in grade and localization in the Japanese and Americans, being severer in the Japanese and affecting primarily the small brain vessels, while beginning in the vessels of the circle of Willis in the Americans (58). Perhaps the ascertainment of senile dementia was less complete in Japan than in the United States since demented old people in Japan will be cared for more often at home or in private institutions. The main reason for the discrepancy, however, is seen by Shinfuku (76) in the traditional respectful attitude of the Japanese toward old age. The favorable human and social climate prevents the manifestation of senile dementia. Larsson et al. (50), however, do not believe in a manifestation-provoking effect of personal relations, social conditions or somatic diseases. These factors only influence the necessity of hospitalization. There is no doubt that events such as severe somatic disease, changes of milieu, or death of a near relative can make an aged person decompensate and thus shift him from a condition of sufficient adaptation into the pathologic group of senile dementia.

ALZHEIMER'S DISEASE

Frequency

The few frequency figures reported have to be accepted with caution since certainly quite a part of Alzheimer cases remains unascertained. Sjögren et al. (80) estimated the average morbidity risk for Alzheimer's and Pick's disease together in Sweden to be 0.1%, and their share in the whole group of dementias is 10%. The systematically collected series contained fewer Alzheimer's patients (36) than Pick's patients (44). Eighteen cases in each group were verified by autopsy and histological examination. The Alzheimer patients predominantly originated from the Stockholm area, the Pick patients from the Göteborg area. However, in the rest of Europe and in the United States, Alzheimer's disease is more frequent or more frequently diagnosed than Pick's disease, the ratio being roughly four to one, while in Asia Alzheimer's disease seems to be rare; Verhaardt and Tumbelaka (86) could not find a single case in China and Indonesia, Shinfuku (77) in 1965 published the 16th case ever observed in Japan. The females predominate among patients, but in extensive kinships the sex distribution among affected persons is even.

Empirical Risk Figures

Only about 10 to 15% of Alzheimer patients have a homologue family history. Thus the majority of cases is sporadic. In a few cases the family anamneses might be incomplete, but there are very carefully studied pedigrees without secondary cases (e.g. Koch (48)). In 1967 we traced in the literature 33 families with one or more patients verified anatomically. Another three or four families have been added in the meantime. Twelve families were observed only clinically. The disease mostly runs through several generations in direct line, but in seven families sibs only were affected.

Sjögren et al. (80) were the first who studied a small but systematically collected series of 36 Alzheimer patients (18 verified histopathologically).

The morbidity risk for the parents was 10±4%, and for the siblings 3.8±2.1%. However, the absolute numbers are small and the secondary cases include senile dementia and "Pick-Alzheimer-Syndrome."

The series observed by Constantinidis et al. (15) consists of 67 patients. The morbidity risk for senile and presenile dementias altogether is 10.6±2.5% for the parents and 9.5±2.0% for the siblings, for Alzheimer's disease alone 1.4±1.0% and 3.3±1.2% respectively. The reproduction of the Alzheimer patients (2.1 offspring) and the senile demented patients (2.4) is lower than that of the arteriosclerotic demented patients (2.6) and the general population (3.1).

The intrafamilial similarity in age of onset, age of death, clinical symptomatology and histopathology is considerable (9, 51, 52, 53). But there are differences too (50), and the great similarity might be an artifact, dissimilar illnesses not being mentioned or not acknowledged as variants of the same basic disturbance.

Until now very few authors extended the clinical examination to unaffected family members and ventured prognostic predictions. Ruggeri et al. (71) found mild but distinct EEG abnormalities, suggesting some cortical process, in the 11-year-old daughter of a female patient. Feldman et al. (22) suspected that three out of 14 unaffected family members would become ill; one of these developed Alzheimer's disease one year later. It was not so much the objective test results that had been abnormal, but the general impression.

Two female probably monozygotic twin pairs are known, one concordant (51), the other one discordant (18). Environmental factors are blamed for the discordance; the relevant ones, however, could not be identified as the life histories of the sisters were extremely different in every respect.

Mode of Inheritance

The majority of authors favors some form of dominance. The disease mostly runs through several generations in direct line; families with siblings only affected are rare, and parental consanguinity was stated but twice (53, 54). However, the high percentage of sporadic cases and the low familial morbidity risks in the series do not fit well into the dominance picture. Even when including all cases of senile dementia—which is certainly not correct—the morbidity risk for the close relatives does not surpass 10%. Thus polygenic inheritance with threshold effect has to be considered (52, 67, 80), along with heterogeneity. Especially atypical forms with characteristic neurologic features and clinical and histopathological pecularities might be caused by a single gene. The dichotomy, proposed earlier, of precocious atypical cases with positive heredity, and presenile, classical cases without heredity cannot be maintained. It is true, the majority of hereditary cases shows early onset, but is this not due to bias? The younger demented patients are more often subjected to a histopathological and genetic examination; the older the patient is, the less questionable the diagnosis seems to be. Classical presenile Alzheimer patients with a family history exist indeed and there might be senile cases too. Constantinidis et al. (15) suggest dominant heredity in presenile Alzheimer's disease and recessive inheritance in "alzheimerized" senile dementia.

Environment

The influence of environmental factors is judged to be low, though perhaps higher than in Pick's disease. Although they might trigger the disposition, this suggestion is purely hypothetical.

PICK'S DISEASE

Frequency

Pick's disease occurs in all races and nations (73), but with different frequency (see page 11).

Empirical Risk Figures

About 15 to 25% of the patients show a hereditary taint. In 1967 we compiled from the literature 22 familial cases with at least one patient verified by histopathological examination. Very remarkable is the extensive kindred described and followed up by Verhaart (87), Sanders, Schenk and van Veen (72), Schenk (74). Of 27 patients in five generations no less than 11 were dissected. In 1939 the authors had tried to trace specific premorbid symptoms and to make predictions for the "healthy" family members. Twenty years later (74), 12 predictions turned out to be correct (six affected, six unaffected) whereas five were wrong (one "sick person" had remained healthy and four "healthy persons" had fallen ill).

The series of Sjögren et al. (80) (see page 11) contained 44 patients with Pick's disease, 18 of them confirmed by autopsy. The morbidity risk was $19\pm5\%$ for the parents and $6.8\pm2.9\%$ for the siblings.

In a monozygotic twin pair (anthropologic zygosity diagnosis (6)), the co-twin of the proposita was not affected, whereas her father, father's father and two father's siblings were.

Mode of Inheritance

The hypothesis of dominance has much in favor—the illness often occurs in several generations without a break. In the family described by Sanders, Schenk and co-workers the illness ran through five generations in direct line; each affected person had a likewise affected parent. In the series of Sjögren et al. (80), however, at least 50% of the patients did not have an affected parent and the morbidity risk in parents and siblings was too low for simple dominance. Of course the manifestation might have been incomplete as suggested by the twin pair mentioned above, and secondary cases exhibiting but minor symptoms might have been missed.

Heterogeneity is supported by the fact that the symptomatology of Pick's disease is quite similar within families, but varies between families. Polygenic inheritance is not so much in the discussion.

The dichotomic classification into a group with early onset, atypical symptomatology, and positive heredity and a group with presenile onset, classical symptomatology, and negative heredity is justified no more than in Alzheimer's disease, and the intrafamilial similarity might have been exaggerated here as well as in the earlier discussion. (See pages 12 and 13).

Environment

No conclusive information on the role of environmental factors is available. Alcoholism, for example, might be a trigger of the disposition as well as the first symptom of a personality change, and there might be mere coincidence. The intricate entanglement of alcohol abuse, possible mercury intoxication, accidents and a diversity of neurologic and psychiatric symptoms is demonstrated in a case of Grünthal and Heimann (29). The autopic diagnosis of Pick's disease was a perfect surprise to everybody. In general, environmental factors are felt to be of little importance.

RELATIONS OF NORMAL OLD AGE, SENILE DEMENTIA, ALZHEIMER'S DISEASE AND PICK'S DISEASE TO EACH OTHER AND TO OTHER NEUROPSYCHIATRIC DISORDERS

Possible relations among the various disorders of old age have always been under discussion. Is there a continuous range of variation from normal old age over senile dementia to the presenile dementias? Is there an inner connection between any two of them? Or do all of them have different bases?

Alzheimer and Pick themselves thought the states called after them to be variations of senile dementia with early manifestation and special localization. But sometimes they doubted this. The morphological changes in the brain—primary atrophy, senile plaques, Alzheimer's neurofibrillary changes—are the same in physiological old age, senile dementia, and Alzheimer's disease, at least when looked upon in the light microscope. This of course does not exclude differences to be discovered by electron microscopic and biochemical techniques (75). Swollen nerve cells and argentophilic globes are characteristic but not specific for Pick's disease. The central nervous system, disposing only over a restricted number of reactions, obviously answers different stimuli in the same way.

At the present state of knowledge the neuropathological differences between normal old age and senile dementia seem to be quantitative rather than qualitative and between senile dementia and Alzheimer's disease quantitative and topographic. However, extent and localization of the brain changes do by no means coincide strictly with severity and quality of the clinical symptoms. There is considerable overlapping and sometimes the discrimination is better on clinical than on anatomical grounds. Thus Grünthal (28) observed an extremely low brain weight in a normal old woman, and nearly normal brain weights in patients with senile dementia. Mommsen and Bunsen showed a considerable brain atrophy though their intellectual capacities were well preserved till their last days (9).

Kallmann as well as Strömgren conclude from the family data that senile dementia does not represent the extreme end of physiological old age. Sjögren argues that, in particular, mild dementias representing intermediate states between physiological old age and senile dementia are lacking in the families of severely demented patients. Thus the popular statement "everybody gets his senile dementia, provided he lives long enough" fortunately lacks support.

A common basis of senile dementia and Alzheimer's disease has been suspected more often by pathologists than by clinicians. Neumann and Cohn (60), though considering Alzheimer's disease as an entity of its own, attribute about 40% of senile dementia to it. Delay and Brion (19) too assume senile cases of presenile dementias. Grünthal and Wenger (30), Arab (5), Tissot (85), and Albert (2) suspect senile dementia altogether of being Alzheimer's disease. Constantinidis (14), though favoring a principal unity of Alzheimer's and senile dementia, suggests dominant inheritance for presenile Alzheimer's disease and recessivity for late onset "alzheimerized" senile dementia. Lauter (52) advocates the identity of the two states from a clinical point of view and explains the clinical and neuropathological differences as age-specific and not etiology-specific. Pratt (67) assumes polygenic inheritance with a shared predisposition both to senile dementia and Alzheimer's disease.

Pick's disease has always stood a little bit apart. Occasionally it has been compared with Lissauer's focal paralysis and Alzheimer's disease with general paralysis. Thus the two illnesses have been regarded as the diffuse or circumscribed manifestation of the same basic process. A very few anatomical descriptions of "Pick-Alzheimer intermediate cases" tried to support this view. However, strong objections have been brought forward against this interpretation and at present Pick's disease is considered rather as a systematic disease. With respect to the irregularity of the anatomical lesions, one is tempted to think of some biochemical system rather than an anatomical one.

The genetic point of view might be summarized as follows: In all three dementias the percentage of familial cases is small. The empirical risk figures for the near relatives are low but clearly higher than the average morbidity risk. Therefore the assumption of a hereditary disposition is justified. On the other hand, environmental influences might operate, perhaps in the form of minor irritations, repeated throughout lifetime.

Single pedigrees of Alzheimer's or Pick's disease often show classical Mendelian dominance. The family studies in systematically collected series of patients, however, suggest polygenic inheritance and heterogeneity. The family data do not support an identical etiology of senile dementia, Alzheimer's disease and Pick's disease. In particular, the differences in geographic distribution and in empirical morbidity risks are against this hypothesis. No family with one Pick and one Alzheimer patient is known. The majority of the familial secondary cases is of the same kind. Senile and presenile dementias of different clinical types do occur in the families, but autoptic findings are lacking in most of them.

Some patients with Pick's disease or Alzheimer's disease exhibit in addition the symptomatology of some systematic heredodegeneration such as amyotrophic lateral sclerosis, cerebellar ataxia, chorea Huntington, or a variety of neurologic or psychiatric disturbances. Coincidence by mere chance can be excluded. The hypothesis of a "broad mutation" is more than doubtful as these combinations were found only in the propositi, but never in their families. These combined states probably can be explained best as atypical consequences of the basic processes underlying Pick's and Alzheimer's disease. The extensiveness and topography of the primary brain lesions might be the cause of the secondary degeneration of dependent systems.

SCHIZOPHRENIC AND AFFECTIVE PSYCHOSES OF OLD AGE

Old age modifies and colors preexisting psychoses. Among others Müller (57, 58) and Ciompi (11, 12) have devoted a series of studies to the outcome of preexisting psychoses in old age and they, as well as Strömgren (84), emphasize that mental disorders in old age are not always organic, progredient, and malignant, but often improve, the symptomatology getting milder, more uniform and less productive.

Here we are interested only in psychoses with first onset in old age. They very often show atypical clinical pictures and therefore are difficult to classify. Late schizophrenias appear most often as paranoid psychoses (70), but not too seldom, show depressive symptoms (81). On the other side, involutional melancholia often exhibits paranoid features. A state at first imposing as endogenous depression may develop organic symptomatology, and some emotional instability thought to be arteriosclerotic might end in a more or less classical depression.

Correlations between organic brain damage—atrophic or vascular—and the so-called functional psychoses, between senile dementia and other psychiatric disorders, have been discussed abundantly from a clinical point of view, sometimes including anatomical aspects (e.g., Post (65); Müller and Ciompi (58), in particular chapter IV with contributions by Post, Ciompi, Garrone and Albert). But as far as we can see, genetic viewpoints have rarely been included, and when they have been included, mention has been made just in marginal notes.

Sjögren (79) stated a lower hereditary load in old age psychoses than in the psychoses of younger age. However he only touches upon genetic problems and just states the percentage of patients with one or more affected relatives without further differentiation.

Bleuler (7), having found about the same morbidity risk in the families of schizophrenics with late and with early onset, concluded that the majority of the late schizophrenias is genetically identical with or closely related to the early ones. Roth (70) and Kay and Roth (45) consider a great part of the schizophrenic and paranoid psychoses with late onset to be "true" schizophrenias manifesting themselves so late because of a high resistance and/or severe stress experience of the individual concerned. They advocate a multifactorial etiology with genetic factors and nongenetic components such as sensory impairment and human isolation contributing to the onset of the psychosis.

Kay (44), however, stated lower familial risk figures for schizophrenia and affective psychoses in paranoid psychoses with onset over 59 years of age. Though the clinical picture of the cases with and without a family history was the same, he judged part of the latter to be based on an exacerbation and accentuation of premorbid personality traits, which are unfavorable for the task of coping successfully with the manifold somatic impairments and psychological stresses arising from getting and being old, and which, in interaction with non-genetic factors, develop into a psychotic state.

Thus, the schizophrenic and paranoid psychoses of old age clearly show genetic relations to the whole group of schizophrenia, but obviously heterogeneous and non-genetic factors play a more important role than in the early onset cases.

The same is true for the melancholias of the involutional and senile period. They have a lot in common with the "classical" manic-depressive and depressive psychoses, but they also show certain differences. In most series the familial load with affective psychoses is a bit lower than in the patients with early onset manic-depressive psychosis, though clearly higher than the average morbidity risk; the familial incidence of schizophrenia is somewhat increased (4, 82, 83).

Hopkinson and Levy (34), in a study into the families of affective patients with onset in different years of age, observed the familial morbidity risks to drop abruptly in patients with onset in the fifth decade.

Roth (69), Kay (44), and Kay et al. (46) subdivided a population of affective patients over 60 years of age according to onset before and after age 60. No corresponding genetic subdivision emerged, as the majority of secondary cases in both groups had fallen ill before age 50. Physical illness and psychic stress, however, occurred more often in the patients of the late onset group. Obviously severer stress is needed to make persons psychotic who have resisted the manifestation of the hereditary disposition successfully till their 60th year of life. Kay feels that the affective psychoses with late onset are very heterogeneous under clinical, prognostic and genetical aspects, the percentage of hereditary cases being less than 50%.

Funding (24, 25) studied 145 paranoid propositi with the dismission diagnoses of schizophrenia, manic-depressive psychosis, atypical psychosis, paranoid psychosis, psychogenic psychosis. This clinically heterogeneous series turned out to be genetically heterogeneous as well, which was to be expected. In the families the morbidity risk for psychoses altogether was as high as in the families of schizophrenics and manic-depressives. However the great majority of secondary cases were senile, psychogenic and unspecified mental disorders, whereas the morbidity risk for schizophrenia (2.5% in the siblings, 1% in the parents and 1.4% in the children) and affective psychoses (1.6% in the siblings, 1.9% in the parents and 0.9% in the children) was but slightly increased. The average morbidity risk for schizophrenia is 0.85%, for manic-depressive psychosis 0.4 to 0.8%.

Kallmann (38) himself called attention to the heterogeneity of his series of 96 twin pairs with involutional psychoses. There are nearly no classical depressives, but a great many atypical melancholias and probably a few schizophrenias and organic states. The importance of heredity is shown by the concordance rate of 61% in the monozygotic twins against 6% in the dizygotic twins.

In conclusion, there is no doubt that the etiology of the psychoses among the aged is heterogeneous and multifactorial. Endogenous and exogenous factors, organic and psychodynamic processes are involved, contributing a varying share to the individual case. The genetic basis underlying psychoses with early onset is the same in at least a part of the late onset psychoses. However somatic changes and psychoreactive mechanisms seem to play a more important role. Some old age psychoses might result from an intensification of premorbid personality traits, which, in interaction with organic changes and emotional stress, result in the psychotic breakdown.

Kallmann considers old age itself as the main requirement since cumulative strain arising from increasingly conspicuous signs of aging, fear of invalidism, diminution of efficiency and adaptability, loneliness by death of friends and relatives, etc., triggers genetic dispositions and, on the other hand, gives the senile psychoses their particular coloring.

REFERENCES

1. ÅKESSON, H. O. 1969. A population study of senile and arteriosclerotic psychoses. *Hum. Heredity.*, 19:546.
2. ALBERT, E. 1964. Senile Demenz und Alzheimer'sche Krankheit als Ausdruck des gleichen Krankheitsgeschehens. *Fortschr. Neurol. Psychiat.*, 32:625.
3. ALZHEIMER, A. 1907. Über eine eigenartige Erkrankung der Hirnrinde. 37.Vers. südwestdeutscher Irrenärzte in Tübingen am 3./4. Nov. 1906. *Zbl. Nervenheilk.*, 18:177.
4. ANGST, J. 1966. Zur Ätiologie und Nosologie endogener depressiver Psychosen.

Monogr. Gesamtgeb. Neurol. Psychiat. 112. Berlin-Heidelberg-New York: Springer.

5. ARAB, A. 1960. Unité nosologique entre démence sénile et maladie d'Alzheimer d'après une étude statistique et anatomo-clinique. Sist. nerv., 12:189.
6. BECKER, P. E. 1948. Genetische und klinische Fragen bei Pick'scher Krankheit. (Mitteilung eines diskordanten eineiigen Zwillingspaares.) Nervenarzt., 19:355.
7. BLEULER, M. 1943. Die spätschizophrenen Krankheitsbilder. Fortschr. Neurol., 15: 259.
8. BLUM, J. E., JARVIK, L. F., and CLARK, E. T. 1970. Rate of change on selective tests of intelligence: A twenty-year longitudinal study of ageing. J. Geront., 25:171.
9. BRAUNMÜHL, A., VON. 1957. Alterserkrankungen des Zentralnervensystems. In: Uehlingen, E. von (Ed.), Handbuch d. speziellen pathologischen Anatomie u. Histologie, Bd. XIII/1.A. Berlin: Springer.
10. Ciba Foundation Colloquia on Ageing. 1955-1959. Vol. I-V. London: Churchill.
11. CIOMPI, L. 1972. Allgemeine Psychopathologie des Alters. In: Kisker, K. P., Meyer, J. E., Müller, M., and Strömgrem, E. (Eds.) Psychiatrie der Gegenwart, Bd.II/2. Berlin-Heidelberg: Springer.
12. CIOMPI, L., and MÜLLER, C . 1969. Katamnestische Untersuchungen zur Altersentwicklung psychischer Krankheiten. Nervenarzt., 40:349.
13. COHEN, B. 1965. Family patterns of longevity and mortality. In: Neel, J. V., Shaw, M. W. and Schull, W. J. (Eds.) Genetics and the Epidemiology of Chronic Diseases. Washington, D.C.: U.S. Dept. of Health and Welfare.
14 CONSTANTINIDIS, J. 1968. Correlations between the age of onset of dysmnesia and the degree of cerebral degeneration. In: Müller, Ch., and Ciompi, L. (Eds.) Senile Dementia. Bern-Stuttgart: Hans Huber.
15. CONSTANTINIDIS, J., GARRONE, G., and D'AJURIAGUERRA, J. 1962. L'hérédité des démences de l'âge avancé. Encéphale, 4:301.
16. CRESSERI, A. 1948. L'ereditarietà della demenza senile. Boll. Soc. ital. Biol. sper., 24:200.
17. CURTIS, H. 0. 1966. Biological Mechanisms of Aging. Springfield, Ill.: Charles C Thomas.
18. DAVIDSON, E. A., and ROBERTSON, E. E. 1955. Alzheimer's disease with Acne rosacea in one of identical twins. J. Neurol. Neurosurg. Psychiat., 18:72.
19. DELAY, J., and BRION, S. 1962. Les démences tardives. Paris: Masson.
20. ESSEN-MÖLLER, E. 1956. Individual traits and morbidity in a Swedish rural population. Acta Psychiat. Scand. Suppl., 100:1.
21. ESSEN-MÖLLER, E. 1961. A current field study in the mental disorders in Sweden. In: Hoch, P., and Zubin, J. (Eds.), Comparative Epidemiology of the Mental Disorders. New York: Grune & Stratton.
22. FELDMAN, G., CHANDLER, A., LEVY, L., and GLASER, H. 1963. Familial Alzheimer's Disease. Neurology, 13:811.
23. FROLKIS, V. V. 1970. On the regulatory mechanism of molecular genetic alterations during aging. Exp. Geront., 5:37.
24. FUNDING, T. 1961. Genetics of paranoid psychosis in later life. Acta Psychiat. Scand., 37:267.
25. FUNDING, T. 1963. Paranoid psychosis in later life. Sociology and prognosis. Acta Psychiat. Scand. Suppl., 169:356.
26. GALTON, F. 1889. Natural Inheritance. London: Macmillan.
27. GOLDSTEIN, S. 1966. Jewish mortality and survival patterns: Providence, Rhode Island, 1962-1964. Eugen. Quart., 13:48.
28. GRÜNTHAL, E. 1927. Klinisch-anatomisch vergleichende Untersuchungen über den Greisenblödsinn. Z. ges. Neurol. Psychiat., 111:763.

29. GRÜNTHAL, E., and HEIMANN, H. 1954. Symptomenbild der amyotrophischen Lateralsklerose bei chronischer Quecksilbervergiftung oder Polyneuritis bei chronischem Alkoholismus, Quecksilverintoxikation und Pick'scher Atrophie? Z. Unfallmed. Berufskr., 47:177.

30. GRÜNTHAL, E. and WENGER, O. 1939. Nachweis von Erblichkeit bei der Alzheimer'schen Krankheit nebst Bemerkungen über den Altersvorgang im Gehirn. Mschr. Psychiat. Neurol., 101:8.

31. HARVALD, B., and HAUGE, M. 1958. A catamnestic investigation of Danish twins. A survey of 3,100 paris. Acta Genet., (Basel) 8:287.

32. HAUGE, M., HARVALD, B., FISCHER, M., GOTLIEB-JENSEN, K., JUEL-NIELSEN, N., RAEBILD, I., SHAPIRO, R., and VIDEBACH, T. 1968. The Danish twin register. A. Ge. Me. Ge., 17:315.

33. HEUSCHERT, D. 1963. EEG-Untersuchungen an eineiigen Zwillingen im höheren Lebensalter. Z. Menschl. Vererb.-u.Konst.-Lehre, 37:128.

34. HOPKINSON, G., and LEY, P. 1969. A genetic study of affective disorder. Brit. J. Psychiat., 115:917.

35. JARVIK, L. F. 1963. Senescence and chromosomal changes. Lancet, I:114.

36. JARVIK, L. F., KALLMANN, F. J., and FALEK, A. 1962. Intellectual changes in aged twins. J. Geront., 17:289.

37. JARVIK, L. F., KENNETH, PH.D., ALTSHULER, Z., KATO, T., and BLUMER, B. 1971. Organic brain syndrome and chromosome loss in aged twins. Dis. Nerv. Syst., 32:159.

38. KALLMANN, F. J. 1952. The genetics of psychoses. Analysis of 1,232 twin index families. Comptes Rend. I. Congr. Mond. de Psychiat., Paris, 1950: Hermann.

39. KALLMANN, F. J. 1956. Genetic aspects of mental disorders in later life. In: Kaplan, O. J. (Ed.) Mental Disorders in Later Life. Stanford: Stanford University Press.

40. KALLMANN, F. J. 1956. The genetics of aging. In: The Neurologic and Psychiatric Aspects of the Disorders of Aging. Vol. XXXV, Proc. Ass. Res. Nerv. Ment. Dis. Baltimore: Williams & Wilkins.

41. KALLMANN, F. J. 1961. Genetic factors in aging: Comparative and longitudinal observations on a senescent twin population. In: Hoch, P. H., and Zubin, J. (Eds.) Psychopathology of Aging. New York: Grune & Stratton.

42. KALLMANN, F. J., FEINGOLD, L., and BONDY, E. 1951. Comparative adaptational, social and psychometric data on the life histories of senescent twin pairs. Am. J. Hum. Genet., 3:65.

43. KALLMANN, F. J., and SANDER, G. 1949. Twin studies on senescence. Am. J. Psychiat., 106:29.

44. KAY, D. 1959. Observations on the natural history and genetics of old age psychosis. Proc. Roy. Soc. Med., 52:791.

45. KAY, D., and ROTH, M. 1961. Environmental and hereditary factors in the schizophrenias of old age ("late paraphrenia") and their bearing on the general problem of causation in schizophrenia. J. Ment. Sci., 107:649.

46. KAY, W., ROTH, M., and HOPKINS, B. 1955. Affective disorders arising in the senium. I. Their association with organic cerebral degeneration. J. Ment. Sci., 101:302.

47. KNUSSMANN, R. 1968. Entwicklung, Konstitution, Geschlecht. In: Becker, P. E. (Ed.) Handbuch d. Humangenetik, Bd.I/1. Stuttgart: Thieme.

48. KOCH, G. 1941. Zur Erbpathologie der Alzheimer'schen Krankheit. Erbarzt, 9:31.

49. KOCH, G. 1957. Ergebnisse aus der Nachuntersuchung der Berliner Zwillingsserie nach 20-25 Jahren. Acta Genet., (Basel) 7:47.

50. LARSSON, T., SJÖGREN, T., and JACOBSON, G. 1963. Senile dementia. Acta Psychiat. Scand. Suppl., 167:1.

51. LAUTER, H. 1961. Genealogische Erhebungen in einer Familie mit Alzheimer'scher Krankheit. *Arch. Psychiat. Nervenkr.*, 202:126.
52. LAUTER, H. 1970. Über Spätformen der Alzheimer'schen Krankheit und ihre Beziehung zur senilen Demenz. *Psychiat. Clin.*, 3:169.
53. LOEWENBERG, K., and WAGGONER, R. W. 1934. Familial organic psychosis (Alzheimer's type). *Arch. Neurol. Psychiat.*, 31:737.
54. MCMENEMEY, W. H., WORSTER-DROUGHT, C., FLIND, J., and WILLIAMS, H. G. 1939. *J. Neurol. Psychiat.*, London, 2:293.
55. V.MANSVELT, J. 1954. *Pick's Disease.* (A syndrome of lobar cerebral atrophy; its clinico-anatomical and histopathological types). Thesis. Utrecht: Enschede.
56. MEGGENDORFER, F. 1925. Über familiengeschichtliche Untersuchungen bei arteriosklerotischer und seniler Demenz. *Zbl. ges. Neurol. Psychiat.*, 40:359.
57. MÜLLER, CH. 1967. *Alterspsychiatrie.* Stuttgart: Thieme.
58. MÜLLER, CH., and CIOMPI, L. 1968. (Eds.) *Senile Dementia.* Bern/Stuttgart: Hans Huber.
59. NAHMAN, S., and RABINOWICZ, TH. 1963. Considérations sur un cas familial de maladie d'Alzheimer. *Encéphale*, 4:366.
60. NEUMANN, M. A., and COHN, R. 1953. Incidence of Alzheimer's disease in a large mental hospital. Relation to senile psychosis and psychosis with cerebral arteriosclerosis. *Arch. Neurol. Psychiat.*, (Chic.) 69:615.
61. NIELSEN, J. 1962. Geronto-psychiatric period-prevalence investigation in a geographically delimited population. *Acta Psychiat. Scand.*, 38:307.
62. NIELSEN, J. 1968. Chromosomes in senile dementia. In: Müller, Ch., and Ciompi, L. (Eds.) *Senile Dementia.* Stuttgart/Bern: Hans Huber.
63. PEARSON, K., and LEE, A. 1903. On the laws of inheritance in man. I. Inheritance of physical characters. *Biometrika*, 2:357.
64. PICK, A. 1906. Über einen weiteren Symptomenkomplex im Rahmen der Dementia senilis, bedingt durch umschriebene stärkere Hirnatrophie (gemischte Apraxie). *Mschr. Psychiat. Neurol.*, 19:97.
65. POST, F. 1962. *The Significance of Affective Symptoms in Old Age.* London: Oxford University Press.
66. PRATT, R. T. C. 1967. *The Genetics of Neurological Disorders.* London: Oxford Univ. Press.
67. PRATT, R. T. C. 1970. The genetics of Alzheimer's disease. In Wolstenholme, G. E. W., and O'Connor, M. (Eds.) *Ciba Foundation Symposium on Alzheimer's Disease and Related Conditions.* London: Churchill.
68. RESCH, J. A., OKABE, N., and KIMOTO, K. 1969. Cerebral atherosclerosis. *Geriatrics*, 24:111.
69. ROTH, M. 1955. The natural history of mental disorder in old age. *J. Ment. Sci.*, 101:281.
70. ROTH, M. 1957. Interaction of genetic and environmental factors in the causation of schizophrenia. In: Richter, D. (Ed.) *Schizophrenia.* London-New York: Pergamon Press.
71. RUGGERI, R., DE MAIO, D., and CANEVINI, P. 1963. Su di un caso di morbo di Alzheimer-Perusini a carattere eredo-familiare insorto in giovane età. *G. Psichiat. Neuropat.*, 91:715.
72. SANDERS, J., SCHENK, V. W. D., and VAN VEEN, P. 1939. A family with Pick's disease. *Verh. Kon. Nederl. Akad. van Wetenschapen*, Sect 2, No. 3, 38:1.
73. SCHENK, V. W. D. 1952. Maladie de Pick. *Comptes Rend. Congr. Mond. de Psychiat.*, Paris 1950, Vol. II. Paris: Hermann
74. SCHENK, V. W. D. 1959. Re-examination of a family with Pick's disease. *Ann. Hum. Genet.*, 23:325.
75. SHELANSKI, M. L., and TAYLOR, E. W. 1970. Biochemistry of neurofilaments and

neurotubules. In: Woltsenholme, G. E. W., and O'Connor, M. (Eds.) *Ciba Foundation Symposium on Alzheimer's Disease and Related Conditions.* London: Churchill.

76. SHINFUKU, N. 1954. Mental disorders of the aged in Japan. *Yonago Acta Med.,* 1:115.
77. SHINFUKU, N. 1966. An autopsy case of Alzheimer's disease. *Exc. Med. Psychiat.,* 19:223. (Original paper 1965 in Japanese).
78. SJÖGREN, H. 1956. Neuro-psychiatric studies in presenile and senile diseases, based on a material of 1,000 cases. *Acta Psychiat. Scand. Suppl.,* 106:9.
79. SJÖGREN, H. 1964. Paraphrenic, melancholic and psychoneurotic states in the presenile-senile period of life. A study of 949 patients in the functional division. *Acta Psychiat. Scand. Suppl.,* 176:1.
80. SJÖGREN, T., SJÖGREN, H., and LINDGREN, A. G. H. 1952. *Morbus Alzheimer and Morbus Pick.* A genetic, clinical and patho-anatomical study. Copenhagen: Munksgaard.
81. SLATER, E. 1953. *Psychotic and Neurotic Illness in Twins.* Spec. Rep. Ser. Med. Res. Coun. 278. London: Her Majesty's Stationary Office.
82. STENSTEDT, A. 1959. Involutional melancholia. An etiologic, clinical and social study of endogenous depression in later life with special reference to genetic factors. *Acta Psychiat. Scand. Suppl.,* 127:5.
83. STENSTEDT, A. 1961. The etiology of involutional melancholia. *Acta Psychiat. Scand. Suppl.,* 162:39.
84. STRÖMGREN, E. 1964. Recent studies on prevalence of mental disorders in the aged. In: Hansen, P. (Ed.) *Age with a Future.* Proc. 6. Int. Congr. Geront. Copenhagen: Munksgaard.
85. TISSOT, R. 1968. On the nosological identity of senile dementia and of Alzheimer's disease. In: Müller, Ch., and Ciompi, L. (Eds.) *Senile Dementia.* Bern-Stuttgart: Hans Huber.
86. VERHAART and TUMBELAKA. 1952. Quoted after Schenk, V. W. D.
87. VERHAART, W. J. C. 1931. Over de ziekte van Pick. Ned. T. Geneesk. 74: (1930), 5586. *Ref. Zbl. ges. Neurol. Psychiat.,* 59:485.
88. VERSCHUER, O., VON. 1954. *Wirksame Faktoren im Leben des Menschen.* Beobachtungen and ein- und zweieiigen Zwillingen durch 25 Jahre. Wiesbaden: Steiner.
89. WALFORD, R. L. 1969. *The Immunologic Theory of Aging.* Copenhagen: Munksgaard.
90. ZERBIN-RÜDIN, E. 1967. Endogene Psychosen. In: Becker, P. E. (Ed.) *Handbuch der Humangenetik,* Bd.V/2. Stuttgart: Thieme:
91. ZERBIN-RÜDIN, E. 1967. Hirnatrophische Prozesse. In: Becker, P. E. (Ed.) *Handbuch der Humangenetik,* Bd.V/2. Stuttgart: Thieme.
92. ZERBIN-RÜDIN, E. 1972. Genetische Aspekte der Erkrankungen des höheren Lebensalters. In: Kisker, K. P., Meyer, J. E., Müller, M., and Strömgren, E. (Eds.) *Psychiatrie der Gegenwart.* Berlin-Heildelberg-New York: Springer.

2

EPIDEMIOLOGY

N. JUEL-NIELSEN

*Professor of Psychiatry, Odense University,
Odense, Denmark*

INTRODUCTION

For quite a long time, it has been a well established fact that life expectancy at birth has increased during the present century by approximately 40 years in all developing countries. In most of these countries the old age groups, 65 years and over, now constitute 10 to 12% of the general population, a figure which represents a doubling since 1900. More recently, it has become clear that the average length of life for people who have reached the age of 65 has increased only slightly, the increase being one or two years during the same period.

Modern countries are thus faced with a development which, due to the improved medical and social care for infants, children and adolescents, leads to more people attaining old age but does not enable them to live much longer than previously. The value of care and prevention of illness in the aged should, naturally, not be measured solely by statistics of life expectancy and mortality rates but should also be evaluated from the more qualitative point of view—life in old age should be worth living. If, however, a community really wants to plan and organize care for the large proportion of the population which is comprised of the aged, statistical information from epidemiological studies cannot be dispensed with, but may even be necessary and very useful as a basis for initiating such efforts.

HOSPITAL STUDIES

The quantitative importance of mental disorders in old age has been substantiated by a great number of reports, primarily demonstrating the increasing impact these disorders have on society by placing pressure on its medical and social institutions. A great number of beds in psychiatric institutions are occupied by patients belonging to the old age group and the need for nursing homes, day hospitals and other psychiatric services for the aged seems to be increasing. Census studies of patients in psychiatric institutions in Denmark in 1957, 1962 and 1967 (8) showed that the percentage of patients 60 years and over increased from 43% in 1957 to 50% in 1962 and 53% in 1967.

The distribution of the old-age population (65+) in institutions in Denmark in 1967, grouped according to main diagnoses and rate per 100,000, is shown in Table 1.

During the 10 year period studied, the rates for schizophrenia in old-age remained practically unchanged for males, while a definite increase can be seen for females (see Table 2). In the case of organic disorders there was an increase for both sexes, particularly females (see Table 3).

TABLE 1

Old-age Population in Psychiatric Institutions in 1967,
Grouped According to Main Diagnoses and
Rates Per 100,000

Schizophrenia	Manic-depressive psychosis	Organic disorders	Reactive conditions	Other conditions	Total
377	77	398	54	25	873

TABLE 2

Old-age Population Suffering from Schizophrenia

	MALES		FEMALES	
Census Year	1957	1967	1957	1967
Rate per 100,000	297	301	416	347

TABLE 3

Old-age Population Suffering from Organic Disorders

	MALES		FEMALES	
Census Year	1957	1967	1957	1967
Rate per 100,000	212	338	247	447

The increase of patients aging in psychiatric institutions had been anticipated, but an analysis of the data revealed that the conditions were rather different for psychiatric hospitals and for psychiatric wards in general hospitals. In psychiatric hospitals the increase was primarily due to the fact that a great number of schizophrenic patients had simply grown old in the hospital. In accordance with the general observation that the combination of pharmacological therapy and rehabilitation measures tends to keep many schizophrenic patients out of hospital, the total rates for schizophrenics in hospital showed a decreasing trend of an almost linear nature, but during the ten-year period concerned, it appears that the majority of schizophrenics in hospital had been admitted a great many years earlier, particularly during periods of economic depression, unemployment and poor social provision. Many of these patients had lost touch with their former communities and could not be discharged and rehabilitated. Only a very small proportion of the increase of old aged patients could be accounted for by patients who had been admitted to hospital late in life; for those patients the duration of their stay in hospital was relatively short, as it was possible to admit them either to nursing homes or to old age homes under psychiatric supervision. The remainder simply died in hospital shortly after admission.

In the psychiatric wards of general hospitals, particularly in Copenhagen, only 27% of the patients were aged 60 years and over in 1957, but in 1962 the figure had increased to 50%—the same as in mental hospitals. This phenomenon aroused interest because several psychiatric wards had been established, or planned, in general hospitals and one could fear that these new psychiatric institutions were in danger of being rapidly converted into predominantly psycho-geriatric wards. The census study in 1967 showed, however, that the previous increase had been practically stopped, the percentage of old patients aged 60 and over was still 50, which was due to an altered policy in the intervening period, during which a number of psychiatric nursing homes, serving the Copenhagen area, had been established.

Psycho-geriatric patients are admitted not only to psychiatric institutions, but also to other wards in general hospitals, surgical and decided geriatric wards. Another Danish study (7), surveying the conditions in a Danish county, showed that within a year 2% of the population aged 60 and over came into contact with a medical institution entirely or predominantly on account of a mental disorder, but only 0.5% of these got in touch with a psychiatric institution. From the point of view of the community this 2%, which is comprised of those who are admitted to psychiatric institutions as well as those admitted to other medical institutions, represents the heavy end of the problems connected with the occurrence of mental disorders in the old age group of the general population. As stated by Kay, Beamish and Roth (9), numerous reports have made it plain that medical services deal only with the visible point of the "iceberg" of mental disorders.

POPULATION STUDIES

How is the state of affairs in the population in general, that is, among the clientele of the general practitioner? How many people in the age groups concerned present a mental disorder of some kind, how great is the real need for examination and treatment by psychiatrists, and how many of these elderly patients should be treated at home by the general practitioner in collaboration with the various social agents in the community? Answers to some of these questions are of fundamental importance if the community, within the boundaries of practical possibility, is to fulfill the need for care, treatment and preventive measures in psycho-geriatrics in the most radical way.

Despite the fact that the magnitude of the problems related to mental disorders in the aged is generally recognized, very few epidemiological investigations of mental disorders of the aged in a population have been performed. Furthermore, these investigations have been carried out in relatively few countries, primarily in Scandinavia and the United Kingdom.

Epidemiological studies of the frequency of mental disorders in old age in well defined communities have been performed in Scandinavian countries by Bremer (1), Essen-Möller (3), Sjögren and Larsson (16), Nielsen (11), and Hagnell (5), in the U.K. by Primrose (14), Kay, Beamish and Roth (9, 10), Garside, Kay and Roth (4) and Parsons (12).

Some of these studies survey only the aged population, either 60 and over or 65 and over; others are entire population studies, from which some results relating to the mental health in elderly people can be extracted for comparison. The population studies in the U.K. deal with urban areas, whereas the Scandinavian studies deal with rural communities which, in some cases, were located in remote and rather isolated areas.

The epidemiological approach differs. Some investigators have recorded the frequency of mental disorders present in the elderly at a point in time, by making a census based either on examinations of all members of the defined population or on investigations of a sample drawn at random from the elderly population in the community. Such measurements of the frequency of mental disorders—usually termed *point prevalence* rates—are of particular interest in the planning and organization of care and the treatment of persons suffering from a chronic disorder, whereas they are of limited value in relation to planning for disorders of short duration. Prevalence figures may be used for various purposes, such as ascertaining the proportion of the population in need of some kind of care or treatment, the need for beds in hospitals and nursing homes, or the need for providing other kinds of facilities for the old age population.

Incidence studies, as used by other investigators, provide frequency rates consisting of the total number of new cases of mental disorders occurring within a specified period of time, and are also of great value in the planning of services in the community. Unfortunately, some of the investigators have calculated so-called "period prevalence" rates, which are based on case-recording within periods ranging from six months to five years, a procedure which results in figures which cannot be directly compared with the true prevalence and incidence rates from other studies.

Finally, these studies of mental disorders in old age differ widely with regard to the diagnostic concepts and criteria for classification used by the various investigators. Consequently a detailed tabulation of the results of these studies is of limited value. Comparisons, in particular of the diagnostic sub-groups, are not only difficult to evaluate, but may even create confusion and doubt with regard to the value of epidemiological studies of mental disorder.

However, when these reservations have been made, some of the main results of the studies can be evaluated as being not only fairly reliable, but also meaningful, especially when seen from the more practical viewpoint of planning and organizing psycho-geriatric care in a community.

First of all, these epidemiological studies confirm that the frequency of mental disorders in the elderly population is high. In the studies referred to, the *total prevalence rates for mental disorders* in old age range from 25 to 40 percent. Most studies confirm also that the prevalence of neuroses in old age is high. Such figures depend primarily on the narrow or wide diagnostic classification used by the investigator, and in particular whether cases of mild mental deterioration, neurotic or personality disorders have been included or not. Ciompi (2) has estimated that it is safe to conclude that some 25% of the aged population presents some kind of mental disorder which, in about one third of the cases, must be classified as a severe disorder. From a practical point of view, it is obvious that even though a person included in an epidemiological survey can be classified in psychiatric terms, this does not necessarily mean that he is in need of psychiatric attention or other forms of care. Post (13) has suggested that 11% of the aged population is in need of some kind of care.

The most reliable figures which can be derived from these studies are undoubtedly the prevalence rates for psychoses in old age. In the studies by Bremer, Essen-Möller, Primrose, Kay et al., Nielsen and

TABLE 4

Prevalence Rates for Psychoses in Old Age Population

Bremer	Essen-Möller	Primrose	Kay et al.	Nielsen	Parsons
6.7	6.1	5.9	8.0	6.8	7.0

Parsons, the prevalence for *all forms of psychoses,* severe senile and arteriosclerotic psychoses, other organic syndromes and functional disorders, varied only from 6 to 8%, indicating that, despite the discrepancies between these studies, this figure seems to represent a consistent and reliable measurement of the core of mental disorders in old age (see Table 4).

MANAGEMENT IMPLICATIONS

Assuming that the problems related to mental disorders concern one fourth of the aged population, and that one third of these disorders are of a severe nature (primarily psychotic disorders), the following question arises: How should the community, represented by medical and social institutions, psychiatrists and general practitioners, deal with these problems?

As already pointed out, only a small proportion of these elderly patients requires admission to an institution, although, as also mentioned, the percentage of beds occupied by the aged in such places is increasing. In a recent Danish prevalence study by Rinder Bollerup (15), comprised of 626 persons aged 70 years, only 7 cases, 1.1%, were in an institution. Of these, five were in a nursing home and two attended a psychiatric hospital as day patients on the census day, whereas the remaining aged population in the community was at home.

This perhaps surprising finding corresponds to the results and conclusions of an earlier Danish prevalence study (7), of persons aged 60 and over in a rural population. When trying to assess the proportion of elderly people who required the attention of a psychiatrist, it was found that 15% of the aged population fell into that category, but only 1% presented a mental disorder that required admission to an institution. Of the remaining 14%, 8% had actually availed themselves of the community psychiatric service existing in the area and the remainder had, in the investigator's opinion, been in need of doing so at one time. The 14% could, with advantage, be cared for in their homes, provided a close cooperation between psychiatrists, general practitioners and social agents was in existence in the community.

CONCLUSIONS

The results and experiences, which can be derived from the epidemiological studies surveyed in this chapter lead to the conclusion that even though the frequency of mental disorders in elderly people is high (it involves at least one fourth of the aged population), probably no more than 10 to 15%, primarily those with psychotic disorders, is in need of medical, and especially psychiatric, assistance. Only approximately 1% requires admission to psychiatric institutions or nursing homes.

The limited number of epidemiological studies of mental disorders in old age which has been performed in relatively few countries will probably be supplemented by new studies in progress not only in the U.K. and Scandinavia, but also in Germany, Switzerland and other European countries.

In a recent report from The Society of Clinical Psychiatrists entitled *The Organisation of Psychogeriatrics* (6), the need for research in this field is stressed and especially the need for research of a statistical or epidemiological nature is emphasized. It maintains that some of the research projects are so urgent, extensive and basic as to require government sponsorship.

The society puts forward the following recommendation with which one can entirely agree:

> Regional Hospital Boards as the planning authority are responsible for the medical service to the aged. The Society is of the opinion that every Regional Hospital Board must provide a full service to the

aged in Mental Hospitals either within a comprehensive service for geriatrics and psychogeriatrics or, if it fails to develop such a service, in a separate psychogeriatric service. The present tendency to leave the aged in Mental Hospitals largely without any organized service is to be deplored.

REFERENCES

1. BREMER, J. 1951. A social psychiatric investigation of a small community in Northern Norway. *Acta Psychiat. Scand. Suppl.*, 62.
2. CIOMPI, L. 1972. Allgemeine Psychopathologie des Alters. In: *Psychiatrie der Gegenwart*, Band II/Teil 2, 1001-1036. Berlin-Heidelberg-New York: Springer Verlag.
3. ESSEN-MÖLLER, E. 1956. Individual traits and morbidity in a Swedish rural population. *Acta Psychiat. Scand. Suppl.*, 100.
4. GARSIDE, R. R., KAY, D. W. K., and ROTH, M. 1965. Old age mental disorders in Newcastle-upon-Tyne. Part III: A factorial study of medical, psychiatric and social characteristics. *Brit. J. Psychiat.* III:193-946.
5. HAGNELL, O. 1966. *A Prospective Study of the Incidence of Mental Disorders*. Stockholm: Svenska Bokförlaget.
6. HOWELLS, J. G. (Ed.). 1971. *The Organization of Psychogeriatrics*. England: Society of Clinical Psychiatrists Report.
7. JUEL-NIELSEN, N. 1965. Some Results and Experiences from Recent Epidemiological Investigations in Denmark. Report on the Symposium held by the Royal College of Physicians, London.
8. JUEL-NIELSEN, N., and STRÖMGREN, E. 1969. Ten years later. A comparison between census studies of patients in psychiatric institutions in Denmark in 1957, 1962, and 1967. *Acta Jutland.* XLI:2, Kobenhavn: Munksgaard.
9. KAY, D. W. K., BEAMISH, P., and ROTH, M. 1964. Old age mental disorders in Newcastle-upon-Tyne. Part I: A study of prevalence. *Brit. J. Psychiat.*, 110: 146-158.
10. KAY, D. W. K., BEAMISH, P., and ROTH, M. 1964. Old age mental disorders in Newcastle-upon-Tyne. Part II: A study of possible social and medical causes. *Brit. J. Psychiat.* 110:668-682.
11. NIELSEN, J. 1962. Geronto-psychiatric period-prevalence investigation in a geographically delimited population. *Acta Psychiat. Scand.*, 38:307-330.
12. PARSONS, P. L. 1965. Mental health of Swanseas old folk. *Brit. J. Prev. Soc. Med.* 19:43-47.
13. POST, F. 1959. Mental health in old age. *Publ. Hlth.* (London), 73:412-153.
14. PRIMROSE, E. J. R. 1962. *Psychological Illness: A Community Study* Tavistock Publications, London.
15. RINDER BOLLERUP, T. 1972. *Nord. Psykiat. Tidskr.* 29:42.
16. SJOGREN, T., and LARSSON, T. 1959. The changing age-structure in Sweden and its impact on mental illness. *Bull. Wld. Hlth. Org.* 21:569-582.

3
ANTHROPOLOGICAL ASPECTS

Marvin K. Opler

Professor of Social Psychiatry, School of Medicine
Professor of Anthropology and Sociology
The Graduate School, State University of New York
at Buffalo, N.Y.

INTRODUCTION

The attitudes toward aging vary considerably among the cultures of the world. Anyone who has read the classical Chinese manuals on filial piety will quickly recognize that great age is accorded tremendous respect. In ancient Japan, also, Shintoistic beliefs ascribed virtue to the ancestors, and a widespread festival, called the *Bon-odori,* is still a time when the villagers dress up in gay apparel and dance to assure their collective progenitors that the village is thriving at the time of harvest. Also, while the ancient Hebrews believed that evildoers died young, the Greeks in their mythology and in one common proverb stated that, "Those who die young are beloved by the gods" (4). The Middle Eastern tradition with which the ancient Hebrews were connected views old age as the summit of life, bringing status and prestige, particularly to the male; in fact, the title, "Sheik," which we equate with chief and other such terms, simply meant "old man" in its original translation (13).

In nonliterate cultures one can also find that the division of labor in society often accords differing roles to people according to their age and sex. The Siriono of Eastern Bolivia as reported by Allan Holmberg are constantly in fear of hunger and travel through jungle terrain seeking

food. Both sexes may work at tasks of carrying burdens, dressing or cooking game, or locating vegetable foods in a kind of general interdependency
of both sexes. Since it is the very young and very old who do not produce, the Siriono decide to cherish children, but to neglect the aged who
are even abandoned (5).

In certain cultures which the author has studied, the elderly may be
respected for their age and its attendant experience. For example, among
the Ute Indians one addresses older brothers and cousins by one term
and younger brothers and cousins by a quite different word. Separate
terms are also used for younger and older sisters as well as for older and
younger aunts and uncles. The Navajo likewise address older brothers
and younger by quite different terms, as well as older and younger sisters, but do not extend the principle to other kin. Both they and the
Eastern Apache tribes, however, have beliefs that include the idea that
older shamans or curers may "wear out" their supernatural curing power
and hence become dangerous, even to younger family relatives. Thus, they
express some ambivalence toward the elders who may in other settings
be respected for their wealth of experience (10). The Hopi Indians, who
are linguistically related to the Ute, also see to it that youth respect the
aged and they claim that this was once a time to which one could look
forward. In addition to such variations, there are tribal groups, for example in East Africa, where age-set systems along with such items as
clan membership establish the status and role of the individual (3).

One of the first cross-cultural studies of the aged in primitive societies
was done by Leo Simmons in 1945 (15). Using 71 cultures, he compiled
an extensive list of traits embodying attitudes toward the aged along with
some general socio-environmental aspects of the societies. In analyzing
relationships between the two factors, he concludes that there is tremendous variation, as we have stated above through single examples, ranging
from deeply reverential attitudes to rejection and even abandonment.
One must remember, however, as with the Siriono, that in some societies
the aged may be abandoned or even killed rather than allowed to die from
exposure or starvation. When we look back upon the Siriono beliefs, it is
obvious that an infant may be carried in this foraging economy, whereas
the elderly person presents, literally, a greater burden. Simmons noticed
that the actual prestige accorded age was highest in those societies which
fell in the middle range of socioeconomic development, so that the Siriono, whose existence is on the barest subsistence level, consider the aged
as burdens just as we, in our so-called modern, urban and civilized
society with all its advanced technology, are nevertheless noted for our

rejection of the aged while suffering from a "guilty conscience" about their actual treatment.

There have been very few studies, like Simmons', which suggest anything like an evolutionary progression linking the attitudes toward the aged with the treatment accorded them. The psychiatric and social literature has tended, rather, to discuss individual countries or cultures only as specific cases. For example, this author might report having visited psychiatric installations in Denmark devoted to the aged in which great effort was expended upon both their physical care and the preservation of their individuality.

THE APPROACH TO PSYCHO-GERIATRICS

It is thought best in this chapter to exclude the special problems of senility which have a purely biological origin. Our reason for so doing is that there seems to be no set correlation by age between chronological age and such things as hardening of the arteries. We have worked with Indian informants, such as Buckskin Charlie of the Southern Ute Indians during the period in which he reached and passed the age of 100 with no impairment of his mental faculties, although he was sorely beset with advanced stages of tuberculosis of the lungs near the end. As all know, other persons show "wear and tear" in relatively younger age brackets such as the decade of the 40s or 50s. Because of this lack of a firm correlation between chronological old age and biological aging processes, we prefer to work chiefly with the cultural variables (including social classes where they occur) in a more direct relationship with the cultural concepts about aging, the attitudes toward the care of the aged, or their rejection, and the questions concerning the psychodynamics of an aging continuum.

For example, it has been pointed out in our society that persons who do not plan for the enjoyable aspects of retirement suddenly may be confronted, after their busy lives, with a sense of futility and worthlessness. There are case histories where this lack of interests, hobbies, and friendly social contacts leaves the individual all the more isolated and alienated. In the Midtown Manhattan Research Study, for which the author was a principal investigator, it was found that both men and women in the central Manhattan borough of New York City showed a positive correlation between aging, even within the limit of 60 years, and progressively worsening mental health (12). One construction on this fact is aging, but the other is neglect of antecedent psychiatric problems. What we mean is that, in our society, people find it perfectly rational to get physical and dental care periodically, but psychiatric problems are usually not attended to until they become a kind of "clear and present danger." Or, to put this another way, individuals may seek biological remedies for psychosomatic ailments such as migraine headache, asthma, peptic ulcer and the like, without ever dreaming that therapeutic interventions of a more psychological sort might lay their psycho-biological problems to rest.

A second aspect of the approach to psycho-geriatrics must include the fact that cultures themselves are often in a transitional status which reflects into the activities of their older people. The Eskimos are a case in point. When the author some time ago was studying Alaskan Eskimos on a V. Stefansson fellowship from Columbia University, the Alaskan Eskimos were just beginning to change in culture from earlier classical or original models. In the terminology of anthropology, Alaskan Eskimo culture was beginning to be more "acculturated" than, for example, the Greenland Eskimos. Classical Eskimo literature describes Eskimo attitudes toward aging in their far northern climate somewhat in the same manner as the Siriono who are naked in the jungles of Eastern Bolivia. That is, the ancient Eskimo often abandoned the very old and infirm because of their dead weight in a highly mobile hunting and gathering society. The Eskimo also formerly believed in a kind of reincarnation of each person with the added belief that if one died in a decrepit and elderly ailing state, that person's health would be beset with afflictions in the next re-incarnation. There were other mythological beliefs to buttress up this abandonment of the very old. For example, in the Sedna Myth, the Eskimo justified another custom, namely that of carefully gathering up the bones of slain and eaten sea mammals, such as seals, and casting them back into the sea in the belief that they, too, would be reincarnated in baby seals and thus replenish this important source of food supply.

At the time I was studying Alaskan Eskimos, we noticed that the mentally ill sent down to the receiving hospital for Alaskans, in Portland, Oregon (the Morningside Clinic and Hospital which received Eskimos, Tlingits, Tsimshians, frontier Whites, etc., from the Northern Territory), included no cases of senile dementias, but had several with physical impairments, who were middle-aged, such as hunchbacks, accident cases and the like. At this time the elderly Eskimos were still putting an end to their current existences, easily achieved by exposing oneself to the elements, with a favorite method being jumping into icy waters and dying in "deep freeze" in a matter of minutes. One would hardly call this "suicide" (though people ignorant of Eskimo beliefs and attitudes tossed that term around frequently), since such elderly persons were happily and voluntarily assigning themselves a healthy new life in their next reincarnation.

The author has conferred with A. McElroy on transitional beliefs among the Eskimo of today where the conditions in the state of Alaska or around Frobisher Bay have changed markedly. Of signal importance is that the elderly now receive old age pensions and hence add to the cash economy of a family group. Secondly, the Eskimos who always widely practiced adoption both of infants and of young children still continue this practice so that younger people grow up side by side with the elderly; indeed the elderly find such young individuals belonging to them powerful impediments against feeling that they are getting to be old and isolated. Thirdly, the hunting and gathering mobility is rapidly changing over into a widespread condition of urbanization, and in the new cash economy older men may busy themselves carving soapstone art objects or may find more sedentary employment just as older women may. Still a fourth factor is that marriage, which has always been somewhat brittle among the Eskimo, now frequently eventuates in later marital liaisons with younger mates, and this in turn means that there will again be younger employed children around and also in some instances increasing birth rates. Thus, the Eskimo have moved far from the simple hunting and gathering subsistence level of the Siriono, though the men still go off to hunt and fish, both for economic supplement and for recreation.

It can be seen from the case of the modern Eskimo that the position of the aged has improved in recent years. On the other hand, it can be claimed that in our own still more modernized urban society, the position of the aged has worsened, except for such individual national situations, e.g. as we have mentioned for care in Denmark. A chief detriment to the emotional and physical health of the elderly is our cultural attitude toward them in the so-called "affluent societies."

As Dr. K. Wolff has stated, our century is the "century of youth" (16). He attributes this emphasis to our social and economic goals, based on continuous competition, the value of working compulsively, and our strenuous efforts to improve social status. He feels we have left little time for the values of recreation, relaxation and the beauty of the natural world, adding that the arts such as music, painting and literature are considered in the American *ethos* as time-wasters. He likewise holds that family life is slighted, and that the new mores stress sexual experimentation rather than love relationships.

In commenting upon this bleak picture of a world ridden with tension, competition and the compulsion to work, we would add that the large numbers of young people in our population have made them a highly important consumer market; that the economic inflation of the most advanced nations has, at the same time, made the elderly, in situations other than the more marginal Eskimo economics, a more prudently spending population; and that the lack of subsidization of the arts and weak protection of natural ecological resources have conspired to exaggerate the very factors which Dr. Wolff mentions. In other words, this is indeed a century of youth, but in addition the urbanization and economic processes have shoved the aged into a more dependent role. The attempts to ward off these effects, like the Senior Citizens clubs in the United States, are really open only to the relatively more affluent and leisurely older people. However, certain cultural groups in the United States have organized not only day care and nursery schools for children of working mothers, but have promoted the maintenance of recreational clubs and associations for the elderly.

When the author was studying cultural groups in the Midtown Manhattan Mental Health Research Study, we found that the Czech-Americans had organized in their community centers and in their social clubs called *Sokols* age-graded organizations from the kindergarten age to the grandparental generation including for each a wide variety of social, athletic, recreational and artistic activities. Once yearly, on Randall's Island, the Czechs put on an athletic event in which males and females of each age group from grandchild to grandfather and grandmother perform in gymnastics, singing, marching, etc. There were, as a matter of fact, 100 delegate organizations in Bohemian National Hall, theatricals put on additionally by the Jan Huss House, and in decent weather Czech picnics for all ages in every available park space of greater New York.

Obviously, psychological and cultural approaches to geriatrics must include knowledge of already existing community resources if the Danish and Czech-American cases are any use as criteria. However, there are other cultural examples where neither the society nor its subcultures have provided the mechanisms for treating the elderly with decency and respect.

It must also be remembered that aging is on the specific watershed of the life continuum which ties in with cultural conceptions concerning illness and death. Societies which include techniques for the prevention of illness and disability at the far end of this continuum are rare indeed. It was, therefore, striking to see in the Danish institution of geriatrics in Copenhagen a considerable number of modern medical facilities. There was correction therapy for diabetes and the recognition of the needs for pedicure, since lower extremities are sometimes affected. One also noted physical and hydrotherapy, exercise machines (somewhat like stationary bicycles), proper attention to diet and outside exercise (like simple walking in parks and gardens), and also specific corrective therapies for particular residents. On the psychological side, one was even more impressed by the arts and crafts, the latter including very clever forms of toy-making for little children. There was little need for direct psychiatric referral because clubs and games mitigated the frequent irascibility of aged persons who are in other circumstances bored or neglected. Club rooms and craft workshops were brightly or pleasantly decorated so that one hardly felt the heavy aura of the usual "institution." Most delightful were the individual rooms, each one decorated with the favorite possessions of its owner, and all containing family pictures or personally selected art, or both. There was a good deal of population movement between this center and both the relatives and friends outside. We view such efforts as constructive, appropriate, and preventive since attention is paid to the psychological needs and individuality of each person. The economics of such an effort is that younger working family members do not feel trapped by medical and nursing necessities of their older relatives and consequently are free to work, travel, and enjoy their separate existences, as well as their relationship to the older family member. In the Czech community, where clubs performed such functions in their community center in New York, it was frequently said that the total family was better off and the elderly more secure even in their situation where the elders slept at home and visited the center on day or evening schedules.

The American experience with nursing homes, which are largely impersonal economic ventures when conducted privately, has a number of built-in difficulties such as inadequate screening techniques for licensing, the profit motive, and a general lack of training in the medical and psychological aspects of the aging process. Institutions run on "social work" principles and often under religious auspices, such as the Jewish or the Catholic, are felt to be doing a better job because they are charitably subsidized and better able to hire and supervise professional personnel. Further, the uniform religious label sometimes, though not always, provides a cohesiveness in cultural background which makes the resident more secure in his surroundings. During the Midtown Studies in New York City, although we found few national subcultural communities as well-organized as the Czechs to develop geriatric resources, it was nevertheless apparent that the better the community was organized for its own mutual benefit, the more it accomplished towards this desirable end. There were also subcultural differences in the strength of family bonds outside the framework of institutional intervention. The Southern Italians, or Italo-Americans had a pattern of matrilocality with the daughter's mother often living with the daughter's family. Irish-Americans also emphasized matri-centered households; and the Western or Bohemian Czechs differed in their emphases upon the women of the household handling the family budget from the Eastern or Slovakian Czechs who were patriarchal and patrilineal in emphasis. We use the word matri-centered to signify cultures in which there is more egalitarian emphasis on the status of women. Obviously, since females typically have longer life spans than males in modern societies, the matri-centered cultures tend to handle the problems of the elderly with greater concern for their welfare.

Obviously, also, the range of these attitudes toward aging in different cultures, varying from such acculturating peoples as the modern Eskimo down to ethnic minority groups in the center of Manhattan, strongly implies that cultural or subcultural groups either facilitate or impede the emotional problems associated with geriatrics. Of course, these traditional attitudes interweave with the individual case and that in turn may reflect highly individualistic or special physical conditions or needs. Take, for example, the case of an elderly widow who has always had the benefit of a wide circle of relatives who respect and cherish her. Under modern urban conditions of the small nuclear family and widespread job mobility, this matriarch may find that younger relatives who are starting out economically are forced to move to other locales, thus reducing the natural emotional supplies she had formerly enjoyed. As she goes from grandmother to great-grandmother status, this isolation may be increased except for holiday occasions and the like. Finally, at the very time when physical resources are waning, emotional isolation is increased. We have commented above on the manner in which Danish geriatrics institutions meet this problem squarely. We have also noted how the modernizing Eskimo woman of advancing years may adopt younger children as a safeguard against future isolation, and support them with old-age pension increments.

Thus, some societies have naturally evolved means for safeguarding the aged which are not institutional in character (e.g. the modernizing Eskimo). Others, like the Danish, carefully plan total institutional safeguards which have a real touch of humanness in their make-up. Still others, like the Czech-Americans of Midtown Manhattan, set up day care programs for the aged in the form of social and recreational interest groups and further support this with kinds of formalized activities as in their age-graded *Sokols* in New York City. Since the Czech culture is extremely good at forming well-developed organized means for promoting this function, we find in the Midtown Studies that they safeguarded the aging process far better than the neighboring ethnic enclaves of the Hungarian-Americans and German-Americans who bordered their area. If one knows these ethnic and subcultural differences, one can utilize them in planning community resources. But beyond this, we feel, the subcultural variability in organizing services for the aged plus the increasing life span of humans in urban society calls for overall planning of the Danish variety.

To concretize what is meant by the necessity of planning for the aged, one can simply consider cases in the United States where the whole matter is left up to the individual entrepreneurship of developing profit-making "nursing homes." Various studies have shown that many of these are improperly organized from health and recreational standpoints. The matriarch or patriarch who falls within the confines of the worst of these may lose all zest for life, become bedridden and dependent to a larger extent sooner than necessary. In addition a second argument for the Danish plan is that extreme old age may beset a segment of this population and thus require more medical and expert intervention to alleviate misery and pain.

Finally, there is the less-aged and infirm category in which zest is lacking less because of the wearing down of the biological mechanisms than for intrinsic psychological reasons. This category includes persons who may retire from more active existences only to find that they have not planned for a final period of leisure or separation from work. It is well-known that the psychiatric categories of senility may actually span several of the old age decades, and taint these with irascibility or irritability. We have clinically found that such "seniles" may range from ages as young as the upper 40s through the 80s and may refer to people who have had a running psychological battle with younger family members, reaching back into the past. Or, one could consider Freud's own classic case of Anna O. who had both hysterical and at least one schizophrenic episode which was apparently overcome. Anna went on in her life to be a highly successful innovator in the field of social work, following remission of her symptoms. Nevertheless, at the height of her troubles earlier in life, she capitulated to hysteria because of the difficult pressure of submerging her own career in order to enact the dutiful guise of a daughter devoted to a demanding and aged mother. It is our belief that more family therapy is required in geriatrics cases, where the family members are as contiguous as were those of Anna.

The approach to psycho-geriatrics, therefore, must include the gamut of factors which comprise the social and cultural, the psychological, the biological or medical, and, of course, the recreational. More will be said of this in the following section.

CROSS-CULTURAL APPROACHES TO THE CARE OF THE AGED

Having just stated that the factors affecting the elderly must include the social and cultural as well as the psychological, it is important to discuss the cultural evolutionary continuum which may affect such care. We have already indicated that while a good many hunting and gathering societies find difficulties in coping with the biological impediments of aging, they may, like the Eskimo, develop methods for abandoning the very old and infirm through such religious beliefs as the notion of their re-incarnation into a new life. Similarly, the Siriono of a jungle climate abandon or kill the aged with less emphasis upon moral values simply to prevent the aged from experiencing the unpleasant consequences of starvation. But these are extreme examples from extreme climates. My own fieldwork among Ute, Paiute and Eastern Apache tribes discloses that these hunters and gatherers actually have value systems which include respect for the aged. While these peoples simultaneously express ambivalence towards older family members through such concepts as the belief that shamans may overuse their power and hence become a source of danger for relatives, they feel that age has the connotations of experience and knowledge in most instances. We are not suggesting that there is a kind of linear evolution in the attitudes toward the elderly because there may be further historical variations involved. For example, the settled agricultural Hopi Indians of Arizona are linguistically closely related to the Ute and Paiute, and Hopi beliefs on this level show a close relationship to those of the related linguistic groups (10).

From an ethical point of view, one can say that hunting and gathering peoples are generally not harsh in their attitudes towards older tribal members, and neither are early agriculturalists or tribes which practice animal husbandry. The reader is reminded again of the Middle Eastern tradition which often viewed old age, as among the ancient Hebrews or the Sheikdoms of the Middle East, as an important status for humans. Again we are reminded of Leo Simmons' study which pointed out that prestige was accorded the elderly in those societies which fell in the middle range of socioeconomic development (15). On the other hand, our so-called modern Protestant ethic tends to remove social supports from aging so that, possibly, even our recent emphases upon the importance of youth culture may be thematically linked with notions of "doing your own thing" and individualistically making one's way in the social order. Hence, perhaps, the result is our relative neglect of the problems of the elderly except in such instances as in Scandinavian countries, where planned programs have been devised by experts.

A social and cultural continuum concerning attitudes or themes in cultures no doubt will relate to the presence or absence of psychological burdens which age connotes. It is usually assumed in our psychiatric nomenclature that depression is the phenomenon which besets the elderly, regardless of cultural background. Yet we know that the epidemiology of depression itself shows great variations in modern settings, to which we should add that there are multivariant "masks of depression." Our habits of naming things in psychiatry in a wholly ethnocentric way has, indeed, led to some overemphases on terms like "agitated depression," or "involutional melancholia" of a given life stage past middle age. Such notions are excessively rigid in addition to being ethnocentric. For example an anthropologist well versed in transcultural psychiatry would be quick to point out that such disorders as *Latah* among the Javanese of Indonesia, or the so-called *Imu* illness of the Ainu of Hokkaido both have a higher prevalence among women past the child-bearing age who in addition have been caught up in further conditions of psychological stress. In the first type, *Latah*, the woman may show evidence of a kind of compulsion to pun obscenely; in the second, *Imu*, these women are often upset by any kind of startle reaction such as a sudden noise or a harsh command, whereupon they become prone to a kind of catatonic-like manneristic behavior which can be either a slavish imitation of the orders from others (versus even imitating the movements of another person) or enacting negativistically the very opposite behavior as if in obstinacy. Throughout Malaysia, as a matter of fact, and among certain well-known tribes in northeastern Siberia, these syndromes which sometimes go under the misnomer of Arctic Hysteria are very frequent. We mention these specific ailments as cultural types in this context because they happen to have both an age and sex distribution. There is some additional evidence that the so-called "confusional states" of various parts of Africa are also transcultural cousins to the above (9). We should also add that in modern countries like the United States masked depression happens to be the most prevalent form of affective state disorder, although it is not ordinarily even noticed, unfortunately, by the average untrained person until it matures into more overt forms of extremely hypomanic behavior or its "depth of depression" opposite (11).

Any psychiatrist knows of the relationship between depression and hypomania or the fact that depressive states contain large components of hostility and aggression. Further, those who have affective disorders sometimes have exaggerated expectations of the "object world." Edith Jacobson describes a case with a loving but domineering mother whose early sexual and aggressive prohibitions led to compensatory high degree of glorification and admiration for her love objects, making her further vulnerable to deep narcissistic injuries. Such persons may move into acting-out phases to restore deflated self-esteem in our culture (6). But in the so-called primitive civilizations, we must remember, relationships are more diffuse within a larger body of kindred, in contrast with our small, nuclear family of parents and children. Consequently, we suggest, acting-out phases to restore deflated self-esteem in our culture (6). But settlement, the encampment, the band or the kindred group. A woman of the Luya tribe in Kenya had periodic spells of acting-out followed by remissions, and in the hypomanic phases flamboyantly enacted the role of a seductive adolescent girl or produced disturbances by excited babbling or even a clattering of pots and pans. These confusional states with much more socially unaccepted acting-out than we condone in our society obviously had a cathartic value for her since they were, indeed, followed by remission back to normal conduct. We introduce these elements of a somewhat aggressive and uncurbed mode of behavior because we note that throughout Malaysia adult males are known for sheer aggressive behavior exemplified in the well-known syndrome of running amok. In contrast, Arctic Hysteria among the Eskimo may be the mode of disturbance common for women in particular (those past child-bearing years).

We have just referred to these syndromes as disorders of disturbed communication because they are just that. For example Jurgen Ruesch furnishes a table in his book on disturbed communication in our society in which he takes the life period of later adulthood (45-65, approximately) and states that normal functioning in the output of information, as in teaching or in participation in decision-making groups, may become transformed into a realization of failure to implement self-chosen ideals (14). As a further illustration of what may be involved, we speak in the United States of the generation gap between adults on the one hand and adolescents and youth on the other. But in the United States, all too frequently, we view this from the vantage point of the young people, whereas it should be added that those in later adulthood may suffer from an interference in communication with this younger generation. We therefore feel that the isolation and separation of the aged from children and youth is artificial and arbitrary, and doubtless causes harm. Again, we may refer back to the Eskimo efforts of adults to consolidate their social position with the young through such modalities as adoption.

Ruesch also tabulates an age of retirement (from 65 on, approximately). The great hazard for this more advanced age group is inactivity and isolation. If there is sudden withdrawal from participation in communication networks, he holds that the lack of stimulation may be overwhelming. We are reminded of the age-graded societies in the East African cattle-raising areas which formalize a system, much like the age-grading in the Czech *Sokols,* whereby those in later adulthood or in the age of retirement do have specific and honorable functions in the culture.

What has apparently happened in modern, urbanized societies is that family structure has changed remarkably, undercutting such "privileges" of the aging process. For one thing the family has changed from extended family types in human history to the small nuclear family. One hundred years ago, in the United States, the family was composed of many generational levels ordinarily living under one roof. Since that was one phase of the Industrial Revolution we can set the larger contrast of an earlier family form, engaged in agriculture more predominantly, living in intergenerational groupings, and certainly less dependent upon outside agencies for the production and processing of food, the making of clothing, the maintenance and repair of family homesteads, and the relationship of these family networks to other similar large bodies in the surrounding community. In large part, these economic shifts to dependency on manufactured goods and services and the gradual displacement of small entrepreneurial farming have transformed the family into a small nuclear unit of parents and children, with a generation gap increasing as the latter must early in the game find their own social and economic identities. The metropolis has sprung into being. Modes of mass communication and more highly technique-ridden educational systems with ever-increasing specialization have supplanted the educational and informational media of former times. Thus the family has changed markedly—in location, in size, in economic dependency, and in the intergenerational conflict of its values and ideologies. All this has made later adulthood stages more vulnerable to the attendant processes of economic dislocations, intergenerational conflicts, the obsolescence of values—at least from the majority point of view—and the hazards of interferences with any possible identifications with the younger generation, plus isolation, boredom, or sheer neglect.

It is clear that cross-cultural approaches to the care of the aged must begin with the independent variable of cultural, subcultural and class attitudes towards the aging process. This independent variable relates immediately to the kinds of psychological stress systems to which the elderly are exposed. The dependent variable, consequently, becomes the psychodynamics and defense mechanisms used by the elderly in response to the first two types of factors. This is not to say that the culture patterns and the cultural attitudes produce a rigid mold for all individuals. Individualized life experiences occur within every culture, subculture and social class. Therefore, the psychological stress systems will vary, even though they statistically may show a neat bell-shaped distribution. With the psychodynamics, the situation is the same, largely because of the complexity of our human material, because of spare adjustive "machinery" which every person has, and also because of the way in which the defense system has possibly been overused. We are thus interested in epidemiological approaches which will throw the most light upon the central tendencies in the care or neglect of the aged as well as upon possible variations from these central tendencies. Epidemiology becomes important because it can quantify matters like the amounts of psychological stress and the amounts of consequential disturbance. The finding we have already reported for the Midtown Manhattan Study, namely that mental health disabilities increased by age, immediately implies that in our cities we have not yet solved the problem of the care of the aged in any respectable sense.

The treatment of the aged in psychiatric settings like hospitals can include individual and group psychotherapy, milieu therapy, and outpatient work. But, as we have pointed out above, it would be disastrous to fail to recognize cultural, subcultural and class differences in designing programs or developing individualized plans for treatment.

Because the terms, culture and subculture, embody the whole range of group responses to clusters of events, anthropologists often refer to the cultural beliefs, attitudes and behavioral patterns which events call forth. In fact, when we say responses, we therefore must include both cognitive and emotional patterns of the person responding. We could use other terms, such as "mind set," or allude to cultural definitions of the situation. The various cultural patterns and themes may therefore help or hinder the individual responding to series of events, whether these be beneficial or harmful in his cognitive and emotional processes. For such reasons we feel that terms like culture, subculture, and class contain the conditions of existence which make psychological stresses either more or less probable.

THE PSYCHODYNAMICS OF THE AGING PROCESS

Having indicated that culture, subculture and class are highly formative independent variables which may induce or abate psychological stresses for the individual, it is important next to scrutinize the most probable range of psychodynamic processes that respond to the cultural induction of stress (8). As we have stated above in connection with the Midtown Manhattan Mental Health Study, aging itself can be a hazardous process. Yet we have indicated by examples from the modernizing conditions among the Eskimo or by the national programs of intervention such as Denmark's that the hazards can be mitigated, again, by cultural arrangements. Culture, subculture and class taken together therefore provide a vast arc of possibilities, not just for individuals singly but for groups of given ages. The further fact that nations and cultures are formed in the crucible of history can make us perhaps less pessimistic about the deplorable conditions of the aged in our own modern civilization.

Turning squarely to the probable psychodynamic processes cross-culturally, we can note in modern societies that psychosomatic illnesses seem to have increased in various age and sex categories. For example, asthma has no age specificity, yet it seems to have increased per population number or in its incidence. On the other hand, rheumatoid arthritis is, indeed, more age-specific to the adult and older population. Peptic ulcer was once more commonly a female ailment, then shifted to the male of the species and is now shifting back, and in addition, there has been a surprising increase of peptic ulcer, which used to be an adult disease, down into a younger aged population. Despite these variations in age and sex distribution, the overall increase taken together would seem to indicate that psychosomatic disorders are prodromal symptoms of what now has come to be known as masked depression (11).

We have introduced the term masked depression, because the ordinary approaches to the psychodynamics of maturity and old age deal usually with other terms in the European and American psychiatric nomenclature, such as involutional melancholia or, for the still later ages, the disturbances of senescence. Often the writers in psychiatry assume that menopause in women and other middle-aged crises in men bring on as biological events the psychological results of involutional melancholia or agitated depression due to aging or even the specific diseases of senility later on. With these notions of biological causation, crude as they are, we utterly disagree. For instance, as we have pointed out above, certain psychosomatic disorders such as asthma and juvenile diabetes occur, albeit rarely, in children and youth. In like manner, we know that depressions may affect even infants, and R. Spitz through various studies called the infantile reactions to deprivation by his term, anaclitic depression. Adolescents have masked depressions. Nevertheless, the peak point for masked depression classically in many cultures of the world occurs statistically in the group past middle age, including post-menopausal women and males in the parallel age categories (11).

The psychiatric nomenclature on types of depression, of course, runs a gamut from normal grief and reactive depression because of deprivations to such psychotic categories as the depressive states including the manic depressive and the involutional melancholia mentioned above. Masked depression with its prodromal psychosomatic symptoms runs a much larger course from lightly neurotic to psychotic manifestations. The work of S. Lesse, R. Spiegel and others on hostility and acting out as masks of depression is gaining increasing attention in the United States. As an anthropologist, this author has stated for some time that agitated and confusional states reported from African cultures are also probably masked depressions in which both the hostile activity and the excited confusions are defensive modes of behavior which hold back the emergence of depression in these primitive cultures (9). While such psychoanalysts as P. Greenacre and G. Baker have noted that types of infantile abandonment or gaps in mothering destroy the possibility of child or even infantile trust in parents, it remains for the anthropologist to note that such occurrences happen also in nonliterate cultures. In these societies the person who "mothers" may be one other than the biological mother. Later on in the life cycle such persons may show agitated euphoria, confusional states with considerable acting out, and may be the very ones who disturb the village, the encampment or the extended family group with uncontrollable hostile behavior.

In our society, it has been found that masked depression, even though it appears without overt depressive signs at all, is actually the most prevalent form of any of the depressive state disorders. With us, also, it occurs in a broad age range from children to the very old. However, in our culture, the peak of its occurrence goes from what we have called above maturity into old age, including the post-menopausal phase in women. Further, its epidemiology is highest among women; this suggests that gaps in the mothering process place a special burden upon mothers in our own society. Often, the prodromal psychosomatic masks of depression disappear and masked depression itself emerges. Since such cases show considerable vitality and ability to cope with inner conflicts, some of them in our society go through this stage and emerge into remission or abatement of both the psychosomatic and the later psychological symptoms.

For one contrast, the nonliterate cultures typically do not utilize the psychosomatic defenses as frequently as their culture bearers evidence simple hysterical patterns of behavior. Further, in the acting-out stages, persons from nonliterate cultures may show a more florid, if temporary, disturbance. In modern societies, the spouse or parent of opposite sex or some other individual in the nuclear family provides the most convenient target for the hostility. The diffusion of hostility shown by various persons in nonliterate societies is a consequence of the fact that more extended kin groups larger than the nuclear family are available targets. Finally, remissions are more easily achieved in nonliterate cultures exactly because of the florid acting out, whereas such catharsis is far more limited in modern societies because of our various impediments and blockages or social constraints preventing a honest and direct expression of inner turmoil and feeling.

Although nonliterate societies handle the problems of aging outside institutionalized buildings, modern society typically utilizes nursing homes and mental hospitals for elderly patients. In one study of two geriatric populations in mental hospitals the authors found two groups. The first consisted of patients who had grown old in the hospital while receiving merely custodial care and who could have been more suitably accommodated in better nursing homes had the communities provided these. The second group had less physical disability and could even take care of themselves in a ward setting with less dependency on nursing staff for day-to-day basic needs. Another group, outside the mental hospitals, consisted of persons in nursing homes who had suffered a severe physical disability but who were at the same time the most elderly of all three groups (1). As a consequence of this study and others like it, psychiatrists in the United States believe that elderly patients are unnecessarily admitted to mental hospitals, including some who are merely feeble and non-psychotic but with physical illnesses. In one of the most ambitious studies of aging and mental disorders, conducted in San Francisco (7), the authors reach a similar conclusion, namely that pressures from the external world have an effect upon the self-assessment of older people. Age-linked stresses or loss of social role resulting from widowhood or retirement are precipitants of conflict only when the individual lacks other important sources of social recognition or morale. As Helene Deutsch observed long ago in 1945 of women's psychic adjustment in the menopausal phase, this depends upon her own psychological assets or liabilities and her own opinion of the real meaning of her existence (2).

In other words the psychodynamics of the aging process depend upon cultural attitudes towards elderly persons as a category of human beings which can in turn influence their treatment as well as their self-assessments. There are obviously cultures in which aging and even the illnesses of the elderly constitute less of a hazard. There are also other societies which penalize the elderly or neglect them or hide them away in mental hospitals under neglectful procedures of custodial care. Perhaps, in addition to the various social minorities which we constantly allude to in modern society, such as deprived racial groups, women, and those of lower socioeconomic status, we shall have to include the elderly, for whom the nuclear family makes less and less provision. The wasteful economics of such neglect stands in sharp contrast with the social costs required for progressive programs such as tiny Denmark has already instituted.

REFERENCES

1. BURVILL, P. W., GRUENBERG, E. M., and SOLOMON, M. 1971. Comparative study of elderly Dutchess County patients in mental hospitals and nursing homes. *Soc. Psychiat.*, 6:61-65.
2. DEUTSCH, H. 1945. *The Psychology of Women: A Psychoanalytic Interpretation*, Vol. II. New York: Grune and Stratton.
3. GULLIVER, P. H. 1969. *Tradition and Transition in East Africa*. Berkeley and Los Angeles: University of California Press.
4. GUTHRIE, W. K. C. 1952. *Orpheus and Greek Religion*. London: Methuen.
5. HOLMBERG, A. 1969. *Nomads of the Long Bow: The Siriono of Eastern Bolivia*. Garden City, New York: Natural History Press.

6. JACOBSON, E. 1971. *Depression: Comparative Studies of Normal, Neurotic, and Psychotic Conditions.* New York: International Universities Press.
7. LOWENTHAL, M. F. 1967. *Aging and Mental Disorders in San Francisco.* San Francisco: Jossey-Bass Inc., Publishers.
8. OPLER, M. K. 1967. The cultural induction of stress. In: Appley, M. H. and Trumbull, R. (Eds.) *Psychological Stress.* New York: Appleton-Century-Crofts.
9. OPLER, M. K. 1967. Preface to the enlarged edition. In: Opler, M. K., (Ed.) *Culture and Social Psychiatry.* New York: Aldine-Atherton Press.
10. OPLER, M. K. 1971. The Ute and Paiute Indians of the Great Basin Southern Rim. In: Leacock, E. B., and Lurie, N. O. (Eds.) *North American Indians in Historical Perspective.* New York: Random House.
11. OPLER, M. K. 1972. Cultural variations of depression: past and present. In: Lesse, S. (Ed.) *The Multivariant Forms of Depression.* Boston: Little, Brown and Co.
12. OPLER, M. K., et al. 1962. *Mental Health in the Metropolis.* (Vol. 1 of the Midtown Manhattan Research Study). New York: McGraw-Hill.
13. PATAI, R. 1959. *Sex and Family in the Bible and the Middle East.* New York: Doubleday Dolphin Books.
14. RUESCH, J. 1957. *Disturbed Communication.* New York: W. W. Norton and Co., Inc.
15. SIMMONS, L. 1945. *The Role of the Aged in Primitive Society.* New Haven: Yale University Press.
16. WOLFF, K. 1963. *Geriatric Psychiatry.* Springfield, Illinois: Charles C Thomas.

4

PATHOLOGY OF DEMENTIA

RICHARD G. BERRY, M.D.

Professor of Neurology and Pathology (Neuropathology)
Jefferson Medical College of Thomas Jefferson University
Philadelphia, Pa.

INTRODUCTION

Dementia is a clinical syndrome of manifold origins. As such, the underlying pathology varies amongst disease groups and often amongst the individual patients within each group.

In its simplest forms dementia describes the deterioration of mental processes. New facts can no longer be stored. Lost is the ability to retrieve and synthesize past or present facts and experiences in order to plan for the future. At times, especially early in the disease, old established experiences, habits and memory may not be involved. Confusion of time, of physical environment and of the patient's relation to the environment becomes a cardinal manifestation of dementia. This implies amongst other things effect on memory, especially for recent events. In some cases confabulation is a prominent feature of the demented state. The personality—the patient's intellectual functioning, his awareness of his place in his own social environs, his response to interpersonal and environmental stimuli—deteriorates to the level of a "vegetative" existence.

The use of such almost self-evident but vague concepts forewarns of the inherent difficulties of defining *the* pathology of dementia. We shall review the morphologic substrate encountered in the brain in the more common dementing processes. In so doing, a brief summary of the morphology of the central nervous system as it can be affected in

51

dementing processes will be followed by an attempt to find a common denominator in the pathology of these disease entities. The final sections will describe in more detail those individual diseases, the cardinal symptom of which is a disintegration of memory, intellect and premorbid personality.

Inherent in the term dementia is the implication of an insidiously progressive deterioration of the "mind." Some cases of dementia with sudden onset and apparent lack of progression can, however, serve as examples from which generalizations may be allowed. This presentation, nevertheless, will emphasize the chronic progressive dementias, especially of the presenium and senility.

GENERAL FEATURES IN PATHOLOGY OF DEMENTIA

Cerebral Atrophy and Aging

The normal adult human brain weighs between 1200 and 1400 grams, showing a positive correlation with body length. There is a general belief that atrophy of the brain (in the absence of focal vascular disease) is correlated with age, and specifically that brain weight declines in the decades of the senium, with a 5% weight loss by age 70, to 20% loss in the 10th decade (52). Although individual examples abound showing this is not invariable, statistical evaluation of large samples demonstrates the general trend (80). Seldom, however, has the agonal period been adequately investigated to elucidate such variables as terminal anoxia and its consequent cerebral edema with both its effect on brain weight and cellular details (45, 52, 85). Cerebral atrophy is characterized by widened sulci and narrowed gyri, the latter on cut section show a thinning of the cortical mantle. The amount of white matter in the centrum semi-ovale may be quite deficient when compared with a normal specimen and under these circumstances the corpus callosum is thin. There is a symmetric dilatation of the ventricular system, especially the frontal and inferior horns of the lateral ventricles. With this increase in ventricular and subarachnoid space an increase in cerebrospinal fluid is present—the picture of an *hydrocephalus ex vacuo.*

In the severe atrophy of subsequently described disease processes, proliferation of fibrous glia in the grey or white matter of the atrophied specimen confers a rubbery consistency to palpation and a resistance to cutting, the basis of the descriptive term *sclerosis.*

Histologic Structure and Reactions of Central Nervous System

Histologic, cytologic and ultrastructural details of the nervous system reemphasize the functional significance of the neuron, its perikaryon, dendritic and axonal extensions. The concept of the astrocyte as a supporting structure for the neuron has been enlarged to include metabolic as well as mechanical support. Not only do its stellate processes stretch from pia to capillary and seemingly hold the neuron suspended within this glia (Virchow: glue) but through the ubiquitous cytoplasm of the astrocyte the neuron receives nutrition from the capillary. Through it, also, the products of neuronal metabolism are removed. The astrocyte functions to lay down fibrillary scars when the neuron or its components are damaged. The oligodendrocytes are concerned in the development and maintenance of the myelin sheath. Through their pulsatile properties they may also aid in the nutrition of the neuronal parikaryon (68). The elements of the reticuloendothelial system, the intrinsic microglia of light microscopy, and the pericytes of the capillaries, as well as the circulating blood monocytes, serve to remove the detritus from cellular damage. Current concepts of the phagocytic elements of the central nervous system are discussed by Vaughn and Skoff (90).

The Normal Neuron and Aging

The neuron, although of many sizes and shapes, can be simplified for descriptive purposes into a globular or pyramidal shaped perikaryon as conventionally demonstrated in the Nissl stains. Unfortunately much of the essential complexity of the cell is lost in this classical method and we tend to lose sight of the essence of neuronal activity. The perikaryon as thus seen is only a small part of the cell. Myriad processes (dendrites) enlarge the functional surface of the cell itself and upon these dendrites even smaller spine-like processes further extend the surface available for contact with other cells (69). The efferent extension, the axon, may be more than a meter in length and often includes more area than the perikaryon. The myelin sheath, a lipid-protein laminated complex derived from oligodendrocytes, ensheaths the axon. Synaptic contacts between axon and dendrite and cell perikaryon are being intensively studied in multidisciplinary approaches (5, 13). The average number of synapses associated with one mammalian cortical neuron has been estimated at 10^4 or 10^5 (13). It is at this synaptic level of cell function that some of the earliest detectable ultrastructural changes in dementias can be demonstrated (3, 24, 25).

The neuron contains organelles common to all cells, but especially characteristic are clumps of basophilic material (*Nissl bodies*) and argyrophilic fibrils. Rough endoplasmic reticulum accumulates into the optically visible ribonucleic acid (RNA) of the Nissl substance, a reflection of the protein manufacture that is essential to this highly specialized cell. Protein is constantly transported from the perikaryon down the axon (93, 94). One (fast) component moves at rates up to 500 mm. per day, and a slower component moves with a rate of 1 - 10 mm. per day. The fast component probably represents ultrastructural vesicles and/or mitochondria rather than neurotubular protein (27). In its specialization, however, the neuron has lost the ability to regenerate its perikaryon after the neonatal period. (Binucleated cells in some of the degenerative conditions may indicate abortive efforts in this direction.) In addition to the Nissl substance there are fibrils which have an affinity for silver (argyrophilic *neurofibrils*). With the resolution of the light microscope, under certain conditions of metabolic damage, these fine fibrils appear to condense and coalesce with evolution of Alzheimer's *neurofibrillary tangles*. (Plate I, a. b). These tangles within neurons may be found in varying numbers in the hippocampus with the advent of the senium (21, 101). They are found in greatly increased numbers in many areas of the brain in the disease of the presenium which bears Alzheimer's name, and in the dementia of the senium itself. They can be recognized even in hematoxylin-eosin preparations by their often flame-shaped or swirling refringent basophilic appearance. Similar tangles occur in other disease conditions but these lack the characteristic ultrastructural appearance described below.

The optically apparent argyrophilic neurofibrils apparently are not true constituents of the neuron but represent condensations of other structures of the cell body. With the electron microscope two filamentous structures appear: *neurofilaments,* 100 Å wide filaments of indefinite length, and *neurotubules,* 240 Å wide straight unbranched hollow tubules identical to similar organelles in cells outside the nervous system, and possibly related to the structural stability of the cell (64). The Alzheimer neurofibrillary tangles, as observed with the electron microscope, are abnormally twisted or constricted tubules. They are 200 to 220 Å in width with periodic constrictions to 100 Å every 200 Å in length and are always intracellular in location (86). Abnormal neuronal protein metabolism apparently produces these dystrophic neurofilaments (70, 86). Although amyloid-like material has been seen in these tangles with light microscopy, none is evident with the electron microscope. The reader

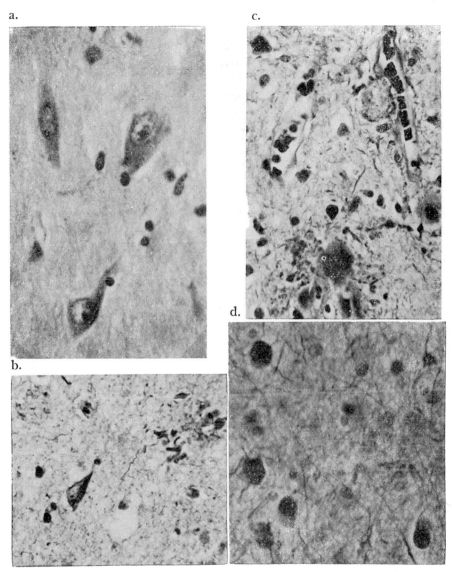

PLATE I

a. Alzheimer's disease: Hippocampus. Neurofibrillary tangles in lower neuron. The arrow points to granulovacoular change present in upper two neurons and in one to right of centre. Hematoxylin-eosin. X40 obj.

b. Alzheimer's disease: Cerebral cortex. Neurofibrillary tangles in central neuron. Senile plaques in upper left and right. Silver stain. X40 obj.

c. Alzheimer's disease: Senile plaques. Note the amyloid core (purple in original) in the large plaque below centre, and in the smaller on right border. Another paler plaque adjoins the capillary in upper right corner. Argyrophilic club-like and filamentous forms in margin of plaques are degenerating neurites. Silver and periodic acid Schiff. X40 obj.

d. Pick's disease. Argyrophilic Pick bodies in all neurons in field. Note cluster of activated astrocytes just left of centre. Holmes silver. X40 obj.

should consult Hirano (29) and Schochet (71) for succinct and lucid descriptions of the tangles.

Other significant age related structures within the neuron are accumulations of insoluble lipid protein complexes—lipochrome granules (*lipofuscin* or "wear and tear" pigment). Both the number of cells involved and the number of granules increase with aging, except for the cerebellar Purkinje cell which is spared. They are also found, sometimes as the principal light microscopic feature of neuronal disease, in some of the lipid storage diseases (see below) and are quantitatively increased in many of the dementing processes. With the light these stain for lipids, are acid fast, fluorescent, and periodic acid Schiff (PAS) positive, as well as showing considerable acid phosphatase activity indicating their kinship to lysosomes. The electron microscope shows them as "membrane bound conglomerates of lipid globules, osmophilic granules, and lamellar material" (71). They accumulate at the expense of ribonucleic acid, although little other optical evidence of damage to the perikaryon is usually seen in the normal aging process (16, 32).

With aging, specifically in the hippocampus, another striking change often occurs in the neuronal perikaryon. Varying small silver positive granules are found surrounded by clear spaces—the *granulovacuolar* change of Simchowicz (Plate Ia). Thus far the ultrastructural appearance of these membrane bound granules has added no clue as to their origin, although Hirano (29) notes their resemblance to lysosomes, and hints at an autophagic phenomenon, A significant correlation between the numbers of cells affected by granulovacuolar change and dementia is demonstrable (4, 100).

Glial Reactions

In addition to the function of *astrocytes* in normal metabolism of the neuron their reactions to neuronal damage forms an important part of the morphologic picture of most dementing diseases. At times primary astrocytic hyperplasia appears as the only optically visible disease process (75, 76). This may represent a primary reaction of the astrocyte to a noxious influence, or it may be that neuronal damage is too subtle to be discerned with available light microscopic technics. Degenerative changes seen as cytoplasmic swelling of the astrocyte and resulting in spongy degeneration may thus be primary, but more frequently a similar vacuolar degeneration of the neuron is also present. (Plate II, a-c).

In certain metabolic encephalopathies, especially those concerned with liver disease, a characteristic degenerative change occurs in these macroglia. Large naked vesiculated and other irregularly shaped, reniform astrocytes are observed in the basal nuclei and elsewhere in the cerebral grey matter. (Plate II, d) These *Alzheimer type II* astrocytes are present in many other conditions as indicators of cerebral damage.

When the neuron or its processes suffer damage, the astroglia hypertrophy and form glial fibers. This may be so extensive as to impart a palpable rubbery firmness of the CNS tissue to which the term *gliotic sclerosis* is applied.

Neuropil

The neuropil contains the innumerable glial processes, and the axons and dendrites of the neurons with the capillaries coursing through. The electron microscope demonstrates little more than a 250Å extracellular space in the cortex. Degenerative changes as a *status spongiosus* with rarefaction and microcystic spaces in this neuropil are demonstrated to be swelling of the astrocytic and neuronal processes in many dementias (75).

A spongy loosening of tissue with prominent vesicle containing fluid is the picture of status spongiosus (Plate II, a-c). It is a nonspecific reaction to many noxious influences, which result in degeneration or "selective partial necrosis" of any of the central nervous system tissue elements, neuronal or glial. Inflammations, vascular disease and trauma, which cause destruction of all tissue elements and thus are nonselective result in a "spongionecrosis," with microglia (phagocytic) activity as a prominent feature. Seitelberger (75) separates the spongy states along the lines of predominate damage:

(1) *Neuronal type* from extensive loss of neurons or from the loss of reparative powers of the glia, a "glial insufficiency." Such a status spongiosus will be present in Pick's disease, some cases of Alzheimer's disease, and the storage neuroaxonal dystrophies.

(2) *Gliogenic type*: most frequently an astrocytic status spongiosus or "glial dystrophy," in which regressive changes occur in the astrocytes and they can no longer function normally in their transport duties. The regular, sequential changes in these glia are from an hypertrophic proliferative phase through a regressive phase (classically clasmatodendrosis) with disintegration of their processes; lacunae develop upon the dissolution of the cell body. Lastly, in a "defective phase" the fibrillary astrocytes are incapable of their duty to substitute for the tissue defect.

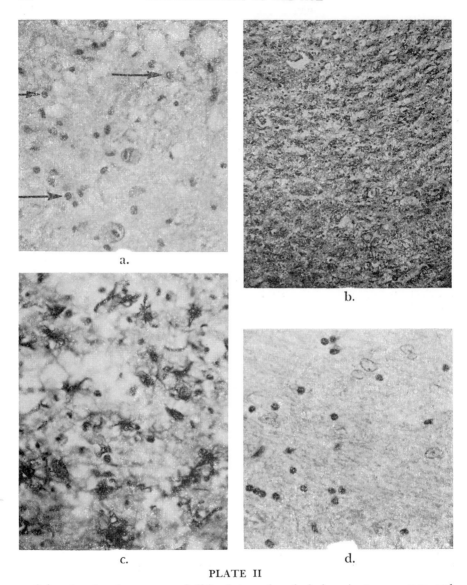

a.

b.

c.   d.

PLATE II

a. Subacute sclerozing panencephalitis: Intranuclear inclusions in two neurons and three oligodendroglia (arrows). The lower neuron has two inclusion bodies to the right of the nucleolus. Note the vacuolar spongy degeneration in the upper half of the picture. Hematoxylin-eosin. X40 obj.

b. Jakob-Creutzfeldt disease: Spongy degeneration in cerebral cortex. Practically no neurons are visible. Vacuolization of tissue, hypertrophy and hyperplasia of astrocytes replace the normal cortical pattern. Holzer. X10 obj.

c. High power of IIb: Hypertrophied fibrous astrocytes with vacuolization of background tissue. Holzer. X40 obj.

d. Hepatic encephalopathy: Alzheimer's type II astrocytes. Large clear, irregular or bilobed naked nuclei in basal ganglia. Hematoxylin-eosin. X40 obj.

Neurons and oligodendroglia thus become embedded in astrocytic fibrils around the vacuoles. Under these circumstances of primary astroglial dystrophy the neuron is secondarily damaged and disintegrates. Seitelberger (76) conceives of Jakob-Creutzfeldt disease as such a glio-neuronal dystrophy. In Wilson's disease the glioneuronal dystrophy is combined with disturbed vascular permeability. Other metabolic varieties associated with hepatic diseases and alcoholism (probably a disturbed protein metabolism) produce astrocytic and thus neuronal damage (62). When primary disorders of vessel permeability or other noxious influences result in defective oligodendroglial metabolism, the effect is principally on the myelin sheath and thus the white matter shows the brunt of damage.

In some conditions of infancy globular spheroidal or elongated eosinophilic swellings of varying argyrophilia can be observed as *neuronal dystrophies* (12). Similar discontinuous axonal swellings or retraction bulbs occur adjacent to areas of necrosis of whatever cause in grey or white matter. They are seen as an accompaniment of aging and in experimental vitamin E deficiency in the nucleus gracilis (7, 10, 20, 35, 63). Neuroaxonal dystrophy may thus be a physiologic degenerative phenomenon of the central nervous system but it is also a focal reflection of certain degenerative diseases—such as Hallervorden Spatz disease or infantile neuroaxonal dystrophy (35). The age-related loci are consistently in the posterior column nuclei and substantia nigra. Such lesions in these nuclei have also been correlated with chronic alcoholism, liver disease, and Parkinsonism (41, 76).

In the senium and in Alzheimer's disease, an argyrophilic condensation appears in the cortex and less frequently in other grey masses. These *senile plaques* have a core of amyloid material as they mature (15, 53) (Plate Ib, c). The club-like argyrophilic and basophilic processes which surround the core have been demonstrated with the electron microscope to consist of degenerated axons, dendrites and glial processes. Often astrocytic and microglial nuclei can be seen in close proximity. The relationship of the reticulo-endothelial (microglial) cells to an immune response has been postulated (40, 86).

Myelin

The myelin sheath can be damaged secondarily from direct ischemic or inflammatory reaction or from damage to the oligodendrocyte. When a neuron succumbs to acute or subacute injury or its axon is severed in the process of *Wallerian degeneration* the distal axon and its myelin sheath cannot survive; physical and chemical alterations occur in the myelin leading eventually to cholesterol and neutral fats to be phagocytized by scavenger cells. A *demyelinating disease,* on the other hand, implies a destruction of the myelin by primary attack on the myelin sheath itself with relative preservation of the axon. In conditions of unknown origin, but frequently genetically determined, an inability of the neuron to adequately maintain its axon (a *dying back process)* is accompanied by a slow distal loss of axon and its accompanying myelin sheath.

Blood Vessels

Arteriosclerosis of the large vessels is often indicted as a cause of dementia. Scattered foci of encephalomalacia of sufficient area to destroy many nerve cells can cause mental deterioration (4, 18). The clinical course with sudden onset, local signs, and tendency to partial remissions is unlike the relentless progression of the presenile dementias. The clinical diagnosis is all too often encountered in psychiatric hospitals. Our experience, in keeping with many neuropathologists (58), indicates a much less frequent association of arteriosclerosis with dementia. Much more often the classical changes of Alzheimer's disease or its senile counterpart are demonstrable without significant vascular disease either in the form of great vessel damage or parenchymal softenings. White matter softening and degeneration of myelin due to cerebral arteriosclerosis on rare occasions may be associated with dementia as in the so-called Binswanger's disease (61).

In *small artery disease,* as encountered in hypertensive cardiovascular disease, multiple small cortical scars may be sufficiently widespread to cause dementia. In a similar manner a dementia can be associated with the small leptomeningeal arterial disease of cerebral Buerger's disease, or of systemic lupus erythematosus. Hypotensive episodes and subsequent watershed lesions, junctional between main territories of vascular supply, can mimic the small vessel disease (89).

More frequently leptomeningeal and cortical vessels are the site of a hyaline degeneration which stains with light microscope technics specifically for *amyloid* (73). Although the association of this *congophilic angiopathy* with the senile plaques of Alzheimer's disease has been discounted by some (49, 86), it has been our experience that the association is not infrequent, and at times the changes in the neuropil with light microscopy do appear as a dyshoria or disturbance in vascular permeability.

Focal Versus Diffuse Pathology

A search for a single focal lesion to account for the symptoms of dementia has been fruitless. Although certain well defined areas in the human forebrain have relatively specific functions as in speech and motor activity, the higher cognitive functions are less clearly confined (8, 65, 66). There is more evidence that the total working of the brain is an essential feature of "normalcy." Put another way, it is more evident that the loss of numbers of neurons rather than the specific location of the lost neurons is the significant feature which produces the symptoms of dementia (33). Blessed, Tomlinson and Roth (1) have demonstrated that in cerebrovascular disease when over 50 cubic centimeters of tissue are damaged there is a steep proportional rise in the symptoms of dementia. There is a quantitative rather than qualitative gradation when senile plaques, as a reflection of neuronal damage, are equated against stages of dementia. The symptoms of Alzheimer's disease are thought by some to be related to degenerative changes in the limbic system, thalamus, hypothalamus and mesencephalon. A "clear threshold effect can be demonstrated in the relationship between plaques and dementia" (85). The thalamic nuclei, anterior, medial dorsal, and medial pulvinar (92) and the hippocampus (61) are essential for the recording and retrieval of recent events. It is probable that the retention of other cognitive functions is more related to number of functioning neurons than to the location of those lost.

Summary

To summarize, age correlated manifestations of cellular degeneration on a microscopic level are: diffuse lipofuscin pigment degeneration; neurofibrillary tangles; senile plaques and granulovacuolar change in the hippocampus; neuroaxonal dystrophy of the nucleus gracilis. Although the hippocampal changes have been suggested as a cause of the minor memory defects of the normal senium, clinical signs or symptoms have seldom been correlated with the dystrophic changes of the nucleus gracilis.

Because the central nervous system has only limited methods of reacting to noxious agents it can be assumed that the substrate of dementia will have no single morphologic criterion. Just as the causes are manifold, the reactions are nonspecific. We can summarize by saying that neuronal degeneration—diffuse through the cerebrum but affecting especially frontal, medial temporal and parietal cortex and probably anterior thalamus—can cause deterioration of mental activity. If the destruction is progressive, the dementia will be progressive. The causative stimuli may be infectious or metabolic, hereditary or without a known etiology. Multiple vascular lesions can result in such a clinical picture, as can expanding lesions be they neoplastic or traumatic (subdural hematoma). The reaction of other central nervous system elements such as the glial cells is usually secondary to the neuronal damage but some apparently primary glial diseases can result in neuronal degeneration. With loss of neurons and shrinkage from gliosis, atrophy will result if the process is of long enough duration.

In the following pages, morphologically specific "dementias" will be briefly described.

DEMENTIAS OF ADULT LIFE

Introduction

The most common pathological findings in dementias in adult life and in the older age groups are the diffuse atrophy and the microscopic changes of Alzheimer's disease and its histologic corrolary, senile dementia. Jakob-Creutzfeldt disease and Pick's disease are less common, the former possibly more frequently encountered than the latter. There is little difference histologically between Alzheimer's disease and "simple" senile dementia and for that reason they will be discussed together. In all three entities exciting new insight has been recorded in ultrastructural studies in the past decade, and in Jakob-Creutzfeldt disease in the demonstration of an infectious origin in some cases. Several useful reviews have appeared recently (71, 76, 78, 88) and a symposium on Alzheimer's disease (99) gives a stimulating and comprehensive discussion of that entity. Other less common causes of presenile dementias will be mentioned in passing.

In childhood and adolescence dementia results from diffuse neuronal degeneration of an infectious process, from neuronal "storage" disease, from diffuse degeneration of the white matter as a leukoencephalopathy (various forms of "Schilder's disease"), myoclonic epilepsy with Lafora bodies, and from the rare dystrophies of axons (infantile neuroaxonal dystrophy), Alexander's disease, juvenile Huntington's chorea. In many of these, recent biochemical investigations have determined a genetic metabolic defect as the basis of the disorder. Adult forms of some of these conditions, although infrequent, must be considered in discussing "presenile dementias."

Adult Amaurotic Familial Idiocy, Kuf's Disease, Neuronal Ceroid-Lipofuscinosis

The genetically determined neuronal storage diseases, or cerebral lipidoses, are best known for their infantile variety (Tay Sach's (GM_2) neurolipidosis). The adult variety (Kuf's disease) and the Batten type of amaurotic idiocy must be re-evaluated in the light of recent clinical and ultrastructural investigations (6, 28, 102). In Kuf's disease there is no increase in the sphingolipid ganglioside. The uniform cerebral atrophy occurs at the expense of the middle layers of the cortex. A pseudolaminar pinkish appearance in the grey mantle results, sometimes accompanied by a status spongiosus. Secondary myelin degeneration can cause a shrinkage of the white matter with a notable thinning of the corpus callosum. The microscopic appearance of those neurons which remain is that of cells with insoluble PAS-positive pigment granules similar to the aging pigment in normal neurons. Varying from dust like particles to larger discrete spherical granules these lipofuscins are insoluble lipid and protein complexes akin to ceroid in other viscera. The ultrastructure is that of "curvilinear bodies" (103) as contrasted with the "membranous cytoplasmic bodies" of Tay Sach's disease. The nature of the underlying genetic deficit is unknown. A defect in peroxidation of polyunsaturated fatty acids may be at fault (102). There is no evidence of a lysosomal disease such as is found in the gangliosidoses. It is not probable that "the mere presence of these pigments is responsible for the clinical signs . . . or for the cell loss. . . . The nerve cell death is the result of progressive loss of cytoplasmic constituents" reflected by reduced neuronal cytoplasm especially prominent in the dendrites (102).

Adult Leukoencephalopathies

Adult forms of *metachromatic leukodystrophy* have been recorded (1). In this lipid storage disease the white matter of the cerebral hemispheres shows a loss of myelin and a variable loss of axons. Oligodendrocytes disappear. In the demyelinated areas and especially at the margins of the diffuse lesions clumps of brown to red staining granules appear when the tissue is stained with the usual Nissl aniline dyes such as cresyl violet or toluidine blue. Similarly, metachromatic staining material can be demonstrated in neurones. There is a mild to moderate proliferation of astrocytic fibres. A defect in the enzyme aryl-sulfatase-A causes an accumulation of the metachromatic staining sulfatide, which is a ganglioside of large molecular weight containing the sulfate radical. The brain is atrophic, and on sectioning the ventricles are symmetrically dilated, at the expense of the white matter. The centrum semiovale is shrunken, greyish and may show cysts of varying sizes where the myelin and axons have been destroyed. The metachromatic material is also found in peripheral nerve and kidney, occasionally in other viscera.

Other forms of leukoencephalopathies can occur in the adult with accompanying dementia. In the most common *demyelinating disease,* multiple sclerosis, the degree of dementia is probably correlated with the quantity of myelin destruction. The deterioration of intellect and personality is most prominent in that variety termed transitional or diffuse-disseminated sclerosis in which coalescent plaques of multiple sclerosis destroy much of the white matter (Plate IVb).

White matter degeneration on the basis of *vascular* disease with multifocal degeneration especially of the subcortical white matter occurs in the form of *Binswanger's encephalopathy* (61). The pathological process is manifested by incomplete softening and demyelination in the cerebral, usually occipital, white matter. It is debatable whether this white matter destruction results from hypotensive episodes, or from poor perfusion of junctional areas between ganglionic white matter vessels and the cortical penetrating vessels. A more diffuse leukoencephalopathy with a vascular origin has been described (47).

Subacute and Chronic Infections

The presumed infectious disease termed subacute sclerozing leukoencephalitis because of its characteristic white matter demyelination with remarkable fibrous astroglial proliferation, was earlier described as a form of lethargic encephalitis with inclusion bodies. The same process was separately termed a panencephalitis because of the inflammatory response in both grey and white matter. This disease, although most common in childhood, may affect young adults or the middle aged. In recent years the most popular term has been *subacute sclerozing panencephalitis.* A measles-like virus has been identified by culture and serological technics in many of these cases (36).

As the recent term implies the disease is that of an inflammatory process, diffusely spread throughout the cortex, subcortical grey masses and brain stem with demyelination and gliosis of the white matter. The brain is atrophic both in cortex and white matter with dilated ventricles and the firm rubbery feel of gliosis. The microscopic picture is one of loss of neurones and gliosis of the grey matter with rod shaped proliferated microglia and variable lymphocyte and plasma cell response in the perivascular spaces and scattered in the overlying meninges. There is a moth-eaten appearance to severe diffuse demyelination of the white matter with fibrous gliosis in the demyelinated areas. At times the sub-cortical arcuate myelinated fibres are relatively spared. In the nucleus of those oligodendrocytes and neurones which remain, eosinophilic inclusion bodies with a clear halo around them and with peripherally displaced nuclear chromatin can be identified (Plate IIa).

The most frequent and most devastating infectious disease to culmin-ate in dementia until recent decades was the tertiary parenchymatous central nervous system form of syphilis—*general paresis* or general paral-ysis of the insane. Present day treatment (hopefully) has relegated this disease to the status of an historical curiosity—a single untreated case has been seen in this laboratory in the past twenty years. The older textbooks give thoroughly adequate descriptions of the gross appearance and histo-pathology. The essential picture is that of cortical disarray with neuronal loss. There is a proliferation of astrocytes, rod-shaped microglia and moderate lympho-plasma cell response around the apparently increased vessels, associated with a mild chronic meningeal exudate. In the treated case, this gives way to absence of inflammatory response with the de-vastated cortex and proliferation of glial fibres of a nonspecific cortical atrophy, sometimes associated with superimposed senile cerebral changes (22).

Trauma

The brain of a boxer with *dementia pugilistica* (punch drunk syn-drome) (traumatic progressive encephalopathy) has seldom been sub-mitted to definitive morphologic examination. In those cases examined other superimposed disease states such as general paresis, the nutritional disturbances of chronic alcoholism, or senile dementias make the relation of the dementia to trauma difficult to delineate. Cases with a Pick's disease pattern (55) or neurofibrillary tangles and senile plaques may have repetitive trauma as the initiating cause with a disturbed colloidal state of the brain and small vessel disease at fault; but these lesions may be coincidental findings (46). A reasonable explanation, in some cases, for intellectual decline subsequent to head injury is afforded by Strich (83, 84). In acute head trauma accompanied by dementia, she was able to demonstrate white matter destruction at the expense of both axons and myelin sheaths with secondary atrophy of the thalamus. Whether the underlying cause is cerebral edema or mechanical shearing has not been determined.

PRESENILE AND SENILE DEMENTIAS

Alzheimer's Disease and Senile Dementia

By far the most commonly observed pathological alterations associated with dementia in either the presenium or in patients over the age of 65 years are the characteristic changes of neurofibrillary tangles in neurons and senile plaques in the neuropil that constitute the morphologic substrate of Alzheimer's disease. Although identical changes can be seen in many aging brains without recorded evidence of dementia these are usually limited to the hippocampus and when scattered in other portions of the cortex are always less extensive than in those patients with documented dementia. In fact a good correlation exists between the degree of dementia and the number of senile plaques and neurofibrillary tangles (4), especially in the amygdala and Ammon's horn of the hippocampus (11, 85).

The histopathology is qualitatively the same in senile dementia and in Alzheimer's disease. It will be described in the following paragraphs as in Alzheimer's disease with the minor differences noted in passing. The difference in locations of senile plaques, however, is an indication that Alzheimer's is not a presenile form of senile dementia (79).

The etiology of Alzheimer's disease is unknown. It is more frequently encountered in women and occasional familial examples are on record.

The *gross appearance* of the brain is that of symmetric atrophy of the frontal, parietal and especially the hippocampal gyri. The weight of the brain can vary from 900 or 1000 grams to an almost normal 1200-1300 grams. In general the patients with Alzheimer's disease have smaller brains than those with simple senile dementia. The small gyri and widened sulci are less striking than in Pick's. The pattern tends to be more diffuse than that of Pick's disease and the firm gliotic feel of the latter brain is less in evidence. The degree of arteriosclerosis of the circle of Willis or leptomeningeal vessels is not significant. In fact, Sourander and Sjögren (79) found a negative correlation between Alzheimer's disease and atherosclerosis. The cerebellum and brain stem are usually not remarkable. Cut sections show symmetric ventricular dilatation of varying severity but the inferior horn of the ventricles is usually quite dilated at the expense of the hippocampal complex. In general the patient with Alzheimer's disease, in contrast to senile dementia, shows a more focal disturbance in the setting of a diffuse disease; temporal and limbic areas are more prone to atrophy (11, 79, 85).

The diagnostic *histopathology* is diffusely present through much of the cortex and, to a lesser extent, the diencephalon, with the mesial temporal cortex, especially the hippocampus and amygdala, bearing the brunt of the histologic change (34, 85).

The normal alignment of the cortex is lost with varying numbers of shrunken neurons scattered seemingly at random in the thin mantle that remains. Upon occasion the vessels are more prominent than normal both in apparent numbers and because their thicker homogeneous walls stand out, especially in the upper layers. There is no hematogenous inflammatory response. Large naked clear astrocytic nuclei are scattered throughout the cortex and a moderate number of fibrous astrocytes can be identified especially with such stains as phosphotungistic acid hematoxylin (PTAH) or the Holzer technic. Although some degree of spongy degeneration can at times be seen, this is not so frequently present as in Pick's and much less evident than in Jakob-Creutzfeldt disease. The cortical fibrous gliosis characteristic of Pick's disease is much less striking in Alzheimer's disease, and, in turn, less evident in senile dementia (18).

In the neurons that remain, neurofibrillary tangles are often present, especially in Ammon's horn of the hippocampus. They tend to be scattered and sometimes in need of diligent search in the neocortex in senile dementia, but are much more prevalent in Alzheimer's disease. Many neurons in Ammon's horn, both those with obvious tangles and those without, show the granulovacuolar change of Simchowicz (Plate I, a-c).

Although the neurofibrillary tangles and the granulovacuolar change may be most obvious in the hippocampus-limbic system, and sparse in the neocortex, the senile plaques tend to be ubiquitous in the neocortex. Rarely they may even seem to spread into the immediately subjacent white matter. These plaques can be identified in hematoxylin eosin stains when older because of their prominent eosinophilic amyloid core, but to appreciate their number periodic acid Schiff (PAS) or, less dramatically, silver stains are most useful (Plate I, b, c). With electron microscopy Terry (86) finds them even more frequent in the neuropil of the cortex than is appreciated with light microscopy, with scarcely a spot free from some evidence of their presence.

The role of amyloid degeneration of cerebral vessels in the pathogenesis of Alzheimer's disease on the basis of present evidence must be considered coincidental. It is tempting to speculate on light microscopic findings that some cases have a disturbance in the permeability of small vessels, that the congophilic material present in the vessel wall extends into the peri-vascular neuropil and enters the core of the senile plaques, and that an altered immune response mediated by the reticulo-endothelial cells of the central nervous system and its vessels is at fault, with neuronal tangles secondary. Thus far the lack of ultrastructural evidence of damage to vessel walls and the observation by some investigators that vessels are not related to most plaques or that they are secondarily damaged make this hypothesis quite tenuous. At present the primary lesion appears to be in the neuron, with the plaques secondary (see below).

The contrary impression which we have gained—of the frequent association of senile plaques with capillaries—can partially be explained by the demonstration by Kraft (40) (see also Polak (67)) that the average size of senile plaques seen with the light microscope equals the average distance between capillaries in the grey matter. In fact serial sectioning showed only 3.2% of the plaques not related to capillaries. He suggested that microglial cells in addition to vascular reticulo-endothelial cells participate in the formation of the amyloid in senile plaques (40).

Schwartz found with light microscopic technics including fluorescence, (but without confirmation by electron microscopy) that amyloidosis in aging is a total body reaction. He would thus de-emphasize the specificity of Alzheimer's disease as a primary brain disease (73). This concept, which should be testable with other patient populations, has thus far not been confirmed.

Senile plaques vary in light microscopic appearances (15, 31, 53). Some are minute foci of condensed eosinophilic material which is PAS positive or which shows slight clubbing of silver positive neurites. Others show dense cores of amyloid material with rays of club-like processes and glial nuclei or debris. Those which do not have a central core are described as primitive; those composed almost entirely of amyloid are considered to be burned out plaques with few and abnormal neurites.

The ultrastructure of these plaques confirms the presence of amyloid. This is usually not related to vessels, or if vessels show amyloid degeneration, there is no reaction to this substance on the part of the brain parenchyma. The corona of argyrophilic material seen in light microscopy consists for the most part of synaptic boutons, dense bodies, twisted tubules and neurofilaments many of which are contained within degenerating dendritic neuronal processes (86). The amyloid core in scanning electron microscopy has a fluffy "tissue paper flower or sea sponge" appearance. It has protein as its chief component with small amounts of carbohydrate, some of which can be attributed to myelin (59).

The origin of the characteristic histopathology of Alzheimer's disease remains in doubt. The twisted tubules encountered as the ultrastructural basis for the neurofibrillary tangles of light microscopy are of undetermined origin but for some reason replace the normal straight neurotubules. Terry and Wisniewski (86) suggest that the tangle, being a manifestation of altered tubular protein, causes normal axoplasmic flow to be reduced and a form of "dying back" results. The neuronal processes (axon and dendrites) degenerate to cause the senile plaque. Amyloid deposition in the plaque is a secondary phenomenon. In the altered neurons lipofuscin may be increased and other organelles may be diminished but there is no apparent relation of these elements to the tangles. Although light microscopy identified an amyloid-like structure within the neurons in Alzheimer's disease (15, 73) no ultrastructural confirmation of intraneuronal amyloid has ever been forthcoming (70, 97). Thus far the answer has not yielded to experimental attempts to reproduce identical intraneuronal twisted tubules with aluminum cream, spindle inhibitors, etc., although with the light microscope a picture similar to neurofibrillary tangles may result (98).

Nor are the origins of the granulovacuolar changes entirely clear; there is evidence that such are altered lysosomes or autophagic organelles but the pathogenesis is unknown (29).

More apparent success is noted in the experimental reproduction of the senile plaques (97). The size is proportional to the extent of neuronal damage. Undercutting the cortex (that is, severing the neurites related to the damaged cells) increases the number and size of these plaques. It is thus postulated that the human senile plaque can result either from "neuronal incompetence and Wallerian degeneration or as a cortical form of dying back process" (97).

The consistent severity of damage as manifested by loss of neurons and damage to others in the hippocampus and amygdaloid nucleus correlates well with other observations that lesions in the limbic system result in the loss of ability to permanently record and store incoming information but with, at first, intact memory of the distant past (60). The loss of neurons throughout the neocortex again justifies the concept that intellectual deterioration corresponds to the amount of tissue destroyed rather than to specific sites affected. The thalamic lesions may be secondary, but the probability remains that this body is also intimately concerned with maintaining intellectual integrity.

Pick's Disease (Lobar Sclerosis)

Pick's disease is a relatively rare condition compared to Alzheimer's disease. We see morphologically confirmed cases in the ratio of about 1 to 40. There is an hereditary tendency and a slight preponderance of women, 6 to 5 according to van Mansvelt (48). It usually occurs in the 5th or 6th decades and has a slow progression. The clinical picture may be difficult to distinguish from Alzheimer's disease but there are more often focal symptoms such as aphasia and apraxia. Personality deterioration occurs early compared to memory defects, a reversal of Alzheimer's symptomatology. The diagnosis is based essentially on the circumscribed character of the atrophy, and its extreme degree compared to the more generalized atrophy of senile dementia and Alzheimer's disease (81). Neurofibrillary tangles and senile plaques are not a feature of the disease although rarely the combination of circumscribed lobar sclerosis and the microscopic appearance of Alzheimer's disease suggest a combined process.

The *gross appearance* of the brain is diagnostic, and is implied in the term Pick's lobar sclerosis or atrophy (Plate III). The brain is rubbery firm to touch. Usually the atrophy is symmetric. The frontal (and especially mesial orbital region), temporal and parietal lobes are involved, separately or together. The process usually spares the occipital lobe (especially the visual cortex), the post central gyrus, the caudal part of the paracentral lobule, Heschl's (acoustic) cortex and the posterior part of the superior temporal gyrus. The cortical atrophy is frequently so pronounced as to give a "knife blade" appearance to the gyri. The brain stem and cerebellum are less evidently involved (81).

On coronal section the affected cortex is thin, often brownish in color and resistant to cutting. The white matter, especially in the gyri, is thin and firm. The frontal horns of the ventricles are dilated. Because the head of the caudate often is atrophic, there may be an appearance reminiscent of Huntington's chorea. The oral portions of the putamen and globus pallidus are atrophied, differentiating from the more posterior involvement in Huntington's chorea. The pallor of the substantia nigra resembles that of Parkinsonism. The reader is referred to Spatz (81), Neumann (56), and van Mansvelt (48) for detailed historical reviews of Pick's disease, and to Wiśniewski et al. (96) for an up-to-date account of the histology and ultrastructure.

The essential *microscopic features* of this disease are the cell loss, cortical disarray and gliosis especially apparent in the superficial layers with the fourth layer relatively resistant. The marked astroglial fibre

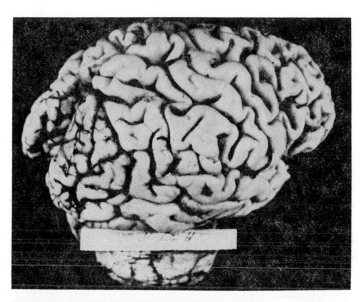

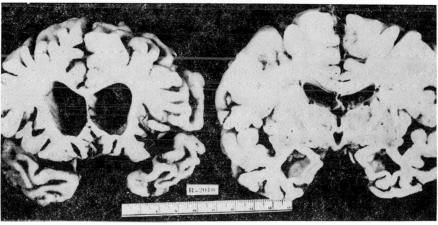

PLATE III

Pick's disease: Marked atrophy of frontal and anterior temporal lobes, sparing Rolandic gyri and posterior half of superior temporal gyri. Meninges have been removed.

proliferation, especially in the subpial and subependymal zones and often in the subcortical white matter is far more apparent than in Alzheimer's disease, and often occurs as a spongioform reaction. In the atrophic caudate nucleus both small and large cells are affected, contrasting with the small cell degeneration of Huntington's chorea.

In many cases swollen cells containing the characteristic argyrophilic Pick's bodies are seen (Plate I, d). They are present early in the disease process and are easier to find adjacent to the degenerated cortex with its pyknotic atrophic cells and fragmented axons. These argyrophilic inclusions are especially common in Ammon's horn and hippocampus. The Pick's bodies are lacking, however, in about half the cases.

With Nissl stains the cells with inclusions appear similar to chromatolytic neurons; with hematoxylin-eosin the inclusions are faintly basophilic. They tend to be globular and to push the nucleus and Nissl granules to one side. They resemble the chromatolysis of proximal axon degeneration (81, 95, 96).

Usually argyrophilic and spheroidal, they occasionally contain small lacunes or even granulovacuolar bodies (71). They do not stain with Masson's trichrome or phosphotungistic acid hematoxylin and, because fibrils are randomly arranged, they do not stain with Congo red nor are they birefringent. With the electron microscope Pick bodies are circumscribed but unbound condensed neurofilaments ringed by short normal neurotubules with scattered other organelles (96). Normal endoplasmic reticulum is severely depleted in the neurons (71, 72). The twisted tubules characteristic of Alzheimer's disease which were found in two recent cases (72) presumably result from coincidental neurofibrillary tangles (96). Most cases studied do not show them.

The *pathogenesis* of the lesions in Pick's disease is unknown. The cases which lack argyrophilic inclusions are those with the more striking subcortical gliosis, an observation that suggested to Neumann (56) two types of Pick's disease. In the first type with prominent neuronal swelling and argyrophilic bodies, a primary disease of neurons was postulated; in the second type the subcortical gliosis was thought to result from a primary disease of astrocytes.

To Spatz (81) Pick's disease is one form of the large group of frequently genetic, systemic atrophies (abiotrophies) of which amyotrophic lateral sclerosis and hereditary spinocerebellar ataxias belong. The essential feature is the inability of certain systematized groups of neurons to maintain their axons during the lifetime of the body. The result is a centripedal atrophy, a "dying back" process. The perikaryon manifests first a swelling and chromatolysis; later, as an end stage, it becomes shrunken and pyknotic as the axon degeneration progresses toward the cell body.

The close resemblance to central chromatolysis on electron microscopic findings has in a sense confirmed Spatz's and Williams' interpretation of light microscopic appearance of the typical Pick's cell. Wiśniewski et al. (96) have demonstrated quantitative gradations between the ballooned cells with and without Pick's bodies. These authors, however, doubt that primary neuronal degeneration is at fault. They believe the characteristic reaction results from damage to the neuronal processes, axonal, or more likely dendritic, and that the chromatolytic pattern may be a reflection of transneuronal degeneration. The etiology of the disease itself remains unknown.

Jakob-Creutzfeldt Disease (Presenile Spongiform Encephalopathy)

On the eve of the monumental demonstrations that a filterable "slow" virus could be isolated from patients with *Jakob-Creutzfeldt disease* (2,23) and that virus particles could be seen with the electron microscope (43, 91), Kirschbaum (38) published a monograph dealing with this fulminating form of presenile spongiform encephalopathy. He was a student of Jakob, and, although admitting priority in publication to Creutzfeldt for the first clinical pathological description, he prefers to give credit to his mentor Jakob for recognizing the significance of the syndrome and elucidating this special degenerative process, separating it from other senile and vascular lesions. In evaluating some 150 cases from the literature and various laboratories, including many of the pathological specimens he himself had examined, Kirschbaum asserted that Jakob-Creutzfeldt disease is "not a unified disease concept but a nonspecific process" characterized by neuronal losses and astrogliosis as invariable findings, with status spongiosus incidental (38).

The clinical picture is that of a subacute dementia with myoclonus. There is no sex predilection and sporadic cases are usual, hereditary predispositions being noted in not more than 10% of the cases (38, 39). Jakob-Creutzfeld disease has an earlier onset and a more rapid course than either Alzheimer's or Pick's disease. The duration is usually a few months, rarely up to 1½ or 2 years. Prominent neurologic signs and characteristic periodic sharp wave electroencephalographic abnormalities further differentiate it from the other two presenile dementias.

The constellation of the neurologic signs reflecting the location of the damage affords a division into three main varieties of the disease: 1) frontopyramidal (Jakob spastic pseudosclerosis, with or without amyotrophy); 2) occipital-parietal (Heidenhain's variety) (in which form the slow virus has been identified); and 3) a diffuse cerebral and basal ganglia form, some with thalamic, occasionally cerebellar, predilection.

The variable constellation of signs, symptoms and pathology, without a definite etiologic agent demonstrable until recently, has resulted in a profusion of synonyms which have tended to compound the confusion. First called a subacute disseminated polioencephalomyelopathy with spastic pseudosclerosis by Jakob, it was called by Spielmeyer (Creutzfeldt's teacher) Creutzfeldt-Jakob disease and then variously corticostriatospinal degeneration; presenile dementia with cortical blindness or Heidenhain's syndrome; Jones-Nevin syndrome—subacute vascular encephalopathy with mental disorder, focal disturbances and myoclonic epilepsy; subacute progresive encephalopathy with bulbar myoclonus; "subacute spongiform encephalopathy" attributable to vascular dysfunction; and most recently subacute presenile spongiform viral encephalopathy. The diversity of clinical signs is a manifestation of the varied sites of maximal pathology and thus far no reason for the predilection can be ascertained (2). Helpful reviews of the clinical and pathologic features of this disease will be found in Kirschbaum (38, 39) and in Beck (2).

The *gross appearance* of the brain varies from the usual picture with slight atrophy and a relatively normal appearance to rather prominent diffuse atrophy and firmness with evidence of spongy cortical degeneration.

The *microscopic appearance* is that of a nonspecific loss of neurons frequently in the mid and lower half of the cortex, and a glial proliferation with hypertrophic fibrous astrocytes. The astroglial reaction is a prominent pattern even when neurons seem little or not involved, and is principally in the first and lower cortical laminae. Although Kirschbaum (38) considers spongy degeneration "incidental" and present in only two-thirds of the cases, its characteristic appearance is reflected in the synonyms appended above. With light microscopy this varies from mild vacuolar degeneration of individual neurons and astrocytes to a pronounced vacuolar dissolution of cortical tissue (Plate II b, c).

The sites of damage are not only the cortex but caudate and putamen. The globus pallidus is less involved. Thalamic damage is most severe in medialis and pulvinar but spares specific relay nuclei (50). The cord in many cases shows a pattern similar to amyotrophic lateral sclerosis. Neurofibrillary tangles and senile plaques are not a part of the picture. Recently, however, kuru-like cerebellar plaques have been described (10, 91). Inflammatory lesions are lacking. Disease of blood vessels is usually absent although Torack (87) found thickening of the vascular basement membrane in one case and primary astroglial damage in his second. The morphologic similarities between Jakob-Creutzfeldt disease and the ischemic cortical lesions noted in patients with hypotensive episodes, during which there is an inability to adequately perfuse the brain, has suggested functional vascular damage as a cause of the disease (14, 58).

The *status spongiosus* characteristic of the disease is found in the electron microscope to be due to distended cell processes, astrocytic, dendritic or both, although some investigators have not observed vacuolated neuronal perikaryon or distended dendrites and find preterminal axons and presynaptic nerve endings of abnormal synapses (3). The demonstration of both neuronal and astrocytic involvement (26, 37) argues against a primary astrocytic disease, a gliogenous status spongiosus (19, 77) in which the neuronal and vascular wall lesions are secondary to the glial damage.

The demonstration of a slow virus in Jacob-Creutzfeldt disease, at least of the Heidenhain variety, has afforded an animal model to further elucidate the *pathogenesis* of the lesions.

From the ultrastructure of the experimentally induced diseases in chimpanzees, an hypothesis has evolved to explain the characteritic spongiform encephalopathy. The vacuoles in the neuronal perikaryon, dendrites and axons show abnormal arrays of ruptured, curled, and irregular membranes as well as irregular vesicular structures in and around the clear spaces. The main defect leading to neuronal degeneration would thus appear to be altered plasma membranes, conceivably ruptured virus membrane. Focal cytoplasmic clearings in glia and neuron are present adjacent to these ruptured membranes leading to fusion of adjacent cells, and the vacuolar degeneration results (44). Astrocytes react by swelling and proliferation (3, 42, 43, 44).

To summarize in the patient with Jakob-Creutzfeldt disease, a subacute dementia with myoclonus and rather characteristic EEG findings, there may be little gross abnormality in the brain but microscopically there is a characteristic triad of neuronal loss with the remaining cells often vacuolated, intense fibrous astroglial proliferation and a spongy degeneration of the grey matter. A filterable virus has been isolated and serially transferred to chimpanzees which in turn show the characteristic pathology. The primary site of the disease appears to be the processes of neurons and astrocytes with the spongy degeneration intracytoplasmic. The varied clinical manifestations which have produced proliferating subgroups result from variable site of major pathologic damage due to an as yet undiscovered pathoclytic factor.

Huntington's Chorea

Huntington's chorea must be considered in the differential diagnosis of presenile dementias. This disease inherited "in a single autosomal dominant fashion with complete penetrance" usually occurs at an early period in adult life, about age 35, with a standard deviation of about twelve years according to Myriantopoulos (54). The duration of the illness is in the neighborhood of sixteen years. Schizophrenic-like symptoms or intellectual deterioration can appear long before the characteristic choreo-athetotic dyskinesias.

The gross appearance of the coronally cut brain with its striatal (caudate and putamen) atrophy and excavation of the frontal horns of the ventricles is diagnostic (Plate IV, a). There is varying atrophy of the cerebral cortex, usually in the frontal lobe, of the subthalamic nucleus and usually of the corpus callosum. The striatal atrophy is principally at the expense of the small cells with the head of the caudate and the middle and posterior portion of the putamen especially damaged. There is a remarkable proliferation of astrocytes in the atrophic caudate. The damage may be so severe as to mimic the status spongiosus of Pick's disease (51). The middle layers of the cortex are usually more involved but in the several members of families we have had the opportunity to examine there was no constancy of cortical involvement amongst siblings, nor was correlation noted between duration of dementia or its degree and the gross cortical atrophy.

The histologic similarity between Huntington's and Pick's is discussed by McMenemey (51) but he emphasizes the more frequent sparing of the caudal putamen in Pick's disease and the relative sparing of the large cells of the caudate nucleus in Huntington's chorea. We have been impressed by the involvement of the anterior and central nucleus of the thalamus in Huntington's, a feature which McMenemey notes occurs when the striatum is severely involved.

Miscellaneous Neurofibrillary Dementias

The *amyotrophic lateral sclerosis-Parkinson dementia* complex of Guam (17, 30), as the names imply, combine, in this geographically limited constellation of diseases, neurofibrillary and granulovacuolar neuronal changes with the essential features of a motor neuron disease.

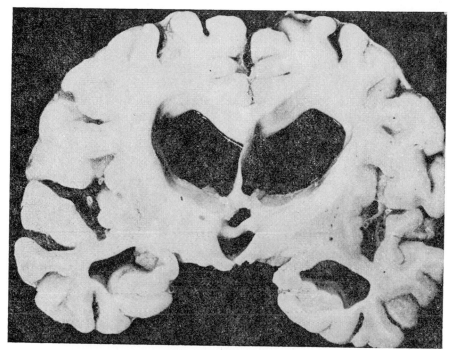

a.

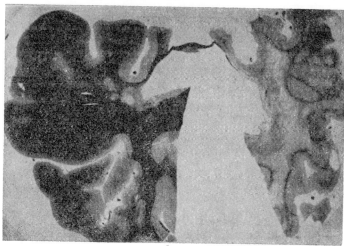

b.

PLATE IV

a. Huntington's chorea: Dilated ventricles, especially at the expense of the atrophied caudate nucleus.

b. Diffuse-disseminated sclerosis. (Weigert-myelin sheath stain). In the right hemisphere there is diffuse demyelination with preserved arcuate fibres. The left hemisphere shows characteristic Periventricular plaques of multiple sclerosis. The atrophic corpus callosum is the thin band between the two hemispheres.

Clinical pathologic correlates suggest that the dementia is more related to loss of cortical and hippocampal neurons than to the presence of the neurofibrillary tangles. The tangles in this disease appear to be the abnormal twisted tubules characteristic of Alzheimer's disease (98, 71). Identical tangles are present in the post encephalitic Parkinsonism. With the light microscope, tangles in brain stem and mesencephalon characterize the degenerative changes of *progressive supranuclear ophthalmoplegia* (82), a condition which Seitelberger (76) considers a variation of Alzheimer's disease.

SUMMARY

Dementia is a syndrome associated with many diseases which have in common a diffuse loss of neuronal function. It may be reversible in certain systemic metabolic disturbances with little or no recognizable morphologic damage. Under other metabolic conditions such as the nutritional disturbance of Wernicke-Korsakoff syndrome it may be stationary, or partially reversible, with a loss of recent memory. Such cases frequently show focal morphologic damage in the limbic-anterior thalamic systems.

Progressive dementias at any stage in post natal development are associated with morphologic evidence of progressive loss of neurons and their connections. The loss is usually diffuse, but frequently there is also a maximal focus of insult, often hippocampal, frontal and temporal lobes. The medial groups of thalamic nuclei are usually involved, their function as projection or association areas making this a logical finding. The histopathologic changes encountered, although often characteristic, are a reflection of the underlying disease; they are not the disease itself.

The multidisciplinary approaches to neuronal and glial function and disease, including viral, immunologic and ultrastructural studies, have lead to more sophisticated speculation and testable hypotheses, which in turn promise further enlightenment of the underlying morphologic changes characteristic of dementing conditions. With the help of the resolution of the electron microscope, study of subtle changes in synaptic contacts between neurons may soon lead us to more sophisticated therapeutic attempts than are now available.

REFERENCES

1. AUSTIN, J., ARMSTRONG, D., FOUCH, S., MITCHELL, C., STUMPF, D., SHEARER, L., and BRINER O. 1968. Metachromatic leukodystrophy (MLD): VIII. MLD in adults: Diagnosis and pathogenesis. *Arch. Neurol.* 12:225.

2. BECK, E., MATTHEWS, W. B., STEVENS, D. L., ALPERS, M. P., ASHER, D. M., GAJ-DUSEK, D. C., and GIBBS, C. J., JR. 1969. Creutzfeldt-Jakob disease. The neuropathology of a transmission experiment. *Brain*, 92:699.

3. BIGNAMI, A., and FORNO, L. S. 1970. Status spongiosus in Jakob-Creutzfeldt disease. Electron microscopic study of a cortical biopsy. *Brain*, 93:89.

4. BLESSED, G., TOMLISON,, B. E., and ROTH, M. 1968. The association between quantitative measures of dementia and of senile change in the cerebral grey matter of elderly subjects. *Brit. J. Psychiat.*, 114:797.

5. BLOOM, F. E., IVERSEN, L. L., and SCHMITT, F. O. 1970. Macromolecules in synaptic function. *Neurosciences Res. Prog. Bull.*, 8:329.

6. BOEHME, D. H., COTTRELL, J. C., LEONBERG, S. C., and ZEMAN, W. 1971. A dominant form of neuronal ceroid-lipofuscinosis. *Brain*, 94:745.

7. BRANON, W., McCORMICK, W., and LAMPERT, P. 1967. Axonal dystrophy in the gracile nucleus of man. *Acta Neuropath.*, 9:1.

8. CHAPMAN, L. F., and WOLFF, H. G. 1959. The cerebral hemispheres and the highest integrative functions of man. *Arch. Neurol.*, 1:357.

9. CHOU, S. M., and HARTMANN, H. A. 1964. Axonal lesions and waltzing syndrome after IDPN administration in rats. *Acta Neuropath.*, 3:428

10. CHOU, S. M., and MARTIN, J. C. 1971. Kuru plaques in a case of Creutzfeldt-Jakob disease. *Acta Neuropath.*, 17:150.

11. CORSELLIS, J. A. N. 1970. The limbic areas in Alzheimer's disease and in other conditions associated with dementia. In: Wolstenholme, G. E. W., and O'Connor, M. (Eds.) *Alzheimer's Disease and Related Conditions*. London: J. and A. Churchill.

12. COWEN, D., and OLMSTEAD, E. V. 1963. Infantile neuroaxonal dystrophy. *J. Neuropath. Exp. Neurol.*, 22:175.

13. CRAGG, B. C. 1972. Plasticity of synapses. In: Bourne, G. H. (Ed.) *The Structure and Function of Nervous Tissue*, Vol. 4. New York: Academic Press.

14. CROMPTON, M. R. 1963. A case of subacute spongiform encephalopathy supporting a vascular pathogenesis. *Acta Neuropath.*, 2:291.

15. DIVRY, P. 1952. La pathochimie générale et cellulaire des processes séniles et préséniles. *Proc. I Int. Cong. Neuropath.*, Rome, Vol. 2. Turin: Rosenberg and Sellier.

16. EINARSON, L. 1962. Cellular structure in the central nervous system of vitamin E-deficient monkeys. In: Shock, N. W. (Ed.) *Biological Aspects of Aging*. New York: Columbia University Press.

17. ELIZAN, T. S., HIRANO, A., ABRAMS, B. M., NEED, R. L., VAN NUIS, C., and KURLAND, L. T. 1966. Amyotrophic lateral sclerosis and Parkinson-dementia complex of Guam (neurologic re-evaluation). *Arch. Neurol.*, 14:356.

18. FERRARO, A. 1959. Senile psychosis and presenile psychoses. In: Arieti, S. (Ed.) *American Handbook of Psychiatry*, Vol. 2. New York: Basic Books.

19. FOLEY, J. M., and DENNY-BROWN, D. 1955. Subacute progressive encephalopathy with bulbar myoclonus. *Excerpta Med.* VIII, 8:782.

20. FUJISAWA, K. 1967. An unique type of axonal alteration (so-called axonal dys? trophy) as seen in Goll's nucleus of 277 cases of controls. *Acta Neuropath.*, 8:255.

21. GELLERSTEDT, N. 1933. Zur Kenntnis der Hirnveränderungen bei der normalen Altersinvolution. *Arbeiten aus dem Pathologischen Institut, Upsala Lakforh.*, 38:193.

22. GIANASCOL, A. J., WEICKHARDT, G. D., and NEUMANN, M. A. 1954. Penicillin treatment of general paresis. *Am. J. of Syph.*, 38:251.

23. GIBBS, C. J., GAJDUSEK, D. C., ASHER, D. M. et al. 1968. Creutzfeldt-Jakob disease (spongiform encephalopathy): Transmission to the chimpanzee. *Science*, 161:388.

24. GONATAS, N. K. 1967. Anoxic and synaptic lesions in neuropsychiatric disorders. *Nature*, 214:352.
25. GONATAS, N. K., and GAMBETTI, P. 1970. The pathology of the synapse in Alzheimer's disease. In: Wolstenholme, G. E. W., and O'Connor, M. (Eds.) *Alzheimer's Disease and Related Conditions.* London: J. and A. Churchill.
26. GONATAS, N. K., TERRY, R. D., and WEISS, M. 1965. Electron microscopy study in two cases of Jakob-Creutzfeldt disease. *J. Neuropath. Exp. Neurol.*, 24:575.
27. GRAFSTEIN, B., McEWEN, B. S., SHELANSKI, M. L. 1970. Axonal transport of neurotubule protein. *Nature*, 227:289.
28. HERMAN, M. M., RUBINSTEIN, L. J., and McKHANN, G. M. 1971. Additional electron microscopic observations on two cases of Batten-Spielmeyer-Vogt disease (neuronal ceroid-lipofuscinosis). *Acta Neuropath.*, 17:85.
29. HIRANO, A. 1970. Neurofibullary changes in conditions related to Alzheimer's disease. In: Wolstenholme, G. E. W. and O'Connor, M. (Eds.) *Alzheimer's Disease and Related Conditions.* London: J. and A. Churchill.
30. HIRANO, A., MALAMUD, N., ELIZAN, T. W. and KURLAND, L. T. 1966. Amyotrophic lateral sclerosis and Parkinsonism-dementia complex on Guam. *Arch. Neurol.*, 15:35.
31. HIRANO, A., and ZIMMERMAN, H. M. 1962. Alzheimer's neurofibrillary changes: A topographic study. *Arch. Neurol.*, 7:227.
32. HYDEN, H. 1955. Nucleic acids and proteins. In: Elliott, Page and Quastel (Eds.) *Neurochemistry.* Springfield: Charles C Thomas.
33. JACOB, H. 1970. Muscular twitchings in Alzheimer's disease. In: Wolstenholme, G. E. W. and O'Connor, M. (Eds.) *Alzheimer's Disease and Related Conditions.* London: J. and A. Churchill.
34. JAMADA, M., and MEHRAEIN, P. 1968. Verteilungsmuster der senilen Veränderungen im Gehirn. *Arch. Psychiat. Nervenkr.*, 211:308.
35. JELLINGER, K. 1968. Neuroaxonale dystrophien. In: *Verhandlungen der Deutschen Gesellschaft für Pathologie.* Stuttgart: Gustav Fischer Verlag.
36. JOHNSON, R. T., and JOHNSON, K. P. 1969. Slow and chronic virus infections of the nervous system. In: Plum, F. (Ed.) *Recent Advances in Neurology*, Vol. 6, Philadelphia: F. A. Davis Co.
37. KIDD, M. 1967. Some electron microscopical observations on status spongiosus. *Acta Neuropath. Suppl.*, 3:137.
38. KIRSCHBAUM, W. R. 1968. *Jakob-Creutzfeldt Disease.* New York: Elsevier Publ. Co.
39. KIRSCHBAUM, W. R. 1971. Jakob-Cruetzfeldt Disease. In: Minckler, J. (Ed.) *Pathology of the Nervous System.* New York: McGraw-Hill.
40. KRAFT, G. 1971. Licht- und polarisationsoptische Untersuchungen über die Frage der Gefässbeziehungen seniler Hirndrusen. *Aerzt. Forsch.*, 23:176.
41. LAMPERT, P. W. 1967. A comparative electron microscopic study of reactive, degenerating, regenerating and dystrophic axons. *J. Neuropath. Exp. Neurol.*, 26:345.
42. LAMPERT, P. W., EARLE, K. M., GIBBS, C. J., and GAJDUSEK, D. C. 1969. Experimental Kuru encephalopathy in chimpanzees and spider monkeys. *J. Neuropath. Exp. Neurol.*, 28:353.
43. LAMPERT, P. W., GAJDUSEK, D. C., and GIBBS, C. J. 1971. Experimental spongiform encephalopathy (Creutzfeldt-Jakob disease in chimpanzees). *J. Neuropath. Exp. Neurol.*, 30:20.
44. LAMPERT, P., HOOKS, J., GIBBS, C. J., and GAJDUSEK, D. C. 1971. Altered plasma membranes in experimental scrapie. *Acta Neuropath.*, 19:81.
45. LINDENBERG, R. 1956. Morphotropic and morphostatic neurobiosis. *Am. J. Path.*, 32:1147.

46. LINDENBERG, R. 1971. Trauma. In Minckler, J. (Ed.) *Pathology of the Nervous System*, Vol. II, New York: McGraw Hill.
47. MANI, K. S., McMENEMEY, W. H., and CUMINGS, J. N. 1964. Ischaemic leucoencephalopathy. *Conf. Neurol.*, 24:404.
48. MANSVELT, J. VAN. 1954. *Pick's Disease, A Syndrome of Lobar Cerebral Atrophy.* Enschede, Van Der Loeff.
49. MARGOLIS, G. 1959. Senile cerebral disease. *Lab. Invest.*, 8:335.
50. MARTIN, J. J. 1967. Les lésions de la couche optique dans la maladie de Creutzfeldt-Jakob et les formes apparentées. *Acta Neuropath.*, suppl. 5:92.
51. McMENEMEY, W. H. 1963. The dementias and progressive disease of the basal ganglia. In: Blackwood, W. (Ed.) *Greenfield's Neuropathology.* Baltimore: Williams and Wilkins.
52. MINCKLER, T. M., and BOYD, E. 1068. Physical growth of the nervous system and its coverings. In: Minckler, J. (Ed.) *Pathology of the Nervous System*, Vol. I, New York: McGraw-Hill.
53. MOREL, F., and WILDI, E. 1952. General and cellular pathochemistry of senile and presenile alterations of the brain. *Proc. I Int. Congr. Neuropath.*, Rome, Vol. 2. Turin: Rosenberg and Sellier.
54. MYRIANTHOPOULOS, N. C. 1966. Review Article: Huntington's chorea. *J. Med. Genet.*, 3:298.
55. NEUBURGER, K. T., SINTON, D. W., and DENST, J. 1959. Cerebral atrophy associated with boxing. *Arch. Neurol. Psych.*, 81:403.
56. NEUMANN, M. A. 1949. Pick's disease. *J. Neuropath. Exp. Neurol.*, 8:255.
57. NEUMANN, M. A., and COHN, R 1953. Incidence of Alzheimer's disease in large mental hospital; relation to senile psychosis and psychosis with cerebral arteriosclerosis. *Arch. Neurol. Psychiat.*, 69:615.
58. NEVIN, S., McMENEMEY, W. H., BEHRMAN, S., and JONES, D. P. 1960. Subacute spongioform encephalopathy—a subacute form of encephalopathy attributable to vascular dysfunction. *Brain*, 83:519.
59. NIKAIDO, T., AUSTIN, J., RINEHART, R., TRUEB, L., HUTCHINSON, J., STUKENBROK, H. and MILES, B. 1971. Studies in ageing of the brain. I. Isolation and preliminary characterization of Alzheimer plaques and cores. *Arch. Neurol.* 25:198.
60. OJEMANN, R. G. 1966. Correlations between specific human brain lesions and memory changes. *Neurosciences Res. Prog. Bull.*, Suppl., 4:1.
61. OLSZEWSKI, J. 1962. Subcortical arteriosclerotic encephalopathy. *Wld. Neurol.*, 3:359.
62. PENTSCHEW, A. 1969. Multidimensional neuropathology. In: Walsh, F. B. and Hoyt, W. F. (Eds.) *Clinical Neuro-Ophthalmology.* Baltimore: Williams and Wilkins.
63. PENTSCHEW, A., and SCHWARZ, K. 1962. Systemic axonal dystrophy in vitamin E deficient adult rats. *Acta Neuropath.*, 1:313.
64. PETERS, A. 1968. The morphology of axons of the central nervous system. In: Bourne, G. H. (Ed.) *The Structure and Function of Nervous Tissue*, Vol. 1. New York: Academic Press.
65. PIERCY, M. 1964. The effects of cerebral lesions on intellectual function: a review of current research trends. *Brit. J. Psychiat.*, 110:310.
66. PLUM, F., and POSNER, J. B. 1972. *Diagnosis of Stupor and Coma.* 2nd edition (Contemporary Neurol. Series). Philadelphia: R. A. Davis.
67. POLAK, M. 1970. General discussion. In: Wolstenholme, G. E. W. and O'Connor, M. (Eds.) *Alzheimer's Disease and Retired Conditions.* London: J. and A. Churchill.
68. POMERAT, C. M., HENDELMAN, W. J., RAIBORN, C. W., and MASSY, J. F. 1966. Dynamic activities of nervous tissue in vitro. In: Hyden, H. (Ed.) *The Neuron.* New York: Elsevier.

69. RAMON-MOLINER, E. 1968. The morphology of dendrites. In: Bourne, G. H. (Ed.) *The Structure and Function of Nervous Tissue*, Vol. I. New York: Academic Press.

70. SCHLOTE, W. 1968. Polarisationsoptisch differenzierbare Stadien der intraneuronalen "Amyloid" bildung bei Morbus Alzheimer. *Verh. Deutsch. Ges. Path.*, 52:204.

71. SCHOCHET, S. S., JR. 1972. Neuronal inclusions. In: Bourne, G. H. (Ed.) *The Structure and Function of Nervous Tissue*, Vol. IV. New York: Academic Press.

72. SCHOCHET, S. S., JR., LAMBERT, P. W., and LINDENBURG, R. 1968. Fine structure of the Pick and Hirano bodies in a case of Pick's disease. *Acta Neuropath.*, 11:330.

73. SCHWARTZ, P. 1970. *Amyloidosis*. Springfield: Thomas.

74. SIEDLER, H., and MALAMUD, N. 1963. Creutzfeldt-Jakob's disease. Clinicopathologic report of 15 cases and review of literature. *J. Neuropath. Exp. Neurol.*, 22:381.

75. SEITELBERGER, F. 1967. The problem of status spongiosus. In: Klatzo, I., and Seitelberger, F. (Eds.) *Brain Edema*. New York: Springer-Verlag.

76. SEITELBERGER, F. 1968. Allgemeine Neuropathologie der Alterns- und Aufbrauchkrankheiten des Gehirns. *Verh. d. Dtsch. Ges. f. Path.*, 52:32.

77. SLUGA, E., and SEITELBERGER, F. 1967. Beitrag zur spongiösen Encephalopathie. *Acta Neuropath.*, Suppl., 3:60.

78. SMITH, W. T. 1970. The pathology of the organic dementias. In: Williams, D. (Ed.) *Modern Trends in Neurology*, No. 5. New York: Appleton-Century-Crofts.

79. SOURANDER, P., and SJÖGREN, H. 1970. The concept of Alzheimer's disease and its clinical implications. In: Wolstenholme, G. E. W. and O'Connor, M. (Eds.) *Alzheimer's Disease and Related Conditions*. London: J. and A. Churchill.

80. SPAHN, W., and DUSTMANN, H. O. 1965. The weight of the human brain and its dependence on age, height, cause of death and occupation. *Dtsch. Z. ges. gerichtl. Med.* 56:299.

81. SPATZ, H. 1952. La Maladie de Pick, les atrophies systematisées progressives et la sénescence cérébrale prématurée localisée. *Proc. I Int. Congr. Neuropath.*, Rome, Vol. 2. Turin: Rosenberg and Sellier.

82. STEELE, J. C., RICHARDSON, J. C., and OLSZEWSKI, J. 1964. Progressive supranuclear palsy. *Arch. Neurol.* 10:333.

83. STRICH, S. J. 1956. Diffuse degeneration of cerebral white matter in severe dementia following head injury. *J. Neuropath., Neurosurg. Psychiat.*, 19:163.

84. STRICH, S. J. 1961. Shearing of nerve fibres as a cause of brain damage due to head injury. *Lancet*, ii:443.

85. TARISKA, I. 1970. Circumscribed cerebral atrophy in Alzheimer's disease: a pathological study. In: Wolstenholme, G. E. W., and O'Connor, M. (Eds.) *Alzheimer's Disease and Related Conditions*. London: J. and A. Churchill.

86. TERRY, R. D., and WISNIEWSKI, H. 1970. The ultrastructure of the neurofibrillary tangle and the senile plaque. In Wolstenholme, G. E. W., and O'Connor, M. (Eds.) *Alzheimer's Disease and Related Conditions*. London: J. and A. Churchill.

87. TORACK, R. M. 1969. Ultrastructural and histochemical studies of cortical biopsies in subacute dementia. *Acta Neuropath.*, 13:43.

88. TORACK, R. M. 1971. Studies in the pathology of dementia. In: Wells, C. E. (Ed.) *Dementia*. Philadelphia: F. A. Davis.

89. TORVIK, A., ENDRESEN, G. K. M., ABRAHAMSEN, A. F., and GODAL, H. C. 1971. Progressive dementia caused by an unusual type of generalized small vessel thrombosis. *Acta neurol. scand.*, 47:137.

90. VAUGHN, J. E., and SKOFF, R. P. 1972. Neuroglia in experimentally altered central nervous system. In: Bourne, G. H. (Ed.) *The Structure and Function of Nervous Tissue*, Vol. V. New York: Academic Press.
91. VERNON, M. L., HORTA-BARBOS, L., FUCCILLO, D. A., et al. 1970. Virus-like particles and nucleo-protein-type filaments in brain tissue from two patients with Creutzfeldt-Jakob disease. *Lancet*, i:964.
92. VICTOR, M., ADAMS, R. D., and COLLINS, G. H. 1971. *The Wernicke-Korsakoff Syndrome.* (Contemporary Neurology Series). Philadelphia: F. A. Davis.
93. WEISS, P. 1967. Neuronal dynamics. *Neurosciences Res. Prog. Bull.*, Vol. 5:371.
94. WEISS, P., and HISCOE, H. B. 1948. Experiments on the mechanism of nerve growth. *J. Exp. Zool.*, 107:315.
95. WILLIAMS, H. 1935. The peculiar cells of Pick's disease. *Arch. Neurol. Psychiat.*, 35:508.
96. WIŚNIEWSKI, H. M., COBLENTZ, J. M., and TERRY, R. D. 1972. Pick's disease (a clinical and ultrastructural study). *Arch. Neurol.*, 26:97.
97. WISNIEWSKI, H., and TERRY, R. D. 1970. An experimental approach to the morphogenesis of neurofibrillary degeneration and the argyrophilic plaque. In: Wolstenholme, G. E. W. and O'Connor, M. (Eds.) *Alzheimer's Disease and Related Conditions*. London: J. and A. Churchill.
98. WISNIEWSKI, H., TERRY, R. D., and HIRANO, A. 1970. Neurofibrillary pathology. *J. Neuropath. Exp. Neurol.*, 29:163.
99. WOLSTENHOLME, G. E. W., and O'CONNOR, M. 1970. *Alzheimer's Disease and Related Conditions*. London: J. and A. Churchill.
100. WOODARD, J. S. 1962. Clinicopathologic significance of granulovacuolar degeneration in Alzheimer's disease. *J. Neuropath. Exp. Neurol.*, 21:85.
101. WOODARD, J. S. 1966. Alzheimer's disease in late adult life. *Am. J. Path.*, 49:1157.
102. ZEMAN, W., DONAHUE, S., DYKEN, P., and GREEN, J. 1970. The neuronal ceroidlipofuscinoses (Batten-Vogt syndrome). In: Vinken, P. J. and Bruyn, G. W. (Eds.) *Handbook of Clinical Neurology*. Vol. 10. Amsterdam: North Holland Publ. Co.
103. ZEMAN, W., and DYKEN, P. 1969. Neuronal ceroid-lipofuscinosis (Batten's Disease). Relationship to amaurotic familial idiocy? *Pediat.*, 44:570.

5

CONCOMITANT PHYSICAL STATES

W. Ferguson Anderson,
O.B.E., M.D., F.R.C.P.

Professor of Geriatric Medicine
University of Glasgow, Scotland

and

R. Davidson, M.B., M.R.C.Psych., D.P.M.

Consultant Psychiatrist
Woodilee Hospital, Lenzie, Scotland

Illness in the elderly may consist of impairment of physical, mental, or social health. In very many cases, all three types of disease coexist and require appropriate diagnosis, assessment, and management, but even when only one type is identifiable as a disease entity, it is usual to find that the aetiology encompasses the other factors as well. Physical, mental and social factors cannot be ignored by anyone involved in the care of the elderly and, although they can be separated in theory, in practice they are inextricably entwined.

SOCIAL FACTORS

The close relationship between psychiatric disorder and social conditions has long been recognized, and the use of psychiatric social workers in the psychiatric team has been, for many years, a tangible expression of this. Social isolation has been shown to be a determining factor in the suicide rate in London (50), suicide occurring more frequently in areas where divorce and illegitimacy rates suggest social disintegration. Batchelor and Napier (4) reported that feelings of loneliness were the commonest psychological precursors of attempted suicide in old age. Busse (9) stated that it appears that the social economic level affects the frequency of depressive episodes, the lower income group of elderly subjects having a considerably greater incidence of depression. It is well known that social isolation increases the chances of admission to a mental hospital, especially among the elderly. Two-thirds of beds in mental hospitals occupied by people over 65 are taken up by single, widowed, or divorced people.

Macmillan (34) has noted that when an old person lives in isolation, deterioration—either psychological because of lack of interest, antagonism, self-pity or resentment on the part of relatives, or actual, because of solitude—sets in. He feels that when the emotional needs of the old person have been unsatisfied for any length of time senile deterioration with subsequent onset of senile psychosis begins. Depression following retirement is a frequently encountered condition and preparation for this important social change late in life can probably avert a number of breakdowns.

Although social factors are of vital importance in many other psychiatric states, the relationship between physical disease and social conditions has not, perhaps, been given adequate recognition by geriatricians, general physicians, and surgeons. Accidents in the home, malnutrition, dehydration, incontinence, constipation, infections, and "bad feet" are only some of the states that may result from unfavorable living conditions and which may lead to psychiatric complications. The publicity attached to the dangers of hypothermia has possibly done most in recent years to draw everyone's attention to the need to think of the old person in his social setting.

INTERACTION OF PHYSICAL AND MENTAL DISEASE

Before the complex interrelationship between physical and mental disease in older people can be considered, it must be noted that the physical condition of a "normal" old person in the absence of recognizable disease appears to change with age mainly in the direction of loss of reserve capacity of organs; thus a difference between the performance of young and old persons can only be demonstrated when some test which draws on the reserve is applied. Many authors have in fact noted an élite of the elderly—people who reach advanced age with few stigmata of aging. There seems in such cases where physical health has been well maintained to be a corresponding quality of mental ability.

Busse (7) stated that the brain of the normal young adult is estimated to contain some 12 million neurons and that during the latter half of the life span it appears that a great many neurons die with each day that passes. The brain decreases in size and weight, so that brain weight at 75 years of age is 56% of the original weight. As with other organs, this progressive loss is not evident in many elderly persons unless tested to the limit, and the explanation lies in the ability of the brain to compensate for the impairment of function. Busse showed that highly intelligent persons reveal considerably less decline in their overall ability than those having lower intellectual capacities. The intellectual loss is greatest in the individuals who can least afford such declines.

There is less reserve capacity in the older person in time of mental stress than in the young individual. This shows itself in the normal reduction of adaptability and increasing rigidity of thought and attitude as age advances; the older person learns to defend himself by avoiding the mental stress involved in change. At the very time when multiple insults occur, such as loss of status and security, retirement, sudden change in the way of life by bereavement, and increased worry because of physical frailty, there is less mental reserve with which to face the challenge. But this is true not only of the brain but of the other organs of the body, and one can see that the tendency is for the aging person to seek uniformity and economy in physical activity so as to avoid the stress of change.

Mental disease is not, of course, confined to impairment of intellect and, in practice, unhealthy or abnormal emotional states are of greater importance. Emotion is much more difficult to measure than intellect and we can only assume from common experience, rather than from scientific study, that people become less emotional from adolescence onwards. Thus we may find elderly people bearing with fortitude situations which would occasion great distress in the young. It may well be, however, that while accepting many difficulties with equanimity, they leave themselves little in reserve and, in consequence, when pushed too far, their breakdown is catastrophic. Physical illness may well be the factor that precipitates such a breakdown.

In a study of the mental health of people 55 years and over at the Rutherglen Consultative Health Centre, emotional disturbance regarded as outside the normal reaction to the vicissitudes of life was observed in 53 (13.3%) of 400 physically healthy men, 72 (17.8%) of 404 physically healthy women, 78 (31.2%) of 250 physically ill men and 68 (38.2%) of 178 women with physical illness. The incidence of emotional disturbance was significantly greater in those with physical disease than in those who were physically healthy. Furthermore, physical illness was high in the order of primary causes of emotional disturbance, as the data for the 131 emotionally disturbed men revealed. In these men, physical ill health, adverse home environment, bereavement, ill health of a relative, neglectful children, compulsory retirement and financial difficulty comprised, in that order, the main causes of emotional disturbance. In women, the causes were the same, but the order was slightly different, adverse home environment being first, and compulsory retirement not being mentioned. Post (44) and Mayer-Gross et al. (36) have also commented on physical ill health as a cause of mental disturbance in older people.

Unhappiness due to bereavement is well recognized among the elderly, and Wilson (61) found bereavement associated with isolation. She felt that a most effective method of preventing social isolation and loneliness in old people is through support given at the time of greatest grief, encouraging the intake of an adequate diet, and ensuring that the elderly do not become completely cut off from their family, friends and neighbors, and that some interest be found for them. Wilson (61) stressed that all cases of terminal illness where the caring relatives are elderly should be reported to the Health Visitor, who can offer help to the patient and his family.

Neglectful children are not commonly found, but if a patient is mentally deteriorating in old age the attitude of relatives may change. At first they will accept the responsibility willingly, but gradually, as the older person causes more trouble and is difficult to handle, a partial, converted to complete, rejection takes place. These feelings are brought on by such incidents as wandering, nocturnal restlessness and incontinence, or aggressive talk and behavior. It is essential when hearing the old person's story to also interview, separately, the relatives. Such a procedure gives much more satisfactory information.

The physician has a clear responsibility to treat related emotional disturbance as effectively as he treats physical disease. As would be anticipated, there is a high incidence of physical and psycho-social illness in the aging segment of the population and, thus, screening procedures for selected diseases are relegated to a second place in contrast to the absolute necessity for an unhurried assessment with regard to the care of the whole patient. Further emphasis for this view is encouraged by a random sample of people 65 years and over carried out from the Rutherglen Centre as part of a nutritional survey on behalf of the Department of Health and Social Security and the Home and Health Department for Scotland. This study showed that 32% of the men and 42% of the women were in psychological or social need, that women over 74 years were a particularly vulnerable group, and that the greatest proportion of this need was unknown before the assessment. The major mental problem was reactive depression as evidenced by slowing of responses, restlessness, sleep upset and fluctuation of mood (24).

A longitudinal investigation of volunteers who were aged 60 years or over at the beginning of the study was described by Busse (8). When initially screened and accepted these people were believed to be relatively free of disease and were functioning at an acceptable level in the community. An increase in the severity of cardiovascular disease had little effect on intellectual functioning and on tests of immediate memory. Cardiovascular disease did produce a significantly extended reaction time. As in other studies, it was noted that approximately one-third of elderly persons cannot be relied upon to give an accurate assessment of their physical health. A sudden decline in intelligence and an alteration in the EEG suggested the onset of a process of deterioration and approaching death. When studied longitudinally, the importance of physical health as a factor in depression became increasingly evident. This longitudinal study provided little support for the disengagement theory; relatively active elderly subjects were more likely to maintain morale than those who were inactive.

Post (46), in discussing the relationship of affective illness in the elderly to physical health, stated that the coexistence in the same person of physical and mental disorders tends to be discovered more frequently than can be explained by chance. This has been shown in the case of subjects suffering from severe neurosis and psychotic disorders by Lovett Doust (31) and confirmed for somewhat younger men with milder psychological disturbances by Roessler and Greenfield (48). Sainsbury (51) noted that physical illness was a prominent feature of elderly suicides, and many workers have confirmed a strong association between depressive illnesses requiring hospitalization and physical ill health.

According to Post (45) a high proportion, 60% to 80%, of cases of depression in elderly persons appears to have been precipitated by incisive events, almost always losses in the wider sense of the word. Acute physical stress, such as operations, acute illnesses or exacerbations of chronic disorders, has been confirmed as the most common aetiological factors by many authors.

The physician practising geriatric medicine must familiarize himself with this background of information and must realize the prime importance of early diagnosis in his patients. This means a complete break with established medical tradition—that some form of ascertainment or seeking out of illness must be put into operation. This has been confirmed by the studies of Williamson (60) in Edinburgh on illness unreported to the family doctor.

PHYSICAL STATES IN THE PSYCHIATRIC PATIENT

Many studies have shown the significant element of physical disorder in the abnormalities found in mental hospital patients. Burvill (6) studied recent admissions over the age of 60 and long-stay patients in a similar age group in Western Australia. Of 85 consecutive admissions to mental hospital, 9 had disability in two or more physical systems, 7 had cataracts, and 6 had moderate or severe defects of hearing. Of the long-stay patients, 8% were partially or completely bedfast or chairfast, and a further 11% needed the help of another person or some mechanical device to enable them to walk; 18% had persistent urinary or double incontinence; 16% had disability in two or more physical systems; 25% were on drugs for their physical state.

Herridge (20) reviewed 209 admissions to a general hospital psychiatric department and found that in 5% the principal diagnosis was major physical illness discovered on admission. In a further 21% a physical illness contributed to the onset of the psychiatric illness, and in 8% physical illness resulted from the psychiatric illness. In another 16% unrelated physical illness was found.

In a review of 100 consecutive female admissions aged over 65 to a mental hospital, Morris (37) found that the following physical illnesses had been diagnosed on admission: hypertension (greater than 200/110)—11 cases; cataract—eight cases; cardiac failure—six cases; cerebral thrombosis—six cases; arthritis—five cases; bronchitis—three cases; pernicious anemia—two cases; diabetes—two cases; deafness—two cases; and one case each of gastric ulcer, asthma, psoriasis, subacute combined degeneration of the cord, syphilis, angina pectoris, mitral disease, peripheral neuritis, cerebral tumor, and vaginal prolapse.

Some studies have been concerned with relating physical states to psychiatric diagnoses. Gibson (16) reviewed 100 consecutive admissions to two mental hospitals serving an industrial population. He subdivided his cases according to psychiatric diagnosis and found that of the 45 cases with affective disorder (43 with depression, 2 with hypomania), 28 had some physical illness. Of those whose first episode of mental illness had occurred before the age of 60, nine had physical illness and 14 did not; of those having their first attack after the age of 60, 17 had physical illness and five did not. In the latter group of 22 patients, he noted 12 with either clinical or electrocardiographic evidence of coronary artery disease. When he studied the 55 cases in his series who were not affectively ill and who were having their first admission to mental hospital after the age of 60, he discovered only eight cases with evidence of coronary artery disease, and, of these, four were associated with arteriosclerotic psychosis. These differences were statistically significant. He went on to discuss the importance of this finding in relation to the use of electro-convulsive therapy and he stated that there was no correlation between the type of the affective disorder and the physical illness.

Gibson's group of 14 cases of arteriosclerotic psychosis contained 11 with evidence of a cerebrovascular accident, six with evidence of renal involvement, seven with hypertension and four with coronary artery disease. The patients with senile psychosis, numbering 11, included six cases of physical illness—three had auricular fibrillation, one was deaf, one was diabetic, and one had a large goiter. In ten cases of paraphrenia there were three patients with deafness, one with blindness, and one with both blindness and deafness. In 11 cases of delirium all had physical disease except one case in which no physical disease was discovered. Eight of this group died and three (including the one with no known physical disease) recovered. Six of the cases, including one who recovered, were over 80 years of age.

Simon and Tallery (55) studied 534 patients over 60 admitted to psychiatric observation wards in San Francisco for their first psychiatric admission. They found that four-fifths had moderate or severe physical disability; physical illness serious enough to interfere with function was diagnosed in 441 patients and only 84 patients (16%) had no physical illness. The most common physical illnesses found were heart disease, malnutrition, congestive heart failure, stroke, hypertension, serious respiratory infection—including pneumonia and active pulmonary tuberculosis—peripheral neuritis, and cancer. Moderate or severe visual impairment was found in 18% and moderate or severe hearing impairment in 11%. Although there was no significant difference between men and women in overall disability rating, severe disability occurred to a greater degree in the men. Men had significantly more respiratory infections and strokes, especially the younger men, while women had significantly more diabetes, fractures and visual defects. Men in the age group 60-69 had significantly more heart disease than women in the same group, although women, as a whole, had more heart disease and more congestive heart failure than did older men. The younger men also had proportionately more peripheral neuritis, malnutrition, and cirrhosis of the liver. Intelligence testing was attempted in 88% of cases; 19% of the total sample proved to be inaccessible. Scores above the median tended to be made by patients with respiratory infection, peripheral neuritis, malnutrition and cirrhosis of the liver; scores below the median tended to be made by patients with congestive heart failure, stroke, diabetes, cancer, poor vision, and poor hearing. The group with fractures had the same number of scores above and below the median.

Psychiatrically, the patients studied by Simon and Tallery were grouped into acute brain syndrome (delirium), chronic brain syndrome (dementia), and psychogenic (functional) disorder comprising depressive, paranoid, and alcoholic states. They found that acute brain syndrome was strongly associated with physical illness and disability; patients with chronic brain syndrome alone were significantly less disabled than patients with both chronic brain syndrome and acute brain syndrome; and patients with chronic brain syndrome plus a psychogenic disorder were significantly less ill than patients with chronic brain syndrome alone. The presence of a psychogenic disorder, alone or combined with organic brain disease, was associated with a good physical status more often than with a poor one.

Taking all the physical illnesses together, the pattern produced was 33% with both acute and chronic brain syndrome, 22% with chronic brain syndrome only, 8% with acute brain syndrome only, 2% with acute and chronic brain syndrome combined with psychogenic disorder, 6% with chronic brain syndrome and a psychogenic disorder, and 26% with a psychogenic disorder only (15% being alcoholic states and 11% other psychogenic states). For every physical illness, with the exception of peripheral neuritis and cirrhosis of the liver, the main association was with combined acute and chronic brain syndrome without psychogenic disorder. Patients with chronic brain syndrome had twice as much heart disease as patients with psychogenic disorder and a greater proportion of hypertension; this contrasts with the findings of Roth and Kay (49) which were confirmed by Gibson (16). Of the group with a diagnosis of paranoid disorder, with or without organic brain disease, 8% had moderate deafness and none was totally deaf; 11% had moderate visual impairment and none was blind. Among the patients with affective disorder, with or without organic brain disease, 3% had moderate or severe deafness and 2% had severe visual impairment. For the total sample, the corresponding figures were 13% with moderate or severe hearing defects and 4% with moderate or severe visual defects. These figures suggest that, while sensory defect occurs more frequently in paranoid than in affective cases, only visual impairment occurs more frequently than in the general run of elderly psychiatric admissions. This finding also contrasts with those of Kay and Roth (29), who found in their study of late paraphrenia that the general health of these patients was normal for their age, that exceptionally good health sometimes was noted, and that serious physical disease was uncommon. Visual defect was no more common than in control groups of comparable age and seemed to be only occasionally a cause of persecutory ideas. Impairment of hearing, however, was markedly more common among paraphrenics than among affective and organic cases; in one group, 40% were deaf to some degree, 15% being severely impaired.

Kay and Roth (29) also studied the incidence of focal cerebral disease in paraphrenics and found that it seldom occurred. Of 99 patients aged over 60, only eight had some evidence of cerebral disease or injury. The onset of the organic condition was generally well before the start of the paraphrenic psychosis. Five patients had pyramidal signs: one a congenital weakness and deformity of a hand combined with petit mal attacks; one a hemiplegia due to head injury in childhood; one a hemiparesis and expressive dysphasia following a fracture of the skull eight years earlier; one a facial paresis due to a small hemorrhage causing transient lameness 28 years previously; and one a history of several small strokes over the previous ten years with no residual neurological findings. Moreover, two patients had coarse senile tremors and one had developed epileptiform seizures soon after the onset of the psychosis. Kay and Roth conclude that paraphrenia occasionally arises in the presence of focal brain damage, the only effect of which may be to increase susceptibility to the psychosis in predisposed individuals.

Herbert and Jacobson (18) studied 47 cases of late paraphrenia admitted to hospital. Of these, only two were males, one of whom had a chronic lung condition and some evidence of Parkinsonism—he died 18 months after admission to hospital. Of the 45 women, 15 had cardiovascular disease, ten had arthritis, two had respiratory disease, one had endocrine disease, one had neurological disease, one had a skin disease, four had nutritional disease (including anemia), and four had other illnesses. In 21 cases there was a visual defect and in 12 of these critical visual defects in both eyes were present. Four cases had total blindness, four cases had near blindness in both eyes, nine cases had severe loss of vision in one eye, and four cases had moderate loss of vision due to cataracts. In 18 cases there was auditory loss—ten cases had total or almost total deafness and eight cases had moderate deafness. There was combined visual and auditory loss in ten cases. Excluding minor defects, there was a total of 39 cases with either visual or auditory loss or both out of the 45 cases.

These findings differ from those of Kay and Roth in that there is a high incidence of physical disorder. Herbert and Jacobson, in discussing this difference, pointed out that they studied admissions aged 65 and over while Kay and Roth included in their series of 99 patients 41 who were under 65. They presumed that, with increasing age, physical and social factors present a different picture. They felt that the role of physical illness in paraphrenia should not be underestimated and they pointed out that elderly people with physical disabilities must restrict their social communication with a tendency, as a result, to diminish social contact and responsiveness. They agreed with Kay and Roth that, for younger paraphrenics, physical illness is rare and disturbances affecting the balance and regularity of domestic life are commoner, but they stressed the need for careful exploration of even minor ailments. They noted that visual and auditory hallucinations were often stimulated by perceptual impairment: "The flashing of lights, the movements of threatening figures, the sounds of radio, the disturbances of ominous machinery, and many of the hallucinatory experiences could be partly attributed to these perceptual defects" (18). They also found that deafness accompanied by tinnitus was associated with machinery, lorries, and so on. Herbert and Jacobson had little doubt that the aging process aggravated the misinterpretation of common experiences due to visual or auditory loss. The lack of the critical company of others, they pointed out, which would correct misinterpreted experience, as well as the loss of warm emotional relationships as helplessness increases, seems logical grounds for thinking that physical illness, blindness, and deafness are causally connected with the psychosis.

It is apparent that there is much conflict in the evidence available in regard to the linking of psychiatric diagnosis with physical illness in patients admitted to hospital because of mental disorder in old age. Writers seem to be agreed on the close association between delirium (acute brain syndrome) and physical disorder but this is largely a matter of agreed definition. There is no clear agreement on the question of which of the other psychiatric classifications is most involved with physical disorder (although paraphrenia is generally thought to be least involved), nor on the extent to which late paraphrenia is associated with physical illness and sensory defect.

PHYSICAL STATES IN PSYCHIATRIC PATIENTS IN THE COMMUNITY

The psychiatrically ill person who is admitted to hospital is, of course, selected in a variety of ways and may not be representative of all people with psychiatric disorder. In the same way, the person who remains at home, whether ill or not, has been affected by some sort of selection procedure. It is common experience that, in domiciliary practice, many patients are seen by the psychiatrist who might benefit from being seen by the geriatric physician, and vice versa. The admission of an elderly patient to a psychiatric hospital rather than to a geriatric unit may depend on which consultant sees the patient first, or which consultant has the stronger personality (if both become involved), or simply on the facilities available in hospital. Clearly the studies quoted above of patients admitted to psychiatric units are affected by unknown selection procedures and it is not certain what findings would emerge for hospital patients as a whole were a comprehensive service for all elderly admissions available.

In the setting of an urban area served by a joint psycho-geriatric assessment unit as well as by separate psychiatric and geriatric services, one of the present authors has found that of 82 cases seen at home as psychiatric consultations, 32 had sufficient evidence of accompanying physical disorder to warrant admission to the psycho-geriatric unit. Even this proportion might have been exceeded had the total service facilities to the elderly allowed of ideal placement in every case. It is obviously of value, therefore, to have studies carried out in the community on a random sample of old people who have not been referred for hospital admission and have not, therefore, been subjected to screening on the basis of the services available.

Kay, Beamish, and Roth (27) carried out such a study on persons over 65 and their findings are of major interest. Physical disability (not including sensory defect) of moderate or severe degree was found in 29% of the sample. Of those who were psychiatrically normal, 16% had such a disability, while 66% of those with organic mental disease and 41% of those with functional (psychogenic) mental disease were so affected. In addition, a second moderate or severe disability occurred in 7% of the sample: 2% in the psychiatrically normal; 17% in the organic psychiatric group; and 12% in the functional group. Chronic disability of any grade (still excluding sensory defect) occurred in 23%, deafness was found in 37%, and visual defect was noted in 27%. Incontinence of urine was found in 19%, liability to falls was noted in 29%, and cerebrovascular disease was diagnosed in 4%. Twenty-seven percent of the sample had been inpatients in a general hospital within the previous five years, and 60% of the sample had seen their doctor in the past three months.

The organic psychiatric group (acute or chronic brain syndrome) showed the highest prevalence of physical illness. There were statistically significant differences between the normal, organic, and functional groups with respect to physical disability, deafness, incontinence of urine, liability to falls, seeing their doctor, and needing home nursing care. Differences between the groups as to admission to general hospital and need for home help were also (although less) significant. Nursing care at home was being provided for 6% of the sample, and home help was being provided for 9%.

The cases involved in this study differ from the hospital cases in that the majority of psychiatric disorders were only of mild degree. Half of the 29 cases of organic psychiatric disorder were considered not to be severely deteriorated, and two-thirds of the functional disorders consisted of mild or chronic neuroses or character disorders.

The authors concluded that in the organic psychiatric group, age was an important factor, since over half of the subjects were over 75. They emphasized the strong association with physical disease or disability and pointed out that the disability was usually a direct consequence of focal brain damage or peripheral sensory defects. They commented that the association of sensory defects with organic mental states is too strong to be explained simply in terms of the age of the subjects and they suggest, therefore, that defects of sight and hearing may sometimes play a part in the production of the mental symptoms by reducing contact with the outside world. Extracerebral disease was present in a minority of cases and might have contributed to the mental disturbance. Among arteriosclerotic cases, they found that the other disease was often serious (diabetes mellitus, prostatic disease, hypertensive heart failure, chronic rheumatoid arthritis); they did not find serious disease in their cases of senile dementia but found on follow-up that two cases had improved mentally, apparently as a result of improvement in general physical condition. They found three cases in which the psychosis was a result of extracerebral disease (one case of malignant disease, one case of pernicious anemia, one case of malnutrition) producing cerebral changes.

In the functional group, physical disability again emerged as the most important single factor. Since disability may be largely subjective, the researchers examined the possibility that it was a consequence of the patients' abnormal mood. An objective assessment of disability was compared with the patient's own assessment and, while a number had to be changed from "moderate" to "mild," and one from "mild" to "moderate," the relative disability of the groups was little changed. Twenty-one percent of the normal group did not complain of any physical disability at all compared with 12.5% of the functional group; 25% of the normal group had a disability graded as moderate or severe, compared with 50% of the functional group.

The results showed that the association between physical illness and affective disorder found in patients admitted to mental hospital by Kay and Roth (28) was of general validity, and they commented that, although Busse and Dovenmeuhle (10) found that, generally, neurotics and normals do not differ in physical disability but the neurotics have more physical complaints, one must bear in mind that in affective disorder in old age exaggerated hypochondriacal complaints may effectively camouflage serious physical illness. "It seems indeed that these two aspects of illness—somatic and psychiatric—may at times, and in certain subjects, be so closely interdependent as to make it impossible to unravel cause and effect. With increasing age, psychosomatic disability in this sense may well be increasingly common" (27).

PHYSIQUE IN ELDERLY PSYCHIATRIC PATIENTS

A study of the constitution of elderly psychiatric patients by Patch, Post and Slater (41) revealed some interesting information about physique. One hundred fifty-eight patients (106 women and 52 men), who had been admitted to a psychiatric unit when aged 60 or over, were studied by anthropometry. Both in men and in women there was a significant association between outcome and one physical measure. The variable for women was chest width, narrowness being associated with favorable outcome; no explanation was proposed. The variable for men was weight; the lower the weight on admission, the better was the outcome. A similar correlation was found between outcome and measures of skinfold fat. It was found (although not proved statistically) that those who gained more weight tended to make more satisfactory and better sustained recoveries; the likely association with malnutrition was pointed out but there was no correlation with any diagnostic grouping, such as depression, and no obvious reason for the finding of this association only in men.

In relation to diagnosis, the most significant finding was that the physical differences known to exist between younger depressives and schizophrenics were absent in corresponding elderly patients. This suggested that factors associated with aging bring on these disorders in persons of a different constitution from young depressives or schizophrenics. This confirmed the findings of other workers (14, 15, 26, 43, 56) that there is much less hereditary loading among older depressives than among those with an earlier onset of depression. Although no significant correlation was found between physique and psychiatric diagnosis, a significant correlation was discovered in women between greater height and more neurotic features in the premorbid personality. An association was found between the diagnosis of dementia (and the presence of organic psychiatric features) and lower measures of height and biacromial width but it was considered that this was due to the association of both these factors with greater age. In depressives, organic mental features were correlated with a poor outcome, especially after six months; these patients, however, were of relatively heterogeneous premorbid personality, suggesting that organic processes may precipitate depressions in a variety of constitutions.

THE ELECTROENCEPHALOGRAM IN THE AGED

Maggs and Turton (35) studied the electroencephalographic variations in a group of people over 60 living normally at home and two groups of depressives, one containing patients whose initial illness occurred before 60 and one containing patients with an onset after 60. No definite difference in the record type was found between the three groups although there was a trend towards more abnormalities in the late onset depressives. The blood-pressure level and the age of the patient when the record was taken had no effect on the type of EEG or the percentage of abnormalities. The considerable number of abnormal records and large number of borderline records found in all three groups were thought to be an expression of a general aging process.

An increase in the amount of slow wave activity in people over 70 was found by Davis (13) and in males over 75 by Obrist (40). Hoch and Kubis (21), and McAdam and McClatchey (33) found close correlations between intellectual deterioration and electroencephalographic abnormality, which Luce and Rothschild (32) found 12% abnormal records in functional cases compared with 75% in organic cases. However, other workers (30, 54, 59) have not found this correlation and Sheridan et al. (52) point out that records often change within a few months in the elderly.

PHYSICAL CAUSES OF MENTAL CONFUSION

In order to stress the importance of the symptom of mental confusion in an older person analogy can be drawn with the "fit" or convulsion of the infant, and a thorough attempt must be made to make a proper diagnosis in such cases. Elderly people with impaired reserve of mental capacity become confused on occasions when a younger individual would not suffer this symptom. Fecal impaction, urinary retention, cardiac failure, anemia, uremia and infectious disease, e.g. pneumonia, are among the common causes.

Metabolic diseases, such as diabetes mellitus, may present with signs of mental upset, and this may also be associated with the treatment of this condition, as a patient on oral anti-diabetic substances may enter a phase where this therapy is no longer required and hypoglycemia may have insidiously occurred. Hypothyroidism is a cause of mental disorder in older people, and it always seems extraordinary that apathy may also be a feature of hyperthyroidism which may on rare occasions present with an onset of acute delirium. Elderly people with mental illness may be worth investigating more completely for hypocalcemia or hypercalcemia. Anderson, Cooper and Naylor (3) described two elderly patients who, suffering from manic-depressive psychosis (depressive reaction), had hypercalcemia from vitamin D intoxication concurrently. These patients developed hypernatremia, with severe potassium and water depletion. Hypercalcemia was pronounced, but both patients recovered quickly and their depressive symptoms resolved following water and potassium repletion and corticosteroid therapy. From this work it can be noted that it is easy to overlook vitamin D intoxication unless the plasma calcium is estimated regularly in patients receiving more than a few thousand units of vitamin D per day. This subject is important because of the reportedly high incidence of osteomalacia in elderly women.

Judge (25) has recently reported that potassium deficiency among older people may produce depression, apathy, weakness, paranoid ideas and disturbance of sleep rhythm, and that this type of deficiency can occur in two separate ways: (1) The diet being taken by the elderly person may not contain enough potassium. The intake may be less than 60 m.-equiv./day. Some of these people will show normal serum levels of potassium, but many will reveal improvement in mood and become more alert and active when given potassium supplementation. (2) The second type of potassium deficiency may occur in persons who are taking just enough potassium in their diet, but a secondary deficiency is produced because of an attack of diarrhea and vomiting, an acute infection or a small cerebrovascular accident. In addition, such persons may take a purgative or be given a diuretic and thus a potassium deficiency will be induced resulting in loss of muscle power, which, by the way, can be easily and accurately measured and the response to treatment thereby followed. These people tend to have a low serum potassium. It is likely too that vitamin C deficiency may be associated with apathy.

Brackenridge and McDonald (5) examined venous blood samples from 80 women patients over 60 years of age with psychiatric disorders and from 66 controls. They found that magnesium and potassium concentration in the red blood cells was elevated in certain psychiatric disorders, namely toxic confusional states, senile dementia (with or without impaired parietal lobe function), and chronic schizophrenia. Raised plasma magnesium concentration was also found in chronic schizophrenia. In mentally normal subjects they found strong linear correlations between duration of institutionalization and erythrocyte potassium and water content, but, in the psychiatric patients, this correlation was noted only in patients with senile dementia.

Cox, Pearson and Speight (12) measured total body water, extracellular fluid, total exchangeable sodium and potassium, renin substrate and renin activity in 22 elderly patients suffering from depression, ten elderly patients with dementia, and 11 younger controls. In both depression and dementia there was a loss of potassium and retention of sodium; the plasma levels of these electrolytes were normal and the changes were mainly intracellular. They concluded that, in depression, there is a loss of potassium from the cell with a corresponding entry of sodium, whereas, in dementia, there is an actual loss of cells together with potassium loss from living cells which may be the initial stage in cell breakdown. These authors also showed that there is total body weight increase in dementia due to retention of intracellular fluid and decrease of total body weight in depression.

The role of vitamin B_{12} deficiency is the subject of some controversy. Strachan and Henderson (57, 58) have studied this and folate deficiency.

Hunter and Matthews (22) have also studied vitamin B_{12} deficiency and both sets of workers recommend serum vitamin B_{12} assays in psychiatric patients. Their work followed a very long-standing interest in the relationship between pernicious anemia and mental illness which had been revived following the introduction of liver therapy (42, 47).

Screening of psychiatric patients for vitamin B_{12} deficiency was recommended by Herbert (19) but the method used was careful examination of the peripheral blood film instead of serum assays.

Shulman (53) studied 117 patients (110 of them over the age of 60) in a mental hospital by the same method and concluded that this was a useful and practical procedure in selecting patients for further investigation. He thought that, in an acute psychiatric unit, this might lead to selective serum assays in as many as 35% of the new admissions but had some doubts about the value of such investigations until more is known about the clinical significance of low serum vitamin B_{12} levels in psychiatric patients. After following the response of ten patients to treatment with vitamin B_{12}, he concluded that, on the available evidence from the literature, routine serum vitamin B_{12} estimation in all psychiatric patients could not be justified. He did, however, recommend careful hematological screening, especially for patients with organic confusional states and senile and presenile dementia of unknown origin.

Buxton, Davison, Hyams, and Irvine (11) studied 40 mentally normal patients and 40 patients suffering from persistent confusion or dementia without obvious cause. They concluded that it was unlikely that unsuspected pernicious anemia or pre-pernicious anemia is a sufficiently common cause of mental disturbance to justify routine screening. They commented that the screening of large numbers of psychiatric patients by Henderson and Strachan revealed an incidence of pernicious anemia similar to that found in the general population.

O'Brien (39) described the aetiological factors of dementia. Certain conditions such as vitamin B_{12} deficiency, myxoedema and syphilis are treatable while rarer causes include subdural hematoma and third ventricle cysts. Communicating or low-pressure hydrocephalus classically presents as an episodically progressive dementia associated with retardation, ataxia of gait and pyramidal tract signs. In advanced stages akinetic mutism and extrapyramidal signs may be found. The cerebrospinal fluid pressure is in the normal range and pneumoencephalography shows gross dilation of the ventricle system with failure of air to reach the subarachnoid space over the convexity of the hemispheres. There is usually a deterioration in the patient's condition after air-encephalography in marked contrast to the reaction seen in Alzheimer's disease. Provided that there is a free communication between the basal cistern and the lumbar theca, patients should show improvement following repeated lumbar puncture.

Treatment by ventriculo-atrial shunting can produce a most dramatic result and this has led to a search for this condition in many patients presenting with dementia. A number of special tests are now available which help in the diagnosis of this condition. Isotope cisternography is the most widely used special test. Here radioactive iodinated human serum albumin (RISHA) is injected into the lumbar theca and diffuses throughout the subarachnoid space. In normal subjects the RISHA spreads over the surface of the hemisphere from the basal cistern with little or none entering the ventricular system because of the normal flow of cerebrospinal fluid from the ventricles to the basal cisterns and then over the surface of the brain to the arachnoid villi in the longitudinal sinus. In patients with communicating hydrocephalus little or no RISHA reaches the surface because of the extra-ventricular block of cerebrospinal fluid pathways, and heavy concentration appears in the ventricles. The scan should be done at 24 and 48 hours to be of value in this differentiation. When the RISHA enters the ventricles only the absorption of RISHA into the bloodstream is delayed and the 24 hour RISHA plasma level remains low in comparison to the normal. This difference can be used as an additional test. Other tests of value include observation of the patient following repeated lumbar puncture, which is equivalent to ventriculo-atrial shunting, and a test which depends on the absorption rate of cerebrospinal fluid when the pressure is artificially increased in the lumbar region.

O'Brien suggested that there was a need for 1) a method of determining the role of vascular disease in any individual with dementia—this would be with a view to treatment even if vascular disease was not the major aetiological factor, since in dementia very small changes in performance make a big difference in social and domestic welfare; 2) biochemical studies in the endeavor to understand the basic biochemical changes associated with the aging process; 3) the elucidation of further treatable causes of dementia otherwise unrecognized—the best recent example was communicating hydrocephalus.

DRUGS AND THE AGED

Drugs such as digitalis, benzhexol, barbiturates, and phenothiazines may produce confusional states. Fluphenazine has been blamed for causing severe depression, and there seems no way of predicting which patients are liable to develop phenothiazine-induced depression. Anti-hypertensive drugs, e.g. methyldopa, have also been reported to produce depression, and in the upper age range from 60 on there is less indication for such therapy. A history of transient loss of power of arm or leg or aphasia, symptoms of severe headache or hypertensive cardiac failure would be among the reasons for using preparations such as methyldopa. In the absence of some such indication the use of such drugs in the very old might well be reserved for those whose diastolic pressure is above 120 mm./Hg. The work of Gibson and O'Hare (17) has drawn particular attention to the dangers of medication in the patient's own home.

MENTAL BARRIERS TO REHABILITATION

The elderly, especially those with brain damage due to stroke, are prone to fear and anxiety through faulty comprehension or perception of situations which would not disturb a person with an undamaged brain. Adams and Hurwitz (2) in 1963, writing about the mental barriers to rehabilitation, demonstrated that faulty comprehension was one of the problems accompanied by a lack of understanding on the part of medical and nursing staff. Hurwitz (23), discussing the factors on which stroke patients' prognosis and eventual placement will depend, has drawn up a list of physical and higher integrative functions which determine the patient's fate. He has also shown that past attainments, as well as the part played by relatives and the hospital and community services, determine the eventual outcome. Among the physical factors are degree of paralysis, discriminative sensory loss, joint position sense loss, postural hypotension, incontinence of urine, and cardiac and respiratory reserve. The need to look for dementia, language disturbance, neglect or denial of hemiparesis, motor perseveration, memory loss for immediate events, apraxia, catastrophic reactions and depression are stressed with regard to the higher integrative functions.

This careful complete assessment of the stroke patient and the intimate and accurate diagnosis of the neurological deficit have improved the outlook for such people. Adams (1) compared the results of his rehabilitation in 710 hemiplegic patients treated between 1948 and 1956 with 729 such patients treated between 1959 and 1963. In the first group 42% regained independence in walking and self-care; in the second series 59% reached this stage. Those remaining chronic invalids consisted of 38% in the first series and 26% in the second. It took many years for the doctor to realize that the patient with the stroke might also be so depressed that he had no desire to get better, and that without a distinct and separate therapy for his depression he was unlikely to benefit from rehabilitation. Rehabilitation must be considered from the aspect of physical factors, mental health and social circumstances.

HISTORY TAKING WITH THE ELDERLY

As people grow older the concept of a single pathology has to fade into the background and the realization of the common occurrence of multiple pathology takes its place. Many previous illnesses may have occurred, the onset of this particular one may well be insidious, and thus the doctor must learn to spend time in taking a history from his patient. The history may be misleading; for example, the patient may fail to direct her complaints to the organ that is affected. The older woman may complain of pain in the neck or high up in the chest but may not mention any abdominal pain, when in fact investigation reveals a gastric ulcer on the lesser curvature. Because of that she may have been labelled as neurotic. The doctor must beware of disbelieving his patient if the symptoms do not fit neatly into a diagnostic category of which he has previous knowledge and experience, while a common disease may be present in an unusual way. This is in essence the art of geriatric medicine, to realize that often there will be no logical description of disease. Frequently the elderly patient, having suffered loss of status, of income, of companionship, of husband or wife, and of confidence may drone out in a monotone what seems to be a series of disasters.

Denial of disease in the older person—"This cannot have happened to me"—is not uncommon and may play a part in the late reporting of illness which is so common in older people. They may be unwilling to admit they are ill and to report this illness to their doctor. There is a lack of adaptation to decline in physical attributes which may influence the concept of self and result in loss of personal identity. This would explain denial of illness and depression; the drive and ambition of the younger person are lost.

Many elderly people have a phobia of organic disease, and this is an indication for investigation, diagnosis and reassurance. In this welter of emotional overtone the importance of accurate diagnosis must be stressed, and the physical illness must be discovered.

While there is abundant confirmation that the elderly mentally ill require comprehensive physical hematological and biochemical investigation, there is also suggestive evidence that there is need to improve by every possible means their mental health. Newman (38) has given a reasoned theory to account for some cases of incontinence. He believes that it may be the result of rejection by society. This theory is based on observation of what happened to young healthy adults, e.g. prisoners of war, who, placed in darkened rooms and given food at irregular intervals so that day and night were indistinguishable, became incontinent. They felt completely rejected by their relatives and friends. Newman certainly associates incontinence in the elderly with isolation, humiliation and privation, and states that a greater understanding of their needs might reduce the dimensions of the problem.

CONCLUSION

In old age the process of aging is intertwined with pathological changes, and these affect not only the brain but many other organs of the body. Mental illness in the elderly is commonly associated with physical illness and on occasion the physical illness is remediable with consequent cure of the mental upset. Collaboration between geriatric and psychiatric services is essential to the majority of elderly patients. The real psycho-geriatric unit in which geriatric physician and psychiatrist share duties and responsibilities is the best situation for full assessment and for forging links with local authority services. Long-term care organized on the same basis will almost certainly be the pattern of future care for many, if not most, of the elderly who require hospital services.

REFERENCES

1. ADAMS, G. F. 1967. Problems in the treatment of hemiplegia. *Geront. Clin.*, 9, 285.
2. ADAMS, G. F. and HURWITZ, L. J. 1963. Mental barriers to recovery from strokes. *Lancet.*, 2, 533.
3. ANDERSON, D. C., COOPER, A. F. and NAYLOR, G. T. 1968. Vitamin D. intoxication with hypernatraemia, potassium and water depletion and mental depression. *Brit. Med. J.*, 4, 744.
4. BATCHELOR, I. R. C. and NAPIER, M. B. 1953. Attempted suicide in old age. *Brit. Med. J.*, 2, 1186.
5. BRACKENRIDGE, C. J., and McDONALD, C. 1969. The concentrations of magnesium and potassium in erythrocytes and plasma of geriatric patients with psychiatric disorders. *Med. J. Australia.*, 2:390.
6. BURVILL, P. W. 1970. Physical illness in the elderly. *Geront. Clin.*, 12:288.
7. BUSSE, E. W. 1965. The early detection of ageing. *Bull. N.Y. Acad. Med.*, 41:1090.
8. BUSSE, E. W. 1966. The effects of ageing upon the central nervous system. Abstracts of papers presented at the 7th International Congress of Gerontology, Vienna. p. 40.

9. Busse, E. W. 1969. Psychophysiological reactions and psychoneurotic disorders related to physical changes in the elderly. *8th International Congress of Gerontology. Proceedings*, 1:195. Washington, D.C.

10. Busse, E. W., and Dovenmeuhle, R. H. 1960. Neurotic symptoms and predisposition in ageing people. *J. Amer. Geriat. Soc.*, 8:328.

11. Buxton, P. K., Davison, W., Hyams, D. E., and Irvine, W. J. 1969. Vitamin B₁₂ status in mentally disturbed elderly patients. *Geront. Clin.*, 11:22.

12. Cox, J. R., Pearson, R. E., and Speight, C. J. 1971. Changes in sodium, potassium and body fluid spaces in depression and dementia. *Geront. Clin.*, 13:233.

13. Davis, P. S. 1941. The electroencephalogram in old age. *Dis. Nerv. Syst.*, 2:77.

14. Freudenberg, R. K., and Robertson, J. P. S. 1956. Personal stresses in relation to psychiatric illness. *Proc. Roy. Soc. Med.*, 49:1034.

15. Funding, T. 1961. Genetics of paranoid psychoses in later life. *Acta Psychiat. Scand.*, 37:207.

16. Gibson, A. C. 1961. Psychosis occurring in the senium. *J. Ment. Sci.*, 107:921.

17. Gibson, Iris I. J. M., and O'Hare, Margaret M. 1968. Prescription of drugs for old people at home. *Geront. Clin.*, 10:217.

18. Herbert, M. E., and Jacobson, S. 1967. Late paraphrenia. *Brit. J. Psychiat.*, 113:461.

19. Herbert, V. 1959. *The Megaloblastic Anaemias*. New York and London: Grune and Stratton.

20. Herridge, C. F. 1960. Physical disorders in psychiatric illness. *Lancet*, 2:949.

21. Hoch, P., and Kubis, J. 1941. Electroencephalographic studies in organic psychosis. *Amer. J. Psychiat.*, 98:404.

22. Hunter, R., and Matthews, D. M. 1965. Mental symptoms in vitamin B₁₂ deficiency. 2:738.

23. Hurwitz, L. J. 1969. Management of major strokes. *Brit. Med. J.*, 3:699.

24. Judge, T. G. 1968a. *Semmelweiss Centenary Meeting of the Hungarian Association of Gerontology*. Budapest. Abstracts.

25. Judge, T. G. 1968b. *Proceedings of the 5th European Meeting of Clinical Gerontology*. Brussels, p. 295 and personal communication.

26. Kay, D. W. K. 1959. Observations on the natural history and genetics of old age psychosis: a Stockholm material, 1931-1937. *Proc. Roy. Soc. Med.*, 52:791.

27. Kay, D. W. K., Beamish, P., and Roth, M. 1964. Old age mental disorders in Newcastle upon Tyne *Brit. J. Psychiat.*, 110:682.

28. Kay, D. W. K., and Roth, M. 1955. Physical accompaniments of mental disorder in old age. *Lancet*, 2:740.

29. Kay, D. W. K., and Roth, M. 1961. Environmental and hereditary factors in the schizophrenias of old age ("late paraphrenia") and their bearing on the general problem of causation of schizophrenia. *J. Ment. Sci.*, 107:649.

30. Liberson, W. T., and Seguin, C. A. 1945. Brain waves and clinical features in arteriosclerotic and senile mental patients. *Psychosomat. Med.*, 7:30.

31. Lovett Doust, J. W. 1952. Psychiatric aspects of somatic immunity. *Brit. J. Soc. Med.*, 6:49.

32. Luce, R. A., and Rothschild, D. 1953. Correlation of electroencephalographic and clinical observations in psychiatric patients over 65. *J. Geront.*, 8:167.

33. McAdam, W. and McClatchey, W. T. 1952. Electroencephalogram in aged patients of mental hospital. *J. Ment. Sci.*, 98:711.

34. Macmillan, D. 1960. Preventative geriatrics. *Lancet*, 2:1439.

35. Maggs, R., and Turton, E. C. 1956. Some EEG findings in old age and their relationship to affective disorder. *J. Ment. Sci.*, 102:812.

36. Mayer-Gross, W., Slater, E., and Roth, M. 1960. *Clinical Psychiatry*. London: Cassells.

37. MORRIS, P. A. 1962. A survey of 100 female senile admissions to a mental hospital. *J. Ment. Sci.,* 108:801.
38. NEWMAN, J. L. 1969. The prevention of incontinence. *8th International Congress of Gerontology. Proceedings,* 2:75. Washington, D.C.
39. O'BRIEN, M. D. 1971. Some neurological aspects of dementia. *Geront. Clin.,* 13:339.
40. OBRIST, W. D. 1951. The electroencephalogram of normal male subjects over age 75. *J. Geront.* 6:130. Supplement No. 3 (Abstract).
41. PATCH, I. C. L., POST, F., and SLATER, P. 1965. Constitution and the psychiatry of old age. *Brit. J. Psychiat.,* 3:405.
42. PHILLIPS, N. R. 1931. Mental disorders associated with pernicious anaemia. *J. Ment. Sci.,* 77:549.
43. POST, F. 1962. The significance of affective symptoms in old age: a follow-up study of one hundred patients. *Maudsley Monograph No. 10.* London: Oxford University Press.
44. POST, F. 1965. Diagnosis and management of paranoid syndromes. In *Psychiatric Disorders in the Aged.* Manchester: Geigy, U.K.
45. POST, F. 1968. The factor of ageing in affective illness. In *Recent Developments in Affective Disorders.* Ed. Coppen, A., and Walk, A. *Brit. J. Psychiat.,* Spec. Pub. No. 2.
46. POST, F. 1969. The relationship to physical health of the affective illnesses in the elderly. *8th International Congress of Gerontology. Proceedings,* 1:198. Washington, D.C.
47. RICHARDSON, W. 1929. Pernicious anaemia. Results of its treatment with liver or its derivatives in 67 cases. *New Eng. J. Med.,* 200:540.
48. ROESSLER, R., and GREENFIELD, N. S. 1961. Incidence of somatic disease in psychiatric patients. *Psychosom. Med.,* 23:413.
49. ROTH, M., and KAY, D. W. K. 1956. Affective disorder arising in the senium. *J. Ment. Sci.,* 102:141.
50. SAINSBURY, P. 1955. *Suicide in London.* London: Chapman.
51. SAINSBURY, P. 1962. Suicide in later life. *Geront. Clin.,* 4:161.
52. SHERIDAN, F. P., YEAGER, C. L., OLIVER, W. A., and SIMON, A. 1955. Electroencephalography as diagnostic and prognostic aid in studying senescent individual. Preliminary report. *J. Geront.,* 10:53.
53. SHULMAN, R. 1967. A survey of vitamin B_{12} deficiency in an elderly psychiatric population. *Brit. J. Psychiat.,* 113:241.
54. SILVERMAN, A. J., BUSSE, E. W., BARNES, R. H., FROST, L. L., and THALER, M. B. 1953. Studies on processes of aging: Physiologic influences of psychic functioning in elderly people *Geriatrics,* 8:270.
55. SIMON, A., and TALLERY, J. E. 1965. The role of physical illness in geriatric mental disorders. In *Psychiatric Disorders in the Aged.* Manchester: Geigy, U.K.
56. STENSTEDT, A. 1959. Involutional melancholia. An etiologic, clinical and social study of endogenous depression in later life, with special reference to genetic factors. *Acta Psychiat. et Neurol. Scand.* Supp. 127, 34:1.
57. STRACHAN, R. W., and HENDERSON, J. G. 1965. Psychiatric syndromes due to avitaminosis. B_{12} with normal blood and marrow. *Q. J. Med.,* 34:303.
58. STRACHAN, R. W., and HENDERSON, J. G. 1967. Dementia and folate deficiency. *Q. J. Med.,* 36:189.
59. STRAUSS, H., and GREENSTEIN, L. 1948. Electroencephalogram in cerebrovascular disease. *Arch. Neurol. and Psychiat.,* 59:395.
60. WILLIAMSON, J. 1966. Ageing in modern society. Paper presented to Royal Society of Health, Edinburgh, 9 November.
61. WILSON, F. G. 1970. Social isolation and bereavement. *Lancet,* 2:1356.

6

PSYCHOLOGY OF AGING:
Basic Findings and Some Psychiatric Applications

JAMES L. FOZARD

Research Psychologist, Veterans Administration Normative Aging Study and Principal Research Associate in Psychiatry, Harvard Medical School, Boston, Mass.

and

JOHN C. THOMAS, JR.

Research Associate in Psychiatry, Harvard Medical School, and Associate in Psychology, Massachusetts General Hospital, Boston, Mass.

"At fifteen, I set my mind on learning; at thirty, I stood firm to my purpose; at forty, I acted with discretion; at fifty, I knew Ming (Decree of Heaven)! at sixty, I comprehended truth; and now at seventy, I can follow my heart's desire without transgressing the sense of justice."—Confucius, *The Analects of Confucius*. Trans. Arthur Waley. London: Allen and Unwin, 1938.

Some of the research reported was supported by the Boston Veterans Administration Outpatient Clinic Normative Aging Study, Benjamin Bell, M.D., Director; National Institute of Health Grant HD 05699; and the Council for Tobacco Research-U.S.A.

INTRODUCTION

Aging, both as a phenomenon and as a subject of scientific study, bears certain resemblances to the weather. Both affect everyone, including those who study them. As natural phenomena, both are generally thought to be universal, and, within broad limits, there does not seem to be much that anybody can do about either of them. People never seem to tire of discussing these topics, nor of listening to pronouncements and predictions about them, especially when the latter have an optimistic tone.

As in the case of meteorologists, gerontologists perform the scientific task of description better than those of correlation, prediction and application. Individual variations in basic behavioral and biological systems of the organism are very substantial indeed, and accurate predictions of an individual's aging are diffcult to make, just as the complexities of meteorological patterns restrict the success of prediction of local weather conditions. The development of palliative measures for the problems posed by aging is more advanced than technologies of intervention in the aging process, just as in meteorology, the technology of items such as unbrellas and rainware is more advanced than that of cloud seeding.

The generalizations about aging made in the whimsical analogy above are particularly applicable to the psychology of aging, in which variations in basic psychological processes associated with aging are measured. In the present chapter, we will see that there are significant age-related changes in certain aspects of behavior that have practical implications for psychiatry. With some possible exceptions in extreme senility, there is little evidence, however, that there is a single pattern of personality, abilities, interests, or style of problem solving and thinking that uniquely characterizes old people. If anything, individual differences in psychological characteristics may be more pronounced in old age than in younger adulthood. Many of the functional problems dealt with in clinical practice with older persons involve syndromes such as hypochondriasis or depression. These in turn may be associated with illness, institutionalization, or loss of social roles. While the incidence of such crisis-inducing events may increase with advancing age, there is little evidence that the responses to such crises by elderly individuals are more stereotyped than is the case with young and middle-aged adults. Aside from clinical problems, there is good documentation that there are many equally successful ways of adapting to the psychological stresses and problems of aging. The point is that diagnoses and planning of programs of therapy for older patients will require the same degree of attention to individual differences as would be expected for younger patients.

In the material that follows, the status of chronological age as a variable in psychology will first be discussed. Second, a simple model will be presented which attempts to organize the data to be presented on aging. Third, information on age differences in measures of personality, abilities, and interests will be summarized, followed by data from more controlled tests of sensory and perceptual functioning and memory and decision processes made in the psychological laboratory. The predictive power of age and social class will be compared. Finally, some general implications and recommendations for practice will be made.

THE CONTEXTS OF PSYCHOLOGICAL AGING

An adequate psychological description of aging requires an understanding of the relationships between psychological assessments of age and biological and social indices of age, as well as calendar age. Little progress has been made in any of these areas; the reasons are instructive to the clinician.

Physiological Bases for Psychological Aging

Biologists consider aging to be a universal, irreversible process that is detrimental to the organism (e.g., Strehler, 158). Aging is correlated with, but not equivalent to, calendar age. At the level of behavior of interest to the psychiatrist, it is difficult to find straighforward examples of psychological aging that are independent of disease processes as implied by the definition. Aging of the nervous and endocrine systems would be the most obvious biological bases for psychological aging. Nevertheless, it is very difficult to measure neurological aging, e.g., to obtain estimates of the rate of cell depopulation in nonmitotic neurons that are not complicated by variations in the degree of cerebral atherosclerosis and other disease states or by variations in environmental insult (30). This situation occurs in part because cells in the nervous system are so sensitive to anoxia (30, 168).

Studies that relate age to various neurological diseases have not been too helpful in defining normal aging of the nervous system. Certain degenerative morphological changes accompany several diseases of the nervous system: " . . . neurofibrillary degeneration, senile plaques, and granulo-vasculary degeneration . . ." occur in individuals with Alzheimer's disease, senile dementia, and Down's Syndrome (168, p. 259). The etiology of Down's Syndrome is different from the other two mentioned, and the typical age of onset of the degenerative changes in all the diseases mentioned is not the same. Thus, while there is little doubt that diseases of the nervous system are clearly related to behavior disorders observed in older patients, there is little evidence, either clinical or experimental, which relates behavior to possible changes in the tissues of the nervous system that occur independently of disease (e.g., Yoshikawa, Hirai and Morimatsu (191)).

The comparisons of resting electroencephalograms of persons over 65 years of age with those of younger persons have revealed various differences, particularly in the frequency and abundance of the alpha rhythm. (See Obrist and Busse (131), and Thompson and Marsh (163), for complete reviews of the literature.) There is little evidence that such age-related changes in the pattern of electrical activity of the brain are related to the variations in the cognitive functioning (132) or adjustment of elderly persons living in the community (33).

The slowing of response speed with advancing age is probably the most reliably documented behavioral phenomenon observed either within the laboratory or in everyday life. It occurs in very healthy individuals (16, 160). Attempts have been made to relate response time to patterns of activity in the brain, particularly age-related changes in alpha rhythm (e. g., see Surwillo, 159). One recent attempt to delineate the relationship between response time and the alpha rhythm frequency was reported by Woodruff (187) who used a biofeedback technique to train young and elderly subjects to increase or decrease their average alpha frequency by two hz. Concomitant measures of their simple reaction times indicated that the response times became shorter with increased alpha frequency and longer with lower frequency. Data from subjects who heard non-contingent feedback based on a prerecorded signal rather than their own brain waves showed no changes in average reaction times. While the data failed to support Surwillo's interesting hypothesis that alpha rhythm is a master timing mechanism of behavior (159), they did clearly demonstrate a plasticity of the nervous system that would not be expected from the simple biological definition of aging. This technique also provides one possible means of determining the limits of relationships between behavioral and neurological function and suggests that some of the effects of "age" on response time may be manipulated experimentally.

There have been many other attempts to relate nervous system and endocrine system functioning to behavior. For example, Nowlin (129) reports that the deceleration of heart rate typically observed in young patients during the time elapsing between an alerting signal and the presentation of a critical signal for a simple manual reaction is not observed in older subjects. This age effect appears to be independent of the absolute difference level in systolic and diastolic blood pressure. The practical significance of these findings for psychiatry is not yet clear and a discussion of them is beyond the scope of the present chapter. Excellent reviews are available in Thompson and Marsh (163), Cohen and Shmavonian (49) and several chapters in Welford and Birren's text (180).

Functional Indices of Aging

The information presented above carries with it the implication that chronological age *per se* is not completely satisfactory as a vehicle for describing the behavioral or psychological ages of an individual. Nor does calendar age provide an entirely satisfactory basis for relating the biological to the psychological aging processes.

The problems of relating age to behavior are not simply empirical. Establishing correlations between behavior and chronological age, or using the latter as a basis for specifying subgroups of subjects within which to seek relationships between behavioral and biological indices, will not by itself provide an understanding of ontogenetic development. The passage of time does not provide a satisfactory scientific explanation of aging. Ideally, the psychologist interested in studying aging would want to be able to manipulate conditions which make an individual appear young or old (9, 106, 114). As pointed out by Kerlinger (109), chronological age is an assigned or organismic variable, and as such it cannot be varied or arbitrarily assigned in an experiment.

To improve our understanding of aging for both scientific and practical purposes, indices of aging have been proposed that are based on functional assessments of an individual rather than his chronological age. Examples for scientific purposes in biology (51, 60, 70, 94, 133), psychology (15, 91), and sociology (141, 142) exist as do indices oriented toward practical purposes such as assessments of fitness for various occupations (75, 112). Of particular interest to physicians is Comfort's (51) proposal to evaluate and measure some 55 biological and behavioral correlates of age in an individual, as a first step in developing interventive medical procedures.

Most of the proposals for indices of psychological age are based on assessments in performance of psychomotor speed and problem-solving abilities because these measures seem to show the most consistent changes with age. In Birren's (15) hierarchy of indices of aging, psychological age falls between biological and social age and would index the adaptability of an individual to his environment as well as his ability to master it.

A common assumption in constructing indices of aging is that an individual has several "ages," and that the proper description of an individual's "age" is based on a relationship among the various correlates of chronological age. Thus, Comfort's (51) working assumption was that a study of the patterns among the correlates of aging would provide a basis for developing a composite index of aging as well as providing a basis for intervention.

As part of an interdisciplinary effort to develop a family of biological and behavioral "ages" (59, 130), Fozard (71) obtained one estimate of chronological age based on scores from the 12 subtests of the General Aptitude Test Battery (164) and another based on the Cattell Sixteen Personality Factor Questionnaire (43). It was possible to compare the predicted ages of the subjects obtained by these two sets of measures to other estimates of age available on the same subjects based on sets of measures of clinical medicine (32), physical anthropometry (58), clinical audiometry (13), and sociological measure of occupational and family roles (142).

Some idea of the importance of the psychological measures that were used to generate the six estimates of age is shown in Table 1, which summarizes the results of a stepwise multiple regression analysis using all the 31 predictors for the six disciplines to predict the ages of 969 males at time of examination. The 12 variables selected account for about 65% of the variance in chronological age (30-87 years). The column labeled "R^2" indicates the relative contribution percentage of variance accounted for by each variable and the column labeled "simple r with age" indicates the correlation of the variables with chronological age. The column labeled "rx Beta" is the product of the Beta weight associated with each variable in the equation and age.

Within rounding error the sums of these products (known as Hoffman weights) is equal to the total R^2 of .65. One may sum the weights associated with the variables in various ways to see the relative contributions of those variables to the prediction of age. For example the contribution of the two psychological measures, Disassemble and Surgency, together accounts for .10/.65 of the accountable variance.

Table 1 indicates that of the various measures employed in these analyses, the amount of greyness in the hair as rated on a five point scale accounts for more of the variance in predicted age than all of the other measures combined. Considering now the psychological assessments, finger dexterity as measured by the Disassemble test was the second most im-

Table 1

Contribution (R²) of 12 Behavioral and Biological
Measures to the Prediction of Chronological Age
of 969 Healthy Males

Measure[a]	R^2	Simple r with Age	r x Beta
Grayness of hair	.40	.63	.22
Dissassemble test score	.06	—.45	.08
Speech reception loss	.06	.35	.04
Forced expiratory volume	.02	—.38	.07
Length of ear	.03	.30	.04
Percent hemoglobin	.02	—.17	.02
Chances for advancement in company	.01	—.29	.04
Perceived position in company hierarchy	.02	.17	.02
Surgency-desurgency score	.01	—.23	.02
Expected age of retirement	.01	.23	.03
Plan to remain with same company	.01	.22	.02
Hearing loss for 8,000 hz tone	.01	.38	.04
Total	.65		

[a] $F_{(12,473)} = 72.43$, $p < .01$

portant of all predictors while the measure of Surgency-Desurgency (a trait of happy-go-lucky vs. taciturn-sober) was less important.

The 12 measures shown in Table 1 are all unrelated to variations in education and socioeconomic status and, with the exception of their relationships to age, are unrelated to one another—with age controlled, none of the partial correlations among them was as large as 0.25, except for that between measures of hearing. The table undoubtedly underestimates the importance of variables commonly associated with aging such as glucose tolerance and cholesterol, since subjects in this sample had been screened for health (14). Nevertheless, Burney's (32) analysis of the longitudinal follow up of these subjects' health indicated that the patterns of the predictors of the ages of the subjects were surprisingly stable over a five-year period.

The findings from this study are consistent with the proposition that an individual has many "ages" and that aging processes in different behavioral and biological systems are independent of one another over a good part of the adult life span. They argue against the proposition that if a subject appears "old" by one criterion, he is necessarily old by others. The implication is that individual variations in abilities, personality, interests, etc., are not related to age in any simple way.

The work on constructing indices of aging is still quite new. Hopefully it will help clarify such issues as the shifts in the relative importance of genetic and environmental influences for psychological descriptions of an individual over his adult years. Such shifts might be expected to occur as one approaches the end of life, but as indicated by Rose and Bell in their analysis of predictors of longevity, the relationships among social, physical, and genetic predictors of longevity are complex indeed. They find in their study, for example, that in the case of advanced longevity, physical predictors are more important, while the contrary was true in the case of moderate longevity (143).

Implications for Physicians

Most of the research reviewed in this chapter is based on average trends obtained from groups of individuals who are grouped according to chronological age. We have seen that there are many other variables that may also be used to classify individuals in an attempt to thereby predict behavior: socioeconomic status, health, education, life-styles, and race are other such classifying variables. The relative importance of chronological age as a predictor of psychological characteristics will vary according to what is being measured, whether the study is longitudinal or cross-sectional, at what points in the life span the assessment is made, the epoch in which the assessment is made, and even the culturally determined expectations of the investigators making the observations. Certainly, secular trends in education, health, industrial technology, nutrition, and drug use are rapid enough so that what might be attributed to age may more appropriately be attributed to the epoch in which an individual experienced his early development. Accordingly, the interests and attitudes of an individual may say more about the environment in which he was raised than about his age as such.

Another caution that should be kept in mind is that although age often exhibits a fair degree of relationship to measures of ability, personality, and neurological functioning, there are still large individual differences remaining between persons within a given age group.

The purpose of taking an individual's age into account should be to help the clinician suit his treatments to the individual. Thus, it should constantly be kept in mind that people of all ages, including the elderly, still are very much individuals. In this chapter, average trends are often presented. The reader must always add the caution to himself that there is large variability around these main trends. If the reader treats all elderly people as if they were stereotyped oldsters, then one major purpose of the chapter will be defeated.

In fact, psychiatrists, who often deal intensively with individuals over a long span of time, might contribute substantially to the literature on aging with presentations of case histories. Naturally, a clinician aware of the experimental findings and methodology in this area will be in an optimal position to make such contributions.

MODEL OF PSYCHOLOGICAL AGING

The organism and its environment are best viewed as a unit for many kinds of analysis. The usefulness of a certain biological or psychological characteristic depends on the particular environment that constitutes the organism's ecological niche. Which is better—gills or lungs? Which is more adaptive—legs or wings? The absurdity of such questions is apparent; the adaptiveness of a physical characteristic depends upon the environment of the organism. The same is true of human psychological characteristics. Whether it is "better" to be aggressive or to be passive or even how perfect one's memory should be are questions that cannot be answered without knowledge both of the environment and of the other characteristics of the person. The results of sensory deprivation experiments (e.g., Heron (92)) attest to the psychological dependence of the organism on its environment.

No environment, however, stays completely constant; the organism must adapt to the changes within his own environment. By testing the ability of a system to adapt to new input, we can discover more about the capacity and health of a system than by observing it in an already adapted state.

For example, a glucose tolerance test will much more readily reveal a pathological condition than observing the static blood sugar level. Similarly, psychological tests which force the person to learn new material—i.e., adapt—much more readily uncover a reduced capacity to handle information than observations or tests of the person's preexisting knowledge.

Usually, when we measure the adaptive capacity of some system we are interested not only in whether or not the system adapts but also in the speed with which this adaptation takes place. For any individual who is not on the verge of death, an increased work load followed by a rest will eventually result in the heart rate returning to its pre-exercise level. An overweight, elderly man and an Olympic miler are alike in that respect. Where they differ tremendously is in the speed with which this happens. Similarly, unless there is some tremendously serious neurological deficit, most humans can eventually respond in a reaction time task, can eventually learn some new material, can eventually change their values. What seems to characterize many types of psychological impairment is the speed with which these various tasks can be accomplished.

In most everyday, in milieu situations, we can conceptualize the organism-environment unit as making its decisions based on some information about past experience. Typically, as an individual grows older and stays within a particular social and occupational context, he relies less on his own central internal memory and more on the external environment to provide memory, or presort data or reduce the information processing load. One way this can be accomplished is to use other people's judgments (17). As a person stays in a certain context he may in addition learn many specific helpful facts about the social and physical space around him. His processing capacity can therefore be less devoted to dealing with the minutiae (178). As a person ages, his own purely internal information-processing capacity may be reduced (38, 176). It is perfectly possible, however, that the total processing capacity of the organism-environment unit will go up with age (178). Evidence concerning the efficiency of workers suggests that in some cases improvement continues throughout adult life. Conductors and concert musicians provide several examples. Crossman (55) showed a cigar maker to continue improving his speed of operation over a 20-year span. Clay (46), reported in Welford (176), measured the speed of print shop workers and found that performance often increased with age—in some jobs even into the 60s.

Lehman's (117) study of major accomplishments in various fields indicates that occupations requiring or allowing external support such as army and navy commanders, politics, and finance peak relatively late (55 to 69). Occupations requiring a moderate dependence on environment, e. g., chemistry, typically show peak productivity earlier (30 to 34). However, when one considers very original work in mathematics and science and artistic creation in which the individual is almost totally dependent on his own resources, the peak is even earlier, in the 20s. One may speculate that as newer external memory devices such as tape recorders and computers become better interfaced with the human, the peak ages of productivity in these latter fields may occur later in life.

On the other hand, because of the older individual's relatively greater reliance on the environment, it is not at all surprising that sometimes changes which may seem minor to younger people can be lethal to elderly individuals. (See Blenkner (20) for a review.) In a very real sense, taking a person away from the social and physical milieu in which he operates reduces the capacity of the organism-environment unit to function on all levels. The extent of this reduction and the length of time before a new organism-environment unit of comparable capacity can be established varies with age.

The beginnings of an ecological theory of aging are outlined by Lawton and Nahemow (115). Their chapter not only documents the tremendous effects of environment, as evidenced by a review of the literature, but points out the importance of designing an environment which is just beyond the current capabilities of the organism. An environment which requires of the organism too much adaptation results in unhappiness and stress, and perhaps withdrawal. Conversely, an environment with too few demands allows the organism to become complacent and to deteriorate. Lawton and Nahemow also point out that the effects of an environmental change can depend upon whether that change was self-initiated or imposed from the outside. This macroscopic effect is mirrored in the laboratory studies to be discussed later. In responding in memory or reaction time tasks, the effectiveness of all people, and particularly the aged, depends on the degree of control over the situation that the individual himself exercises.

In this chapter, we will review findings that at first seem disparate. Some studies will claim age-related changes in intellectual and emotive functioning which are relatively severe and begin relatively soon after early adulthood. Other studies will claim that many kinds of functions remain amazingly intact over the major portion of a normal life span. If, however, we consider the organism and his environment as a biological unit, a consistency between the results of these two types of studies can be seen. In general, studies measuring the organism's adaptability to new situations apart from his own environment show larger, earlier, age-related changes or differences. We shall term such studies *in vacuo*. On the other hand, studies of the functions of the organism within his own environment show relatively small age-related differences or changes and in many cases advancing age is correlated with improvement. We shall term such studies *in milieu*. Even if there were *no* age-related changes in the central nervous system, established psychological principles of learning would indicate that the greater experience of the older individual would result in continued improvement of performance *within* his own environment but lessened ability to adapt to a very different environment.

AGE DIFFERENCES AND AGE CHANGES IN ABILITIES

One of the best established findings in the psychology of aging is that there are age differences in performance on tests of intelligence and aptitude. Typically, older adults perform more poorly than do younger ones. The standardization data for the Wechsler Adult Intelligence Scale provide an example (124). The Wechsler Scale consists of eleven subtests measuring vocabulary, factual information, problem solving, and measures of perceptual motor speed in the selecting and copying of non-verbal symbols. The single score that summarizes performance on the tests is called the intelligence quotient, or IQ, and is based on a weighted sum of subtest scores. In order to establish the test norms, Wechsler administered the test to a sample of persons in the United States that represented the appropriate proportions of males and females, occupational groups, educational levels, income, rural vs. urban living, etc., as well as age.

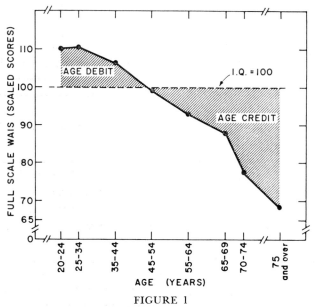

FIGURE 1

The number of points required to obtain an Intelligence Quotient of 100 in the Wechsler Adult Intelligence Scale for individuals in various age cohorts. From *Cognitive Processes in Maturity and Old Age* by Jack Botwinick, published by Springer, 1967. Reproduced by permission.

As expected, age was importantly related to overall performance. For purposes of computing an IQ, Wechsler therefore created separate tables of norms for different age groupings. The result is that a person's score is automatically compared to the average of his age peers. The age adjustments are illustrated in Figure 1 (from Botwinick, 23).

The vertical axis indicates the weighted sum of the scores from the eleven subtests. The horizontal axis shows the age groups used by Wechsler in establishing his normal values. The function shows the number of points needed for the mean IQ, 100 points, for people in various age groups. Clearly, the number of points required for an IQ of 100 decreases with advancing age. The data illustrated in the figure have resulted in a great deal of speculation about what the age differences mean and how they are to be interpreted. For example, is it true that scores on all of the subtests decline with advancing age, in the way suggested by Figure 1, and if so, do they decline uniformly? The following paragraphs summarize the major findings relating age to abilities such as those used in the Wechsler Scale.

Differential Effects of Age on Various Abilities

An important finding is that all abilities are not equally affected by age. In the Wechsler scales, for example, data from both longitudinal and cross-sectional studies indicate that there are virtually no age differences in performance on the vocabulary tests, and indeed, in some studies in which the effect of educational level is controlled, vocabulary is found to increase rather than decline with age.

Botwinick (23) summarizes the results of ten studies of Wechsler subtest scores with older populations and finds that older individuals (all over 60) did best on the information, vocabulary, and comprehension tests. They did fairly well on arithmetic, similarities, digit span, and picture completion. Their worst scores were on object assembly, block design, picture arrangement, and the digit symbol substitution task.

The Wechsler subtest showing the strongest and most consistent age decline in performance is the Digit Symbol Test. In this test, an individual is given a code in which the digits zero through nine are uniquely paired with geometric symbols such as a square, cross, etc. The subject is presented with several rows of digits and next to each he is to copy the appropriate geometric symbol. The code is in front of him at all times; his score is the total number of symbols correctly written in the alloted time.

Differences in the familiarity of the test materials may help to account for the differing effects of age on the vocabulary and on the digit symbol tests. In the case of vocabulary, the opportunities to learn and to use words should increase with age. An older subject should, accordingly, be more likely to know one of the words on the test list. In the Digit Symbol Test, on the other hand, the subject is required to learn and to utilize an arbitrary pairing of associations between geometric symbols and digits. The chances are remote that the skills tapped by the digit symbol subtest are used in everyday life.

Analyses of several kinds of test materials used in intelligence tests have led Cattell (41) to postulate two classes of intelligence: crystallized, as measured by those tests which rely on an individual's accumulated intellectual experiences, and fluid, as measured by his ability to adapt to new situations and solve unfamiliar problems. Considerable data now exist that support this interpretation (76, 91, 95, 127, 147). The vocabulary items test crystallized intelligence, while the digit symbol substitution task tests fluid intelligence. An individual's fluid intelligence is hypothesized by Cattell to peak early in adulthood; crystallized intelligence, to peak late.

Another explanation of the differential effects of age on performance in the two tasks is suggested by the fact that the requirements of the two tasks are not the same. In the case of the vocabulary subtest, the subject's only task is to define the target word. He does not have to use the word in a sentence nor to contrast its definition with that of another word. Also, the amount of time he takes to define a word is not considered in the scoring. An individual's score on the Digit Symbol Test, on the other hand, is based on the speed, as well as the accuracy, of his responses and response time is known to increase with age.

The two explanations just described are not mutually exclusive, and various experiments and analyses of the differential effects with age in performance on intelligence tests have suggested that all the factors considered by them are involved. For example, cross-sectional studies have shown that when a person is required to use words in some way other than simply defining them, age differences do appear. Thus, in the analysis of the vocabulary test of the General Aptitude Test Battery, small but statistically significant declines in performance with age are found (75, 164). In this timed test, the subject must select the synonym or antonym of the target word. Also, studies by Elias and Kinsbourne (66) have indicated that when subjects must categorize or select symbolic or verbal stimuli equated for difficulty, then equivalent age differences in performance occur with both classes of stimuli. These data suggest that the difference between age trends in subtests is not due to differences in material but to the requirements of each task.

The cross-sectional and longitudinal age declines found in the digit symbol task have also been analyzed. The age-related declines in performance could result in part from age differences in the speed of copying the unfamiliar symbols, from the difficulties in learning the codes—i. e., the pairing of the symbols and the letters—or differences in the cautiousness of subjects in looking up to confirm their choices before they write. The analysis by Jarvik, Kallmann, Lorge and Falek (101c) of the correlations among the subtests of Wechsler's scale show that performance on it is related both to differences in ease of learning new associations and to the speed of repetitive movements.

Schonfield's (153) research helps to distinguish among the alternatives —only a small part of the observed differences in performance can be attributed to age-related differences in speed of copying, cautiousness, or in the difficulty of writing the symbols. Rather, the age differences in the ease of recalling and selecting the correct codes seem to be most important.

When in the Life Span Do Changes Occur?

At what point in the adult age span do abilities measured in the psychometric assessments reach their peak, how long are they stable, and at which point do they decline? Evidence presented earlier indicates that the question must be answered separately for different abilities. The answer to the question is also different for longitudinal and cross-sectional data.

Estimates of the age at which IQ and verbal abilities reach a maximum has changed radically over the years. Green's (83) review points out that cross-sectional estimates of the typical age of maximum abilities increased from the early teens in World War I to the midtwenties in 1955. Green cites evidence which indicates that the bulk of this shift may be attributed to increases in the average amount of formal education. Numerous studies point to the same finding. (See Baltes and Lavouvie (10) or Nesselroade, Schaie, and Baltes (127) for a review.) A secondary reason may be associated with cohort differences in the familiarity with modern testing procedures.

Longitudinal studies have typically shown that age differences in abilities are less than in cross-sectional studies, and they indicate that the point of decline occurs later in life. Since educational levels vary across generations the maximum average level of abilities also varies with the cohort. Volunteer subjects in longitudinal studies are typically more highly selected than those in a general population; this can also affect estimates of age changes.

The same factors that influence the age at which maximum scores are achieved on ability tests also affect the length of the period of stability and point of decline on performance across the adult years. In addition, individual differences in tested ability are important. In their review, Riegel and Riegel conclude that, "Superior individuals show a faster rate of growth and a slower rate of decline; inferior subjects generally show slower rate of growth and a faster rate of decline . . . This holds consistently for tasks relying on unfamiliar material and new choices" (139, p. 313).

There is accumulating evidence for the existence of a discontinuous and abrupt drop in performance on ability tests in the periods ranging from a few months to about five years or more prior to death. Previous scores of surviving individuals are higher on the average than the scores of those who died. "In their study of elderly twins, Jarvik and Falek (101a) found that persons who have any decline in vocabulary scores or a yearly decrement in excess of 10% on the Similarities and 2% on the Digit Symbols Subtests were more likely to die within five years than coevals who survived longer than five years. The association between "critical loss" in scores and mortality was confirmed in a longitudinal analysis (Jarvik and Blum (101b)) which also revealed that the critical loss predicted mortality over a range of chronological ages and differences in genetic background. Case studies reported by Jarvik and Blum indicate that deterioration in cardiovascular status is associated with the change. Because the evidence supporting the concept of critical loss is based upon differences in mortality and morbidity of the members of monozygotic and dizygotic twin pairs, the association described by these writers is particularly compelling.

A related phenomenon, reported by Riegel, Riegel, and Meyer (140), shows that those individuals who resisted retesting in a longitudinal study of intelligence had lower initial scores than those who cooperated on the retesting. Both factors operate to bias the estimate of age decline in abilities. In the case of cross-sectional analyses, the estimates of age declines are probably underestimated because those persons who refuse to cooperate or who are near the end of their lives are probably less likely to be included in a sample. Longitudinal estimates of abilities are also selectively biased, because longer-lived individuals tend to have higher abilities.

Longitudinal studies of gifted individuals or healthy old persons (e. g., Bayley and Oden (11); Blum, Jarvik, and Clark (21); Granick and Birren (81)) would, according to this view, have underestimated the amount of decline in the population (139, p. 312).

Practical Applications

Practical applications for psychiatrists of the research on age-related differences in abilities are in three areas: (a) assessment of competence for employment and for living in a community as opposed to an institutional setting; (b) identification of certain patterns of brain damage and assessment of therapeutic programs; and (c) diagnosis of terminal stages of life, assuming that there is a baseline measure.

One of the psychiatrist's tasks is to decide whether psychometric assessments of abilities will be useful in the diagnosis and treatment of a psychiatric problem. He must also know how to make the best use of these assessments.

The variety of assessment procedures and the diversity of problems encountered in practice and research make it difficult to prepare a list of specific do's and don't's with regard to psychological testing. There are, however, two basic principles which are useful when evaluating the need for, or the significance of, an objective assessment of abilities. The first principle is that an individual's IQ or his profile of scores on a battery of ability tests only has meaning with respect to the expected values obtained by representatives of some reference group. The critical question to ask is: To whom is a person being compared? The more difficult it is to decide whether an individual is "typical" of those persons in a reference group, the more difficult it is to interpret his score. The evidence presented in this chapter has indicated that comparisons of the performance of elderly persons to the norms of a reference group of young, usually Caucasian, individuals who are optimally placed in a competitive industrial society will show them frequently at a disadvantage, just as in the case of representatives of delinquents, the institutionalized, or other disadvantaged groups. This comments is not intended as an attack against the use of objective assessments of ability, but rather against the uncritical applications of standards.

The second principle is that the utility of measures of abilities (or of any assessment procedure) in a practical clinical setting needs to be determined by some empirical procedure. No matter how technically excellent an instrument may be, and no matter how applicable the reference group norms seem, the value of the assessment procedure still needs to be empirically established. This principle is simply a restatement of the concept of validity in the use of tests. For example, in order to find out if a minimum level of intellectual ability is necessary for success- ful functioning outside of an institutional setting, it is necessary to correlate a measure of "successful functioning outside of an institution" with a measure of intelligence. Chances are that the major difficulty in answering such a question will be in obtaining a measure of "successful functioning."

Once stated, the principle of validity seems obvious enough, but it is often ignored or overlooked. The experience of the writers, as well as a reading of some popular attacks on the use of psychological tests in education and industry (e. g., Whyte 182), suggests that the attacks on the validity of the tests are misplaced; more frequently, the difficulty is in identifying and measuring the objectives of the testing program. In practical situations where difficult decisions about the relationship be- tween treatments and outcome criteria are being determined, the data from measuring instruments stand out as the single most visible source of information available, leading sometimes to the over-reliance on them by those who seek objective evidence and to an uncritical attack on them by others who may be angered by the failure of the "tests" to accomplish things for which they were never intended.

Vocational counseling. When using measures of ability for purposes of vocational counseling, one must remember that the relationships between measures of performance on the job and the measures of abilities estab- lished for young workers may not be appropriate for older workers (12, 74, 75, 161). Technological changes in work routines or the elimination of jobs through automation often have a relatively greater impact on the older worker, who experiences considerable difficulty in finding work that relies on his previous experience. One important use of aptitude tests is to help the older individual assess his potential skills for occupations other than those in which he has had extensive experience.

Appropriate employment has tremendous consequences for the mental health of the individual. Feelings of self- esteem and purposefulness are closely linked to an individual's work role; for middle-aged individuals in particular, the salience of the work role to an individual probably in- creases as children grow up and patterns of interest crystallize.

An objective assessment of abilities and a proper interpretation of them may themselves be of considerable therapeutic importance. Older persons who experience depression resulting from loss of jobs or from difficulty in finding employment may rationalize their difficulties, in part, by assuming that their abilities are not as good as they once were, or that they are not "as good" as younger persons with whom they may be competing for jobs. Misconceptions about the decline of abilities with age may have the psychological quality of a self-fulfilling prophesy. Although the evidence is scant, Green's (83) review of available research suggests that there is little objective evidence that directly links age *per se* to success or failure on a job. One possible exception is the occupation of air traffic controller. In this instance, persons between 34 and 52 had a failure rate in the training program of the Federal Aviation Administration Academy that was three times that of younger trainees, even though almost all trainees had had some previous experience. However, the stress and the demands to cope with an ever-changing flow of information characterize this job as unique (48).

In contrast, Welford (178) has suggested why the very same age-related changes in functioning that may reduce scores on standardized tests could produce improvements in executive abilities. Again, the validity of a test as a predictor of occupational fitness depends very much on the demands of the occupation, as implied by the model of aging presented earlier.

Diagnosis of brain damage. The most widespread application of ability tests in geropsychiatry is in the diagnosis of organic brain syndrome. The primary symptoms are impairment of recent memory, disorientation, and impairment of intellectual functioning. As indicated in Prien's (137) recent review, one complication of assessing brain syndrome is that patients are frequently difficult to test, with the result that it is difficult to isolate the effects of brain disease independently of the possible effects of poor motivation, fatigue, or communication difficulties. Whatever the shortcomings related to the use of objective measures of abilities, they are usually better than the informal clinical assessments frequently used to diagnose brain diseases—an unvalidated series of questions relating to orientation and memory for recent events, which are particularly unfair to persons who are in an institutional setting (96).

The complications of illness and the presence of functional psychiatric disorders not only render the diagnosis of brain syndrome difficult, but they also make the selection and evaluation of chemotherapies difficult. Behavioral improvement could occur from the administration of psychotropic drugs which relieve symptoms of depression or agitation, or improvement could come from drugs which influence cerebral circulation which presumably have a more direct bearing on brain function. Reviews by Prien (137) and in Wolstenhome and O'Connor (186) contain an extensive summary of research on the treatment of brain disease by chemotherapies. A frequently noted shortcoming of research in this area is the failure to include placebo controls. From the point of view of using individual, group, or milieu therapy, such shortcomings may be regarded as failures to fully utilize nonsomatic therapies. One use of ability measures has been to assess the effects of hyperbaric-oxygenation therapy. The value of the therapy is in some dispute, partly because of issues relating to patient selection, placebo effects, and the measures of abilities used. A useful summary is by Jacobs, Winter, Alvis, and Small (99).

The shortcomings in the diagnosis and treatment of organic brain syndrome in the elderly result in part from the readiness of clinicians to "give up" on elderly psychiatric patients, but they also reflect the more general difficulty involved in diagnosing brain damage. The similarities between the symptoms of aging and diseases of the nervous system have been pointed out by many authorities (see Welford and Birren (180) for several examples). Recently, considerable effort has been made to simplify and improve the quality of behavioral assessments of brain damage by the application of the concept of "biological keys" to the selection and organization of behavioral tests used to identify damage (150). This procedure requires cross validation and its application to older subjects is yet to be demonstrated. It shows considerable promise in simplifying the use of behavioral assessments in diagnosing brain damage and may make it more practical to use objective assessments more routinely to identify organic brain disorders in the elderly.

Prediction of impending death. Kral (113) has distinguished between two types of memory dysfunction in senescence: a benign type in which an unreliability of recall is temporary—i. e., the individual can recall the same material at one time but not at another; and a malignant type for which the cardinal symptom is failure to recall recent events. The general health and functioning of individuals with the malignant type of memory disorder consistently showed a shortened survival time and an increased death rate, regardless of other complications (over a three-year period of their study). These data, along with the information from the study of rate of decline of intelligence test scores described earlier (139, 101b), suggest that measures of intellectual functioning are important predictors of mortality and health. The possibilities of reversing the symptoms or for alleviating them are largely unexplored.

PERSONALITY AND ADJUSTMENT

Allport's (4) classic analysis of some fifty definitions of personality showed that this concept is not a simple one. Chown provides a succinct and practical definition: ". . . the gestalt of an individual's attitude, emotions, motivations and activity patterns—the impression a man makes on others and the impression he makes on himself" (44, p. 134). Personality includes an individual's perception of himself as well as the perception of him by others. With respect to aging and personality, Botwinick's remark seems apt: "The world changes for the older person because on the one hand he has changed; on the other hand, people often respond differently to him than they did when he was young" (24, p. 250).

Little systematic treatment of personality changes associated with aging is provided by either the major psychoanalytic or trait theories (see Hall and Lindzey, 89, for example). One notable exception is Erikson's extension of psychoanalytic theory (67); another is the theory of disengagement (57). Cattell (40) has speculated on possible changes in personality traits with age, but in a recently revised handbook for the Cattell Sixteen Personality Factor Questionnaire, Cattell, Eber and Tatsuoka (43) restricted their discussion of age to a presentation of formulae for "correcting" an individual's score on several of the 16 personality scales for which Sealy and Cattell found age-related differences. As a result, the relative position of an adult's scores on each of the bipolar scales may be compared to the values of a single adult reference group with an average age of 35 years. Scores on almost half of Cattell's personality scales are systematically affected by variations in education or socioeconomic status; some of those so affected also vary with age (73). Accordingly the practice of adjusting certain scores of the scale to some idealized age may not be more justifiable than some adjustment to a standard level of education or social class. Because the distributions of years of formal education and social class vary with cohorts of different ages, reference values for men and women which classify scores according to age and education would be the most valuable.

In any case, the ignoring of age by most theories of personality (see Hall and Lindzey, 89, for examples) and by most available "norms" for psychological instruments for personality measurement reflects the widely held belief that personality is believed to be stable over the adult years. From the material to be presented, it is equally clear that the expression of an individual's personality varies considerably in successive stages of adult life.

Theoretical accounts of personality development over the course of adult years have certain common tasks. First, they must relate the description of both the stable and the changing elements of personality to the different epochs of an individual's life that are psychologically important. (The process of identifying the important stages of development is, of course, not independent of the personality characteristics that are considered by particular theories.) Second, they must identify the relative importance of contemporary and antecedent factors, both intrinsic and extrinsic to the organism, for the description of an individual's personality.

As suggested by Urban and Lago (165), one's hypothesis about the importance of contemporary and antecedent factors as determinants of personality is especially important in clinical practice. The degree to which diagnosed psychopathology is viewed as the result of the accumulation of premorbid processes as opposed to the results of a response to contemporary stress may determine whether a choice of psychiatric treatment for an elderly patient would be different than that for a younger one (see Cameron (36); Rothschild (49); and Busse and Pfeiffer (35)). There is no single account of personality in the adult years that is completely satisfactory for either theoretical or practical purposes; the differences among contemporary views of personality and aging, accordingly, provide the more interesting information.

Erikson's (67) extension of psychoanalytic theories of personality specifies issues that seem particularly salient in different stages of life: for the young adult, coming to terms with intimacy was hypothesized to be most important; for the mature adult, generativity; and for the old adult, integrity and acceptance. Erikson's theory is oriented toward internal dynamics of personality and emphasizes the relative importance of antecedent events for descriptions of personality (see Slater 154, for another account of personality and aging based on psychoanalytic theory). Determining the relative degrees of continuity and specificity of the personality processes throughout the life span is the major task in evaluating this theory as well as in applying predictions from it to an individual's behavior. In fact, there has been considerable difficulty in describing and measuring the dominant personality processes postulated by the theory by means of interviews and projective instruments (87).

In contrast to Erikson's theory, the disengagement theory of Cumming and Henry (57) emphasizes the importance of changes in social roles with advancing age as important determiners of personality. Evaluations of the predictions about personality made by disengagement theory provide little evidence for a single dominant personality process in old age. Cumming and Henry's original formulation was that older individuals naturally withdraw from the world of people and things and become progressively more content to live in the present and relax. Results of tests and interviews with subjects in the Kansas City Study, as well as those of subsequent investigators, indeed suggest that older people have fewer and sometimes less intense social and personal interactions, but whether the withdrawal is voluntary or not is widely disputed (see Chown 44, and Maddox 121, 122 for reviews). A later refinement of the theory postulated two basic methods by which individuals of different temperaments adapt to changing social roles. For example, the "impinger," basically brash and lively, depends more on feedback from others than the "selector," who is reserved and self-sufficient (56).

Both psychoanalytical and social formulations of the stages of psychological development require a systematic description of the roles occupied by an individual in various stages of his life span. Lowenthal and her colleagues (119) classify stages of adult life according to whether the current stage represents an increment in activity (marriage, first job, children, etc.) or a decrement (child leaving home, widowhood, retirement). Roles are also classified according to their content—e.g., whether they are instrumental or social-affective—and their timing—e.g., whether they are scheduled or unscheduled (retirement vs. widowhood). This multiple classification of roles provides a framework for interpreting how personality is involved in adapting to the stages of life.

In applying the model, Lowenthal classifies both the activities associated with the roles and the expressed goals of an individual as either constrictive or incremental. The individual's behavior is then interpreted in terms of the congruence of roles and goals. The congruence of an individual's goals and his behavior in one epoch, along with an analysis of the types of expected transition (as incremental or decremental), allows one to anticipate the manner in which he will adapt to the next epoch in his psychological development. Simply to adopt the behavior appropriate to a new role may have more than one consequence. For example, a person who evidences both constricted behavior and goals in one epoch might not be well adapted during an incremental transition, e.g., to marry and to have children. In contrast, a person with expansive preexisting goals and restrictive behavior in one stage of life may achieve congruence between behavior and goals in a later stage involving an incremental transition simply by adopting the behavior appropriate to the later stage, e.g., the teenager who gets married and/or gets his first job. In this way, Lowenthal accounts for the frequent observation of psychiatrists that it is possible for an individual to be better adjusted in one period of his life than in another. It is also possible for an individual to facilitate a transition by adapting his goals to the possibilities associated with a new situation, e.g., a potential retiree who restricts his occupational (instrumental) goals and emphasizes social (affective) goals.

Within the framework of Lowenthal's analysis, persons moving toward expansion when facing a decremental transition are most relevant to the present discussion. As one extreme example, Lowenthal cites the example of the woman who, facing both the imminent death of her husband and the prospect of an empty nest, developed plans for training for a new career (thereby exhibiting what Lowenthal calls transcendence). Other behavioral possibilities for the expansive individual facing decremental transitions include disengagement, denial (the retiree who haunts his former place of employment), or escapism (the potential retiree who excessively plans his postretirement activities). A parallel analysis is made for the person with constrictive goals facing an incremental transition (119).

Personality Assessment with Questionnaires and Projective Tests

Some psychological evaluations of personality are based on responses to objective questionnaires or structured interviews—i.e., those in which the alternative responses to a query are established in advance. Others are based on projective assessments—i.e., the individual's interpretation of ambiguous stimuli, such as an ink blot (the Rorschach Test), or scenes depicting persons in various social situations (the Thematic Apperception Test), or the loosely structured questions in an open-ended interview. Projective instruments are predicated on the idea that such stimulus material provides an index of the strength of unconscious needs and motives not readily revealed by self-report procedures.

There is controversy among psychologists and psychiatrists concerning the value of psychological instruments for describing personality, as well as the relative merits of objective and projective instruments. As a practical matter, correlations between measures of adjustment, happiness, or other measures which might be expected to be related to differences in personality measured by the instruments have often been disappointingly small, partly because of problems associated with measuring personality and partly because of difficulties related to specifying and measuring the criterion, e.g., adjustment or happiness. Even more importantly, the adaptiveness of a personality characteristic, as pointed out by Lowenthal (119), depends upon the environment of the individual. Any attempt therefore to find a relation between personality and a criterion such as happiness, which fails to include environmental variables, is doomed to failure. Personality descriptions based on projective assessment procedures depend considerably more on the interpretations of the user and typically have less desirable psychometric properties than do the objective measures. On the other hand, some psychiatrists and psychologists feel that the self-report procedures provide relatively little information, and that the results can easily be faked, and so forth. These technical issues complicate the assessment of age differences in personality beyond the complexities of distinguishing the effects of age on personality from those of socioeconomic status or genetic factors.

The most consistently observed age difference measured by the Cattell Questionnaire occurs in Factor F. With older age there is a shift away from surgency toward desurgency (43, 73, 80). The surgent person is described as enthusiastic and happy-go-lucky, as opposed to the desurgent type, who is sober, serious and often glum. Cattell (39) characterizes the trend toward desurgency as representing the adopting by an individual of an increasing "load of care" associated with aging. Rose (142) suggests that the trend is associated with decreasing occupational ambitions. Trends toward lower impulsivity, a tendency to shy away from responses of anger, and lowered levels of energy with older age, that have been noted in scores on the Minnesota Multiphasic Personality Inventory (MMPI) (155), may be related to the age trend observed in Factor F. The age trend observed in the Normative Aging Study sample is unrelated to social class differences and other measures of ability and personality that correlate with age (71).

Two traits showing an increase with age are a tendency for an increase in self-sufficiency (Factor Q2), as opposed to a group dependency, and an increase of self-sentiment (Factor Q3), which is defined in terms of a tendency to show increase in persistence and a seeking of socially approved behavior, as opposed to poor self-sentiment or lack of persistence. With respect to the latter factor, Cattell and Eber (12) hypothesize that the degree to which one shows high self-sentiment represents the extent to which he has crystallized for himself a clear, consistent, admired pattern of socially-approved behavior to which he tries to conform. The age differences probably are not unique to particular social class groups (73). Some of the age differences noted in the three examples may reflect cohort differences, particularly the self-sufficiency dimension (141, 151).

Both cross sectional and longitudinal age trends have been observed with the Allport-Vernon-Lindzey Scale of Values. In the male sample of the Normative Aging Study, an increase with age was observed in the social value. The increase in altruistic or philanthropic love may reflect greater accumulated experiences with age as well as an increased need for older persons to relate to others. A parallel tendency has been noted in an analysis of items from the MMPI (44). The trend was not observed in a twenty-year follow-up of a highly educated cohort of engaged couples that was in its 20s in the period of 1935-38 (108). A trend toward an increase with age in religious values was found by Kelly and in the Normative Aging Study. The trend could of course be peculiar to the cohort studied by Kelly.

There is a tendency for older persons to be more introverted, a finding that has been documented in several measuring instruments. In the Strong Vocational Interest Blank (37), this tendency is reflected in the preference of older men for occupations that are individualistic rather than group oriented, and for a decrease in the tendency to prefer artistic occupations (73). The tendency toward introversion has also been identified in assessments of personality based on projective tests, such as the Rorschach, by Ames (5), in a longitudinal study.

All of the examples just given are for scores that fall in a normal range. Age trends in the Minnesota Multiphasic Personality Inventory, which is specifically devised to measure neurotic and psychotic tendencies, indicate little psychopathology that cannot be accounted for in terms of changes of health status. Aaronson (1) examined the effects of age on the peaks of the profiles and found the relative incidence of peaks in the Depression Scale increased with age while those for the Psychopath Scale decreased. Hypochondriasis was particularly prevalent among the middle age groups. Slater and Scarr (155) examined MMPI scales collected on a sample of 211 high socioeconomic status subjects at the New England Age Center and found older individuals to have higher intellectual control as opposed to impulsivity.

There are many other studies which could be cited. Most point in the same general direction. Typically, such tests characterize the older individual as higher in introversion, rigidity, control, and lower on impulsivity, activity, heterosexuality, and need for achievement.

The projective tests have also been used extensively to describe age differences in personality. Eisdorfer (63) reports that when differences in intelligence are controlled, responses to the Rorschach by elderly subjects do not vary from those of younger ones. Veroff, Atkinson, Feld, and Gurin (166) studied responses to the Thematic Apperception Test pictures in a national sample of American men and women aged 21-65. They found that need for achievement was lower among the older men and need for power was higher. Among women, need for affiliation and need for power were lower among the older women.

Extensive work on personality in the second half of life is presented by Neugarten and Associates (128). They studied Thematic Apperception Test stories in both cross-sectional and longitudinal comparisons; they found lower ego energy in affect-intensity, and lower activity-energy level with increasing age. A group of 144 subjects was divided into eighteen cells of eight each on the basis of sex, age (40-49, 50-59, 64-71), and social class (upper middle and above, lower middle, and upper lower). These persons were from the larger Kansas City Study. All were living in their own homes. Older subjects introduced fewer characters, introduced less conflict, exhibited lower activity-energy levels, and showed lower affect-intensity. A five-year follow up showed change in the direction of lowered energy level.

Further studies analyzed the Thematic Apperception Test stories of 287 men and women, aged 40 to 70, from the Kansas City Study. A cross-sectional comparison indicated that the older groups were more magical and less reality bound, and that their ego functioning and defense were more regressive.

These three studies just summarized are of particular interest because measures of the actual level of adjustment in the community were also available on the same subjects. In her summary of the studies on this subject population, Neugarten concluded that large age-related personality differences were found when the investigation was of intrapsychic mechanisms or ways of adapting. In contrast, few age differences were found when the investigation concerned the level of adjustment of the same individuals. The degree to which these results imply ontogenetic changes in personality with age is not clear; there is evidence, however, that as a group, older individuals are less "mature" in their methods of adaptation than young adults. On the other hand, older individuals are at least as likely to be adjusted.

The foregoing review has emphasized those aspects of personality that correlate with differences in age. There are, of course, many measured traits that show no relationship to age. A frequently observed example is an orientation towards people vs. things as measured by the Cyclothymia-schizothymia scale (Factor A) of the Cattell Questionnaire and the personal service oriented vs. product- or process-oriented occupation on the Strong Vocational Interest Blank (174). Some, but not all, of the traits that do not vary with age do vary systematically with socioeconomic status.

Figure 2 was constructed to provide an overall impression of the relative

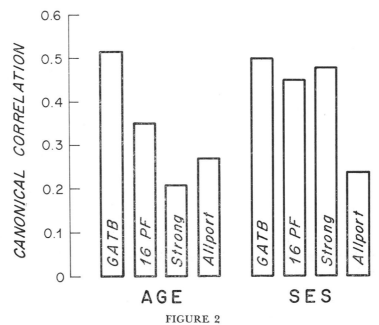

FIGURE 2

Canonical correlations are shown between age or socioeconomic status (SES) group-ings and scores on the 12 subtests of the General Aptitude Test Battery (GATB), the 16 primary scales of the Cattell Sixteen Personality Factor Questionnaire (16 PF), five interest factors scores from the Strong Vocational Interest Blank (Strong) and the six scores from the Allport-Vernon-Lindzey Scale of Values (Allport). There were six age groups the midpoints of which are 33, 38, 43, 48, 53, and 59 years respectively, and four SES groups, Warner Levels 1-2 (upper middle), 3 (middle), 4 (lower middle), and 5-7 (working class). Calculations are based on data from the United States Veterans Administration Normative Aging Study.

importance of variations in chronological age and socioeconomic status for describing patterns of abilities, personality, interests and values. The figure is based on responses of the same subjects to each of four instruments: the General Aptitude Test Battery; the Cattell 16 Personality Factor Question-naire instrument; the Strong Vocational Interest Blank; and the Allport-Vernon-Lindzey Scale of Values.

The vertical axis displays the magnitude of the canonical correlation between performance on the set of all the measures contained in each instrument on the one hand, and six age groups (median ages of 33, 38, 43, 48, 53, and 59) or the four socioeconomic class groups (upper middle, middle, lower middle, and working class) on the other. Canonical corre-lations are interpreted in the same way as simple correlation coefficients, i.e., the amount of shared variance between the two sets of measures is equal to the square root of the correlation coefficient. The size of the correlations between the ability and personality scores and age and SES is about the same. Age is considerably less powerful than SES in predicting interests. The figure suggests that, overall, socioeconomic status is slightly more important than age. Other results from the analysis indicate that the contributions of age and socioeconomic status were statistically independent. In practical terms this means that the amount of accountable variance is doubled when both factors are taken into account. Finally, the point should be stressed that age and SES together only account for about 50% of the variance in the ability and personality scores.

There has been less longitudinal research with studies of personality than with measures of ability. Recent research by Schaie and Marquette (151) serves as a vivid reminder that age-related differences may be affected by cohort differences and changes in scores may result from greater familiarity with the test materials on successive testings. Subjects, grouped into seven-year cohorts with mean years of birth ranging from 1889 to 1931, first were tested in 1956, and again in 1963 and 1970. Data from retesting of subjects were compared to those from independent samples tested just once. There were significant differences on all measures due to differences between generations. For example, a questionnaire measuring social responsibility in 1963 showed a cross-sectional decline in responsibility from age 39 onwards, but the same questionnaire given to comparable subjects in 1970 showed a cross-sectional increase up to 60 years. Substantial effects of the previous testing were also noted even though this testing had taken place seven years earlier. Significant effects of retesting were found for all four measures used. Investigators conducting longitudinal studies utilizing repeated measures *are not* safe in assuming that long intervals between tests prevent prior exposure effects. Changing sociocultural factors between 1963 and 1970 seem to have produced changes in some factors as well.

Results of another recent study by Woodruff and Birren (188) further demonstrate how cohort differences and age interact in determining scores on one test of adjustment, the California Personality Inventory. Young adults who responded to this inventory in the early 1940s were retested 20 years later. On the second testing, they first responded to the questionnaire on the basis of their present reactions as adults, and then responded to it a second time, attempting to respond as they believed they had 20 years earlier. Another cohort of adults (some of them the grown children of the older subjects) also responded to the questionnaire at the time of the second testing. There was very little difference between the scores of the older adults on the two test occasions. However, when the adult subjects in the older cohort group responded to the questionnaire as they thought they had 20 years earlier, they responded in about the same way as did the individuals in the younger cohort. The responses for the youngsters indicated "poorer adjustment" than was found for the older cohorts when tested 20 years earlier. Accordingly, the results show that while there was longitudinal stability in the scores, there were substantial generational differences in typical responses to the questions which affect younger and older individuals.

A study by Kelly (108) also reports a 20-year follow-up on a number of personality and interest measures. The group subjects were engaged couples, who, at the time of original testing, were students. Kelly concluded that stability over the adult range rather than change was the more typical result. Responses to the Strong Vocational Interest Blank Scales and the Allport-Vernon-Lindzey Scale of Values were the most stable, while those measuring general attitudes showed the greatest change.

The conclusion from these three studies is that questionnaires measuring cognitive styles, rigidity and attitudes may be most likely to change with time in subjects of all ages while other items like values and occupational interests are not as likely to change. Despite the relative abundance of data, we must conclude with Schaie and Marquette (151) that because of generational differences and the lack of adequate norms for instruments, the delineation of age and cohort effects on personality development is just beginning.

Life Styles and Adjustment

Much of the research summarized above described individuals along a number of relatively independent dimensions of personality. Assigning scores to people in this way somehow misses the gestalt of personality, and several investigators have instead tried to classify the overall mode of adjustment of the older individual. Naturally, not everyone belonging to a given type is alike in all or even most respects. However, these types do provide some insight into the variety of major strategies that individuals may use to deal with the problems of aging.

Buhler (31) categorized interview data and found that old people could be satisfied with life either by reflecting on the past, relaxing in the present or by continued fulfilling activity. One group of unhappy oldsters was characterized as being dissatisfied with the past but unable to do anything about it. Another group was found to feel guilty and frustrated at what they considered to be meaningless lives. A similar study by Reichard, Livson and Peterson (138) was based on interview data of 87 men aged 55 to 84. The clusters of traits they found fell into five groups: a) the mature philosophical men; b) the rocking chair men seemingly glad to have time to relax; c) the armored men who try to keep active at all costs and use this as a defense against old age and death. These first three groups were accepting of aging. Group "d" was labelled aggressive and seemed to blame others for their disappointments and frustrations. Those in Group "c" were intrapunitive, depressed and gloomy. Twenty-three of the 87 men did not fit neatly into any of these categories.

Neugarten and associates (128) followed up Reichard's work on participants in the Kansas City Study. They found six types per sex. All but 18 of their 88 subjects fell into one of these groups. The groups common to the sexes were: a) the integrated who were high on most positive personality variables; b) the "defended" group who were aggressive and full of energy; c) the passive-dependent group who were like Reichard's rocking chair men; d) the unintegrated group who were low on almost all personality measures. There were two further groups of men: One group was characterized as introspective, timid, stable, high on super-ego control but "lacked" internalization of institutional values. The other group of men was fearful of failure and becoming dependent on others. One group of women had feelings of inferiority and self-doubt and was over-controlled and dissatisfied. Another group of women similarly was self-doubting but very aggressive and competitive.

Three conclusions may be drawn from this research. First, there are several patterns of successful aging. Second, there is continuity across age in the way that individuals adapt. Neugarten's subjects seemed to use styles that continued from the 50s to the 70s. The third conclusion is that adjustment to life as measured by life satisfaction measures and self-report of happiness was poorly related to differences in personality types. As reported earlier, Neugarten found that many persons who evidenced pathological affect and thinking showed no change in social competence (128).

Motivation and Emotion as Expressions of Personality

Chown's definition of personality encompasses the emotions and motivations of an individual. Evidence presented earlier in the chapter indicates that lowered impulsivity and emotionality are frequently associated with advancing age. Other studies (see Atchley 7, for a review) indicate a decreased interest in food on the part of some older persons. Such a finding could reflect both loss of sensitivity of taste and smell with advancing age and some loss of interest in the social activities related to eating.

A well documented finding is a decrease in sexual activity with advancing age (e.g., Kinsey, Pomeroy, and Martin 110). This decrease in sexual activity is partly due to decreased sexual drive. However, Atchley's discussion of the research of Masters and Johnson (123) concerning the sexual performance of older individuals also emphasizes the importance of psychosocial factors such as boredom with one's partner, fear of failure, or preoccupation with economic or other pursuits. Masters and Johnson argue that such factors may be far more important than changes in biological drive in determining the decline in sexual activity observed with advancing age.

The point of this example, as well as the one just before it, is that physiological changes in old age *per se* are not a particularly critical variable in describing personality. As Atchley puts it in his review: ". . . motivation in later life can be expected to be a product of reduced drives and changes in opportunity for good attainment" (7, p. 91).

One of the important generalizations of the material on motivation, as well as of that on life-styles and adjustment, is that an individual's degree of "motivation" cannot be considered independently of the situation in which he finds himself. This suggests that managers of living institutions for the elderly have many possibilities for improving the quality of life for residents over the level frequently observed. In one excellent study, Filer and O'Connell (69) demonstrated that when elderly patients in a rehabilitation hospital were clearly reinforced for behavior related to self-management of medication, dependability in keeping appointments, etc. by rewards valued by patients (such as increased privacy), they improved their behavior far more than other patients who did not recieve such reinforcement. One implication of the results of the Filer-O'Connell research is that motivation may be increased by the creation of goals. A second is that the deteriorated behavior and apathy of elderly persons frequently observed in institutions are fostered in part by the climate of the institution itself. Numerous suggestions for improving the "motivation" of the elderly have been made by various authorities, e.g., Lindsley (118), Kastenbaum (104), and Labouvie, Hoyer, Baltes and Baltes (114).

Personality Change and Health

Changes in an individual's perception of himself or in others' perception of him often occur as a result of alterations in his state of health. Increases in sensitivity to somatic complaints and susceptibility to depression, as measured on instruments such as the Minnesota Multiphasic Personality Inventory, have been observed in retrospective studies of individuals who develop heart diseases such as myocardial infarctions and angina pectoris.

Changes in self-perception and responses to personality questionnaires might be expected to occur with the development of heart disease, but there is also a growing body of evidence that some of the characteristics of personality are associated with the development of heart disease. In his summary of a number of studies using the Cattell Sixteen Personality Factor Questionnaire, Jenkins (102) concludes that patients with heart disease show tendencies toward less surgency (Factor F), increased sensitivity (Factor I), greater self-sentiment (Q3), and lower ego strength (C) than their coevals. This list contains the three scales associated with age that were described earlier in the discussion of the Cattell instrument.

Another constellation of behavior characteristics involving extremes of ambitiousness, competitiveness, impatience and alertness has been related to greater prevalence and incidence of clinical coronary disease (146). Interview-based assessments of Type A or B personality have been successfully mimicked by questionnaires and behavior tests (22, 103) in about 75% of the cases. The personality type is only moderately related to traits measured on the Cattell instrument: Type A individuals are more surgent (Factor F), more shrewd (Factor N), and more outgoing and sociable (Factor A). It is quite clear that psychiatric evaluation and intervention in such nonclinical cases may have important implications for a psychology of aging as well as for the prevention of disease.

Summary and Conclusions about Ability and Personality

To the extent that results of the preceding sections may be true despite some methodological flaws, we may generalize as follows:

1. There is some reason to believe that mental abilities will deteriorate as the individual gets past 50, particularly to the extent that tasks are speeded and to the extent that the test is neutral or even interfered with by the individual's previous experience outside the test situation.

2. Personality is remarkably stable over the adult years in most respects.

3. There is evidence that individuals tend to appear more rigid in their thinking as they get older.

4. Individuals who are older now are more likely to be introverted, more controlled, less flexible, less energetic, lower on surgency, and have lower needs for achievement and heterosexuality than people who are now young.

5. There is no such thing as *the* "old personality." People cope with the problems and benefits of old age in different ways depending on their life experiences, their economic resources, their health and their cognitive capacities. There are a number of different types of individuals who are old.

6. Those tests which measure the individual's cognitive or personal level of how well-adapted he is to *his* environment show little decrement with age. On the other hand, tests of the individual's ability *to adapt* indicate increasingly maladaptive modes among older cohorts and with increasing age.

7. Age, on any measure, is a weak variable. That is, age itself does not tell us very much about the individual that could not be discovered much more accurately with even minimal psychological testing.

The implications of these findings depend to some extent on the type of application the psychiatrist is involved in. Age is such a weak predictor of personality that almost any decision about an individual, e.g., his prognosis, preferred method of treatment, or competency, should not be justified by his age. One would definitely not be justified in denying psychotherapy to an individual since the "old" are "more rigid" and therefore less likely to benefit.

On the other hand, the administrator dealing with people of varying ages can expect that groups of people of various ages are probably going to react somewhat differently to changes in procedure, changes in personnel, etc. For group reactions (which confound cohort differences with age differences in the same way that most of the studies do), it is probably reasonable to expect the older group to be more introversive, to have more primitive defense mechanisms, less surgency, lower needs for achievement, less cognitive ability, and to be less able to cope with changes in their environment.

SENSORY, PERCEPTUAL AND MOTOR FACTORS IN COGNITIVE CHANGE

Methodological Issues

The study of peripheral changes in sensory and perceptual functioning with age is important for two reasons. First, there are situations such as night driving that require a substantial degree of sensory acuity. Second, we cannot adequately judge the age-related impairment or improvement in central decision-making processes unless we are able to parcel out the changes in the periphery. Any experiment or test of higher mental processes still requires the subject to perceive some aspects of the environment and to respond to it. Slow-downs in the sensory or motor functions may be partially responsible for changes seen in cognitive activities. Unfortunately studies of sensory functions have not always been carried out in such a way that central slowing could be distinguished from peripheral slowing. Not only do peripheral factors influence central factors, but nearly any so-called perceptual experiment will involve central factors—personality and motivation can influence tests of "simple perception."

For example, imagine a truck driver in his 60s who has been noticing a decline in his night vision. But he only has five more years until retirement, and he has no prospects for another job. His company has volunteered him to participate in an experiment on dark adaptation. He is brought into a room of total darkness and the doctor says, "O.K., Mr. Jones, now I want you to look straight ahead and as soon as you see a light, I want you to tell me." After a few moments, he sees a light . . . or does he? Sometimes it's there; sometimes not. Of course, he wants to be honest but there does seem to be a light there, so he reports seeing a light.

On the other hand, imagine a young truck driver in the same company who has been worried about voices and dream images that bother him on long trips, particularly when he supplements his coffee with amphetamines. Now he is brought into a totally dark room and the doctor says to him, "Now look straight ahead and whenever you see a light, tell me." Now he sees a very dim light . . . or does he? What if the doctor's trying to trick him and there really isn't any light there?

In these hypothetical examples, the method employed attempts to establish an absolute threshold. Such a procedure is very sensitive to a person's biases. Experimental psychologists have developed better techniques which separate a person's biases from his perceptions. One method of doing this is to use a forced-choice procedure. In this method, the experimenter always presents a light on every trial; sometimes on the left, sometimes on the right. The subject must tell which side the light is on. Below the threshold, the subject will only be correct half the time. Although the superiority of this and other methods over the absolute threshold method used with the truck drivers is well-documented, many of the studies of perceptual functioning as related to age have used the inferior method. This is particularly unfortunate since we have already seen evidence indicating that older subjects are more cautious, rigid, and less impulsive. These characteristics, in and of themselves, would simulate poorer perceptual abilities in older subjects when the method of absolute thresholds is used. Even when one uses the superior methods, however, there is one further problem—differentiating central from peripheral factors. Even in a simple discrimination, the subject still must make a central probabilistic judgment about whether the light is on the right or left. An organic impairment in this central processor could result in fewer correct decisions. Appropriate experimental and statistical methods could help separate central factors as well.

It is a well-established psychological principle that perception, or at least reports of perception, are influenced by expectations. Glance quickly at the phrase below.

Paris

in the

the springtime

Most people misread this phrase. Furthermore, based on current psychological theory there is every reason to believe that the more experience one has had with the English language—i.e., the older one is—the more likely one is to misperceive the phrase. In most laboratory experiments, the investigator, in his efforts to make the sequence unpredictable and *neutral,* actually *violates* the expectations built up by years of experience.

One is tempted to believe that these methodological difficulties are quite small for fundamental visual and auditory perception; many studies of age-related diseases of the eye and ear have clear physiological bases and the effects of possible age-related differences in expectations are not important. However, methodological difficulties do exist.

The importance of differential environmental effects on even the simplest auditory functions can hardly be overestimated. Comparisons of the average audiograms of individuals living in a relatively noisy environment compared to those of age peers in a less noisy one show that accumulated trauma associated with prolonged exposure to industrialized environments may indeed make a substantial amount of difference in hearing loss associated with "aging." See Figure 3.

The point of the preceding discussion about methodological difficulties is that the conclusions of much of the research on sensory and motor changes with age, while true, may have multiple causes.

Specific Perceptual Deficits

Vision. The research on simple visual sensation can be easily summarized. Bearing in mind the preceding cautions about methodology,

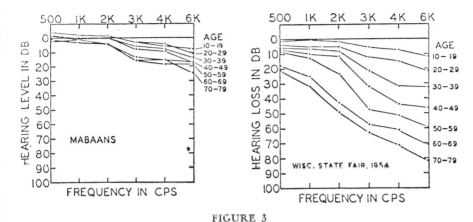

FIGURE 3

Hearing loss for pure tones of different frequencies for men in a nonindustrialized (Maaban) and industrialized society. Data in left panel from Rosen et al. in the *Annals of Otology*, etc. (1962). Right panel from the Wisconsin State Fair, Glorig and Nixon (1964). Reprinted with permission.

one can simply say it seems that old people are worse on every tested visual function. Older individuals have smaller peripheral vision (185), are more affected by glare (184), have higher thresholds (88), have poorer dark adaptation (120), are worse at color matching (79), visual acuity (93), flicker fusion (53), accommodation (77), and contrast sensitivity (28).

To what extent are these perceptual deficits secondary consequences of physical change in the eye itself? Welford (116), after reviewing many studies on age-related differences in perception, concludes that ". . . it seems fairly clear that difficulty of visual perception in later middle and old age is not solely due to readily observable and commonly recognized changes in the eye."

Welford cites a study by Weston (181) showing that although low levels of illumination increase the age differences in time taken to tell the location of the gap in the Landoll rings, there is no level of illumination which would completely eliminate the difference. Since these reaction times were already corrected for differences in motor time, there must be some residual age difference in decision time which cannot be accounted for in terms of lower levels of illumination reaching the eye or increased response time. Experiments by Gregory and his co-workers, cited in Welford (176), used signal detection theory (82) to help differentiate central from peripheral problems. Gregory (84, 85) and Gregory and Cane (86) have suggested that at least part of the problems of perception in older people must be accounted for in terms of increased noise level, not in terms of lower level of effective illumination. Let I stand for the intensity of light and $\triangle$ I be the Just Noticeable Difference (JND), the smallest increase in illumination that a subject can note. $\triangle$ I is proportional to I for both young and old subjects, but older subjects need proportional increases in $\triangle$ I with I over and above what young people need. The higher the level of illumination, the greater the increase in $\triangle$ I. If the reason for poorer perception in old people were merely a lowered effective level of illumination due to the increased opacity of the eye, then we would expect the same constant increase in $\triangle$ I at all levels of illumination.

There have also been a number of studies showing complex perception to be less accurate and less flexible among older subjects. Botwinick, Robbin, and Brinley (26), used a reversible figure of an old woman/young lady and found that the older subjects had more difficulty seeing the perception other than their initial perception. Heath and Orbach (90) also found fewer reversals for a Necker cube for older subjects. Jalavisto (100) found that older subjects were less likely to switch eyes in retinal rivalry situations than younger subjects. Welford (176) reports an experiment by Speakman which indicates that the decrease in the number of reversals by older subjects reported when looking at a reversible staircase figure cannot be accounted for by lower levels of illumination reaching the retina. Eisdorfer (62) looked at the relation between visual acuity and Rorschach responses of older subjects. He did not find, in this case, any relation between the visual acuity and the Rorschach scores.

Thus, the evidence from those studies which have attempted to parcel out central from peripheral effects indicates that a major part of age-related deficits in visual perception is of central origin.

There have also been a number of studies dealing with visual illusions. Here, older subjects' responses are qualitatively more similar to those of children than to those of young adults. On some illusions, older adults are *more* reality oriented than younger adults and on some illusions the older are *less* accurate. For example, Wapner, Werner, and Comalli (169) showed that subjects 65-80, like children 6-14, are less veridical in the Muller-Lyer illusion. Comalli, Wapner, and Werner (50) present evidence that older subjects were less influenced in their perception of the vertical by their own body position. Qualitatively, their performance is more like youngsters from 6 to 14. For those age groups, apparent vertical is very slightly to the same side as body tilt. With adults from 16 to 50, there is a much larger error toward the side opposite their own body tilt. Wozniak and Eisner (190) point out other similarities of perception between the very young and the aged that differentiate them from young and middle-aged adults.

Audition. As with vision, there seems to be a general loss of sensory capability with age. Pitch discrimination is worse among older subjects (111); auditory acuity is worse (157). Perception of speech is also worse for the elderly, though the *greatest* hearing loss for sounds occurs at frequencies above those used in speech. The decrement in speech perception apparently has central as well as peripheral components. Pestalozza and Shore (134) compared the discrimination loss in old patients to a group of young patients whose audiometric hearing losses were about equivalent. The discrimination for older subjects was 9 to 20% worse than for the young subjects. Farrimond (68) found that older subjects' ability to "hear" speech sounds depends not only on audiometry data but also on their vocabulary.

Weiss (175) looked at several kinds of hearing loss as a function of health. Five groups of subjects were studied: a young group; a normal old group; a hypertensive group; the asymptotic and/or subclinical disease group; and the "apparent disease" group. All old groups showed differential hearing loss at the high frequency end of audiometry tests. The difference in hearing loss between the two ears was greatest for the disease group, least for the young group. The subjects were also tested for click perception. All subjects were first given a test in which they had their own threshold for 2,000 clicks/second measured diotically. A click discrimination measure was taken for each subject at 30 db. above his own threshold. (Clicks were presented either singly or doubly and the subject had to tell which.) Results indicate that young and old men do not differ from each other but that these groups differ from less healthy older men. The correlations show that this is *not* due to peripheral factors, at least as measured in audiograms. Each subject was then given a train of clicks from 1 to 10 and asked to tell how many he had heard. Though age was significant, there was no significant correlation between two-click discrimination and performance on this test. Results of such studies indicate that even "simple" perceptual tasks show a substantial involvement by high centers. Functional hearing loss hardly seems to be solely dependent on changes in the peripheral organs.

In aging research, one is often left with the impression of inevitable and continuous decline. On the other hand, Figure 3 indicates that the amount of hearing loss expected with age can differ considerably depending on (apparently) the amount of stress and noise that one is subjected to. Eighty-year-old Mabaans, who live in a non-noisy environment in which hypertension, coronary thrombosis, and duodenal ulcers are virtually unknown, show a hearing loss comparable to that found in 25-year olds in an industrialized area of our country (144). It is possible that part of the difference between the groups is due to differences in selective pressures in two cultures, but the data are certainly suggestive that much of what is considered to be "primary" aging may not be, at least in the case of hearing.

Other Senses. Studies of age-related differences in the other sensory capabilities have not been common. Thresholds of touch sensation (101) increase with age. Cooper, Bilash, and Zubek (52) found lowered taste sensitivity with increasing age. Pain sensitivity also seems to decrease with age (152). Vibrational sensitivity also declines (54).

Motor Factors

Although maximum muscular strength is often attained at a fairly young age (47), there is little evidence that this peripheral factor accounts for much of the age-related slow-down in psycho-motor tasks. Welford (176), after reviewing a number of studies, concluded that the time required to make unguided movements of a few inches does not change much with age. Rather, it seems that the decision and guiding of movements slow down. Thus, two basic conclusions can be drawn from the work on peripheral mechanisms: First, there seems to be a decline in most sensory abilities with age, although most such studies are of cross-sectional rather than longitudinal nature. Secondly, these "peripheral" deficits cannot wholly account for the failures in more complex central processing. In fact, what evidence exists suggests the opposite—that much of the reduction in "perception" is not due to problems in the mechanics of the neural apparatus at the end organs but rather is a by-product of central processing problems. In particular, many studies indicate that older individuals may have a "noiser" central processor.

PSYCHOLOGICAL PROCESSES IN DECISION-MAKING, MEMORY, AND PROBLEM-SOLVING

The efficacy of an individual's adaptation to the physical and social world around him is indexed in part by his performance on standardized psychological tests such as those described earlier. Such instruments are of limited usefulness. Tests of abilities, for example, though efficacious in determining whether or not a person can obtain correct solutions to problems, are typically unsuited to revealing the processes that underlie performance.

In order to discover basic differences in psychological processes between individuals of different ages, the psychologist studies performance in laboratory situations. Although psychologists occasionally study affective processes such as aggression and love in the laboratory, adult age has seldom, if ever, been considered as a variable in such studies. Consequently, the following discussion will deal only with laboratory studies of cognition, i.e., the processes by which people of various ages make decisions, remember, and solve problems.

Discrete and Continuous Reaction Time Studies

Reaction time tasks explore one of the most pervasive features of aging—behavioral slowing. In a discrete reaction time task, a stimulus is presented and a simple response is required of the subject; furthermore, the relation between the stimulus and the response is typically straightforward. The subject is allowed to "recover" from his response and get set before the next stimulus is presented. In a *simple reaction time* task, there is only one response for the subject; i.e., he does not have to make a decision after perceiving the stimulus. He is merely to respond as quickly as possible after the onset of the stimulus. In a *choice reaction time* task, the subject must make a response that is contingent on which stimulus is presented. For example, the subject's task may be to push a right hand lever if a green light comes on and a left hand lever if a red light comes on. Studies of age differences indicate that older subjects are generally slower than younger on both simple and choice reaction time tasks. Though the reader may agree that such tasks may be well-controlled, he is apt to be puzzled as to why psychologists should bother to study such a simple task. What light can such studies shed on the processes involved in a person's day-to-day interactions with his social and physical environment?

There are three reasons for the concern with reaction time studies. First, the age-related slowing of reaction time cannot be attributed to a slow-down in the transmission time of peripheral nerves to and from the brain (25, 176). The large part of the slow-down seems to be due to the decision-making component of reaction time. One possible importance of reaction time studies stems from this fact. Any *complex* process involves *many* decisions. If each decision is slowed down by a fraction of a second, then the total slow-down can be quite considerable.

Secondly, information decays quite rapidly from the very short auditory and visual stores and from primary memory (8, 173). A slow-down in processing thus means that in attempting to rehearse or process items in these stores, more items may be lost from memory for the older subjects. A quantitative time difference in processing rate can lead to a quantitative difference in number of items processed. This could lead to a qualitative difference in complex tasks, since the older subjects may not be able to work with as many factors "simultaneously" and thus may be forced to oversimplify a problem more than a younger subject. Any age-related differences in decision or basic processing time may thus underlie an age-related difference in memory and problem solving capabilities.

The third reason a slow-down may be important is motivational. A person who takes longer to complete a task may be more likely to quit or start over before finishing. Assuming older and younger individuals are equally motivated, then an underlying quantitative slow-down of psychological processes could again result in a qualitative performance deficit.

The major results of studies on age-related differences in reaction time studies can be succinctly summarized. Older subjects have longer simple reaction time; for example, oldsters take longer to make a motor response such as pushing a button to the onset of a tone or light (25, 78).

Choice reaction time studies reveal larger age differences than simple reaction time studies (25). As the number of alternative stimuli and responses increases, the size of the age-related differences in reaction times also increases (see Welford (177), for a review). Generally, cross-sectional studies indicate gradual increases in reaction times from the twenties to the fifties and more dramatic differences thereafter.

It should be kept in mind that the results summarized are average trends which obscure large individual differences. For example, measurements of two-choice reaction times taken on healthy men aged 25-75 years revealed the usual age-related difference in response latency—an analysis of variance indicated that the age trends observed were statistically significant. Age differences only accounted for 5% of the total variance in reaction time, while individual differences, apart from age, accounted for 86% of the total variance (172).

Although there is a general slow-down of response speed with age, the results of many studies in which various parameters of the reaction time task may have been varied indicate that old and young subjects react similarly to variations in the task. Generally, however, as the task is made more difficult, the discrepancy in response latency between old and young subjects increases. Practice, in contrast, reduces the time taken to respond for both. With long-continued practice, the age differences become vanishingly small (126).

A variety of hypotheses has been advanced to account for the age-related differences in reaction time. Perhaps the most interesting hypothesis is that the alpha rhythm underlies the slow-down in reaction time (159). The status of this hypothesis is still somewhat in doubt. The relative speeds of different individuals' reaction times are not perfectly correlated with the rank order of their alpha rhythm frequencies.

In her doctoral dissertation, Woodruff (187) used instrumental conditioning techniques (biofeedback) to train old and young to increase the frequency of their alpha rhythm and found correlated decreases in reaction times. The implications of these results, if generalizable, are quite important. If an old person's processing time can be decreased with training without a concomitant loss in accuracy, then perhaps the age-related decrements found in most laboratory tasks can be reduced.

Several investigators (16, 18, 177) have speculated on the possible causes of age-related slow-downs in reaction time. Such notions typically postulate a weakening with age in the relative strength of the neural representation of a signal to the general background activity in the brain. Another possibility is that older subjects are more cautious; they integrate information over a longer period of time, not because they must, but because they wish to in order to avoid making errors. Welford (116) discusses this possibility, but concludes that caution cannot wholly account for age-related differences in speed. Results of a variety of studies of decision-making and remembering from our own laboratory tend to confirm his conclusion. In nearly every case, older subjects are slower and in addition, make at least as many errors as the younger subjects (71, 148, 162).

Continuous reaction tasks. In the discrete reaction time task, the subject can finish the processing of one stimulus before the next one is presented. However, many situations in real life require one to continually or continuously respond to an ever-changing array of data. Differences in how old and young subjects perform on such tasks are of both theoretical and practical importance.

The overall rate of processing one can maintain in a continuous task depends not only on how long it takes for each signal to be processed but also on the extent of overlap that can be tolerated among the various processes of perceiving, deciding, and responding. It is conceivable that older subjects might be slower at each of these subprocesses but be able to organize their information processing activities in such an efficient manner that they could compensate and thus be as fast as or even faster than young subjects in monitoring a series of signals. Alternatively, however, we might hypothesize that the necessity to use partially overlapping information-processing would be even more confusing to older subjects, since one activity could interfere more with others than would be the case for younger subjects. In fact, results indicate the older subjects generally seem to do relatively worse on continuous responding tasks than they do in discrete reaction time tasks (72, 107, 176).

Performance decrements in continuous tasks are more difficult to analyze than is the case for discrete tasks. Continuous tasks have not been as extensively studied as discrete tasks, but to the extent that they have, the same general results are found. As task complexity increases, the age *differences* also tend to increase but the *ratio* of performance measures stays constant (176).

In summary, reaction time generally becomes slower with increasing age. The explanation for why this is so has not been completely specified; however, a variety of artifactual, peripheral and attitudinal explanations have been ruled out. The cause of the age-related slowing in reaction time seems to be in a lowered speed of central decision-making, possibly because of lowered neural efficiency.

In attempting to apply these findings, it is important to keep in mind that individual differences in reaction time within an age group are usually larger than the differences between age groups. Another caution is that while there is some evidence for longitudinal change in reaction time (183), most studies of reaction time are cross-sectional.

As suggested by Birren (16), anyone who lives long enough will experience a slowing of response speed. Behavioral slowing with advancing age may come not so much from primary aging, but rather with the slowing of behavior resulting from other variables that may be correlated with age, such as a breakdown in health or a lowering of muscle tone. For example, Botwinick and Thompson (27) found age-related differences in reaction time between healthy males 68-86 years of age and athletic males aged 19-22, but not between the older subjects and a group of non-athletic young males. The finding could be due either to age-related differences in general muscle tone or to cerebral blood circulation or both. In a more recent study, Abrahams (2) found that young and middle-aged males without heart diseases but identified as having coronary prone per-

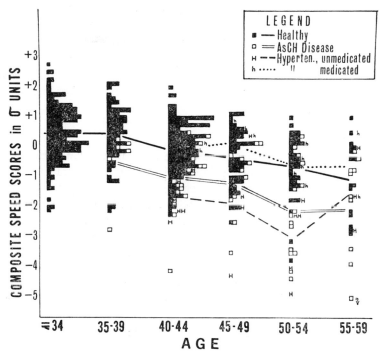

FIGURE 4

Distributions of composite response speeds (in standard score units) for men in six age groups. The speed estimates were obtained by summing response time on various perceptual motor tasks. The distributions show the relative speeds of healthy subjects and those with arteriosclerotic or coronary heart disease (ASCH Disease), and individuals diagnosed as having hypertension. From Chapter 20 by Walter Spieth in *Behavior, Aging and the Nervous System*, edited by A. T. Welford and J. E. Birren, published by Springer, 1965. Reproduced with permission.

sonality characteristics were slower on both simple and complex reaction time tasks than were age controls without these personality traits.

Spieth (156) constructed a composite index of response speed by summing response times from a variety of speeded perceptual-motor and problem-solving tasks. The subjects were airline pilots ranging in age from the 30s to the 60s. The distribution of the response speed measures for subjects within each of four age groups is shown in Figure 4, which is reproduced from Spieth's article. The distributions show that the slowest response speeds observed occurred in those subjects who had a history of coronary heart disease or hypertension. Note also that the pilots in each group whose hypertension was controlled by medication performed about as well as healthy coevals.

In summary then, the most important applications of studies of speed of decision-making may be to identify variations in health status that covary to some extent with age. Perhaps behavioral slowing associated with disease may be corrected to some extent by medication, instrumental conditioning, and psychotherapy.

Studies of Memory

A failing memory is perhaps one of the commonest complaints of older people, and it is also a widely held belief that one's learning capacity diminishes after the late teens or early twenties. Many people believe that for some kinds of learning, such as foreign languages, tennis or ice skating, even *earlier* exposure is necessary if high levels of competence are to be reached. In real life, there are many factors confounded with learning *ability,* such as motivation and the other responsibilities of the learner; therefore, it is difficult to draw sound conclusions from naturalistic observations. Nevertheless, evaluating learning functions of adults of various ages is extremely important, particularly now, when the knowledge requirements of nearly all occupations are changing rapidly. It is for these reasons that many psychologists have studied age differences in memory.

In order to make sense of the literature on memory and age, it is necessary to distinguish at least three kinds of memory: Primary, Secondary and Tertiary. If a person is given a five digit number like "57653" and immediately asked to repeat it, he can do so by reading out the contents of what psychologists usually term "Primary Memory" (173). The capacity of the Primary Memory is limited to only a few items. Information seems to decay rather rapidly from Primary Memory unless rehearsed. If one makes no conscious effort to learn or rehearse the five digit number mentioned above, then a few minutes later he will be quite unlikely to remember it. Psychologists prevent rehearsal of items in Primary Memory experimentally by requiring the subject to do some other task which takes his full attention. The forward digit span test is primarily a measure of the Primary Memory capacity. The time taken to recall items from Primary Memory is somewhat longer with older subjects (171), but the number of items that can be held and retrieved from Primary Memory is very minimally related to age (161). Primary Memory capacity is thus not the type of memory capacity that older people typically complain about.

If a student discovered, 15 minutes before a French exam, that there was a list of 30 new vocabulary words that he had not known about but that he would be tested on, and then by cramming managed to write them on the exam, he would be recalling information from Secondary Memory. Thirty items is far too many to hold in Primary Memory. Secondary Memory is the type of memory typically tested in the laboratory studies of verbal learning in which subjects are given rather arbitrary lists of words or nonsense syllables to memorize. It is also what would be involved in remembering a list of eight items to buy at the grocery on the way home from work (assuming one's work was demanding enough so that the individual could not repeat the list to himself for eight hours!). It is unlikely that our French student would remember these vocabulary words for long after the exam if he studied them no further. Secondary Memory is only a semi-permanent store.

This use of Secondary Memory is, of course, exactly the kind of memory that older subjects feel they are losing. The exact age at which a lessened Secondary Memory capability first begins and the overall degree of loss associated with age will depend upon the exact type of material to be learned, the selection of subjects, the timing of events, the pre-learning instructions and other factors. This general finding though—decreasing Secondary Memory capacity with increasing age—seems well-established (23, 176). The finding that older subjects have trouble with material in Secondary Memory is not limited to attempts to recall the material. Older subjects aslo take longer and make more errors when asked to decide whether a given item is in a memorized list (71).

There are several variables that seem to reliably affect the estimates of the size of the age differences. In general, making the task more difficult increases the age differences. Unfortunately, many of the studies which have attempted to determine more precisely the locus of age-related differences in Secondary Memory did not adequately control for task difficulty, thus resulting in ambiguities of interpretation. It does seem, however, that older subjects do better when the learning is slowly paced (23). If the stimuli are presented too quickly or the responses must be forthcoming too quickly, then older subjects seem particularly hurt. This is not terribly surprising in view of the results cited in the previous two sections on reaction time measures.

Although numerous attempts have been made to discover whether older subjects seem to have particular difficulties in storing information in Secondary Memory or in retrieving information from it, a definitive answer is yet to be forthcoming. There are reasons apart from storage or retrieval that older subjects may not perform as well on Secondary Memory tasks. The older subjects in our study, as well as those in a Russian study (98) claim that one strategy they have acquired with age is to be quite selective about what they bother to learn. If this is true, then the typical useless information taught to subjects in the laboratory may be made difficult by the generally adaptive habit of attempting to learn only those items which are useful. Eisdorfer (64) has also suggested that older subjects have reduced motivation to recall recent events. This possibility has not been sufficiently explored, perhaps because older volunteer subjects are certainly "trying hard" as far as they are able. In any case, motivational differences seem quite unlikely as a basis for the total age-related differences found in Secondary Memory capacity. Many older subjects are quite concerned during interviews about losing this capacity and the subjects also mention forgetting things they *do* want to remember.

Most of the studies of age-related deficits in Secondary Memory are of a cross-sectional nature. Consequently, the older subjects have, typically, had less formal education, and the education they have had is generally less recent. There may be certain strategies for attempting to learn in the somewhat similar and contrived situations of school and laboratory. Younger subjects have had more, and more recent practice with these strategies. Bower (29) reviews evidence that various kinds of mnemonic systems can improve memory performance in college students quite substantially. Hulicka and Grossman (97) found that older subjects were far less likely than younger ones to use good strategies under neutral instructions and still somewhat less likely to use them even when specifically instructed to do so. If improvements in memory function in the older subjects would result from teaching them or convincing them to use mnemonic systems, greater practical benefits could follow.

One further possibility is that older subjects are more anxious in laboratory learning situations and that this interferes with their learning abilities. Powell, Eisdorfer, and Bogdonoff (136) found that older subjects do have higher levels of free fatty acids in the blood during learning, and this may be indicative of higher anxiety levels. However, there is no independent way to measure whether equal levels of free fatty acids in the blood mean functionally equal levels of anxiety in young and old subjects. In a later study, Eisdorfer (63) found that the use of propanonol, which reduces the autonomic concomitants of anxiety, increased the learning efficiency of older subjects. He did not, however, include in this study a control group of younger subjects whose performance may also have been improved. In addition, Ansello (6) found that when the learning task itself was very easy, old and young subjects did not differ in performance, suggesting that if age differences in anxiety produce learning decrements, the anxiety differences must be partially caused by learning difficulties and not by the laboratory situation *per se,* or the fact that the subject is about to engage in something labelled a "learning experiment."

Our immediate impressions of how quickly another person can learn are probably based principally on our assessments of the person's Secondary Memory capabilities. Thus, the Secondary Memory loss associated with age can be particularly damaging to the older individual's chances of getting accepted for a new job, a new training program, or a new method of psychotherapy.

In contrast to the deficit that seems to begin relatively early in Secondary Memory, the person's store of long-held knowledge, his Tertiary Memory, seems to change little with age. Except in cases of definite pathology, a person's motor skills, language habits, and memory for remote experiences seem to hold up fairly well with increasing age. It is difficult to estimate the probability that an item will be lost from Tertiary Memory (170).

Studies in our laboratories indicate that the time required to retrieve a name from Tertiary Memory increases slightly with age (162, 171). The estimated time to retrieve a name includes corrections for the time taken to perceive the stimulus and organize a response. The age-related increase in retrieval time from Tertiary Memory is far less than the increase in time to retrieve items from Secondary Memory (171). The age differences exist, moreover, only on the first of several successive occasions that the item is recalled. The magnitude of the relative differences with age in retrieval time from Secondary and Tertiary Memory is consistent with our subjects' own comments about their "problems" with their memories. It is also relevant to the distinction made earlier between the extent to which an organism *has adapted* (Tertiary Memory) and *can adapt* (Secondary Memory). In closing this section on memory, perhaps it needs to be reemphasized that the typical age differences found are only differences in the speed with which certain processes take place. You *can* teach an old dog new tricks, but on the average, it takes longer.

Problem-Solving

In an ever-changing society, the ability to deal with new situations becomes increasingly important. Positions of decision-making and responsibility are often held by older individuals. It is therefore of considerable interest to determine the extent to which people of various ages can solve problems. Again, general findings can be quickly summarized; it should be kept in mind, however, that these results are uniformly based on cross-sectional results. In problem-solving skills, particularly, the differences in the quality of education, the emphasis upon the ability to solve problems (as opposed to rote memorization), and the likely level of education of one's parents and peer groups would all favor the younger subjects. Welford (176) and Botwinick (23) both summarize a number of studies in the ability to think logically and solve problems. The overall results of the various studies reviewed revealed that in comparison to young subjects, older subjects were more likely to make logical errors and to experience greater difficulty in solving problems. The more difficult the problem, then, generally, the larger the absolute age difference in performance. The extent to which these differences are due to personality factors, memory factors, or the speed with which subjects can learn the subtleties of the task has not yet been determined.

CONCLUSIONS

As Kastenbaum (105) has documented in a recent popular article, old age has a terrible reputation. And indeed, physicians responsible for the physical and mental health of older individuals are likely, on the basis of their everyday professional experience, to have good reason to be pessimistic about old age. The chances of overcoming chronic diseases apparently associated with old age or of undoing the effects of 60 years of a patient's accumulated unfortunate encounters with life make his task a difficult one under the best of circumstances. The psychiatrist treating the elderly patient finds himself in something of a different situation than the dermatologist who, as the old joke goes, sees patients who never get well but who never get sick enough to die, or the pediatrician whose patients are, for the most part, healthy kids. In comparison to the psychiatric treatment of young adults, the geropsychiatrist is relatively hard pressed to find the environmental supports or personal resources in his patient which will facilitate psychotherapy. Moreover, some orthodox psychiatric views do not provide much encouragement for his efforts, emphasizing at the practical level diagnosis and ward management, and, at the theoretical level, the importance of overcoming the accumulated effects of years of psychological development.

Yet one reason that old age has such a terrible reputation is that age is often blamed for things that ought better to be attributed to illnesses, for many of which, the elderly do not enjoy a monopoly, or to environmental deprivation associated with institutional settings or lack of opportunity to maintain a satisfactory style of life.

One important purpose of the present chapter is to see that the reputation—both good and bad—of old age is shared as it should be with other determinants of behavior.

The expectation that old age would have a bad reputation among psychiatrists, just as it does for many other people, and the real possibility that the reputation of old age is only partly deserved were, therefore, the two basic themes that dictated the choice of material reviewed in the present chapter. In contrast to many other chapters in this book which deal more specifically with the diagnosis, treatment, and management of specific psychiatric and neurological disorders, the present chapter has emphasized the normal range of variations in abilities, personality, and cognitive processes that are associated with age. Accordingly, we have included a description of some of those psychological characteristics that do not appear to change over the adult years as well as a summary of those which do. With respect to psychological characteristics which do correlate with age, we have attempted to distinguish between the effects of calendar age on behavior and the effects of other variables, many which covary with age: socioeconomic status, secular shifts in education, values, income distributions, and the prevalence of certain kinds of diseases.

The material reviewed in the present chapter is consistent with the general conclusion that it is usually uninformative or misleading to talk about age-related changes in psychological processes independently of the specific process being considered, the situation in which it is being described, and the societal epoch in which the effect is described. These themes were repeated in our discussions of abilities, personality and adjustment, and cognitive performance as well as in our discussion of efforts to construct psychological and biological age scales.

The following paragraphs emphasize and summarize some of the major ideas discussed in the chapter.

At our present level of biological sophistication, there is no practical way to "stop aging," either by genetic or environmental manipulation. All individuals age and many of the psychological results of aging are not considered favorable. The degree to which the rate of aging, known to be different for different individuals, may be altered to practical advantage is also unclear. There seems to be only suggestive evidence of how one might slow down the aging process. Faster aging can apparently be produced by higher caloric intake (167), radiation (94), and, at least in laboratory animals, by stress (135). Although the life-styles of some purportedly long-lived groups of people include physical exercise, high altitude, low psychological stress, and low caloric intake (116), care must be taken in deriving prescriptions for patients from these facts. Even for rats, for example, it appears that whether exercise regimens produce increased or decreased survival rates depends upon the age at which they begin exercising (61). In this study, rats whose exercise program began before they were 400 days old outsurvived their littermates. Rats whose exercise programs began later than 400 days, on the other hand, showed mortality rates higher than those of their littermates. Obviously, the relevance of this work to humans needs further clarification.

Some negative behavioral attributes that are associated with an individual's age may be better attributed to his environment. According to this view, changes in the environment may, on the average, help many individuals. The cross-cultural comparison of hearing loss for individuals in different environments provides one obvious example. One possible way to slow down the detrimental hearing loss often associated with age, then, may be to diminish noise pollution.

We also saw that part of the neurological damage which seems to accompany age seems to be related to cardiovascular problems (2, 156). Aside from the still relatively unexplored possibilities of psychotherapy for individuals with coronary prone personality, medication for hypertension may diminish the functional differences in the intellectual functioning of those with and without hypertension.

Hypoxygenation is frequently implicated as a source of age-related decline in intellectual functioning. Some recent studies have reported that hyperoxygenation treatment may cause partial remission of mental deterioration associated with aging. If such results prove reliable with further refinements in technique, then this treatment could help relieve some of the behavioral symptoms of senility. Aside from the methodological issues that complicate these results, one may also question their logic; the long-range effects of increased oxygen consumption in experimental animals seems to be faster aging; it is not clear what the long-range effects of repeated hyperbaric treatments might be (independently of the well known short-term risks). In general, however, future improvements in the prevention and treatment of poor blood circulation to the brain will probably produce, as secondary benefits, a lessened effect of "aging" on intellectual performance.

According to recent popular reports, drugs may also have detrimental long-range effects on the central nervous system. Further study is needed for firm conclusions, however. Unfortunately, most prescription drugs on the market have not had any kind of research done on their long-range effects on humans. Many possible detrimental effects on higher mental processes may not be easily discoverable in animal research either because the animals are incapable of highly intelligent behavior in the first place, or because their life span is too short to show the effects of a really long-range process. It is possible then that a number of drugs might be detrimental to neural functioning without any present knowledge of this fact.

There are also a number of nonphysical factors which may influence the speed of any observed age decrement in intellectual abilities. Results on standard intelligence tests by Bayley and Oden (11) seem to indicate that subjects who continue their education for longer may retain their abilities more than those whose education stops early. This evidence is only suggestive, but hardly surprising.

Barring gross organic impairment, an individual does not, at any age, show a complete incapacity to learn. Although studies reviewed in this chapter suggest that it takes longer for older individuals to learn, subjects do learn if sufficiently motivated and given enough time. No one can therefore validly be excluded from therapy because they are too old to change their behavior. We know of very little research with adequate controls in which different psychiatric treatment methods have been compared directly in patients of different ages. To the extent that the data on learning in experimental and industrial situations can be compared to therapy situations, there is some suggestion that older individuals will do relatively better under non-directive rather than directive therapies compared to younger subjects. The evidence from the laboratory also suggests that older subjects, relative to younger ones, will be more sensitive to different treatments. That is, the difference in success between the optimal and nonoptimal conditions will be greater for older than for younger subjects. Other data from industrial situations suggest that age as such is not critical in adapting. Chown (45) in particular found that variations in many measures of personal rigidity that were important to job performance and adaptability were correlated more highly with intelligence than with age.

One implication of extreme importance in the literature on personality in the elderly is that there are many successful styles of adjustment in old age. There is a disconcerting tendency in some of the current literature on personality to unabashedly assume that some personality traits are "better" than others with no references made to the environmental conditions under which these traits are "better." For example, it is "better" to be extroverted, flexible, committed, liberal, etc. In fact, such lists of supposed "good" traits may reflect the values of the individuals who created them more clearly than those of potential patients. Although older individuals can eventually learn and change their behavior patterns, one might well ask whether it might not be more economical and ethical to help a patient change definite problem behaviors within the constraints of his own style rather than trying to change the patient's style to more nearly match that of the therapist's own ideal of the mature personality.

Perhaps the single most important point to keep in mind from this chapter is that the interdependence between an individual and his environment generally increases with age. The growing interaction between the organism and its environment is important to considerations of psychological characteristics in two ways. First, the extent to which a study measures abilities, attitudes, and interests similar to those of importance to the individual functioning within his own ecological niche largely determines the observed size of any age differences. Second, the validity of a psychological test, and more broadly, the usefulness of a person's abilities, attitudes or traits depend upon the environment in which he is to exist. These are examples of ways one should consider both the role of the environment and the actual behavior. Behavior should not be evaluated without reference to the environment.

On the other hand, individuals should not be totally evaluated by the environment in which they find themselves, irrespective of their actual behavior! There is a danger that people may be labelled as senile and therefore be seen as senile merely bcause they are aged patients with behavioral difficulties. Even trained professionals may sometimes experience difficulty in recognizing normal people as being normal if these normal people are labelled as "schizophrenic" and observed in the environment of a psychiatric ward (145). Only when health care professionals and the general public interact with older individuals as individuals, regardless of their labels, and learn to interpret behavior with regard to the environmental context in which it occurs, can we say, along with Rabbi Ben Ezra, "Grow old along with me—the best is yet to be."

The references cited below are by no means exhaustive of the literature on the psychology of aging. The interested reader will find an excellent cumulative bibliography on aging compiled by Dr. N. W. Shock and published in part in each issue of the *Journal of Gerontology*. Another good cumulative source is the *Psychological Abstracts* published by the American Psychological Association, Washington D.C. Periodic reviews appear in the *Annual Reviews of Psychology,* published by Annual Reviews,

Inc., Palo Alto, California. Several good recent book reviews are available, many of which were cited in the present chapter. *The Psychology of Adult Development and Age,* edited by C. Eisdorfer and M. P. Lawton, published by the American Psychological Association, contains many excellent critical reviews of material on the psychology of aging. Another excellent source of information is the three-volume *Age and Society* by Matilda Riley and her associates which was published by the Russell Sage Foundation in New York. Other basic sources were cited at appropriate places in the text.

REFERENCES

1. AARONSON, B. S. 1958. Age and sex influences on MMPI profile peak distributions on an abnormal population. *J. Cons. Psychol.,* 22:203-206.
2. ABRAHAMS, P. 1972. Psychomotor performance, cardiovascular functioning, and coronary-prone behavior. (Abstract.) *Gerontologist,* 12:57.
3. ACORD, L. D. 1972. Hallucinogenic drugs and brain damage. *Milit. Med.,* 137 (1): 18-19.
4. ALLPORT, G. W. 1937. *Personality: A Psychological Interpretation.* New York: Holt.
5. AMES, L. B. 1960. Age changes in the Rorschach responses of individual elderly subjects. *J. Genet. Psychol.,* 97:287-315.
6. ANSELLO, E. F. 1972. Verbal learning, memory, and aging. (Abstract.) *Gerontologist,* 12:54.
7. ATCHLEY, R. C. 1972. *The Social Forces in Later Life.* Belmont, California: Wadsworth Publishing Company.
8. AVERBACH, E., and CORIELL, A. S. 1961. Short-term memory in vision. *Bell System Tech.,* 40 (4):309-328.
9. BALTES, P. B., and GOULET, L. R. 1972. Exploration of developmental variables by manipulation and simulation of age differences in behavior. *Hum. Develop.,* 14:149-170.
10. BALTES, P. B., and LABOUVIE, G. V. 1973. Adult development of intellectual performance: description, explanation, modification. In: Eisdorfer, C., and Lawton, M. P. (Eds.) *The Psychology of Adult Development and Aging.* Washington, D.C.: American Psychological Association.
11. BAYLEY, N., and ODEN, M. H. 1955. The maintenance of intellectual ability in gifted adults. *J. Geront.,* 10:91-107.
12. BELBIN, E., and BELBIN, R. M. 1968. New careers in middle age. In Neugarten, Bernice (Ed.) *Middle Age and Aging: A Reader in Social Psychology.* Chicago: University of Chicago Press.
13. BELL, B. 1972. Auditory functional age. *Aging and Human Development,* 3 (2): 183-187.
14. BELL, B., ROSE, C., and DAMON, A. 1972. The normative aging study: an interdisciplinary, longitudinal study of aging. *Aging and Human Development,* 3 (1):5-17.
15. BIRREN, J. E. 1959. Principles of research on aging. In Birren, J. E. (Ed.). *Handbook of Aging and the Individual: Psychological and Biological Aspects.* Chicago: University of Chicago Press.
16. BIRREN, J. E. 1964. *The Psychology of Aging.* Englewood Cliffs, New Jersey: Prentice Hall.

17. BIRREN, J. E. 1969. Age and decision strategies. In: Welford, A. T. (Ed.) *Interdisciplinary Topics in Gerontology*. New York: Karger, Basel, 4.
18. BIRREN, J. E. 1970. Toward an experimental psychology of aging. *Amer. Psychol.*, 25:124-135.
19. BIRREN, J. E., CARDON, P. V., JR., and PHILLIPS, SHIRLEY, L. 1963. Reaction time as a function of the cardiac cycle in young adults. *Science*, 140:195-196.
20. BLENKER, M. 1967. Environmental change and the aging individual. *Gerontologist*, 7:101-105.
21. BLUM, J. E., JARVIK, L. R., and CLARK, E. T. 1970. Rate of change on selective tests of intelligence: a twenty-year longitudinal study of aging. *J. Geront.*, 25: 171-176.
22. BORTNER, R. W., and ROSENMAN, R. H. 1967. The measurement of pattern *A* Behavior. *J. Chron. Dis.*, 20:525-533.
23. BOTWINICK, J. 1967. *Cognitive Processes in Maturity and Old Age*. New York: Springer.
24. BOTWINICK, J. 1970. Geropsychology. *Ann. Rev. Psychol.*, 11:239-272.
25. BOTWINICK, J. 1973. *Behavior and Aging*. New York: Springer.
26. BOTWINICK, J., ROBBIN, J. S., and BRINLEY, J. F. 1959. Reorganization of perceptions with age. *J. Geront.*, 14.
27. BOTWINICK, J., and THOMPSON, L. W. 1968. Age differences in reaction time: an artifact? *Gerontologist*, 25-28.
28. BOUMA, P. J. 1947. Perception on the road when visibility is low. *Philips Tech. Rev.*, 9:149-157.
29. BOWER, G. 1972. A selective review of organizational factors in memory. In: Tulving, E., and Donaldson, W. (Eds.) *Organization of Memory*. New York: Academic Press.
30. BRODY, H. 1972. *Aging in the Central Nervous System*. Kiev: 9th International Congress of Gerontology, abstracts, 1:228.
31. BUHLER, C. 1961. Old age and fulfillment of life with considerations of the use of time in old age. *Acta Psychol.*, 19:126-148.
32. BURNEY, S. 1972. Morbidity and mortality in a healthy aging male population— a 10-year survey. (Abstract.) *Gerontologist*, 12:49.
33. BUSSE, E. W., and OBRIST, W. D. 1963. Presenescent electroencephalographic changes in the elderly. *Postgrad. Med.*, 34:179-182.
34. BUSSE, E. W., and OBRIST, W. D. 1965. Presenescent electroencephalographic changes in normal subjects. *J. Geront.*, 20:315-320.
35. BUSSE, E., and PFEIFFER, E. 1969. *Behavior and Adaptation in Later Life*. Boston: Little Brown.
36. CAMERON, N. 1956. Neuroses of later maturity. In: Kaplan, O. J. (Ed.) *Mental Disorders in Later Life*. Stanford, California: Stanford University Press.
37. CAMPBELL, D. P. 1971. *Handbook for the Strong Vocational Interest Blank*. Stanford, California: Stanford University.
38. CATTELL, R. B. 1941. Some theoretical issues in adult intelligence testing. *Psychol. Bull.*, 38:592.
39. CATTELL, R. B. 1950. *Personality: A Systematic Theoretical and Factual Study*. New York: McGraw-Hill.
40. CATTELL, R. B. 1957. A universal index for psychological factors. *Psychologica*, 1:74-85.
41. CATTELL, R. B. 1963. Theory of fluid and crystallized intelligence: a critical experiment. *J. Educational Psychology*, 54:1-22.
42. CATTELL, R. B., and EBER, H. W. 1964. *Handbook for the Sixteen Personality Factor Questionnaire*. Champaign, Illinois: Institute for Personality and Ability Testing.

43. CATTELL, R. B., EBER, H. W., and TATSUOKA, M. M. 1970. *Handbook for the Sixteen Personality Factor Questionnaire*. Champaign, Ilinois: Institute for Personaity and Abiity Testing.

44. CHOWN, SHEILA M. 1968. Personality and aging. In Schaie, K. Warner (Ed.) *Theory and Methods of Research on Aging*. Morgantown, West Virginia: West Virginia University.

45. CHOWN, S. M. 1972. The effect of flexibility-rigidity and age on adaptability in job performance. *Industr. Geront.*, 13:105-124.

46. CLAY, HILARY M. 1958. A study of performance in relation to age at two printing works. *J. Geront.*, 11:1956b, 417-424.

47. CLEMENT, F. 1972. The physical strength decline. Remarks about the effect of some influent factors. *Proceedings of the Ninth International Congress of Gerontology*, 2:254.

48. COBB, B. B., LAY, D. C., and BOURDET, N. M. 1971. The relationship between chronological age and aptitude test measures of advanced-level air traffic controllers. *Federal Aviation Report No. FAA-AM-71-36*.

49. COHEN, S. I., and SHMAVONIAN, B. M. 1967. Catecholamines, vasomotor conditioning, and aging. In: Gitman, L. (Ed.) *Endocrines and Aging*. Springfield, Illinois: Charles C Thomas.

50. COMALLI, P. E., JR., WAPNER, S., and WERNER, H. 1959. Perception of verticality in middle and old age. *J. Psychol.*, 47:259-266.

51. COMFORT, A. 1969. Test battery to measure aging in man. *Lancet*, ii:1411-1414.

52. COOPER, R. M., BILASH, I., and ZUBEK, J. P. 1959. The effect of age on taste sensitivity, *J. Geront.*, 14:56-58.

53. COOPINGER, N. W. 1955. The relationship between critical flicker frequency and chronological age for varying levels of stimulus brightness. *J. Geront.*, 10:48-52.

54. COSH, J. A. 1953. Studies on the nature of vibration sense. *Clin. Sci.*, 12:131-151.

55. CROSSMAN, E. R. F. W. 1959. A theory of acquisition of speed skill. *Ergonomics*, 2:153-166.

56. CUMMING, E. (1964). New thoughts on the theory of disengagement. In: Kastenbaum, R. (Ed.) *New Thoughts on Old Age*. New York: Springer.

57. CUMMING, E., and HENRY, W. 1961. *Growing Old: The Process of Disengagement*. New York: Basic Books.

58. DAMON, A. 1972. Predicting age from body measurements and observations. *Aging and Human Development*, 3, 169-174.

59. DEMPSTER, A. P. 1972. Functional age and age-related measures. *Aging and Human Development*, 3, 195-196.

60. DILMAN, V. 1972. Biological age and its determination in the light of elevation mechanisms of aging. *Proceedings of the 9th International Congress of Gerontology*, 2:319-322.

61. EDDINGTON, D. W., COSMAS, A. C., and McCAFFERTY, W. B. 1972. Exercise and longevity: evidence for a threshold age. *J. Geront.*, 27 (3)341-343.

62. EISDORFER, C. 1960. Rorschach rigidity and sensory decrement in a senescent population. *J. Geront.*, 15:188-190.

63. EISDORFER, C. 1963. Rorschach performance and intellectual functioning in the aged. *J. Geront.*, 18:358-363.

64. EISDORFER, C. 1965. Verbal learning and response time in the aged. *J. Genet. Psychol.* 107:15-22.

65. EISDORFER, C. 1968. Arousal and performance: experiments in verbal learning and tentative theory. In: Talland, G. A. (Ed.) *Human Aging and Behavior*. New York: Academic Press.

66. ELIAS, M. F., and KINSBOURNE, M. 1972. Time course of identity and category matching by spatial orientation. *J. Exp. Psychol.*, 95:177-183.

67. ERIKSON, E. 1950. *Childhood and Society*. New York: Norton.
68. FARRIMOND, T. 1961. Prediction of speech hearing loss for older industrial workers. *Gerontologia*, 5:65-87.
69. FILER, R. N., and O'CONNELL, D. D. 1964. Motivation of aging persons in an institutional setting. *J. Geront.*, 19:15-22.
70. FINCH, C. E. 1972. The brain as a site for cellular pacemakers of aging. *9th International Congress of Gerontology Abstracts*, 1:100.
71. FOZARD, J. L. 1972. Predicting age in the adult years from psychological assessments of abilities and personality. *Aging and Human Development*, 3:175-182.
72. FOZARD, J. L., CARR, G. D., TALLAND, G. A., and ERWIN, D. E. 1971. Effects of information load, sensory modality, and age on paced inspection performance. *Quart J. Exp. Psychol.*, 23:304-310.
73. FOZARD, J. L., and NUTTALL, R. L. 1971a. Effects of age and socioeconomic status differences on the Sixteen Personality Factor Questionnaire. *Proceeding of the 79th Annual Meeting of the American Psychological Association*, 495-496.
74. FOZARD, J. L., and NUTTALL, R. L. 1971b. General aptitude test battery scores by age and socioeconomic status. *J. Appl. Psychol.*, 55:372-379.
75. FOZARD, J. L., and NUTTALL, R. L. 1972. General Aptitude Test Battery scores for men in different age and socioeconomic status groups. In: Shatto, G. (Ed.) *Employment of the Middle-Aged*. Springfield, Illinois: Charles C Thomas.
76. FOZARD, J. L., NUTTALL, R. L., and WAUGH, N. C. 1972. Age-related differences in mental performance. *Aging and Human Development*, 3:19-43.
77. FRIEDENWALD, J. S. 1952. The eye. In: Lansing, A. I. (Ed.) *Cowdry's Problems of Aging*. Baltimore: Williams and Wilkins, (third edition).
78. GALTON, F. 1889. On instruments for (1) testing perception of differences of tint and for (2) determining reaction time. *J. Anthrop. Inst.* 19:27-29.
79. GILBERT, J. G. 1957. Age changes in color matching. *J. Geront.* 12:210-215.
80. GOODWIN, K. S., and SCHAIE, K. W. 1969. Age differences in personality structure. *Proceedings of the 77th Annual Convention of the American Psychological Association*, 4:713-714.
81. GRANICK, S., and BIRREN, J. E. 1969. Cognitive functioning of survivors: 12 year follow-up of healthy aged. *Proceedings of the Eighth International Congress of Gerontology*, 2.
82. GREEN, D. M., and SWETS, J. A. 1966. *Signal Detection Theory and Psychophysics*. New York: Wiley.
83. GREEN, R. F. 1972. Age, intelligence and learning. *Industr. Geront.*, 12:29-41.
84. GREGORY, R. L. 1955 A note on summation time of the eye indicated by signal/noise discrimination. *Quart. J. Psychol.*, 7:147-148.
85. GREGORY, R. L. 1956. An experimental treatment of vision as an information source and noisy channel. In: Cherry, C. (Ed.) *Information Theory: 3rd London Symposium*. London: Methuen.
86. GREGORY, R. L., and CANE, V. 1955. A statistical information theory of visual thresholds. *Nature*, 186:1272.
87. GRUEN, W. 1964. Adult Personality: an empirical study of Erikson's theory of ego development. In: Neugarten, B. L. (Ed.) *Personality in Middle and Late Life*. New York: Atherton Press, 1964, 1-14.
88. GUTH, S. K., EASTMAN. A. A., and McNELIS, J. F. 1956. Lighting for older workers. *Illumination Engineering*, 51:656-660.
89. HALL, C. S., and LINDZEY, G. 1957. *Theories of Personality*. New York: Wiley.
90. HEATH, H. A., and ORBACH, J. 1963. Reversibility of the Necker cube: IV responses of elderly people. *Perceptual and Motor Skills*, 17:625-626.
91. HERON, A., and CHOWN, S. 1967. *Age and Function*. Boston: Little, Brown.
92. HERON, W. 1957. The pathology of boredom. *Scientific American*, 196:52.

93. HIRSCH, M. J. 1960. Data cited by Weymouth, F. W. Effect of age on visual acuity. In: Hirsch, M. J., and Wick, R. F. (Eds.) *Vision of the Aging Patient.* Philadelphia: Chilton.

94. HOLLINGSWORTH, J .W., HASHIZUME, A., and JABLON, S. 1965. Correlation between tests of aging in Hiroshima subjects—an attempt to define "physiological age." *Yale J. Biol. Med.,* 38:11-26.

95. HORN, J. L., and CATTELL, R. B. 1967. Age differences in fluid and crystallized intelligence. *Acta Psychol.,* 26:210-220.

96. HULICKA, I. 1967. Age changes and age differences in memory functioning. *Gerontologist,* 7:46-54.

97. HULICKA, I., and GROSSMAN, J. 1967. Age-group comparisons for the use of mediators in paired-associate learning. *J. Geront.,* 22:46-51.

98. ISTOMINA, Z. I., SAMAKHOVALOVA, V. I., and PREBAZHENSKAYA, I. N. 1967. Memory in elderly individuals engaged in intellectual professions. *Sov. Psychol.,* 6:30-37.

99. JACOBS, E. A., WINTER, P. M., ALVIS, H. J., and SMALL, S. M. 1971. Hyperoxygenation effect on cognitive functioning in the aged. *New Engl. J. Med.,* 32:159-170.

100. JALAVISTO, E. 1964. The phenomenon of retinal rivalry in the aged. *Gerontologia,* 9:1-8.

101. JALAVISTO, E., ORMA, L., and TARVAST, M. 1951. Aging and relation between stimulus intensity and duration in corneal sensitivity. *Acta Physiol. Scand.* 23:224-233.

101a. JARVIK, L. F., and FALEK, A. 1963. Intellectual stability and survival in the aged. *J. Geront.* 18:173-176.

101b. JARVIK, L. F., and BLUM, J. E. 1971. Cognitive declines as predictors of mortality in twin pairs: a twenty year longitudinal study of aging. In: Palmore, E., and Jeffers, F. C. (Eds.) *Prediction of Life Span.* Lexington, Massachusetts: D. C. Heath.

101c. JARVIK, L. F., KALLMANN, F. J., LORGE, I., and FALEK, A. 1962. Longitudinal study of intellectual changes in senescent twins. In Tibbitts, C., and Donahue, W. (Eds.), *Social and Psychological Aspects of Aging.* New York: Columbia University Press.

102. JENKINS, C. D. 1971. Psychological and social precursors of coronary disease. *Med. Progr.,* 284:244-256, 284:307-316.

103. JENKINS, C. D., ROSEMAN, R. H., and FRIEDMAN, M. 1967. Development of an objective psychological test for the determination of the coronary-prone behavior pattern in employed men. *J. Chron. Dis.,* 20:371-379.

104. KASTELBAUM, R. 1968. Perspectives on the development and modification of behavior in the aged: a developmental-field perspective. *Gerontologist,* 8:280-283.

105. KASTENBAUM, R. 1971. Getting there ahead of time. *Psychology Today,* 5:52-58.

106. KASTENBAUM, R., DERBIN, V., SABATINI, P., and ARTT, S. 1972 (May). "The Ages of Me": Toward personal and interpersonal definitions of functional aging. *Aging and Human Development,* 3:197-212.

107. KAY, H. 1968. Learning and aging. In Schaie, K. W. (Ed.) *Theory and Methods of Research on Aging.* Morgantown, W. Virginia: W. Virginia University Press, 61-82.

108. KELLY, E. L. 1955. Consistency of the adult personality. *Am. Psychol.,* 10.

109. KERLINGER, F. N. 1964. Foundations of Behavioral Research *Educational and Psychological Inquiry.* New York: Holt, Rinehart & Winston.

110. KINSEY, A. C., POMEROY, W. B., and MARTIN, C. E. 1948. *Sexual Behavior in the Human Male.* Philadelphia: Saunders.

111. KONIG, E. 1957. Pitch discrimination and age. *Acta Oto-laryng.* (Stockholm), 48: 475-489.

112. KOYL, L. F. 1970. A technique for measuring functional criteria in placement and retirement practices. In: Sheppard, H. L. (Ed.) *Towards an Industrial Gerontology*. Cambridge: Schenkman.

113. KRAL, V. A. 1966. Memory loss in the aged. *Dis. Nerv. Syst.* (Monograph supplement), 27:51-54.

114. LABOUVIE, G. V., HOYER, W. J., BALTES, P. B., and BALTES, M. M. (in press). Operant analysis of intellectual behavior in old age. *Human Development*, 15.

115. LAWTON, M. P., and NAHEMOW, L. 1972. Ecology and the aging process. In Eisdorfer, C. and Lawton, M. P. (Eds.), *The Psychology of Adult Development and Aging*. Washington, D.C.: American Psychological Association.

116. LEAF, A. 1973. Every day is a gift when you are over 100. *National Geographic*, 92-119.

117. LEHMAN, H. C. 1953. *Age and Achievement*. Published for the American Philosophical Society. London: Oxford University Press.

118. LINDSLEY, O. R. 1964. Geriatric behavioral prosthetics. In: Kastenbaum, R. (Ed.) *New Thoughts on Old Age*, 41-60. New York: Springer.

119. LOWENTHAL, M. F. 1971. Intentionality: Toward a framework for the study of adaptation in adulthood. *Aging and Human Development*, 2:79-95.

120. MCFARLAND, R. A., DOMEY, R. G., WARREN, A. B., and WARD, D. C. 1960. Dark adaptation as a function of age: I. A statistical analysis. *J. Geront.*, 15:149-154.

121. MADDOX, G. L. 1970a. Fact and artifact: evidence bearing on disengagement theory. In: Palmore, E. (Ed.) *Normal Aging*. Durham, N.C.: Duke University Press.

122. MADDOX, G. L. 1970b. Persistence of life style among the elderly. In: Palmore, E. (Ed.) *Normal Aging*. Durham, N.C.: Duke University Press.

123. MASTERS, W. H., and JOHNSON, V. 1966. *Human Sexual Response*. Boston: Little, Brown.

124. MATARAZZO, J. D. 1972. *Wechsler's Measurement and Appraisal of Adult Intelligence*. (Fifth edition). Baltimore, Maryland: Williams & Wilkins.

125. MILES, R. A., DOMEY, R. G., WARREN, A. B., and WARD, D. C. 1960. Dark adaptation as a function of age: I. A statistical analysis. *J. Geront.*, 15:149-154.

126. MURRELL, F. H. 1970. The effect of extensive practice on age differences in reaction time. *J. Geront.*, 25:268-274.

127. NESSELROADE, J. R., SCHUIE, K. W. and BALTES, P. B. 1972. Ontogenetic and generational components of structural and quantitative change in adult cognitive behavior. *J. Geront.*, 27:222-228.

128. NEUGARTEN, B. L. and ASSOCIATES 1964. *Personality in Middle and Late Life*. New York: Atherton Press.

129. NOWLIN, J. V. 1972. Age-related differences in cardiovascular response during reaction time experiments. Paper presented at the American Psychological Society Meeting, Honolulu, Hawaii, September, 1972.

130. NUTTALL, R. L. 1972. The strategy of functional age research. *Aging and Human Development*, 3, 2:149-152.

131. OBRIST, W. D. and BUSSE, E. W. 1965. The electroencephalogram in old age. In: Wilson, W. W. (Ed.), *Applications of Electroencephalography in Psychiatry: A Symposium*. Durham: Duke University Press.

132. OBRIST, W. D., BUSSE, E. W., EISDORFER, C. and KLEEMEIER, R. W. 1962. Relation of the electroencephalogram to intellectual function in senescence. *J. Geront.*, 17:197-206.

133. ORDY, J. M. and SCHJEIDE, O. A. 1972. Biological age and its determination: an interdisciplinary study. *Proceedings of the 9th International Congress of Gerontology*, 2:315-318.

134. PESTALOZZA, G. and SHORE, I. 1955. Clinical evaluation of presbycusis on basis of different tests of auditory function. *Laryngoscope*, 65:1136-1163.
135. PETER, C. P., MAKINODAN, T., and PETERSON, W. J. 1972. Effect of surgical, physical and chemical insults on the life-span and pathology of a strain of mice with long life-span. Paper presented at the 9th International Congress of Gerontology, Kiev, July, 1972.
136. POWELL, A. H., JR., EISDORFER, C., and BOGDONOFF, M. D. 1964. Physiologic response patterns observed in a learning task. *Arch. Gen. Psych.*, 10:192-195.
137. PRIEN, R. F. 1972. Chronic organic brain syndrome. Veterans Administration Department of Medicine and Surgery, Washington, D.C.
138. REICHARD, S., LIVSON, F., and PETERSON, P. G. 1962. *Aging and Personality*. New York: Wiley.
139. RIEGEL, K. F., and RIEGEL, R. M. 1972. Development, drop and death. *Develop. Psychol.*, 6.906-919.
140. RIEGEL, K. F., RIEGEL, R. M., and MEYER, G. 1968. The prediction of retest resisters in research on aging. *J. Geront.*, 23:370-374.
141. RILEY, M. W. 1971. Social gerontology and the age stratification of society. *Gerontologist*, 11:79 87.
142. ROSE, C. L. 1972. The measurement of social age. *Aging and Development*, 2, 153-168.
143. ROSE, C. L., and BELL, B. 1971. *Predicting Longevity: Methodology and Critique*. Lexington, Mass.: D. C. Heath & Co.
144. ROSEN, S., PLESTER, D., ELMOFTY, E., and ROSEN, H. V. 1964. High speed audiometry in presbycusis: a comparative study of the Mabaans in the Sudan with urban populations. *Arch. Oto-laryng.*, 79:18-32.
145. ROSENHAN, D. L. 1973. On being sane in insane places. *Science*, 250-258.
146. ROSENMAN, R. H. et al. 1964. A predictive study of coronary heart disease: the Western Collaborative Group Study. *J.A.M.A.*, 189:15-26.
147. ROSS, J. E. 1970. A measure of "crystallized intelligence" in the General Aptitude Test Battery. *Am. Psychol.*, 25:820 (Abstract).
148. ROSS, J. E., WAUGH, N. C., THOMAS, J. C., and FOZARD, J. L. 1972. Age differences in stimulus and response repetition effects in choice reaction time. Paper presented at the Psychonomic Society Meeting, St. Louis, November 1972.
149. ROTHSCHILD, D. 1956. Senile psychoses and psychoses with cerebral arteriosclerosis. In: Kaplan, O. J. (Ed.) *Mental Disorders in Later Life*. Stanford, California: Stanford University Press.
150. RUSSELL, E. W., NEURINGER, C., and GOLDSTEIN, G. 1970. *Assessment of Brain Damage*. New York: Wiley-Interscience.
151. SCHAIE, K. W., and MARQUETTE, B. W. 1971. Personality in maturity and old age. In Dreger, R. M. (Ed.) *Multivariate Personality Research: Contributions to the Understanding of Personality in Honor of R. B. Cattell*. Baton Rouge, La.: Claitor.
152. SCHLUDERMANN, E., and ZUBEK, J. P. 1962. Effect of age on pain sensitivity. *Perceptual and Motor Skills*, 14:295-301.
153. SCHONFIELD, D. 1969. Age and remembering. *Proceedings of Seminars* 1968-69. Durham, N. C.: Center for the Study of Aging and Human Development.
154. SLATER, P. E. 1964. Prolegomena to a psychoanalytic theory of aging and death. In: Kastenbaum, R. (Ed.) *New Thoughts on Old Age*, 19-40. New York: Springer.
155. SLATER, P. E. and SCARR, H. A. 1964. Personality in old age. *Genet. Psychol. Monogr.*, 70:229-269.
156. SPIETH, W. 1965. Slowness of task performance and cardiovascular diseases. In: Welford, A. T., and Birren, J. E. (Eds.) *Behavior, Aging, and the Nervous System*. Springfield, Ill.: Charles C Thomas.

157. SPOOR, A. 1967. Presbycusis values in relation to noise-induced hearing loss. *International Audiology*, 6:48-57.
158. STREHLER, B. L. 1962. *Time, Cells, and Aging*. New York: Academic Press.
159. SURWILLO, W. W. 1968. Timing of behavior in senescence and the role of the central nervous system. In: Talland, G. A. (Ed.) *Human Aging and Behavior*. New York: Academic Press.
160. SZAFRAN, J. 1968. Psychophysiological studies of aging in pilots. In: Talland, G. A. (Ed.) *Human Aging and Behavior*. New York: Academic Press.
161. TALLAND, G. A. 1965. Three estimates of the word span and their stability over the adult years. *Quart. J. Exp. Psychol.*, 17:301-307.
162. THOMAS, J. C., and MARSH, G. R. 1972. Remembering the names of pictured objects. *Gerontologist*, 12:54. (Abstract.)
163. THOMPSON, L. W. 1973. Psychophysiological studies of aging. In: Eisdorfer, C., and Lawton, M. P. (Eds.) *The Psychology of Adult Development and Aging*. Washington, D.C.: American Psychological Association.
164. UNITED STATES DEPARTMENT OF LABOR. 1967. Manual for the General Aptitude Test Battery, Section III. Development. Washington, D.C.: U.S. Government Printing Offices, October 1967.
165. URBAN, H. B., and LAGO, D. J. 1972. Life-history antecedents in psychiatric disorders of the aging. Paper presented at the Gerontology Society Meeting, San Juan, Puerto Rico, December, 1972.
166. VEROFF, J., ATKINSON, J. W., FELD, S. C., and GURIN, G. 1960. The use of thematic apperception to assess motivation in a nationwide interview study. *Psychol. Monogr.*, 74:12 (Whole No. 499).
167. VISKUM, P. 1972. Obesity in a normal population and department for long term treatment. 9th International Congress of Gerontology, Kiev, 1972, 3:408.
168. VOGEL, F. S. 1969. The brain and time. In: Busse, E. W., and Pfeiffer, E. (Eds.) *Behavior and Adaptation in Late Life*. Boston: Little, Brown & Co.
169. WAPNER, S., WERNER, H., and COMALLI, P. E., JR. 1960. Perception of part-whole relationships in middle and old age. *J. Geront.*, 15:412-416.
170. WARRINGTON, E. K., and SILBERSTEIN, M. 1970. A questionnaire technique for investigating long term memory. *Quart. J. Exp. Psychol.*, 22:508-512.
171. WAUGH, N. C. 1972. Recalling names from primary and secondary memory. *Gerontologist*, 12:54 (Abstract).
172. WAUGH, N. C., FOZARD, J. L., TALLAND, G. A., and ERWIN, D. E. 1973. Effects of age and stimulus repetition of two-choice reaction time. *J. Geront.*, 28:466-470.
173. WAUGH, N. C., and NORMAN, D. A. 1965. Primary memory. *Psychol. Rev.*, 72:89-104.
174. WEINERT, J. R., ROSS, J. E., FOZARD, J. L., and NUTTALL, R. L. 1971. The stability of vocational interests across age, education and social class. Paper presented at the Gerontological Society Meeting, Houston, October 1971.
175. WEISS, A. D. 1963. Auditory perception in aging. In: Birren, J. E., Butler, R. N., Greenouse, S. W., Sokoloff, L., and Yarrow, M. R. (Eds.) *Human Aging: A Biological and Behavioral Study*. Public Health Service Publication No. 986. Washington: U.S. Government Printing Office.
176. WELFORD, A. T. 1958. *Aging and Human Skill*. New York: Oxford University Press.
177. WELFORD, A. T. 1959. Psychomotor performance. In: Birren, J. E. (Ed.) *Handbook of Aging and the Individual*. Chicago: University of Chicago Press.
178. WELFORD, A. T. 1969. Age and skill: motor, intellectual and social. In: Welford, A. T. (Ed.) *Interdisciplinary Topics in Gerontology*, 4:1-22.
179. WELFORD, A. T. 1970. Age changes in discrimination, choice and the control of

movement: nine years on. *Proceedings of the Eighth International Congress of Gerontology*, I, Washington, D.C. International Association of Gerontology.

180. WELFORD, A. T., and BIRREN, J. E. (Eds.). 1965. *Behavior, Aging and the Nervous System*. Springfield, Ill.: C. C Thomas.

181. WESTON, H. C. 1949. On age and illumination in relation to visual performance. *Transactions of the Illuminating Engineering Society*, London, 14:281-297.

182. WHYTE, W. H., JR. 1956. *The Organization Man*. Garden City, N.Y.: Doubleday.

183. WILKIE, F. A., and EISDORFER, C. 1972. Components of Reaction Time Change in Old Age. Presented at the American Psychological Association Meeting, Honolulu, Hawaii, September 1972.

186. WOLSTENHOLME, G. E. W., and O'CONNOR, M. (Eds.). 1970. *Alzheimer's Disease and Related Conditions*. London: Churchill.

184. WOLF, E. 1960. Glare and age. *Arch Opthalm.* 64:502-514.

185. WOLF, E. 1967. Studies on the shrinkage of the visual field with age. In: *Night Visibility*, Highway Research Record Number 164, 1-7.

187. WOODRUFF, D. S. 1972. Biofeedback control of the EEG alpha rhythm and its effect on reaction time in the young and old. Doctoral Dissertation, University of Southern California.

188. WOODRUFF, D. S. and BIRREN, J. E. 1972. Age changes and cohort differences in personality. *Develop. Psychol.* 6:252-259.

189. WOODRUFF, D. S. and BIRREN, J. E. 1972. Biofeedback control of the EEG rhythm and its effect on reaction time in the young and old. 9th International Congress of Gerontology abstracts, 3:413.

190. WOZNIAK, R. H. and EISNER, H. 1972. Human performance and verbal control in the aging process. Paper presented at the 9th International Congress of Gerontology, Kiev, July, 1972.

191. YOSHIKAWA, M., HIRAI, S., and MORIMATSU, M. 1972. A clinicopathological study of dementia in the aged. Paper presented at the 9th International Congress of Gerontology, Kiev, July, 1972.

7

NOSOLOGY

KLAUS BERGMANN, M.D., CH.B., D.P.M.,
M.R.C.PSYCH.

Lecturer in Psychogeriatric Medicine
Department of Psychological Medicine
Newcastle General Hospital
Newcastle upon Tyne, England.

"Old age seems the only disease; all others run into this one."
R. W. Emerson, Essays, Circles, (1841).

INTRODUCTION

The act of growing old itself seems to be a sufficient cause for depression and fear, and deterioration of the mind is often seen as a normal part of ageing.

The nineteenth century saw the rise of systematic psychiatry and the advent of attempts at systematic classification of known psychiatric phenomena. The special phenomena of ageing were included within a broad concept of dementia, which also embraced chronic hypomanic and schizophrenic states, and yet as early as 1806 Pinel (25), having included senile dementia with these other conditions, paradoxically described it as "childishness of old age." Esquirol (9) emphasized that in his study of age-related admissions to hospital 20-50 seemed to be the peak period for psychiatric admissions. He noted further that for a hospital population the frequency of suicide decreased in old age and his conclusion was that the elderly person, due to his feeling of powerlessness, became calmer, ideas and desires lost their strength, and imagination was set at rest. He concluded that, apart from senile dementia, other psychiatric disorders faded as old age approached.

Henry Maudsley (22), as would be expected of such an acute clinical observer, produced some very profound observations. He described senile insanity and gave a good clinical description of the amnestic syndrome, pointing to the impairment of recent memory and preferential preservation of past memory ("the memory is long-sighted, so to speak"), but he saw senile insanity as continuous with the symptoms of a failing mind natural to old age; he implied that these pass gradually but continuously into senile insanity. He noted the relationship between this condition and post-mortem findings such as atheromatous vessels and decay of the brain with shrunken convolutions. His classification did not distinguish them from the "melancholics" and the "maniacs" of younger age groups who were also said to pass into a state of dementia. However, he gave a description of senile melancholia as a form of senile insanity. Agitated depression was described and his statement about this is of interest. He said, "They are remarkably quick in perception and exact in memory" and went on to say that "excitement rises to such a height . . . that they die at last from exhaustion." Prognosis was seen as being uniformly unfavourable.

At the turn of the century further impetus was brought to the organic psychosyndromes of old age by neuropathological studies which differentiated neuro-syphilis, arteriosclerotic vascular disease, and degenerative senile brain disease. An excellent historical review of the developments in this field, both clinically and neuropathologically, was given by Rothschild (33). He was also one of the strongest protagonists for the belief that the severity of the neuropathological changes bore little relationship to the severity of "mental alterations," and expressed the view that "different persons vary greatly in their ability to withstand cerebral damage, so the factor of individual mental vulnerability must be taken into consideration . . . this opens up many fields for study, for example, unfavourable hereditary or constitutional tendencies and unfavourable personality characteristics or situational stress." He extended this thesis and stated that even the impairment of memory is due not to organic changes alone, but also to psychologically determined mechanisms. This type of approach is reflected also by social psychiatrists such as MacMillan (21) who denies the existence of senile dementia because it is a therapeutically nihilistic concept. Views such as this would then regard each elderly individual under a variety of stresses as unique and not subject to classification in groups.

When the functional disorders of old age are considered, such as the affective disorders and those disorders resembling, to some extent at least, the schizophrenias found in younger age groups, then several viewpoints can be taken: firstly, that they are not different from similar mental illnesses arising in younger people and therefore do not require separate classification; secondly, that the conditions, although they show different colourings, are all aspects of a central degenerative process and their differentiation is purely descriptive; lastly, that classification may be attempted because different clinical descriptions are found to be diagnostically meaningful, and the special effects of ageing make their differentiation from younger age groups valuable.

THE DIFFERENTIATION OF DISEASE ENTITIES

Roth (30) pointed out that "most of the classical accounts of mental disorder of old age (4, 17) confine themselves to the presenile and arteriosclerotic psychosis." He goes on to observe that the writers evidently regarded other illnesses as numerically insignificant in relation to degenerative disorders peculiar to old age. Even as recently as 1956 Nordman (24) stated that, though certain symptoms were reversible and their removal might bring about a remission, they constituted merely a "superimposition" upon "the general picture of old age psychosis."

Roth defined clearly 5 descriptively distinct groups as follows:

1) *Affective psychosis* - in this category he classified all cases "whose admission to hospital had been occasioned by a sustained depressive or manic symptom complex."

2) *Late paraphrenia* - the patients he put in this group were "those with well organized systems of paranoid delusions with or without auditory hallucinations, existing in a setting of a well preserved personality and affective response."

3) *Arteriosclerotic psychosis* - patients classified in this group were "those (i) in whom dementia was associated with focal signs and symptoms indicate of cerebrovascular disease, or (ii) in whom a remittent or markedly fluctuating course at some stage of the dementing process was combined with any one of the following features: emotional incontinence, the preservation of insight, or epileptiform siezures."

4) *Senile psychosis* - the definition given was of "a condition with a history of gradual and continually progressive failure in the common activities of everyday life and a clinical picture dominated by failure of memory and intellect and disorganization of a personality where these were not attributable to specific causes. . . ."

5) *Acute confusion* - this was defined as "any condition of rapidly evolving clouding of consciousness produced by some extraneous cause or appearing for no discoverable reason. . . ."

It can be seen that these definitions, although implicating particular types of cerebral disease, implied no foreknowledge of cerebral pathology and were descriptive and clinical in their basis. It would be expected that if all these conditions were merely a colouring of the same underlying morbid process, then with the passage of time they would tend to merge into each other with regard to their course and prognosis. Roth examined three major criteria: discharge from mental hospital, current inpatient status, and death. All groups of patients were examined at 6 months and 2 years after admission. At 6 months all diagnostic groups described had different outcomes for discharge, current inpatient status, or death, but between organic and functional groups wide differences could be observed so that, for instance, of those patients with affective psychosis after the advent of E.C.T. more than 60% were discharged at 6 months follow-up period, whereas more than 60% of those patients who were admitted with a diagnosis of senile psychosis were dead. At 2 years the difference had widened: nearly 70% of patients with affective psychosis had been discharged and more than 80% of patients with senile psychosis had died. Of those patients with acute confusion at 2 years, half were dead and the other half had been discharged. The paraphrenics fared well for survival, but not for discharge, and patients with arteriosclerotic psychosis, whose prognosis at 6 months had been somewhat better than those of senile psychosis, approximated more to the outcome seen in senile psychosis at the 2-year follow-up.

MORTALITY AND CAUSES OF DEATH

Kay (13) showed that the organic psychosis had an increased mortality at least five times as high as that of the general population, whereas those patients diagnosed as paraphrenia or manic depressive psychoses showed no different mortality from the general population when specific causes of death due to mental disease had been excluded. Patients with late affective disorder, however, showed twice the mortality that might be expected mainly from the effects of cerebrovascular disorder. When the causes of death were examined for both patients with functional psychoses and those with organic psychosyndromes, in the latter group the cause of death was much more frequently of a non-specific type, whereas in the former group specific diagnoses could more readily be given.

THE ORGANIC PSYCHOSYNDROMES

In this section it is proposed to discuss the chronic organic psycho-syndromes, especially those conditions described above as senile or arterio-sclerotic psychosis. Two major questions arise with regard to these con-ditions:

1) Are different forms of brain damage related to a descriptive clinical picture?

2) Is the degree of brain damage related to the clinical severity of the disease?

Roth (30) showed the clinical and prognostic distinctions between organic and functional psychosyndromes. However, it has to be said that although senile and arteriosclerotic psychosis showed differences in their need for continued hospitalization and their mortality at 6 months, after 2 years had elapsed the outcomes for both these conditions came to resemble each other and it could be argued that they are but manifesta-tions of the same aging process expressed in terms of parenchymal and vascular change. Nevertheless, it is of some importance to decide whether a clinical separation into arteriosclerotic or senile psychosis is justifiable on neuropathological grounds. Such a distinction is not purely of aca-demic interest, but must surely be one of the necessary requirements before any rationally based therapeutic trial or investigations into pos-sible "causes" can be undertaken. All too often vaso-dilators are tested indiscriminately on people with parenchymatous brain disease and it has been found that parenchymatous "replacement" of R.N.A. (5) in fact worked best in those subjects whose organic psychosyndrome had a clinical component suggestive of vascular disease. Thus, clear definitions of clinical populations corresponding to an underlying neuropathological picture are most essential for the progress of any future therapeutic research in this field.

Corsellis (7) used Roth's criteria (*see above*) to assign, from the clinical notes, a diagnosis to 300 mental hospital patients over the age of 65 who came to autopsy. He quantified various types of cerebro-vascular change and parenchymatous degeneration in each brain and demonstrated the relationship between the extent of various types of brain damage found on neuropathological examination and the clinical picture described in life-time (*see Figure 1*). It can be seen from this Figure that the type of brain damage found in those cases in whom there had been clinical grounds for diagnosing arteriosclerotic psychosis (labelled "vascular" in

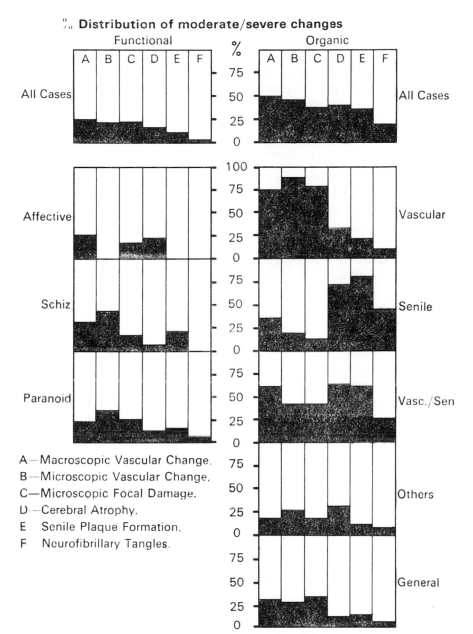

FIG. 1 — The incidence of cerebral changes in 300 mental hospital patients.
Mean age at death: 70 years.

the Figure) was of predominantly a vascular type; in those cases with senile psychosis (labelled "senile" in the Figure), degenerative changes predominated. Where the clinical picture seemed to contain some features of both types of disorder, neuropathological changes were more widely distributed. It can also be seen that patients with functional disorders, though still showing some evidence of brain damage, could be distinguished clearly from the organic psychosyndromes.

Clinical and Pathological Quantification

More detailed descriptions of quantitative relationships between brain damage and their clinical features have been given by Blessed (3), Tomlinson (36), and Roth (31). In these studies, clinical features such as disturbed behavior, inability to cope with day-to-day life, emotional upset, deterioration of personality, and disturbance of memory and orientation were all scored in such a way that the degree of clinical impairment for each patient could be numerically represented. Neuropathological quantification was carried out by counting senile plaques to indicate the extent of degenerative disease and measuring volume of softening to indicate the extent of arteriosclerotic damage. A further advantageous feature of this group of studies was the fact that they were prospective in nature, clinical diagnoses and assessments being done before death and neuropathological findings being reported "blind" without knowledge of the clinical features.

Figure 2 shows the close relationship between the dementia score (indicating disturbances of behavior and ability to cope) and the mean plaque count in patients diagnosed clinically as having senile dementia. For subjects diagnosed clinically as arteriosclerotic dementia, a similar relationship could be observed between the dementia score and the volume of softening (see Figure 3). From these results it could be seen that about 80% of all patients diagnosed clinically as senile dementia had a mean plaque count of more than 12 per high power field and only 11% of those patients who were presumed to be not demented had a mean plaque count of more than 12 per high power field and even these patients did not have as high a plaque count as the senile dementia group. Similarly, 73% of subjects diagnosed clinically as arteriosclerotic had a total of more than 50 ml. of softening.

Blessed (2) showed that by increasing the number of clinical criteria required to diagnose arteriosclerotic dementia, a greater degree of accuracy could be obtained. The clinical features of arteriosclerotic demen-

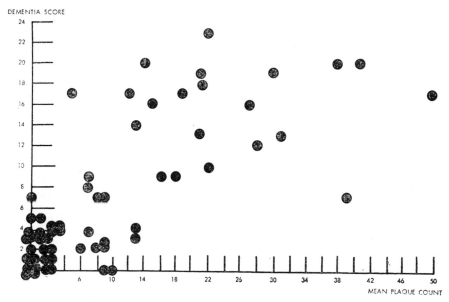

FIG. 2 — Relationship of dementia score to mean plaque count in 60 aged subjects. The higher the score the greater the degree of dementia.

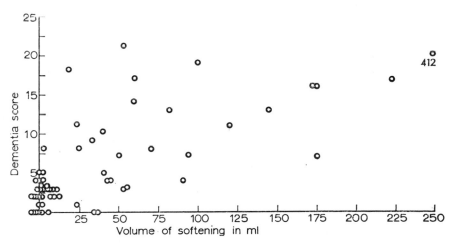

FIG. 3 — Relationship of dementia score to volume of softening in 22 arteriosclerotic dements and 38 control subjects. r=+0.69 p<.001.

tia which were considered in making the diagnosis were the history of a stroke, with localized variability of course, epileptic fits, preservation of insight, and emotional incontinence. If patients were scored 1 point for each of the above features then the means for the following groups were:

I   Senile Dementia   = 1.45 items
II   Mixed Senile and Arteriosclerotic Dementia = 2.7   items
III   Arteriosclerotic Dementia   = 4.30 items

In these cases, the clinical diagnosis corresponded to the neuropathological picture. Furthermore, by using two instead of one of the above criteria the accuracy of diagnosis could be increased from about 50% to 78%.

It would therefore seem justified, on the basis of present information, to assume that the role of brain damage in the clinical picture of organic psychosyndromes is of major importance, while accepting and recognizing that it by no means accounts for all the variance in behavioral ratings between the demented and non-demented subject.

Senility or Dementia?

With respect to senile dementia, however, further arguments need to be considered. One is that all elderly people are potential senile dements. As no one has yet been able to point to distinct qualitative differences between normal age changes and those ascribed to senile dementia, it could be assumed that in time all elderly people would succumb to senile dementia were they to live sufficiently long.

Kay et al. (16), examining the incidence of organic psychosyndromes in community residents, showed that even among the Over 80's only 22% could be diagnosed as suffering from organic psychosyndrome. Genetic studies (Kalman (11) and Larson et al. (19)) suggested that senile dementia was a distinct entity. Larson et al. (19) have suggested that its mode of inheritance is as a dominant gene inherited as a "Mono-hybrid autosomal dominant." They calculated that in the general population the frequency of persons with a deviant gene would be in the order of 12%. Constantinides et al. (6) concluded that senile dementia was a recessive or polygenically inherited condition. Their assessment of the families of probands, was not as thorough as the family histories were gathered from hospital records and not field studies. Nielsen (23), examining a hospital population, suggested the association of chromosomal abnormalities with senile dementia and Jarvik (10), studying community residents, reported the statistically significant relationship between memory loss and cognitive impairment and hypodiploidy.

The facts discussed in the above section seem to suggest that senile dementia is a disease entity rather than an extreme variation of a normal process. Lauter and Meyer (20) suggested that there is no fundamental criterion by which the pre-senile form of dementia originally described as Alzheimer's disease can be distinguished from later forms of dementia. In both conditions neuropathological Alzheimer change of a similar type was found and clinically the so-called *werkzeugstörungen* occurred. They concluded "this leads to the hypothesis that senile dementia and Alzheimer's Disease are simply different age manifestations of one disease entity. They further suggested that only the term Alzheimer's dementia should be used, with the addition of pre-senile or senile according to the age at onset.

FUNCTIONAL PSYCHOSYNDROMES

There are no clinical descriptions of functional psychosyndromes which refer exclusively to the senium. The process of aging influences functional psychosyndromes in respect of their clinical picture and course, genetic and family history, and association with exogenous stresses. An understanding of these differences is important in the use of nosological descriptions of functional psychiatric disorder in old age.

Schizophrenia

Schizophrenia beginning in old age is commonly called paraphrenia. The essential feature is a delusional state arising in clear consciousness. The delusion may arise suddenly in the manner of a primary delusion or gradually, blend imperceptibly from an irritable, hostile paranoid personality development to an undoubted delusional illness. Auditory hallucinations are frequently present and deafness is more commonly found in elderly paraphrenics. Genetically, Kay (14) established that the relatives of paraphrenic probands were more at risk for schizophrenia than normal subjects but showed a lesser genetic susceptibility than younger schizophrenics. Kay (15) sums up the recent views concerning schizophrenia and schizophrenia-like states in the elderly and concludes that "chronic paranoid hallucinatory psychoses that arise late in life are schizophrenias from the descriptive point of view." His review also pointed out that there may be favorable factors at work to postpone the illness until later life, including a lesser genetic susceptibility. It is suggested that, in common with symptomatic schizophrenias in earlier life, focal cerebral lesions may be of importance and that these accumulate in the senium. The prognosis of the illness is poor in that it persists without remission, but it does not affect the life-span of the patient and preservation of the personality and capacity to cope is often found. Indeed, above average drive and ability may sometimes be evident.

Depressions

Depression occurring in later life was considered a clinically distinct disease entity. A clinical picture of involutional depression is described by Post (28): "agitation rather than retardation, almost grandiose and often religious delusions of guilt or self-reproach, bizarre hypochondriacal delusions, especially of nihilistic quality (Cotard's syndrome). Moreover, involutional melancholia is said to arise in a special type of personality—rigid, emotionally brittle, introverted, bigoted and sexually inhibited. . . ." Post points out that there is now little evidence to point to the validity of this syndrome except possibly for the relative differences in younger and older depressives with regard to psychomotor agitation more commonly found in the aged and retardation in the younger depressives. However, late onset depressions do have certain characteristics: their more frequent association with physical ill health (32), an association with cerebro-vascular disease (13), and an impairment in the maintenance of clinical recovery for a large proportion of elderly depressives who were followed up (27).

Post (29), reporting on a more recent series of depressive patients treated with a more effective and wider range of therapy, believed that in spite of the fact that his patients were more unfavorably placed prognostically than those in his earlier series, it was possible to confirm the impression that both short-term and long-term outlook of the elderly patients with affective disorder had been improved through the introduction of antidepressant drugs. The genetics of late onset affective disorder suggest that there is a lesser risk of affective illness in the first degree relatives of late onset probands (12, 35).

NEUROTIC DISORDER

The clinical picture of neurotic disorder in later life does not differ remarkably from that found in younger patients. However, certain conditions seem to be relatively infrequent.

Obsessional neurosis (26) rarely starts in the senium and out of 300 elderly subjects seen in a random sample of community residents not one had a clear-cut obsessional neurosis starting in the senium (1). That is not to say that obsessional symptoms may not be prominent in the coloring of both depressive illness, reactive depression and mixed depressive and anxiety states.

It would be dangerous to make a primary diagnosis of *hysteria* in elderly patients showing conversion or dissociative symptoms. Ernst (8), in following up a group of hysterics treated in earlier life, did not find any that persisted into the senium with hysterical or behavioral disturbance.

Late onset neurotic disorder beginning after the age of 65 appears to have certain characteristics which differentiate it from the more long-standing neurosis (1). Late onset neurosis is compatible with a relatively undisturbed early history. In later life a greater association with physical ill health, especially cardio-vascular disorder, is found. The longstanding elderly neurotic seems to suffer relatively little from his or her disorder even when symptoms may be florid. The patient with neurotic disorder beginning in the senium suffers more acutely from loneliness, difficulty in self-care, and lack of hobbies and recreations. In spite of this, the clinical picture is less florid and is usually an admixture of neurotic depression or anxiety. Phobic features may often be present arising out of irrational extension of limitations imposed by physical ill health. For example, patients who have suffered syncopal or hypotensive collapses due to acute myocardial ischaemia may become totally housebound during the convalescence and on recovery and are afraid to go out in spite of good exercise tolerance and reassurance from relatives and medical attendants.

The main characteristic of neurotic disorder occurring in the senium is that it remains relatively silent, manifesting itself mainly by social disabilities and a stepwise reduction in the quality of life.

THE CLASSIFICATION OF PSYCHOGERIATRIC DISORDERS

Only the two most widely accepted systems will be discussed and these are the International Classification of Disease (1967) referred to as I.C.D.-8 (Manual of the International Statistical Classification of Diseases, Injuries, and Causes of Death, 1965 revision, Geneva, World Health Organization, 1967) and the Diagnostic and Statistical Manual of the American Psychiatric Association (Second Edition D.S.M. II 1968).

I.C.D.-8

The I.C.D. will be discussed in conjunction with the Glossary of Mental Disorders (studies on medical and population subjects No. 22, General Registry Office, H.M.S.O. 1968). This latter population provides explanation and operational definitions which supplement and expand the mental illness section of the I.C.D.

Organic Psychosyndromes: Senile dementia (I.C.D. 290.0). This diagnosis is defined operationally firstly by making it a diagnosis for dementia occurring after the age of 65, and secondly applying the criteria of exclusion of any other forms of cerebral pathology.

Arteriosclerotic Dementia: (293.0). This definition, in contrast to the one above, includes a satisfactory clinical description consistent with the type discussed in the preceding section.

Delirious States (Acute Confusion). The main problem arises when delirious states are considered. These have no classificatory status at all and this is most unsatisfactory. They have to be included in the category "Psychosis associated with other cerebral or other physical conditions" (I.C.D. 293.0-293.9 and 294.0-294.9). This method of classification gives no possibility of distinguishing mental impairment of acute or sub-acute onset from chronic dementing syndromes of symptomatic origin. For instance, a patient with an acute delirium due to hepatic failure could not be distinguished from a patient with a dementia arising as an end process from hepatolenticular degeneration. Another example might be the acute or long term consequences of coal gas poisoning which could not be distinguished by referring to the I.C.D. classification. Disease entities listed under 294.0-.9 leave out, for instance, neoplastic disease, B_{12} deficiency and collagen disorders. A further point of criticism is that it is not clear whether symptomatic or exogenous psychoses in clear consciousness should or should not be excluded, as in some sub-categories certain types of exogenous psychoses are excluded whereas in other categories this is left as a moot point.

Functional Psychosyndromes. Paraphrenia is classed with paranoid states as an "involutional paraphrenia" (I.C.D. 297.1). The separation from other schizophrenic syndromes is maintained in spite of the fact that strong evidence has been adduced for the acceptance of paraphrenia as a form of schizophrenia (15).

Involutional Melancholia: (I.C.D. 296.0). This is still accepted as a disease entity. The disease is said to begin between the age of 45 and 65. This leaves the patient whose depression begins after the age of 65 in rather an unfortunate and isolated position! The arguments against such a concept have been rehearsed by Post (28) and seem to the author to be convincing. There might, however, be more justification for the introduction of a category of "late onset depression" defined operationally as depressive psychosis arising for the first time after a certain age, as it has been demonstrated that such depressions have characteristic features which differentiate them from the recurrent manic depressive disorder of earlier life.

The Diagnostic and Statistical Manual of the American Psychiatric Association

Until 1968 the Diagnostic Manual (DSM I) differed quite substantially from the I.C.D., especially with regard to organic psychosyndromes. American usage referred to these under two headings:

1) *Acute brain syndrome*: this condition was synonymous with the acute confusional or delirious state.
2) *Chronic brain syndrome*: this term referred to the conditions which are commonly described as dementias or organic psychoses. Aetiological factors, where known, could be added to the description. For instance, Simon and Malamud (34), in describing the relationship between clinical diagnosis and autopsy findings, used the term chronic brain syndrome and qualified where appropriate with "senile brain disease," "arteriosclerotic brain disease," or "combined senile and arteriosclerotic brain disease." D.S.M. II (1968) approximates closely to I.C.D.-8. Important distinguishing features do remain. There is a curious distinction between psychotic and non-psychotic brain disease, the definition of psychotic being made according to the severity of the functional impairment. A distinction of greater use and considerable elegance that is employed is the distinction between acute and chronic syndromes of any sort. These are defined after the fourth classificatory numeral by x 1 (acute) and x 2 (chronic), a practice that might well be adopted more widely.

World Health Organization Classification

A recent report of a W.H.O. Scientific Group No. 507 (37) entitled *Psychogeriatrics* deals fully with the question of diagnosis and classification (pp. 12-17) and has helpful suggestions to make. The authors note especially the difficulties in the psychogeriatric field which arise from combining diagnoses from descriptive, aetiological and developmental sources, and the fact that these all co-exist. They recommend the proposal for psychogeriatric nosological classification which meets many of the problems which have been raised in the preceding paragraphs.

Proposed Psychogeriatric Classification of W.H.O. Scientific Group

1. Atrophic senile psychosis
   (a) (mild) psycho-organic syndrome
   (b) moderate senile dementia
   (c) severe senile dementia

2. Arteriosclerotic psychosis and other cerebrovascular diseases
   (a) mild psycho-organic syndrome
   (b) moderate psycho-organic syndrome
   (c) severe psycho-organic syndrome

3. Acute confusional state

4. Presenile dementia
   (a) Alzheimer syndrome
   (b) Pick's disease

5. Affective psychosis
   (a) late depression
   (b) late mania

6. Schizophrenia
   (a) late schizophrenia

7. Paranoid syndrome (paraphrenia)

8. Neurosis (acute psychogenic reaction, reactive development)

9. Changes of personality occurring in old age.

Some minor objections to this classification might include the view that the qualifications to neurosis which occur in parenthesis preempt any other view about the origin of neurosis in old age and one doubts the value of being able to distinguish between "a psychogenic reaction" and a "reactive development." Section 9, "changes of personality occurring in old age," raises some problems. Can we be absolutely certain that this is not just an accentuation of a previous personality trait? Is this to be defined in the presence of organic psychosyndrome? Or, only if organic psychosyndromes are absent? Is it to be distinguished in some fundamental way from the I.C.D. categories of personality disorder?

In the region of the organic psychosyndromes one or two ambiguities still remain. One example of this is that, in spite of the fact that leading authorities within the psychogeriatric field agree about the essential continuity of senile psychosis and Alzheimer's disease, one is classified under the broad heading of "Atrophic Senile Psychosis" and the other under the broad heading of "Pre-senile Dementia." The author's personal feeling is that, with respect to the organic psychosyndromes, it might be best if the term "psychosis" were abandoned. The report on psychogeriatrics also comes out very strongly in favor of a classification of organic psychosyndromes, not only according to pathology but according to degrees of severity. This is of the greatest value as a case has often been made for the different clinical course of at least some forms of mild psychosyndrome (18), such as "Benign Senescent Forgetfulness." The use of the term "acute confusion" is an advance on the I.C.D. classification of "psychosis," though it might be argued that a definition of whether the confusion is associated with cerebral disease, systemic disease, or both would be of the greatest of value for research purposes.

CONCLUSIONS

Precision in diagnosis is of the greatest importance in psychogeriatrics. The helplessness of the elderly patient unfortunately allows caring agencies in the hospital and in the community to act too freely on a mistaken assessment.

The elderly patient remains a unique individual, characterized by a multiplicity of physical and psychiatric symptoms, in whom one single nosological description would be totally inadequate. A formulation is therefore required, but one in which the various diagnoses that could be made have to be ranked in some sort of hierarchy (Kay and Roth unpublished communication). In general, such a hierarchy would have at its top the organic psychosyndromes, followed by functional psychoses, neuroses, and personality disorders. The elderly patient however, may often present because of an emotional or psychotic reaction rather than because of an early or relatively mild dementia, and therefore it is to be recommended that the major presenting psychiatric feature should be recorded in its own right and that precipitating stresses, social, emotional and physical, should be listed where possible.

REFERENCES

1. BERGMANN, K. 1971. The neuroses of old age. In: Kay, D. W. K., and Walk, A. (Eds.) *Recent Developments in Psychogeriatrics. A Symposium.* Ashford, Kent: Headley Bros.

2. BLESSED, G. (unpublished observation) cited in BERGMANN. 1969. Mental aspects of Cerebrovascular disease. *Report of a Symposium on the Sixth and Seventh Ages of Man. J. Roy. Coll. Gen. Practit.* Supplement No. 1, XVIII (No. 84).

3. BLESSED, G., TOMLINSON, B. E., and ROTH, M. 1968. The association between quantitative measures of dementia and of senile change in the cerebral grey matter of elderly subjects. *Brit. J. Psychiat.*, 114:797-811.

4. BLEULER, E. (1916). Cited in ROTH, M. 1955. The natural history of mental disorders arising in the senium. *J. Ment. Sci.*, 101:281-310.

5. CAMERON, D. E., SOLYOM, L., SVED, S., and WAINRIB, B. 1963. Effects of intravenous administration of ribonucleic acid upon failure of memory for recent events in presenile and aged individuals. *Recent Advances in Biological Psychiatry*, 5:365.

6. COSTANTINIDIS, J., GARRONE, G., and AJURIAGUERRA, J. DE. 1962. L'hérédité des démences de l'âge avancé. *Encéphale* (Paris), 51:301-44.

7. CORSELLIS, J. A. N. 1962. *Mental Illness and the Ageing Brain.* Maudsley Monographs No. 9. London: Oxford University Press.

8. ERNST, K. 1959. *Die Prognose der Neurosen.* Monographien Heft 85. Berlin: Springer-Verlag.

9. ESQUIROL, J. E. D. 1838. De la Folie. p. 33 in *Des Maladies Mentales.* Paris: Baillière.

10. JARVIK, L. (In press). *Proceedings of the Vth International Congress of Psychiatry.* 1971, Mexico.

11. KALLMANN, F. J. 1956. Genetic aspects of mental disorders in later life. In: Kaplan, O. J. (Ed.) *Mental Disorders in Later Life.* Stanford: Stanford University Press. Second edition, Chp. III, p. 26.

12. KAY, D. W. K. 1959. Observations on the natural history and genetics of old age psychosis: a Stockholm material, 1931-1937. *Procy Roy. Soc. Med.*, 52:791-4.

13. KAY, D. W. K. 1962. Outcome and cause of death in mental disorders of old age: a long-term follow-up of functional and organic psychoses. *Acta Psychiat. Scand.*, 38:249-76.

14. KAY, D. W. K. 1963. Late paraphrenia and its bearing on the aetiology of schizophrenia. *Acta Psychiat. Scand.*, 39:159-69.

15. KAY, D. W. K. 1972. Schizophrenia and schizophrenia-like states in the elderly. *Brit. J. Hosp. Med.* October 1972, 369-376.

16. KAY, D. W. K., BERGMANN, K., FOSTER, E. M., McKECHNIE, A. A., and ROTH. M. 1970. Mental illness and hospital usage in the elderly: A random sample followed up. *Comprehen. Psychiat.*, 11, No. 1.

17. KRAEPELIN, E. (1909). Cited in ROTH, M. 1955. The natural history of mental disorders arising in the senium. *J. Ment. Sci.*, 101:281-301.

18. KRAL, V. A. 1962. Senescent forgetfulness: benign and malignant. *Canad. Med. Assoc. J.*, 86:257.

19. LARSSON, T., SJÖGREN, T., and JACOBSON, G. 1963. Senile dementia. *Acta Psychiat. Scand.*, 39, Supplement. 1967.

20. LAUTER, H., and MEYER, J. E. 1968. Clinical and nosological concepts of senile dementia. In: Müller, Ch., and Ciompi, L. (Eds.) *Senile Dementia.* Bern, Stuttgart: Hans Huber. pp. 13-36.

21. MACMILLAN, D. 1967. Problems of a geriatric mental health service. *Brit. J. Psychiat.*, 113:175-181.

22. MAUDSLEY, H. 1879. Senile Insanity. In: *Pathology of Mind.* London: MacMillan. p. 472, third edition.

23. NIELSEN, J. 1968. Chromosomes in senile dementia. *Brit. J. Psychiat.*, 114:303-309.

24. NORDMAN. (1956). Cited in K (fl, D. W. K. 1959. Observations on the natural history and genetics of old age psychosis: a Stockholm material, 1931-1937. *Proc. Roy. Soc. Med.* 52:791-4.

25. PINEL, P. H. 1806. *A Treatise on Insanity*. Transl. by Davis, D. D., Sheffield, 1806.
26. POLLITT, J. 1957. Natural history of obsessional states *Brit. Med. J.* i:194-198.
27. POST, F. 1962. *The Significance of Affective Symptoms in Old Age*. Maudsley Monograph, No. 10. London: Oxford University Press.
28. POST, F. 1968. The factor of aging in affective illness. In: Coppen, A., and Walk, A. (Eds.) *Recent Developments in Affective Disorders. A Symposium*. Ashford, Kent: Headley Bros., Chp. IX, p. 105.
29. POST, F. (In press). *Proceedings of the Vth International Congress of Psychiatry*. 1971, Mexico.
30. ROTH, M. 1955. The natural history of mental disorders arising in the senium. *J. Ment. Sci.*, 101:281-301.
31. ROTH, M. 1971. Classification and aetiology in mental disorders of old age: some recent developments In: Kay, D. W. K., and Walk, A. (Eds.) *Recent Developments in Psychogeriatrics. A Symposium*. Ashford, Kent: Headley Bross., Chp. I, p. 1-18,
32. ROTH, M., and KAY, D. W. K. 1956. Affective disorders arising in the senium II. Physical disability as an aetiological factor. *J. Ment. Sci.*, 102:141-150.
33. ROTHSCHILD, D. 1956. Senile psychoses and psychoses with cerebral arteriosclerosis. In: Kaplan, O. J. (Ed.) *Mental Disorders in Later Life*. Stanford: Stanford University Press. Chp. XI, p. 289.
34. SIMON, A., and MALAMUD, N. 1965. Comparison of clinical and neuropathological findings in geriatric mental illness. *Psychiatric Disorders in the Aged*. p. 322. Symposium World Psychiatric Association. Manchester: Geigy (U.K.) Ltd.
35. STENSTEDT, A. 1959. Involutional melancholia: an aetiological, clinical and social study of endogenous depression in later life with special reference to genetic factors. *Acta Psychiat. Scand.* 34, Supplement 127.
36. TOMLINSON, B. E., BLESSED, G., and ROTH, M. 1968. Observations on the brains of non-demented old people. *J. Neurol. Sci.*, 7:331-56.
37. W.H.O. 1972. Psychogeriatrics. Report of a W.H.O. Scientific Group. *Wld. Hlth. Org. Techn. Rep. Ser.* 1972, No 507.

8

A CONTRIBUTION TO NOSOLOGY
FROM THE U.S.S.R.

Professor E. Ya. Sternberg

Institute of Psychiatry, Academy of Medical Sciences,
Moscow, U.S.S.R.

INTRODUCTION

The increasing practical and theoretical problems of gerontological psychiatry have stimulated interest among many Soviet psychiatrists. A number of research studies have been carried out in this special field against a background of a worldwide increase of aged mental patients. The many studies undertaken in different countries make it clear that this increase depends mainly upon the fact that the whole population lives longer, and not on a rise in the prevalence rate of mental disorders. An analysis of mental patients on the register of psychiatric dispensaries in Moscow has shown, for instance, that the percentage of registered patients in the age group of 60 and older approximately corresponds to the percentage of the same age groups in the whole population.

The aging process should also have influenced the increase of disorders directly related to senility, i.e. the increase of mental disorders due to organic brain lesions, and the psychoses of old age. An additional factor is that the changes in the organization of mental health services make it possible for a greater number of patients with an onset of illness in adolescence and middle age to live up to senescence. Consequently, the research problems facing psychiatry of old age are concerned not only with the traditional studies of mental disorders whose pathology is linked with old age, but also with the study of an increasing number of patients who become ill at an earlier age and live up to old age; these disorders may show diverse forms in the different age periods.

The main trend in the research studies of gerontological psychiatry, and in general psychiatry, in the U.S.S.R. is clinico-biological. The purpose of such clinical studies in this field consists in attempting to define, by clinical analysis of the psychopathology, the expression, the development, and the outcome of mental disorders of old age. Furthermore, by analyzing the constitution and the genetic background of the patients, as well as their physical, psychological and social conditions, an attempt is made to create a clinical and nosological classification of mental disorders of old age. This could serve as a basis for eventual biological studies of pathogenesis, as well as for the organization of more effective therapeutic and prophylactic services.

The fulfillment of the above research in gerontological psychiatry has all the necessary organization. The leading research institutes of the country have special geriatric departments and groups conducting such studies in accordance with a unified plan. Some of the professional departments of psychiatry in medical schools have concentrated on the studies of gerontopsychiatric problems. In recent years gerontopsychiatric research has extended to out-patient groups of aged mental patients on the register of psychiatric dispensaries. Such overall epidemiological studies of mental patients over 60 years of age are conducted at present in our Institute by M. G. Shchirina.

The contemporary state of the study of mental disorders of old age is unsatisfactory in many ways. There are significant discrepancies in concepts related to all the nosological groupings of disorders in old age. Up till now many problems of classification of organic dementia of old age, particularly those relating to the limits of mental disorders brought about by cerebrovascular diseases, are disputable.

Again, for decades and up to the present, such problems as the nosological independence, the nature and limits of the "functional" aging (involutional) psychoses have not been solved. Indefinite too are the approaches to the possibility of a late manifestation of endogenous psychoses, i.e. the possible relation of endogenous psychoses to such conditions as late affective, delusional and hallucinatory-delusional psychoses. The literature existing in this field indicates that the difficulties arising in relation to the diagnosis and classification of these forms are often related to the different evaluation of those factors which color the specific psychic disorders of old age. Many authors, especially of the German school in the first decades of this century, assessed the psychopathological features of late psychoses as proof of their special nosological nature. However, subsequent studies gave more weight to the general aging factors which naturally influence the clinical picture of any mental disorder at this age period.

The Soviet studies on this central question of a nosological identification of psychoses in senescence are by their methodological trend related to studies concerned with the general pathology and general psychopathology expressed in mental disturbances in old age.

Some Soviet psychiatrists (S. G. Zhislin (17), E. Ya Sternberg (11, 13), etc.) have attempted to compare those conditions which are different causally, but are similar in symptomatology, as they appear in the so-called involutional period or senescence. They also tried to define the general features of the psychopathological structure of different syndromes, i.e. those features which are due to the influence of the "age factor." This general "age factor" was studied as it occurred in different syndromes in old age.

The present report deals mainly with the clinical studies of the psychoses of old age, endogenous psychoses (which may occur in younger age groups also) and involutional psychoses (that are said to occur in the aged only), and organic brain processes leading to dementia. A discussion concerning the complicated problems of "borderline" conditions, i.e. neurotic, psychopathic and psychosomatic disorders of old age, would require a special study and would go beyond the purpose of this presentation.

ENDOGENOUS PSYCHOSES

The Aging Factor and Depression

The psychopathological structure of depressive syndromes seen in different periods of old age were carefully studied. It was established that such traits of depressions as mild anxiety in the depressive mood, a relatively mild expression of motor retardation, the existence of internal anxiety, agitation, fears or anxious verbigeration and prevalence of depressive ideas of reference and diffuse paranoid ideas, ideas of self-accusation and guilt, or a tendency to anxious-hypochondriacal fears, etc. not only are found in "involutional" melancholia, but may be seen in different disorders, occurring in the involutional period. In depressive states of senescence, also relatively irrespective of the cause of the disease, there are other features characterizing the structure of the depressive syndrome: different degrees of apathy, resignation, dissatisfaction, irritability, moroseness, grumbling, a feeling of undeserved mortification, etc.

Depressions of senescence are not usually accompanied by a depressive self-evaluation or a depressive reconsideration of the past. In the opinion of the patients the present situation is reflected not as a deserved punishment, but rather as an undeserved misfortune, as an unhappy contrast with the past. In a gloomy-pessimistic perception of the present (especially of one's health and financial state), the past appears in a positive light. As an individual becomes older, ideas of self-abasement, self-accusation and guilt become less frequent, whereas somatic complaints, hypochondriacal fears concerning health, and ideas of financial difficulties, impoverishment, professional and social incompetence become more apparent. There are grounds for assuming that these aging features are signs of a "shallowing" of depression. Depressions in the aged, more than in younger people, involve self-evaluation related to changes of mental activity, with an increased personality rigidity and a characteristic typical of old age—the "reassessment of values."

The Aging Factor and Delusional State

The factors depending on aging in delusional disorders, which to different degrees may be seen in different mental disturbances of old age, are related to the development of a predilective content. The crystallization of delusions in the young is preceded by changes in mental activity, which to different extents involve the personality, its self-consciousness, the feeling of the active "I," etc. The development of delusions in old age occurs as a rule on the backgrounds of certain characterological shifts: an increasing distrust and suspiciousness, a tendency to an illusional perception, of reference, etc.

Delusions are a rather frequent mental disorder of old age and are most usually expressed in delusions of interpretation, or, if the disease progresses, in confabulation. Both forms of delusions are related to "morbid types of mental activity" which, in 1912, were considered by Kraepelin (6) to be characteristic in disorders of the old which, to a lesser degree, are accompanied by "radical general mental changes." General features related to aging (irrespective of their nosology) are reflected in the content of delusions. The later the onset of the psychotic manifestations, the more shallow are the delusions. They become more concrete and petty, and lose their "large scale," mysteriousness and incomparability with realistic dangers. These "ordinary" and plausible delusions are as a rule directed towards concrete people in the surroundings of the patient. The frequent delusions of jealousy and detriment occurring in old age reflect, in a certain way, the ideas of preserving what has been achieved and acquired. Expansive forms of delusions, ideas of grandeur, over-estimation of one self are mainly concerned with the past are not directed towards the future. Thus, the aging modifications in the psychopathological structure of delusional syndromes are also in correlation with the achieved stage of the ontogenetic development of mental activity and with the soundness of the personality structure.

The Aging Factor and Hallucinatory States

It has been possible to demonstrate some psychopathological traits of hallucinatory disturbances characteristic of mental disorders of old age. Genuine hallucinations, and especially auditory hallucinosis, prevail over pseudo-hallucinations which are accompanied by a certain feeling of alienation of mental activity. In psychoses of old age the specific frequency of olfactory and tactile deception increases, pointing not only to a "peripheric localization," but also to the central significance for the self-evaluation of a patient.

The Aging Factor and Schizophrenia

A comparative study of the clinical expression of schizophrenia at different stages of development was undertaken during recent years in the Institute of Psychiatry of the Academy of Medical Sciences (8).

This study has shown that only in middle age are there the most typical psychopathological syndromes, the most characteristic signs of a defect (negative symptoms), and the most obvious diversity of development. It is possible that for this reason the clinical picture of psychosis of middle age becomes the basis of defining discrete forms of mental disorders. In relation to mental disturbances of middle age, it is permissible to speak of typical symptoms and syndromes of schizophrenia, of "symptoms of the first range," as outlined by K. Schneider (9), as signs of special diagnostic significance.

In schizophrenic psychoses of old age the range of expression of syndromes gradually narrows. Such conditions as florid hebephrenic and catatonic states, oneiroid changes of consciousness, and polymorphic terminal states are practically never encountered.

The schizophrenic symptomatology of old age is characterized by the psychopathologic features described above, together with "small-scale" paranoid conditions: the "age content" already described, auditory hallucinosis, hallucinatory and confabulatory delusional (paraphrenic) syndromes, etc. The "negative" schizophrenic symptomatology may lose its typical middle-age character. For instance, schizophrenic personality disorders may be modified by nonspecific traits of accentuated aging and a mild organic decline of the personality. Such shifts have been seen in a relatively large number of clinical cases and are correlated with the age of the onset (R.A. Nadzharov, E.Ya, Sternberg, 7).

Such specific changes of the mental disorders are, in our opinion, the clinical expression of internal factors created by the influence of a complex of biological, psychological, and social processes typical for each age group ("the age factor"). That is why, on the one hand, we see certain differences in the symptomatology of the same disease being due to the age of onset, and, on the other hand, we see an element which is "typical" for each age group being seen in different disorders occurring in the same age periods. This may be an explanation for the "levelling" of nosological differences in old age which leads to obvious diagnostic and nosological difficulties.

CONCLUSIONS

The main conclusions which can be made from the above-mentioned phenomena are the following: 1) the existence of clinical and psychopathological features of all mental disorders of old age was to a great extent the same as for psychoses of middle age; this finding should naturally be taken into consideration in diagnostic work and in an attempt to create a classification of psychoses in the aged; 2) the findings also support that the expression of mental disorders in old age is determined not only by the nature of the disease, but also by changes in the mental activity related to biological aging.

Similar conclusions were reached by a comparative study of different mental disorders (mainly of endogenous psychoses) occurring at different age levels: in childhood, adolescence, middle age, and senescence. The purpose of such studies was to investigate the role of the age factor in determining the clinical picture at the different stages of development.

In discussing the significance of the "age factor" for the clinical manifestation of mental disorders it is necessary to stress the purely empirical and conventional sense in which it is being used here. Its direct biological determination is hardly possible at present; in clinical practice we speak conventionally of the "age factor" to indicate its role in the clinical picture, but in the pathogenetic sense significant groups of symptoms—biological, psychological and social—are involved in different morbid processes.

INVOLUTIONAL PSYCHOSES

The question of the pathogenetic significances of age factors and the basic involutive processes is central to the oldest and most disputed problem of gerontological psychiatry—the problem of the "independent" aging or involutional psychoses. The approach of clinicians to this group of mental disorders has undergone significant fluctuations with time. Although such diseases were widely diagnosed in the past, during the last decades there has been a distinct tendency to narrowing this concept. At the present time, German psychiatry on the whole does not acknowledge the existence of such disorders. Soviet and Anglo-American psychiatrists, though to different degrees, still diagnose such diseases. Our personal opinion based on studies undertaken in the past years may be summarized as follows.

Follow-up studies of involutional psychoses, and in particular of involutional melancholia (i.e. anxious-delusional depressions), have provided sufficient grounds for narrowing the meaning of those concepts. These studies demonstrated that diagnosis based only on the age of the onset and its apparently typical clinical picture requires significant reconsideration. It appears that the majority of the cases of depression with anxiety and agitation or anxiety and delusion manifesting in the involutional or even later age proceed periodically in the form of repeated attacks. The repeated attacks have a tendency to complicate the clinical picture with the appearance of indisputable signs of schizophrenia. Or, vice versa, there is a tendency towards a simplification of the attacks which eventually become depressive or acquire a circular character. The follow-up studies permit one to allocate a large number of such cases, which were primarily qualified as involutional melancholia, to episodic forms of schizophrenia or to a late manifestation of endogenous affective psychosis. Such conclusions are substantiated also by family studies. The genetical similarity of affective and affective-delusional psychoses of old age to endogenous diseases is indisputable at the present time.

However, a study of this group of psychoses does not allow us at the present time to allocate them wholly to the group of endogenous psychoses. There are rare clinical forms which at the present state of our knowledge should occupy a special place in the classification of mental disorders of old age where the causal relation to the process of age involution appears to be quite probable. At the moment we qualify such forms as "involutional melancholia." We allocate to these forms protracted depressions with anxiety and delusions developing over five to ten years and more, which have a tendency to a "rigidity" of symptomatology with an exclusive monotonous and stereotyped clinical picture. With time there is a very gradual regression of symptoms, as the disease develops into a terminal state of psychic weakness without, however, symptoms of crude dementia. The development and outcome of such cases of "rigid involutional melancholia" are confirmed by the anatomical findings. The morphological picture in these cases displays diffuse, but not sharply expressed, dystrophical brain changes. With Bumke (3), Weitbrecht (16) and others, we presume that these forms occupy a transitional place between endogenous and organic processes.

ORGANIC STATES

In order to outline the future trends in research, we thought it expedient to discuss briefly the classification of those forms of disorders the nature of which is still unclear. The essence of many protracted delusional and hallucinatory delusional psychoses which develop in individuals with cerebral vascular disorders has not been studied in depth.

An unconditional allocation of these forms to the group of vascular psychoses proper presents certain difficulties, not only because of an absence of a distinct parallelism between the vascular process and the development of mental disorders, but also because frequently the clinical picture is similar to that seen in endogenous psychoses (the so-called endoform psychoses of Alsen and Ekman (1)). A family study of patients with such endoform psychoses (as well as of their premorbid traits) displayed with convincing proof the important role of genetical and constitutional factors in the development of such disorders. These studies demonstrated a hereditary loading with endogenous psychoses and the existence of clear-cut personality anomalies in the premorbid history of such patients.

On the other hand, the vascular process, although developing as a rule with an expressed arterial hypertension, is characterized by a relatively weak progress. In many cases, the differential diagnosis of these forms from late endogenous psychoses is difficult. It may be stressed that the symptomatology of these organic psychoses, unlike that of endogenous psychoses, displays a certain incompleteness, partiality and "simplicity." As rule there is no tendency to a complication of the clinical picture, as often happens in endogenous psychoses, but the clinical picture remains at a certain level, for instance that of verbal hallucinosis. More frequently there are exogenous episodes with changed consciousness. Characteristic of these forms is a late development of dementia with a simultaneous regress of psychotic symptomatology. The clinical picture of dementia is frequently accompanied by vascular and senile traits. The nosological nature of these forms is as yet unclear. Quite possibly this is a combined group, where along with those provoked by vascular lesions there are special varieties of constitutionally conditioned organic (vascular) psychoses.

Similar nosographic questions arise in relation to the "senile" (affective, delusional, hallucinatory-delusional) psychoses which sometimes proceed during many years with psychic disturbances resembling those in endogenous psychoses. However, the psychotic symtomatology of these conditions gradually decreases and is replaced by a global dementia of slow progress, similar, although not identical, to senile dementia. Such "senile psychoses" were described by psychiatrists of the past century, but were eliminated from the classification in 1912 by Spielmeyer (10). Even then the principal question was how to divide the different groups or "families" of mental disorders. These boundaries served as the basis for the classification of K. Schneider (9), well-known in contemporary German psychiatry. He clearly divides the group of endogenous disorders from the "somatically conditioned" psychoses. Studies of a certain group of psychoses in atrophical and vascular processes of old age have shown that in the elderly these boundaries become less rigid and distinct, as a result of which, according to Jacob (5), different intermediate "endogenous-organic" forms occur. These forms call for a very thorough and detailed study in future investigations.

The special character of the nosological problem in gerontopsychiatry and the necessity for a special approach to the elimination from the classification of clinico-nosological entities in old age follow not only from a presumed intermediate nature of these psychoses, but also from a special concern with the problem of boundaries between mental diseases and non-morbid changes of mental activity.

It is evident that there is a similarity between the main morphological signs of a physiological age involution of the brain and pathological atrophical processes, and there is also a similarity between the decline of mental activity occurring in the process of normal aging and the initial stages of dementia. Similarly, changes of the human personality also occur in old age, as well as "senile psychopathization" in the initial period of the dementing processes. In both cases, there is a quantitative difference in thinking processes only up to a certain time, but it is difficult to distinguish clearly between "health" and "disease," i.e. between normal decline due to aging and pathological changes occurring in the aged. Personality changes accompanying the process of physiological aging and personality shifts in the initial stage of organic brain disorders of the elderly display similar paths of development. As a rule, after the initial stage of a sharpening of the previous character traits (in atrophical process, the sharpening of character traits acquires a grotesque form), there is a gradual levelling of personality features, an erasing of individual characteristics.

The famous Soviet pathologist I.V. Davidovskiy, in his monograph "Gerontology," (4) discussed in detail the question of conditions intermediate between disease and health in old age. I.V. Davidovskiy posed a very important concept for gerontological psychiatry, the concept of "ailments" of the elderly, of conditions morbid by nature which, however, are completely determined by the biological processes of aging and which are conditioned by the "very essence of senescence," but without which "senescence does not actually exist." I.V. Davidovskiy differentiates from these "natural" morbid conditions certain nosological forms, "diseases of the aged" proper. Clinical studies point to the possibility that such serious states as a mild organic decline of mental activity (called mild dementia by Anglo-American authors), as well as some forms of non-psychotic depressions and delusional disorders in the aged, could receive a more adequate interpretation under this theory. A detailed study of such specific changes of mental disorders seen in the elderly is also an essential issue for future gerontopsychiatric investigations.

CONCLUSIONS

The issues that have been discussed here may lead to a solution of the old disputed question of the nosological nature of psychoses in old age. It has become evident that the allocation of psychoses of old age to endogenous psychoses cannot be based only on the dissimilarity to the clinical picture of disturbances seen in middle age. Neither can a definition of special, nosologically independent psychoses at any age be based only on the clinico-psychopathological specificity of the clinical picture because it may be caused by the non-specific influence of the "age factor," and not by the causal nature of the disorder.

Another conclusion is that the solution of nosographical problems of gerontological psychiatry depends first of all upon clinical studies at a high methodological level. These studies should focus on the "psychiatry of development" and take into consideration the development and outcome of disorders, with maximum use of anamnestic and follow-up studies and a deeper analysis of the psychopathological structure of different syndromes. Of special importance appears to be the constitutional and genetic background of patients suffering from late psychoses; their special study acquires great significance for the understanding of their essence.

On the basis of the concepts outlined, it should be stressed that mental disorders of old age do not arise from psychological processes of aging. The phenomena of psychic aging distinguished by psychologists is, in our opinion, determined by the processes of biological involution and reflects the same changes in the internal factors of the organism and brain activity which condition similar phenomena in the aging properties of psychopathological disorders. These two levels may coexist but are genetically unrelated. Often and without sufficient methological inquiry, pathogenetic significance in its narrow sense is being allocated to different psychological, social, situational, etc. factors, which are common in old age (for instance, isolation, loss of a spouse, retirement, loss of social status, etc.). To a certain extent, epidemiological studies correct this impression. They have shown, for instance, that aged patients registered in psychoneurological dispensaries do not differ significantly in marital and social status from individuals of the same age group in the population.

The classification of mental disorders of old age has been repeatedly discussed in Soviet psychiatry (2, 15). A detailed classificational schema, submitted to the WHO Seminar in 1968 (Moscow), was specially related to the diagnosis and classification of disorders of old age. Without going into the details of this classification, which was published by the WHO, it would perhaps be expedient to stress some of the principal issues of systematization in gerontopsychiatry which were reflected in it.

At the present stage of our knowledge, the classification of mental disorders of old age is impossible on the basis of one criterion only (clinical, aetiological, anatomical, or other). Any systematization has inevitably an eclectic and pragmatic character, i.e. along with aetiologically or anatomically distinct forms, they also include such criteria which are determined only by clinical and psychopathological signs, or where the elimination of disease remains either transient or presumed.

Taking into consideration the increasing number of patients whose disorder has had an onset in youth and who live till senescence, as well an increase of the life-span, and increasing late manifestations or exacerbations of mental disorders, we divided the disorders into two large groups:

1) a group of disorders occurring primarily or only in old age, i.e. pathogenetically related to involutive (aging) processes;

2) a group of disorders which can be encountered not only involution and senescense, but also in earlier age periods, in endogenous psychoses.

The systematization of the latter group is, of course, less difficult, inasmuch as it coincides with the general classification of mental disorders. However, because of the changes in the age structure of the population, this group includes also some insufficiently studied forms which are of great interest to psychiatry in general and to gerontopsychiatry in particular. Such states as late depression, late forms of epilepsy, special forms of neurotic and psychopathic conditions, oligophrenia in old age, symptomatic and somatogenic psychoses in old age, mental disorders in brain tumors, etc. can be included in this group. This division of mental disorders encountered exclusively in old age can be accepted only with some reservations. *Firstly*, even in those forms of diseases which are mainly exclusive to old age, a direct and distinct pathogenetic connection between the aging pathological process and mental dysfunction may be seen only in crude organic, destructive brain lesions, and mainly in atrophical processes. In the psychotic forms of aging diseases the determination of such pathogenetic connection is being made only on the grounds of purely clinical correlations. *Secondly*, serious difficulties are met in an attempt to distinguish the causal role of aging from the influence of old age on late manifestations of such disorders as schizophrenia or cyclothymia, which may have an onset at any age. Future studies may solve the question of whether there is a genuine pathogenetic significance in the first group, while age has only a provocative or pathoplastic significance in the second.

REFERENCES

1. ALSEN, V., and ECKMANN, F. 1961. Depressive Bilder in der zweiten Lebenshälfte. *Arch. Psychiat. Nervenkrankh.*, 201:483.
2. AVERBUCH, Y. S. 1969. *Rasstrojstva psychitscheskoy dejatelnosti ve posdnem wosraste.* Leningrad: Medizina.
3. BUMKE, O. 1948. *Lehrbuch der Geistenskrankheiten.* 7. Aufl. München: J. F. Bergmann.
4. DAVIDOWSKI, I. W. 1966. *Gerontologia.* Moscow: Medizina.
5. JACOB, H. 1960. Differentialdiagnose perniciöser Involutionspsychosen, präseniler Psychosen und Psychosen bei Involutionspellagra. *Arch. Psychiat. Nervenkrankh.*, 201:17.
6. KRAEPELIN, E. 1912. Über paranoide Erkrankungen. *Ztschr. ges. Neurol. Psychiat.*, II:617.
7. NADZHAROW, R. A., and STERNBERG, E. Ya. 1970. Die Bedeutung der Berücksichtigung des Altersfaktors für die psychopathologische, klinische und nosologische Forschung in der Psychiatri. *Schweiz, Arch. Neurol. Psychiat.*, 106:1-159.

8. NADZHAROW, R. A., STERNBERG, E. YA., and VRONO, M. S. 1969. Nekotorije woprossi psychiatritscheskoj nozologii ve wostrastnom aspekte. In: *Materiali V. sjesda nevropat.i psychiat.*, v.2, 321, Moscow.

9. SCHNEIDER, K. 1971. *Klinische Psychopathologie.* 9.Aufl. Stuttgart: G. Thieme.

10. SPIELMEYER, W. 1912. Die Psychosen des Rückbildungs und Greisenalters. In: *Aschaffenburgs Handb.d.Psychiat.*, Bd. 5, Leipzig-Wien.

11. STERNBERG, E. YA. 1968. Zur Frage der funktionellen Rückbildungspsychosen. *Wissensch.Z.d.Humboldt-Universität*, I, 325. Berlin.

12. STERNBERG, E. YA. 1970. K psychopathologii i psychologii posdnewo wosrasta. In: *Diagnostika i klassifiskazia psych. sabolewanii posdn-wosrasta. Leningrad*, 228.

13. STERNBERG, E. YA. 1972. Über psychotische ("funktionelle") Frühstadien seniler Geistesstörungen. *Psychiat. Neurol. Med. Psychol.*, 24:6-315.

14. STERNBERG, E. YA., and SHCHIRINA, M. G. 1969. Geriatric aspects of anxiety. *Brit. J. Psychiat.*, spec. public. No. 3, 102.

15. STERNBERG, E. YA., SHCHIRINA, M. G., and CHUMSKY, N. G. 1970. K woprossu o klassifikazii psychitscheskych sabolewanii posdnewo wosrasta. In: *Diagnostika i klassifikazia psych. sabolew. posdn. worasta*, Leningrad, 192.

16. WEITBRECHT, H. J. 1963. *Psychiatrie im Grundriss.* Berlin-Göttingen-Heidelberg: Springer-Verl.

17. ZHISLIN, S. G. 1965. *Ostcherki klinitschekoj psychiatrii.* Moscow: Medizina.

9

NEUROSES AND CHARACTER DISORDERS

David Blau, M.D.

Assistant Clinical Professor of Psychiatry
Harvard Medical School, Cambridge, Mass.

and

Martin A. Berezin, M.D.

Associate Clinical Professor of Psychiatry
Harvard Medical School, Cambridge, Mass.

INTRODUCTION

During the past thirty years the emotionally ill aged have been receiving a greater amount of attention than ever before (36, 37, 40). The psychiatric literature has multiplied greatly and reflects the interests and priorities of mental health workers. Mental health workers are not without their own biases and prejudices. Frequently their values and attitudes mirror those of society at large, and are not the product of objectivity or scientific detachment. Many stereotypes and myths have been put into scientific language which tends to give them greater credence and to inhibit the further investigation and understanding of the emotional problems of older people.

Myths of the older person developing increasing rigidity and inflexibility are often accepted without question and used to rationalize the approach of therapeutic nihilism. The indiscriminate application of diag-

nostic labels based on the assumption of underlying organic brain pathology also tends to promote pessimism and to discourage psychotherapy as
a form of appropriate treatment. Assumptions that the aged as a group
withdraw silently and without pain, into the enveloping blackness of
senescence and death are not unusual, and lead to the feeling that either
nothing needs to be done since the aged do not suffer, or that nothing
can be done for the relief of emotional illness in the aged since they are
beyond help.

It is our purpose to describe a sample of non-psychotic older persons
who have appeared for help over the years and to examine some of the
myths and stereotypes about the aged in the light of our experiences.
These patients were all treated with psychotherapy and were mainly outpatients who were ambulatory and living in their own homes. They were
60 years of age and older and may have had mild amounts of organic
impairment, but were generally in good physical health.

Diagnostically, our patients were either suffering from symptom or character neuroses. By neuroses we refer to those disorders resulting from impaired effectiveness in functioning which are the result of unconscious
intrapsychic conflicts and the attempts to resolve those conflicts which may
lead to symptom formation or to an alteration in the entire personality.
These disorders involve the return of infantile repressed wishes and the
mobilization of defenses which fail to maintain the repression, resulting
in a return of the repressed.

In some cases the patients had suffered from lifelong emotional problems, while others had led satisfactory and gratifying lives until certain
changes occurred in their later years to impair their ability to cope with
everyday problems. The changes we refer to included physical alterations,
object loss, and various narcissistic injuries and mortifications associated
with aging, which produced added stress and resulted in a neurotic dis-
equilibrium.

In our experience, many of these older patients were treatable by analyt-
ically oriented psychotherapy, but they were often neglected and ignored.
A great deal of needless suffering and unhappiness results from the failure
to attend to the needs of the non-psychotic older person. Much more
interest and concern has been demonstrated for the institutionalized
aged than for the ambulatory neurotic older person. The institutionalized
group has received the major share of society's concern and contains many
severely disturbed individuals with considerable amount of organic impairment (10), but does not necessarily reflect the usual or typical problems of older people in the community. Only about five percent of the

population over age 65 are in institutions, and yet the major focus of mental health workers has been on this group. By contrast, the majority of psychiatrists who work with younger people are concerned with the non-psychotic and non-institutionalized group of patients. Clearly, the tendency to focus almost exclusively on the more disturbed older patients is not just a matter of mental health priorities but seems to represent a "blind spot" which extends throughout society and is reflected in the patients psychiatrists select for treatment.

The mental health clinics and the average private psychiatric practitioner see a very small number of older people (1). Generally, colleagues in private practice report that their older patients are frequently the parents of professionals in the mental health field who have been advised to seek treatment by their children. If financial considerations are a major influence, then we would expect to see older people at public mental health clinics, but this is not usually the case. Social agencies frequently do have a large elderly clientele, but often they consist of many severely disturbed individuals with multiple and chronic problems.

Are there great numbers of non-psychotic older people in the general population who are suffering and untreated? A survey by Busse (14) of a group of socially well-adjusted volunteers 60 years of age and older revealed that at least 25 percent suffered from neuroses and an additional 20 percent had a mixture of neurotic and psychotic difficulties. In this group of volunteers, there was evidence that many of them suffered from neuroses that presumably were unrecognized and untreated by their physicians.

Where careful investigations of the aged have been conducted, every variety of neuroses and behavioral disorder has been observed in the aged (16). Reports of various kinds of hysterics (3, 21), including those with primitive oral problems (11), narcissistic characters (48), conversion reactions (39, 45), sexual problems (6, 21), and even delinquency in the aged have all been described (47). Psychosomatic disorders are extremely common and frequently are associated with underlying depression (43). A large group of aged patients with multiple chronic physical complaints has been studied and an effective course of treatment suggested (32).

Where mental health workers have been interested in the problems of older people, a larger number of patients are evaluated and treated. For example, the Boston Society for Gerontologic Psychiatry has stimulated a greater interest in the emotional problems of older people in the psychiatric world. This organization is composed of workers from the fields of psychiatry, psychology, medicine, social work, and nursing. Through seminars and teaching programs a number of mental health workers have been alerted to the psychological problems of older people. Newspaper articles and television programs have acquainted the general public with the treatment potential of the older person. As a consequence of this kind of interest, many workers have become aware of the large numbers of individuals suffering from non-psychotic disorders and are more involved in their treatment. In private practice more people are being referred with relatively acute neurotic disorders. Experience with the treatment of such patients indicates that they respond as well as younger patients with comparable disorders.

STEREOTYPED ATTITUDES TOWARD THE AGED

The Stereotype of Rigidity

Although there have been scattered reports about the favorable results of treating old people with psychotherapy (3, 11, 16, 20, 21, 24, 27, 32, 35, 45, 48), there remains a core of resistance and pessimism which bears inspection. It would appear that the myths and social beliefs about the rigidity of older people have been so accepted, that experiences which are contrary to these beliefs are ignored or discounted as unusual situations which are the exceptions to the rule.

Freud (19), who was able to see through the surface to the inner depths of man, was pessimistic about the treatment of older people. He felt that when people became old they were no longer flexible and that a certain rigidity occurred which precluded their treatment. Although he was in his late forties at the time he wrote about his feelings, there was no evidence that he himself displayed this kind of rigidity. In fact, he continued to display an active curiosity and a capacity to rethink old problems and produce new insights all of his life. Freud, however, was correct that certain compulsive personalities frequently become more rigid and unyielding as they age, but the aged, as a group, do not necessarily show this characteristic (3).

The Stereotype of Homogeneity

One of the many temptations that the authors of this article and other writers are also confronted with is the issue of whether to generalize and to deal with the aged as though they are a homogeneous group faced with similar problems and all utilizing similar methods to deal with them.

Considering the group of people 60 years of age and older who seek psychiatric treatment will quickly demonstrate that they have a wide spectrum of problems that do not all appear to be closely related. A 65-year-old man with marital problems who is physically well and able to work is far different from an octogenarian in a nursing home who resents following a prescribed routine after a lifetime of independence and who has many physical infirmities. A woman in her mid-70s, who is distressed that she has recently lost her spouse but is alert and active, is very different from a woman in her 70s with mild memory changes who has become very depressed at the changes she perceives inside herself. While these individuals may have certain similarities, the differences between them are most striking and the temptation to generalize about the aged and their emotional problems must be handled with considerable caution.

The Stereotype of Untreatability

Why should professionals spend time with such a group of older people? Our own clinical experience, as well as the experience of others, confirms the treatability of many older people. Many older people are not rigid but, quite the contrary, have come to treatment after much soul-searching and are eager to show what they know of life and themselves, as well as to relieve their current distress.

Frequently they do not perceive of themselves as old, and they continue to seek the gratification of unfulfilled unconscious infantile and adult wishes. These old unconscious wishes and drives are frequently undiminished by time and still urgently require attention (2). Often they have made connections between current symptoms and past experiences, and have a capacity for flexibility and insight that is rare in younger people (34). Two examples will be given.

Case 1

In a second interview, a man of 75, who had considerable anxiety about his body and fears of dying of cancer, spoke of a mild conversion symptom he had recently developed. He then quickly connected it with his brother who had died years before and had displayed a similar disability as part of his terminal illness. He then said he felt it had to do with his feelings about losing his brother who had protected him most of his adult life. Even as a child he had prevented him from being assaulted by other children. This man was almost aware at this point that he currently felt vulnerable and needed a protector. Shortly after this he made arrangements to live with a young and protective relative and felt much less anxious and concerned about his body. He arrived at this solution, based on an understanding of his own needs, after a total of four interviews.

Case 2

A 65-year-old man with many somatic complaints commented in his second interview that he recently felt distressed, as though his stomach was very full and he was suffering from indigestion. When asked why he might have suddenly developed such a feeling, he recalled that he was annoyed with his wife for not having his entire meal ready at his usual supper hour. Instead, she gave him each part that was ready as she prepared it. He felt neglected and annoyed with her and realized that a few hours later he was suffering from stomach distress.

In the same interview he reported a sudden sensation that he was dying of heart trouble, which had occurred a few days after he experienced the initial gastrointestinal distress. He had become quite frightened at the sense of pressure in his chest and was seen by his physician who found no evidence of organic heart disease. The patient, in thinking over that evening, realized that he had been very annoyed that his wife had gone to bed early, and again when he felt neglected he developed somatic symptoms. As he made these connections between various upsetting events and his bodily sensations, he recalled that he had become dizzy and fainted once when he recently visited a racetrack. He then remarked that his former business partner was a man who gambled a great deal. As a result of losses, this man withdrew large sums of money from their business and eventually bankrupted the company. The patient said he was angry at his former partner and embarrassed that people might see him at the racetrack and think he, too, was a heavy gambler. He said, with a smile, "Perhaps I associated the gambling of my partner with my recent trip to the racetrack and felt very ashamed and that's why I felt faint."

This man was quite quickly able to make connections between past events and current difficulties, as well as to appreciate that current feelings of annoyance could produce a variety of distressing symptoms. He left this interview saying that he felt better and thanked the therapist for having spent so much time talking with him. He seemed genuinely pleased that he could make sense of the distressing feelings he was experiencing and was hopeful about the future. He remarked that his internist had felt he was too tense and advised him to relax, but never suggested that he see a psychiatrist. He did not say it, but was probably aware that his internist was pessimistic about treating someone his age with psychotherapy. His therapist knew that this internist usually would refer younger patients with similar problems for psychotherapy but did not consider it for older people.

The "Wastebasketing" Syndrome

Clinical experience in treating the aged shows this group to be as amenable to psychotherapy as any other age group with similar disorders. Despite the publication of many reports which indicate positive results, a persistent attitude of pessimism is almost universally held. The most common stereotype about the aged with emotional problems is that these problems are the result of aging and are biological in nature. A young person with feelings of depression is considered to be unhappy and is rarely told that it is related to organic processes or to his age. An older person with feelings of depression is frequently assumed to have senile or arteriosclerotic brain changes. People often assume that all emotional symptoms are part of the aging process and are inevitable. While many symptoms are related to the processes of aging, they are not necessarily inevitable, progressive, or irreversible. Recent memory defects, for example, may be associated with emotional difficulty and are reversible with treatment. Depressed patients sometimes show these defects, which disappear when the depression is lifted.

Rationalizations for the Pessimistic Attitude Concerning the Aged

Why does this pessimism regarding the aged persist in the face of experience to the contrary? Unconscious determinants play a major role in shaping the attitude of society toward the aged (9). The residual ambivalence of younger people for their parents often is given full and direct expression when parents are old and less powerful. Challenging and critical comments are frequently made by adult children in very similar fashion to the way adolescents sometimes deal with their parents. At times children are as controlling and disapproving of their parents as they felt was the case when they were growing up. Often the roles are reversed and the opportunity arises to act out old grievances with little fear of retaliation. At times it appears that society as a whole has joined together to express this ambivalence.

In a recent discussion (9) of laws concerning the obligation to financially support aged persons, it was pointed out that most laws were written in very vague fashion and reflected the ambivalence of society about providing an adequate and comfortable life for older people. This vagueness could be traced back historically four centuries and was not the result of recent changes in family ties, but seemed to reflect a much longer trend in human development.

When we examine the substandard housing and inadequate pensions meted out to the elderly, we must consider the possibility that the young are "acting out" their childhood feelings of deprivation and frustration on their aged parents. However, further elaboration of this issue is not germane to our major topic.

The Myth of Family Rejection

Although society may ignore and reject older people and devalue the aged in general, it is not uncommon for aged people to feel that devoted relatives may be ignoring them or are disinterested. This is especially true of the depressed aged who suffer from inner feelings of impoverishment and neglect. Often sociological studies of the aged imply that a modern cultural pattern, in which children do not assume filial duties, is responsible for the large amount of illness and institutionalization of the aged. This view is not necessarily borne out by investigation (10) and stems, in part, from the desire to attribute the problems to reasons beyond the scope of the individual and to reinforce the view that emotional illness does not exist in the aged. Families, in these instances, are used as sociological "scapegoats." This is not to say that cases of neglect and poor relationships do not exist. Frequently the reasons are not so difficult to understand and do not necessarily involve sociological issues, but rather the personalities of the individuals involved and their lifelong patterns of interaction. A clinical example of the myth of family rejection follows.

Case 3

A widowed woman of 78 frequently berated her children for not visiting her and loudly complained that they were ungrateful. The neighbors were sympathetic and concerned and, at times, contacted the children. They were surprised to learn that there were occasional visits and frequent telephone calls, as well as some financial support given to this woman by her relatives. The children explained that their mother had always been a difficult woman who often initiated arguments over very minor issues and generally seemed to be uncomfortable with them and distrustful.

In the ensuing years the neighbors have discovered that this woman tended to be rather seclusive and frequently refused to answer her door when they visited. They have also learned that she has been involved in several law suits in recent years for the kind of minimal inconveniences that are generally accepted as part of the vicissitudes and frustrations of everyday life. Gradually the neighbors have noticed that this woman is never pleased or satisfied with their efforts to assist her. Some of her neighbors are themselves elderly people, and it has been revealing to hear them initially accept the prevailing view of filial neglect, and then to hear them observe that they would hate to be the children of this woman who is so difficult and suspicious.

Obviously, long standing problems can be easily mistaken for recent disturbances or be considered the result of environmental influences if the myths and stereotypes concerning the aged are accepted without question.

Other Attitudes

Other factors also contribute to the pessimism about the aging person. We are aware of the premium placed on youthfulness and the importance of physical attractiveness. Psychiatric residents are usually much more interested in treating good looking young people with whom they can identify. Aged persons, on the other hand, are often viewed as suffering from a condition to be avoided, as though they had a contagious disease. The term 'gerontophobia' has been coined by Bunzel (12) to describe the common fear of contact and dealing with aging persons. Thompson (44) expresses these feelings quite graphically:

> Also, there are special countertransference problems when we work with old people. If it is frightening during one's own analysis to consider the loss of bodily integrity, or the vulnerability of dependency, or anger at parents, it appears to be doubly or trebly difficult to deal with such feelings when they are aroused during the treatment of a woman past 70 (p.65).

Many younger people fear that they may be depleted by contact with the aged, whom they see as consuming and devouring and offering little in return. Stories and legends about old men being restored by attractive young women unconsciously suggest that the younger person in the relationship does the giving and the older person does all the taking. Here we can see the operation of the younger person's infantile attitude of greed and devouring being projected onto the aged.

For physicians, in particular, the desire to cure and restore patients to full health is severely challenged by older patients with various chronic infirmities. Such patients will destroy feelings of omnipotence and produce narcissistic injury in physicians who feel that they must restore all their patients to health. Often the aged person has more modest goals than the physician who cares for him.

Still other reasons for pessimism may be advanced. An attitude of pessimism implies that nothing further can be done and that everything else that is attempted will fail. Such an attitude precludes further efforts as unnecessary and creates the illusion that nothing more is required. Many of the myths and stereotypes concerning the aged are actually adaptive for society as a whole. They imply that, rather than waste efforts in unrewarding ways, one should turn to more fruitful areas. In this way guilt is assuaged and painful work is avoided. Man often uses myths and stereotypes (9) to avoid unpleasant tasks requiring emotional investment and falls back on fantasies which avoid facing the obvious human suffering which can so casually be written off as senility and attributed to changes occurring at the highly impersonal cellular level.

The relatives of aged persons often do not seek assistance for an emotionally distressed older person. Although it may be argued that this occurs because relatives are not professionally trained to recognize symptoms, this does not account for the fact that the relatives of a disturbed person are among the last to recognize that assistance is required. Emotional factors frequently play an important role in the failure to appreciate the illness. For example, an aged spouse might be attached to the disturbed patient in an intense symbiotic relationship and require the emotional support and presence of the patient for his own security.

Children, too, may fear recognizing the illness and the possibility of assuming emotional responsibility for an aged parent. In spite of the ambivalence that many children feel for their parents, and despite pre-oedipal and oedipal wishes to replace parents, many children are very unhappy about assuming the role of parents themselves and caring for their aged relatives. It is not uncommon to see the burden shifted from one child to another because each one fears the wish of unconsciously displacing the parent, and prefers to remain a child. Under these circumstances, it is not surprising to find that family members in frequent contact with emotionally upset older people are often the last ones to consciously notice such distress.

SYMPTOMATOLOGY

How are the emotional problems of the non-psychotic aged manifest? What kind of treatment and goals can be established? Are there specific disorders which are particularly connected with aging?

There seems to be some evidence that most people who are aged 60 and older suffer from non-disabling periodic feelings of depression. Busse (13), who studied a large group living in the community, concluded that recurrent periods of depression were very common and occurred in individuals who had not experienced depression in their younger days. He felt that these depressions were due to loss of self-esteem and feelings of weakness and inability to obtain narcissistic supplies. He concluded that the aging process itself was responsible for these affective states, and he pointed out that guilt and other manifestations of neurotic and psychotic depressions were not present in these people. He felt that these patients differed from those usually encountered in clinical practice. In this "normal" group with depression, moderate numbers had associated insomnia and constipation, symptoms which are so commonly found in depressed patients.

We do not know from Busse's studies whether these mild cyclical depressions are restricted to the aged, or whether they may be universal for all age groups from the time of puberty. Clinically we frequently observe such depressions in adolescence and consider them to be an important part of psychological development rather than a pathological entity (28). Further longitudinal studies of all adult age groups might supply the answer as to whether these mild, almost ubiquitous cyclical depressions are present only after the age of 60.

People do not usually seek psychiatric attention for these mild symptoms, perhaps because they are aware that mild states of depression are common and normal throughout life and must be endured and experienced. However, occasionally patients do present themselves to physicians and clinics with these mild depressions and are quite concerned about whether this is a premonitory sign that they will become severely disturbed. They may be reassured with the information that mild feelings of depression are ubiquitous for older people, and even for younger people, and are not necessarily of pathological significance. In a similar way, some adolescents are unaware that feelings of depression and minor mood alterations are a normal part of this developmental stage and will need some reassurance that these feelings are part of their growth.

More severe alterations in mood are very common and neurotic depressive reactions are a common psychological affliction of the aged, but the entire spectrum of neurotic illness can be seen. Confounding and complicating the problem of diagnosis is the frequent occurrence of mild confusion and recent memory alterations in those patients who are depressed. At times this "organic impairment," which was earlier referred to as pathognomonic for organic brain syndrome, seems to clear when the depression lifts. For others, signs of confusion, disorientation and memory loss remain after the depression lifts and suggest the depressive reaction may be produced by the patient's unconscious perception of these organic changes which have taken place. A trial of therapy and observation is recommended with these patients, since it is difficult to know what the main operant factors are in any given situation without careful investigation.

Authorities are divided about the determinants of neurotic reactions in the aged. Some emphasize specific factors, such as concern about death (42). Others stress the premorbid personality (3) and still others stress the importance of the loss of significant objects (31). Decreasing capacity to adapt, with increasing lack of flexibility of the ego, is also mentioned (20). Problems with feelings of helplessness and weakness are stressed by others (24). Diminished ability to make new object ties and replace old ones is also emphasized (31). Many talk about the effect on the aged person of narcissistic injuries, including changes in appearance, sexual ability and physical health (14). Others see the early relationships as crucial to the issue of being able to withstand and tolerate feelings of anxiety and depression (49, 50).

Psychiatrists have their own special areas of interest and emphasis regarding the aged. Some stress the ego and defense, others the instinctual drives and gratification, and others the superego and its rigidity. At times the adaptive functions of the ego have been emphasized as central to the understanding of mechanisms like denial, isolation, and regression (52). Still others focus on the ego ideal and the superego as crucial to the understanding of the aged (31). What seems especially notable is that all of these factors are relevant, and that in any given case they may all play significant roles to some degree. The importance of certain factors will be greater in some situations than others. In the very old and feeble the issue of helplessness and feelings of vulnerability will more likely be crucial. In some younger patients these same issues will also be important, but by and large these will be individuals who were concerned with helplessness and feelings of vulnerability prior to old age.

The danger in generalizing about the "core problems" of the aged and reducing them to issues like adaptation and survival is that this hardly does justice to the broad spectrum of patients in their sixties and seventies who are interested in instinctual gratification and can relate to objects, make contributions and, obviously, have the potential for more than survival. Many of these patients are grappling with desires and feelings exactly like those found in younger people (2).

At times the persistence of unconscious attitudes and fantasies from much earlier life is striking (3). It is not always easy to know what significance to attach to them (18). We do not know whether these attitudes carry the same value and meaning throughout life or represent the individual's characteristic style of reaction to all conflicts and vicissitudes. For example, a coquettish and flirtatious girl may be looking for an object for sexual gratification or to supply other needs. An elderly woman may behave in the same fashion in order to obtain sexual gratification, too, or to get a feeling of still being lovable, or to obtain basic oral supplies from men, or for protection against loneliness and death, or even for assistance with realistic needs, as well as to be able to show she still has control over her objects. The same style of behavior may have different purposes at different periods in life. The primary goal of the clinician is to assess the dynamic unconscious needs and conflicts of the individual which are concealed beneath the characteristic styles of coping between the intrapsychic and external world.

Clinical Illustrations of Psychodynamics

Some clinical illustrations follow, which provide an understanding of how a dynamic approach can be useful.

Case 4

A 62-year-old widowed female complained of feeling depressed for several months and was referred by her former employer, who felt that she had changed recently from a happy productive worker to a complaining, sad-looking woman who was unable to work. The patient complained to the psychiatrist of difficulty in sleeping; she felt sad and expressed concern that very few people were interested in her. She had divorced her husband years before and he was now dead. Her only son was killed in the Second World War. A niece, who was her only living relative, seemed mainly interested in borrowing money from her. The psychiatrist encouraged her to begin psychotherapy on a twice-weekly basis, and she agreed and began to relate her history chronologically.

She was the youngest of two girls. At an early age she developed heart trouble and for many years was not permitted to go to school with other children. She was often physically restricted and spent months at bed rest. Her mother warned her that she might die if she was too active. Despite these early physical and educational restrictions, she did very well in school when she could return. Over the opposition of her mother, she attended college and graduated with honors. For several years after graduation she taught school. In her mid-twenties she married and had a great deal of trouble with her husband who refused to work and often was physically abusive. One child resulted from this marriage.

After 23 years the patient finally divorced her husband. When her son was drafted into the military service, she went to work for a laboratory where she was recognized as a person gifted in administration and science. While holding this job, she was notified of the death of her son in combat. She later developed a very close relationship with the director, a prominent scientist, who was 18 years her junior, and they both fell in love. He asked her to marry him, although he was 37 and she was 55. When she refused, because of the difference in their ages, he became interested in a younger woman and subsequently married her.

The patient then left this position but kept in touch with this man and his wife. She accepted a job as the administrative director of a medical project where she became very much involved in her work. When she wanted to study a certain medical problem on her own, she requested a leave of absence to pursue this research. The director refused because he needed her assistance in his own work. The patient took this as a sign that he did not respect her ideas or really want her, and she felt crushed. On the other hand, he became quite concerned when he observed she was depressed and advised her to seek psychotherapy. Within a few weeks of beginning psychotherapy she became aware that she had again fallen in love with her employer. This time her employer was unaware of it and did not reciprocate these feelings, and she felt rejected. Shortly afterwards she wrote a letter of resignation and felt an upsurge of feelings of rejection from earlier experiences with her mother and husband.

Her mother emerged as a punitive woman concerned with sin and literally threatening her with hell. On occasion she was forced to leave the house, as a small child, and was told she would be placed in an orphan home, until she promised that she would be obedient in the future. In therapy she quickly developed a very positive, dependent attachment to the therapist and in a dream made clear references to wanting someone to help her put the pieces of her life together. In another dream she felt as though she was being pulled in at least four different directions and expressed surprise that a person of 62 could be in so much conflict.

She presented concerns on many levels. She felt unappreciated. She felt weak and spoke of wanting a male therapist who would be big and solid and could protect her. She also wanted psychological treatment in order to prevent future problems. Shortly after this she mentioned her fear of death, and especially the fear of a feeling of completely disappearing. She experienced a sense of pressure to publish her ideas and to write an autobiography so that she would not be forgotten. Her recitation of past events also served the purpose of leaving a part of herself with the therapist so she would not be forgotten. She associated to a poem about blue flowers and said she knew the therapist's name meant "blue" in German and it reminded her of forget-me-nots.

Repressed feelings and experiences began to emerge in connection with the wish to be remembered, and to be remembered as an admirable person. The other side of her that she regarded as less attractive also began to appear at this time with associated feelings of guilt.

Her past sins began to emerge. She had not been kind to her mother and had refused her financial support when she was old. She had murderous feelings toward her husband. She had some childhood sexual experiences and she envied her sister who was close to her father. Next came conscious erotic feelings which were transferred to the therapist and caused her embarrassment when she once asked for an "apartment" instead of an "appointment." This occurred as she was leaving treatment for a long trip and led to wishes for physical contact with both parents. She then realized that she had always been a very lonely person and that it was caused by having been so aloof.

She remained away for eight months but wrote occasionally and seemed to be feeling better, but asked to return and discuss some residual problems.

The residual problems took the form of feelings that the therapist was in love with her. She also had developed some fears of women pushing carriages. Her fears cleared rapidly and were replaced by sadness when the therapist pointed out she was talking about her dead husband and son. This led her to expose the fantasy which she had always held that her son was still alive and could be returned to her by the therapist. She became increasingly demanding of the therapist's time and attention and clearly expected him to be the all-giving, good, and powerful mother. He insisted that she needed a job and to make friends and pressed her to consider her realistic needs rather than rely on magical expectations. This led her to express much anger at inconsiderate and demanding doctors.

Again she returned to her erotic fantasies but appreciated that, although she had in fact had sexual opportunities, she had been celibate for 19 years. She then recalled a sexual experience at the age of seven with a little boy of six, and how her mother had discovered her and refused to allow her to visit him again and severely punished her. This led her to recall several other traumatic sexual incidents in latency. Prior to her experience at seven she had been very natural with boys and men; after this she was frightened of them. Over a period of several weeks she recalled how her mother had threatened to send her to an orphan asylum because of the incident with the little boy and had made her pack a bag to go. She felt that her mother never approved of her actions after this, and when she developed heart trouble at seven, after her sexual experience, she really believed she was being punished and would die.

When she had worked through these old fears, she became interested in obtaining work. She thought of taking care of small children and she obtained employment as a nurse for newborn babies and for small children whose parents were away. She connected her fears of death, which were lifelong, with violating her mother's injunctions about having sex, giving birth, and working hard. She tried to get the therapist to forbid her to work so much, just as her mother had forbade too much activity. She then worked for the next 15 months and was seen on a gradually decreasing basis.

During this time she was twice approached sexually by men, and on both occasions refused them with some feelings of anxiety. She appreciated that she would be too upset if she gave in to these men and had casual affairs. Instead, she led a busy life and had several close friendships and felt satisfied with her life.

When she was 65 years of age, she began to have increasing trouble with pulmonary infections and developed shortness of breath. An extensive medical workup revealed that she had a congenital cardiac defect which was the source of her illness as a child. The therapist visited her in the hospital on several occasions and talked with her about a very difficult choice she faced. She had been told that she could live a restricted life or could have surgery and possibly return to her previous level of activity. She weighed the choices and decided she would rather be dead than inactive. She was sent to a famous research center where she was again studied and warned that the risks were very great for someone her age and that surgery was inadvisable. She told them that she knew the risks but preferred to take the chance for a complete recovery. Surgery was performed and a septal defect was successfully repaired. However, she died of postoperative pulmonary complications.

A letter she wrote to the therapist eight days before her death revealed her feelings about herself and her treatment and showed her to be composed and thoughtful when confronted with the reality of death. It has been frequently observed (46) that people who are really dying face it with more composure than those around them.

Her letter reads:

Dear Dr. X:

The diagnostic tests were finished last Thursday and confirmed those made at the Y Hospital. Additional tests showed that my lung function is within normal limits. In spite of this they advised against an operation solely because of my age. When they learned that I was willing to take the additional risks they feel may be involved, they reconsidered and the operation is scheduled for Tuesday, September 20th.

I've been here two weeks tomorrow and the more I learn of their program and experience, their competent care and the understanding friendliness of all the personnel, from the porter who brought up my suitcase to Dr. A, chief surgeon, the more fortunate I feel to be here.

After the operation I shall be in an observation room for quite a number of days. It differs from the usual recovery room in that it is located in this corridor in familiar surroundings, and while there are no visiting hours, relatives or close friends may go in for brief periods when treatment allows. My friends, and I have more than I realized, are rallying around and I am sure of seeing some familiar faces.

I guess I truly was more afraid of not getting the operation than of getting it because now that it is assured I feel quite at peace. Of course I am afraid and will be glad when it is over, but deep within me I know that whatever the outcome, I am in the right place at the right time. That I have been able to achieve this feeling is the outcome of my work with you.

Discussion of Case 4

In this case the patient had to deal with bodily illness, the loss of familiar and sustaining objects, decreasing physical attractiveness, lifelong concerns about death and rejection, and a rigid and prohibiting conscience derived from a strict mother. She was forced to seek a new way to earn her living in her sixties and felt rejected by men and unloved by her mother. She yearned for warmth and affectionate contact and wanted to love and care for children again. Some of her concerns seemed to be reminiscent of involutional aged women some 10 to 15 years younger. She also had to deal with the problems of again becoming an invalid as she had been in childhood and with the likelihood that she might not recover this time. She struggled with the desire to be remembered and to leave her mark, and she succeeded in this by being described in this chapter.

She treated the therapist as though he were her potential lover, husband, son, father, and mother. She endowed him with magical powers, including being able to restore her dead son. In addition, she saw him as a real person with all the deficiencies people have, and she even forgave him for making two appointments with two patients for the same hour. On occasion, the transference almost became a psychotic one, but usually these distortions could be managed and quickly reversed.

Case 5

In contrast to the woman in Case 4, who was such a richly complex person, a 74-year-old woman was seen with signs of an agitated depression. She was restless and had difficulty with her appetite. She felt that something had happened to her memory and worried about it. She found herself forgetting where she put things in her own apartment and noticed one day, to her mortification, that she was not wearing a dress but was leaving in her slip. At times she would forget her purchases in a store or not take her change. Her husband, who was still working, found that he had to spend a great deal of time with her and was now cooking and cleaning the apartment because his wife could not take care of it.

The patient was happily married and had two successful children whom she loved and was proud of. She still was having satisfactory sexual experiences with her husband who was in his late seventies. She had several living siblings who often visited her and were quite attentive. Until about a year before, she was considered a very alert and bright person who had helped her husband in his business. She was considered to have a good sense of humor and had many friends. She had been active in social organizations most of her life.

Psychological testing indicated a moderate degree of organic impairment in a woman who had previously been of superior intelligence. Neurological studies indicated the presence of a diffuse organic process involving large areas of the cortex. A review of the situation indicated that she began experiencing feelings of depression about a year before, as she became aware of changes in her memory. As her trouble became progressively worse, she became more and more depressed about her intellectual deficit. She had always valued her ability to think and was particulary proud of being so bright. She spoke of the fact that nowadays she would have gone to college like her grandchildren, but in her younger days bright girls were not given this opportunity.

Discussion of Case 5

Dynamically, this woman was a compulsive character who thought everything over several times before making any decision and carefully weighed all of the possibilities. She was not inclined to be swayed by emotions but was always a logical and reasonable person who used her capacity to think for adaptive, defensive and narcissistic gratification. Consequently, she was quite distressed when she began to experience changes in cognitive functioning and her entire character structure seemed threatened.

Supportive therapy, medication, supervision and a recreational program helped this woman for over a year, but eventually she required complete custodial care as her organic impairment became even more severe.

The next case history demonstrates the restoration of a previously successful equilibrium as the goal of therapy.

Case 6

For other patients, a return to previously successful methods of coping with their lives can be achieved with the assistance of psychotherapy. A 61-year-old married businessman was referred by his son after he failed to respond to electroshock, psychiatric hospitalization, and medication. He looked quite depressed and said he had been unable to work for the past two months. In the past he enjoyed working and had been in business for himself for 34 years. He reported attacks of anxiety two or three times a day and felt as though he was going to die.

He described his wife as a woman who "wouldn't cooperate" and said she was grouchy and made him nervous. She had never wanted children, although they had six, and had generally refused to have sexual relations. Since her last pregnancy, fifteen years ago, she had completely refused sex and also would not attend social functions with her husband. The latter was a gregarious man who enjoyed attending dances and club meetings with his wife. On at least three occasions he left home in order to frighten her into submission, but he relented each time and returned.

He had been a part-time musician for many years and enjoyed playing until a fellow musician died about seven years before. Five or six years ago he began seeing the widow of a friend and commenced an affair with her. She went with him to dances and meetings and enjoyed sex. He thought if his wife died he could marry her, but his wife was in good health. About two years ago he terminated his love affair. At that time his married daughter was abandoned by her husband. He had been quite distressed about this and stopped seeing his girl friend then.

His recent feelings of depression seemed to follow the departure of his oldest son to Vietnam, where he was to remain for a year. He mentioned that he himself had a previous episode of depression many years before when he was rejected for military service on physical grounds, although he had not wanted to go. Since the patient denied all concern about his son's safety or any guilt about escaping the service himself, this area seemed fruitless to pursue. There were, however, two pleasures that he had enjoyed and abandoned—sex and music—and these areas were then the focus of attention. He mentioned that his older brother was a noted musician, and some of the competition between them came out to a mild degree. Turning to the issue of sexuality, he felt that he was wrong to be still interested in his girl friend and that he was too old. To his surprise the therapist told him that it seemed quite natural to him that he was still interested and, in view of his wife's problems, quite understandable. He then became worried that his children would find out about his girl friend if he resumed the affair.

Fortunately, he often came to the office with his second son, who once asked to talk with the therapist and said that his mother was a cold woman who was only interested in keeping the house clean and in cooking. The son knew of his father's girl friend and approved, although he wondered why his father stayed with his mother. He spoke warmly and sympathetically of his father. Later, the therapist told the patient that his son knew all about the situation and was not critical.

The patient was pleased and indicated he would resume seeing his girl friend who also enjoyed music and shared many interests with him.

Discussion of Case 6

This man was a guilty, obsessional character who many times had to atone for his sins. He felt guilty that he had escaped the draft and feared something might happen to his son in the service, so he made his own sacrifice, giving up the pleasure of work and social activity. Guilt over his own sexual interests made him give that up when his daughter's husband left her. Guilt over the death of a fellow musician caused him to give up playing. Encouraging him to permit himself more pleasure was quite effective, coupled with the discovery that others did not have the cruel and judgmental superego that he did, helped him to be more charitable about himself.

After two months of weekly psychotherapy he returned to work and resumed his social life. In the past year he has not suffered any serious difficulties, and has had no further contact with the therapist. He did call once to say that he was fine and was pleased with the way things had turned out. In this case the therapist felt that this man had led a fairly successful and satisfactory life until recent years and helped to support and encourage the reestablishment of those defenses and gratifications which had been of help in the past.

It must be emphasized that at times there is no way to restore previously successful defenses and gratifications, so that a new style of adjustment must be attempted, or the patient must accept certain limitations in coping with the aging process. These new adaptations may appear regressive and cause much concern to the outsider, but often they are adaptive and useful to the patient (52).

Case 7

A 74-year-old widow complained of feelings of depression; she felt like crying. She had thoughts about death and was afraid to be alone in her own home. She would then call her children and complain that she felt fearful and blue. Further investigation revealed that she had been well until a few months before, when she took her usual summer vacation and learned of the death, by suicide, of a young girl who lived in the area. She became anxious and sad and was frightened to be alone after that.

Psychotherapy was begun on a once-a-week basis, and shortly afterwards, associating to the girl's death on vacation, she recalled, with some sadness, the unexpected death of her older sister many years before. She spoke of how unprepared she was for this loss and how she had been so close to her sister. She also spoke of her older daughter who had lived with the patient until she recently married. She missed her and found it particularly difficult since she was now living in another country and could not visit very often. At the same time, a previously devoted son who lived near the patient was very involved in the establishment of a new business. The patient understood that he could not visit as often as he had before, but she still missed his attention. A second daughter currently had a full-time job and her visits to her mother had decreased because of her schedule.

A review of the patient's relationship with her husband, who had died almost 10 years before, revealed that she had usually been in the store with him and helped manage the business. After her husband's death, she helped her son. When he sold the family business a few years before, she felt there was very little left for her to do. She had prided herself on being an astute and capable businesswoman and now had lost this source of pleasure as well as losing the previously close relationship with her children.

Interestingly enough, there was evidence that this woman had always avoided being alone and that she worked in her husband's business as much for his companionship as anything else. When her last child left home and she was alone, she found a boarder to live with her. This arrangement worked well until the boarder went away for a long summer vacation. Thus, after hearing about a depressed girl who killed herself, she returned to her own empty home and became depressed and anxious.

In reviewing the situation, it did not appear feasible to change this woman's attitude. She had avoided being alone all of her life, and in spite of protests that she did not want to interfere in her children's lives, she was very pleased when the therapist spoke to them about her need for companionship. At first a woman was found to live with the patient, but she correctly noted that her companion was a disturbed person herself who needed care and fired her. Instead, her children and grandchildren took turns remaining with her, particularly at night when she was most fearful. Following the return of her boarder and tangible signs from her family of their concern, she began to feel more comfortable. The therapist pointed out that she needed companionship and recomended her joining a local social organization for older people. She did and was pleased at the friendliness of the group.

In a period of three months this woman was feeling comfortable again. After the first month she no longer needed family members to remain with her. She was also assisted by an antidepressant drug. After some four months of visits, she began to plan for her usual summer vacation when she could meet many of her old friends. She asked for consent about this plan and received the therapist's encouragement to enjoy herself. She did take her antidepressant medication with her, consisting of a homeopathic dose of one pill daily, which represented an important symbolic tie to her doctor. She has remained well for the past two-and-a-half years, but has phoned on two occasions to say that she felt sad and recognized the reasons during the conversations. On the first occasion she returned from a trip to learn of the death of an old friend and was encouraged to contact the friend's family and express her sympathy. She also was told that sadness, under the circumstances, was a highly appropriate feeling. She really wanted to know if it marked the return of her depression, and was relieved to find that it did not. A second call took place when her boarder again was away. She said she felt anxious and knew this was the reason, and she would find someone to stay with her temporarily.

On several other occasions, when about to make trips, she contacted the therapist to mention her plans and to obtain encouragement. After each trip she has called to report that she had a pleasant time and to inquire about the health of the therapist and his family. She has never met his family and seems more interested in the therapist remaining in good health and being available, should she require assistance.

Discussion of Case 7

This patient presents the type of feelings of depression and anxiety described by Zetzel (50) as "depressive anxiety." This kind of anxiety is different from signal anxiety or traumatic anxiety and is related to the primitive anxiety of the helpless and dependent young child who fears the loss of parental support and love. This variety of anxiety is related to the fear of object loss in a vulnerable person and is more likely to appear during the process of aging when feelings of helplessness and weakness return. Zetzel contrasts this primitive depression with the normal mood alterations of the aged and the milder clinical depressions seen in practice. In her view, the capacity to handle inevitable losses and to accept one's realistic limitations are determined by the early life experience of the individual with his objects.

In the case described above there appeared to be lifelong concerns about being left alone, which were never visible as long as the patient had her husband and children around her. Fears of death and concerns about aggression seemed to have been lurking in the background. Anger that her family was less attentive in recent years was vigorously denied, as well as all concerns about her own death. As sustaining and supporting objects were lost and feelings of vulnerability increased, she became more and more distressed. The therapist (52), under these circumstances, becomes more of a "real" object and replaces the previously sheltering objects. This patient had the need to maintain contact with the therapist and to obtain permission for her actions much as a child might with parents. In this way she felt loved and received the support and protection she felt she required.

This is very similar to the transference described by Goldfarb (22) in his work with institutionalized older people who often are brain damaged and physically ill, and feel very helpless and weak. The patients he described were in their seventies and eighties, and anxiety was a prominent feature in their complaints. He saw his patients' behavior as motivated by the desire to secure help and restore a feeling of power and mastery. This was achieved in treatment by permitting the patient to feel that he could defeat the powerful therapist, or through the feeling the patient could take in (introject) the powerful therapist and use the internalized new-found power from the object to again secure a feeling of mastery. No attempt was made to work through the transference or to disturb the fantasies of these patients who felt so vulnerable, since these transference fantasies were essential to alleviate anxiety. The therapist did not "role play," but tried to permit the patient's unconscious needs to be met.

Working in an institutional setting with a staff who obviously look up to the therapist may further enhance the magical powers and expectations that such patients seem to expect from the contact and lend even more credence to the omnipotent transference fantasies. Persons treating border-line and psychotic patients often are aware of their tendency to search for powerful supportive figures whom they can introject in order to achieve a reduction in anxiety. Patients who are less disturbed may be treated in a more classic therapeutic approach in which the powerful, omnipotent, pregenital transference is less of a factor and a genuine therapeutic alliance is achieved.

Varieties of Reactions to Loss

In contrast with many of the patients clinically described in this paper who experienced marked feelings of depression, there are in the aged other varieties of reactions to loss and threatened loss which are not necessarily accompanied by depressive affect (5). Stern (43) described a group of patients who, following a loss, somatized their feelings of bereavement. They displayed little overt grief or guilt about the person who died and tended to idealize him, but frequently treated living people with great hostility as though displacing the angry feelings onto them in order to preserve the positive image of the lost person. This group did not appear to be severely disturbed. Lipsitt (32) has described a group of patients with numerous somatic complaints who were carefully studied. Many of these patients were depressed, but some were masochistic characters who required their physical dysfunctions. Others were unrecognized as depressions because of their somatic complaints and responded well to psychiatric treatment when properly evaluated.

At times confusion, disorientation, recent memory changes, and other signs of "organic" impairment may occur around the time of a loss. Some of these patients, when treated with psychotherapy, with the feelings about the loss worked through, may show reversal of the organic signs, while others do not improve. A clinical trial of psychotherapy seems indicated in cases where the "organic" impairment appears related to traumatic events, such as a loss.

There follows a case history which demonstrates the development of a paranoid and organic reaction as part of the attempt to cope with a recent loss.

Case 8

A 74-year-old retired man was agitated, confused and suspicious. He had lost weight and had little appetite. He slept poorly and had a worried expression on his face. His memory for recent events was impaired. He was extremely fearful that he would be disgraced by an investigation of his past income tax returns and would be sent to prison. He felt that government agents were spying upon him to get the necessary criminal evidence against him. He believed his food might be poisoned by them. He tried to decrease his food consumption and consequently lost a moderate amount of weight.

Since the death of his wife three years before, he had lived with a devoted housekeeper who was quite worried about his agitation and fearfulness. His relatives had noticed a gradual change following the death of his wife. Prior to her death he was an alert and vigorous man who worked every day and enjoyed intellectual pursuits. After her death he began to withdraw, lost interest in his business and retired. Discussion of his paranoid concerns elicited the information that his wife was his bookkeeper and had always prepared his income tax returns. In talking about her, he spoke of her devotion, her painful death from cancer, and his distress at her loss. He was unable to utter a single critical remark about her, except obliquely in his references to his income tax returns being improper.

The therapist pointed out that he was angry with his wife for dying and leaving him to fend for himself, but could not admit such feelings and chose to express it through paranoid concerns about the income tax returns she had filed. Shortly after this interpretation, his paranoid concerns disappeared, but he continued to be agitated. He then began to talk about older men still having sexual feelings. He felt that younger people were unaware that the elderly had such feelings. With some encouragement, he finally said that his housekeeper treated him like a little boy and that he was an adult man. He resented the fact that she bathed him and washed his genitals and insisted on helping him urinate by holding his penis. He often felt aroused by her actions but could not tell her that he wanted her to stop. A discreet word by the therapist to the housekeeper caused her to stop stimulating him. As a result, the patient became much less agitated and more cooperative. His recent memory loss was not improved to any great extent, but his behavior improved and he was much more amiable and contented.

Discussion of Case 8

In the therapy, which lasted less than six months and was conducted on a weekly basis, the therapist was seen as being like the patient's younger and powerful brother, who was a famous medical specialist. The patient disparaged specialists and their minute areas of concern. He pointed out that he had worked to finance his brother through medical school, but that he had put himself through graduate school by working while attending classes. This attitude was caused by obvious feelings of sibling rivalry still visible after seventy years of struggle. Despite this rivalry present in the transference, and despite the patient's organic impairment, the therapist's words were considered and had an obvious therapeutic impact.

This aged patient's continued sexual interests and feelings really should come as no surprise to those who have been closely involved with patients who are willing to express their feelings to a sympathetic person (6). In this case, the patient felt as though he was instructing his younger brother who was so knowledgeable about so many things but still could learn a few things from him. He expressed the feeling that society in general denied the sexual interests of the aged, or made them feel that such feelings were inappropriate. He felt, justifiably, that this attitude needed correction.

General Discussion of the Dynamics of Aging

In this chapter we have not distinguished between endogenous and exogenous depressions. Often this distinction depends on the point of view and knowledge of the observer. Frequently, losses and changes which produce depressive feelings are overlooked by mental health workers because they are not dramatic in nature but reflect the patient's inner concerns that slow but perceptible changes are occurring as part of the aging process (30). For example, the gradual loss of hearing, hair and vision, and the increasing aches and pains of arthritis are responsible for more feelings of discomfort, gloom and anxiety than are the more apparent major traumatic events. Minor narcissistic injuries can produce more serious symptoms than significant external events. What is perhaps equally distressing about these minor slights is that they are doubly narcissistically injurious since they frequently elicit mocking, teasing, unsympathetic responses in those who unconsciously perceive the importance of these changes, whereas those suffering from major external trauma are generally accorded a much more sympathetic and understanding response.

The ability to handle both external losses and the narcissistically perceived internal and external changes without becoming seriously disturbed is at the crux of normal versus pathological aging. The normal aged must expect to sustain mild feelings of depression and anxiety without any fear of the deepening of the process (49, 50). The ability to experience depression, grief and anxiety passively as an affect depends on the early life experiences (50). In aging, certain aspirations must be reduced if the individual is to live with himself comfortably and still maintain pride and obtain gratification from continuing accomplishments. Often those individuals who are unable to reduce their aspirations to reasonable levels in old age were obsessive-compulsive characters premorbidly and developed severe depressions in old age as they continued to expect the same level of performance in old age and failed to meet these standards.

The following case history demonstrates the problems of a person with an obsessive-compulsive character and his unfulfilled aspirations.

Case 9

A 65-year-old man developed some numbness in his right hand and was found to have marked arteriosclerotic narrowing of his major carotid vessels. He had been a hard-working man who was very proud of his ability to earn money and his reputation as a businessman. Gradually, as he developed some mild memory impairment, he became severely agitated about it, but insisted on working and driving his car. He finally was asked by his associates to leave his business, and he was forced to relinquish his driver's license after a number of accidents. He became progressively more depressed and was constantly preoccupied with the subject of his finances. He spent much of his time making investments and often took risks hoping to make a great deal of money. Then he was forced by his family to give over the management of his funds to a guardian.

At each step he fought against recognizing his impairment and insisted that he was capable of continuing his life as he previously lived it. At times he cried about his fate, refused to eat and spoke of wanting to die. He recounted many past experiences in which he had made mistakes and felt extremely guilty, seeing his current life situation as part of the punishment for his misdeeds. He was especially saddened by the knowledge that his oldest son had many severe emotional problems and would never be as successful as his father in the business world. Some people who recognize that they are unable to perform as they once did can be pleased knowing that someone they love will do well and carry on in their place. This man seemed to have lost this solution, and he could only dwell on his past failures and present infirmities. He had never reduced his aspirations and continued to expect an impossible level of achievement as he grew older. Even past success had the taste of cold ashes.

ISSUES OF PSYCHOTHERAPY

For many older people, reminiscing about the past is a highly important form of maintaining mental health and avoiding serious depression (33). As a rule, the older person thinks about a period of success and pleasure in the days when he or she was vigorous and youthful. In these reminiscences, physical attractiveness, vigor, sexual potency and former achievements are central themes. Such a recollection often is a mixture of fantasy and reality, but it usually enhances the self-image. At times, creative activity in old age may follow such reviews and reminiscences, leaving a permanent contribution for society and a sense of immortality for the contributor (15).

Many of the older patients treated by psychiatrists talk primarily about past achievements and avoid the current reality which is usually less attractive. They often emphasize that only the past was worthwhile, and that there really isn't anything current that wasn't achieved in the past in another, more attractive form, all of which derides current reality and causes antagonism from younger people who feel narcissistically injured by these comments. At times, it is possible to use these reminiscences of past accomplishments to point out that the older person has achieved a great deal and is entitled to care and gratification on the basis of these past contributions. Frequently, patients who are in conflict about their dependent needs will cease struggling and relax when such an approach is used (7). Even certain obsessional patients with rigid standards will agree that their past excellence merits special consideration in old age and that they can take pride in their past record.

No discussion of the issues of psychotherapy with the aged would be complete without mentioning the subject of death. Concerns about death are frequently encountered in work with older people. Certain therapists have given death a special place in the psychology of aging (34, 42). Not all writers agree as to the unconscious meaning of death. There is controversy about whether it represents a narcissistic injury, such as a castration threat (26), or is seen in terms of oral rage, killing and incorporation of objects (42). In recent years there has been a growing interest in the subject of death and how people deal with it as a real event, as well as the symbolic experience. Elderly people seem able to talk about it and to view it realistically when it is close to them (46). On the other hand, younger people seem much more concerned when they have to discuss the subject and are frequently distressed by it. This leads us to consider the special anxieties and problems created for the therapist who chooses to work with the aged.

Certain Countertransference Issues

The requisite attitude for treating the geriatric patient has been a subject of considerable interest (16, 25, 35, 38, 40, 41, 44). Many have stressed the need for working through one's own conflicts and feelings about parents and grandparents (16, 44). Flexibility is often mentioned (52), including the need to see patients on schedules other than the 50-minute hour, and even to see them in their own homes when necessary. The inexperienced therapist often believes that the aged are no longer interested in sex, an attitude which is widely held by society and is responsible for considerable distress in older people who have retained their interest and their ability, but are made to feel ashamed (6). The therapist must be prepared to accept sexual feelings in the aged as in any other group.

Those who work with the aged are frequently aware that it is draining and demanding work. Younger therapists are often made anxious by having to deal with the patient's concerns about death and general feelings of decline and helplessness. Regressive behavior is very threatening, and the prospect of increasing dependence is one of the most serious threats in a culture firmly rooted in valuing independence and individual freedom. Despite these problems, increasing numbers of people are becoming concerned with the issues and problems of the aged. Many are surprised that the aged do not greet them with open arms when they offer to help.

Sometimes a great deal of giving is expected before the elderly person is convinced of the genuineness of the therapist's interest. This is particularly so when the elderly person does not select the therapist, but is brought by concerned relatives or friends.

Less experienced therapists often respond to these pressures by wanting to do too much for their patients and meeting their needs by concrete offers of interest and concern (8). The general rule that one does not introduce more parameters than are necessary for carrying out the therapy seems relevant.

The aged often display an impoverishment of libido and an inability to make new object relations (31). Frequently the depressed aged are regarded as "disengaged" because they fail to make contact with people in their environment (17). An active and interested therapist usually can overcome such inertia if he is willing to reach out to the older person and is willing to "give" in an emotional sense. To offer one's interest, assistance and understanding is usually recognized by patients as much more precious than any tangible gifts. Therapists have to learn the value of a sincere offer of genuine involvement. Since it happens so infrequently, it is not surprising that the elderly may hesitate before recognizing it.

The Nature and Resolution of the Transference

The quality of the transference is of great importance in the treatment of the aged, as it is with any group of patients. Although certain authors feel that a specific type of transference is established by the aged (23, 34), this is not our belief. The type of transference established by patients of any age group has more to do with their early object ties and level of maturity than with their chronological age. Helpless, dependent and clinging patients may be found from childhood to old age. Individuals seeking powerful and protective parental figures may be found in every age group.

The most mature and well integrated individuals will utilize psychotherapy to achieve insight about themselves, taking away from treatment added inner strength to cope with the vicissitudes of life. For a great number of patients contact with the therapist assumes a different role. Many seek real replacements for lost or ungratifying objects. Others seek the powerful benevolence of omnipotent parents who can restore the childhood sense of security and comfort. Only an accurate appraisal of the nature and quality of the transference will establish how to bring treatment to a close. Although there are always regressive aspects in the transference, and even the most mature individuals have remnants of the most primitive relationships, it is still possible to see that certain patients will have a solid bedrock of emotional development and will be able to make their own way when the transference has been examined and worked through. For others, who are more fragile, the therapist will have to remain a source of strength and understanding, who continues to be available when the occasion arises.

SUMMARY

This chapter emphasizes the importance of understanding and treating the aged with neuroses and character disorders. This group is often neglected by mental health workers, and yet the aged with these emotional problems form a far larger group than the psychotic aged who receive a greater share of attention. Stereotyped attitudes and commonly accepted myths regarding the aged encourage an attitude of therapeutic nihilism and pessimism. The unconscious motivation for ignoring the obvious distress of older people is discussed. Certain specific myths, such as the "rigidity" of the aged, the tendency to "wastebasket" and to view all pathology as organic or caused by aging alone are discussed. The fear of the devouring older person is also explored, as well as the myth of "family rejection."

A number of clinical examples are given of the types of emotional problems frequently seen among the non-institutionalized older population. The dynamic understanding and management of each case is described. A trial of observation and psychotherapy is recommended in all situations, since even "organic" signs may be reversed. Generalizations concerning the aged as a group are avoided as leading to further stereotyping and the discouragement of scientific investigation. Individual assessment and understanding are emphasized. The persistence of unconscious attitudes, fantasies and wishes from childhood is pointed out, but they may not always carry the same value and meaning throughout life.

Certain patients achieve insight through treatment, along with a greater capacity to enjoy life than they had before. Others are comforted by the relationship with the therapist for both its "real" and unconscious meanings. Some require assistance in accepting and tolerating more regressive behavior, while some patients need help in accepting and assimilating their changing feelings about their goals, objects and sexuality in old age.

Reminiscences are emphasized as important sources of elevating self-esteem. Concerns about death and common countertransference problems in work with the aged are examined. The need to be flexible but not to "lean over backwards" is emphasized. Patients understand a genuine offer of involvement and concern as the most precious gift.

REFERENCES

1. BAHN, A. K., CONWELL, M., and HURLEY, P. 1965. Survey of private psychiatric practice. *Arch. Gen. Psychiat.*, 12:295.
2. BEREZIN, M. A. 1963. Some intrapsychic aspects of aging. In: Zinberg, N. E., and Kaufman, I. (Eds.) *Normal Psychology of the Aging Process*. New York: International Universities Press.
3. BEREZIN, M. A. 1967. Persistence of early emotional problems in a seventy-year-old woman: Discussion. *J. Geriat. Psychiat.* 1:61.
4. BEREZIN, M. A. 1969. Sex and old age: a review of the literature. *J. Geriat. Psychiat.*, 2:131.
5. BEREZIN, M. A. 1970. Partial grief in family members and others who care for the elderly patient. *J. Geriat. Psychiat.*, 4:53.
6. BEREZIN, M. A. 1972. Psychodynamic considerations of aging and the aged: an overview. *Am. J. Psychiat.*, 128:1483.
7. BLAU, D. 1967. Medical management, psychotherapy, and aging: Discussion. *J. Geriat. Psychiat.*, 1:98.
8. BLAU, D. 1967. The loneliness and death of an old man: three years of psychotherapy of an eighty-one-year-old depressed patient: Discussion. *J. Geriat. Psychiat.*, 1:38.
9. BLAU, D. 1972. Responsibility for the care of the geriatric patient: legal, psychological, and ethical issues: Discussion. *J. Geriat. Psychiat.*, 5:21.
10. BLAU, D., ARTH, M. J., KETTELL, M. E., et al. 1962. Psychosocial reasons for geriatric hospitalization. In: Tibbitts, C., and Donahue, W. (Eds.) *Social and Psychological Aspects of Aging*. New York: Columbia University Press.
11. BROOKS, L. 1969. A case of eroticized transference in a 73-year-old woman. *J. Geriat. Psychiat.* 2:150.
12. BUNZEL, J. T. 1972. Note on the history of a concept—gerontophobia. *Gerontologist*, 12:116.
13. BUSSE, E., BARNES, R. H., SILVERMAN, A. J., et al. 1955. Studies of the processes of aging. X: The strengths and weaknesses of psychic functioning in the aged. *Am. J. Psychiat.*, 111:896.
14. BUSSE, E., DOVENMUEHLE, R. H., and BROWN, R. G. 1960. Psychoneurotic reactions of the aged. *Geriatrics*, 15:97.
15. BUTLER, R. N. 1967. The destiny of creativity in later life: studies of creative people and the creative process. In: Levin, S., and Kahana, R. J. (Eds.) *Psychodynamic Studies on Aging: Creativity, Reminiscing, and Dying*. New York: International Universities Press.
16. CAMERON, N. 1965. Neuroses of later maturity. In: Kaplan, O. J. (Ed.) *Mental Disorders in Later Life*. 2nd ed. Stanford, Calif.: Stanford University Press.
17. CUMMING, E., and HENRY, W. E. 1961. *Growing Old*. New York: Basic Books.
18. FREUD, A. 1965. *Normality and Pathology in Childhood: Assessments of Development*. New York: International Universities Press.
19. FREUD, S. 1904. On psychotherapy. *Standard Edition*. 7. London: Hogarth Press.
20. GITELSON, M. 1948. The emotional problems of elderly people. *Geriatrics*. 3:135.
21. GITELSON, M. 1965. A transference reaction in a sixty-six-year-old woman. In: Berezin, M. A., and Cath, S. H. (Eds.), *Geriatric Psychiatry: Grief, Loss, and Emotional Disorders in the Aging Process*. New York: International Universities Press.

22. GOLDFARB, A. I. 1955. IV. One aspect of the psychodynamics of the therapeutic situation with aged patients. *Psychoanalytic Rev.,* 42:180.
23. GOLDFARB, A. I. 1959. Depression, brain damage, and chronic illness of the aged. Psychiatric diagnosis and treatment. *J. Chronic Dis.,* 9:220.
24. GOLDFARB, A. I. 1959. Minor maladjustments in the aged. In: Arieti, S. (Ed.) *American Handbook of Psychiatry.* New York: Basic Books.
25. GOLDFARB, A. I., and TURNER, H. 1953. Psychotherapy of aged persons. II. Utilization and effectiveness of "brief" therapy. *Am. J. Psychiat.* 109:916.
26. GROTJAHN, M. 1940. Psychoanalytic investigation of a seventy-one-year-old man with senile dementia. *Psychoanal. Quart.,* 9:80.
27. GROTJAHN, M. 1955. Analytic psychotherapy with the elderly. I. The sociological background of aging in America. *Psychoanal. Rev.,* 42:419.
28. JACOBSON, E. 1961. Adolescent moods. *The Psychoanalytic Study of the Child,* 16:164.
29. JONES, H. E., and KAPLAN, O. J. 1956. Psychological aspects of mental disorders in later life. In: Kaplan, O. J. (Ed.) *Mental Disorders in Later Life.* 2nd ed. Stanford, Calif.: Stanford University Press.
30. LEVIN, S. 1965. Depression in the aged. In: Berezin, M. A., and Cath, S. H. (Eds.) *Geriatric Psychiatry: Grief, Loss, and Emotional Disorders in the Aging Process.* New York: International Universities Press.
31. LEVIN, S. 1965. Some comments on the distribution of narcissistic and object libido in the aged. *Int. J. Psychoanal.,* 46:200.
32. LIPSITT, D. R. 1958. The "rotating" patient: A challenge to psychiatrists. *J. Geriat. Psychiat.,* 2:51.
33. McMAHON, A. W., JR., and RHUDICK, P. J. 1967. Reminiscing in the aged. An adaptational response. In: Levin, S., and Kahana, R. J. (Eds) *Psychodynamic Studies on Aging: Creativity, Reminiscing, and Dying.* New York: International Universities Press.
34. MEERLOO, J. M. 1955. Transference and resistance in geriatric psychotherapy. *Psychoanal. Rev.* 42:72.
35. MEERLOO, J. M. 1961. Modes of psychotherapy in the aged. *J. Am. Geriat. Soc.,* 9:225.
36. MOSS, R. M. 1965. Aging—A survey of the psychiatric literature. 1950-1960. In: Berezin, M. A., and Cath, S. H. (Eds.) *Geriatric Psychiatry: Grief, Loss, and Emotional Disorders in the Aging Process.* New York: International Universities Press.
37. MOSS, R. M. 1967. Aging—A survey of the psychiatric literature. 1961-1964. In: Levin, S., and Kahana, R. J. (Eds) *Psychodynamic Studies on Aging: Creativity, Reminiscing, and Dying.* New York: International Universities Press.
38. MULLAN, H. 1961. The personality of those who care for the aging. *Gerontologist,* 1:42.
39. PAYNE, E. C., JR. 1967. Medical management, psychotherapy and aging: Discussion. *J. Geriat. Psychiat.,* 1:90.
40. RECHTSCHAFFEN, A. 1959. Psychotherapy with geriatric patients: A review of the literature. *J. Gerontology,* 14:73.
41. ROCKWELL, F. V. 1956. Psychotherapy in the older individual. In: Kaplan, O. J. (Ed.) *Mental Disorders in Later Life.* 2nd ed. Stanford, Calif.: Stanford University Press.
42. SEGAL, H. 1958. Fear of death. Notes on the analysis of an old man. *Int. J. Psychoanal.,* 39:178.
43. STERN, K., WILLIAMS, M. G., and PRADOS, M. 1951. Grief reactions in later life. *Am. J. Psychiat.,* 108:289.

44. THOMPSON, P. W. 1967. Persistence of early emotional problems in a seventy-year-old woman: Discussion. *J. Geriat. Psychiat.*, 1:62.
45. WAYNE, G. J. 1953. Modified psychoanalytic therapy in senescence. *Psychoanal. Rev.*, 40:99.
46. WEISMAN, A. D., and HACKETT, T. P. 1967. Denial as a social act. In: Levin, S. and Kahana, R. J. (Eds.) *Psychodynamic Studies on Aging: Creativity, Reminiscing, and Dying* New York: International Universities Press.
47. WHISKIN, F. E. 1968. Delinquency in the aged. *J. Geriat. Psychiat.*, 1:242.
48. ZARSKY, E. L., and BLAU, D. 1970. The understanding and management of narcissistic regression and dependency in an elderly woman observed over an extended period of time. *J. Geriat. Psychiat.*, 3:160.
49. ZETZEL, E. R. 1949. Anxiety and the capacity to bear it. *Int. J. Psychoanal.*, 30:1.
50. ZETZEL, E. R. 1965. Dynamics of the metapsychology of the aging process. In: Berezin, M. A., and Cath, S. H. (Eds.) *Geriatric Psychiatry: Grief, Loss, and Emotional Disorders in the Aging Process*. New York: International Universities Press.
51. ZINBERG, N. E. 1963. The relationship of regressive phenomena to the aging process. In: Zinberg, N. E., and Kaufman, I. (Eds.) *Normal Psychology of the Aging Process*. New York: International Universities Press.
52. ZINBERG, N. E. 1965. Special problems of gerontologic psychiatry. In: Berezin, M. A., and Cath, S. H. (Eds.) *Geriatric Psychiatry: Grief, Loss, and Emotional Disorders in the Aging Process*. New York: International Universities Press.
53. ZINBERG, N. E., and KAUFMAN, I. 1963. Cultural and personality factors associated with aging: An introduction. In: Zinberg, N. E., and Kaufman, I. (Eds.) *Normal Psychology of the Aging Process*. New York: International Universities Press.

10

PSYCHOPATHOLOGY

JACK WEINBERG, M.D.

Clinical Director, Illinois State Psychiatric Institute,
Professor of Psychiatry, University of Illinois College of Medicine,
Chicago, Ill.

INTRODUCTION

There are realities that transcend the truth. Paradoxical though this may seem it is not so to anyone who has heard the words of the emotionally ill . . . the poetry of the anguished mentality which becomes its credo, its reality. The 81-year-old confused and incontinent woman, whose delusion is that she is pregnant, clings to what is to her a reality despite all objectively true findings to the contrary. For truth is objective, while reality is subjective, varying with the individual and becoming clear to anyone willing and able to interpret its meaning. What the old woman was saying was that she harbored her own regressed self within herself and was about to deliver it. If senility is the "second childhood," then she was pregnant with it and at the point of delivery. Viewed from this perspective, her delusion makes sense—her method of expressing it, poetry.

To understand the uniqueness of each person's reality, the young and the old, is the very essence of psychological skill which must deal not only with the individual variance, but also with the shifting and altering quality of this subjective state as the human being grows, develops and ages. Each period in the life span of man forces on him a different reality, based on the altered physiology and the extent of the richness of the human experience. Old age can become an expression of the summation of the human experience, and therein "lies the rub." It can be rich, varied, color-

234

ful and, in turn, enriching; conversely, it may be impoverished or empty and serve only to emphasize the futility of life and its meaning to many of the old. However, no matter what one's experiences may be, there is a need for an elaboration upon one's experiences which tend to distort the objective truth, but which add to the uniqueness of the reality which the individual wishes to convey. It is by far more real, for it delineates more clearly to the observer the actual personality of the observed. It is a more "real" reflection of the personality structure of the communicating person than the actual facts warrant or state. What emerges is a romanticized version of events, a dramatization of the facts: the good becomes magnificent, the sad—tragic. It is a poetic interpretation of one's experiences which, in turn, need interpretation by the listener.

Furthermore, we who are engaged in the field of mental illness and health are quite aware of the permutations of time. We work with emotions that have their origins in the person's dim forgotten or repressed past, but which make themselves ferociously felt in the present. No sooner does the patient express an emotion, a feeling, than it is related to his past. His dreams know of no time dimension—they permeate all three and operate as if the individual organism has no cognizance of that which we know as temporal. What is needed most, therefore, in working with the emotionally ill elderly is an understanding of their manifest behavior in the light of their lifelong experiences and affected as it may be by accrued deficits—both extrinsic and intrinsic.

Much too much has already been written on the subject, yet much too much has either been ignored or simply misunderstood. My effort is to make the covert overt, the seemingly bizarre understandable, to point out the order inherent in chaos and thus make life bearable for the observer and help the observed.

Behavior is the aggregate of observable responses of the organism in its interrelationships. In its predictable form, it is the usual modality by which an individual handles life situations that may arise. It is usually automatic and more often than not defines the character of the person. It is what one expects of one's contacts with another and upon which one projects a continuum of transactions. While minor deviations from the established patterns are allowed for under certain circumstances, the usual set of expectations is that of stability, if not rigidity. Unfortunately, the predictability of behavior presumes a static quality to the source, the human being, who, of course, is in a constant state of change, development and, hopefully, growth. Added to this dilemma is the subtlety of an ever-increasing spectrum of that which is called normal due both to the greater tolerance by society of more and more deviant behavior and the greater understanding that the helping professions bring to the study and alleviation of the human condition.

In view of the above, I have chosen to address myself to the psychodynamics of what I like to call agedness rather than aging. Aging is an ongoing process, therefore difficult of assessment. Agedness, however, is an assumed stance on the part of the organism that may or may not be due to organ dysfunction, but may be behaviorally characteristic of a unified complex of roles, assigned, ascribed and much too often acquired. It may be both character and pathology. It may be independent of any overt manifestations of organic disease and thus present itself as a mode of coping or adaptive behavior most economical to the character structure of the individual. Behavioristically speaking, one may manifest agedness quite early in one's life, though usually it is characteristic of the later periods of the life cycle. Thus it is the manifest behavior of an individual that should interest us and the latent meaning of its content that should intrigue us. For again it is the understanding of behavior, and not only its origin, that can produce the proper responses in dealing with it and with the problems that may ensue.

PSYCHODYNAMICS IN THE AGED

Many clinicians tend to reify the names of abnormal psychological conditions and thus assume their reality as entities. A more consistent clinical view would, to my mind, regard diagnoses as names given to sets of extreme variation of different kinds of behavior. The behavioral modalities subsumed under a diagnostic category are not describable as unitary. It is not the diagnoses that have a reality reference, but rather the behavioral variations the diagnoses describe. In any type of class of behavior one will see extremes, and the laws that govern and describe those extremes also govern and describe the nonpathological functioning. Thus, the idea of continuity between normal and abnormal can be established and have meaning.

We can further assume that no one behavior is unique to a diagnostic category; therefore, individual symptoms are not reliable indices of a psychopathological grouping. When precise and definite etiological factors are isolated and the pathogenesis is well understood, the disease entity itself may certainly be used to define a target population. However, most studies on the psychopathological conditions of aging do not define etiological or pathogenic factors solely, and lacking such forces, lead some of us to what may be described as empirical conclusions on behavioral patterns.

Perception-psychopathology relationships in old age are a case in point. While some regard perception as an independent variable and direct our attention to the effect of disordered perception on personality development and consequent behavior, others view psychopathological conditions as independent variables and regard the perceptual behavior as outcomes or effects. I, for one, an adherent to the latter notion, have long since postulated the *exclusion of stimuli* in later life as an outcome or effect of a psychopathological, if not psychodynamic, condition.

Perception, of course, refers to a perceptual act that transforms a physical stimulus into psychological information. Complex processes are involved in this transformation: reception of the stimulus, registration, the processing of the registered information and the checking of the information against continued input. Eventually, the human organismal organization is meant to interpret all of the above in the light of its life experiences and effect action. Thus, sensory, cognitive, conceptual, affective and motor processes are all linked with each other in any given perceptual act. Most of us have long since recognized the crucial significance of perception, its central role in the development of those modulatory and controlling structures designated as the ego or, as I like to call it, the problem-solving self. For the perceptual act reflects the psychological point of contact between a person and his internal and external milieu. Its principal function is to convey information from his environment for integration with other psychological functioning such as memory, judgment and anticipation. Obviously, too, it also receives and carries information about the nature and consequences of the perceiver's actions. Perception is, thus, a central ingredient in effective adaptation, in the fitting-in process between the individual and his environment.

As the individual develops and moves towards active mastery, he can no longer depend on the instrumentality of others as in infancy, childhood, and adolescence, but must amplify and coordinate the executive potential of his own body parts, which cease to be independent information and pleasure receptors, and take up their collaborative, productive functions. In later life, due to intrinsic and extrinsic vectors, recapitulation of early developmental sequences may take place, moving the individual from productivity to receptivity and, in effect, to dependence on the mastery or the instrumentality of others, an adaptive approach which, in the belief of some, is characterized by gross coercive dependence and/or by the disruption of proper ego functioning.

The threat of organic deficits or destruction within, plus the welling-up of heretofore unacceptable but controlled impulses and the all too frequent deterioration of the individual's socioeconomic status, tax the adaptive capacities of the ego to the utmost. To master the threat of dissolution of its boundaries and to ward off any break with reality, the aging organism, having at its disposal a lowered psychic energy supply and being unable to deal with all stimuli, begins to exclude them from awareness. While, of course, the nature of the receiving organ obviously influences reception, we have seen that perception is not a passive process. The physical stimulus is organized and transformed at the point of reception, and I like to believe that it never goes beyond the point of the sensory receptor.

The infant, too, is faced by the problem of too many stimuli and little ego development to help him cope with them. The very young, however, can and do take refuge in sleep or withdrawal to allow a gradual exposure to the clamor and the slow, measured, developmental integration of stimuli and the evolvement of acceptable responses to them. Then, too, the very young are helped by supportive figures who are ever ready to supply ego judgment and strength to the struggling new organism. Neither of these elements is available to the aging individual nor are they acceptable—hence, the exclusion.

Though it may be argued by some that the mechanism of exclusion of stimuli is identical to the familiar mechanism of denial, it is my belief that this defense is rather different. Denial, in my view, implies that a stimulus has been received, cathected and invested in, and then cathexis is withdrawn. Not so with the exclusion of stimuli. A stimulus may be blocked at the point of entry by a threshold lowered only for those stimuli relevant to one's narcissism, by which, at this point, I mean survival value. The problem is how to assess the rate and extent of the exclusion experimentally so as to utilize this mechanism as a psychobiological measure of aging.

Based on the above assumptions and on the assumption that our society is neglectful, if not hostile, to the needs of the aged, I have allowed myself psychodynamic formulations on some aspects of their behavior.

The sensory organs envelop each individual with personal spatial boundaries within which messages may be perceived, and which may differ in dimensions and scope for each organ. Tactile language would therefore be the closest and, unless invited or eagerly yearned for, the most encroaching and threatening of all stimuli received. Thermal, olfactory, aural, and visual stimuli, in that order, provide ever-increasing spatial territoriality for meaningful messages of increasing complexity to reach the human being, for him to decode and to give the proper response. Each of these personal spaces may have a "Do Not Trespass" sign, not discernible to others but well delineated for the comfort of each organism.

When cultural determinants are added to these biologically determined boundaries, the problem becomes even more complex. Unless invited, encroachment on one's personal space becomes an invasion of one's privacy. Cultural values, biases, and practices tend to decrease the allowable areas of intrusion, inhibit the sending out and receiving of messages, and thus further thwart the language of communication. The transactional reciprocity between the human organism and its circumambience is a thing of beauty to behold. For, ironically enough, as visual and auditory acuity diminish and the environmental language becomes less discernible, the aged themselves join the vast throngs of the invisible and untouchable in our society.

It is not that I am unaware of the effects of organic deficits. My emphasis is on the effects on sensory organ functioning of one's inner perception of the self and one's ambience. While all may agree with what is here stated, the tendency is to arrive at quick closure on the effects of organic deficits, sacrificing a more comprehensive therapeutic effort on the altar of organicity. Thus, in a recent paper concerning the needs of the elderly for tactile relationships, of the need for intimacy and touch, I wrote, "The sensory organ of the aged person's skin often becomes dull, as if in response to an anticipated deprivation. There is no need to feel, if feelings are to be denied." And again: "Visually the older person is more concerned with messages in his environment dealing with movement. Available data suggest that he relies more heavily on visual information channeled through the periphery of the eye, which magnifies movement, than on information received by means of detailed and clear vision. Psychologically it is as if the older person anticipates some external threat to his being and is alert to ward off an offending object, or in search of a supportive figure" (3).

Complicating matters even more is the fact that the behavioral patterns as manifested by the aged are bound to inner secret legends each person has about himself. As psychiatrists, we are engaged in a type of life review of each one of our patients. The life review allows us to perceive the life-style, or more often the life-theme, as Binswanger calls it, of the individual.

The life-theme of a person, as an example, may be of emptiness and a constant search for the filling of the self, as one may encounter in a depressed individual. What is not so apparent, even to an astute observer, is the personal legend, as I like to call it, that pervades our being and motivates our behavior. I use the term legend, for in all of us the concept of the self as a dynamic force, interacting with the environment, is more often than not tinged with wish rather than reality, and is thus distorted and obscured. When the legend of the self is not in concert with the facts as they are, discomfort and disease make their appearance. The legend leads to a romanticizing of the self and a poetic interpretation of reality, which arouse skepticism and even hostility toward the holder of the dream. There are personal realities, therefore, that transcend the obvious truth.

To move on to another dimension, man recognizes that the existing harmony and interrelationships in the world about him bespeak an interdependence between them. The loss of any of the components or systems calls for a new adaptation and adjustment to the whole. The observation of these phenomena, added to man's own life experience from infancy to maturation in a complex society, makes it quite apparent to him that he cannot exist isolated from other interacting individuals. He can manage to do so for a given period of time, particularly when there is hope that the isolation will eventually end. He cannot manage, though, if the isolation is not self-imposed or if there is no hope of its amelioration. This, however, is precisely the situation faced in later life within our culture. The gradual isolation of the aging organism into a state of aloneness is the great tragedy of aging.

I use the term aloneness because it is descriptive of the intensely experienced inner affect related to the gradual isolation that takes place, and is a physical or geographic state. Aloneness, of course, is a result of a number of factors. A very real one is the dispersal and death of friends and members of the family. Each loss necessitates a rearrangement of the equilibrium that had been set up for comfortable functioning. Each loss, too, releases energy previously invested, but which now needs a new object. The aging person searches for a substitute, but there are no candidates. There is no replacement of family and there are no bidders for his friendship. When the aging individual attempts to reestablish equilibrium by attempting to reinvest the freed libido in new objects in the environment, he meets a wall of resistance. Having no place to go, this freed-up energy is turned inward and is either reinvested in organs or organ systems and appears in the guise of somatic complaints, or is experienced as pain and ruminatory recapitulation of a past life experience. The aged then appear to be egocentric, selfish, and preoccupied with inner rumblings of the self.

Within the final span of years, the aged must also face the twin spectrum of physiological losses and eventual death, of which the above are but a part. Losses may be handled by denial, overcompensatory mechanisms, or projection. Grief may be a constant companion which takes on the appearance of depression. Equally common, and most troublesome to respond to, is one method of dealing with losses—projection. It is most often expressed by complaints of the aged that someone is cheating or lying to them, stealing, or taking things away from them. It is a rebuke and an expression of anger at the fact that internal biological losses are being sustained, that mastery over hitherto controlled functions and impulses is threatened, and influence over one's family and environment is waning. The "thiefs, robbers, and cheaters" are usually members of the family, friends, relatives, and caretakers who can least comprehend the accusations made against them, and who in turn respond in anger, resulting in mutual frustration, distrust, and alienation.

Psychodynamically, the above is quite clear. By taking over functions for the aged, we do rob them of mastery and control. While this may be necessary as a protective device to save the aged from their own judgmental deficits, it does not deny the fact that control of their independent actions is being usurped. The response on the part of the aged is either by rage or accusation, hanging on to any vestige of control, or by denial that may be either vigorous or pitiful, depending on the circumstances. Frequently, the aged will begin to cling to many seemingly meaningless objects. Hoarding is not uncommon, whether it be of food, priceless objects, or trifles. This, too, needs to be understood in the light of ever-increasing losses. The more often the aged person loses close friends—others with whom he has shared life experiences—the greater is his need to hold on to inanimate objects with which he has shared common experiences. These objects replace and are substitutes for cherished reunions and memories when very few, if any, friends are left to meet with and reminisce. Chaotic disorder to the observer may represent organizing strength to the observed old person, so that forbearance should be the guiding rule.

Cultural patterns, too, play a great role in determining variables in human behavior. These include not only moral standards and mores but also more subtle patterns of motivation and interpersonal relationships. Variations in judgment and systems of belief, like religion and philosophies, have been integrated with the other cultural patterns, like child-rearing practices, by the cultural anthropologists. As a result of this synthesis, there is now clearer understanding of the effects of one or the other on the individual and on the cultural patterns he has developed. The values the child accepts, introjects, and incorporates into himself have much to do with defining his attitude toward aging people and later toward himself as an aging person. If in our society the aged are perceived as unattractive, unproductive, old-fashioned, useless, querulous, etc., then we in our youth absorb these concepts, make them part of ourselves, and apply them to ourselves in later life. Clearly a built-in system of self-depreciation or denial and dynamic processes determine behavior.

We need, therefore, to examine some specifics of our culture and its value system, along with their continued effects on behavior long after their usefulness to the organism has become anachronistic. No easy assessment of what is defined as culture is available, but this could best be understood by Kluckhohn's approach to the problem (1). According to her, there are five questions that man, regardless of the level of sophistication of his culture, asks himself, whether he is aware of it or not. These questions can be answered within a given spectrum and while each society may relate to the entire spectrum, it is the inordinate emphasis that is placed on one of these answers that determines the society's value system, its child-rearing practices, its behavior, and its treatment of the aged. A brief examination of one or two of these questions may illustrate my point.

What is man's relationship to time? Which of the three time orientations, past, present, or future, does he value most? There is, of course, no question that we as Americans, or those who attempt to emulate our culture, value the future. Our future mindedness makes planners of us all. Nothing is left to chance, not even a spontaneous good time. We are so busy planning for the future that, when the future catches up with us and becomes the present, we cannot enjoy it because we are again busy planning for the future. As a result, we cannot have a good time and enjoy the present. We seldom sit anywhere without feeling that we should be somewhere else. How does this affect older persons? Not only are they people without a future and hence not ones to invest in, but having incorporated the valued time orientation, they, the only group in our society meant to do so, are incapable of enjoying the present, while the hope for a better future is a mirage in the twilight of life.

Another question: *What type of personality is valued most?* The "being" —the individual who is mainly concerned with feelings, impulses, and desires of the moment; the "being in becoming"—most interested in inner development and the fullest realization of aspects of personality; or the "doing"—the one principally concerned with action, achievement, and getting things done? It is not too difficult to recognize ourselves in this configuration. We are the doers. While the Mexican mother, valuing the "being" orientation, may happily enjoy her child from day to day, the "doing" mother is too often concerned with his progress. His achievements are a measure of her competence as a mother, an efficient manager, and a force in the community. Doing, too, must have a by-product discernible to one of our senses. We unconsciously depreciate the contemplative aspects of life. One does nothing when one reads or thinks.

Here, again, we can readily recognize the impact of such an orientation on the aging organism. The old have stopped doing, are alien in our eyes and depreciated in their own. Nor have they prepared their lives for a contemplative existence. The effects are often quite devastating, resulting frequently in restlessness and purposeless agitation.

CLINICAL STATES

The specific mental disturbances seen in the older years may be divided into two major categories: (1) organic, in which there is some demonstrable pathology in the brain, and (2) functional personality disorders, in which there seems to be nothing wrong from an organic viewpoint. Under organic disturbances are to be classed the many cases of cerebral arteriosclerosis. The physical symptoms are dizziness, tremors, unsteady gait, tingling sensations, and so forth. Emotionally there appear apprehension, panic, restlessness, sleeplessness, disturbance in consciousness and thinking, memory defects, delusions of threats of bodily harm, nightmares, and depression. There may occur actual violence against people, even against those closest to the individual. All of these symptoms reflect the reaction of the personality to the inwardly perceived threat to its integrity, and the extreme fight that it puts up to master it.

Presenile Syndromes

Alzheimer's disease and Pick's disease, which occur in middle age, are known as presenile psychoses. The onset is in the forties or fifties and is characterized organically by marked diffuse changes in the brain. Psychologically they present symptoms of marked failure of memory, rapidly developing confusion and disorientation, speech difficulties, and complete dementia. Even in these undeniably organic diseases, the individual in the early phases manifests emotional responses and reactions indicative of his struggle against the threat of overwhelming destruction. The individual often overcompensates by euphoric overactivity, grandiose business plans, sexual deviations, and general uninhibited behavior.

The Senile Psychosis

This has been called the "final caricature of old age." It is insidious in onset and may therefore be neglected until it it too late. It begins with a gradual decline in initiative, loss of interest in things which normally are of importance, reversal of the sleep rhythm, failure of memory, concentration and comprehension, and general deterioration with final confusion and formation of delusions. This constitutes a gradual breakdown of the personality into what may be called a second childhood, but minus the charms and easy acceptability of the first.

Infectious disease, acute or chronic, and vitamin deficiencies may bring with them disturbances in the mental functioning of the aging person. There may be delirious types of reaction which in the aged are more sustained than is the case in younger years.

Among the gross functional disturbances seen in the later years are the following:

Involutional Melancholia

This most common disorder of middle life was formerly thought of as a direct result of the female menopause, or "change of life." In reality, it tends to appear in both women and men as a first attack of mental illness, in women between the ages of 40 and 55 and in men between the ages of 50 and 60. In the female the symptoms that present themselves are: nervousness, menstrual disturbances, flushes and chills, excitability, fatigability, weeping and depression, irritability, sleeplessness, memory defects, inability to concentrate, headaches and other vague and indefinite pains. Men show the following: hot flashes, emotional instability with sudden uncontrollable shifts in mood, tendency to break into tears, periods of irritability and sudden anger, physical and mental fatigability, difficulty in concentration, hypochondriacal complaints, and impatience. As the illness progresses, both sexes show marked anxiety, an agitated type of depression, delusions of guilt, and attempts at self-destruction.

Simple Depression

This is another common disorder of the later years. It is characterized by general feelings of desolation and isolation which, in a measure, reflect the reality of the life situation. Feelings of unworthiness, of guilt, and self-punishing attitudes are the rule and psychologically constitute a reaction to the resentment and hostility which these patients feel toward their environment and fellow human beings, but which, for many reasons, they cannot express. Because of this inability, they turn their resentment and hostility inward and tend to be self-depreciatory and self-destructive.

Paranoid States

Paranoid states are characterized by feelings of persecution and apprehension. It is easy for the older person to develop ideas that people and the world are hostile to him and wish to destroy him.

Primarily, however, paranoid states are the result of the resurgence in an individual of primitive hostile impulses toward the world and the people in it, both of which are beginning to fail him. To the average person such hostility is unacceptable and the only defense against it is to project it outward. The individual's hostile ideas thus become delusions of persecution. It is simpler to say that one is hated and not wanted because one is old, than to admit to oneself and others that one is incapable of coping with overwhelming odds.

The Neuroses

The neuroses occupy a conspicuous place in the disorders of later life. The incidence of the neuroses is by far greater than is that of the psychoses, yet little attention is being paid to them because in the neuroses there is no total break with reality. Much too often neuroses have been thought of as precursors to a general physical decline. Nothing could be further from the truth. A neurosis may occur at any period in life and is indicative of a failure in adaptation. Among the common neuroses in later life, the following are the most conspicuous.

Hypochondriasis

Hypochondriasis is the inordinate preocupation with one's bodily functions and is an especially common disorder seen in the aged of present-day culture. The symptoms are directed mostly to the organs of ingestion, digestion, and evacuation, that is, to the gastrointestinal tract, and also to the heart and circulatory system. This does not mean, however, that the reproductive system or the muscles, bones and joints are excluded from attention. Hypochondriacal over-concern is often mitigated by the reeducation in the range of activities permitted by one's own physical limitations, and by conventions in certain socioeconomic groups which accept an excessive concern with bodily functions as normal behavior. However, with fewer worthwhile things to hold the attention and to divert one from self-concern, it becomes easier to notice and to talk about minor ailments and accidents. In general, the older a person grows, the more experience he has had with illness, operations and accidents, whether his own or those of other people, and the easier it is for him to feel himself to be ill or in danger. Then, too, bodily concern helps to save face when one is beset by failures. "I am ill and therefore I cannot . . .," is a rationalization that is more universally acceptable than the truthful but prestige-shattering, "I cannot."

Despite the fact that heart conditions are more numerous and more often fatal than gastrointestinal disease, the elderly person is usually much more concerned with the latter. Psychologically it is believed that this is tied in with an unconscious expression of the person's dependency needs. It is an expression of a desire to be taken care of, just as one had been taken care of when one was young and when a great deal of attention centered about the feeding, digestive and evacuation processes of the infant. The responsiveness of the gastrointestinal tract at all ages to emotional disturbances, to anxiety, to conflict, to apprehension, to frustration and to unhappiness is by now well recognized. By his unconscious utilization of the resulting physical symptoms, the older person often attempts to regain attention, affection, and domination.

Anxiety States

Anxiety states are not entirely new experiences for older people. In all probability they have experienced similar reactions, perhaps rather frequently, whenever their security had been threatened or whenever they faced emotional deprivation. Since insecurity and realistic anxiety-producing situations are more common in later life, anxiety states can easily arise. An anxiety neurosis is characterized by increased muscular tension with difficulty in relaxation and sleeping, disturbances in the regular rhythm of the heart, gastrointestinal tract and urinary system disturbances, tremors, headaches, excessive perspiration, increased irritability, and a vague sense of impending doom. At times acute anxiety may arise because of guilt feelings resulting from hostility toward one's family when it fails to understand and meet the needs of the older person.

In any event, anxiety is not without its compensating elements. It has long been recognized as a danger signal for something more serious that may supervene. It has a dynamic quality that bespeaks treatability. It is by far better than the seemingly less distressing attempts at withdrawal from any experiencing of feelings, with its attendant fantasy-formation and possible total divorce from reality.

Chronic Fatigue States

These states are at times difficult to diagnose in the aging individual because it is normal for elderly people to tire more quickly and easily and to recover more slowly and imcompletely than younger ones. Also, as a rule, sleep in older people is shorter and less sound, and they awaken feeling less refreshed and at times irritable. Fatigue can, however, be a result of emotional frustration. Whenever the prospect of gratification is small, a person is apt to tire quickly and to remain so until something interesting turns up. Since prospects for gratifying experience wane with the years, easy fatigability is therefore common in this age group.

It is a mistake to meet these fatigue states in older people with advice for rest cures or prolonged vacations. Very often it is these very prolonged vacations or rests that produce lethargy and fatigue. A balanced diet of rest, recreation, and occupation gives a starting point for a successful therapeutic effort. One cannot overstress the need for some occupation and satisfying accomplishment geared to the physical limitations of the person involved as a definite therapeutic aid for fatigue based on emotional factors.

Compulsive Disorders

Compulsive disorders and patterns in later life are similar to those occurring in earlier life. The compulsive individual can be recognized by his overconscientiousness, perfectionism, orderliness, overattention to details, and doubts about himself and his adequacy. While some of these character traits may be considered as quite praiseworthy, they can readily become troublesome symptoms that undermine the person's efficiency and immobilize him. Such symptoms may take the form of excessive cleanliness and orderliness, and endless and inflexible rituals to guard against mistakes, danger, or evil thoughts. There may be endless counting, the compulsion to do certain things over and over again, checking and re-checking of gas jets, locks, faucets, rituals in food, dress, excretion, and evacuation, excessive washing of hands, etc. Compulsions, like anxieties, have some protective aspects to them. Repeated acts of a penitential or conciliatory character may appear in elderly people as a result of or as a protection against erratic, hostile, or vindictive fantasies which arouse guilt in them.

Any attempt to stop these compulsive acts may arouse acute and intolerable anxiety. It must be recognized that these symptoms constitute a last-ditch effort on the part of the individual to ward off complete disintegration. The attack, therefore, should be directed at the environment and not at the symptoms themselves. The treatment of symptoms should be attempted only by a skilled therapist who is thoroughly familiar with psychodynamics and aware of the possible dangers involved in treatment.

Hysterical Neuroses

Such neuroses are not too common in the later years. The classical hysterical picture of the giving-up of function of a part of the body, such as in hysterical paralysis, blindness or deafness, so that the rest of the organism can continue to function unimpaired is relatively rare in the elderly. What one does see is a form of exaggeration of minor physical symptoms which may be present.

Sexual Behavior

Studies uniformly agree that proper health and proper environment (i.e., availability of partners and, thus, sanction by society) are the most important factors for continued activity of sexual intercourse. This, of course, means that an essential or fundamental fit between behavior and environment exists. When such a fit does not exist, it is brought about by changing behavior to fit the environment or by changing the environment to fit the habitual or accustomed mode of behavior.

Whether environment or behavior will be changed to attain this fit depends upon the kind of organism, its developmental level, and other circumstances. As a general principle, it may be said that the organism will modify its immediately given environment to suit itself to the extent it is capable of doing so. Thus, there is a relationship between the state of the organism and its "docility in the face of environmental restrictions," as phrased by Lawton (2).

The more competent the individual is, in terms of health, intelligence, ego strength, and social role performance, the less will be the proportion of behavior variance attributed to objects or conditions around him. With a high degree of competence, he will rise above or bend the environment to suit his needs. However, reduction in competence or deprivation of status heightens his behavioral dependence on external conditions and social organization.

In old age a person's competence—physical, mental, social—is reduced, and he becomes more dependent on the environment. To attain the fit with his environment, he engages in a continuous process of behavior change. This does not mean that he never tries to alter the circumstances about him or never succeeds in doing so. It simply means that environmental change takes place infrequently and to a lesser degree than the frequency and degree that behavior is changed to suit the environment.

No one seems to want to touch the older person. Very few seek physical contact with them. Yet there seem to be instinctual and acquired needs for contactual relationships which are sought by all living organisms. We are all too ready to touch and even caress and pat the young, the cat or the dog, but not the aged. Our physical encounters with them are perfunctory, with no warmth or conviction behind them.

Theirs is a psychological hunger that usually remains ungratified. If sensory organs of the skin of the old become dull, as they so often do, it is as if this were in response to an anticipated deprivation. There is no need to feel, if feelings are to be denied. It is an unspoken grievance that needs to be redressed.

In the absence of opportunity for direct sexual gratification, the need for sexual expression may indeed take on many forms. Without thinking of regressive maneuvers related to dynamic formulations of oral, anal, and phallic preoccupation, we should take into consideration the sublimated and socially acceptable expressions such as touch, or tactile contact, which in the younger adult may be acceptable and natural but in the older person is looked upon with curiosity, and often with suspicion and disapproval. The sick old man who reaches out a feeble hand to touch the young female nurse is an "old fool making a pass." The sick younger man with the same gesture may also be making a pass, but he, of course is no "fool." The aged man who reaches out to touch and pat the smooth, inviting skin of a youngster becomes the prototype of the dangerous molester despite the fact that statistically he ranks low on that scale. Nevertheless, it is quite true that the courts may be more lenient with the aged and ascribe their behavior to confusion. (The number of aged molesters is quite negligible when compared to the number of young adult molesters.)

The sexual expressions of the elderly are numerous and diverse. Chronological age is no barrier to the continued sexual life of the old when opportunity and sanction are present. Difficulties arise when, in the absence of the above, sublimated activities are also denied them. Much too often their feeble efforts to establish contactual relationships are misinterpreted and rejected, forcing the old to regressed behavior. Not only must this be understood and placed in proper perspective, but the overt sexual acting out on the part of the elderly must also be understood. In the wake of biological deficits and in the waning moments of one's influence over one's environment, reestablishment of mastery may take on the form of overt sexual acts and aggression.

MANAGEMENT

Remedial measures for all of these difficulties can be gratifying. One must make due allowances for the reduced vigor, agility, and learning capacity of the individual. Beyond that, therapy can be conducted along the lines of therapy at any age level. The skilled therapist who knows the dynamics involved has to be more active and more direct than with other age groups, for the exigencies of time demand shorter methods. This holds as true for therapy directed at the level of personal conflict of insecurity and of rebellion as it does for therapy directed at attitudes, at manipulation of the environment, at social rehabilitation, and so on.

In dealing with the rehabilitation of the mentally ill among the aged, it must be borne in mind that all human beings are to be treated as individuals. While there are character traits and human experiences common to most men and women, the most invariable feature of human beings is their variability. There are no two persons with precisely the same fingerprints, much less any two with exactly the same mind. It is the variance in life experience and in personality, the differences in nuance, which dictate an individual approach to each person. This truth compounds, of course, the difficulties encountered in the treatment of the mentally ill. At the same time, however, it multiplies the challenge and interest of those engaged in rehabilitation.

The question as to what type of therapy is to be employed in treating the older patient is dependent on a number of factors. First of all, one should assess the physical state of the patient, in order to determine how much the aging organism will be able to take. Secondly, one must evaluate the suitability of the individual for therapy from the viewpoint of his earlier adaptation and maladjustments, his capacity for establishing a workable relationship with the therapist, and the degree to which these characteristics are modifiable. Lastly, it is important to determine whether the presenting symptomatology is something new in the life of the individual or whether it is a continuation of a long-existing neurotic personality structure. Obviously, all of these determinations require the services of a trained individual. It is the psychiatrist's responsibility to decide as to the type of treatment to be instituted and who is to do the therapy. When therapy is not directly conducted or supervised by a trained psychiatrist, the following techniques should be of help as general guidelines.

Allow the patient to express himself, to talk about himself and his difficulties. Impatience will be interpreted by the patient as a rejection which cannot be tolerated. The attitude should be one of respectful attention and thoughtful consideration despite the fact that the same problem may arise and be discussed over and over again. Empathy—the ability to place oneself in the patient's place without ever identifying with him, not sympathy, is of the essence. The older person does not wish the other person to sympathize with and pity him. He craves respect which will help him to bolster his self-esteem. An insincere approach will be easily discerned by the patient and is apt to lead to insurmountable barriers.

Allay the anxiety and insecurity of the aging patient insofar as this is possible. This requires of the helping person a genuine fondness for the elderly and a willingness to help them. One must, however, be tactful, for the elderly are proud and do not wish to betray their weakness. Therefore, they should be allowed to gratify their dependency needs in a manner that will not make them feel that they are leaning on another person. A condescending, patronizing attitude on the part of the supporting figure will only accentuate feelings of inadequacy and insecurity.

Patients should be helped into activities which will tend to enhance their attractiveness—physical and mental. When an individual is young, he may be physically attractive. When that fails him, achievement in some field of endeavor or continued productivity on a job can enhance the person's attractiveness. For to be wanted increases one's self-esteem and, as a by-product, one's value to others. At the same time, the elderly must be helped in accepting gracefully a curtailment of activities, when necessary, into something meaningful and gratifying rather than merely out of a job and thus out of life. Plan their daily activity with them, and not for them, when life would otherwise become empty. In addition to knowing the patient's own personal and family situation, one should become thoroughly acquainted with the facilities that the community, the church, and social agencies have established for the elderly population. At times the older person needs literally to be led by the hand to participate. The mere pointing out of the presence of such facilities may not be enough.

Finally, one must bring an optimistic attitude to the psychiatric techniques used in working with older people. One must not get too easily discouraged. One should leave the patient at the end of any interview with the feeling that the contact was a gratifying experience and that something had been accomplished during that hour. Only an understanding of and due consideration for the validity of the feelings of the older person can and will accomplish the desired results.

REFERENCES

1. KLUCKHOHN, F. 1963. Dominant and variant values orientation. In: Kluckhohn, C., and Murray, H. A. (Eds.) *Personality in Nature, Society and Culture.* New York: Alfred A. Knopf.
2. LAWTON, P. 1968. The ecology of social relationships in housing for the elderly. *Gerontologist,* 8:108-115.
3. WEINBERG, J. 1970. Environment, its language and the aging. *J. Am. Geriat. Soc.,* 18, No. 9, 681-686.

11

FAMILY PSYCHOPATHOLOGY

JOHN G. HOWELLS, M.D., F.R.C.PSYCH., D.P.M.

Director, The Institute of Family Psychiatry,
The Ipswich Hospital, Ipswich, England

INTRODUCTION

The aged, like others, are the product of families. From birth to old age the individual is the object of swaying fortunes within this small group, the family. Old age brings no lessening of the family influence and no safety from the perils of its emotional climate. Age brings change—psychological, biological, physical, neurological, and social—but it takes place within a framework, the family, that remains essentially the same. Those changes that produce the aging process have been described elsewhere. Here we will concentrate on the essential framework within which they take place—the family group.

Family psychiatry has as its central tenet that the functional unit in clinical practice be the family rather than the individual. The family, rather than the individual, is the patient. This approach has thrown new light on the psychopathology of emotional states. The individual is seen as one element in a field of emotional forces. Any event in this transaction of forces affects every other element in the system. Each element is a part of the whole, continually responding, advantageously or disadvantageously, to the ebb and flow of the tides of family emotion. The flow of family emotion brings safety or danger, benefit or loss, health or ill health. The individual reflects the changing nature of the forces besetting him. The individual in his early years is especially vulnerable to noxious emotional forces. Hurt here may leave permanent deficit, susceptibilities to special stresses, and a handicap that can worsen with ill fortune or improve with good fortune. The changing fortunes of time play throughout the years on any initial strengths or weaknesses. At last the individual reaches old age. But respite is not yet. To his dying day he has to contend with the still active elemental family life.

In old age are to be found two areas of pathology:

(1) That which he brings with him from earlier years;

(2) That which is the product of the senium.

Naturally the first must be added to, or will react with, the second. The pathology that concerns the psychiatrist is:

(1) That which springs from damage of the encephalon—encephalonosis displaying so-called "mental" symptoms (in truth organic);

(2) That which springs from damage to the psyche—psychonosis that displays so-called "emotional" symptoms (truly psychic). We shall see in the span of the clinical examples that follow, how encephaonosis and psychonosis react the one on the other.

In clinical practice it can also be seen how in the evaluation of pathology there has been much neglect of psychonosis. As in other age groups, psychic pathology emits from the destructive effects of algo-psychic forces or vectors that come from other psychic sources—other people; these other people are, most commonly, members of the family circle.

Turning for a moment, perhaps for respite, into the world of literature, we can find a number of excellent accounts that exemplify the statements above. None is more starkly clear than that of Shakespeare's description of Lear's "madness" which was no madness at all. Lear displayed an advanced dementia of old age, but he was also beset by family ill fortune that established his psychonosis and the anguish arising from this killed him. I will follow Shakespeare in his account.

Lear's decaying physical powers, dementia resulting from senility, are recognized and described by Shakespeare. He says that not only can we expect the "imperfections" of Lear's "rash" personality, but in addition the "unruly waywardness" of old age.

> "The best and soundest of his time hath been
> but rash; then must we look from his age to
> receive not alone the imperfections of
> long-engraffed condition, but therewithal
> the unruly waywardness that infirm and
> choleric years bring with them."
>
> (King Lear, I, i).

Dementia leads to loss of judgment and thus to rash decisions, such as Lear's banishment of his most affectionate daughter and by so doing placing himself in the power of his other unscrupulous children. This loss of judgment, too, is depicted:

> "Oh, Lear, Lear, Lear!
> Beat at this gate that let thy folly in
> And thy dear judgement out!"
>
> (King Lear, I, iv).

One of the cardinal symptoms of dementia is the loss of memory, especially for recent events, and thus inability to recognise people. The King can take the Fool, Edgar and Kent for high justices.

Lear:	"I'll see their trial first. Bring in their evidence.
(To Edgar):	Thou robed man of justice, take thy place.
(To the Fool):	And thou, his yoke-fellow of equity, Bench by his side.
(To Kent):	You are o' th' commission, Sit you too."

> (King Lear, III, vi)

Lear himself can half perceive his disability and has a feeling that he should be able to recognise those about him and remember recent events, which escape him, like blurred images from a dream.

> "I fear I am not in my perfect mind.
> Methinks I should know you, and know this man;
> Yet I am doubtful; for I am mainly ignorant
> What place this is; and all the skill I have
> Remembers not these garments; nor I know not
> Where I did lodge last night."
>
> (King Lear, IV, vii).

Defect of memory and disorientation in time and place lead to confusion—well portrayed here by Shakespeare. Lear's thoughts become incoherent. In his agitated mind images come and go in quick succession with no link between them. He suffers from illusions, misinterpreted phenom-

ena. He imagines himself to be recruiting men for his army and offers enlisting money (press money), he comments on a man handling his bow as
if he were employed to scare crows. Then he thinks he sees a mouse and
wants to catch it with a piece of cheese. In the next instant he grabs his
gauntlet and offers to fight a giant, whilst calling for the foot soldiers with
their brown painted halberds (brown bills). The image of arrow returns
to his mind, and he sees it flying like a bird to the centre of the target
(the clout).

> "There's your press-money. That fellow handles
> his bow like a crowkeeper; draw me a clother's
> yard. Look, look, a mouse! Peace, peace; this
> piece of toasted cheese will do't. There's my
> gauntlet; I'll prove it on a giant. Bring up
> the brown bills. O, well flown, bird! i' the
> clout, i' the clout—hewgh!"
>
> (King Lear, IV, vi).

But when the end comes it is emotion that kills him, not old age. The
emotion released by the death of his beloved Cordelia overwhelms him
and he raves, unable to accept this last terrible blow.

> "No, no, no life!
> Why should a dog, a horse, a rat have life,
> And thou no breath at all?
> Thou'lt come no more,
> Never, never, never, never, never!"
>
> (King Lear, V, iii).

When death comes for him it is a welcome release, as Kent knows when
he stops Edgar's efforts to revive him.

> ". . . O, let him pass! He hates him
> That would upon the rack of this tough world
> Stretch him out longer."
>
> (King Lear, V, iii).

So the old king dies, killed not by his venerable age, but by an emotion,
grief.

Esquirol would have listed grief under the heading of "moral causes."
In his book (1) he presents two tables, one of physical and one of "moral"

causes of dementia. The highest single aetiological factor in the list of physical causes is "progress of age." An analysis of 40 cases for "moral" causes reads as follows:

Disappointed affection	5
Frights	7
Political shocks	8
Disappointed ambition	3
Want	5
Domestic Trials	12

Lear suffered them all, including "want" in his aimless wanderings. But like less exalted mortals, it was his "domestic trials," the damaging family relationships, more than any other single factor, that affected him deeply enough to lead to his death (3).

This damaging family climate now requires further consideration. What are the damaging noxious vectors that arise within it, what damage results, how is this field to be explored, how can the ill-effects of family life be ameliorated?

FAMILY PSYCHOPATHOLOGY AND THE AGED

Family psychiatry demonstrates how algo-psychic vectors arise from clashing attitudes within the family. Painful blows are dealt to the "idea of self" of a family member. But these clashing attitudes do not spring only from the climate of the present family. The most fundamental spring from the preceding families of the two adult family members. Each family member is an epitome of the preceding family from which he springs, carrying with him a psychic self uniquely formed by it, and with the capacity to agree or disagree with the epitomes of other family climates which it will meet in its course through time. From the preceding families come pathological attitudes, coping devices and the indicators of pathology, the symptoms. The climate of the present family depends upon the complementarity of the two preceding families.

Discussion of the family and the aged will be accompanied by a case description that will serve to illustrate many facets of psychopathology, investigation and treatment. A lady of 70 (Mrs. S) presented at the Geriatric In-take Clinic of the Institute of Family Psychiatry, referred for a slow response to convalescence following an embolism in the chest. Her physician discerned that she was depressed and sought assistance for her. It emerged, almost at once, that the embolism had followed a quarrel with her husband in the course of which he begun his habitual angry response to frustration by banging the table. She was admitted to hospital as an emergency because of embolism of the chest. The old lady said "I knew something must give." Her grasp of the significance of emotional events was out of the ordinary and was accompanied by a rare understanding of their effect on her somatic state.

This case history illustrates the clashing attitudes now, their basis in the past, and the aggravating additional stresses.

The Major Clash Now

The old lady gives a clear account of it. Long experience in the up-bringing of her nine children and the many vicissitudes of their families allows her to clearly see her own situation. The last child leaves home, her husband retires, they move to a small apartment, no longer can either deny the mutual disharmony that submersion in child care and long hours of work have allowed them to ignore over the years. I quote from the type-script of the interview:

> . . . after having a family of nine to look after, all of a sudden, my husband and I were left on our own. . . .

> . . . all of a sudden I seemed left with my husband and everything seemed at a dead end. I was easily getting depressed.

> . . . I got a nose bleed . . . well then I have had about three or four since I have been home. Little things gets on my nerves, and if he gets riled with me, he bangs on the table. And I say there is no need to do that. I said "we are in this room. Don't shout, I can't put up with it." When I was younger I should have shouted back perhaps. But my husband is very erratic tempered if you know what I mean.

Again:

> . . . if I upset him he flies up and if I say anything. I might say "well what have I had to look forward to this week, just sitting there looking at you and the four walls. You don't even walk out with me."

And again:

> I conceal my feelings you see and they boil up inside me because I know if I say too much to him he will upset me, you see what I mean.

The old lady can see the process. She has insight. But insight does not solve problems. Insight is never enough. The danger is considerable. Her nose bleeds with stress. She has had a clot in the chest. Members of her family have died with thrombosis as we shall see. She makes the links. She feels in danger when the husband bangs the table.

The Past Makes the Present

The old lady's problem is acute now. But its roots lie in the past—and beyond into the family: a coming together; a long courtship in the days of the depression; she moves away to a better job; he saves his pennies and calls for her; she has already forgotten him; but her father exerts pressure —the boy is respectable; she accepts the father's values—not her own; so the past dictates the choice of her husband; the marriage; the quick disillusionment, as his other, nonrespectable, attitudes emerge; the birth of the first child is marred as the product of him; but she loves children and accepts them as a part of herself and her family and not his; the long submersion in children begins.

She speaks herself of the marriage:

> . . . if he had been a bad man I wouldn't have married him. It was just that I think that at the time I got married, I didn't really want to get married, if you can understand my meaning. At 21 I would have eagerly married. But by the time the six years was round I regretted it. I didn't want it and four months afterwards I was very unhappy.

> . . . He treated me very well. But I just didn't want him enough for anything to happen at all between us. I had a good job in London, and wanted to go back to it, you see. But I had been with him so long, that Dad said it wasn't fair me keeping him so long, and just end up like this. So I really married through Dad, if you can understand my meaning. . . .

> . . . I liked kiddies, but by the time I married I didn't. . . . I became pregnant right away, you see. . . . It made me miserable.

But the past goes beyond the marriage—to his family. From them he gathered the attitudes she found so difficult to tolerate.

The lack of feeling:

> . . .when we lost a dear one in our family, my brother at 22 and my sister at 26, I really felt it for months after. Whereas my husband lost a sister in hospital and he lost a brother suddenly a few weeks ago and he just carries on the same!

And the quick temper that she fears and finds dangerous:

> . . . His family are rather quick tempered, very quick tempered. As a family they soon fly. He bangs on the table if something upsets him. But of course he doesn't see that when I tell him.

The quick temper again, coming from his family, and its dangers confirmed by experience:

> Yes, he is very firey. So was his mother and his sister, who died with a stroke. She died in a temper, she had had a quarrel just before she died. I remember that.

The husband, if consulted, and he must be consulted, would point to the sexual frustration. She uses the age-old defence mechanism—illness. She cannot give herself to him in mutual enjoyment. The children are to be desired for themselves alone and bring her the support and interest she needs. She yields after a long siege.

> I just think he comes to bed the nights he wants me. That doesn't worry him. I don't want him. I just don't want him and I told him so. I think it is my general health you see. I can't put up with it. That is telling you frankly. I can't put up with it and go as long as I dare go and then he sort of goes up in the air a mile.

Special Stresses

Old age brings its own special stresses as does any age period. As the years go by, cherished friends and relatives are lost—by death or distance. In a large family losses are inevitable and each brings its grief and strain. The ultimate strain is to be left with a disharmonious spouse.

The treasured daughter who died of multiple sclerosis. The tension from her own family behind it. Does the old lady hint at a psychopathology of multiple sclerosis?

> . . . I found within the last four years I have had rather a lot of trouble. You see, I have brought up nine children. Four years ago I lost a daughter, who was very dear to me, with multiple sclerosis.

> The one with multiple sclerosis, her husband wasn't at all good to her. No; and the doctors at the hospital told me that it was mainly through him and his women that had brought it on.

> . . . I think he broke her spirit really. I could see it, you see. . . .

Then the daughter who went far away to Australia. A very special daughter. Not weak and needing protection, but her "right hand," a support, a replica of a loved mother, a replica of her family and not his:

> She had evidently spoken about going to the others, her brothers and sisters. She hadn't mentioned it to me because I think she knew that it would upset me. You see she was the fifth child born. Therefore, she was my right hand as I told her husband when he married her at nineteen. I said 'you are taking my right hand' and she was the living image of my mother to look at at birth.

The loss is remembered to the day. No clouding of memory here. But a cerebral thrombosis that she so fears could bring a terrible toll to her cerebral functions.

> *Dr.*: And then, when this daughter went to Australia, when was this Mrs. S?
> *Mrs. S*: Oh, it did cut me. It will be two years come the 27th June. This year she will have gone two years.

This daughter spares something for the old man too. For both, there is the compensation of a letter and the satisfaction that all is well.

> Well, we have got a daughter in Australia. My husband reads and all his books seem to be about Australia. She emigrated. That was another pill for me. She had three lovely children that we adored and of course that sort of, well, she went in the June, and that is when I started going down hill. It played on my mind you see. Of course, with the other girl I said well it was God's choosing and I had to let her go. But you were going on your own accord and I may never see you again and that upset me, you know. But I am getting over that because she writes and they are very comfortable and very happy.

Then the last and youngest daughter leaves:

> But the youngest daughter is in Germany. She has been there over a year. Her husband is in the Army and I am worried about her. You see, she is having a baby any day. So maybe that is what has made me depressed the last few days again, if you can understand my meaning. . . .

The last loss leaves her alone with husband—the greatest stress of all.

> . . . four weddings in two years and then all of a sudden my husband and I were there alone after having so much to do. My mind was occupied all the while you see when I had the family.

Experiential Psychopathology

It should be noted that in this account of psychopathology we have been concerned with real events. No attempt has been made to interpret in the light of any psychopathological dogma or school of symbolism. The facts speak for themselves and need no interpretation. The lives of the aged are real. A chain of real events leads to pathology. The life as experienced is what counts. Thus, this approach is termed experiential psychopathology.

FAMILY DIAGNOSIS

This is based on two main questions:

(1) What are the indicators of dysfunction in the individual?
(2) What process in the family sets up the dysfunction?

Elucidating the Indicators

The steps are:

(1) The investigation starts with the presenting indicator. In Mrs. S's case, it was the embolism in the chest.

(2) Then comes a history-taking that allows the geriatric patient to reveal any other subjective indicators of dysfunction, traditionally called the symptoms. These are organic and psychic.

Mrs. S's account fills in the picture, clearly reveals psychic as well as organic pathology and hints at the aetiology within the family. She recalls husband banging on the table, the somatic result, and goes on:

> . . . I suppose that was what caused the terrible pain. They took me away that night. I don't remember it, only waking up in the hospital, you see, the next day. So they must have put me under sedation. Anyway, I was in terrific pain when they took me away in the ambulance. . . .

She has another psychosomatic indicator, her nose bleeds. She knows why, and she fears the implications.

> I said, if you hadn't have upset me, my nose wouldn't bleed, you see.
>
> Sometimes when I get upset my nose bleeds and it worried me because my father died suddenly with cerebral haemorrhage, you see, and he was younger than I am now.

Her account also soon reveals psychic indicators. She is, of course, an organism that reacts as a whole.

> . . . .my whole trouble is nerves. I so easily get upset.

Her terminology, perforce, is simple—"nerves" she calls her psychonosis. But she can see the link with her physical weakness and her attacks of tremor.

> . . . and my nerves got me so low that I was too weak to walk even. . . . The least little thing upsets me and then I shake and then I can't control it. . . .

(3) Mrs. S's account, revealing though it is, must be supplemented by a careful questioning based on a form designed to reveal any dysfunction in the somatic or psychic fields.

(4) Lastly, Mrs. S. is examined for signs, objective to the examiner, of psychic or somatic dysfunction.

(5) If necessary, the above must be supplemented by special somatic or psychic diagnostic procedures. Mrs. S's embolism would certainly call for this.

All the above has been a formal examination and now ends by formulating a diagnosis from the data collected. Briefly, in Mrs. S's case it could be termed "acute psychonosis presenting with embolism of the chest." This can be extended by listing all the somatic and psychic indicators. We are now in the era of somato-psychic medicine and no investigation of any patient is complete without a global assessment that includes both psychic and somatic fields.

The Family Process

The above tells us in what way Mrs. S dysfunctions. But it does not tell us *why* she dysfunctions. Thus, we move now from the individual to the family. The other family members are drawn in, they meet as a group and the procedure of family group diagnosis takes place.

The first part of the investigation was directive; this part is nondirective. The material tumbles out from the family, is analysed under the framework of the 15 family dimensions (2), and the family encouraged to discuss neglected areas.

Mrs. S told us a great deal which was reported under family psychopathology earlier in this chapter. But this is a one-member slanted view of the family. Husband must also be seen, possibly alone initially and then later together with his wife. This must be done with care—a clumsy interview could result in the counterpart of table banging by husband—and this is dangerous to Mrs. S (and perhaps to the husband also).

Once the family process is revealed, a family diagnosis is made, e.g., in the S family a brief formulation might be, "Disharmony in the marital area of the family resulting in acute episodes of family psychonosis superimposed on a state of chronic family psychonosis, and presenting with embolism in one family member." A longer account could tell of the contribution from both preceding families (husband's and wife's families) that led to disharmony in the present family and its course through time to the present. The procedure of family diagnostic together with systematic investigation is discussed in greater detail in *Principles of Family Psychiatry* (2).

FAMILY THERAPY

The above term is used in the sense of treatment of the family by any procedure. Certain principles are basic:

(1) The whole family, in this case Mr. and Mrs. S, must be treated.

(2) The family must be treated in both somatic and psychic areas. Somatic therapy is enormously important, and in Mrs. S's case it was life saving. Drug therapy may be an essential part of psychic therapy also. But with care in the aged, as Mrs. S relates:

> . . . I took one (tablet) and before that had been down a half hour I was like this you see (showing a tremor of the hands). It was overacting the nerves. They were too strong. Each time I had only got it down about a half an hour and I would be like this, the chair and bed would shake and I would have to go and lie on the bed in the next room. . . .

(3) Psychic therapy can be in terms of family psychotherapy or vector therapy, or both.

Family psychotherapy can be applied in three ways:

(1) *Depth psychotherapy* aimed at changing in many ways the essential disharmonious situation in the family. It involves dealing with the effects of the two preceding families (the husband's and wife's families). A number of factors may exclude this possibility: (a) it is immensely time consuming; (b) the number of psychiatrists available for this work could meet the needs of only a few of the aged. Unskilled psychiatric help is danger-

ous, just as bad surgery is worse than no surgery; (c) it may be difficult to justify expenditure of the limited resources when the span of life to run is so short and so many families with young children are denied help; (d) old people do not respond easily, as the process has gone on for so long.

(2) *Focal psychotherapy*. Here small parts of the total situation are dealt with. Usually these are the major attitudes that cause friction in the family, e.g. Mrs. S's reluctance to have intercourse with Mr. S. In the aged, even obvious situations are sometimes difficult to resolve, as they have been so fixed with time. Behind Mrs. S's reluctance to have sexual intercourse is her distaste for Mr. S and that has the deepest of roots.

(3) *Supportive psychotherapy*. This is based on the rationale that certain measures have a tonic effect on the psyche—hope, encouragement, praise, appreciation, sharing of dangers, affection, etc. This should be an essential part of any contact with the aged—even for somatic therapy alone.

Vector therapy has a different rationale. It is based on the observable fact that within and without families there is a pattern of emotional communications—of vectors. Some of these emotional interactions bring pain, anguish and destruction. Some are beneficial and constructive. The aim of vector therapy is to analyse the pattern of interaction within and without the family, to bring relief to the family. Vector therapy is effective only if the evaluation of the interactions is correct. We must know before we change. Are we right in our evaluation that Mr. and Mrs. S are disharmonious together—or does someone else intervene to create disharmony for his or her own purposes? Thus family group diagnosis is an essential preliminary. Careful work in time reveals a basic disharmony between Mr. and Mrs. S. Once the pattern of the emotional vectors is clear, the family interview is then employed to reach a degree of rapport between therapist and family which makes change possible. The family must accept its handicaps with insight, be free of guilt and able to see change as an opportunity for relief. Insight, time, patience, lack of blame are the ingredients for success. Coercion should never enter the scene.

Mr. and Mrs. S have employed vector therapy with success for years. They have simply not met, since they have contrived things so that work has been his abiding passion and the children hers. Life has been tolerable. Time has wrecked the pattern of vector therapy—both the children and work have gone. A new pattern is required, so that the marital interaction operates for as brief a time as possible. Mrs. S as the healthiest of the two (an evaluation supported by her wonderful insight) is already groping for a new pattern, as we shall see in her remarks. Mrs. S is passionate in her need:

I do, I do, just now I do. I need something more than just sitting looking at my husband all the afternoons and evenings.

Mrs. S tries. But surely we can do better than this.

Yes, the only outing I have been having is to the hospital. I have been going to the hospital for the blood pricks, you see, and that has made an outing you see.

Vaunted welfare agencies have not seen fit to help. But at least she has not been presented an analysis! A little practical help instead. . . . Mrs. S reaches for it from the good neighbours rather than the "welfare."

I have asked Mrs. Banks from over the road to come in for a cup of tea. He says well what did you do that for? I said, well, I want company. He said, well, why don't you go over to hers? Well, Mrs. Banks said come over any time you like you see.

The neighbour helped a bit but it is not enough. She attempts a more radical solution.

> Mrs. S: . . . Last year I went to—to work in the canteen serving the young ladies with their meals. I did that for just three or four days a week, if you can understand my meaning, for three weeks. Tuesday, Wednesday, Thursday, Friday, for three consecutive weeks. But then I gave it up because he didn't like it.
>
> Dr.: How did you enjoy those twelve days?
>
> Mrs. S: I was very happy when I went to work.
>
> Dr.: And when you had those twelve days when you were working, you really enjoyed it, did you?
>
> Mrs. S: Yes, I was much better. He said so himself. He told his brothers that I was much better. I did that to forget about my daughter and what she went through, you see. . . .

Mrs. S, weak though she is, in her dire need reaches again for the solution that helped for a brief glowing moment.

I have thought of it again. But at the present stage that I am with my legs I can't get a little job like I had last year when I felt myself getting low. . . .

She tried in another way but failed:

> *Mrs. S:* I could easily write a book. I have always wanted to. I did start to, but when I was ill I got so low that I thought I was just going to fade, you see. So I gave it up and put it on the fire.
>
> *Dr.:* Do you paint?
>
> *Mrs. S:* At school I did. I was the best painter in the school. I have painted since.

So now Mrs. S attends the day hospital to write (about life with nine children) and to paint (she loves to paint children).

She likes the principles of vector therapy, as a long practitioner. The husband has come to see merit in it also. Life begins to glow. And like an old Druidess she puts it all down to the weather.

> *Dr.:* . . . We can help you to have a fuller life. That is the best medicine we can give you.
>
> *Mrs. S:* I think so too. I definitely think so too. It is a beautiful day today, I think you do feel better, everyone does. Even normal people feel better when the sun shines.

CONCLUSION

Psychonosis, with frequent and severe somatic concomitants, is a common feature of old age, as in any other age group. The aged are not immune from family influence and the trauma that often arises in the family. History-taking must embrace a global psychic and somatic evaluation not only of the individual but also of the family. Therapy must be based upon a family evaluation. Psychotherapy may sometimes be indicated. But help is usually best met by vector therapy together with somatic measures as appropriate. These last seem to be in accord with Shakespeare's management of Lear.

At first the vector therapy:

> "O, sir, you are old;
> Nature in you stands on the very verge
> Of her confine. You should be rul'd and led
> By some discretion that discerns your state
> Better than you yourself."
>
> (King Lear, II, iv).

And then the physician prescribes one of the many "simples" (drugs), that will induce sleep and give him rest from the anguish that wears him down.

> "Our foster-nurse of nature is repose,
> The which he lacks; that to provoke in him
> Are many simples operative, whose power
> Will close the eye of anguish."
>
> (King Lear, IV, iv).

REFERENCES

1. ESQUIROL, J. E. D. 1845. *Mental Maladies*. Philadelphia: Lea and Blanchard. (Reprinted in 1965 by Hafner Publishing Co., New York and London.)
2. HOWELLS, J. G. 1975. *Principles of Family Psychiatry*. New York: Brunner/Mazel.
3. HOWELLS, J. G., and OSBORN, M. L. 1973. King Lear—A case of senile dementia. *Hist. Med.*, 5, 2, 30.

12

PSYCHOSOMATIC STATES

Asser Stenback, M.D., M.A.

Professor, Department of Psychiatry
University of Helsinki, Finland

INTRODUCTION

The prevailing view considers old persons as different from middle-aged, whereas the accumulating evidence of gerontological research asserts that the aged are more similar than commonly believed. When dealing with psychological and social aspects of physical disease in high age—psychosomatics in a wide sense—the crucial question is whether the facts and hypotheses established concerning psychosomatic aspects in adults are true also about the aged. This question cannot be answered without reviewing those biological, psychological, and social aspects of aging that may have bearing upon the psychosomatic reaction tendency. Only some pertinent facts will be touched upon.

RELEVANT ASPECTS OF THE PROCESS OF AGING

Biological Aspects

The physiological mechanisms used by psychological factors in the etiology of physical disease are the *autonomic nervous system* and the *hormonal system*. In old age a marked decrease in excitability of the cerebral cortex, hypothalamus, and the reticular formation is observed (36). Likewise, the synthesis of neural transmitters—acetylcholine, norepinephrine, and serotonin—is lowered. These changes imply reduced influence of higher brain regions upon lower ones, including the autonomic system, and upon peripheral organs. This more "sluggish" reaction is to some degree compensated for by a slower inactivation of norepinephrine at the receptor cells, which is the neurochemical explanation for the well-known fact that older people have a prolonged recovery period following stress (89). All these findings indicate a decrease in the general activity and adaptation potential of the autonomic nervous system.

According to present evidence, no essential age changes take place in the hormonal system—with the exception of the gonads. Contrary to previous findings, there is no essential decline in the thyroid and adrenal cortex, nor in the hypothalamic-pituitary function (37). In the peripheral organs, the reduced neural sensitivity is compensated for by increased sensitivity to hormones (which is a part explanation for the well-known observation that the aged react more strongly, e.g. to tricyclic antidepressives) (36).

Psychological Aspects

Among the numerous interesting results of the biological study of aging is the observation that many biological changes in old age are not due to the aging process but to diseases of old age, e.g., atherosclerosis. Another relevant observation is the fact that differences between healthy aged and healthy adults are surprisingly small in many respects (9). These findings concerning *biological aging* have implications for psychological functions.

The stereotype of the aged as more or less demented cannot be upheld anymore. Different studies on dementia in high age have shown a ratio of at most one to ten. This points to a normal capacity for experience of strains and stresses, losses and frustrations in most aged. This normal intelligence level, however, does not imply that emotional reactivity and the cognitive appraisal of his life situation are the same in the elderly as in the adult. Some evidence indicates less intense emotional reactivity (21), contradicted by a study which showed higher anxiety scores in aged over 65 than in the age group of 45 to 65 (41). Higher frequency of chronic disease, more losses in personal relationships, e.g. widowhood, changes in social position, e.g. retirement and pre-retirement, and fact and feeling of approaching death are factors distinguishing the life situation of the elderly from that of the middle-aged. When the life situation is different, there are reasons to expect that the psychological make-up is different, too.

In two epidemiological field studies (5, 48), the high frequency of *depression* in old age was the most striking finding. Both studies found about 30 percent depressive persons in the aged population. This frequency is so high that the stereotype of the demented aged may be replaced by the depressed aged. There is a close relationship between depression and physical disease, to which more attention will be given in connection with the discussion of the "giving up-withdrawal" concept.

A striking difference between middle-aged and elderly persons can be observed in the prevalence of *Behavior Pattern A* described by Friedman and Rosenman (35) and found by them in higher frequency in patients with coronary heart disease. The mere enumeration of the most characteristic features suffices to convince that this behavior pattern is not as frequently present in the aged population as in the middle-aged. The authors described Behavior Pattern A as: " (1) an intense, sustained drive to achieve self-selected but usually poorly defined goals, (2) profound inclination and eagerness to compete, (3) persistent desire for recognition and advancement, (4) continuous involvement in multiple and divers functions constantly subject to time restrictions (deadlines), (5) habitual propensity to accelerate the rate of execution of many physical and mental functions, and (6) extraordinary mental and physical alertness." This behavior pattern is a *behavior* pattern and as such not a description of a particular personality. Behavior is always the outcome of biological, personality, and social factors. The different social situation of the aged, along with biological factors, suffices to account for the absence of Behavior Pattern A as a prevalent phenomenon in high age. Conversely, the fear of failure, rather than need for achievement, is characteristic of the aged, particularly the depressed aged. Eisdorfer (23) gives a vivid picture of the plight of the aged:

> "Younger individuals tend, by and large, to be achievement oriented; given the opportunity, they will strive. However, individuals of any age who have had experience with failure begin to fear this experience. With age, individuals become increasingly familiar with loss and failure—vision and hearing loss is common, illness becomes more common, retirement is experienced, children leave home, loved ones die. All of these factors contribute to an increased expectation and, indeed, fear of failure. Thus, many aged individuals may be accurately characterized as motivated by a tendency to avoid failure rather than to strive for success. In the balance, the cost of striving becomes too high for many; the benefits of success are less important than the impact of failure. Thus, the emotionally aroused older person may withdraw psychologically from a competitive situation."

This description is in many cases true, but if the attitude described becomes the general attitude to life, it is a *"giving up-withdrawal"* attitude and, as such, one of the main psychological causes of the higher frequency of physical disease in high age.

Social Aspects

As will be presented later in detail, there are three main psychological mechanisms in the development of psychosomatic disease: emotional arousal, sustained hyperactivity, and the giving up-withdrawal reaction. Pathogenic emotional arousal comprises mainly anxiety and aggression. The common source of intense prolonged anxiety is insecurity related to the future. Frequently, this insecurity arises from lack of subsistence and absence of dependable human relations. It falls to many aged to live isolated and without opportunity to get immediate help. Although old age pension systems have been built up during the last decades, the income so obtained does not always reach the subsistence level.

One of the most conspicuous differences between the social situation of the aged and that of the middle-aged is the relationship to work. The aged live in a leisure society which has replaced the work society. Sustained activity is not only not required anymore, it is even to a large extent impossible due to lack of social roles. Against popularly held belief, retirement mostly does not affect health in a harmful way (56, 85). Finding even 24.1 percent improvement of health since retirement, Ryser and Sheldon (75) suggested that the process of retirement relieves tension and reduces somatic symptoms despite transient anxiety-provoking situations.

These findings indicating no harmful impact of retirement upon health during the years immediately after retirement, however, say nothing about the long-range effects. Although the leisure society of the aged relieves him from sustained overactivity and its noxious sequels, the elderly may little by little begin to suffer from the enforced inactivity and the absence of social roles for the retired. When to this plight, due to macrosocial factors, bereavement of spouse, children, and friends is added (66), the effect may be a damaging increase in the giving up-withdrawal tendency. The giving up-withdrawal behavior is always an outcome of both personality tendencies and outer social reality. Eitner (24, 25) put forward the societal measures to be taken in order to build up a society in which the elderly may find outlets for his activity needs, and so avoid the *hypokinetoses* due to lack of physical and mental activity: obesity, hypertension, heart insufficiency, and others.

The *disengagement theory* (19) has aroused a lively discussion about the nature of the psychosocial aging process. Contrary to the *activity theory* of aging, the disengagement theory maintains that a gradual disengagement from the social world normally takes place with age. This implies that relinquishment of the work role of the middle-aged does not give rise to feelings of boredom and dejection, but is in accordance with inner needs of the elderly. Although recognizing particularly the heuristic value of the disengagement theory, most authors taking part in the debate have rejected the disengagement theory as a general theory of psychosocial aging (54). This is also in agreement with biological views of continuing activity and rest as prerequisites of physical well-being.

PSYCHOSOMATIC DISEASES

Although repeated warnings have been leveled against designation of some particular diseases as "psychosomatic," this usage has not disappeared. The reason for disapproval of the term "psychosomatic disease" is obvious: psychological and social factors are at work in all diseases; hence, allocation of some diseases to the group of psychosomatic seems not wholly justifiable. Nevertheless, some diseases, particularly those without infectious, toxic or physical injury in the etiology, have drawn the attention of psychosomatic research to such a degree that they stand out as psychosomatic. Somewhat arbitrarily, the following diseases have been sorted out for presentation: peptic ulcer, ulcerative colitis, bronchial asthma, rheumatoid arthritis, hyperthroidism, diabetes mellitus, essential hypertension, myocardial infarction, and stroke. A separate discussion will be given to atherosclerosis.

Peptic Ulcer

Peptic ulcer includes both gastric ulcer and duodenal ulcer. Although gastric ulcer tends to appear 5 to 10 years later than duodenal ulcer, the incidence of both types of peptic ulcer at age 60 and over is only about 5 percent of the total incidence (46, 78). Although lesions due to aging and atherosclerosis play a part in peptic ulcer in high age (78), there is, nevertheless, a great number of acute "stress ulcers" which at autopsy do not show induration and fibrosis characteristic of chronic ulcers (11).

Ulcerative Colitis

The frequency of ulcerative colitis is highest in the two first decades of life (26). Nevertheless, Paulley (68) reported acute cases of ulcerative colitis in elderly patients. These patients, who managed to live over 60 years without any symptoms of colitis, had personalities with sensitive character traits like those adult patients with ulcerative colitis described earlier (28) and fell ill in circumstances in which they had suffered the loss of an extremely important object relationship.

Bronchial Asthma

Bronchial asthma is so commonly regarded as a disease of the younger age groups that the diagnosis is reluctantly approached or missed in the older patient manifesting the symptoms for the first time (39). According to Tuft (87), asthma begins in 5 to 13 percent of persons more than 50 years old and in 2 percent of those more than 60 years. Although allergic factors are of progressively less importance in the older, asthma is the same disease in the old as in the young. Rees (62) found 78 percent of the precipitating factors in elderly patients to be psychological.

Rheumatoid Arthritis

Rheumatoid arthritis has a rather high prevalence in old age: 10 percent of all cases are 60 or over (27), but the incidence is low. Most cases begin in the age period of 40 to 55, while only about 5 percent fall ill after 60 years of age (10). In a study of 100 patients with rheumatoid arthritis, Rimón (73) did not find any differences between the few patients falling ill after 60 and the rest. One elderly patient got her arthritis after unemployment, another after the family home had to be sold. As to psychological factors in the etiology of rheumatoid arthritis, Rimón's main findings pointed to two types of the disease, one with slow onset and genetic disposition, the other with acute onset and psychodynamic conflict. Frequently, rheumatoid arthritis and osteoarthrosis (also called osteoarthritis) are likely to be intermingled. There is no evidence indicating psychosomatic correlations in osteoarthrosis, which is a common ailment in high age: after 60 years of age, 15 percent of men and 25 percent of women have symptoms.

Hyperthyroidism

Hyperthyroidism has for a long time been known as a disease which may develop in close connection with severe emotional stress. Nevertheless, conclusive evidence for hyperthyroidism as a psychosomatic disease is hard to get at. In a review paper, Mason (57) stated that inclusion of the pituitary-thyroid system in the psychoendocrine system is not yet possible, but neither can it be refuted. In spite of this lack of evidence, clinicians not biased against a psychosomatic etiology tend to regard hyperthyroidism as the outcome of a process in which long-standing emotional stress is an essential component. Dongier et al. (22) predicted the rate of thyroid secretion with reasonable accuracy from a psychodynamic assessment according to which higher secretion rates have to be found in patients characterized by early premature striving for independence, denial of hostility, tendency to get affection by compulsive doing for others, and feebleness of the defenses making for anxiety-proneness. As to the relation of hyperthyroidism and age, hyperthyroidism has its peak incidence between 20 and 60 years of age (93), whereas the incidence of diabetes mellitus is highest between 50 and 80 years (83). It is well known that the clinical picture of hyperthyroidism in high age is somewhat different, or "masked" (6, 92). The frequently found decrease in the metabolic rate is mainly due to decrease in metabolic mass, primarily because of reduction of the muscle tissue (34, 80).

Diabetes Mellitus

Diabetes mellitus is a disease with two main types of onset: one related to growth in childhood and adolescence, "growth-onset diabetes," the other beginning later in life, particularly after 50 years of age, called "maturity-onset diabetes." In East Germany about 75 percent of the patients with diabetes are 50 or over; 23.9 percent of all diabetes patients are past 70 (64). Diabetes mellitus is considered genetically due to a recessive gene. This does not preclude the possibility of emotional factors as contributive etiology. Epinephrine, which is secreted in times of fear and anxiety, inhibits insulin secretion (52). Growth hormone, corticosteroids, and thyroxine have the same effect. In a normal population the blood sugar increases with age, whereas no similar trend can be observed in plasma insulin (7). The destruction of pancreatic islets in the mostly severer growth onset diabetes is much more extensive than in maturity-onset diabetes. In the former there is insulin deficiency, whereas in the latter only the pancreatic reserve is decresed. As to etiology of diabetes mellitus, Hinkle (45) has in many clinical and experimental studies made the psychosomatic hypothesis trustworthy, further confirmed by Danowski (20) and Slawson et al. (82). This hypothesis is in accordance with the generally accepted view that all kinds of severe stress upon the body bring to light a diabetic state if a predisposition exists: high caloric intake, obesity, pregnancy, infection, hyperthyroidism, and others (92). According to Alexander (3), prolonged sympathetic activation chronically strains the carbohydrate regulatory mechanism until collapse occurs. Sometimes acute emotional stresses cause the onset of diabetes (20), but mostly these acute emotional factors are seen prior to acidosis and coma (45, 86).

Essential Hypertension

Essential hypertension is characteristically a disease of the latter part of life. The prevalence figures for the white population in United States at age 60 to 64 are as follows: systolic blood pressure above 150 mm hg in males 34.9 percent, and in females 39.8; diastolic blood pressure above 100 mm in males 14.9 percent and in females 14.9 (58). From age 40-45 to 60-64, the number of people with elevated blood pressure has doubled. Essential hypertension as a disease of the latter part of life does not imply that it begins in old age. On the contrary, the onset of hypertension after the age of 65 is unlikely (59).

Myocardial Infarction

Myocardial infarction, like stroke, in most cases develops on the basis of atherosclerosis. Although atherosclerosis is a prerequisite for coronary heart disease, additional pathogenic factors are at work. In their comprehensive survey on psychosomatics and epidemiology of myocardial infarction, Hahn et al. (38) stated that in the multifactorial etiology there is both an accumulation of *risk factors* during a long time and *acute events* producing the final infarction. As to risk factors, the Western Collaborative Group Study has brought up the well-known *Behavior Pattern A* described above (35). While giving some acknowledgement, the critics of the Behavior Pattern A maintain that Friedman and Rosenman's findings are valid only in patients belonging to the higher socioeconomic strata. Dividing coronary disease patients into subgroups by age, Miller (63) found statistically significant differences in behavior patterns between patients above 55 years (mean age 63) and below 55 (mean age 45). In a study of 100 patients with coronary heart disease and 113 patients without, all subjects being 65 or older, Brown and Ritzmann (12) reported more stress and competitive drive in the coronary patients, confirming the general finding of Friedman and Rosenman.

Stroke

Stroke is the common name for cerebrovascular disease due to hemorrhage, thrombosis, and embolism. Stroke is almost exclusively a disease of old age. In a Swedish hospital region, the percentage of stroke patients aged 60 and over was 81.0 (81), and of all deaths due to stroke, the portion of the same age group was 94 percent (51). Nobody will question the massive organic pathology in stroke, of which, in addition to atherosclerosis, two-thirds have arterial hypertension and 10 to 30 percent diabetes mellitus (33).

Nevertheless, the final blow causing the stroke may be an emotional conflict or other acute stress. Among 32 men with stroke (out of whom 22 were 60 years or older), Adler et al. (2) found "pressured" personality pattern in 30. These patients got the stroke mostly in a setting in which they were reacting with a feeling of anger, hopelessness, and sometimes shame when they felt they were not performing up to their own standards. This personality pattern and the life situation resemble those of the coronary. However, in spite of the common atherosclerotic basis of myocardial infarction and stroke, there are obvious differences. In a comparative study of these two conditions, Bull (13) drew attention to the following facts: myocardial infarction appears at younger age; the male/female ratio at the age of 40 is 10 to 1; no association between stroke and smoking has been observed. Is one reason the lack of sympathetic control of the cerebral vessels, unlike the coronary arteries?

Atherosclerosis

Atherosclerosis is the most prevalent and severe disease in old age. To many it appears so massively organic that, when discussing etiology, only genetic, toxic and like factors can be taken into consideration. When weighing the attempts to correlate atherosclerosis and psychological factors carried out by epidemiological methods, Heydén (44) concluded that the evidence is inadequate for establishing correlation. On the other hand, Russek (74) and Moses (65) took a stand in favour of psychological factors as significant determinants, along with a number of other factors. "Stress" is frequently mentioned as a risk factor in the literature.

For ethical reasons there is no possibility for using humans in long-term experimental studies. Animal studies have unequivocally proved that psychosocial factors can produce atherosclerotic changes. Henry and co-workers (42) exposed mice to six months of social confrontation leading frequently to vigorous fights. Significantly more atherosclerotic changes in heart, aorta and kidneys were found in the stimulated animals compared with the controls. By atherogenic diet, stressed animals got more hypercholesterolemia and coronary atherosclerosis than non-stressed animals (74).

Although hemodynamic and thrombogenetic factors bear upon atherosclerotic changes in arteries, disturbances in the lipid metabolism are viewed as the most crucial factor. In this *atherogenic lipid metabolism,* the role of *free fatty acids (FFA)* has been emphasized. The formation of FFA is to a high degree under sympathetic control. All forms of stress producing increase in catecholamines mobilize FFA. If FFA is not utilized in the muscles, a rapid synthesis of endogenous triglycerides takes place. In case of atherosclerotic development, plasma triglycerides will be deposited in the arterial wall. From the psychosomatic point of view, two parts in this metabolic process are of significance.

First, the formation of FFA is increased during all kinds of stress, both emotional arousal and sustained overactivity. Second, physical inactivity resulting from a giving up-withdrawal setting prevents utilization of FFA in the muscles and, in this way, supports the disposition of fat in the arterial wall.

The relationship between the metabolism of FFA and stress is not the only area in which stress factors may influence lipid metabolism (17). Russek (74) listed a number of harmful factors such as excessive eating, excessive drinking, smoking, no exercise, sense of time urgency and obesity (all of which are related to emotional tension), and then proceeded to call atherosclerosis a Maladaptation Syndrome. After discussing the relationship of emotional stress, FFA and atherosclerosis, Carruthers (17) concluded: "This hypothesis suggests that in modern society wrath, reinforced by sloth and gluttony, is the deadliest of the seven sins."

MECHANISMS IN PSYCHOSOMATIC DISEASE

Although emotional reactions imply a high degree of parallelism between psychological and physiological mechanisms, the cognitive appraisal of life events always takes place not only before the pathological excitation of the visceral organs and the muscles involved in emotions, but also before the autonomic and humoral activation preceding these pathological processes (4). This fact implies justification for the view that psychological factors influence physiological processes. Without stating more reasons, Table 1 is presented as a general outline.

Physiological Mechanisms

The central nervous system exerts its influence upon the organism by means of three effector systems: the somatic nerves subserving the skeletal-

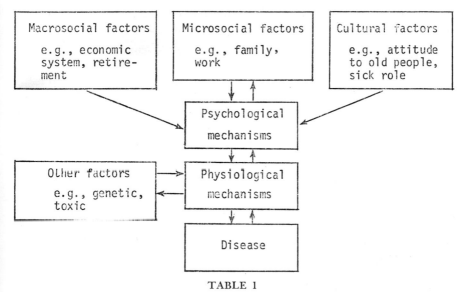

TABLE 1

General outline of relationship between psychological and social factors and psychosomatic disease.

muscular function, the autonomic nervous system, and the neuroendocrine or hormonal system. The skeletal-muscular system is primarily concerned with the interactions of the organism with the external environment and has no direct relationship to psychosomatic disease (but it does to conversion hysteria).

Neurogenic and Humoral Mechanisms in Hypertension

A number of scholars subscribe to the neurogenic hypothesis of essential hypertension according to which hypertension is due primarily to overactivity of the autonomic nervous system and only secondarily to hormonal changes. This overactivity produces a higher hemodynamic pressure which, if continuing for years, will change the structure and diameter of the blood vessels. The autonomic overactivity will readily be associated with an excitation of the adrenal cortex, mediated via epinephrine secretion and the anterior pituitary, leading to sodium retention and aldosteronism. When the arteriolar damage becomes worse, renal damage ensues, finally resulting in renal hypertension. In this way the autonomic system, as well as the endocrine system, is involved in the development

of essential hypertension. This hypothesis seems to be in complete agreement with the age distribution of hypertension reported above.

Inflammation

Peptic ulcer, ulcerative colitis, rheumatoid arthritis, and bronchial asthma are all disease processes under the regulatory influence of the autonomic and hormonal systems. In addition, the local mechanism of *inflammation* is crucially significant in development of these diseases. Inflammatiou
is an unspecific process, and can be elicited not only by infectious, toxic
and like agents but also by emotional factors (79) which H. G. Wolff
(94), among others, has demonstrated in numerous experiments. Inflammation is a local reaction of vascular connective tissues to injury. Changes
in parenchymatous cells are secondary to inflammation and are degenerative. Cortisone has an inhibitory effect on increased capillary permeability,
whereas desoxycorticosterone, somatotropin and aldosterone have an opposite effect.

As reported above, peptic ulcer, ulcerative colitis, rheumatoid arthritis,
and bronchial asthma may occur for the first time in high age, but the
incidence is much lower than in middle age. The reason for this decrease
may be the reduction of hormonal secretion (which, however, is unlikely
or uncertain (37)), or it may be reduced neural excitability (36). The most
effective factor, however, may be the reduction in inflammatory potential,
well known to all clinicians. Bürger (14) attributes this slower rate of inflammation to thickening of the capillaries. Nevertheless, this reduction
of the inflammatory potential is not so pronounced that it constitutes a
complete hindrance to inflammatory reactions in old age; new cases of
ulcerative colitis in old age may exemplify this (68).

Ergotrophy and Trophotrophy

Since Eppinger and Hess (31) put forward the theory of sympathicotonia and vagotonia, the concept of the vegetative system as being comprised of two antagonistic main branches has existed. Because the terms
sympathicotonia and vagotonia give undue preponderance to the autonomic nervous system, overlooking the hormonal system and metabolic
processes, Hess (43) coined the new terms ergotrophy (ergon=work, tro-
phein=nourish) and trophotrophy. In an elegant study (57), Mason reviewed previous research and reported new findings concerning the relationship between psychic function and the endocrine system. In his con-
cluding overview, he stated that experimental evidence seems to support

the unifying concept of *catabolism-anabolism* sequence. During the energy-spending catabolism (ergotrophy) secretion of corticosteroids, epinephrine, norepinephrine, growth hormone, and thyroxine predominate, whereas insulin, estrogens, testosterone, and the androgenic metabolites are associated with predominantly anabolic effects in energy metabolism (trophotrophy). Sympathetic activity, catabolism and ergotrophy are related to emotional arousal and sustained overactivity, whereas parasympathetic activity and anabolism predominate in giving up-withdrawal states. Mason's conception based upon sophisticated animal experiments is not only in agreement with Eppinger and Hess (31) and Hess (43) but gives support also to some of the notions reached by Alexander (3) with the aid of clinical experience and psychoanalytic treatment.

Psychological Mechanisms

Like other living organisms, man gets information and acts upon it. Before information is followed by behavior, it will be subjected to cognitive appraisal—what is the "meaning," and to emotional evaluation— good or bad? Only after these psychological activities are carried out will the action to be taken be decided upon and executed. From the psychosomatic point of view, all these processes are of great significance, not only the emotional reaction but also the cognitive appraisal and the decision-making and subsequent striving to reach the accepted goal. The last mentioned and often neglected psychological activity, in psychopathology, is also named conation (conari—to attempt). Emotion and conation are, along with appraisal, the main psychological actions related to psychophysiology. They will be dealt with under the headings of emotional arousal, sustained hyperactivity, and giving up-withdrawal.

Emotional arousal. After basic knowledge of the autonomic nervous system was obtained, psychosomatic medicine developed through fruitful combination of Cannon's "bodily changes in pain, hunger, fear and rage" —later endocrinological findings (79)—and the psychoanalytic views on anxiety and aggression. Keen clinicians have always observed bodily diseases arising after and during deeply disturbing life events, e.g. hyperthyroidism and peptic ulcer. In a long series of experiments, Wolff (94) found pathological changes of inflammatory and hemodynamic nature pointing to the possibility of chronic changes under prolonged emotional upheavals. Prolonged animal experiments have confirmed the supposition that long-standing states of emotional arousal may produce changes indicative of chronic diseases (42, 91).

The mechanism of emotional arousal is also named "fight and flight" (28) because behavior of this kind tends to develop from emotional arousal. Obviously, this outward behavior "fight and flight" adds to physiological arousal but does not make up the core of this state. Emotional arousal may also produce physiological derangement in persons who quietly hold out in difficult life situations, as happens in the immobilized animal which, without fighting or fleeing, develops anatomical lesions as a result of the fear caused by the immobilization (79). The crucial factor is the internal emotional state and not the external behavior.

This psychological mechanism of emotional arousal is at work in psychosomatic diseases in connection with conflicts, losses, and frustrations, mostly when the emotional disturbance goes on for at least one to three months (84). Peptic ulcer, ulcerative colitis and rheumatoid arthritis typically belong to this group. In the same setting of emotional arousal, myocardial infarction, stroke, and congestive heart failure (69) frequently occur.

Sustained overactivity. Speaking within the psychoanalytical frame of reference, the statement can be made that ego psychology is not yet fully integrated into the theory of psychosomatics. There is a growing discontent with the view of man as a being mainly dominated by emotions only. Not only are micro- and macro-social forces determinants of human behavior, but also those capacities described as belonging to the ego bear in a "dynamic" way upon the individual. Sociological theory views man primarily as a goal-setting and goal-pursuing being (61). According to the "theory of action," action is central to man (67). A broader view of man has been introduced to present-day psychiatry under different headings. Rado (71) speaks of an "action-self" that integrates self-awareness and willed action. Erik Erikson's (32) concept of identity as the privotal force of mind is on the same line. Common to these partly diverse terms is emphasis upon pursuing social and cultural goals. The underlying intrapsychic process is conation, volitional striving, the externally observable activity being outward activity, mostly in the form of *work*. When speaking about "stress," most people do not think only about conflicts, losses and frustrations, but also about excessive work and tight timetables with scarce opportunities for needed rest. The term *sustained overactivity* may be the proper designation for this work stress.

Sustained overactivity is observed particularly in the setting in which essential hypertension tends to develop. Blood pressure reacts sensitively to emotionally upsetting events, but development of chronic hypertension takes place typically in prolonged hard work or work-like activities. Only sustained overactivity can change acute hypertensive reactions and transient hypertension to fixated hypertension with hormonal changes. Hambling (40) described two types of hypertensive patients: one is depicted in a way that resembles the aggressive competitive go-getter (like Behavior Pattern A); the other hypertensive patient type is like the submissive, hard-working subordinate employee. Mostly due to character traits and/or social necessity, both are subjected to a life of sustained overactivity.

This emphasis upon sustained overactivity in development of hypertension must not prevent us from recognizing the close relationship between emotional arousal and acute hypertensive crises. Once sustained overactivity has contributed to permanently elevated blood pressure, strong emotional arousal is harmful. Since hypertension seldom starts in high age, the condition to be most feared in this age is the acute elevation of blood pressure.

Giving up-withdrawal. During the last decade no theoretical formulation in psychosomatics has aroused so lively an interest as the interrelated concepts of giving up, withdrawal and conservation. In two recently published books, there are extensive presentations of the application of these concepts, not only to psychosomatic diseases but to all kinds of physical disease (30, 77). There are two reasons for giving here particular attention to this hypothesis. First, the giving up-withdrawal reaction seems to have special relevance to illness in high age. Secondly, the present writer cannot help feeling that critical analysis is needed so that this original and fruitful theorizing may get that recognition it deserves.

Starting from observations of an infant aged 15 to 21 months (29), the concept of depression-withdrawal (29), withdrawal-conservation (28), and conservation-withdrawal (30) evolved as designations for a specific *biological* state. As the *psychological* counterpart, the term "giving up" has gradually been established (1, 28, 76, 77). "The pathway involves first a psychological appraisal of "giving up," with its concomitant affects of helplessness or hopelessness, which may then be followed or accompanied by conservation-withdrawal as the somatic response" (30). This daring hypothesis states that the psychological giving up and the biological conservation-withdrawal facilitate the development of almost any somatic disease except those designated psychosomatic, which were thought of as caused by the fight-flight mechanism (28). According to the hypothesis, giving up creates an increased vulnerability to disease, allowing or facilitating the onset of disease in the presence of both psychobiological predispositions of the individual and pathogenic elements in the environment. In his first report, Schmale (76) observed giving up-withdrawal reaction prior to the onset of such diverse diseases as acute bronchitis, Laennec's cirrhosis, hyperthyroidism, and aseptic meningitis.

As the heading of this section indicates, the combination term "giving up-withdrawal" has been chosen as the most adequate designation. Giving up describes the more or less conscious decision made by the patient after the cognitive appraisal of the life situation as not worth holding on to. Giving up is primarily giving up of activity in pursuit of adopted life goals. Withdrawal describes the same step from the behavioral and social point of view: withdrawal from goal-directed activity, not only from other people.

Engel's emphatic statement that giving up-withdrawal implies conservation of biological energy (30) seems to be only partly correct. The main biological rhythm of man is the *circadian rhythm* (circa=approximate, dies=day). Within the 24-hour period, a shift from work to rest normally takes place. As Engel pointed out, rest and sleep are conditions of giving up-withdrawal in which physiology of the body changes from ergotrophy to trophotrophy, or from catabolism to anabolism. Man has no prolonged rhythms like hibernation, hence long periods of giving up-withdrawal are unphysiological. Contrary to the statement of Engel, giving up-withdrawal tends to produce depletion of biological energy because energy will increase only during regular catabolic-anabolic sequences (62). Prolonged giving up-withdrawal periods produce prolonged anabolic trophotrophy, which furthers the disease process. It is a self-evident fact that giving up-withdrawal from physical activity is harmful to the organism. Lack of exercise is listed by the American Heart Association as a risk factor in coronary heart disease. Giving up-withdrawal is a pathological factor because it means giving up health-preserving psychic and physical activity.

Engel and Schmale (30) try to differentiate giving up-withdrawal from mental depression. It seems reasonable to suppose that the difference is frequently only in degree of psychological and social derangement. The high frequency of depression in old age, referred to above, gives particular relevance to the study of giving up-withdrawal and its consequences in old age.

INTERACTION OF SOCIAL, PSYCHOLOGICAL AND BIOLOGICAL FACTORS

With its emphasis on factors *preceding* onset of physical disease, this presentation has been deliberately one-sided. In order to get information fitted into an overall view of psychological and social aspects of health and disease in old age, some pertinent findings have to be pointed to.

Functional disturbances have not been dealt with although their practical significance in old age may be even greater than many so-called diseases, e.g. angina pectoris. Because the functional disturbances are partly due to the same factors as the psychosomatic diseases, the information about etiology of psychosomatic diseases is applicable to functional disturbances.

The feedback from physical disease to psychic functioning and social behavior has deliberately been left out of discussion, although these aspects are even more important to health and disease in old age. First, the psychological impact of *organic brain disease* is of tremendous significance. Then other physical diseases, including psychosomatic diseases, contribute in many ways to functional mental disorders in old age. Depression (10, 48, 70), neurosis (8), and particularly hypochondriasis (15) develop often in a vicious interaction circle: somatic disease acts as an etiological factor in psychic disorder, and psychic disorder contributes to somatic deterioration.

Illness behavior (60) which "refers to the ways in which given symptoms may be differentially perceived, evaluated and acted (or not acted) upon by different kinds of persons" covers a wealth of relevant aspects. The rapidly growing information in this area (47) has to be integrated into the excessively biologically oriented geriatrics (50, 53, 55, 88, 90).

The greatest benefit obtained by good knowledge in psychosomatic processes is related to *health behavior*. Health behavior is any activity undertaken by a person believing himself to be healthy for the purpose of preventing disease or detecting it in an asymptomatic stage (47). This definition has to be somewhat modified, at least in old age. A person with a chronic disease, e.g. atherosclerosis, has to view himself more as impaired and/or disabled than as sick, and accordingly he has to adopt the "well role." In spite of his disease, he is entitled to consider himself well and to take part in the well world. In addition, he has not only to prevent himself from getting worse, but also to improve his physical fitness. In doing so, he is in urgent need of knowledge, particularly concerning psychological and social factors giving rise to emotional arousal and giving up-withdrawal reactions which, along with physical environmental factors, are the real enemies to health in old age.

Admittedly, the evidence for psychological and social factors in the etiology of physical disease is not always "hard data." But postponing preventive measures until hard data are available implies delaying needed health education for boundless time, and is hence irresponsible. Like most politics, health politics, too, has to some extent to live on more or less "soft data."

REFERENCES

1. ADAMSON, J. D., and SCHMALE, A. H. 1965. Object loss, giving up, and onset of psychiatric disease. *Psychosom. Med.,* 27:557.
2. ADLER, R., RITCHIE, K., and ENGEL, G. L. 1971. Psychologic processes and ischemic stroke. 1. Observations on 32 men with 35 strokes. *Psychosom. Med.,* 33:1.
3. ALEXANDER, F. 1952. *Psychosomatic Medicine.* London: George Allen and Unwin.
4. ARNOLD, M. B. 1970. Brain function in emotion: a phenomenological analysis. In: Black, P. (Ed.) *Physiological Correlates of Emotion.* New York and London: Academic Press.
5. BALIER, C., BOURGERON, J. P., BOURGERON, G., and FERRY, M. 1968. Enquete sur les besoins medicaux et sociaux des personnes agées du XIII arrondissement de Paris. *Bull. Inst. Nat. Santé Rech. Med.,* 23:439.
6. BARTELS, E. C. 1965. Hyperthyroidism in patients over 65. *Geriatrics,* 20:459.
7. BAYNS, D. R., CROSSLEY, J. M., ABRAMS, M. E., JARRETT, R. J., and KEEN, H. 1969. Oral glucose tolerance and related factors in a normal population sample. I. Blood sugar, plasma insulin, glyceride, and cholesterol measurements and the effects of age and sex. *Brit. Med. J.,* 1:595.
8. BERGMANN, K. 1972. Personality traits and reactions to the stresses of ageing. In: van Praag, H. M., and Kalverboer, A. (Eds.) *Ageing of the Central Nervous System. Biological and Psychological Aspects.* Harlem: De Erven F. Bohn N. V.
9. BIRREN, J. E., BUTLER, R. L., GREENHOUSE, S. W., SOKOLOFF, L., and YARROW, M. R. 1963. *Human Aging: A Biological and Behavioral Study.* Washington: U.S. Government Printing Office.
10. BÖNI, A. 1967. Entzundliche-rheumatische Erkrankungen des Bewegungsapparates. In: Doberauer, W. et al. (Eds.) *Handbuch der praktischen Geriatrie.* Band II. Stuttgart: Ferdinand Enke Verlag.
11. BRADLEY, R. L. 1967. Acute peptic ulcer in the elderly: similarity to stress ulcer. *J. Am. Geriat. Soc.,* 15:254.
12. BROWN, R. C., and RITZMANN, L. 1967. Some factors associated with absence of coronary heart disease in persons aged 65 or older. *J. Am. Geriat. Soc.,* 15:239.
13. BULL, G. M. 1969. A comparative study of myocardial infarction and cerebral vascular accidents. *Geront. Clin.,* 11:193.
14. BURGER, M. 1960. *Altern und Krankheit als Problem der Biomorphose.* Leipzig: VEB Georg Thieme.
15. BUSSE, E. W. 1959. Psychopathology. In: Birren, J. E. (Ed.) *Handbook of Aging and the Individual.* Chicago: University of Chicago Press.
16. CANNON, W. B. 1920. *Bodily Changes in Pain, Hunger, Fear and Rage.* New York and London: Appleton.
17. CARRUTHERS, M. E. 1969. Aggression and atheroma. *Lancet,* 2:1170.
18. CIOMPI, L., and LAI, G. P. 1969. *Depression et vieillesse.* Bern and Stuttgart: Hans Huber.
19. CUMMING, E., and HENRY, W. E. 1961. *Growing Old.* New York: Basic Books.
20. DANOWSKI, T. S. 1963. Emotional stress as a cause of diabetes mellitus. *Diabetes,* 12:183.
21. DEAN, L. R. 1962. Aging and the decline of affect. *J. Geront.* 17:440.

22. DONGIER, M., WITTKOWER, E. D., STEPHENS-NEWSHAM, L., and HOFFMAN, M. M. 1956. Psychophysiological studies in thyroid function. *Psychosom. Med.*, 18:310.
23. EISDORFER, C. 1971. Background and theories of aging. In: Maddox, G. L. (Ed.) *The Future of Aging and the Aged.* Atlanta, Georgia: SNPA Foundation.
24. EITNER, S. 1969. Beziehungen zwischen Altern und perufsspezifischen Erkankungen in geroarbeitsmedizinischer Sicht. *Z. Alternsforsch.*, 22:29.
25. EITNER, S. 1972. Der gegenwärtige Stand der gerohygienischen Forschungsarbeit und Schlussfolgerungen fur die komplexe medizinische, soziale und kulturelle Betreung alternder und älterer Burger. *Z. Alternsforsch.*, 25:209.
26. EKDAHL, P. H. 1968. Carcinoma in ulcerative colitis—especially in relation to age. In: Engel, A., and Larsson, T. (Eds.) *Cancer and Aging.* Stockholm: Nordiska Bokhandelns Förlag.
27. ENGEL, A., and ROBERTS, J. 1966. *Rheumatoid Arthritis in Adults. United States 1960-62.* Public Health Service Publication No. 1,000, Series No. 17.
28. ENGEL, G. L. 1962. *Psychological Development in Health and Disease.* Philadelphia: Saunders.
29. ENGEL, G. L., and REICHSMAN, F. 1956. A study of an infant with a gastric fistula. I. Behavior and the rate of total hydrochloric acid secretion. *J. Am. Psychoanal. Ass.*, 4:428.
30. ENGEL, G. L., and SCHMALE, A. H. 1972. Conservation-withdrawal: a primary regulatory process for organismic homeostasis. In: *Physiology, Emotion and Psychosomatic Illness.* Ciba Foundation Symposium 8 (new series). Amsterdam: Associated Scientific Publishers.
31. EPPINGER, H., and HESS, L. 1909. Zur Pathologie des vegetativen Nervensystems I-III. *Zschr.f.Klin.Med.*, 67:345, 67:203 and 68:231.
32. ERIKSON, E. H. 1950. *Childhood and Society.* New York: W. W. Norton.
33. FLORA, G. C., OMAE, T., and NISHIMORU, K. 1969. Clinical profile of the stroke patient. *Geriatrics*, 24:95.
34. FORBES, G. B., and REINA, J. C. 1970. Adult lean body mass declines with age: some longitudinal observations. *Metab. Clin. Exp.*, 19:653.
35. FRIEDMAN, M., and ROSENMAN, R. H. 1959. Association of specific overt behavior pattern with blood and cardiovascular findings. *J.A.M.A.*, 169:1286.
36. FROLKIS, V. V. 1972. Regulation and adaptation processes in aging. In: Chebotarev, D. F., et al. (Eds.) *The Main Problems of Soviet Gerontology.* Kiev.
37. GUSSECK, D. J. 1972. Endocrine mechanisms and aging. In: Strehler, B. L. (Ed.) *Advances in Gerontological Research,* Vol. 4. New York and London: Academic Press.
38. HAHN, P., NUSSEL, E., and STIELER, M. 1966. Psychosomatik und Epidemiologie des Herzinfarktes. *Psychosom. Med.*, 12:229.
39. HALL, J. W., and HENDERSON, L. L. 1966, Asthma in the aged. *J. Am. Geriat. Soc.*, 14:779.
40. HAMBLING, J. 1955. Essential hypertension. In: O'Neill, D. (Ed.) *Modern Trends in Psychosomatic Medicine.* London: Butterworths.
41. HELANDER, J. 1969. Åldrandet och den tjugotredje artikeln. *Scialt Forum*, No. 5:265.
42. HENRY, J. P., ELY, D. L., STEPHENS, P. M., RATCLIFFE, H. L., SANTISTEBAN, G A., and SHAPIRO, A. P. 1971 The role of psychosocial factors in the development of arteriosclerosis in CBA mice: observations on the heart, kidney, and aorta. *Atherosclerosis*, 14:203.
43. HESS, W. R. 1948. *Das Zwischenhirn.* Basel: Benno Schwabe.
44. HEYDÉN, S. 1969. Environmental factors, (1) Emotional stress. In: Schettler, F. G., and Boyd, G. S. (Eds.) *Atherosclerosis.* Amsterdam: Elsvier.
45. HINKLE, L. E., and WOLF, S. 1952. A summary of experimental evidence relating life stress to diabetes mellitus. *J. Mount Sinai Hosp.*, 19:537.

46. JAMIESON, R. A., SMITH, W. E., and SCOTT, L. D. W. 1949. Peptic ulcer in Glasgow. *Brit. Med. J.,* 1:298.
47. KASL, S. V., and COBB, S. 1966. Health behavior, illness behavior, and sick-role behavior. *Arch. Environ. Hlth.,* 12:246 and 531.
48. KAY, D. W., BEAMISH, P., and ROTH, M. 1964. Old age mental disorders in New-castle-upon-Tyne. Part I. A study of prevalence. *Brit J. Psychiat.,* 110:146.
49. KAY, D. W., ROTH, M., and BEAMISH, P. 1961. *Physical Illness and Psychological and Social Factors in the Psychiatric Disorders of Old Age.* IIIrd World Congress of Psychiatry, Montreal. Vol. 3:122.
50. KUTNER, B., FANSHEL, D., TOGO, A. M., and LANGNER, T. S. 1956. *Five Hundred over Sixty.* New York: Russell Sage Foundation.
51. LARSSON, T. 1967. Mortality from cerebrovascular disease. In: Engel, A., and Larsson, T. (Eds.) *Stroke,* Stockholm: Nordiska Bokhandelns Förlag.
52. LEVINE, R. 1971. New horizons in our knowledge of diabetes mellitus. *J. Am. Geriat. Soc.,* 19:897.
53. LIVSEY, C. G. 1972. Physical illness and family dynamics. In: Lipowski, Z. J. (Eds.) *Psychosocial Aspects of Physical Illness.* Basel: S. Karger.
54. MADDOX, G. 1963. Disengagement theory: A critical evaluation. *Gerontologist,* 4:80.
55. MADDOX, G. 1964. Self-assessment of health status. *J. Chron. Dis.,* 17:449.
56. MARTIN, J., and DORAN, A. 1966. Evidence concerning the relationship between health and retirement. *Sociological Review,* 14:329.
57. MASON, J. W. 1968. Organization of the multiple endocrine responses to avoidance in the monkey. *Psychosom. Med.,* 30:774.
58. MASTER, A. M., DUBLIN, L., and MARKS, H. H. 1950. The normal blood pressure range and its clinical implications. *J.A.M.A.,* 143:1464.
59. MASTER, A. M., LASSER, R. P., and JAFFE, H. L. 1958. Blood pressure in white people over 65 years of age. *Ann. Int. Med.,* 48:284.
60. MECHANIC, D. 1962. The concept of illness behavior. *J. Chron. Dis.,* 15:189.
61. MERTON, R. K. 1957. *Social Theory and Social Structure.* New York: The Free Press.
62. METEEV, D. 1971. Biologische Grundlage des Alterns aus der Sicht des Physiologen. *Z. Alternsforsch.,* 24:117.
63. MILLER, M. B. 1968. Life history of the stroke syndrome. *J. Am. Geriat. Soc.,* 16: 603.
64. MOHNIKE, G. 1967. Klinik des Diabetes mellitus im Alter. In: Doberauer, W. et al. (Eds.) *Handbuch der praktischen Geriatrie.* Band II. Stuttgart: Ferdinand Enke Verlag.
65. MOSES, C. 1967. Is atherosclerosis preventable? In: Brest, A. N., and Moyer, J. H. (Eds.) *Atherosclerotic Vascular Disease.* London: Butterworths.
66. PARKES, C. M. 1970. The psychosomatic effects of bereavement. In: Hill, O. W. (Ed.) *Modern Trends in Psychosomatic Medicine.* London: Butterworths.
67. PARSONS, T., and SHILS, E. A. (Eds.) *Toward a General Theory of Action.* Cambridge, Mass.: Harvard University Press.
68. PAULLEY, J. W. 1972. Psychosomatic and other aspects of ulcerative colitis in the aged. *Mod. Geriat.,* 2:30.
69. PERLMAN, L. V., FERGUSON, S., BERGUM, K., ISENBERG, E. L., and HAMMARSTEN, J. F. 1971. Precipitation of congestive heart failure: social and emotional factors. *Ann. Int. Med.,* 75:1.
70. POST, F. 1962. *The Significance of Affective Symptoms in Old Age.* London: Oxford University Press.
71. RADO, S. 1954. Hedonic control, action-self and the depressive spell. In: Hoch, P. H. and Zubin, J. (Eds.) *Depression.* New York: Grune & Stratton.
72. REES, L., 1956. Psychosomatic aspects of asthma in elderly patients. *J. Psychosom. Res.,* 1:212.

73. RIMÓN, R. 1969. A psychosomatic approach to rheumatoid arthritis. *Acta Rheum. Scand.*, Suppl. No. 13.
74. RUSSEK, H. I. 1967. Role of emotional stress in atherogenesis. In: Brest, A. N., and Moyer, J. H. (Eds.) *Atherosclerotic Vascular Disease*. London: Butterworths.
75. RYSER, C., and SHELDON, A. 1969. Retirement and health. *J. Am. Geriat. Soc.*, 17:180.
76. SCHMALE, A. H. 1958. Relationship of separation and depression to disease. *Psychosom. Med.*, 20:259.
77. SCHMALE, A. H. 1972. Giving up as a final common pathway to changes in health. In: Lipowski, Z. J. (Ed.) *Psychosocial Aspects of Physical Illness*. Basel: S. Karger.
78. SCHUBERT, R., and BASEL, G. 1965. Ulcus ventriculi et duodeni, Konstitution und Altern im Sinne der Biomorphose von Max Burger. *Z. Alternsforsch.*, 18:285.
79. SELYE, H. 1950. *Stress*. Montreal: Acta, Inc. Medical Publishers.
80. SHOCK, N. W., WATKIN, D. M., YIENGST, M. J., NORRIS, A. H., GAFFNEY, G. W., GREGERMAN, R. I., and FALZONE, J. A. 1963. Age differences in the water content of the body as related to basal oxygen consumption in males. *J. Geront.*, 18.1.
81. SJÖSTRÖM, AKE. 1967. Hospitalized cases of stroke in a Swedish hospital region. In: Engel, A., and Larsson, T. (Eds.) *Stroke*. Stockholm: Nordiska Bokhandelns Förlag.
82. SLAWSON, P. F., FLYNN, W. R., and KOLLAR, E. J. 1963. Psychological factors associated with the onset of diabetes mellitus. *J.A.M.A.*, 185:166.
83. SPIEGELMAN, M., and MARKS, H. H. 1946. Age and sex variations in the prevalence and onset of diabetes mellitus. *Am. J. Publ. Hlth.*, 36:26.
84. STENBÄCK, A. 1960. Gastric neurosis, pre-ulcer conflict and personality in duodenal ulcer. *J. Psychosom. Res.*, 4:282.
85. THOMPSON, W. E., and STREIB, K. F. 1958. Situational determinants: health and economic deprivation in retirement. *J. Soc. Issues*, 14:18.
86. TREUTING, T. F. 1962. The role of emotional factors in the etiology and course of diabetes mellitus: A review of the recent literature. *Am. J. Med. Sci.*, 244:93.
87. TUFT, L. 1951. Problems of the geriatric asthmatic and their clinical management. *J.A.M.A.*, 146:1951.
88. TWADDLE, A. C. 1972. The concepts of sick role and illness behavior. In: Lipowski, Z. J. (Ed.) *Psychosocial Aspects of Physical Illness*. Basel: S. Karger.
89. VERKHRATSKY, N. S. 1972. Characteristics of catecholamine metabolism during aging. In: *9th International Congress of Gerontology in Kiev. Reports and Introductory Lectures*. Vol. 1.
90. VERWOERDT, A. 1972. Psychopathological responses to the stress of physical illness. In: Lipowski, Z. J. (Ed.) *Psychological Aspects of Physical Illness*. Basel: S. Karger.
91. VON HOLST, D. 1972. Renal failure as the cause of death in Tupaia belangeri exposed to persistent social stress. *J. Comp. Physiol.*, 78:236.
92. WILLIAMS, R. II. 1962. The pancreas. In: Williams, R. H. (Ed.) *Textbook of Endocrinology*. London: Saunders.
93. WILLIAMS, R. H., and BAKKE, J. L. 1962. The thyroid. In: Williams, R. H. (Ed.) *Textbook of Endocrinology*. London: Saunders.
94. WOLFF, H. G. 1953. *Stress and Disease*. Springfield, Ill.: Charles C Thomas.

13

DEPRESSION AND SUICIDE

EDMUND C. PAYNE, M.D.

Assistant Clinical Professor of Psychiatry
Harvard Medical School, Cambridge, Mass.

INTRODUCTION

The significance of suicide as a public health and clinical problem is underestimated by the general public and the medical profession alike. The number of suicides in Western society exceeds the number of homicides. Especially among the aging, suicide is both common and relatively ignored.

The author recently asked a number of psychiatrists if they could present from their psychotherapy practice a clinical report of the suicidal crisis in an elderly patient. All but one replied that they did not have such material available. Some of these colleagues had practices based in a psychiatric hospital, and one was involved in a research project on suicide. This informal survey suggests that the elderly suicidal patient does not commonly become involved in a psychotherapeutic relationship with a psychiatrist.

The same pattern is seen in the literature on suicide. The patients who appear in published reports of therapeutic work with suicidal crises are drawn primarily from adolescence and early and mid adulthood. Reports on a significant number of patients in the older age range generally appear only in post-mortem clinical studies of successful suicides or in the broad statistical studies based on coroners' reports. These observations are all the more striking when it is realized that the rate of suicide increases dramatically with increasing age.

It is evident from these observations that while the elderly are most at risk from suicide, they are least engaged and benefit to the smallest extent from the therapeutic and succoring resources that are available in society. The reasons for this paradox are not clearly discernible. The explanation may lie in the nature of the suicidal process, in the nature of aging, or in the interrelation between the two. It may reflect the disengagement of the elderly from the social milieu, and their relative ineffectiveness in availing themselves of the resources in the environment. In all likelihood the pessimism that the elderly feel about the predicament of old age, a pessimism often shared by the potentially available people in their environment, plays an important role. Although this pessimism may have tragic consequences, it is, nonetheless, often unfounded.

In this chapter the life circumstances and intrapersonal factors that have been shown to be significantly correlated with suicide in the elderly will be reviewed, in order to try to better understand the despair that leads a man or woman to finally terminate his own life after living it for so long. Also, principles of early detection of the suicidal individual, of management and of treatment will be considered. The answers to the puzzle posed by the failure of available community resources to adequately engage a group so prone to suicide lie in issues of too broad a scope and range to be dealt with in this chapter. Information to answer this question adequately is in all likelihood not available. Nonetheless, greater awareness of the factors associated with increased vulnerability to suicide and of the effective therapeutic approaches that are available may encourage a more effective response to the vicissitudes of aging that generate hopelessness and also to the challenge of suicide prevention.

THE SOCIOLOGICAL POINT OF VIEW

Most investigations of suicidal phenomena have proceeded from one of two points of view, the sociological and the clinical approach. In its extreme position, the sociological viewpoint has asserted that suicide is a phenomenon *sui generis,* fully capable of explanation in terms of the relationship of the individual to his social group (11). The clinical approach to the investigation of suicidal behavior is based on the study of individual cases. Under these circumstances the relation of suicide to mental illness frequently stands out most clearly (33), and the social factors may not be as evident as they are when larger population samples are examined. This is especially true when suicide is studied in the elderly, since assessment of subjective experience and the meaning of life events is of course not possible with the post-mortem studies that characterize this group. The suicidal act represents the convergence of multiple, complex factors, and an explanatory model must attempt to integrate both points of view.

The Sociological Approach

At the turn of the century Emile Durkheim pioneered an approach that revolutionized the study of suicide (11). His unequivocal rejection of extrasocial causation freed the field from the rigid, nineteenth-century, disease-based models in which it had theretofore been encased. By studying the stable differences in suicide rates between various large comparable groups—political and national enclaves, religious affiliations, and marital and family status—he evolved four categories of suicide which were related to the degree of integration of the individual into society, and to the degree of regulation of the individual by society.

Although these categories of egoistic, altruistic, anomic, and fatalistic suicides have been modified by later sociologists, and are now seldom used as inclusive explanatory concepts, the point of view introduced by Durkheim has influenced most subsequent studies. Above all, this approach has firmly established that suicide is not a disease, and that it is not just the outcome of a mental illness, however closely it may be related to a syndrome such as depression. Rather, there are a number of independent factors related to the social and psychological condition of man that converge to find their expression in the act of suicide. Some of these factors which are associated, directly or indirectly, with suicide and aging will be considered in the following sections. As these issues are developed, two areas of concern should be kept in mind. An understanding of the factors correlated with suicide in aging can be helpful in the management of the individual suicidal patient. Of greater importance, however, is the utilization of the insight gained to improve the quality of life for the aging person.

Aging and Suicide

Below the age of forty there are more than seven unsuccessful suicidal attempts for every completed suicide, with an even higher proportion among women (9, 10, 54). This proportion of successful suicides increases with increasing age. Over age sixty the ratio is reversed, and the number of completed suicides exceeds the number of attempts. Among the group most vulnerable to suicide, the elderly, white male, the proportion of accomplished to attempted suicide is over three times that for the entire population at the ages of sixty-three to sixty-nine, and over five times greater at age eighty-five (38). Below the age of forty-five, the percentage of successful suicides in each age group is less than that age group's representation in the total population. This discrepancy constantly widens with decreasing age. Over age fifty, the percentage of suicides in this age group exceeds the group's representation in the population (57). This pattern holds for every special group that is vulnerable to suicide, such as those appearing in psychiatric case registries or receiving a diagnosis of depression. In each special group the rate of suicide is twice as high for the fifty-five or older than for younger groups (15, 40).

A suicidal attempt is more likely to be fatal in a man than in a woman. At age eighty-five the ratio of completed to attempted suicide is twelve times greater for men than for women (38). Men in all age groups use more violent means of suicide, employing shooting or cutting as opposed to poisoning and asphyxiation, which are the methods preferred by women. For both men and women, however, the rate of successful attempts increases with age, and the methods employed become more violent. Older people more frequently resort to leaping from high places, drowning, hanging, and shooting than do the young (2).

Clearly, the suicidal threats and attempts in older people are almost always genuine, and involve a very high degree of risk. Whereas in younger individuals a suicidal threat or gesture may frequently express a wish to manipulate or affect another person engaged in an intensely ambivalent relationship, in the elderly it indicates a much more unambiguous wish to die.

This changing quality of suicidal preoccupations with aging should influence the alertness and willingness to intervene on the part of the front-line health workers who come most into contact with older people. It does not, however, justify greater pessimism regarding the effectiveness of therapeutic intervention.

Occupational and Economic Factors

Increased suicide rates are positively correlated with situations involving stress, instability, and threatened deprivation. The elderly are especially vulnerable to stress involving occupational and economic factors. Contrary to common expectation, suicide rates are low among the habitually poor, but rise among the privileged groups. However, a change in status, such as unexpected poverty, downward social and economic mobility, and unemployment, is highly correlated with an increase in suicide (3, 4, 15, 46). The suicide rate increases during periods of economic depression, with the highest effect in high income groups and the least effect among those with the least to lose (20, 21). The group most vulnerable to an economic depression are those persons in their fifties and sixties who are especially vulnerable to job loss. In contrast, suicide rates show no significant change among the youngest age groups of employed men. Although the full impact of the retirement process is hard to measure, these observations lend support to the expectation that when retirement requires an adjustment to a deteriorating occupational status and to the loss of economic security, the resultant stress is a serious trauma for many of the aging.

Many people experience a peak of depressive affect immediately after retirement. The impact is especially severe when retirement is coupled with poor health or with deprived economic conditions. On the other hand, it is ameliorated when an alternative role permits a sense of worth and social importance to be maintained (55). An alternative role is developed from interests which were present during the working life but which were not fully developed because of lack of sufficient time. These roles are most often expressed through participation in relationships with family and friends, in organizational and religious activities, and in recreational pursuits. Most of these opportunities are related at least in part to reasonable health and reasonable financial security. They are also influenced by the opportunities offered by the milieu for participation. While work supports morale for those with restricted activity patterns, the chances for good morale can be higher with retirement for those elderly persons who have an interest in a variety of activities.

Sainsbury (46) has related the high incidence of suicide among elderly men to their lack of occupation, as well as to their distressing loneliness, and observes that during the war when elderly men are able to obtain employment the incidence of suicide among them shows a greater drop than for younger men.

Loss and Loneliness

Almost all theories, both sociological and psychological, in their formulation of suicide, have stressed the importance of the loss of a centrally important person. The concept of loss has been used broadly to include most of the vicissitudes to which the aging are subject: functional, material, and societal loss, and the loss of mutuality (38). It is clearer usage, however, to restrict the term to the loss of a meaningful, need-fulfilling other person.

The loss of a spouse is one of the most severe traumas to which the aging person is exposed. When the marriage has been a good and stable one, a deep attachment will have developed over the years, and the partner will have become the primary need-satisfying person. Widowhood can then represent intense loneliness, loss of emotional security and interruption of the fulfillment of basic needs, at a time in life when only the most resourceful and least rigid are able to find a replacement that is even partially satisfactory.

Even in the instances in which the marriage has been marked by hostility and conflict, it has still served as protection against loneliness, support for dependent needs, and as a vehicle for the discharge of both libidinal and aggressive instinctual needs. Frequently one or both partners in such a relationship is excessively dependent or emotionally disturbed in other ways. In such a situation, loss of the spouse through divorce, separation, or death may create an even greater instability and disruption of need satisfaction. In addition, the magnitude of the hostility provides a basis for guilt and self-reproach.

Empirical studies support the importance of loss. The suicide rate is higher in areas where more individuals live alone, and where there is a high rate of divorce or widowhood (46). The suicide rate is highest when divorce or separation has occurred, and next highest with widowhood. Although these studies have not been specifically correlated with age, it is probable that divorce remains the most traumatic form of loss in the elderly but that widowhood is a much more important trauma because of its greater frequency. The older male, in particular, has difficulty in adjusting to the loss of his spouse. The rate of suicide following divorce for both men and women is approximately two and a half times greater than the rate of the general population. On the other hand, the rate is three and a half times greater among widowed men but less than 1.3 times greater among widows (57). In contrast, elderly women who were always single are more vulnerable to suicide than men who never married (26).

The vulnerability to suicide is highest in the first year after the loss of a spouse, but remains significantly greater for over five years (5, 28). For the first four years of widowhood, the number of deaths from suicide exceeds the number of deaths from all other causes. An important variable is the degree of interaction with other meaningful people, such as relatives. The rate of suicide among the bereaved is three times higher for those who live alone than for those who live with someone else. Even more striking, among the recently widowed, 80 percent of those who commit suicide are living alone (7).

Predisposition to suicide has also been attributed to another form of loss, the loss that results from failure of parental care, either through loss of the parents or other deprivation in childhood (56, 58). This factor exerts its influence through its formative effect on personality development, and by creating special vulnerability to loss and depression. Its relative importance in the suicides at different ages has not been analyzed, and it is difficult to assess the significance for suicide in the elderly. It is likely to retain some importance, however, even though the cumulative influence of the vicissitudes of aging assumes a relatively greater significance.

The Attitude of Society

The correlations of the frequency of suicide with the characteristics and cultural attitudes and patterns of the society within which the individual lives are among the most reliable data on which we base our understanding of suicide (11, 19, 23, 25, 29, 48, 63). The derivation of individual meanings from broad sociological observations is, however, a difficult and treacherous undertaking. An intuitive expectation is that the esteem in which a person is held or the indifference and hostility with which he is met will play an important part in the development of the despair that makes a suicidal act possible. Clinical impressions from work with suicidal patients have led to the following oversimplified but persuasive statement: "Those commit suicide who want to kill somebody, and those commit suicide who are wished dead by others" (29). The contribution made by the covert hostility and open indifference which the aged not infrequently encounter in contemporary society to the steady increase in frequency in suicide in aging, to the lethality of suicide attempts in aging, and to lack of effective therapeutic engagement is difficult to demonstrate convincingly. Indirect corroboration is supplied, however, by examining settings in which attitudes toward the aging differ from our own. One of the few studies which have examined these variables compared suicide rates in Hongkong in 1922, when ancestor reverence was a part of Chinese culture. Under these conditions, the younger age groups showed higher suicide rates and the older segments of the population showed a lower incidence, a reversal of the patterns seen in Western cultures (63).

The Role of Depression in Suicide

Over the centuries both lay and professional opinion has linked suicide with depressive illness. Clinical studies have supported this connection (2, 33, 36, 40, 41, 44, 47, 48, 61). The percentage of suicidal patients for whom a diagnosis of depression can be established varies widely, depending on the age and sex of the sample study, the severity of the attempt, and whether or not the study was limited to attempted or completed suicides. There seems no doubt, however, that affective illness plays a major role in suicide, and it seems likely that the group at highest risk, those who make the most severe suicide attempts, are those with clinical depressions. The importance of depression increases with advancing age.

Manic depressive psychoses are associated with the highest rates of suicides. The rate increases dramatically with aging. Although 50 percent of these patients become ill before the age of forty, only 8 percent of the suicides occur before this age (40). In a study of 19 patients over sixty years of age who had attempted suicide, all had a definite psychiatric disease, and nine were diagnosed as having a clinical depression. The majority had made serious attempts employing violent means. Another investigation found that 25 percent of younger suicides and 40 percent of those over forty had an affective disorder (47).

Affective disorders have in recent years become one of the more active and exciting areas of psychiatric research. This interest has been stimulated by significant advances in the understanding of genetic and biochemical factors important in the pathogenesis of depression, and by the promise of developing effective pharmacological therapy with an adequate theoretical basis. Because depression does play an important role in suicidal behavior, some current views will be very briefly reviewed, although no effort will be made to systematically examine the rapidly growing literature.

The validity of the dichotomy of "endogenous" and "reactive" depressions, still widely accepted by many psychiatrists, has been severely questioned (reviewed in 16). Longitudinal studies on patients with a diagnosis of endogenous depression, followed throughout their course of hospitalization, have demonstrated that stressful events occur prior to the onset of illness with as high a frequency as in the group diagnosed reactive depression. The apparent absence of a precipitating event, which is a leading diagnostic characteristic of the endogenous group, appears to be an artifact created by the inability of severely depressed patients to give an adequate history early in the course of the illness. The possible exception is the group with a well-established manic-depressive syndrome. This debate concerning the validity of the concept of endogenous depression, with an onset essentially unrelated to stress, is still unresolved (24, 45).

Genetic studies (62) have begun to divide the pure depressive disorder (as opposed to those preceded by other forms of psychiatric illness) into homogeneous groups. Genetic factors have been delineated most clearly in the bi-polar (manic-depressive) affective disorders and in a prototype group ("depressive spectrum disease") characterized by onset before age forty and a predominance of females, along with other features. The possible role of genetic transmission is more obscure in other depressive syndromes. In an essay on suicide in aging, it is pertinent to note that genetic factors seem less clearly delineated in those affective disorders in which the initial episode occurs late in life.

Other research approaches, stimulated initially by the fortuitous observations of the effect of drugs on mood states, have made substantial progress in describing aspects of the neurochemical basis of affective disorders (16, 24, 45). The systems which have been most thoroughly investigated are those which regulate the metabolism and release of the biogenic amines, such as noradrenalin and serotonin, as neurotransmitters. The study of related regulatory mechanisms is just beginning, and so far more questions have been raised than have been definitively answered. Nonetheless, sufficient evidence has accumulated to substantiate a definite biological basis for the major affective disorders.

Two influential points of view exist in regard to psychiatric theory, and their divergence is often expressed in significantly different approaches to the management of psychiatric disorders. Proponents of a psychodynamic or psychosocial point of view make token acknowledgment of the importance of the biological factors, but often de-emphasize them in practice. Those who rely primarily on organic biological theories make verbal acknowledgment of the role of psychosocial factors, but frequently give them only slight or superficial attention when dealing with patients.

Some investigators whose backgrounds combine an appreciation of psychodynamic and psychosocial issues with a sophisticated biochemical and physiological approach (16, 24, 45) have attempted to devise comprehensive theoretical models which integrate biological and genetic data with the organism's response to stress and life events. This effort is encouraged by the finding that the level and the metabolism of brain amine are affected by stress and by early experience (16).

Despite these efforts in the direction of integrating the points of view, the newer genetic and biological discoveries influence the pendulum of scientific opinion and practice to swing from the previous, predominantly psychodynamic bias to a more prominent emphasis on purely biological factors. This swing of opinion can lead to a too narrow preoccupation with organic etiology and methods of treatment. There is abundant evidence already of strong intrapsychic and social resistance to involvement with the sources of unhappiness encountered by the elderly, and these resistances could be augmented by such a trend. It is necessary, therefore, to stress that despite the close correlation of suicide and depression, these are two separate entities. No genetic basis for suicide has been established. Even in samples of depressed patients, a number of variables still significantly differentiate suicidal patients from other depressed patients. Although treatment of the accompanying depression is often a central issue in the management of the suicidal patient, attention to the quality and character of his life is of at least equal importance.

The Role of Physical Illness

The relation of physical illness to suicide in the elderly is difficult to establish with any assurance. Various studies have reported that a large minority of older patients who killed themselves were physically ill (33, 36, 47). However, these were retrospective post-mortem studies, and offered no opportunity for assessing the subjective significance or effect of the illness for the patient. Rather than the illness being the primary cause of the depression, an opposite effect can sometimes obtain. A patient who is depressed will frequently express this affect through rumination about his physical disabilities. On the other hand, many older people who are not depressed will dismiss or minimize the effects of even a serious illness. The clear, logical decision to end one's own life rather than await the termination of a fatal illness is probably a rare event (34).

More commonly, the illness represents a very special kind of stress. The increasing disability that accompanies the chronic illnesses of aging leads to loss of activity, restriction or loss of functions, and inability to engage in important habitual pursuits. Increased dependency, regression, greater helplessness, and social isolation result. All of these factors can contribute to the development of depression, especially when essential characterological defenses are thereby undermined. This is illustrated in the following clinical vignette (34).

A 62-year-old woman was admitted to the hospital with a massive myocardial infarction. Even after her recovery became well established, she continued to have anginal pain, and even more limiting, severe apprehension that the slightest exertion would result in her death. Early conflicts around dependent needs had been intensified when she was sent from home to live with relatives in another country at the age of twelve. She had found marriage and motherhood trying but made a fair adjustment until she underwent a hysterectomy at the age of thirty. Afterward, she had developed a number of somatic complaints and diffuse fears. However, she had still been able to maintain a certain balance and to find a channel for the discharge of many of her impulses through a compulsive program of housework and by working long hours in her garden. An intense, mutual ambivalence had long characterized her relationship with her husband, but as long as she was active, each could satisfy enough of the other's needs and maintain enough distance to make the hostility bearable. The restriction of activity forced her into an unbearably close dependency on him. She gradually developed an agitated depression, tormenting to her husband and herself, and became preoccupied with suicidal impulses.

Other Aspects of Suicide in the Elderly

Attempts to understand the relation of suicide to aging labor under the handicap that most studies are retrospective and usually post-mortem. The paucity of reports on psychotherapy with elderly suicidal people makes difficult any generalizations about the subjective experience of these patients, and renders suspect any assessment of the complex motives that culminate in the final act of suicide. Two recently published studies of patients who made unsuccessful attempts have identified affect states that significantly differentiate suicidal patients from other depressed patients. One found that hopelessness was more frequent in suicidal patients than in other depressed patients (30).

Another group of investigators found that suicidal patients were significantly more angry than other depressed patients (61). Both groups, however, were composed predominantly of younger individuals, and the latter study entirely of women. Indeed, there is some indirect evidence, based on analysis of suicide notes, that intense hostility, both directed outwardly or inward toward the self, is more characteristic of younger and middle-aged suicides than of the elderly (12). When the notes were sorted into the categories of "the wish to kill," "the wish to be killed," and "the wish to die," the notes left by those age sixty and over were characterized predominantly by the wish to die. There is even some evidence that a suicidally preoccupied elderly man who displays overt anger is less likely to make a successful attempt (26).

RECOGNITION OF THE SUICIDAL PATIENT

The readiness and ability of physicians to investigate the existence of suicidal preoccupation or suicidal intent in their patients, and to respond in an active and therapeutic manner, is the single most important element in the prevention of suicide. The importance of this simple yet very often neglected first step can hardly be overemphasized. More than any other therapeutic factor, the recognition by an influential person that the patient is contemplating suicide and that person's wish to prevent this action are critical for preserving the patient's life.

The great majority of suicidal patients are intensely ambivalent about their wish to die. Contrary to popular belief, most are eager to communicate the dilemma with which they are struggling. This readiness was convincingly demonstrated in a retrospective study of 134 completed suicides (39). A series of interviews was held with relatives and other people associated with the person who had killed himself. The investigators discovered that 69 percent of the entire group had communicated suicidal ideas, most frequently in the form of a direct and specific statement of the intent to commit suicide. The frequency of this communication did not vary significantly for sex. age, marital state, socioeconomic status, or religion. More surprisingly, those living alone communicated their suicidal thoughts as frequently as did those living with someone else. Nor were significant differences found when the communications were compared by clinical diagnoses. Over two-thirds of the group had expressed these ideas on more than one occasion. One-quarter of the recipients of these communications felt that the danger was not genuine. More often, even nonprofessionals recognized the presence of a serious disturbance. It is of interest that only 18 percent of the group expressed their concerns to physicians, although at least 50 percent had seen a physician in the preceding year. Only 6 percent were in a hospital at the time of their suicides.

The most common response to the communication of suicidal preoccupations was the feeling of marked tension and dismay on the part of the recipient, often followed by some rejection or denial of the threat. Another pervasive response was a sense of helplessness at being unable to relieve the distress or to act to prevent the suicide.

The Role of the Physician

The patient's primary physician is a vital point of contact in making therapeutic care available to suicidal older people. Of almost equal importance are nurses, social workers, and other members of the therapeutic professions. The responsibility falls on the physician, however, to initiate effective action. Two potential barriers may interfere with his appreciating the seriousness of the suicidal risk. One is the reluctance to recognize intensely distressing emotions in patients that is experienced by most doctors. The other barrier is present if the physician is not sufficiently familiar with the warning signs of a suicidal crisis. Of the two, the former is the more important.

Physicians, like the recipients of suicidal communications described above, often experience a painful emotional tension when they permit a patient to express feelings of fear, despair, or hopelessness. This reaction was observed in a group of physicians treating patients with terminal cancer (35). Their reluctance to investigate their patients' reactions to fatal illness and their consistent tendency to underestimate the degree of the patient's distress were in part based on the wish to protect themselves from sharing their patients' painful feelings. A second important reason was simply a lack of knowledge of how to conduct such an investigation with patients, which led to the fear that the discussion would evoke emotions in their patients which would get out of control and thereby damage the patients.

In a similar fashion, physicians frequently fear that inquiry into the presence of suicidal thoughts will suggest such thoughts to the patient, and push him in the direction of suicide. The patient's actual response is quite different from this expectation, however. A depressed patient is seldom troubled by being asked about the severity of his discouragement, and whether or not he has had any thoughts of harming himself. If he has entertained suicidal thoughts, he will usually express them readily to the physician, with gratitude for the implied offer of help.

In addition to his readiness to inquire into his patient's emotional state, the physician needs to be alert to the signs of depression, the covert indicators of suicidal preoccupation, and the life stresses which are associated with suicide. These more subtle manifestations, rather than the direct expression of suicidal intent, are usually the evidence that his patient first presents to him.

Most physicians readily recognize the signs and symptoms of a severe depression, when it is accompanied by the characteristic retardation of speech, movement, and thought, the sagging posture, the depressed visage, and rumination with failure, unworthiness, poverty, and material loss, or with guilt and the conviction of wrongdoing. The patient with an agitated depression is also easy to recognize even though he exhibits more restlessness in movement and speech, a higher level of anxiety and freer expression of anger rather than psychomotor retardation. Physiological symptoms of anorexia, loss of weight, painful insomnia with early morning awakening, and constipation confirm the diagnosis.

When faced with this clinical picture, most doctors will be alert to the possibility of suicide and will frequently formulate a therapeutic plan. The initial signs of an underlying depression or impending suicidal crisis may be more subtle, however. They may be manifested as increasing agitation and despondency about the progress of physical illness. The patient may express excessively strong emotional reactions to pain or physical disability, or heightened concern about suffering, or fear of dying from what may be a minor illness or operation. The primary indication may be an unrelenting, demanding pressure for the treatment of the physical illness, or an increasing hypochondria (36). In some patients complaints of fatigue and signs of apathy may be the sole presenting manifestations of an underlying depression.

The expression of suicidal intent can take a variety of forms. The following covert communications were among those employed by a group of successful suicides: "I would be better off dead"; "I'm tired of living"; "my family would be better off without me." Also expressed were references to dying before the spouse, statements of "I can't take it any longer," and moves to put one's affairs in order (39).

Evaluation of Risk

When the physician recognizes that his elderly patient is preoccupied with thoughts of suicide, his first task is to evaluate the degree of risk and to begin formulating a plan of management. Recognition that the seriousness of suicide attempts increases with age is a constant consideration.

Certain events in the patient's life alert the physician to more than ordinary risk. Most important is a history of a previous suicide attempt. Depending on the sample studied, 20 to 65 percent of those who eventually commit suicide have a history of a previous attempt (7).

Deteriorating health, increased physical disability, or other unfavorable changes in life circumstances also are signals of potential increased vulnerability. Loss of a spouse by death or divorce can alert the physician to an increased potential for suicide, especially if the patient lives alone.

A serious suicide attempt is more commonly associated with a depression of sufficient severity to produce somatic symptoms. However, the absence of signs of depression is by no means a guarantee against the risk of suicide. The depth of the depression is also not a dependable gauge. The period of greatest risk is often when a depression seems to be lifting or in the early stages before a severe depression has been established rather than in the more advanced stages of an incapacitating depression.

If a dependable working alliance has been established between the patient and physician, the task of evaluation of suicide risk should be shared with the patient. A most important measure of the degree of risk is the patient's own judgment of whether and under what circumstances he can be trusted to not kill himself. An interesting approach has been described (8) in which, after suicidal ideas have been elicited, the patient is asked to make the statement: "No matter what happens, I will not kill myself, accidentally or on purpose, at any time." If the patient can make this statement with confidence, suicide is dismissed as a danger. The patient who will not make this statement is judged to be a serious risk. For other patients, the degree of risk is judged by the qualification that the patient attaches to the statement that he will not kill himself, and the circumstances under which he says the statement will not hold. The authors report no fatalities with 600 such "no suicide decisions" over a five-year span. This approach emphasizes some factors too often neglected: the importance of direct communication with the patient; the importance of actively eliciting the patient's cooperation; and the patient's capacity to accurately estimate his own emotional position when given a method that helps cut through the ambiguities with which he usually cloaks his thoughts.

Such a decision based on active cooperation with the patient provides the physician with important additional information and increases his confidence in the decision. It also serves the important function of strengthening or initiating a therapeutic relationship between the doctor and the patient. The reliability of such decisions, however, depends on favorable circumstances. The physician must feel that the patient is cooperative. If the patient uses alcohol excessively, if a psychotic process is present, if the patient is confused or shows other evidence of serious interference with cognitive processes from organic brain disease, his judgment is unreliable and his statement invalid. When these factors are present, the risk of suicide is greatly increased.

If relatives are available, they should be interviewed by the physician or by a social worker. The information so obtained can aid in judging risk and in planning treatment. Tensions within the family which may have played a role in precipitating the suicidal crisis often are thereby brought to light. The involvement of the family also mobilizes important emotional support for the patient.

Outpatient Management or Hospitalization

The decision to hospitalize the suicidal, elderly patient or alternatively to treat him on an outpatient basis will depend on the physician's assessment of the risk of suicide, balanced by an evaluation of the disruptive effects of uprooting the patient from his accustomed environment. If the risk of suicide seems great, the patient should be treated in a hospital setting. In many cases, however, when the signs are more equivocal, other factors must be considered.

Older individuals have difficulty adapting to a new and strange environment, and a course of action that involves removing them from familiar surroundings is to be undertaken only with caution. It has been observed that the death rate for elderly people is high shortly after admission to homes for the elderly, and even higher following confinement to a mental hospital. In a classic study of the effects of relocation on elderly people (1), it was decisively demonstrated that the death rate substantially and significantly increased in the first three months after a group of old people were moved from a familiar nursing home in which they had adjusted to other nursing homes or other facilities for long-term care. The relocation was necessitated by the closing of the nursing home in which they lived, and thus the decision bore no relation to the health of the patient or to the situation within the family. Those who survived the move best were those who were able to reconcile themselves to the change and deal with it adaptively. The highest death rate occurred among those whose adaptive capacity was impaired by depression, by some psychotic process, or by some other serious emotional disability.

Uprooting and hospitalization can precipitate irreversible regressions or disrupt a fragile engagement with significant people or with other aspects of the environment which the elderly person may have little capacity to reinstitute at a later time. Therefore, these risks too are not to be lightly taken, and must at times be given equal weight with the risk of suicide. The conservative course of hospitalization may sometimes carry a higher risk of morbidity. Outpatient management is to be preferred if a confident and cooperative relationship can be established with the patient and if the special factors increasing risk that were described above are not present. When serious doubt exists, however, priority must be given to the immediate preservation of the patient's life, and hospitalization is the only choice.

METHODS OF TREATMENT

In the majority of cases, the management of the suicidal crisis involves three main considerations. These are: treatment of the underlying depression; keeping the patient alive until treatment can be effective; and amelioration of the psychosocial issues that have contributed to the patient's despair.

Treatment of Depression

Electroconvulsive therapy has traditionally been the mainstay of treatment of depression in the elderly, especially when suicide was a consideration. This not only reflects the effectiveness of this therapeutic modality in this syndrome, but probably also the reluctance of many psychiatrists to seek psychotherapeutic involvement with the elderly. In recent years, with the development of the tricyclic antidepressant drugs, chemotherapy has assumed a growing, and currently probably a preeminent, role (22, 37, 44). Some debate continues over the relative effectiveness of the two approaches. The preponderance of current opinion would probably favor a thorough initial trial of chemotherapy, reserving ECT for those patients who fail to respond. Post (37) reported that 75 percent of a group of 60 patients responded initially to ECT, but suffered a high relapse rate, especially among the women in the group. Initial response to treatment with imipramine was slower, but ultimately 84 percent of the patients on this treatment achieved complete control of symptoms. Symptomatic relapse was not a problem in this group. An extensive literature exists on both electrical and chemotherapeutic treatment of depression, and the subject will not be developed in any more detail at this time.

Keeping the Patient Alive

The most important element in keeping a suicidal patient alive is the wish of a responsible person that he remain alive, expressed in that person's vigilance, and conveyed to the patient by means of the psychotherapeutic relationship. This vigilance is expressed in the initial estimate of the balance between the patient's wish to live and his wish to die. In the hospital setting it is manifested in the continuing attention to this shifting balance and to the patient's reactions to the sometimes minor environmental vicissitudes that can disturb it. Precautionary measures are adjusted in accordance with the changing risk.

In outpatient management it is necessary that the patient know that the therapist is available to him if the suicidal pressure increases. The therapist's vigilance insures that the span of time that elapses between contacts does not exceed the patient's capacity, and that disruptions in the relationship do not occur, so that the patient is not adrift with no one to be concerned about him.

There are two periods in the treatment of the suicidal patient when the risk is greatest. The first of these dangerous periods occurs at the time of initial contact, when arrangements for treatment are being made. The second is during the stage of recovery.

The first period of risk is often encountered when contact is first made with the suicidal patient. As was indicated above, the general physician has the best opportunity to recognize the presence of suicidal risk. If he decides that the danger of suicide is a serious one, he will usually refer the patient to a psychiatrist for evaluation and management, or alternatively discuss hospitalization. At this point the patient is presented with what may be to him a frightening prospect, and at the same time is faced with a transitional period when he is without the care of a vigilant physician. Under these circumstances an immediate suicidal attempt may be precipitated. To avert this danger, the physician must be active in seeing that his recommendation is promptly carried out, and in maintaining contact with the patient until other safe arrangements are made.

The second period of greatest danger occurs when the patient has made progress in his recovery, and appears much better. At this time the vigilance of both the patient and the therapist has often subsided. However, the great majority of seriously suicidal patients who are hospitalized experience some reactivation of the suicidal urge when they leave the hospital on pass or at discharge (31). At this point they leave the protective support of the hospital and again encounter the stresses in the environment which played a role in the original wish to die. There may be a return to conflictual relationships. The lonely person is again alone with his isolation, and the bereaved person with his grief. The protection afforded by the hospital against his self-destructive wishes is no longer present. The positive, supportive transference to the hospital personnel is weakened.

Risk remains high during the first six months to a year following discharge. Every effort should be made to maintain contact with the patient during this period. Most completed suicides subsequent to hospitalization occur in the groups of patients with whom it is not possible to maintain a continuing therapeutic relationship and followup (32). The subsequent rate of suicide shows a higher correlation with this factor than with the severity of the original depression.

At all times during the suicidal crisis, which must be considered as continuing until the patient is reestablished in a relatively stable setting and functioning with reasonable effectiveness and adequate self-esteem, he remains vulnerable to disappointments and especially to loss. Unfortunately, the vicissitudes of living are not suspended during this time. Particularly in the elderly, financial worries, an illness or operation, the death of a friend or relative, or separation from a son or daughter may occur. An increase in suicidal impulses can be anticipated at such times, and must be met with active psychotherapeutic support. During the period of suicidal risk there is particular sensitivity to loss of the therapist, whether temporarily during vacations or permanently as the result of transfer to other work, for the therapist often represents the primary support to the patient's wish to live (18). Depressed and suicidal patients possess an ability to provoke the therapist's anger, discouragement, and wish to rid himself of this burdensome patient. Patients sensitively perceive this usually unconscious wish in the therapist, and may utilize it to reinforce the suicidal impulse.

Social Intervention

A suicidal wish in an elderly patient is usually the culmination of multiple inner and outer problems. Restoration of an inner balance often requires some change in the external social environment. Involvement of a skilled social worker or community agency in the therapeutic plans can be of crucial assistance. The case reported by Haggerty (17) represents an excellent example of the value of such intervention by a social worker.

The 70-year-old man was admitted to a psychiatric hospital following his third suicide attempt in four months. His history showed many features that are characteristic of suicidal crises in the elderly. His mother had died when he was four, and he was reared by an older sister. His father was alcoholic, frequently away from home, and provided little emotional support. Born in a Scandinavian country, he had immigrated in early adulthood. He married a strong, aggressive woman on whom he was dependent. On occasion he had expressed the wish that he die before her. For many years he had periodically experienced depressive moods, had talked of suicide as a valid course of action, and had said that he did not want to live beyond his seventieth year.

Prior to the first suicidal attempt, he had suffered a series of losses. The sister who had reared him had died four years earlier. Arthritis of increasing severity had caused him to move with his wife from his long-time home to a new city in order to live with his daughter. This move away from his friends and acquaintances had resulted in increased social isolation. Finally, a year before his first suicide attempt, his wife had died. Some months after her death he had visited his native country and returned from the trip appearing noticeably more depressed.

During this time he told his internist that life was no longer worth living. A few weeks later he took an overdose of sleeping pills. No psychiatric referral was suggested until after a second attempt at suicide, at the time of the anniversary of his wife's death. Outpatient therapy with antidepressant medication was attempted for two weeks, but a third suicide attempt led finally to hospitalization.

The social worker's initial involvement was with the family, obtaining additional history. As discharge approached, she played an important role in working out the problems of the patient's reintegration into his family, and in helping plan a program of activity to encourage increased socialization. When for a variety of reasons it become too difficult for the daughter to continue having her father live in her home, the work with the social worker helped make a move to a retirement home more acceptable to the patient. After this move, she continued to help work through the resultant difficulties in his relationship with his daughter. Throughout the period of post-hospital readjustment, her relationship with him served as a support that helped offset the pain of his loneliness, and provided a vital bridge that assisted in his reintegration into his environment.

SUMMARY

In this chapter some of the sociological and clinical contributions to the understanding of suicide in the elderly have been reviewed. Attention has been called to the crucial role played in preventing suicide by the physician's willingness to listen to his older patients' despair. The necessity for a comprehensive approach to treatment has been stressed. If there is an active approach to treatment and continued interest in the fate of the suicidal elderly person, the prognosis is good.

Prevention of suicide in the elderly is an important goal. It depends on an active interest in the problems encountered by the elderly, and a willingness to be aware of their distress. The most significant aspect to the study of the phenomenon of suicide in the aging population is the sensitive indicator to the sources of despair with which it provides us. This is the more important morbidity to which we must direct our attention.

REFERENCES

1. ALDRICH, D. K., and MENDKOFF, E. 1968. Relocation of the aged and disabled: a mortality study. In: Neugarten, B. L. (Ed.) *Middle Age and Aging: A Reader in Social Psychology.* Chicago: University of Chicago Press.
2. BATCHELOR, I. R. C. 1957. Suicide in old age. In: Shneidman, E. S. and Farberow, N. L. (Eds.) *Clues to Suicide.* New York: McGraw-Hill.
3. BREED, W. 1963. Occupational mobility and suicide among white males. *Am. Sociological Rev.,* 28:179.
4. BREED, W. 1967. Suicide and loss in social interactions. In: Shneidman, E. S. (Ed.) *Essays in Self-Destruction.* New York: Science House.
5. BUNCH, J. 1972. Recent bereavement and suicide. *J. Psychosom. Res.,* 163:361.
6. DIGGORY, J. S. 1967. The components of personal despair In: Shneidman, E. S. (Ed.) *Essays in Self-Destruction.* New York: Science House.
7. DORPAT, T. L., and RIPLEY, H. S. 1967. The relationship between attempted suicide and committed suicide. *Comprehensive Psychiat.,* 8:74.
8. DRYE, R. C., GOULDING, R. L., and GOULDING, M. E. 1973. No-suicide decisions: patient monitoring of suicidal risk. *Am. J. Psychiat.,* 130:171.
9. DUBLIN, L. 1963. *Suicide.* New York: The Ronald Press.
10. DUBLIN, L. 1968. Suicide: an overview of a health and social problem. *Bull. Suicidol.,* December, 25.
11. DURKHEIM, E. 1951. *Suicide: A Study in Sociology.* New York: The Free Press. Trans. by Spaulding, J. A., and Simpson, G.
12. FARBEROW, N. L., and SHNEIDMAN, E. S. 1957. Suicide and age. In: Shneidman, E. S., and Farberow, N. L. (Eds.) *Clues to Suicide.* New York: McGraw-Hill.
13. FARBEROW, N. L., and SHNEIDMAN, E. S. 1965. A survey of agencies for the prevention of suicide. In: Farberow, N. L., and Shneidman, E. S. (Eds.) *The Cry for Help.* New York: McGraw-Hill.

14. FARBEROW, N. L., and SHNEIDMAN, E. S. (Eds.). 1965. *The Cry for Help*. New York: McGraw-Hill.

15. GARDNER, E. A., BAHN, A. K., and MACK, M. 1964. Suicide and psychiatric care in the aging. *Arch. Gen. Psychiat.*, 10:547.

16. GOODWIN, F. K., and BUNNEY, W. E. 1973. A psychobiological approach to affective illness. *Psychiat. Annals*, 3:19.

17. HAGGERTY, J. 1973. Suicidal behavior in a 70-year-old man: a case report. *J. Geriat. Psychiat.*, 6, No. 1, 43-51.

18. HAVENS, L. L. 1965. The anatomy of a suicide. *New Engl. J. Med.*, 272:401.

19. HENDIN, H. 1964. *Suicide in Scandinavia*. New York: Grune and Stratton.

20. HENRY, A. F., and SHORT, J. F., JR. 1954. *Suicide and Homicide*. Glencoe, Illinois: Free Press.

21. HENRY, A. F., and SHORT, J. F., JR. 1957. The sociology of suicide. In: Shneidman, E. S., and Farberow, N. L. (Eds.) *Clues to Suicide*. New York: McGraw-Hill.

22. HOLLISTER, L. E. 1972. Mental disorders—antianxiety and antidepressant drugs. *New Engl. J. Med.*, 286:1195.

23. KALISH, R. A. 1968. Suicide. *Bull. Suicidol.*, December, 37.

24. KLERMAN, G. L. 1971. Clinical research in depression. *Arch. Gen. Psychiat.*, 24:305.

25. LESTER, G., and LESTER, B. 1971. *Suicide, the Gamble with Death*. New York: Prentice-Hall.

26. LETTERI, D. J. 1973. Empirical prediction of suicidal risk among the aging. *J. Geriat. Psychiat.*, 6, No. 1, 7-42.

27. LITMAN, R. E. 1957. Some aspects of the treatment of the potentially suicidal patient. In: Shneidman, E. S. and Farberow, N. L. (Eds.) *Clues to Suicide*. New York: McGraw-Hill.

28. McMAHON, B., and PUGH, T. 1965. Suicide in the widowed. *Am. J. Epidem.*, 81:23.

29. MEERLOO, J. A. M. 1962. *Suicide and Mass Suicide*. New York: Grune and Stratton.

30. MINKOFF, K., BERGMAN, E., and BECK, A. T. 1973. Hopelessness, depression, and attempted suicide. *Am. J. Psychiat.*, 130:455.

31. MOSS, L. M., and HAMILTON, D. M. 1957. Psychotherapy of the suicidal patient. In: Shneidman, E. S., and Farberow, N. L. (Eds.) *Clues to Suicide*. New York: McGraw-Hill.

32. MOTTO, J. 1965. Suicide attempts: a longitudinal view. *Arch. Gen. Psychiat.*, 13:516.

33. O'NEAL, P., ROBINS, E., and SCHMIDT, E. II. 1956. A psychiatric study of attempted suicide in persons over 60 years of age. *Arch. Neurol. Psychiat.*, 75:275.

34. PAYNE, E. C. 1964. Teaching medical psychotherapy in special clinical settings. In: Zinberg, N. E. (Ed.) *Psychiatry and Medical Practice in a General Hospital*. New York: International Universities Press, Inc.

35. PAYNE, E. C., and KRANT, M. J. 1969. The psychosocial aspects of advanced cancer. *JAMA*, 210:1238.

36. POLLACK, S. 1957. Suicide in a general hospital. In: Shneidman, E. S., and Farberow, N. L. (Eds.) *Clues to Suicide*. New York: McGraw-Hill.

37. POST, F. 1968. The factor of aging in affective illness. In: Coppen, A., and Walk, A. (Eds.) *Recent Developments in Affective Disorders*. Brit. J. Psychiat., Special Publication No. 2, 105.

38. RACHLIS, D. 1970. Suicide and loss adjustment in the aging. *Bull. Suicidol.*, Fall, 23.

39. ROBINS, E., GASSNER, S., KAYES, J., WILKINSON, R. H., and MURPHY, G. E. 1959. The communication of suicidal intent. *Am. J. Psychiat.*, 115:724.

40. ROBINS, E., MURPHY, G. E., WILKINSON, R. H., GASSNER, S., and KAYES, J. 1959. Some clinical considerations in the prevention of suicide, based on a study of 134 successful suicides. *Am. J. Publ. Hlth.*, 49:888.

41. ROBINS, E., and MURPHY, G. E. 1967. The physician's role in the prevention of

suicide. In: Yochelson, L. (Ed.) *Symposium on Suicide*. Washington, D.C.: The George Washington University.

42. ROBINSON, D. S., DAVIS, J. M., NIES, S., RAVAVIS, C. L., and SYLVESTER, D. 1971. Relation of sex and aging to monoamine oxidase activity of human brain, plasma, and platelets. *Arch. Gen. Psychiat.*, 24:536.

43. ROSENBAUM, M. 1967. Recognition of the suicidal individual. In: Yochelson, L. (Ed.) *Symposium on Suicide*. Washington, D.C.: The George Washington University.

44. SABSHIN, M. 1967. The treatment of depression—the major suicidal illness. In: Yochelson, L. (Ed.) *Symposium on Suicide*. Washington, D.C.: The George Washington University.

45. SACHAR, E. J. 1974. Some clinical and biological considerations in depressive illness. *J. Geriat. Psychiat.*, 7, No. 1, 55-69.

46. SAINSBURY, P. 1955. *Suicide in London: An Ecological Study*. London: Chapman and Hall.

47. SAINSBURY, P. 1962. Suicide in later life. *Geront. Clin.*, 4:161.

48. SAINSBURY, P. 1968. Suicide and depression. In: Coppen A., and Walk, S. (Eds.) *Recent Developments in Affective Disorders. Brit. J. Psychiat.*, Special Publication No. 2, 1.

49. SHEIN, H. M., and STONE, A. A. Monitoring and treatment of suicidal potential within the context of psychotherapy. *Comprehensive Psychiat.*, 10:59.

50. SHNEIDMAN, E. S. (Ed.). 1967. *Essays in Self-Destruction*. New York: Science House.

51. SHNEIDMAN, E. S. (Ed.). 1969. *On the Nature of Suicide*. San Francisco: Jossey-Bass.

52. SHNEIDMAN, E. S., and FARBEROW, N. L. 1957. Clues to Suicide. In: Shneidman, E. S., and Farberow, N. L. (Eds.) *Clues to Suicide*. New York: McGraw-Hill.

53. SHNEIDMAN, E. S., and FARBEROW, N. L. (Eds.) 1957. *Clues to Suicide*. New York: McGraw-Hill.

54. SHNEIDMAN, E. S., and FARBEROW, N. L. 1965. Statistical comparisons between attempted and committed suicides. In: Farberow, N. L., and Shneidman, E. S. (Eds.) *The Cry for Help*. New York: McGraw-Hill.

55. SPENCE, D. L. 1966. Patterns of retirement in San Francisco. In: Carp, F. M. (Ed.) *The Retirement Process*. Public Health Service Publication 1778. Washington, D.C.: U.S. Government Printing Office.

56. TABACHNICK, N. 1957. Observations in attempted suicide. In: Shneidman, E. S., and Farberow, N. L. (Eds.) *Clues to Suicide*. New York: McGraw-Hill.

57. TUNAKAN, B. 1972. A ten-year survey of suicide in Omaha-Douglas County, Nebraska. *Neb. Med. J.*, 57:231 and 265.

58. WALTON, H. J. 1958. Suicidal behavior in depressive illness. *J. Ment. Sci.*, 104:884.

59. WAZIRI, R. 1973. Symptomatology of depressive illness in Afghanistan. *Am. J. Psychiat.*, 130:213.

60. WEISMAN, A. D., and WORDEN, J. W. 1972. Risk-rescue rating in suicide assessment. *Arch. Gen. Psychiat.*, 26:553.

61. WEISSMAN, M., FOX, K., and KLERMAN, G. L. 1973. Hostility and depression associated with suicide attempts. *Am. J. Psychiat.*, 130:450.

62. WINOKUR, G., CLAYTON, P., and REICH, T. 1969. *Manic Depressive Illness*. St. Louis: C. V. Mosby Co.

63. YAP, P. M. 1963. Aging and mental health in Hongkong. In: Williams, R. H. (Ed.) *Process of Aging II*. New York: Atherton Press.

64. YOCHELSON, L. (Ed.). 1967. *Symposium on Suicide*. Washington, D.C.: The George Washington University.

14

SEXUAL BEHAVIOR

Eric Pfeiffer, M.D.

Professor of Psychiatry
Duke University School of Medicine

and

Project Director, Older Americans Resources and
Services Program, Duke University Center for the
Study of Aging and Human Development
Durham, North Carolina

THE QUALITY OF SURVIVAL

Survival into old age is becoming increasingly commonplace. As a consequence, the aged themselves and the larger society are becoming increasingly interested in not only the fact of survival but also the quality of survival. This interest is giving rise to action on two fronts. Governmental and private agencies are increasingly concerning themselves with the provision of *services* to the elderly, particularly in the areas of health maintenance, income continuance, job availability, and housing. At the same time, governmental and scientific organizations are increasingly involved in the conduct of research into basic and applied aspects of aging. Some excellent studies on the physiology, psychology, and sociology of old age have already been published (1, 3, 12, 18, 19, 20), and new information is being generated and disseminated regularly.

One facet of the aging experience which has thus far received insufficient attention has been the sexual life of elderly persons. In fact, until recently relatively little scientific information with respect to the range and scope of sexual behavior in the elderly has been available, either to the elderly themselves or to those who must care for and counsel them. But the picture has begun to change, starting with the publication of Kinsey's monumental works (4, 5) and proceeding to the investigations of Masters and Johnson on the human sexual response (9, 10) and more recently to our own publications on the natural history of sexual behavior in old age (14, 15, 16, 17, 21, 22).

Still, information about sexual behavior in the aged lags far behind similar information on adults or adolescents. Psychiatry has contributed much to greater enlightenment and greater frankness in regard to many aspects of human sexuality in our society. Many of the taboos concerning sexuality in adolescence and adulthood have largely been laid aside. Not so the taboo against sex in old age, however. Therefore it is particularly gratifying to the present author to see a chapter on sexual behavior included in a volume on the psychiatry of aged persons.

THE TABOO AGAINST SEX IN OLD AGE

That a taboo against sex in old age still exists cannot be doubted, nor that it constitutes a serious impediment to systematic, in-depth investigations into patterns of sexual behavior in old age. The taboo operates at several different, if clearly related, levels. First, it is evident among potential subjects and their relatives. Aged subjects are difficult to recruit for studies which are clearly labeled sexual in nature. In addition, even when cooperation has been gained, the data which can be collected are generally of a very limited sort. At other times, the aged individuals themselves may be glad to participate in such studies, but relatives who learn of their participation may become "concerned" and insist that the subjects withdraw from the study.

The taboo also operates among physicians and behavioral scientists who are not themselves investigators in such studies. Thus, referring physicians may express "concern" that such studies may prove upsetting to their patients, or they may contend that such matters are essentially private and should not be studied scientifically. As has been pointed out so eloquently by Lief in his several publications, physicians themselves may not be entirely comfortable in dealing with sexual matters since their training in general has but inadequately prepared them to do so (6, 7).

Finally, investigators themselves must learn to overcome a degree of initial hesitancy and embarrassment before they can comfortably inquire into the sexual lives of their elders. For instance, in our studies at Duke we found that it was extremely difficult for young physicians to bring them-selves to inquire into the sexual lives, past or present, of aged women who had remained single all of their lives.

How can we account for this taboo? One frequently stated opinion is that it is merely a hangover from a Victorian Age. But the tenacity with which the taboo persists makes it seem likely that active, present-day proc-esses also exist to maintain it. Our society still holds to the notion that sexual activity should be engaged in primarily for procreative rather than for recreative purposes. In adolescence, in early and middle adulthood, when the production of offspring is at least a possibility, sexual activity can be accepted. But in old age the fiction that sex is being carried on for procreational purposes can no longer be maintained and sex in old age therefore cannot be countenanced.

It is also likely that the taboo against sex in old age is, in part an extension of the incest taboo. Children of all ages experience a great deal of anxiety at the thought or the sight of their parents engaged in sexual activity. Since the elderly constitute the parent generation, the seeming cultural prohibition against active sexual expression among elderly per-sons may be accounted for on this basis.

STEREOTYPES OF SEXUAL BEHAVIOR IN OLD AGE

In our society cultural stereotypes exist about sex in old age which bear little resemblance to the actual data which will be presented below. One of these is the notion that sexual desire and sexual activity cease with the onset of old age. Another is that sexual desire and activity *should* cease to exist with the onset of old age. A third notion is that older persons who say they are still active sexually are either morally perverse or they are lying. Another aspect of the stereotype that older persons have or should have laid their passions to rest is the fact overt expressions of affection or sexual interest among older persons are often met with the harshest kind of ridicule or other disapproval on the part of the grown children of aged adults. In these stereotypes, of course, what constitutes being old is not particularly well defined, ranging all the way from the middle forties to truly advanced old age.

And now let us examine what relationship, if any, these stereotypes have to the actual data regarding sexual behavior in later life.

STUDIES IN HUMAN SEXUAL BEHAVIOR

The Kinsey Studies

Kinsey studied the sexual behavior of 14,084 males and 5,940 females. Included in these large samples were only 106 men and 56 women who were 60 years old and over. Only a very few pages in the two Kinsey volumes (4, 5) are devoted to sexual behavior in the aged. Kinsey himself readily admitted that the aged were under-represented; nevertheless, some interesting findings emerged from these studies.

Basing his conclusions on data from 87 males whose sexual histories were judged to be adequate, Kinsey found that at age 60 only one out of five men was no longer capable of sexual intercourse, but that at age 80 this proportion had risen to three out of four men (4, p. 235). This constitutes a steep decline in the proportion of men still sexually capable over a 20-year age span. Kinsey, however, also concluded that the rate of decline in absolute frequency of sexual outlets (which in his studies include sexual intercourse, masturbation, and nocturnal emissions) on average did not decline any more rapidly in old age than it did at ages between 30 and 60 (4, pp. 220-221). While this may well be true in absolute terms, the relative decline in old age would still appear to be greater. Kinsey also noted that while married men at all ages had a somewhat higher frequency of sexual outlet, single and post-marital males had frequencies only slightly below those of their married counterparts. We will return to this observation in discussing the differential influence of marital status in men and in women, based on the Duke longitudinal data.

Kinsey had even fewer women in his study who were more than 60 years old. His conclusions regarding age-related changes in sexual behavior therefore represent extrapolations from changes observed at younger ages. He noted a gradual decline in frequency of sexual intercourse between ages 20 and 60, but felt that this "must be the product of aging processes in the male" and that there is "little evidence of any aging in the sexual capacities of the females until late in her life" (5, pp. 348-353). We will return to this point also. Kinsey further observed that, in contrast to the men, single and post-marital females had rates of sexual activity which ranked far below those of their married counterparts. Although he deals primarily with women below age 60, we will address ourselves to this point in regard to women above age 60 further on in the paper.

The Masters and Johnson Studies

Masters and Johnson have published two major volumes on human sexual behavior: *Human Sexual Response* and *Human Sexual Inadequacy*

(9, 10). Each of these volumes contains substantial information on the sexual responses of aged persons. In the first, attention was given principally to anatomical and physiological considerations. Masters and Johnson reported that men past age 60 were slower to develop erection, slower to effect intromission, and slower to reach a point of ejaculation. Accompanying physiological signs of sexual excitement, such as sexual blush and muscular tone, were also lessened.

They also reported that among women over age 60 the duration of physiological response to sexual stimulation, as measured by breast engorgement, nipple erection, sex blush over the breasts, increased muscle tone, clitoral and labial engorgement, and vaginal secretions, was clearly diminished over age 60. However, capacity for "sexual performance at orgasmic response levels" was not diminished, especially among women who had regular exposure to "effective stimulation."

In addition to the men and women who participated actively in the laboratory studies, a somewhat larger number of men and women over age 60 were interviewed by Masters and Johnson in regard to their sexual behavior. Interview data were obtained on 133 males above age 60, of whom 71 were in their 60's, 37 in their 70's, and 15 in their 80's.

Masters and Johnson found that "the most important factor in the maintenance of effective sexuality for the aging males is consistency of active sexual expression. When the male is stimulated to high sexual output during his formative years and a similar tenor of activity is established for the 31-40 year age range, his middle-aged and involutional years usually are marked by constantly recurring physiological evidence of maintained sexuality. Certainly it is true for the male geriatric sample that those men currently interested in relatively high levels of sexual expression report similar activity levels from their formative years" (9, p. 263). Newman and Nichols in an earlier study reported a positive correlation between strong sexual feelings in youth and continued sexual interest in old age (11).

Masters and Johnson also obtained interview data on 54 women above the age 60. Thirty-seven of these women were between 61 and 70 years of age, and 17 between 71 and 80. The authors speak more to the point of capacity for sexual intercourse with orgasmic response than to the actual activity or interest levels of these women. They agree with Kinsey that a large part of the post-menopausal sex drive in women is related directly to the sexual habits established during the procreative years. The chapter, however, contains no data on the influence of age, marital status, health status, or sexual capacities of the spouses of these women.

In the second volume (10) Masters and Johnson focus more on the psychological rather than the physiological aspects of sex in old age. They urge the wide dissemination of knowledge, to health professionals and to the aged themselves, of the physiologically modified sexual responses in old age. Unless aging men and their spouses understand these changes, the danger exists that these modifications are interpreted as being signs of an end to sexuality altogether when in fact they only signify a change to a modified form of sexual expression.

The Duke Longitudinal Studies

One important aspect of the Duke longitudinal studies is the fact that they are part of more broadly-based longitudinal studies of how people adapt to growing older: how they adapt physically, socially, psychologically, economically, and so on. Actually, two longitudinal studies are going forward at Duke University. The first of these is a study of 260 community volunteers, men and women, age 60 or over at the time of the beginning of the study in 1954. The overall methodology of this study is well described in several previous publications (2, 8, 12). The second longitudinal study is a study of 502 men and women aged 45 to 69 years of age at the beginning of the study, which was in 1969. The overall methodology of that study is described briefly elsewhere (13). Examinations carried out in the first of these longitudinal studies include the tests, procedures, and examinations listed in Table I, administered to subjects over a two-day period on an ambulatory basis. The procedures carried out on the subjects of the second longitudinal study are generally similar to those in the first, but extend over only a single 8-hour day on an ambulatory basis.

In each of these longitudinal studies, data on sexual behavior were gathered as part of the medical history, and information was sought on the followings topics (possible replies are indicated in parenthesis):

1) Enjoyment of sex relations in younger years (*none, mild, moderate, very much*).
2) Enjoyment of sex relations at present time (*none, mild, moderate, very much*).
3) Sexual feelings in younger years (*absent, weak, moderate, strong*).
4) Sexual feelings at present time (*absent, weak, moderate, strong*).
5) Frequency of sex relations in younger years (*never, once per month, once a week, up to three times a week, more than three times a week*).

TABLE 1

DATA OBTAINED ON SUBJECTS IN STUDY

Social history
Medical history
Psychiatric evaluation
Physical examination
Neurological examination
Ophthalmological examination, including fundus photographs
Audiometry
Electroencephalogram
Electrocardiogram
Ballistocardiogram
Chest x-ray
Microscopic vascular study of bulbar conjunctiva
Laboratory studies
      Urinalysis
      Complete blood counts
      Nonprotein nitrogen determination
      Blood sugar determination
      Serologic test for syphilis
      Serum cholesterol level determination
Full-length photograph against grid
Psychological test data
      Welchsler Adult Intelligence Scale
      Rorschach

6) Frequency of sex relations at present time (*never, once per month, once a week, up to three times a week, more than three times a week*).
7) Awareness of any decline in sexual interest or activity (*yes, no*). If yes, at what age first noted (*5-year age brackets*).
8) If sex relations stopped, when stopped? (*still have, less than year ago, 1-2 years ago, 2-5 years ago, 6-10 years ago, 11-20 years ago, more than 20 years ago*).
9) Reason for stopping sex relations (*not stopped, death of spouse, illness of self, illness of spouse, self lost interest, spouse lost interest, self no longer able to perform sexually, spouse not able to perform sexually, separation or divorced from spouse*).

Pfeiffer, Verwoerdt, Wang and Davis (14, 15, 16, 17, 21, 22) have published a series of papers detailing the findings in regard to sexual behavior from the two longitudinal studies. In this chapter, only a summary of these findings, along with some implications for the practitioner, will be presented.

Perhaps the most important generalization which can be drawn from these studies is the finding that sex continues to play an important role in the lives of many elderly persons (16). Sexual interest and coital activity are by no means rare in persons in their 60's, 70's, and 80's, and by no means unheard-of in persons in their 90's. In one analysis (17) we found that about 80 percent of men whose health, intellectual status, and social functioning were not significantly impaired reported continuing sexual interest at the start of the study. Ten years later the proportion of those still sexually interested had not declined significantly. In this same group of men, 70 percent were still regularly sexually active at the start of the study, but 10 years later this proportion had dropped to 25 percent. Thus there was a growing discrepancy with advancing age between the number still sexually interested and those still sexually active.

Another important finding was the fact that with cross-sectional analysis of the data we found a gradual decline of sexual activity with advancing years, a decline somewhat similar to that projected by Kinsey's findings. However, with a longitudinal analysis it became clear that this gradual decline pattern was not representative of patterns of individuals. Over a 10-year period a group of individuals was followed and the pattern of change in sexual activity for individuals was made up of at least three very distinct patterns. One of these was, in fact, a gradual decline of sexual interest and activity. The other pattern was one of a steady level of sexual interest and activity over the 10-year period of observation, and a third and truly surprising pattern was that for 23 of the men actual increases in sexual interest and activity occurred over the 10-year period of the study (16, 22).

Another finding of general significance which emerged from these several studies was the fact that in virtually every analysis the data for men and for women differed markedly from one another (14, 15, 16, 17, 21, 22). Thus, at every specific age for which data were analyzed, men reported greater sexual interest and activity than did the women of like age. For instance, in the analysis referred to above (17), among women whose health, intellectual status and social functioning were well preserved, only 33 percent (as compared with 80 percent of the men) admitted to continued sexual interest; only 20 percent (as compared with 70 percent for the men) still reported regular sexual activity. As with the men, however, there was no significant decline from these levels in the ensuing 10-year period.

The explanation for this difference between men and women is complex and as yet incomplete. But an examination of the following additional differences between men and women may shed some light on this phenomenon. In the earlier longitudinal study, only 39% of the women, but 82% of the men, studied still had intact marriages (16). Thus the majority of men still had marital partners available; the majority of the women did not. As is well known, women in the U.S. outlive men by approximately 7 years; in addition, women tend to marry men who are on average 4 years their senior; as a result, married women can expect to spend the final 11 years of their lives in widowhood. In addition, if a man becomes widowed, he has ample opportunity to remarry; a widow has almost none. At each successive age level, fewer and fewer men survive for each 100 women, and a good man becomes harder and harder to find.

An additional interesting finding illustrative of the differences between men and women was the fact that the level of sexual activity and interest was essentially *identical* for *married* and *non-married* (includes single, separated, divorced, and widowed) *men;* however, there were major *differences* in level of sexual interest and activity *between married and non-married women,* with only very few of the non-married women reporting any sexual interest or sexual activity (22).

An additional finding which may explain in part the lower level of sexual interest and activity reported by women is the fact that, among men and women asked to give reasons for having ceased sexual relationships in late life, men generally tended to place responsibility for cessation of sexual activity on themselves, while women in general tended to place this responsibility on their husbands. Thus there was congruence between the men and the women that the determining factor for continuity or cessation of sexual activity in a marriage in general was the husband.

Our interpretation of these data has been that age places no limitation on the sexuality of women except that which is related to the limitation age places on the sexuality of their husbands. In short, the availability of a sexually capable and societally sanctioned partner is one of the most important requisites for continued sexual interest and activity among aging women.

How Reliable Are Interview Data on Sexual Behavior?

The question of the reliability of data on sexual behavior obtained by interview has often been raised. The presence of a group of intact couples in the first of these longitudinal studies provided an outstanding opportunity to cross-check the reliability of reporting of sexual data within a marriage. The question of congruence between the two marriage partners was examined from two vantage points (17): (a) Did the two marriage partners agree or disagree on the current frequency of sexual intercourse in their marriage? (b) Did the two marriage partners agree or disagree, in instances where intercourse had already ceased, on who was responsible for stopping intercourse in the marriage? There was agreement of 91% of the responses in regard to the question of presence or absence of sexual activity in the marriage. There was a similar level of agreement between the marriage partners as to who had been responsible for stopping sexual activity in the marriage. These findings have been encouraging to those of us who have utilized interview data to draw conclusions about sexual behavior in late life.

Sexual Behavior in Middle Life

While the studies on individuals 60 years and older provided a certain number of answers to questions, they also raised new questions. What are the antecedents of sexual behavior in old age? Do male-female differences reported in old age already exist in middle age? At what age is decline in sexual functioning noted most commonly, and is this age the same for men and for women? Are specific factors operative in middle age which account for the differences between men and women in reported sexual behavior in old age?

In the studies on sexual behavior of persons aged 46 to 71, many of the observations made on persons over age 60 were confirmed (14, 15). In this age group, too, important differences in sexual behavior between men and women were apparent. At all of the ages at which comparisons were made, men reported both greater sexual interest and activity. While at each 5-year period there was some decline in level of sexual interest and activity, it was also quite clear that during the middle years sex continued to play a very important role in the lives of the vast majority of the subjects studied. Only 6% of the men and 33% of the women said they were no longer interested in sex. Only 12% of the men and only 44% of the women said they no longer had sexual relations. Interestingly, the oldest age group in this study indicated higher levels of sexual involvement than did the next-to-oldest age group. This suggests that this oldest group actually constitutes a group of élite survivors from whose midst less highly advantaged individuals have already been removed by death,

Among the persons in this study, too, who had ceased sexual relations, there was general agreement that it was the man who was responsible for stopping sexual intercourse in the marriage.

From the previous studies we already had some indication that a number of major demographic variables, in particular the age, sex, marital status among women, and previous sexual experience, had considerable effect on the degree of sexual interest and activity. Pfeiffer and Davis also carried out a multiple step-wise regression analysis which examined all the various factors and their independent contribution to the presence or absence of sexual activity and/or interest (14). These analyses indicated that a high level of sexual interest and activity in youth was highly correlated with continued sexual interest and activity in later years. This was true for both men and women, although more markedly so for the men. Thus there would appear to be no validity to the notion that indulgence in sexual activity early in life leads to a "burning out" of sexual interest and activity later in life. Rather, the opposite appears to be true.

Other factors which independently influenced the level of sexual activity and interest in the later years were: age, present physical health status, and social class of the individual. For women, marital status was the principal indicator of current sexual interest or activity.

The overall conclusions which can be drawn from these various studies are that enormous variability exists among individuals and between the sexes in regard to the strength of sexual interest and activity in old age; no specific age has yet been found at which all sexual activity must of necessity cease; and at any given age the availability of a societally sanctioned partner, earlier sexual experience, and good physical health influence in a major way the continuity of a sexual life into old age.

IMPLICATIONS FOR THE PRACTITIONER

What are the implications for the practitioner of the above mentioned findings? First, the practitioner must himself become familiar and comfortable with the idea that many of his aged patients still continue to have or desire an active sex life. Not only may sex still give pleasure to older persons, but sexual problems may also trouble the older persons. Some practitioners are still too ready to dismiss even an allusion to sexual matters as "inappropriate" for an older person and simply avoid discussion of this area of their patients' lives. Counselling an older person or couple successfully on a sexual problem can be very rewarding to the practitioner and his patients. At times the practitioner also has the task of sharing his own understanding of the sexual needs of older persons not only with his patients but also with patients' families, nursing home or hospital administrators, and the general public. In short, the practitioner must seek to educate others and to temper prejudices regarding sexual matters wherever he can.

There is also a great need for individuation. While the practitioner must stand ready to discuss any aspects of sexual behavior with an older person, he must not try to create for the older person any kind of standard of sexual performance the older person should emulate. In counselling the older person, he must take into account the older person's present and previous life-styles, as well as his current interest, desires, and circumstances, in order to allow that person to continue to participate in all of life to the fullest extent possible.

We have discussed sexuality up to now as though it were an activity apart from the general activities of human relatedness. Obviously it is not. It is fully part and parcel of the larger fabric of human interaction; of touch; of affectionate relationships. Older people need these interactions (touch, affection) as much as or more than specific sexual expression. But the taboo against sex in old age robs the older person of this richest measure of human affectionate tactile relationships. An acceptance of the sexual needs of the older person means we accept him as a whole person.

REFERENCES

1. BIRREN, J. E. (Ed.). 1959. *Handbook of Aging and the Individual.* Chicago: University of Chicago Press.
2. BUSSE, E. W. 1966. Longitudinal research—the Duke study. *Proceedings of the 7th International Congress of Gerontology.* Vienna, pp. 283-288, June-July.
3. BUSSE, E. W., and PFEIFFER, E. (Eds.) 1969. *Behavior and Adaptation in Late Life.* Boston: Little, Brown.
4. KINSEY, A. C., POMEROY, W. B., and MARTIN, C. R. 1948. *Sexual Behavior in the Human Male.* Philadelphia: Saunders.
5. KINSEY, A. C., POMEROY, W. B., MARTIN, C. R., and GEBHARD, P. H. 1953. *Sexual Behavior in the Human Female.* Philadelphia: Saunders.
6. LIEF, H. I. 1965. Sex education of medical students and doctors. *Pacif. Med. Surg.,* 73:52-58.
7. LIEF, H. I. 1968. Sex and the medical educator. *J. Am. Med. Wom. Ass.,* 23:195-196.
8. MADDOX, G. L. 1962. A longitudinal multidisciplinary study of human aging: selected methodological issues. *Proc. Soc. Statistics Sect. Am. Statistical Ass.,* 122:280-285.
9. MASTERS, W. H., and JOHNSON, V. E. 1966. *Human Sexual Response.* Boston: Little, Brown.

10. MASTERS, W. H., and JOHNSON, V. E. 1970. *Human Sexual Inadequacy*. Boston: Little, Brown.
11. NEWMAN, G., and NICHOLS, C. R. 1960. Sexual activities and attitudes in older persons. *J.A.M.A.*, 173:33-35.
12. PALMORE, E., (Ed.). 1970. *Normal Aging*. Durham, N.C.: Duke University Press.
13. PFEIFFER, E., and DAVIS, G. L. 1971. The use of leisure time in middle life. *Gerontologist*, 11:187-195, Autumn.
14. PFEIFFER, E., and DAVIS, G. C. 1972. Determinants of sexual behavior in middle and old age. *J. Am. Geriat. Soc.*, 20:151-158.
15. PFEIFFER, E., VERWOERDT, A., and DAVIS, G. C. 1972. Sexual behavior in middle life. *Am. J. Psychiat.*, 128:1262-1267.
16. PFEIFFER, E., VERWOERDT, A., and WANG, H. S. 1968. Sexual behavior in aged men and women. I. Observations on 254 community volunteers. *Arch. Gen. Psychiat.*, 19:641-646.
17. PFEIFFER, E., VERWOERDT, A., and WANG, H. S. 1969. The natural history of sexual behavior in a biologically advantaged group of aged individuals. *J. Geront.*, 24:193-198.
18. RILEY, M. W., and FONER, A. 1968. *Aging and Society*. Volume One: An Inventory of Research Findings. New York: Russell Sage Foundation.
19. SHANAS, E., et al. 1968. *Old People in Three Industrial Societies*. New York: Atherton Press.
20. TIBBITTS, C. (Ed.). 1960. *Handbook of Social Gerontology*. Chicago: University of Chicago Press.
21. VERWOERDT, A., PFEIFFER, E., and WANG, H. S. 1969. Sexual behavior in senescence: I. Changes in sexual activity and interest of aging men and women. *J. Geriat. Psychiat.*, 2:163-180.
22. VERWOERDT, A., PFEIFFER, E., and WANG, H. S. 1969. Sexual behavior in senescence. II. Patterns of sexual activity and interest. *Geriatrics*, 24:137-154.

15

FUNCTIONAL PSYCHOSES

G. E. LANGLEY, M.B., F.R.C. P.ED., M.R.C.PSYCH., D.P.M.

Consultant Psychiatrist, Exe Vale Hospital,
Exminster, Exeter, Devon, England

INTRODUCTION

The occasional psychogeriatrician has to cross two hurdles before he can effectively treat the functional psychoses of old age. Firstly, he must obtain relevant information from a patient in whom communication is likely to be impaired by the processes of aging, sensory deprivation and illness so that a good *interviewing technique* is essential. Secondly, he must cross a self-erected barrier of classification by fitting the observed symptoms and signs into a system that guides him towards effective treatment and a valid prognosis. Clinical method, classification, and treatment will all be dealt with in turn with reference to the literature, but also from the personal viewpoint of one particular clinician, the writer.

CLINICAL METHOD

No psychiatric diagnosis or treatment is better than the quality of the information on which it is based. Psychiatrists accept that the case notes must extend far beyond the conventional history of the present complaint and embrace information about early life, previous personality and family relationships, etc., but this point needs to be made for the benefit of those not trained in the specialty. It is not the purpose of the present chapter to document in detail the techniques of psychiatric history-taking

326

and to a large extent the desired content of a history will become apparent in the discussion of the relevant variables.

History-taking must be followed by an examination and assessment of the patient's mental state, no less than by an examination and investigation of his physical condition. For this purpose each clinician must establish his own, but preferably standardized, simple battery of tests of orientation, memory, etc., bearing in mind that simple questions about the immediate environment are likely to be more productive than some of the more hallowed tests such as "Serial Sevens."

To make adequate personal contact with an elderly, easily fatigued, perhaps forgetful, apathetic, deaf and partially sighted patient and to elicit the depth of information required for a psychiatric diagnosis and appraisal can be a stern test of *clinical technique* and dispassionate patience. For the unwary or hasty, diagnostic error is most likely to be in the direction of underestimating the capacity and/or distress of the patient, to his ultimate detriment. A private, relaxed and unhurried conversation, the acceptance of the necessity for some leading questions, non-personal hearing aids, and a preparedness to communicate by written (if necessary pre-prepared) questions are all required.

It must be recognized that the obstacles to adequate communication are insurmountable in some patients. In untrained workers this is likely to give rise to personal anxiety, perplexity, or hostility as understandable reactions to the frustrations of clinical endeavor. These extreme *communication blocks* can be circumvented by interviewing a third person with close knowledge of the patient, usually a relative, and indeed this can be so profitable that it is to be recommended no matter whether communication with the patient himself is good or poor.

CLASSIFICATION

The work of the clinician is not simply to classify but also (and primarily) to treat and offer a prognosis to those patients who present to his care. As a guide and as a form of shorthand in dealing with the diversity of symptoms seen, he forms in his mind (hopefully) useful classes. These classes have been defined by prior clinical observation and systematic research and are passed from clinician to clinician through the medium of textbook descriptions. Both classifications and descriptions of disease are worthy ends in themselves, but the purpose of arriving at a diagnosis is distinct. This chapter is written as a guide to the process of diagnosis as the first step in determining treatment and prognosis. Additionally, data necessary for the classification of *disease* must be supplemented by that required to arrive at a decision about the total clinical situation, e.g. the diagnosis of depression if the patient is suicidal must be supplemented by relevant information about the support he has available in the community before a decision about his care can be taken.

As systems of *classification* in psychiatry, particularly those concerning the affective states, are open to dispute and imply attitudes with regard to etiology, the author must first make his theoretical standpoint clear in certain areas.

TABLE 1

Psychiatric Disorders of Late Life—Diagnostic Classification

1. Organic: a) Acute
            b) Chronic

2. Affective Psychosis: a) Depressive
                        b) Mania

3. Functional Paranoid States.

4. Neurosis and Personality Disorders.

The classification of mental illness of most value in the psychiatry of late life accepts four broad diagnostic categories, as shown in Table 1. They are not necessarily mutually exclusive. This classification is in part etiological (e.g. in the case of the organic states), but is predominantly based on a grouping of observed symptoms and signs, i.e. a syndrome.

It is important to recognize that symptoms and *syndromes* may both bear the same name, e.g., paranoid symptoms may occur in organic syndromes, but in this case do not imply a functional syndrome. The addition of a mild/severe dimension to all these diagnoses can also profoundly affect the presentation.

This occurrence of similar symptoms in diagnostic groups with different prognoses means that the clinician must approach the problem with a wide *differential diagnosis* in mind before finally placing the patient in one particular diagnostic group. The clinician presented with symptoms of mood disorder must work through a system of classification

TABLE 2

Illnesses Associated with Disorders of Mood

(A) *Depression**

1. (a) Primary affective psychosis—depression.
   (b) Primary affective psychosis precipitated by drugs, e.g. Rauwolfia preparations or infections, e.g. post-influenzal.
   (c) Neurosis—reactive depressive states.

2. (a) Associated with organic cerebral disease, e.g., neoplasm (temporal lobe), G P I, arteriosclerotic dementia.
   (b) Associated with organic non-cerebral disease, e.g. thyrotoxicosis, myxoedema, Vitamin B_{12} deficiencies, non-cerebral neoplasm, urinary infections.

3. As part of a functional paranoid state.

4. Mixed, as part of a multiple diagnosis, e.g. primary depressive illness in a senile dement.

(B) *Mania*

1. Primary affective disorder—mania.

2. Euphoria associated with clouding of consciousness.

3. Frontal lobe euphoria.

* See later remarks with regard to endogenous and reactive depressive states.

such as that shown in Table 2 before arriving at a diagnosis of either a primary mood disorder, e.g. depression, or an alternative illness, e.g. functional paranoid or organic, in another diagnostic category, i.e. with depression as a secondary feature of this illness.

Similar tables can be written for a case presenting with forgetfulness who may suffer from dementia or a depressive pseudo-dementia or with paranoid symptoms, in which latter case the diagnosis may be either organic, depressive or schizophrenic. Although this chapter is not concerned with organic mental states, they are relevant to the need for exclusion. The main characteristics of the main syndromes to be differentiated are described in general terms in Table 3.

Having placed the patient tentatively in one of the main diagnostic groups, the next clinical step is to refine and confirm the diagnosis, arrive at a *prognosis,* establish any need for further investigation, and institute treatment. Leaving aside the organic states to be dealt with elsewhere, the affective psychoses will now be considered in more detail.

TABLE 3

Description of Clinical State in Main Diagnostic Categories

Organic mental states: Marked failure of memory and orientation, intellect, and ability to organize life. Some cases, principally in the arteriosclerotic sub-group, will show an admixture of mood disturbances. Functional incapacity may vary from a mild to a profound disorganization of the personality, with a need for considerable external support, and is usually slowly progressive. Paranoid symptoms may be present.

Affective psychosis

(a) *Depression*: The principal symptoms seen are lowering of mood, anxiety, irritability, insomnia, guilt, self-blame, anorexia, and general withdrawal. There may be associated obsessive, compulsive, histrionic, or hypochondriacal symptoms. Psychomotor responses are slowed, and agitation, the motor component of anxiety, may be seen. Memory, orientation, and intellect are unaffected except that depressive withdrawal may make assessment difficult and give an appearance of "organic" (pseudodementia) type of failure. Paranoid ideation can also occur.

(b) *Mania*: Typically, mania is characterized by euphoria, optimism and excessive cheerfulness. In the elderly it often shows as an acute and persistent irritability with a strong paranoid flavor.

Functional paranoid states: These symptoms attribute hostility and hostile acts to others or may involve grandiose feelings about the self. The ideas are commonly highly organized and persistent but may be less persistent, fleeting and changeable. Some mood disturbance may be associated and some organized paranoid states appear to be associated with minor degrees of organic mental deterioration not amounting to profound dementia. Hallucinations may be present, but in the main thought processes are coherent. Consciousness is clear.

THE AFFECTIVE PSYCHOSES—DEPRESSION

Classification

Primary disorders of mood may center around low or high spirits, being called depressive or manic accordingly. Mania should be reserved for use in this specific sense and not applied to any state of overactivity, e.g. in delirium. Discussions over the *classification of depressive illness* are as old as psychiatry and the debate has moved from the intuitive/descriptive approach into the current statistical/methodological era, but is as yet unfinished. In terms of the depressive illnesses of old age, the present writer finds his clinical intuition leads him to favor the ideas expressed by Post (39). ". . . Every depressive attack is an individual affair. It is not infrequently characterized by different symptom complexes at different times during the life of the same person. On each separate occasion the illness should be regarded as an individual amalgam

TABLE 4

A Classification of Depression in Late Life
(modified from Post (38))

Type	Symptoms
Severe	a) Severe depression with nihilistic, somatic, or paranoid delusions and/ or *guilt and self-blame*. Some anxiety and agitation may be present. b) Severe depression without delusions or guilt or self-blame. Some anxiety may be present.
Intermediate	c) Mild depression with delusions or guilt as above and possibly some histrionicity and complainingness. d) Depressive delusions or guilt without overt depression.
Neurotic	e) Mild depression without delusions or guilt. f) Neither overt depression nor depressive thought content, but with poor sleep and appetite, loss of interest in outside matters, non-delusional pre-occupation with unpleasant internal sensations, tension, or anxiety.

multifactorily compounded of inborn and acquired predispositions to depression, current emotional trauma and existing personality defects, which are themselves, of course, the product of predisposition and life experience." In this present chapter the terms *endogenous* and *reactive* will be avoided because of their etiological implications, but this is not to deny that syndromes of retarded or anxious depression exist (25). Similarly, no mention will be made of the concept of *involutional melancholia* which has been largely discarded in favor of the continuum approach to depressive symptomatology.

A practical classification suggested by Post (39) and based largely on a grading of severity is summarized in Table 4. Sub-parts of this table are grouped and classified as severe, intermediate and neurotic without any particular etiological implication in the label. Depression is defined as severe if both *"distinct quality"* (5) and *"depressive psychomotor activity"* (retardation or agitation) are present together. Mild depression refers to the presence of one or other but not both of these features and depression is regarded as absent when neither of these features is present. It should be explained that "distinct quality" refers to the particular feeling of depression that many depressives state to be distinct from ordinary sadness felt in the face of adversity and disappointment.

No difference in prognosis is implied by this grading of severity and although in Post's study E.C.T. was often used in treating the more severe states, it was used to a significant degree in all grades. Within this broad classification, certain particular modes of presentation bear mention.

Atypical Presentation of Depression

(1) *Depressive pseudo-dementia*: The patient may appear perplexed. Forgetfulness and disorientation mimic an organic mental syndrome. Differentiation from genuine organic syndromes may be difficult, but the onset is often sudden, pre-morbid intelligence often low, and the patient at interview tends to show apathy and disinterestedness rather than give wrong or confabulated replies.

(2) *Hypochondriasis* (35) shows in the form of unjustified complaints or an unwarranted conviction of physical disease, especially if found in a previously uncomplaining patient. Alternatively, it may present with demands for an indulgence in polypharmacy, often with severe intolerance of the drugs prescribed.

(3) Concurrent long standing physical or neurotic illness may be present and may mask a superimposed depression.

(4) Cases may also present with unexplained sub-nutrition and self-neglect, especially in patients living alone.

(5) The quiet uncomplaining patient, perhaps unheeded from the psychiatric viewpoint, in the corner of a general ward, i.e. the too patient patient, may also be depressed.

(6) The histrionic or predominantly anxious patient (including those with phobias) without a previous history of neurosis who presents for the first time over the age of 60 years should be suspect.

(7) Unwarranted and premature retirement blamed on overwork may be an early symptom.

(8) Unreasonable and sometimes repetitive changes of residence or routine can also be motivated by depressive thinking.

In any of these atypical and masked depressive states, change in *sleep pattern,* a *self-deprecatory attitude,* or lessening of activity offers important clues.

If the significance of the differential diagnosis between depression and *dementia* may be discussed at this point, it is worth saying that dubious or early dementia can usually be ignored, especially in the more elderly patients. Patients suffering from depression do not progress to dementia in any greater numbers than do non-depressives. Depressive symptoms may color the organic syndrome, but in this case slowly progressive organic symptoms usually precede the affective component. The emotional lability and "April showers" of an arteriosclerotic dement are usually not regarded as part of the primary depressive syndromes, although needing mention only to be excluded. Such depressive syndromes as do occur simultaneously with an organic picture usually have a shallow feel about them in that the intensity of feeling of a severe primary depressive is not conveyed to the observer. (They may still be worthy of treatment.)

Suicide

Of special importance are those symptoms and other characteristics of the elderly depressed patient that indicate a risk of suicide. Barraclough (4) reviews suicide in the elderly and records that in a study of thirty suicides over the age of 65 years, 87% were mentally ill and in all such cases an affective disorder of some type was present. He noted that the traditional symptoms associated with suicide are agitation, persistent insomnia, feelings of guilt, inadequacy, and delusions of disease. In Barraclough's own sample, insomnia, loss of weight, reduced activities, hypochondriasis, guilt, loss of concentration, anxiety, and agitation were the commonest symptoms and were present in 50% or more of cases. It is important to note that he states that the intensity of the symptoms were not severe and would not of necessity impress doctors or relatives. Many suicides occur after an illness of less than one year's duration and in most cases (83%) there had been a consultation with a doctor within three months of the event. Psychiatric drugs had been prescribed in 80% of cases. Serious physical illness was present in a higher proportion of elderly suicides than would be expected by chance.

In Barraclough's study a significant proportion had lived alone for less than one year. Many of those living alone for short periods did so by reason of the death or admission to hospital of a relative or friend and more rarely because of the break-up of a marriage. The majority of those living alone for a substantial period of five to seven years appeared to do so by choice and it is noted that the reason for suicide may be separate in the two groups, bereavement in the former and super-added illness in the latter. Anniversaries of a significant loss may be dangerous times.

Sainsbury (47) points out that while the suicide rate for elderly men is falling and is still greater than that for females, the rate for females is increasing. Suicide rates are highest in the professional and managerial classes: those with no spouse are more prone than those with a spouse. Suicide rates are lower in wartime and times of social stress.

In addition to the factors mentioned by Barraclough, Sainsbury (47) lists the following as important in the recognition of suicidal depression: a family history of suicide, previous attempts, a history of alcoholism or psychopathic personality in *addition* to the diagnosis of an affective illness and loss of a parent in childhood. The period shortly after discharge from hospital also appears to be a time of greater risk. In summary, these patients have suffered broken relationships in the past and are breaking in the present, either in their spirits or physical health.

The Etiology of Depressive Illness

With the clinical picture clearly in mind, some aspects of etiology may be briefly discussed. Some reference to the multideterminant nature of depressive illness has been made in the remarks on the endogenous v. reactive debate. The autosomal dominant *genetic* factor in the constitution of the depressive is now preferred to the polygenetic theory. This genetic component is least strong in those cases where depression begins for the first time in late life and where there are strong precipitants. A positive family history is found more often in depressives than chance would anticipate, but is not necessarily related to the severity of the subsequent illness.

The effect of environment upon constitution is shown by those depressives who above expectation give a history of loss of one or both parents before the age of 15. The previous personality of the depressive is one of the few things associated with the severity of the depression, as rated in Post's classification. Those with "severe" psychotic depressive illnesses are more likely to have normal personalities than those in the neurotic class, who show neurotic, sexual, and psychopathic deviations in their pre-morbid personality.

Precipitants of depressive illness are very common in the elderly, both Post (38) and Wilson and Lawson (57) quoting a high incidence. They are frequently present even in the group with the highest constitutional loading, but evaluation of precipitating causes is always difficult and precipitants and early symptomatic social disturbance can be easily con-fused. All precipitants must be judged in the light of their personal meaning to the patient and not their significance to the examiner. Denial being a common defence mechanism in depression, many pre-cipitants are not revealed until after recovery or upon questioning a third party. An important group of pharmacological precipitants exists in the form of drugs used in the treatment of hypertension, notably the Rauwolfia alkaloids and Aldomet. Parkinson patients treated with L-Dopa are also at risk. Acute infections, especially influenza and urinary infections, are also important precipitants. Early carcinoma has also been shown to present with a depressive illness.

Recently suggested models for the origin of depressive illness (41) are the *hibernation* model when the environment is inclement and the *domi-nance hierarchy* model. In the latter, any fall in the pecking order lowers mood and would certainly be relevant to many on retirement and in the senium. Mania in old age is more difficult to explain in this model.

At this point some of the non-specific *psychological stresses* experienced by the elderly will be discussed although they are not necessarily relevant only to depression. A large section of present day society values youth, assertion, and acquisition, which characteristics may not be held by the elderly in abundance! Feeling undervalued by society and without a role to play, the elderly may undervalue themselves. Society's neglect and fail-ure to support an old person may be echoed in his own lack of self-care. Anticipatory anxiety in the face of foreseen advancing age, infirmity, or approaching death can precipitate new or resurrect old and previously hidden conflicts, anxiety, and guilt about dependency in both the patient and others. Submission to the will or needs of others in an institution or in the household of another and *dominance/submission problems* at times of role reversal between parents and children or between marriage part-ners may cause anxiety. For example, where the dominant spouse becomes disabled by illness, the other partner may become overwhelmed by his new responsibilities. In the writer's practice the husband of a demented old lady found it very difficult to accept that his wife could no longer find her way to post his letters for him!

Old *family conflicts* may be resurrected where a relative has to go be-cause of illness or age to a household of which he was previously inde-pendent. Admission of an old person to hospital may cause younger rela-tives to grieve in anticipation of loss and, having grieved, experience distress and concern at having to rebuild the recovered invalid into their lives. Repetitive attempts on the part of relatives to search for a cure may be motivated by the need to deny and reject the necessity of continuous care. Recognition by an old person of anxiety and hostility in an attendant relative or the venting of such feelings upon the patient is yet another emotional burden for him to bear. Notably in depression, a sense of loss, particularly after a difficult relationship with the lost one, is important. The loss may be actual or threatened, of a person or a valued ideal, and remains equally potent in its effect. There is a continuous gradation with normal grief and mourning, and an aggressive component is present in both the normal and pathological states, which in the extreme can result in suicide.

Investigation of Depressive Illness

It will be clear from what has been said already that a social and medical as well as psychiatric examination must be undertaken. The task is well suited to the psychiatrist and social worker acting together in a hospital setting with full physical and laboratory investigatory facilities. Much can be achieved in a modern general practice supported by social workers, health visitors, and the laboratory. The high incidence of depression as a secondary feature in neoplastic, endocrine diseases and blood dyscrasias makes a thorough physical appraisal essential in every case.

Prognosis

Extensive studies of the outcome of depressive illness in old age show that clinical presentation is a poor guide to prognosis. There appear to be no symptoms which give a good indication of outcome. Poor results most frequently are due to the recurrence of a remitted illness or to a failure to retain the previous level of health because of the residual depressive or neurotic symptoms. Post's early investigations suggested that factors indicative of good prognosis were: age less than 70, a positive family history, recovery from an earlier attack before the age of 50, extroverted personality with social activities and ideas reaching beyond the family, and an even temperament without psychopathic or dysthymic trends.

Factors indicative of poor prognosis are brain damage, serious physical illness, age over 70, and an illness continuous for two years or more. Later research (39) has suggested that symptoms bear little relation to prognosis and that the main adverse factors are age over 70 and disabling physical illness. Although these two factors are in general adverse, their presence does not necessarily mean a poor outcome in every individual case. Duration of illness of two years or more augurs badly for the outcome, but again not in every case. In Post's cases of intermediate severity, the duration of the illness is a poor guide to outcome. Obsessional symptoms making their first appearance within the setting of depression after the age of 50 tend to remain obtrusive. The presence of confirmed cerebral disease as a special case of severe physical disease deserves special mention as indicating poor prognosis.

In general, depressive states show a considerably better prognosis than organic syndromes. The expectancy of life is, however, somewhat less than that of the mentally unaffected person or the functional paranoid patient of the same age, probably because of the relationship between depression and physical illness (particularly vascular disease) already noted.

Treatment of Depressive Illness

A progressive approach to the individual patient will be described. Associated illness must be treated and any offending drugs withdrawn. The main psychiatric treatments of first choice are *electro-convulsive therapy* and *tricyclic anti-depressants*. The choice between them must depend upon the severity of the illness (the quicker response from E.C.T. being desirable in those most severely disturbed) and response to previous treatment (re-applying a previously "failed" treatment is not always contra-indicated, but should be approached with caution).

Anti-depressant drugs: Presuming that urgent E.C.T. is not required, the first step is to prescribe tricyclic anti-depressants, ultimately in adequate doses but initially, even if only for two or three days, in small doses to guard against unpleasant sequelae. It should be understood from the outset that tricyclic anti-depressants are not euphoriants and will only be effective in the presence of certain as yet largely undetermined biochemical states associated with the more severe and retarded depressions. Broadly speaking, they may be classified into two groups, those which are more sedative such as Amitriptyline hydrochloride 50-150 milligrams daily and those which have little sedative effect such as Iprindole 45-90 milligrams daily. Both tend to be more effective in the retarded depressive rather than the anxious depressive, but are worthy of trial in either group.

By the time a severe illness is established with delusions, drugs are less likely to be effective than E.C.T. Improvement with drugs may not become apparent for two weeks and if no response is shown after four weeks the drug should be discontinued. There is said to be a lower relapse rate after treatment with tricyclic compounds compared with electroplexy. The total duration of treatment after response is a matter for judgment. As these drugs are suppressive rather than curative, the illness will relapse if they are withdrawn too quickly. In practice it is wise to maintain therapy for a minimum of three months after improvement, continuing perhaps to a year or more in those cases where the illness has a tendency to relapse or where social conditions are adverse. Indefinite prescription is not favored by the writer as he has seen many cases relapse after several years of continuous Amitriptyline medication.

Favorable responses are more likely to be seen in those who have been ill for a shorter time, who have previously responded to this class of drugs, and who have more adequate personal and social resources. The genetic factor in etiology and treatment is also shown by the report by Pare (29) that improvement is more likely when there is a family history of response to the same drug in similar clinical circumstances. The response to tricyclic anti-depressants is in general more satisfactory than that to monoamino-oxidase inhibitors in the more severe depressions, especially the retarded depressions. Intravenous infusion of Clomipramine hydrochloride is now possible, but its use in the elderly is limited by the dangers of overloading the circulation. Amitriptyline and Trimipramine may be usefully given in a single (daily) dose at night, in which circumstance, because of the sedative properties of these drugs, night sedation may be reduced or omitted.

The side effects of tricyclic anti-depressants are mostly anti-cholinergic. Those particularly difficult in the elderly are dry mouth, tachycardia (which may aggravate arrythmias or congestive cardiac failure), loss of visual accommodation (precipitating glaucoma), postural hypotension (that may precipitate falls and fractures), and urinary retention. In general, however, and with controlled doses, these effects are not formidable and should not deter the therapist. Jaundice is rare. The tendency of these drugs to simulate ischaemic changes of the E.C.G. should be remembered. Activation of the E.E.G. dysrythmias and fits can occur. Toxic confusional states, although rare, have been reported and are important to remember in the elderly where clouding of consciousness and perceptual anomalies are common.

Electroplexy: The indications for electroplexy are:

    (a) The need for immediate relief of symptoms because of either personal distress or suicidal risk.
    (b) A strong delusional content.
    (c) Failed drug treatment.

Modern techniques of anaesthesia, with premedication and pre-oxygenation, and the administration of a controlled dose of electricity from a calibrated and automatic machine either bi-temporally or to the non-dominant hemisphere make this a safe technique for the elderly. Age is no bar. Cardiovascular disease is a bar only in the presence of recent coronary or severe congestive disease. Acute systemic and respiratory infections should be treated before electroplexy is commenced. For those with some cardiovascular impairment, a well-given anaesthetic and electroplexy twice weekly may be preferable to the continuing and protracted effect of anticholinergic drugs upon the heart.

There is no magic in numbers, but most patients require five to eight biweekly treatments, some more, unless confusion or hypomania intervenes. Attention to the pre treatment environment is important to minimize anxiety and distress to the patient. In the presence of organic mental confusion, E.C.T. should be given with caution and then only in the presence of the uncommonly seen combination with severe affective distress.

The side effects of E.C.T. on a minor level include temporary memory impairment and muscular aches and pains (from depolarising relaxants). Post ictal nausea and vomiting may be relieved by pre-medication with an anti-emetic such as Promethazine 25 milligrams.

More severe side effects include confusional states (rarely) and fractures, especially in the upper lumbar vertebrae, but these should not occur when the fit is properly modified by muscle relaxants. Hypomania is sometimes an undesired sequel in a patient with a manic-depressive constitution. E.C.T. may safely be combined with tricyclic anti-depressants, but it is wise to exercise caution when monoamino inhibitor drugs have been pre scribed. Preferably they should be discontinued before treatment begins. E.C.T., while more immediate in effect, is less likely to prevent recurrences than the tricyclic group of anti-depressants and lithium.

Should the above treatments fail or be contra-indicated, a number of additional anti-depressants and adjuvant treatments are available.

Monoamino-oxidase inhibitors: Scientific evidence for the place of monoamino-oxidase inhibitors (M.O.I.'s) in treatment is conflicting. In general, however, it is thought that they are most effective in those patients suffering from depression, anxiety, and an atypical sleep pattern who also give a history of good pre-morbid personality. Nevertheless, they are worth a trial in any elderly depressive who has failed other treatments, as responsiveness to these drugs can never be predicted with accuracy. Isocarboxazid, 10 milligrams twice or thrice daily, is perhaps the safest, as it is the M.O.I. with the least sympathomimetic effect. The necessary restrictions of diet, alcoholic intake, and certain drugs must be instituted. All patients should carry a warning card. As with other M.O.I.'s, Isocarboxazid can be given immediately after a course of tricyclic anti-depressants without a rest period. Like other anti-depressants, there is a latent period of up to two weeks; if the drug has been ineffective at the end of one month it should be withdrawn. In addition to prescription alone, it may be combined with tricyclic anti-depressants, although this measure is best reserved for those who are resistant to simpler regimes. When so combined the combination is safe, but it is better to use Amitriptyline or Trimipramine rather than Imipramine, for in this latter combination side effects are more frequent. Whilst electroplexy can be added to combined drug regimes, the writer feels it is safer to omit the combination of electroplexy and an M.O.I. in the elderly. Of the other M.O.I.'s, Tranylcypromine is perhaps the most potent, but also the most dangerous because of its strong sympathomimetic effect.

The side effects of treatment with M.O.I.'s of most significance to the elderly are dizziness and hypotension leading to falls; water retention that results in congestive heart failure; muscular irritability that may be mistaken for fits or a small stroke; and peripheral neuropathy which may give rise to unpleasant parasthesiae. The risk of jaundice is now accepted as small.

The need for care before taking certain foods and drugs in combination with M.O.I.'s is now well-known. Again with emphasis on problems most likely to be seen in the elderly, the chief points to note are that M.O.I.'s should not be combined with Imipramine or amphetamine compounds. In the writer's view, there is no indication for amphetamines in the treatment of depression or any other condition. Adverse effects from the combination of M.O.I.'s with Rauwolfia preparations and Alpha-Methyl Dopa should be noted because it is possible that these drugs have been prescribed for hypertension. Well-meaning dietary additions given to a debilitated depressed patient may well include cheese, Marmite, Bovril, broad beans, and alcohol, and these should be specifically guarded against. The potentiation of narcotics, barbiturates, and phenothiazines should be noted, as certainly the latter two drugs are commonly prescribed. Insulin can also be potentiated to the detriment of the elderly diabetic.

Lithium: Lithium is best used in the prophylaxis of relapsing depressive or manic-depressive illnesses, but may also be used in the treatment of depression. It can be prescribed as the salt Lithium Carbonate or in delayed relapse form, Priardel, the latter having the advantage of less gastric irritation and a smoother absorption. In the treatment of depressive (and manic) illness, the response tends to be slower than with other modes of treatment. Because of a danger of an increased toxicity in the presence of sodium and electrolyte imbalance, or renal failure, it is wise to screen all patients prior to the treatment for the presence of such disorders. During treatment, the diet should contain an adequate sodium content. The treatment should commence with Lithium Carbonate 250 milligrams twice or thrice daily or Priardel 400 milligrams twice daily and be increased slowly under laboratory control of the serum lithium level and with due recognition of side effects. Equilibrium with the brain tissue tends to be slow and levels in the brain may be considerably higher or lower than the serum levels, depending on the direction of the gradient. Serum lithium estimations may be commenced approximately two weeks after the beginning of treatment and should in the first instance be at weekly intervals extending to monthly or longer intervals as control is achieved. The serum lithium should be kept to within the therapeutic limits of 1 to 1.5 milli-equivalents per litre. Levels over these figures or the presence of toxic side effects should call for a reduction in the dose. Lower blood levels are ineffective.

Toxicity is most commonly shown by gastro-intestinal effects, including vomiting which may be either local gastric or central in origin, diarrhea and a fine tremor (which is common and of no great significance). A coarse tremor comparable to a "liver flap" is a danger signal. Headache and coma can result if toxicity is extreme. Some thirst and polyuria are quite common side effects and in some cases thyroid enlargement, usually non-active, has been reported after the use of this drug for long periods. A full review of lithium therapy is given by Schou (49).

The point when a depressive illness is regarded as relapsing sufficiently often to warrant protracted lithium therapy is a matter for clinical judgment. Certainly in those cases which repeatedly relapse in less than a year from recovery treatment is worthwhile. In patients who relapse at intervals of two years or more, one must weigh the possible long term complications and the burden of regular surveillance against possible benefit.

A study of patient rejection of Lithium Carbonate (33) suggests that some patients reject this drug because they feel "a brake on creativity . . . an inability to express themselves, with diminished drive and an absence of incentive." It may be that they are less hypomanic on the drug and resent the change to normality. Alternatively, in some subtle way lithium may impair cognitive functioning and although the author cannot confirm this from personal experience there would seem to be at least a theoretical problem here in terms of the use of this drug in the elderly. Other patients dislike lithium because they believe it has a depressive effect on them. It is difficult to exclude coincidence and certainly, in the main, lithium is beneficial rather than harmful, but the possibility of a small group of patients in whom the reaction is adverse must be considered. Many other remittant and relapsing patients accept the treatment gratefully.

Adjuvant treatments: Recent reports suggest that tricyclic anti-depressants are potentiated by small doses of thyroid hormone, even in patients with normal thyroid function (8, 55, 56). In these studies, Amitriptyline 100 milligrams with Liothyronine (T3-40 MCG daily) was shown to be more effective than either Amitriptyline or Liothyronine alone. Similar results have been reported in combination witn Imipramine and in this latter study Liothyronine was given for only two weeks in the hope that once recovery was established the thyroid supplement would no longer be required. No deterioration was observed after the thyroid was withdrawn. Both studies suggest in different ways that slightly higher doses of or longer medication with Liothyronine may be required in women. Interestingly, Coppen states that Liothyronine diminishes the side effects of both Imipramine and L-Tryptophane. Clinicians will know of the dangers of coronary insufficiency that can arise when too much thyroid is given too quickly to elderly patients.

In studying thyroid function in depressives, Whybrow (56) suggests that patients with a faster ankle reflex time prior to treatment show a greater improvement with Imipramine than those with a slower ankle reflex time.

L-Tryptophane: This amino acid is a precursor of Serotonin, one of the neurogenic centrally active monoamines on which anti-depressant drugs operate in the brain. The addition of the precursor to the diet can significantly increase therapeutic response (8) without increasing toxicity. The preparation is given in either capsules or a chocolate flavored mixture, but the dose is rather high and can be nauseating.

This is a useful potentiating technique in many cases. The writer has seen startling improvement in a patient with poor nutrition who was not responding to conventional treatments and it is tempting to speculate that the failure to respond was due to the lack of the basic substrate on which the anti-depressant acts.

Tranquilizers: Anxiety is a common symptom in depressions of late life. While symptomatic treatment of such anxiety with tranquilizers alone is mistaken, it is nevertheless important to give patients symptomatic relief until such time as anti-depressant drugs or E.C.T. are effective. One of the diazepoxide derivatives is best such as Chlordiazepoxide, 10 milligrams t.d.s., Medazepam, 10 milligrams t.d.s., or Oxasepam 10-30 milligrams t.d.s. Diazepam is an alternative, but tends to produce muscular weakness and incoordination. These drugs all exert an effect preferentially upon the limbic system and Parkinsonism is not seen. Phenothiazines are best avoided because of the tendency to produce Parkinsonism, dystonic reactions, and oral dyskinesia which, with continued medication, may become permanent. In some severely agitated depressives, their use may be justified for brief periods, in which case Chlorpromazine 50-100 milligrams t.d.s. is more sedative than one of the Piperazine derivatives such as Perphenazine 4 milligrams t.d.s., which is nevertheless sometimes worth a trial.

Leucotomy: Leucotomy in the past has found favor for the treatment of protracted severe depressive illness in late life, i.e. those over two years duration. Modern localized stereotactic operations may still have a part to play in a few cases, but the development of drug and electro-convulsive therapies has reduced the need for this treatment and it is significant that in a recent follow-up study (39) only one case out of a series of 92 was operated upon. The morbidity rate and risks of personality deterioration after the modern limited operations are acceptably small, providing clinical indications are present.

Psychological treatment: Psychological treatment of the elderly depressive has been left until last for consideration, not because it is least in importance but because it is a separate dimension that can be applied continuously through all other previously mentioned treatments.

In the more severely depressed, agitated, and nihilistic cases, psychotherapy may amount to no more than the therapist's acceptance of disability. The patient is asked to give no more than his ability allows. This may be accompanied by simple and persistent reassurance that the illness will ultimately resolve. Some patients of obsessive disposition must be prevented from provocatively testing out their (dis)ability before they are ready for the task in hand, so that they are saved from repeated, demoralizing failure. As the depression and retardation resolve, many patients have to be encouraged during a phase of anxiety and tension by reassurance and education in the technique of relaxation. A similar period of tension is often seen on return home from hospital and relaxation learned in hospital can be usefully applied.

During the course of a profound depression, it is wise to avoid far-reaching decisions about the future, such as a move of home, the sale of a house, or a change of residence to an area where friends are few. On recovery, many patients will regret decisions made during their illness and find in them a ready-made precipitant for the next breakdown. The therapist must maintain the patient's self-respect at a time when he is more likely to devalue himself. Some recently bereaved patients will need to be helped through the due process of grief. Practical aid and support in the early crisis of bereavement may be followed, when it can be tolerated, by frank discussion of the mixed feelings and loyalties that accompany the sense of loss. Emotional catharsis should be allowed, even if not encouraged, and certainly not suppressed. The therapist's own acceptance of the internalized, aggressive component in depression can often bring relief, although care must be taken that the patient does not feel the interpretation is an aggressive act in itself.

Social support is important both in and out of hospital. Shochet (50) talks of securing the social nutrition of the patient and community activities; day centers and voluntary organizations can all play their part in rehabilitation and prophylaxis.

Prophylaxis and management of suicide and attempted suicide: The fact that patients will attempt suicide and as a consequence intrude themselves into the clinician's practice must be accepted without hostile reaction to the aggressive component in the psychopathology. In any successful or unsuccessful attempt at self-damage, there are components of personal despair and aggression. Views on the right of the suicidal patient to determine his own fate are largely determined in both the patient and the therapist by personal and socio-cultural factors. Nevertheless, they need to be discussed frankly as a topic and few clinicians will deny that a determined patient has this option of self-destruction open to him should he so wish. Hospitalization may be offered if the patient is frightened of his own impulses and wishes help. In some resuscitated cases or in those communicating intent, *providing change can be effected in the life situation (either clinical or social)*, the patient may be better treated without hospital admission. All other techniques having failed, there is a place for compulsory admission to hospital in order to prevent self-harm during the course of what is in essence a treatable and temporary illness.

Socio-medical requirements for suicide prevention have been discussed by Sainsbury (48) and Barraclough (4). The first must be towards improving the old person's physical health, including even minor ailments, so that he has a greater capacity for independence and social activity. Retirement needs to be planned and anticipated so that there is no sudden cessation of the support to self-esteem that comes from role-playing. The general practitioner, the doctor in the emergency room, and physicians concerned with resuscitation must be able to recognize and understand the symptoms of depression, particularly in the high risk cases mentioned above. Most suicides communicate their intent, most often to a doctor. Ready cross referral between all agencies concerned, including social agencies, is a sine qua non.

Any person involved must be able to talk without embarrassment about the problems of death and be able to lead from simple questions on the patient's interests, through to interest in life, and finally to thoughts of or interest in death. A question such as, "Do you ever go to bed not caring whether you wake again or not?" is a useful entrée to more intimate thoughts.

A community based psychiatric service is preferable. The open-door policy in psychiatric hospitals has been shown to reduce rather than increase the incidence of suicide. Organizations in the community which produce immediate aid, such as the Samaritans, are effective and the importance of third party referrals by those who know a patient to be at risk is now recognized. Feedback of information from coroners would alert all clinicians concerned to the problems of their own practice. Relatives have a part to play and must be educated into the danger signals. Psychiatrists, social workers and relatives must realize that the transition from home to hospital, and indeed the reverse, are danger times. Stengel (51) points out that any measures which improve the medical and social preventive services will reduce the suicide rate. After-care must be as thorough as treatment and should aim at maintaining contact (perhaps diminishing in frequency) with the patient during his rehabilitation in the community. This can be an open life line of communication.

THE AFFECTIVE PSYCHOSES—MANIA

Mania produces symptoms which are polar opposite to those seen in depression. It is less common than depression and represents only 5%

to 10% of all referrals for affective disorder. It may share the course of an illness with depressive episodes or occur in isolated attacks, some with a tendency to chronicity. The picture in the elderly tends to be atypical when compared with the more classic picture of the disease described in middle age.

Clinical Picture

(a) *Typical*: There is a sudden onset with psychomotor overactivity, elation of mood, distractibility, and delusions of omnipotent and omniscient content. Self-confidence, self-esteem and feelings of well-being are exaggerated. Behavior may be erotic and irritability may ensue when frustrations occur. Speech is over-productive and may be incoherent as a result of a choice of words according to sound rather than meaning. Magical thinking, aggressive attitudes, and heightened genital libido are manifest. Conflicts and drives tend to be externalized (14).

(b) *Atypical*: Overactivity may not be marked and there is a greater admixture of depressive symptoms. Speech tends to show circumstantiality rather than flights of ideas and paranoid (basically grandiose but sometimes amorous) delusions are more likely. Mild organic features may be seen and there is an associated air of perplexity. A feeling of gaiety tends to be lacking and irritability and, indeed, overt aggression can be marked. Nevertheless, the manner and appearance tend to be youthful.

Differential diagnoses: Euphoria associated with clouding of consciousness, frontal lobe lesions and L-Dopa therapy need to be considered. Some euphoria can also occur in dementing illnesses of both the arteriosclerotic and senile types. A strong paranoid content will suggest paraphrenia, while admixture of depressive symptoms may cause confusion with the diagnosis of depression (with the unfortunate consequence of anti-depressant treatment).

Etiology

Mania being part of the affective psychoses, the etiology is largely that of depression. Constitutional rather than reactive factors are considered predominant, but if "reactive depression" is an acceptable diagnosis there seems to be no reason why "reactive mania" should not be acceptable. The biochemical determinants of mania remain obscure. In the psychoanalytic model (14), the presence of real or threatened loss, as in depression, is regarded as important. From this, hypomania can be seen as defense against depression or as an attempt to resolve a conflict involving aggression by the free expression of aggressive drive against an external object. In the depressive state the conflict is internalized and the aggression self-directed. Certainly the most aggressive old lady that the writer has seen was an elderly manic.

Prognosis

Most manic illnesses beginning in old age subside within six months. Chronic cases are possible but unusual, and have often started before old age. Treatment with lithium (see below) has greatly improved the prognosis for relapsing cases. Attacks of depression during the recovery period (28) are not uncommon, occurring in at least 28% of cases (all ages). Such a change occurring soon after discharge from hospital could have serious consequences unless relatives are forewarned of the action they should take and follow-up facilities are available. There is an unconfirmed suggestion that such reactions may be more common in those cases of mania treated with Haloperidol.

Treatment

The principal drugs used in the treatment of mania are the phenothiazines (Chloropromazine and Thioridazine); the butyrophenone Haloperidol; and the salt, Lithium Carbonate. The carbonic anhydrase inhibitor, Benzanilamide, has been reported effective in the treatment of mania (53). The dose of whatever agent is used is that which achieves control within a reasonable period of time and without producing toxicity. Body weight is relevant to the dose employed.

If urgent control is required, intravenous injections of Chlorpromazine in doses of 25-50 milligrams diluted in 10 c.c.'s of normal saline can be given. Intramuscular Chlorpromazine 50 milligrams can also be given to those who refuse oral medication, but can sometimes lead to unpleasant local reactions. Haloperidol 3-5 milligrams can also be given by intramuscular injections to a non-cooperative patient and some advocate larger starting doses, 10-30 milligrams daily, but this is not without danger of Parkinsonism in the elderly.

There is a danger in the too vigorous use of these medications in the elderly. Chlorpromazine can produce drowsiness and extra pyramidal syndromes, chiefly Parkinsonism. Thioridazine has potent anti-cholinergic effects which may be uncomfortable (dry mouth, constipation), but does

not usually produce Parkisonism. Haloperidol can produce both Parkinsonism and dystonic reactions affecting the eyes and jaw. Akathisia, the
syndrome of restless itchy feet in which the patient is comfortable neither
sitting nor standing and alternates repeatedly between these two states or
simple restlessness, can be produced by any of the above drugs. There
is a danger that the restless activity so produced may be mistaken for
manic overactivity, with the consequence of inappropriate treatment.

Whether anti-Parkinsonism agents should be combined with phenothiazines and other Parkinson-producing drugs from the beginning or
whether they should be reserved for use with high doses or after side
effects have developed is something of a matter of individual clinical
preference. At the very least, if signs of Parkinsonism appear they should
be treated with a single drug or a combination of two anti-Parkinson
drugs. Orphenadrine hydrochlor. 50-100 milligrams t.d.s. is useful and
may be combined with Benzhexol 2 milligrams t.d.s. or Procyclidine
hydrochlor. 5 milligrams t.d.s., but these drugs have their own toxicity.
Reduction in the dose of these drugs when the primary drug is reduced
in dose should not be forgotten.

With the advent of the above mentioned drugs, *electroplexy* is not the
commonplace treatment of mania. In a small number of cases which
are resistant to drugs or where the nature of the disturbance is so severe
as to require early control, electroplexy can be given daily and at this
rate rarely needs to continue beyond four or five treatments, when it
can be either discontinued or tentatively spaced out. There is a danger
that with twice weekly electroplexy in mania more, rather than less,
excitement is produced.

The psychological management of the acutely manic patient can be
difficult, but as in all psychiatry a good relationship is the greatest aid.
Some moderately disturbed patients will need control in their financial
and business lives in order to prevent excesses and if such disturbances
are protracted the patient should be regarded as incapable of managing
his affairs by reason of mental illness as defined within the Mental Health
Act 1959 and in the United Kingdom referred to the Court of Protection.

PARANOID PSYCHOSES

Symptomatology

Persistent persecutory states in the elderly (paraphrenia) must be
studied in relation to the depressive and organic illnesses in old age from

which they must be differentiated, but with which they may share certain symptoms (including paranoid symptoms) in common.

The relationship with paranoia, a term now largely discarded, of paraphrenia and paranoid schizophrenia is one of the speculative issues of psychiatry that will not be debated. Dealing with mental illness only in old age, Roth and Morrissey (46), Kay and Roth (22) and Kay (19) have used late paraphrenia as a descriptive term for an illness characterized by delusions, in the setting of a well preserved intellect and personality, usually associated with hallucinations (in clear consciousness) that are commonly auditory but may be in any modality. Passivity feelings and volitional disorders may be seen, but less commonly. Cases of dementia, sustained confusion, and primary affective disorders in which the delusions are in keeping with the mood state or are understandable in terms of forgetfulness are excluded.

Thus defined, paraphrenia is a limited, circumscribed illness or group of illnesses which certainly does not embrace all paranoid symptoms.

The wider meaning of "paranoid" cannot be better expressed than by quoting Lewis (24). "The paranoid syndrome is one in which there are delusions of self-reference which may be concerned with persecution, grandeur, litigation, jealousy, love, envy, hate, honor or the supernatural (the list is Kolle's) and which cannot be immediately derived from a prevailing morbid state such as mania and depression. It may be a symptomatic condition, a toxic condition or part of a schizophrenic disorder. The adjective 'paranoid' should not be applied to persons, but may be applied to a psychopathic personality characterized by the same features as the paranoid syndrome, except that 'dominant ideas' must be substituted for delusions. Unlike 'paranoiac,' it is a descriptive term carrying no implications about chronicity, permanence, curability, presence of hallucinations, integrity of personality, or etiology. 'Paraphrenia' can be comprehended within 'paranoid.' Recognition of the paranoid syndrome is not a diagnostic act but a preliminary to diagnosis, as would be the recognition of stupor or depersonalization."

From this wider approach, a differential diagnosis of paranoid symptoms analogous to that for depression shown in Table 4 can be drawn up and is illustrated in Table 5.

The significance of the transitory paranoid states lies in their recognition and separation from the paraphrenic group of illnesses and in the need to treat any underlying cause, be it a depressive, manic, toxic or infective state. In addition to any other symptoms which may be

TABLE 5

Differential Diagnosis of Paranoid Symptoms with
Special Reference to Those Seen in Old Age

(1) *Persistent persecutory states* (36) or paraphrenia (45). Characteristics: Paranoid delusions and hallucinations in all modalities, predominantly auditory, in the setting of clear consciousness. Passivity feelings or volitional disorders may be present, primary organic or depressive syndromes are absent. Although regarded as a schizophrenia of late onset, thought disorder, together with flattening and incongruity of affect, is rare.

(2) *Transitory paranoid states,** alcoholic paranoia, Korsakov's psychosis, amphetamine intoxication, psychomimetic drugs, mania, depression, GPI, acute and sub-acute toxic and delirious states with clouding of consciousness, early arteriosclerosis, and senile dementias. The paranoid delusions vary from time to time and are unsystematized.

(3) *Paranoid personality reactions.* These are morbid but not psychotic. There are often psychopathic traits. The word "delusion" must be replaced by "a dominant idea" in Lewis's description. Many such patients live out their lives as eccentric recluses.

 * All ages.

present, the paranoid symptoms themselves in this group tend to be fleeting and poorly organized, changing from one day on examination to another. An irritable manic and a depressive with paranoid ideas may at times be very difficult to distinguish from primary paranoid disorders. In some cases, diagnosis can only be made in retrospect. In the writer's experience, those cases with mixed depressive/paranoid symtomatology in most cases move towards the paraphrenic group as the illness progresses. The organic group of disorders must be sought for by diligent history-taking, examination, and laboratory investigations. Paranoid symptoms in the dementias are usually seen in the early stages of the disease when there is sufficient cerebral capacity left for delusional formation to be possible. Minor "organic" symptoms, especially in patients over 75, should be discounted as they have been shown to rarely proceed to a major dementing illness.

Paranoid personality reactions can also pose difficult diagnostic problems, but by definition personality traits are longstanding and non-progressive. Ideas are overvalued rather than beyond logic and much attention may be paid to litigation or various obscure "causes." These personalities lead odd eccentric lives and are perhaps in danger of neglect as they age and become enfeebled. There is no positive evidence that they develop into paranoid illnesses over a period of time.

The remaining cases to be discussed are those belonging to the *persistent persecutory* or paraphrenic category. The defining characteristics of this group have already been given in some detail. Post (36) attempts a further subdivision into a group with gross schizophrenic character-istics, one with simple paranoid hallucinosis, and an intermediate group. He concludes that these are not three separate entities, but are grada-tions along a continuum. The issue will not be pursued here except to mention later its relevance to prognosis. Those who require a more refined clinical approach are referred to Post (36).

Most elderly paraphrenics are female. Their age range is comparable with elderly depressives, but they tend to be single or living apart from their spouses more than a comparable elderly or depressive population. Compared with elderly depressives, more belong to a low socio-occupa-tional status. Intelligence is not strikingly different from the average although there is a tendency for it to be low. Normal pre-morbid per-sonalities were found only in 26 out of 87 cases and a normal sexual ad-justment was found only in a similar low proportion. Dysthymic ten-dencies in the personalities were found in 15 out of 88 and personal rela-tionships were poor in nearly one-third. Brain damage was present no more often than would be expected in the population at risk; deafness was present in 15 out of 65 and has been shown by Roth to be associated with late paraphrenia. Depressive admixtures during the illness occurred in three-fifths. Life expectancy has been shown by Kay to be that of a normal elderly person (19).

Treatment and Prognosis

Treatment and prognosis will be considered together because they are closely related.

Before the advent of phenothiazine drugs, the prognosis for these cases was poor. From Roth's early work in delineating this syndrome in the elderly, it can be seen that once admitted a substantial proportion spent long periods in mental hospitals. Tolerance by others of their eccentricity was the best that could be expected.

The effect of phenothiazine medication in these cases has been well documented by Post (36) and his results are here quoted. Trifluoperazine was used in gradually increasing doses amounting to 15-25 milligrams daily by the third or fourth week of treatment. Two-thirds of these pa-tients developed Parkinson side effects during drug therapy. In some intractable patients, the dose was increased to 90 milligrams daily but 30 milligrams daily appeared a reasonable limit in elderly patients. Thioridazine was later considered a more suitable drug in a daily maximum dose of 150-600 milligrams. On this regime, fewer depressive mood changes were seen. On both drugs, concomitant depressive symptoms were treated by either tricyclic anti-depressants or electroplexy.

On this regime all but 8 out of 73 patients showed partial or complete remission in the short term. A good long term outcome was shown to accompany patients with the following characteristics: age under 70, immediate response to drug treatment with some insight, married, lower social class, previous non-paranoid personality disorders, good sexual adjustment, good relationship with others (including the doctor), duration of illness of less than one year, cooperation in maintenance therapy. Of these items good relationships and cooperation in maintenance therapy appeared to be of prime importance. In the long term, full remission occurred in 43 out of 71, partial remission in 22 and no remission in 6.

Of the newer psychotropic preparations now available, Fluphenazine decanoate given intramuscularly in doses of 12.5 to 25 milligrams every two or three weeks as a depot preparation by injection and Pimozide 4-6 milligrams *once daily* would seem useful preparations in view of the importance of maintenance therapy and supervision. Pimozide 4-10 milligrams daily appears to be well tolerated in the elderly and has the advantage of being given in a single daily dose.

Social and psychological measures remain important even with physical treatment. Post demonstrated that although those cases showing the greatest degree of schizophrenic disturbance did not respond to a change in environment, those with the lesser degrees often remitted temporarily simply by admission to hospital. The keynote of management of the individual patient should be the maintenance of a personal relationship in a low emotional key. Attempts to convince patients by logic of the folly of their delusions will fail and produce emotional distress. Sympathy at the difficulties they are experiencing can be expressed and medication is often accepted as a "tonic" to fortify them through a period of strain. Occasional supportive visits to outpatients are reassuring, both to the patient himself and to those around him who may be perplexed and frightened by any residual symptoms. Living close to a paranoid psychotic can be a traumatic experience and support to the relatives should not be forgotten.

CONCLUSIONS

The diagnosis, investigation and treatment of functional psychoses in the elderly can require a breadth of knowledge ranging from pure clinical psychiatry outwards into physical and social medicine and social work.

Collaboration with physicians, geriatricians and social workers is required and access to a full range of hospital diagnostic facilities is essential.

The belief that all mental illness over the age of 60 represents the beginning of an organic degenerative process has long since proved to be false, but the clinical difficulties of differentiating the subgroups described are such that functional cases are still referred for treatment under the mistaken impression that they are suffering from either "arteriosclerosis" or "senile degeneration." The increasing size of the elderly population and the ready availability of potent drug therapies mean that this is a fruitful field for activity and interest for all those concerned with the elderly. Social workers and nurses engaged in the community, no less than doctors in both hospitals and the community, should be alert to the development of these syndromes, particularly early depressions and the risk of suicide. Even in the more infrequent cases of paranoid illness it is clear that much suffering to the patient and those in attendance can be prevented.

Many matters of detail have been omitted in this brief review. Those with a further interest are referred particularly to the works of Roth, Kay and Post that have been extensively quoted as the major source of knowledge on these matters in the English literature.

REFERENCES

1. ABRAMS, R., and DORNBUSH, R. L. 1972. Unilateral and bi-lateral electro-convulsive therapy. *Arch. Gen. Psychiat.*, 27:88-91.
2. ALARCON, J. C. DE. 1971. Social causes and social consequences of mental illness in old age. In: Kay, D. W. K., and Walk, A. (Eds.) *Recent Developments in Psycho-Geriatrics*. 75-86. London: Royal Medico Psychological Association.
3. ALARCON, R. DE. 1964. Hypochondriasis and depression in the aged. *Geront. Clin.*, 6:266-277.
4. BARRACLOUGH, B. M. 1968. Suicide in the elderly. In: Kay, D. W. K. and Walk, A. (Eds.) *Recent Developments in Psycho-Geriatrics*. 87-98. London: Royal Medico Psychological Association.
5. BUNCH, J., BARRACLOUGH, B. M., and NELSON, B. 1971. The influence of parental death anniversaries upon suicide rates. *Brit. J. Psychiat.*, 118:621-626.
6. CANNICOTT, S. M. 1962. Unilateral electro-convulsive therapy. *Postgrad. Med. J.*, 38:45.
7. CANNICOTT, S. M., and WAGGONER, R. W. 1967. Unilateral and bi-lateral electro-convulsive therapy. *Arch. Gen. Psychiat.*, 16:229
8. CAPSTIK, A. 1960. Recognition of emotional disturbance and the prevention of suicide. *Brit. Med. J.*, i:1179-1182.
9. CARNEY, M. W. P., et al. 1965. The diagnosis of depressive syndromes and the prediction of E.C.T. response. *Brit. J. Psychiat.*, 111:659-674.
10. COPAS, J. B., FREEMAN-BROWNE, D. L., and ROBIN, A. A. Danger periods for suicide in patients under treatment. *Psychol. Med.*, 1:400-404.
11. COPPEN, A., et al. 1971. Prophylactic lithium in affective disorders. *Lancet*, ii:275-279.

12. COPPEN, A., et al. 1972. Comparative anti-depressant value of L-Tryptophane and Imipramine with and without attempted potentiation by Liothyronine. *Arch. Gen. Psychiat.*, 26:234-241.

13. DOWNING, R. A. 1972. Predictors of Amitriptyline response in out-patient depressives. *J. Nerv. Ment. Dis.*, 154:248-263.

14. FREEMAN, THOMAS. 1971. Observations on Mania. *Int. J. Psychoanaly.*, 52:479-486.

15. GOLDFARB, A. I. 1965. The recognition and therapeutic use of the patient's search for aid. In: *Psychiatric Disorders of the Aged*. Manchester: Geigy, U.K.

16. GOLDFARB, A. I. 1965. The common denominator of differing therapeutic approaches to mental illness in the aged. In: *Psychiatric Disorders of the Aged*. Manchester: Geigy, U. K.

17. GOODWIN, F. K. 1971. Behavioral effects of L-Dopa in man. *Seminars Psychiat.*, 3:477-492.

18. HENDERSON, D., and BATCHELOR, I. R. C. 1962. *Henderson and Gillespie's Textbook of Psychiatry*. London: Oxford University Press.

19. KAY, D. W. K. 1963. Late paraphrenia and its bearing on the etiology of schizophrenia. *Acta Psychiat. Scand.*, 39:159-169.

20. KAY, D. W. K., BEAMISH, P., and ROTH, M. 1964. Old age mental disorders in Newcastle-on-Tyne, Part II: A Study of Possible Social and Medical Causes. *J. Ment. Sci.*, 110:668-682.

21. KAY, D. W. K., and ROTH, M. 1955. Physical accompaniments of mental disorder in old age. *Lancet*, ii:740-745.

22. KAY, D. W. K., and ROTH, M. 1961. Environmental and hereditary factors in the schizophrenia of old age (late paraphrenia). *J. Ment. Sci.*, 107:649-686.

23. KAY, D. W. K., ROTH, M., and HOPKINS, B. 1965. Affective disorders arising in the senium: Their association with organic cerebral degenerations. *J. Ment. Sci.*, 101:302-316.

24. LEWIS, A. 1970. Paranoia and paranoid. A historical perspective. *Psychol. Med.*, 1:2-12.

25. LEWIS, A. 1971. "Endogenous" or "Exogenous": A useful dichotomy? *Psychol. Med.*, 1:191-196.

26. LEWIS, A. J. 1934. Melancholia: A clinical survey of depressive states. *J. Ment. Sci.*, 80:277-278.

27. MAYER-GROSS, et al. 1969. *Clinical Psychiatry*. London: Cassell & Co.

28. MORGAN, H. G. 1972. The incidence of depressive symptoms during recovery from hypomania. *Brit. J. Psychiat.*, 120:537-539.

29. PARE, C. M. B. 1968. Recent advances in the treatment of depression. In: Coppen, A., and Walk, A. (Eds.) *Recent Developments in Affective Disorders*. 137-150. London: Royal Medico Psychological Association.

30. PARE, C. M. B., REES, L., and SAINSBURY, M. J. 1962. The differentiation of two genetically specific types of depression by response to anti-depressant drugs. *Lancet*, ii:1340.

31. PAYKEL, E. S. 1972. Depressive typologies in response to Amitriptyline. *Brit. J. Psychiat.*, 120:147-156.

32. POIDEVIN, D. LE, and NAYLOR, G. J. 1972. Methysergide in mania. *Psychol. Med.*, 2:66-69.

33. POLATIN, PHILIP. 1971. Patient rejection of lithium carbonate prophylaxis. *J. Am. Med. Ass.*, 218:864-866.

34. POST, F. 1962. *The Significance of Affective Symptoms in Old Age*. Maudsley Monograph, 10. London: Oxford University Press.

35. POST, F. 1965. *The Clinical Psychiatry of Late Life*. London: Pergamon.

36. POST, F. 1966. *Persistent Persecutory States in the Elderly*. London: Pergamon.

37. POST, F. 1968. The factor of ageing in affective illness. In: Coppen, A., and

Walk, A. (Eds.) *Recent Developments in Affective Disorders.* 105-116. London: Royal Medico Psychological Association.

38. POST, F. 1971. The diagnostic process. In: Kay, D. W. K., and Walk, A. (Eds.) *Recent Developments in Psycho-Geriatrics.* 63-74. London: Royal Medico Psychological Association.

39. POST, F. 1972. The management and nature of depressive illness in late life: A follow-through study. *Brit. J. Psychiat.,* 121:393-404.

40. POST, F., REES, W. L., and SCHURR, P. H. 1968. An evaluation of bimedial leucotomy. *Brit. J. Psychiat.,* 515:1223-1246.

41. PRICE, J. 1968. The genetics of depressive behavior. In: Coppen, A., and Walk, A. (Eds.) *Recent Developments in Affective Disorders.* 37-54. London: Royal Medico Psychological Association.

42. PRIEN, R. F. 1972. Comparison of lithium carbonate and chlorpromazine in the treatment of mania. *Arch. Gen. Psychiat.,* 26:146-153.

43. PRIEN, R. F. 1972. Relationship between serum lithium level and clinical response in acute mania treated with lithium. *Brit. J. Psychiat.,* 120:409-414.

44. ROGERS, M. P. 1971. Clinical hypothyroidism occurring during lithium treatment. *Am. J. Psychiat.,* 128:158-163.

45. ROTH, M. 1955. The natural history of mental disorders in old age. *J. Ment. Sci.,* 101:281-301.

46. ROTH, M., and MORRISSEY, J. D. 1952. Problems in the diagnosis and classification of mental disorders in old age. *J. Ment. Sci.,* 98:66-80.

47. SAINSBURY, P. 1955. *Suicide in London.* Maudsley Monograph No. 1, London: Chapman and Ford.

48. SAINSBURY, P. 1968. Suicide and depression. In: Coppen, A., and Walk, A. (Eds.) *Recent Developments in Affective Disorders.* 1-13. London: Royal Medico Psychological Association.

49. SCHOU, M. 1968. Lithium in psychiatric therapy and prophylaxis. *J. Psychiat. Res.* 6:67-95.

50. SHOCHET, B. R. 1969. Recognizing the suicidal patient. *Maryland Med. J.* 18/9:65-67.

51. STENGEL, E. 1965. Causation and prevention of suicide in old age. In: *Psychiatric Disorders of the Aged.* Manchester: Geigy.

52. STERNBERG, E. J., and SHCHIRINA, M. G. 1969. Geriatric aspects of anxiety. In: Lader, M. H. (Ed.) *Studies of Anxiety.* 102-104. London: Royal Medico Psychological Association

53. TANINUKAI, H. 1970. Treatment and prophylaxis of manic states with a carbonic anhydrase inhibitor. *Pharmacopsychiat.,* 5:34-43.

54. WALMSLEY, K. 1968. Epidemiology of affective disorders. In: Coppen, A., and Walk, A. (Eds.) *Recent Developments in Affective Disorders.* 27-36. London: Royal Medico Psychological Association.

55. WHEATLEY, DAVID. 1972. Potentiation of Amitriptyline by thyroid hormones. *Arch. Gen. Psychiat.,* 26:229-233.

56. WHYBROW, P. C., COPPEN, A., PRANGE, A. J., and BAILEY, J. E. 1972. Thyroid function in response to liothyronine in depression. *Arch. Gen. Psychiat.,* 26:242-245.

57. WILSON, L. A., and LAWSON, I. R. 1962. Situational depression in the elderly: A study of 23 cases. *Geront. Clin. Addit. Add.,* 4:59-61.

16

CONFUSIONAL STATES
Description and Management

V. A. Kral, M.D., F.R.C.P. (Canada),
F.R.C.Psych. (Eng.)

Clinical Professor of Psychiatry, University of Western Ontario,
London, Ontario, Canada

INTRODUCTION

In geriatric psychiatry the terms "confusion" and "confused" are frequently used with reference to patients with fairly advanced senile and/or arteriosclerotic dementia. The amnestic syndrome of these patients, their short retention span, and severely impaired immediate recall render them unable to pursue goal-directed thinking for any length of time, the main characteristic of any confusional state from the point of view of general psychopathology (6). Disorientation in time and place, misinterpretation of the present situation, and frequently also confabulations aggravate their confused thinking and behavior.

There occurs among the aged still another type of confusion, which differs from the former in certain important respects. It occurs in people who so far have not shown any signs of one of the dementing processes of the senium; it is precipitated by various conditions, the common feature of which is the acute stress which they exert on the aging organism; and it takes, at least in the great majority of cases, an acute course. These features justify the assumption that one is dealing here with a separate nosological entity, for which the term "acute confusional state of the aged" has been proposed (15).

INCIDENCE

The incidence of these acute confusional states of the aged is unknown. The figures reported in geropsychiatric literature, namely 7-10%, represent the prevalence of this condition among aged patients admitted to mental hospitals or psychogeriatric wards and are not representative of its incidence in the aging population at large for which they are certainly too low. The psychiatrists usually see only the most severe cases, who require psychiatric consultation or hospitalization in a psychiatric ward, or those where the condition develops during another psychiatric illness, as during a severe endogenous depression. The less severe confusional states, which develop during a physical illness, frequently clear up within a short time, a few days or even hours, at home or in a general hospital without being seen by a psychiatrist. This would suggest that the overall incidence of this condition may be higher than 7-10%. Robinson, who based his report on "acute delirious reactions of old age" on the case material of a general hospital, mentions an incidence of 20-40% (14).

AETIOLOGY

The conditions which can give rise to the confusional states of the aged are varied. Physical noxae, even if they do not affect the brain directly, such as a fracture of the hip or rib, a surgical intervention performed in local anesthesia, or a mild respiratory or gastrointestinal infection, as well as psychological stresses such as endogenous or reactive depressions following the loss of a husband, personal disappointments, or rejections, or in some cases, enforced relocation, were factors which in our material precipitated an acute confusional state in aged persons.

SYMPTOMATOLOGY

The onset varies, depending on the severity of the stress and apparently also on the stress resistance of the patient. Where the stress is not too severe and the stress resistance relatively high, it may take one or more days before the full clinical picture develops. During these prodromal days, the patient appears depressed, anxious, and perplexed. On the other hand, if the stress is severe or the stress resistance low, or both, it may take only a few hours before the psychosis becomes manifest.

When fully developed, the acute confusional state is characterized by clouding of consciousness and lowered level of awareness with unclear perceptions and illusional misinterpretations. Disorientation in time and place is common, while personal orientation is usually preserved. However, the patient does not grasp the situation in which he finds himself. He may have difficulties recognizing his wife or children and believes himself in a strange and frequently threatening surrounding.

Attention span is reduced. The patient is easily distracted by external and internal stimuli and unable to maintain goal-directed thinking, even for a short period of time. Immediate recall and recent memory are severely impaired. Remote memory is usually preserved, although the patient may have difficulties placing events in the proper order. After the delirious state subsides, there is partial and patchy, but only rarely complete, amnesia for the time of its duration.

Some patients develop hallucinations of smell and taste, along with delusional ideas secondary to these hallucinations. They fear that the food is poisoned and refuse to take food or fluids. Visual and auditory hallucinations are rare. Most patients are anorexic and sleepless. They are restless and anxiously agitated. Some patients show an inverse sleep rhythm: they are drowsy and difficult to arouse in the day time and become manifestly confused and agitated at night.

Neurological examination is usually negative, except for some tremor and ataxia; medically, the patient shows, in addition to the signs of the physical condition which may have caused the confusional state, dehydration with polycythemia and leucocytosis; the temperature is normal or mildly elevated; the spinal fluid negative. Robinson (14) observed abnormal glucose tolerance curves. Where reliable tracings could be obtained, the EEG showed generalized slow wave activity, which reverted to normal after recovery.

In less severe cases the patients may be able to recognize the members of their families and to manage in their familiar surroundings, particularly in the day time, but become lost and disorientated when confronted by strangers or moved to a hospital or from one room to another. While still able to converse rationally for a short while, they become confused when the conversation is extended over a longer period of time. But even in these mild cases there is impairment of recent memory during the duration and patchy amnesia after recovery from the confusional state.

The course of the acute confusional states also varies. The mild ones clear up within a few days (sometimes hours) or weeks. The severe ones, which necessitate admission to a mental hospital, have a less favorable prognosis. Roth (15) found that two years after admission 50% of these severe cases were dead, while the rest were still in hospital. Our own experiences are similar. About 50% of our hospitalized cases cleared up after several weeks or months. Of the remaining 50%, about half died within a year, while the rest developed a clinical picture which was not distinguishable from senile dementia (8, 9). In such cases the level of awareness improves and illusions, hallucinations and delusions gradually recede, while the memory impairment develops into a typical senile amnestic syndrome, with its concomitant behavioral disorder, which progressively deepens. This course is found particularly in patients who had suffered more than one confusional state when under stress, a situation similar to that sometimes found in chronic alcoholics, in whom a Korsakoff's psychosis develops out of a delirium tremens, particularly when the latter has occurred more than once (11).

PATHOLOGY

Pathological findings have so far not contributed much to our understanding of the acute confusional states of the aged. The few post-mortem reports on patients who have died during the acute stage show in the first place the pathological changes typical of the stressor (pneumonia, acute enteritis, etc.), while the brains show either the moderate atrophy and senile plaques commonly found in the brains of aged people, or diffuse swelling and Nissl's acute neuronal cell disease in the cortex and brainstem, with cloudy swelling or liquefaction. However, there does not seem to be as yet any systematic neuropathological study available in the literature dealing specifically with the acute confusional states of the aged. The same applies also regarding the adrenal cortex and the pituitary.

This lack of factual anatomical information is partly compensated for by present-day neuroendocrinological knowledge, which offers some lead to a better understanding of the condition.

Clinically the acute confusional state of the aged represents an acute toxic psychosis, although the nature of the pathogenic toxic substance (or substances) is still unknown. Robinson (14), who stresses the multiplicity of etiological factors, sees the pathogenic background in a breakdown of the carbohydrate metabolism with a consequent failure of the detoxifying function of the liver, which in turn leads to an autogenous toxemia with its effect on cerebral functioning. Kral, on the other hand, sees in the acute confusional states of the aged a reaction of the aged brain to acute stress (10).

Selye has shown that various nocuous stimuli may lead to non-specific morphological, functional, and biochemical changes, the sum of which he calls "stress." They constitute the General Adaptation Syndrome (GAS), which involves largely, but not exclusively, the pituitary-adrenocortical axis. Although the stress changes are primarily adaptive, they may not always be effective or may even become maladaptive and pathogenic (16).

Extensive experimental studies in various centers have documented an actual increase in the ACTH and cortisol level in the plasma in stressful conditions, which parallels the behavioral changes, thus confirming Selye's original conception. On the other hand, recent research seems to indicate a far greater importance of psychobiological factors as the cause of the stress changes than originally assumed by Selye. Mason (13) states that "the primary mediator of stress changes is the emotional arousal of the organism from laboratory animals to man." He suggests that impulses from the amygdala complex and the reticular system in the midbrain reach the CRF producing cells in the hypothalamus. The CRF eventually reaches the anterior pituitary with its portal system, thus activating the pituitary-adenocortical axis.

Experimental studies demonstrated that the mammalian stress-resisting mechanism comprises adeno-pituitary, adrenocortical and adrenomedullary components, as well as nervous hypothalamic functions (4). These studies, furthermore, showed that there is an age-linked decline in adrenocortical function, as well as an age-linked hypothalamic vulnerability (5).

Pathophysiologically, the confusional state seems to represent an acute cerebral decompensation, probably due to an acute failure of the centrencephalic apparatus in the brainstem which is responsible for the level of consciousness and the integration of cognitive and memorial processes with their emotional changes (7).

It would seem possible that in certain individuals the age-linked weakness of the stress-resisting mechanism involves particularly its nervous hypothalamic part and it may well be that these individuals react to the impact of a severe stress with the acute brain syndrome described above.

One will have to assume that in such individuals toxic substance formed in the adrenals as part of the stress changes exert a detrimental effect on the centrencephalic system in the brainstem and thus produce the clinical picture of an acute brain syndrome.

A considerable body of evidence indicates that the corticosteroids, whose level in the circulation increases under conditions of severe stress, may produce behavioral changes, mood swings, euphoria, even hypomania, or alternatively depressions, schizophrenia-like pictures, or confusional states

(2). Furthermore, numerous reports have appeared in the literature on the effect of ACTH and cortisone on the human EEG, in non-epileptic as well as in epileptic patients (3).

Finally, recent reports tend to show that, at least in the experimental animal, glucocorticoid and ACTH injections, as well as acute stress, may lead to neuronal damage in the hypothalamus and the hippocampus (1).

Considering these findings, it would appear possible that the acute confusional state, which develops in some aged subjects under stress, is due to the impact of corticosteroids on the hypothalamus, either because there is an abnormally high level of corticosteroids in the circulation or because the hypothalamus is particularly vulnerable to these steroids or because both conditions exist simultaneously. The origin and nature of the supposed age-linked weakness of the nervous part of the stress-resisting mechanism in these subjects is as yet unknown; it may be hereditary or acquired during the person's lifetime and it may have relevance also for the development of the more chronic mental disorders of the aged, as evidenced by the fact that in a certain, although still unknown, percentage of cases senile dementia is preceded by an acute confusional state which, in turn, is the consequence of an acute physical or mental stress (11).

MANAGEMENT

Treatment of the acute confusional states is possible and effective in a great number of cases. Although one of the etiological factors, the age-linked decline of the aged patients' stress resistance, cannot be changed, etiotropic therapy is still possible, at least in a great number of cases, by treating and eliminating the stressor: repair of a fractured hip, treatment of the pneumonia or other infection by active means and, particularly important for the psychiatrist, treatment of an endogenous depression by means of anti-depressants or even E.C.T. in spite of the present confusion.

In addition to this etiotropic therapy, which of course is not feasible in all cases, one will try to increase the patient's stress resistance. Daily slow infusion of 1000 cc of 5% glucose solution, which also serves to counteract the frequently present dehydration, combined with high vitamin and protein feeding, rendered in our experience the best results. On the symptomatic level, neuroleptics, particularly chlorpromazine in medium dosages of 50-100 mg four times per day or perphenazine 4-8 mg four times per day, were the most helpful in our experience. Our experience with the treatment of the acute confusional states with cortisone is as yet too limited to allow a valid conclusion about its value. However, good results have been reported by others (12).

REFERENCES

1. Aus der Muehlen, K. and Ockenfels, H. 1969. Morphologische Veraenderungen im Diencephalon und Telencephalon nach Stoerungen des Regelkreises Adeno-hypophyse—Nebennierenrinde III. *Zeitschrift f. Zellforschung*, 93:126-141.
2. Cleghorn, R. A. 1965. Hormones and humors. In: *Proceedings of the First International Congress on Hormonal Steroids*, 2:429-441.
3. Glaser, G. H. 1953. On the relationship of adrenal cortical activity and the convulsive state. In: *Epilepsia*, 2:7-14.
4. Grad, B., and Kral, V. A. 1957. The effect of senescence on resistance to stress. I. *J. Geront.*, 12:172-181.
5. Grad, B., Kral, V. A., Payne, R. C., and Berenson, J. 1967. Plasma and urinary corticoids in young and old persons. *J. Geront.*, 22:66-71.
6. Jaspers, K. 1962). *General Psychopathology*. Manchester: Manchester University Press.
7. Kral, V. A. 1959. Amnesia and the amnestic syndrome. *Canad. Psychiat. Ass. J.*, 4:61-68.
8. Kral, V. A. 1962. Stress and mental disorders of the senium. *Med. Serv. J. Canad.*, 18:363-370.
9. Kral, V. A. 1967. Stress reactions in old age. *Laval Med.*, 38:561-566.
10. Kral, V. A. 1971. Stress and senile psychosis. In: Proceedings of the Fifth World Congress of Psychiatry, *Excerpta Medica*.
11. Kral, V. A. 1972. Senile dementia and normal aging. *Canad. Psychiat. Ass. J.*, 17: SS25-SS30.
12. Kral, V. A. 1972. Somatic therapy in old age. In: *Psychiatrie der Gegenwart, Forschung und Praxis*, II/2:1159-1172. Berlin: Springer-Verlag.
13. Mason, J. W. 1971. A re-evaluation of the concept of "non-specificity" in stress theory. *J. Psychiat. Res.*, 8:323-333.
14. Robinson, G. W., Jr. 1956. The toxic delirious reactions of old age. In: Kaplan, O. J. (Ed.) *Mental Disorders in Later Life*. Stanford: Stanford University Press.
15. Roth, M. 1955. The natural history of mental disorders in old age. *J. Ment. Sci.*, 101:281-301.
16. Selye, H. 1950. Stress. The physiology and pathology of exposure to stress. *Montreal Acta Medica Publica*.

17

MENTAL RETARDATION

B. W. RICHARDS, M.R.C.S., F.R.C.PSYCH., D.P.M.

Consultant Psychiatrist, St. Lawrence's Hospital
Caterham, England

AGING AND MORTALITY

Old age has attracted little attention until modern times because most people have died from the hazards of life before attaining it. In 1740 few liveborn babies lived to grow up; in 1970 most of them did.

As the conditions of life improve, more and more people survive into old age and die from causes connected, directly or indirectly, with the process of aging. This is well shown by comparing survival curves of populations living under different conditions (Figure 1). In a progessively more favourable environment, the shape of the curve changes from concave to convex, remains high until later and later ages, and falls with increasing steepness. It comes to assume the shape characteristic of a population in which aging contributes to most deaths and deaths from causes independent of aging are relatively few. The curves also show that it is not true, as many have supposed, that human beings live longer and longer as living conditions become increasingly favourable. On the contrary, more and more people live to about the same age, so that the curves appear to be pegged somewhere between the ages of 70 and 80. This is known as the specific age, which has been defined as the commonest age at death for the species when living under the most favourable conditions. Warm-blooded vertebrates appear to age in this way. The specific age differs in different species, presumably due to different rates of aging: "The length of time that an animal can live under the most favourable conditions is deter-

The Longevity of Animals and of Man

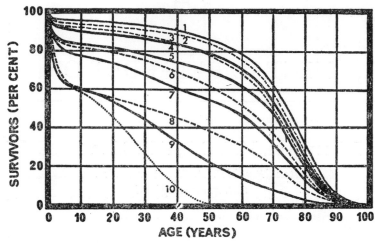

FIGURE 1. Human survival curves, all for females, show the effect of improvements in living conditions. (Comfort, 1965.)

1. New Zealand 1934-8
2. U.S. Whites 1939-41
3. U.S. Whites 1929-31
4. England and Wales 1930-2
5. Italy 1930-2

6. U.S. Whites 1900-2
7. Japan 1926-30
8. Mexico 1930
9. British India 1921-30
10. Stone Age Man (guesswork)

mined by whether, and at what rate, the likelihood of dying increases with age" (2).

The reduction of mortality shown by the series of curves in Figure 1, therefore, represents a progressive change towards the most favourable conditions of living. The reduction is brought about by such developments as improved nutrition and drainage systems, immunization against infectious diseases, and the use of antibiotics and has affected predominantly the young and the very young, that is to say, the reduction in mortality has been largely confined to age-independent (more strictly, aging independent) causes of death. This may be illustrated by comparing exponential curves of 1740 and 1970 deaths. Aging, like a number of other biological phenomena, tends to occur at a rate which is exponential. The 1970 death rate, after the first two decades, is represented by an almost straight-line graph suggesting that aging contributes to nearly all deaths that occur after 20. In 1740 many more deaths are independent of aging not only before the age of 20, but for some years after that.

Life Tables

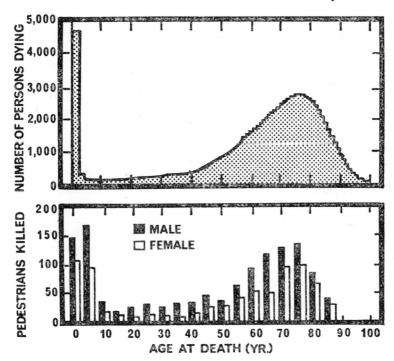

FIGURE 2. Distribution by age of all deaths in a privileged community (top) and of deaths of pedestrians in road accidents. (Comfort, 1965)

The physical and mental changes that accompany aging increase the likelihood of dying from a wide variety of causes, many of which may seem to be totally unconnected, for instance, bronchopneumonia and road accidents. Comfort (2) compared deaths from road accidents with deaths from all causes (Figure 2) to show that, allowing for differences in early life, when aging is not apparent, the peaks are remarkably similar. "In other words, survival as a pedestrian correlates highly with that vigour which declines with age; it is a measure of the ability to see, hear, jump and recover if hit" (2). Thus, the physical and psychological changes which characterise aging include failing senses, less sharp attentiveness, declining agility, reduced powers of resistance, and waning powers of recovery, all of which increase the likelihood of dying from a wide variety of causes.

TABLE 1

Age and Sex-specific Death Rates per 1000, Mentally Handicapped
(St. Lawrence's Hospital) and General Population Compared*

| | MALES | | | FEMALES | | |
Age Group	(a) St. Lawrence's Hospital 1961-65	(b) General population*	(c) Observed/ expected (a/b)	(d) St. Lawrence's Hospital 1961-65	(e) General population*	(f) Observed/ expected (d/e)
10—	12.1	0.75	16.1	10.3	0.13	79.2
20—	18.6	1.01	18.0	14.2	0.15	27.8
30—	8.9	1.47	6.0	10.2	1.05	9.7
40—	13.5	4.06	3.3	18.7	2.75	6.8
50—	20.8	12.69	1.6	30.5	12.06	2.5
60—	32.2	25.28	1.3	36.0	16.89	2.1
70—	107.6	81.18	1.3	60.3	48.36	1.2

* Registrar General's Statistical Review for 1966.

It was observed, above, that in 1740 few liveborn babies lived to grow up. This might have been said in respect to the mentally subnormal population until well into the present century, and to mongols until after the second World War. Table 1 shows that the death rate of the mentally subnormal is appreciably higher than of the general population at all ages. That the lower chance of survival for the mentally subnormal is not due to a more rapid rate and earlier onset of aging is suggested by the fact that the excess mortality is greatest in the youngest age group and the difference in death rates, between subnormal and normal populations (Table 1), diminishes quite rapidly with increasing age (columns c and f). Table 2 reveals that the more severe the degree of mental handicap, the less the chance of survival. These statistical findings imply that the excess mortality in most mentally subnormal subjects is independent of aging and is caused by risks of death directly associated with mental subnormality. It may therefore be concluded that the process of aging is approximately similar to that which occurs in the normal population.

The one exception to this is mongolism. Mongols have a particularly high mortality in infancy, but between the ages of 10 and 40 years, the death rate resembles that of other mentally subnormal subjects of similar grade. After 40, however, mortality rises steeply (Table 3) and the proportion of mongols that reach the age of 60 is very small. (The writer has seen one mongol who died in her seventieth year. She proved to be a mosaic.) The degree to which the death rate of mongols exceeds that of non-mongols of similar mental grade definitely increases with increasing

TABLE 2

Age Specific Death Rates per Thousand of Mentally Handicapped Patients at St. Lawrence's Hospital, 1955-67, Mongols Excluded. (Sexes Combined. Numbers Dying in Parenthesis)

Degree of sub.

Age Group	(260) Severe	(341) Moderate	(115) Mild
5 — 9	153.8	10.9	—
10 — 19	58.4	4.2	4.8
20 — 29	79.1	7.4	3.7
30 — 39	51.0	6.7	5.4
40 — 49	59.6	15.8	11.0
50 59	104.8	18.0	43.5
60 — 69	206.9	33.5	40.7
70 — 79	111.1	106.4	50.5
80 — 89	—	165.9	66.6

TABLE 3

Mongols: Age-specific Death Rates per 1000 at Risk Compared with Normal Population

Age Group	(a) At Risk 1955-72	(b) Died	(c) Death Rate per 1,000	(d) RGO, 1966*	(e) Observed/ expected (c/d)
5—	134	1	7.5	0.37	20.3
10—	699	8	11.4	0.46	24.9
20—	937	7	7.5	0.76	9.9
30—	767	7	9.1	1.25	7.3
40—	394	6	15.2	3.46	4.5
50—	187	12	64.2	12.46	5.2
60—	57	5	87.8	24.79	3.4
Total	3,175	46	14.5	11.72**	

* Registrar General's Statistical Review for 1966.
** Includes oldest age groups, not included in table.

age. This could be explained by assuming a more rapid rate of aging in mongols. This assumption receives some support from observations of brain pathology. Struwe (16) was the first to report senile plaques in a mongol of 37 years. Jervis (4) described personality change and mental deterioration in three mongols aged 37, 42 and 47 years. Neuropathological changes showed numerous senile plaques, neuronal degeneration, neurofibrillary, and Alzheimer changes. The same author (4) found signs of senile dementia during life in five of 16 mongols examined during the fifth decade. Malamud (8) examined 20 of 251 mongols that had died between the ages of 37 and 66 years and found that "in all of them there were neuropathologic changes characteristic of Alzheimer's disease." Owen, Dawson and Losin found physical and mental signs of aging in 19 mongols examined after the age 35 years and Sylvester (17) found neuropathological changes characteristic of senility in all 20 brains examined. Death had occurred before the age of 60 in all of them. Recently, Ohara (13) described electron microscopic appearances of senile changes in the brains of eight mongols.

PREVALENCE AND DISTRIBUTION

Death is the most serious and inevitable consequence of aging, but is usually preceded by a period of time, which may be many years, during which declining intelligence, impairment of memory, and other sources of mental impoverishment or of physical deterioration reduce employ- ability and social competence. As described above, improving conditions of life have greatly increased the proportion of people who survive to reach the age range within which such disabilities commonly become man- ifest. Old age amongst the severely subnormal, for instance, was rare until after the second World War and their care has now become a serious practical problem for the first time.

Table 4 records the prevalence of mental subnormality in Bristol, England, on January 1st, 1969 (9). There are two striking features about this table: first, the fall in prevalence with increasing age which results from a higher death rate, at all ages, than occurs in the normal popula- tion; and secondly, the increasing proportion of subnormal subjects in institutions. The proportion living in the community starts to fall be- fore the age of 20 years and very few remain at large after 60. Under the age of 20 years there are twice as many in the community as in hospital. At 55 and over, there are six times as many in institutions. Thus, growing old bears two major risks for the mentally subnormal: death and admission to an institution. They are not usually admitted in order to die. Although admission may sometimes be on the grounds of physical or mental deterioration, more often it results from the in- firmity or death of relatives who have cared for them and who, in the past, would have outlived them.

TABLE 4

Numbers of Mentally Subnormal by Age, in Bristol on 1st January, 1969 (Midwinter, 1972) in the Community and in Hospital

Age group	—4	5—	10—	20—	30—	40—	50—	60—	70—	Total
Community	33	103	179	171	97	63	28	14	4	692
Hospital	11	42	124	148	128	143	149	89	58	892
% Hospital	25	29	40.9	45.3	56.9	69.4	84.9	86.4	94.0	56.3

TABLE 5a

Percentage of All Mentally Handicapped Patients in Institutions in England and Wales,* Aged 50 Years and Over

Subjects	1954	YEAR 1963	1970
Male	6.7	15.4	20.3
Female	12.5	23.8	28.7
Persons	9.4	19.3	24.0

* Dept. Hlth Soc. Security (1972).

TABLE 5b

Resident Mentally Handicapped: Rate per 100,000 Population at 55 Years and Over

	1954	1963	1970
Male	50	103	124
Female	60	98	107
Persons	56	100	114

Examination of hospital statistics reveals the change in age structure in favor of the aged over the years (Table 5). The proportion of resident patients over the age of 55 years has nearly trebled since 1954, from about nine percent to almost 25 percent. The increase is also large when expressed as a rate per 100,000 of the total population. National statistics of all mentally handicapped patients resident in institutions (Table 6) reveal that of those at 55 years or older, the proportion that is severely subnormal has increased by about 20 percent between 1954 and 1970, the proportion of mildly subnormal being correspondingly reduced.

TABLE 6

Resident Mentally Handicapped: Degree of Mental Handicap
(Percent) of Patients of 55 Years and Over

Grade	YEAR		
	1954	1963	1970
Severe	35.9	55.6	56.1
Mild	64.1	44.4	43.9
All	100.0	100.0	100.0

In summary, the chance of survival of the mentally handicapped population has steadily improved over the last 20 years or so. This improvement has affected all mental grades. The number surviving into old age is now sufficient to present a serious problem of their care.

The place of residence of the mentally handicapped is greatly influenced by age—most of the young live in the community and nearly all the elderly are in institutions. This effect is so striking that death and admission to an institution may be regarded as by far the most important consequences of aging for the mentally handicapped population.

CHARACTERISTICS OF THE AGED

Mortality is selective insofar as the physically unfit have less chance of survival and a higher proportion of them die before they grow old. This selective process is more striking in the subnormal than in the normal population because, amongst the former, the proportion with physical handicaps is considerable. These severely subnormal, even in the absence of physical handicap, have less chance of survival than the mildly handicapped. For these reasons, the young and the old are two very different types of population (Table 7). Amongst the young are many severely spastic and incontinent patients and many requiring assistance in feeding, washing, or dressing.

Patients of 55 and over are, typically, ambulant, without epilepsy or other physical handicaps, able to talk, feed, wash and dress, continent, quiet, and without behavior disorders. They tend to be somewhat apathetic, especially males, and to have very restricted interests unless stimulated. This description applies to a large proportion of the aged subnormal, but this population has undergone a gradual change, which may be continuing, towards a lower grade of patient (see Table 6)

TABLE 7

Mentally Handicapped Patients by Age and Degree of Incapacity.
Percentage Distribution of 63,385 (all) Resident Patients in
England and Wales at the End of 1970*

Disability		—5	5—	10—	Age group (yrs.) 15—	20—	35—	55—	65—
A	Severe	76	43	30	18	10	8	8	11
	Mild	10	9	10	9	8	8	10	15
I	Severe	94	71	54	36	22	12	8	10
	Mild	3	14	14	11	11	9	8	8
F	Severe	93	75	59	39	26	14	8	9
	Mild	6	20	24	22	20	19	16	17
	None	1	5	17	39	51	67	76	74
No behavior difficulties		82	57	52	52	58	71	82	85

A: Non-ambulant (severe) or partially ambulant (mild). I: Incontinent. F: Feeding difficulties.
* Dept. Hlth Soc. Security (1972).

as an increasing proportion of the severely subnormal have survived.
Although, therefore, the aged present, in many respects, fewer care and
management problems than the young, the difference between them has
diminished somewhat during the last 16 years.

INTELLIGENCE AND COMPETENCE

The aged subnormal have not been extensively studied. It is well-
known that aging is accompanied by decline in certain abilities, some
of which affect scores on items included in mental tests, particularly performance items, whereas vocabulary and information hold up rather
well (5, 19). Longitudinal and cross-sectional studies of normal populations have indicated that the decline is related to original intelligence
level in that, on the average, the higher the original level, the later the
onset and the less the degree of the decline (1, 11, 15, 18).

Kaplan (6) carried out mental tests on 66 patients, selecting those
over 45 years of age who had previously been tested. They varied in age
from 48 to over 70 and in I.Q. from 50 to 69. They were tested on the
1916 revision of the Stanford Binet. He found the average decline in
Mental Age to be 6.65 months. There was considerable variability and
some patients gained. There was no significant difference in losses be-

tween those with Intelligence Quotients from 50-59 and 60-69. Vocabulary survived well. Kaplan concluded that morons appeared to retain such capacities as they have about as well as the normal population. He pointed out, however, that they have less to lose. He also commented that "The Binet does not emphasize speed to any pronounced degree, and it therefore misses, to a large extent, the marked slowing down in mental reaction which qualitative observations reveal."

As far as the evidence goes, then, mentally subnormal subjects age in the same way and, with the exception of mongols, at about the same rate as the normal population. Their mental powers seem also to decline in the same way, as measured by intelligence tests. In behavior, they tend to become slower, less excitable, and quieter, and to narrow their interests as occurs with the normal population.

The point made by Kaplan that they have less to lose and the findings from normal population studies, that there is a tendency for losses to be of earlier onset and greater in degree the lower the original I.Q., might lead one to expect a noticeable loss of employability and reduction of social competence. There is a paucity of information on these matters, but the experience of the present writer and of others professionally concerned with subnormal persons in institutions and in the community provides no evidence that it is particularly common for previously employable subnormal persons to become unemployable owing to deterioration before the usual retiring age. One reason for this may be that those in institutions are living in a protected environment and doing jobs below their capacity. Those living in the community are also doing, in most instances, simple jobs demanding little of them, such as sweeping leaves, collecting refuse, or doing sweeping, cleaning, or portering jobs in factories, domestic jobs in schools and nursing homes, and so on. Whether in institutions or in the community, their lives tend to be limited to the same activities and situations year after year, the same people and entertainments, and they are not obliged to adapt to new situations or to apply their minds to the unfamiliar and the unexpected. Under these conditions, they survive fairly well.

As observed above, most of the aged subnormal are resident in institutions, usually large ones. The question of their suitability for living with families in the community or in hostels arises because of the national policy in England (as well as in other countries), likely to be put into practice during the next two decades, of providing such accommodation for a large proportion of the mentally subnormal.

Most of the aged subnormal seem to be suitable for residence in hostels or homes of some kind. There are many now in institutions, however, who are so accustomed to the way of life they have been leading that they might not welcome the change. Most of them could have been admitted to hostels in the first instance. Those in large hospitals are accustomed to many and frequent entertainments and outings and, in connection with hostels, arrangements would have to be made for a stimulating social life.

An investigation of the suitability of aged institutional patients for foster homes or nursing homes was carried out by O'Connor, Justice and Warren (12) in the U.S.A. They studied 463 patients of 60 years and over at Pacific State Hospital, California. They found that only 5.6 percent were frequently hyperactive, 4.5 percent were aggressive, and 7.8 percent could not communicate intelligibly. On the basis of clearly defined criteria, it was judged that 76 percent were eligible for transfer to foster homes or nursing homes. "Eligibility was related to higher intelligence, passivity, few physical handicaps or behavior problems and the ability to do work tasks." The results of mental tests are not given, but evidently a high proportion of these patients of 60 years or more were employable and socially acceptable. Incidentally, the authors were surprised at the increased proportion of lower grade elderly patients, compared to an earlier investigation at the same institution.

The Census of Mentally Handicapped in Hospitals in England and Wales at the end of 1970 (3) revealed that 72 percent of those in the 55-64 years age group were employed or occupied in some way. At 65 and over, 62 percent were employed in some way. A proportion of the remainder had some kind of handicap, such as deafness or blindness, and some, no doubt, might have been employed had facilities been more adequate. With regard to behavior of the severely handicapped (severely subnormal), six percent in the 55-64 years age group were reported to have severe behavior difficulties, while three percent needed much assistance in feeding, washing, and dressing. At 65 and over these percentages were five and three respectively. At 20-34, they were 13 percent and four percent. Among the mildly handicapped (subnormal), six and three percent respectively of the 55-64 and 65 and over age groups had severe behavior difficulties.

The available statistics concern, chiefly, mentally handicapped persons in hospital. Few statistics are available for those in the community but, as observed above, nearly all the elderly subnormal that have been ascertained either when elderly or when young by the Mental Health Department of Local Authorities have become resident in institutions.

The population of mentally subnormal subjects discussed in this chapter consists, by definition, of those ascertained, at some time in their lives, by the various Mental Health Departments. It includes the untrainable, those that have attended training centers, and those resident in institutions. It also includes those who started education at schools for the educationally subnormal and who, sometime before the age of 16, were considered no longer educable and were reported to Mental Health Departments. Finally, it includes those who successfully completed their education at schools for the educationally subnormal (ESN schools) but, later in life, were found in need of supervision and reported to Mental Health Authorities.

It does not include those educated at ESN schools who proved sufficiently educationally and socially competent to escape the attention of Mental Health Departments. The population attending ESN schools, nearly all in the I.Q. range of 50-70, are administrativey divided and differently defined according to whether they succeed or fail, which no doubt is socially desirable and administratively convenient, but they are fundamentally the same population. Those that succeed, who are a considerable proportion of the mildly handicapped (that is, mentally subnormal as opposed to severely subnormal), are lost sight of after leaving school and obtaining employment. No doubt they undergo aging in the same manner as the subnormal persons in institutions, but they are subject to very different conditions. Many are married and have responsibilities, and there is a paucity of information about them in old age. It may be that they receive the same treatment as others of the geriatric population, large numbers of whom occupy beds in a variety of hospitals and homes. As they may share the same qualities of senility, they may not easily be distinguishable from the rest. There is, therefore, no reliable information about the proportion of the mentally subnormal population that may be rendered socially incompetent before retiring age by symptoms of senility or whether, in fact, senility does weigh more heavily upon the subnormal than upon the normal population, living under more or less similar conditions.

Some enquiries in other countries suggest that aging does not cause social or psychiatric problems more frequently or seriously among the aged subnormal than among the aged normal population, and perhaps less so. According to Kaplan (7) those disturbances specifically associated with old age occur in those whose intelligence is least reduced (I.Q. 70-90) although they do also occur to a lesser extent in those in the 50-70 I.Q. range.

Moser (10) investigated 476 mentally subnormal patients who had, on one or more occasions, been hospitalized at the Psychiatric University Clinic of Lausanne, and who, at the time of the study, were (or would have been) 65 years old or more. These subjects had been hospitalized during the period 1873-97. Those still living were followed up after 1963. Eighty-eight were still living and the author examined 87 of them. The sample examined is, therefore, biased, being selected for survival and for attendance at a psychiatric clinic. About three-quarters were subnormal ("Debile"). About 70 percent had been employed, either full or part time, until at least the age of 60 years. Psychiatric disorders were not especially common. Schizophrenia and depressive psychosis were rather rare in this material. Those that had had hysterical symptoms, character or behavior disturbances tended to improve with age.

The author (10) questioned the subjects concerning their happiness, worries, fear of death, and so on. Most patients were satisfied with their situation and lived for the day. When asked whether in their thoughts and daydreams they were more concerned with past, present, or future, most of them (93%) were concerned with the practical problems of the moment. The fact of old age and of approaching death did not occupy the minds of most of them or cause anxiety.

The author also investigated the incidence of "the psycho-organic syndrome," which he described as follows: Mild, disturbance of attention, and (or) concentration and (or) slight emotional lability; Moderate, disturbance of memory and (or) occasional disorientation and (or) emotional lability; Severe, the full picture of senile dementia, with disorientation in space and time, loss of memory, confabulation and emotional lability. Twenty-three percent had none, 37 percent mild, 15 percent moderate and six percent severe symptoms. The remainder, for various reasons, could not be assessed. Those with mild symptoms were actually better adjusted than those without. The author points out that these figures refer to the survivors in the sample, and the sample is confined to those who, for some reason, have been hospitalized at least once. (About 80 percent of those interviewed were in the 65-74 age range, the remainder being older.)

Amongst other facts of interest in this exhaustive investigation is the sex incidence (56 percent male) and the civil state, the proportion married or widowed being much below that of the general population, men in the sample being more often married than women.

It is evident that many members of this sample, although, properly speaking, belonging to the mentally subnormal population, would not have been reported to the Mental Health Departments in this country. Account must also be taken of the very different conditions prevailing in Switzerland 60 years ago, when the subjects investigated were young adults, from those of Great Britain today.

The typical mentally subnormal man in his sixties is spared many of the indignities, fears, and miseries of more intelligent people. He is less likely to be conscious of a diminishing hold on the fabric of reality. He held no positions of power or influence to relinquish. He was never numbered amongst those who go south in winter. He does not, therefore, have to watch over the progressive impoverishment of a once richer life and has, perhaps, fewer sources of regret for the past and of anxiety for the future. The change in his way of life that attends old age is less radical for him than for those more highly gifted. It may be for these reasons that psychiatric disorders are not particularly common among them (if the rather scanty evidence available is to be trusted), there being few psychogenic influences that would contribute to their occurrence.

One radical change in their circumstances which they are not spared is admission to an institution or hostel. This usually takes place, however, before the age of fifty. It occurs also to the normal population of aged persons at a later age and amongst these, as mentioned above, may be many mentally subnormal persons who have not been ascertained as such.

CONCLUSION

It must again be emphasized that there has been no investigation of a truly representative sample of the aged subnormal in this country and statements about them are based upon the study of selected samples or upon the results of enquiries abroad, where conditions and definitions may differ. Such information and evidence as exist suggest that they are rather less liable to psychiatric disorders than others and that those who survive to a late age do not dement more seriously than more gifted people. The apparent mental stability and the finding of Moser (10) that psycho-organic symptoms of mild degree do not upset them unduly must be considered in the light of the limited demands that have always been made upon them, the absence of mental stress or of the need, as they age, to reduce radically their range of interests and responsibilities, with the accompanying sense of a shrinking role in life and of increasing isolation (particularly if these changes are forced upon a person sooner than necessary).

It is no doubt important for the aged subnormal to continue to exercise such abilities as they have and not to relinquish contact with the world about them. Like all old people, they require a familiar environment, whether it be people, employment, or entertainment, and need to continue doing for themselves, as long as possible, whatever they have been accustomed to do. Many may need to be coaxed and encouraged to prevent withdrawal and growing apathy. Company and occupation are important. Physical health is a necessary foundation for an active life and such minor disabilities as corns of the feet can be crippling.

Most of the mentally subnormal are fortunately placed in that retirement need not be determined by official regulation but may depend on the physical and mental health of the person. It may also be gradual so that it occurs as insidiously as aging itself.

All the aged, sooner or later, require residence where they are partly or wholly cared for, in residential accommodation either large or small. The type of residence most suitable may vary somewhat from case to case and will depend upon the degree of management and care required.

REFERENCES

1. BUTCHER, H. J. 1968. *Human Intelligence: Its Nature and Assessment.* London: Methuen and Co.
2. COMFORT, A. 1965. In: *The Process of Ageing.* London: Weidenfeld and Nicolson.
3. DEPARTMENT OF HEALTH AND SOCIAL SERVICES. 1972. Census of Mentally Handicapped in Hospital in England and Wales at the End of 1970. *Statist. Res. Rep. Ser. No. 3.* London: H.M.S.O.
4. JERVIS, G. A. 1948. Early senile dementias in mongoloid idiocy. *Am. J. Psychiat.,* 105:102-106.
5. JONES, H. E., and CONRAD, H. S. 1933. The growth and decline of intelligence: a study of a homogeneous group. *Genet. Psychol. Monogr.,* 13:223-298.
6. KAPLAN, O. J. 1943. Mental decline in older morons. *Am. J. Ment. Defic.* 47:277-285.
7. KAPLAN, O. J. 1956. The aged subnormal. In: Kaplan, O. J. (Ed.) *Mental Disorders in Later Life.* Stanford (California): Stanford University Press.
8. MALAMUD, N. 1964. Neuropathology. In: Stevens, H. A., and Heber, R. (Eds.) *Mental Retardation.* Chicago: University of Chicago Press. pp. 429-452.
9. MIDWINTER, R. E. 1972. Mental subnormality in Bristol. *J. Ment. Defic. Res.,* 16:48-56.
10. MOSER, A. 1971. *Die Langfristige Entwicklung oligophrener.* Berlin: Springer-Verlag.

11. NISBET, J. D. 1957. Intelligence and age: Retesting with twenty-four years interval. *Brit. J. Educ. Psychol.*, 27:190-198.
12. O'CONNOR, GAIL, JUSTICE, R. S., and WARREN, N. 1970. The aged mentally retarded: institution or community care? *Am. J. Ment. Defic.*, 75:354-360.
13. OHARA, P. T. 1972. Electron Microscopical Study of the Brain in Down's Syndrome. *Brain*, 95:681-684.
14. OWENS, D., DAWSON, J. C., and LOSIN, S. 1971. Alzheimer's disease in Down's Syndrome. *Am. J. Ment. Defic.* 75:606.
15. OWENS, W. A. 1966. Age and mental abilities: A second adult follow-up. *J. Educ. Psychol.*, 57:311-325.
16. STRUWE, F. 1929. Histopathologische Untersuchungen über Entstehung und Wesen der senilen Plaques. *Z. Ges. Neurol. Psychiatr.*, 122:291-307.
17. SYLVESTER, P. E. 1972. Personal communication.
18. VOGT, O. 1951. Study of the ageing of the nerve. *J. Gerontol.*, 6.
19. WECHSLER, D. 1958. *The Measurement and Appraisal of Adult Intelligence.* (4th ed.). London: Baillière, Tindall and Cox.

18

THE ASSESSMENT CENTER

R. A. ROBINSON, M.B., M.R.C.P.(E), F.R.C.PSYCH., D.P.M.

Senior Lecturer, University Department of Psychiatry, Western General Hospital, Edinburgh, Scotland

INTRODUCTION

Though in recent years the initial screening and investigation of the medical geriatric patient have become progressively more intensive and successful, there has been little comparable development on the psychiatric side.

Yet all investigators are agreed on the frequent association of physical and mental illness in the elderly (1); the increasing use of powerful drugs means that iatrogenic causes of mental symptoms are more likely (15); and with the availability of specialized diagnostic techniques, evidence is accumulating to suggest that some forms of deficiency or depletion are much more common hazards than has been realized (12). It remains to be shown how much relevance the existence of such states has for the mental health of elderly people in general. There is no doubt that in many cases they are primarily responsible for psychiatric breakdown (24). It is perhaps not too fanciful to suggest that the commonest cause of mental handicap in old age is physical disorder.

In a recent study it was found that of 50 consecutive admissions to a Psychiatric Geriatric Unit, 22 had significant deficiencies of either vitamin B_{12} or folic acid or both (20). It was not possible to prove absolutely that the deficiencies were causally related to psychiatric illness, though comparison with a control group showed that the presence of such abnormality was associated with mental hospital admission and not with diet or age. Osteomalacia and magnesium and potassium deficiencies presenting with mental symptoms have also been described (21). The common factor in these was malabsorption syndrome, though it was largely by accident and only after considerable delay that the collaboration of specialists in several different fields revealed the true nature of the illnesses. The psychiatric disorders responded completely to replacement therapy.

It may be argued that these cases represent only a small proportion of psychiatric practice and that "hard cases make bad law." But even a few such problems, multiplied nationally or internationally, represent a formidable total. Moreover, it is from such atypical presentations that we learn best and our knowledge is most rapidly advanced. Only the active cooperation of physicians and psychiatrists can promote the exchange and cross-fertilization of knowledge which the solution of these mutual concerns urgently demands.

The associated topic of "misplacement" has attracted a great deal of attention (14). Partly as a result of its consequent visibility, it seems that this problem is now not serious in numerical terms (16). But because of the present general inadequacy of resources and our failure in the past to conceptualize and organize properly the services which do exist, it is inevitable that a great deal of "overlap" occurs. It is the patient in this middle group who tends to fare worst at the present time. In such a situation it is not surprising that facilities have become blocked by immovable and apparently irremediable patients whose needs have neither been fully understood nor met.

It is in order to deal with these interrelated problems that the notion of the "psycho-geriatric" patient has evolved.

ASSESSMENT CENTERS

General

The Psychiatric Geriatric Assessment Center, conceived at least fifteen years ago and blessed by the World Health Organization (27), has suffered a prolonged gestation. Though fully conceptualized by Kay (13), it has only recently been legitimized in Scotland (9) and in England (5). This tardy acceptance arises from a variety of causes (20). Its consequences are that only a few models are yet available for comparative study (3, 7, 11, 17, 26). The account which follows draws on the author's experience of a unit based on a psychiatric hospital (18, 19, 20). But the locus of such assessment is of less importance than the availability of appropriate personnel and facilities.

The elderly organic patient with his multiple physical and social pathologies may have to be investigated in many different directions before the rehabilitative therapies can be of significant or permanent benefit. Geriatric psychiatry is pre-eminently the field where a multidisciplinary attack is essential in diagnosis, treatment and placement. In practice, the necessity for specialized investigation and the continuing collaboration of the geriatrician probably means that the center will best be sited in relation to a geriatric unit of a district or general hospital. The Social Work Department clearly will also have a vital role to play in assessment, in the development of policy, in the provision of community services, and in the collection of "feed-back." The representatives of these disciplines will then together form a team which can be readily identified by patients, general practitioners and other workers in the field as a group committed to the older persons' mental and physical health and welfare. The united energies of such a team will ensure the development of appropriate philosophies of action, teaching and training.

Severe organic brain disease occurs in about 5% of elderly people; milder cases account for a further 5%. Many of these do not present serious behavioral problems and are maintained by their families without assistance. In the past, probably less than 1% have had psychiatric care.

But the changing age structure of our population will result in a substantial increase of the elderly, particularly of those over 75 years. As the members of this group will be the main consumers of hospital and residential services it is of vital importance that they be maintained in the community so long as their physical and mental health permits. When this is no longer possible they should be placed in a supportive environment appropriate to their needs.

The functions of such an assessment unit should therefore include consultation; investigation, assessment and diagnosis; treatment and rehabilitation; placement and continuing care. It has already been proved in many centers that such a policy ensures that a diminishing proportion of patients requires long-term institutional care and that the most economic use is made of existing facilities.

Ascertainment and Assessment in the Community

The family doctor holds the main responsibility for providing medical and psychiatric needs and for enlisting hospital and social services where these are indicated. If he is backed by the resources of a health center and served by district nurses and health visitors, he is well equipped to deal personally with many of the problems which will arise. "High risk" registers have been shown to be an effective means of screening practice populations. It is known that the most vulnerable patients are found within the group of those who are over 75 years, female, living alone, recently bereaved, recently discharged from hospital, solitary, house bound, physically handicapped or with a previous history of psychiatric breakdown. Regular visiting of these individuals by the nursing team and the prompt evaluation and treatment by the practitioner of those brought to his notice represent an invaluable preventive function (25).

If such primary medical care is not effective or where the psychiatric upset is greater than can be managed in a home setting, then the resources of the assessment center may have to be invoked. This will usually be decided by means of a "domiciliary" visit from a member of the assessment center team.

Pre-admission home visiting is particularly valuable for the organic case. The behavior of such patients at out-patient clinic is often a deceptive indication of their capacities. The significance of the occasion may convey itself even to the brain damaged person and may affect his performance in either direction. A much more realistic view is usually obtained in the patient's home, where, moreover, the obvious presence of social stresses or intergenerational tensions may help to elucidate the problem.

Ideally this home visit should be made by a doctor. However, in some instances the crisis will have been precipitated by social rather than medical events, for example in the case where disability has been exposed by the illness or death of a supporting relative. Experience has shown that in these circumstances a well trained member of the unit team—a community nurse or social worker—who has a detailed knowledge of aims and methods can make an adequate preliminary evaluation and effectively provide the vital link between general practitioner and hospital doctor. If this alternative is chosen in appropriate cases, it should be initiated only after discussion—often by telephone—between the doctors concerned; and of course a personal evaluation by the specialist is essential at some point.

The action recommended as a result of the home visit might be one of several possibilities.

(1) The arrangement of community support sufficient to enable the patient to remain at home.
(2) Attendance at an out-patient clinic for additional medical and psychiatric evaluation.
(3) Attendance as a day patient. This has the advantage of allowing a longer period of skilled observation and investigation.
(4) Admission to the assessment center.
(5) A combination of these.

It will be found in practice that the two most important variables which determine whether a patient requires admission, or attendance on one or more occasions, is the quality of home support available together with the amount and type of physical disability. The degree of psychiatric disturbance, in itself an important factor, is dependent in many cases on these correlates.

The ideal to be pursued is the availability of a range of options. Where flexibility of judgment about optimum placement becomes possible, best use will be made of the services available.

Selection of Patients

The original conception of an assessment center was to deal more effectively with that "misplaced" group of patients whose needs at first referral could not be clearly defined as simply "psychiatric" or "geriatric." However, some observers have argued that misplacement is merely a measure of inadequacy of services (2); that where appropriate psychiatric and geriatric facilities exist, there will be little difficulty in directing patients to the proper service and thus few demarcation disputes. While there is some justification for this view, it overlooks the need for thorough medical assessment—unless it is intended to have parallel investigations in both streams, an expensive proposition.

The policy suggested here is that all organic psychiatric illness in the elderly should have the benefit of medical screening at an early stage. Separation into psychiatric and geriatric streams is only justifiable when this has been done. In this conception, the assessment center will thus deal with all those patients who would in the past have been referred to the psychiatric service. Whether functional cases are included will depend to a large extent on local organization—there is certainly less need in this case for medical procedures. But there is much evidence to suggest that it is again the presence of physical complications which determines whether the functional case requires in-patient care. The straightforward depressive or paraphrenic can often be handled nowadays as an out-patient or day-patient. The toxic confusional state is eminently suitable for treatment in such a center; the medical procedures required are often easily determined and readily applied; enlightened management is the most significant determinant of outcome.

In the writer's view, therefore, the assessment center should provide a comprehensive service for the full range of psychiatric illness in the elderly. It is vital in this field to catch the interest and enthusiasm of staff members by every means available. The inclusion of functional illness ensures that there is a rapid turnover rate for a significant pro-portion of the referrals. This provides at once satisfaction and consola-tion, particularly for the nursing staff, who are thus able to accept philosophically the slower turnover or even chronicity of the somewhat larger group of organic cases. In such an inclusive program there is ample scope for the use of every nursing skill. The toxic confusional state can provide, in presentation, some of the most challenging, and in solution, the most satisfying problems in clinical medicine and nursing. As a result there will be diminishing problems in recruitment of com-petent staff of all categories.

This structure also means that the organizational problems of the service can be tackled in a comprehensive fashion along the lines which have proved so successful in geriatric medicine; that research programs both clinical and operational can be more broadly orientated; and that specialized knowledge and skills relevant to the understanding of old age syndromes may be more readily acquired and taught.

It will be appreciated that this somewhat idealized concept is at vari-ance with the policy of the Department of Health and Social Security (6). However, it is accepted that national plans must be determined to some extent by matters of expediency. The principles outlined above may be applied even within the fragmented service which the policy document recommends. In this case the identification of a responsible team com-mitted to the integration of district psychiatric services for the elderly, wherever they may be situated, is an overriding imperative.

EVALUATION AND ESTIMATION

It has already been emphasized that investigation will be required in medical, psychiatric and social dimensions. Given the present gaps in our knowledge of old age and its requirements, the assessment center should have an important research function. Most effective use of the information elicited will be made if provision is available for a computerized data collection system.

Medical

The medical facilities should be equipped to supply diagnostic services such as clinical laboratory, radiology and neuropathology. Remedial services—occupational therapy, physiotherapy and speech therapy—have also a valuable evaluative function. This also applies to a lesser extent to audiology, dentistry, optics, chiropody and hair-dressing, all of which should be available. Other essential services which will be called on though not necessarily placed in the unit should include neurology, electroencephalography and other specialized methods of cerebral investigation.

The basic laboratory investigations which should be applied to every patient are:

Hematology: Hb., M.C.H.C., P.C.V., W.B.C., E.S.R., and blood film.

Biochemistry: Blood sugar, Urea, Sodium, Potassium, Chloride, Bicarbonate. Alkaline Phosphatase, Calcium and Phosphorus. Fecal occult blood. Urinalysis.

Bacteriology: W.R., M.S.U. Culture.

Radiology: X-ray chest.

This may seem to be an elaborate and expensive battery, but these tests have been shown to be an essential requirement in geriatric assessment. There seems no logical reason why the organic psychiatric case should not be equally favored.

Psychiatric

The emphasis on the historical development of the patient and his illness is one of the distinguishing features of psychiatry and one on which we are most dependent. The organic patient can seldom give us the quality of information which we require. It is often from his behavior and its reflection of his affective and intellectual state rather than from his talk that we must derive much of our knowledge.

The technique of interviewing the elderly subject must be adapted to his peculiar problems and sensitivities. The attempt to elicit the essential details of previous history, onset and progression of symptoms and present complaints will often be foiled by amnesic difficulties. Too firm pressure at this stage may permanently damage the therapeutic relationship. We must allow the patient to find his own pace—to guide him gently towards reminiscence rather than pose a series of questions. His failure to respond correctly to such demands may confirm his feelings of inadequacy and will hardly advance our knowledge. Even if his talk is irrelevant it enables us to note his spontaneous thought content and pre-occupations—in these the percipient ear will often detect useful cues.

Though it is clearly desirable to base diagnostic and prognostic decisions on standardized case taking procedures, these must be modified and augmented for the brain damaged or confused patient. One of the features which may lead us into error is the variability of his performance. Thus the stress of the traditional doctor-patient interview may influence his responses depending on such factors as temperament, education and social aptitudes. It is a common experience that verbal fluency is often well preserved into an advanced stage of behavioral impairment.

Behavioral Rating Scale

Careful and continuing observation in a variety of situations is the key to accurate assessment in such conditions. Significant alterations of behavior and coping ability must be noted, together with the provoking circumstances and our interpretation of their interrelationships. Such observations are quantifiable.

Thus some of the defects inherent in the inertial observer may be overcome by invoking all members of the unit team in diagnostic, assessment and placement decisions and recording their observations in the form of a Behavioral Rating Scale (Table 1). More detailed instructions in its use are given elsewhere (22).

There is advantage in assigning each patient on admission to a particular nurse, who will then be primarily responsible for such reporting. This has the additional therapeutic benefit of giving the patient a stable figure to whom he can relate and orientate himself. A major and clinically important attribute of such a scale is that the co-operation of the subject is not required. Evaluation can thus proceed even though he is inaccessible in consequence of his abnormal mental state, sensory deficits or extreme physical debility.

Psychological

The psychiatrist faced with a diagnostic problem cannot yet rely too firmly on psychological aid. Dementia is one of those words, freely but loosely used, and difficult to define accurately in useful clinical terms. In the past, too much emphasis has been placed on its purely intellectual implications. In some recent studies, even fairly simple clinical assessments —including personality and behavioral variables—have given better correlations with performance and prognosis than have conventional psychometrics (10).

The role of the psychologist is seen additionally in the wider context of furthering the development of the program both in its diagnostic and therapeutic aspects and in his capacity as a specialist in human relationships. He may also be able to contribute to the architectural planning of facilities and to the development of a "prosthetic environment."

We need to develop rating scales for a variety of functions, which will have international acceptability and validity. We require more reliable methods of measuring the effects of drugs and other treatments on course and outcome of illness. We need to know more about the effect of previous personality and life-style on behavior in dementia. We need to know what personality structures best withstand the impact of illness in old age; which psychological mechanisms offer best protection for the older person in adversity, and whether these can be strengthened and taught; and which forms of support are most acceptable and effective.

A more traditional use of the psychologist's skills can be seen in the interpretation of the effects and localization of brain damage on the phenomenology of aging and their correlation with other studies. For the majority of patients with established intellectual impairment a simple questionnaire can give reliable judgments about current performance and long range prognosis (20).

The *Intellectual Rating Scale* (Table 2) has the advantage of allowing a normal conversational approach which does not involve too obviously a test situation. The scored questions are introduced casually along with others which are clearly friendly and innocuous. The arithmetical problems are introduced at a later stage when the subject is at ease and his confidence and co-operation have been gained. On the basis of the scores obtained, subjects can be assigned with a considerable degree of accuracy to mildly, moderately and severely impaired classes.

Group Assessment

The majority of these assessments and estimations ought to be avalaible within a week of admission. They may then be brought together and eval-

TABLE 1

Crichton Royal Geriatric Behavioral Rating Scale

Mobility	Orientation	Communication	Co-operation	Restlessness	Dressing
Fully ambulant (including stairs).	Complete.	Always clear and retains information.	Actively cooperative.	None.	Dresses correctly unaided.
Usually independent (not stairs).	Orientated in ward and identifies persons correctly.	Can indicate needs. Can understand simple verbal directions. Can deal with simple information.	Passively cooperative.	Intermittent.	Dressing imperfect but adequate
Walks with supervision.	Misidentifies persons and surroundings but can find way about.	Understands simple verbal and nonverbal information but does not indicate needs.	Requires frequent encourage- ment and/or persuasion.	Persistent by day.	Dressing adequate with minimum supervision.
Walks with artificial aids or under careful supervision.	Cannot find way to bed or to toilet without assistance.	Cannot understand simple verbal or non-verbal information but retains some expressive ability.	Rejects assistance and shows some independent but poorly directed activity.	Persistent by day with frequent nocturnal restlessness.	Dressing inadequate unless continually supervised.
Bedfast or mainly so.	Lost.	No effective contact.	Completely resistive or withdrawn.	Constant.	Unable to dress or retain clothing because of mental impairment.

Feeding	Continence	Sleep	Mood	
			Objective	Subjective
Feeds correctly unaided at appropriate times.	Fully continent.	Normal (hypnotic not required).	Normal and stable affective response and appearance.	Well-being or euphoria.
Feeds adequately with minimum supervision.	Nocturnal incontinence unless toileted. Occasional accidents. (Urine or feces.)	Requires occasional hypnotic; or occasionally restless.	Fair affective response; or not always appropriate or stable.	Self-reproachful, listless, dejected, indecisive, lacks interest. (Not completely well though no specific complaints.)
Does not feed adequately unless continually supervised.	Continent by day if regularly toileted.	Sleeps well with regular hypnotic; or usually restless for a period every night.	Marked blunting or impairment of mood or inappropriate-ness of affect.	Marked somatic or hypochon-driacal concern. Pre-occupation.
Defective feeding because of physical handicap or poor appetite.	Urinary incontinence in spite of regular toileting.	Occasionally disturbed in spite of regular standard hypnotic.	Emotional liability or incontinence. Retarded, lacks spontaneity but can respond.	Severe retardation or agitation, marked withdrawal though responds to questioning.
Unable to feed because of mental impairment.	Regularly/ frequently doubly incontinent.	Disturbed even with heavier sedation.	Hallucinations or nihilistic delusions of guilt or somatic dysfunction.	Suicidal or death wishes. Mute or agitated to the point of incoherence.

TABLE 2.

INTELLECTUAL RATING SCALE

NAME: Regd. No.: DATE:	AGE: E.E.G. No.:	DIAGNOSIS: Date 1st Adm.: Duration of Illness:	TOTAL SCORE	Range -4 to 17
TEMPORAL ORIENTATION	Day? Month? Date? Year?	SCORE 0, ½ or 1.		
ESTIMATE OF AGE	Patient's own estimate. (Correct if within 5 years)	SCORE 0 or 1.		
DURATION OF STAY IN HOSP.	Accept if within correct time sense (i.e. days, weeks or months)	SCORE 0 or 1.		
REMOTE MEMORY	Place of birth? School attended? Teacher's name?	SCORE 0, ½ or 1.		
STATUS	Whether realizes that he is a patient, ill, in hospital.	SCORE 0 or 1.		
INTERVIEW SITUATION	Whether realizes purpose of interview, and identifies role or profession of doctor.	SCORE 0 or 1.		
APPRECIATION OF FAILING ABILITIES	Spontaneous mention during interview (poor memory, calculation, etc.)	SCORE 0 or 1.		
RAPPORT		SCORE 0 or 1.		
ATTENTION & CONCENTRATION		SCORE 0 or 1.		
CURRENT AFFAIRS	Name of Queen?	SCORE 0 or 1.		
SERIAL SEVENS	100-7 = 93: -7 = 86: -7 = 79: -7 =72 SCORE 0, ½ or 1.			
1d in 1/-d	SCORE 0 or 1 ‖ 3d in 1/-d │ SCORE 0 or 1‖ 3d in 3/9 │ SCORE 0 or 1.			
ACTIVITY & PRODUCTIVITY	Scored on basis A. Generally interested & of Nurses' active when supervised. SCORE 0 or 1. Report. B. Spontaneous production, caring for others, etc. SCORE 0 or 1.			
HABITS	'Ditto' - Feeding, Dressing, Washing, Toilet SCORE 0, ½ or 1.			
			PLUS SCORE	Possible Total 17

MOOD	⎫	CONFABULATION	⎫	
TALK	⎪	EMOTIONAL LABILITY	⎪	
HALLUCINATIONS	⎬ Noted briefly but not scored.	CONFUSED UNDER STRESS	⎬ Substract one point for each item present	
DELUSIONS	⎭	MISIDENTIFIES RELATIVES	⎭	
			MINUS SCORE	Possible Total -4

Range: -4 to 2   = Severe deterioration.

3 to 9 = = Moderate deterioration.

10 to 16 = Mild deterioration.

uated at a case conference representing all the personnel who have been involved.

As a result of this multidisciplinary exercise a generally agreed formulation, prognostic statement and tentative placement decision can usually be reached. The proceedings should be recorded and will thus provide a valuable addition to the case notes. The results of this method of pooled group observations are, for the organic patient, much superior to the traditional interview. It has the additional advantage of providing an unrivalled teaching and learning situation.

Such group interaction and process is vital in the development of morale and high operational standards. Staffing quotas must allow time and opportunity for them in various forms. These groups offer a common ground where staff of all the disciplines involved, both hospital and community based, can contribute their special knowledge and expertise, can discuss their mutual problems and responsibilities and can plan the therapeutic and continuation program for the individual case.

TREATMENT

Only the main principles of therapy will be outlined here. A more detailed account will be found elsewhere (23).

Sedative and tranquilizing drugs should play only a limited and minor role in the treatment of the organic psychiatric case. More important is the provision of a suitable milieu. This depends firstly on the surroundings which should be as comfortable and as non-institutional as possible. For example, it is an advantage to have separate night and day accommodation. The visible presence of beds serves only to focus the attention on sickness and infirmity and presents unnecessary hazards and distractions. It depends also on "atmosphere" which should be active, cheerful, supporting and non-threatening. Ward design and routines should be adapted to the needs and idiosyncrasies of the patients, and not the reverse. Fundamental to this is the understanding of the patient, the gaining of his confidence and the improvement of his morale and independence, particularly by rehabilitative therapies.

"Attitude therapy" provides a useful philosophical and practical approach. One must continually ask oneself (8) "why does the patient behave like this? What meaning has his behavior in relation to his present situation, his history and experiences?"

The environment should be permissive insofar as is consistent with safety and sanitation. All patients should be dressed in their own clothes and no one confined to bed except for medical illness. There need be no segregation of the sexes. Day time incontinence can be largely avoided by regular toileting and should never be accepted solely as a consequence of dementia unless urological examination has failed to show an adequate physical cause.

For the restless wandering patient, a recurrent problem, there are two possible solutions, sedation or acceptance. In choosing the latter course one is supported by the knowledge that a full program, occupational and social, seldom fails to attract attention and interest and thus diminishes perplexity and anxiety, the basis of this agitation. Free ambulation has its hazards, but fractures are avoidable if footwear, floors and furnishings are of appropriate design. Such a regime demands qualities of personality and leadership, particularly in the nurse in charge.

Treatment is thus firmly based on a general understanding of the interplay of the historical, dynamic, social and physical factors involved in the individual case. Only then can more specific medical and psychiatric measures achieve maximum effect.

REHABILITATION

A selection of all the remedial services will be required in each case both during the initial investigative phase and thereafter for an extended period, depending on response and prognosis. Occupational therapy should supply the basic framework of the unit program. A wide variety of group and individual tasks, pastimes, games and "Activities of Daily Living" will be required (4).

Apart from its obvious contribution to re-learning and rehabilitation, occupational therapy, in the widest application of the term, stimulates interest, diminishes restlessness and gives patients a sense of achievement and some control of the environment. It should not be reserved therefore for the compliant person with favorable prognosis, but must have an integrating role in the treatment of all.

It provides for the staff a focus for the development and application of management and assessment skills. Performance in a variety of situations is an important index of competence, indicated by initiative, persistence and success or failure at different levels of complexity.

DISCHARGE AND PLACEMENT

At all stages in investigation and treatment, therapeutic goals and prognosis should be in mind. Assessment should be a flexible and continuing process and discharge potential kept under constant review. The general stereotype of the organic psychiatric patient includes the need for continuous hospitalization. It has been shown that with an active and progressive program of treatment and rehabilitation, together with adequate back-up facilities and community support, a minority will require permanent care. The average stay should not be much in excess of 4-6 weeks.

An overall discharge rate of at least 70% is possible. The residue is heavily weighted by organic cases, but even of these 40% should leave hospital. Functional cases should approach 100% discharge rate. Toxic confusional states occupy an intermediate position at about 75%, for many florid conditions subside to reveal an underlying dementia.

Discharge rates will clearly depend on admission criteria. If demand is regulated by chronicity or crisis, turnover will be low and the service will inevitably become blocked. If, however, an active policy is directed to the detection of the early case and preventive rather than custodial principles, there is every expectation that performance will equal the output of general psychiatric or medical wards.

Such a high turnover unit should be able to return 50% of its intake to the community from which they came—though additional social and follow-up support will often be required. The provision of suitable living accommodation in the form of old persons' flatlets or sheltered housing will be an essential pre-requisite for some of these. Others may be "boarded out" or placed in "group homes." Many will benefit from supportive services—laundry, home helps, meals on wheels, lunch clubs or attendance at old age clubs or day centers—and may require regular attendance from health visitor or district nurse.

Residential home placement, including local authority homes, voluntary homes and hostels for the mentally confused, will be appropriate for a further 25%. The remaining 25% will require long term hospital care, either psychiatric or geriatric. The choice should depend on the anticipated needs of the patient. If security and the control of disturbed behavior is paramount a psychiatric facility should be chosen. If the patient, though severely intellectually impaired, is manageable and the primary requirement is for basic nursing care, then geriatric accommodation is preferable.

It is essential that there be a wide range of options for placement and support and that assessment includes measures for matching the individual to the most appropriate situation. It has been shown that with experience and the evaluative and predictive procedures described, a high degree of accuracy of placement can be assured.

OUT-PATIENT SERVICES

Health services are in general orientated to episodic care. In all forms of geriatric illness the wider concept of continuity of care is essential. Though many of these conditions are responsive to treatment, their occurrence in the aging organism implies that review and support, sometimes over an extended period, will be required if the patient is to be maintained at an optimum level of functioning.

It must be emphasized therefore that the center's responsibility includes the family or social unit and does not end simply with the patient's discharge. There should be no attempt to clear beds by implied threat or by time limit. It is clearly anti-therapeutic to force a placement in an unwilling or non-supporting situation. In practice, it is found that by the flexible use of experimental discharge, supportive measures for relatives both emotional and practical, holiday or "intermittent" admissions, and attendance at day hospital or out-patient clinic, it is rarely necessary to retain a person in hospital for reasons other than his mental or physical state. Such an extended program will require experienced case-workers of sound judgment, and the monitoring of information from practitioners, district nurses and health visitors.

The value of day care for psychiatric and geriatric patients is now well established. There has been less experience in the psycho-geriatric field. However, evidence is accumulating to show that such a facility is manageable and provides an effective alternative to in-patient care. Of particular importance in the management of the confused patient is the provision of a reliable transport service with attendant nurse who will supervise his collection and return and provide continuing liaison between family and hospital.

It is not necessary for in-patient accommodation and day hospital to be separately sited. Indeed considerable advantage can be gained from the combination of both facilities, provided that the day area is sufficiently spacious. Both groups have similar needs and it is desirable that they are under the care of a unified staff. In this way the most economic and flexible use can be made of investigative and remedial services and patients can be easily transferred either way should their condition improve or deteriorate, or should the initial prescription prove to have been incorrect. Frequency of attendance will be determined both by the needs of the patient and relatives and by the pressures on the service. It will be found that many will require to come daily, at least initially.

The availability of day care ensures that many patients can be fully investigated and treated without the need for in-patient observation; that the admission of others with progressive impairment can be postponed or even permanently avoided; that through it some in-patients can achieve earlier discharge; and that relief can be offered to relatives during the stresses of chronic illness.

The place of the orthodox out-patient clinic in the care of the organic psychiatric patient is less easily determined. The complexity of transport in a large city can render attendance exhausting for the patient and thus misleading for the doctor. It would seem logical for the psychiatrist to arrange his clinics at the health centers of the district. In this way a group of patients, both new referrals and return cases, could be seen in company with their practitioners and ancillary workers. Such an arrangement would strengthen community links, allow easy exchange of information and provide a valuable teaching situation.

CONCLUSION

In the past the care of the elderly confused patient has attracted low priority, has been associated with poor therapeutic expectations and low prestige. It has now been demonstrated in a few centers that a more optimistic and active approach can transform this negative image. The present concern about existing facilities and the increasing interest shown by government, administration and the public is helping to improve professional attitudes.

The functioning of such a treatment and rehabilitative service makes great emotional and physical demands on the personnel involved. If it is to be successful much care must be given to the selection of staff of all categories. Apart from training grades, recruitment to the unit should be voluntary. This vocational selection must be supported by responsibility and emotional and intellectual satisfaction if personnel of adequate experience and ability are to be attracted.

There should be free communication at all levels; the development of philosophies and strategies of care should be a group process. The psychiatrist in charge should be prepared therefore to devote a considerable proportion of his time and energy to intra-mural activities of this sort.

The type and scope of the program which has been described, together with the progressive identification of needs which it will demonstrate, will hopefully lead to the more appropriate and generous provision of resources of all kinds.

NOTE: A service based on the concepts outlined above is at present under development at the Royal Victoria Hospital, Edinburgh, Scotland.

REFERENCES

1. ANDERSON, W. F. 1971. The interrelationship between physical and mental disease in the elderly. In: Recent Developments in Psychogeriatrics. *Brit. J. Psychiat.*, Special Publ. No. 6.
2. ANDREWS, J., BARDON, D., GANDER, D. R., GIBSON, K. B., MALLETT, B. L., and ROBINSON, K. V. 1972. Planning of Psycho-Geriatric Care. *Geront. Clin.*, 14:100-109.

3. ARIE, T. 1971. Morale and the planning of psychogeriatric services. *Brit. Med. J.* 3:166-170.
4. BERESFORD COOKE, K. 1964. Occupational therapy in the psychiatric geriatric unit, Crichton Royal. *J. Occup. Therap.* May/June.
5. Department of Health and Social Security. 1970. *Psycho-geriatric Assessment Unit.* H.M. (70) 11. London.
6. Department of Health and Social Security. 1972. *Services for Mental Illness Related to Old Age.* H.M. (72) 71. London.
7. DONOVAN, J. F., WILLIAMS, I. E. I., and WILSON, T. S. 1971. A fully integrated psychogeriatric service. In: Recent Developments in Psychogeriatrics. *Brit. J. Psychiat.*, Special Publ. No. 6.
8. GINSBERG, R. 1955. Attitude therapy in geriatric ward psychiatry. *J. Am. Geriat. Soc.*, 3:7.
9. H.M.S.O. 1970. Services for the elderly with mental disorder. Edinburgh.
10. IRVING, G., ROBINSON, R. A., and McADAM, W 1970. The validity of some cognitive tests in the diagnosis of dementia. *Brit. J. Psychiat.*, 117:149-156.
11. JEFF, O., and ROTH, M. 1969. The new psychogeriatric unit at Newcastle General Hospital. *J. Occup. Therap.*, October.
12. JUDGE, T. G. 1969. *Proceedings of 5th European Meeting of Clinical Gerontology, Brussels.* p. 295.
13. KAY, D. W. K., ROTH, M., and HALL, M. R. P. 1966. Special problems of the aged and the organisation of hospital services. *Brit. Med. J.*, 2:967-972.
14. KIDD, C. B. 1962. Misplacement of the elderly in hospital. *Brit. Med. J.*, 2:1491.
15. LEAROYD, B. M. 1972 Psychotropic drugs and the elderly patient *Med. J. Aust.*, I: 1131-1133.
16. MEZEY, A. G., HODKINSON, H. M., and EVANS, G. J. 1968. The elderly in the wrong unit. *Brit. Med. J.*, 3:16-18.
17. MORTON, E. V. B., BARBER, M. E., and MacMILLAN, D. 1968. The joint assessment and early treatment unit in psychogeriatric care. *Geront. Clin.*, 10:65-73.
18. ROBINSON, R. A. 1962. The practice of a psychiatric geriatric unit. *Geront. Clin.*, Additamentum, pp. 1-19. Basel/New York: Karger.
19. ROBINSON, R. A. 1965. A psychiatric geriatric unit. In: "Psychiatric disorders in the aged." Report on the symposium held by the World Psychiatric Association. London: pp. 186-205. Geigy.
20. ROBINSON, R. A. 1969. The prevention and rehabilitation of mental illness in the elderly. *Interdisc. Top. Geront.* 3:89-102. Basel/New York: Karger.
21. ROBINSON, R. A. 1969. *The confused elderly. In: Centrepiece: Collected Conference reports: Scottish Hospital Centre.* Edinburgh.
22. ROBINSON, R. A. 1971. Assessment scales in a Psycho-Geriatric Unit. In: Stocker, G., Kuhn, R. A., Hall, P., Becker, G., and van der Veen, E. (Eds.) *Assessment in Cerebrovascular Insufficiency.* Stuttgart: Georg Thelme Verlag.
23. ROBINSON, R. A. 1972. The role of drug therapy in geriatric psychiatry. In: Anderson, W. F., and Judge, T. G. (Eds.) *Geriatric Medicine.* London and New York: Academic Press.
24. SIMON, A., and TALLERY, J. E. 1965. The role of physical illness in geriatric mental disorder. Report on the Symposium held by the World Psychiatric Association. London: Geigy. Pp. 154-170.
25. STOKOE, I. H. 1971. Care of the elderly. *Update Plus.* September.
26. WHITEHEAD, J. A. 1965. A comprehensive psychogeriatric service. *Lancet*, 55:583-6.
27. World Health Organization. 1959. Mental Health Problems of Aging and the Aged. *W.H.O. Techn. Rep. Ser.*, 171:49.

19

PSYCHOMETRIC TECHNIQUES

R. Douglass Savage, B.A., Ph.D., F.B.Ps.S.

Senior Lecturer in Applied Psychology
University of Newcastle upon Tyne, England

INTRODUCTION

It is always a difficult problem to attempt to do justice to all the contributors in an area and, at the same time, to present a picture of recent developments in a field which highlights only the practical applications and implications for the practicing clinician—medical or psychological. This chapter, nevertheless, will try to fulfill the requirements of this series by answering the basic question, "If a clinical colleague is unfamiliar with my field, what does he need to know in order to be up to date in the subject?" My brief clearly stated, indeed emphasized, that each chapter should not be simply an exhaustive review of the literature, but provide important up to date material relevant to clinical practice, the bias being practical rather than academic. Although it is difficult to separate these two aspects when considering psychometric techniques, I will attempt to present the major assessment techniques, the background to their development, their uses and abuses. Broadly speaking, I will cover techniques for investigating Intellectual functioning and Personality characteristics, as well as Social and Personal adjustment. Within each area, I will discuss the background to the work and outline some of the recent methods of psychometric investigation suitable for investigations of the aged.

The whole problem of psychometric assessment in the aged, like that at other levels, revolves around the definition and measurement of normality and abnormality and the spread of any characteristic in the relevant population. It is gratifying to be able to say that our understanding of the processes and changes in behavioral functioning in the aged has increased considerably in the last 15-20 years. One will recall the contributions of Roth and his associates (86, 87), who have stressed the natural history and classification of mental disorders in old age based on clinical practice and methodology. The work of Havighurst and his colleagues (51, 52) has attempted to define and measure successful aging on the basis of a study of public opinion concerning the activities of older people. More recent developments in personality measurement from the work of Cattell (24) and Eysenck (35), not to mention the previous work on projective techniques, such as the Rorschach and the Thematic Apperception, have all pointed to the importance of age changes in personality. Our understanding of behavioral skilled performance has been vastly improved by the work of Welford (111, 112, 113) and his co-workers. Most attention in psychometric terms, however, has been given to the investigation of intellectual aspects of functioning in the aged by Birren (6, 8), Botwinick (11), Savage et al. (89, 92) and several others.

Nevertheless, as this chapter will illustrate, and as a more comprehensive review by Savage (90) showed, we still lack normative data on many psychological or behavioral aspects of old age and a number of significant behavioral and practical problems still remain unsolved in this area. As Professor P.B. Medawar (70), in his address to a Ciba Foundation Colloquia on Aging, stated, "nothing is clearer evidence of the immaturity of gerontological science than the tentative and probationary character of its systems of definitions and measurements." Despite passages in Plato's *Republic* and from Cicero's *De Senectute,* gerontology in any real scientific sense dates only from about 1950.

For those wishing to delve further into this fascinating area I may at this point be excused a few major references. There have been a number of comprehensive reviews of various aspects of old age by Kubo (62), Cowdry (29), Granick (42), Watson (107) and Kaplan (58). *The Handbook of Aging and the Individual* edited by Birren (6) and Anderson's (4) *Psychological Aspects of Aging* may be regarded as the initial attempts to organize the inaccessible and complex literature in this area. Research workers are considerably indebted to the *Annual Review of Psychology,* chapters by Shock (98), Lorge (66), Birren (7), Chown and Heron (27) and Botwinick (12) on aging and the aged and the books by Heron and Chown, *Age and Function* (54), *Clinical Psychiatry of Late Life* by Post (81), *Clinical Psychiatry* by Slater and Roth (100), *Life Span Develop-*

mental Psychology by Goulet and Baltes (41), *Recent Developments in Psychogeriatrics* by Kay and Walk (59), and *Intellectual Functioning in the Aged* by Savage et al. (92) to name a few.

Over the past 15-20 years, increasing attention has been paid to aging and old age in terms of psychological or behavioral development. There has been a considerable output of research and further concern for the problems of old age, spurred perhaps more by actual or potential economic necessity than ethical or academic virtue. However, one must be thankful for any motivating initiative for work in this area is essential. As the United Nations Organization for Economic Co operation and Development stated in 1962, "The capacity for the medical department to assist in promoting the health and working efficiency of people in all grades would be considerably enlarged were it possible to develop simple and practical measures for the assessment of functional age." In addition to this, work on the aged has a vital contribution to make to many theoretical and practical issues in general psychology.

INTELLECTUAL ASSESSMENT

There have been numerous publications on the effects of age on cognitive functioning which illustrate how this area is beset with difficulties and how a radical rethinking of the situation is only just emerging. The theoretical and practical problems are now being revealed and adequately tackled; until recently, the measures available to assess cognitive functioning in the elderly were far from satisfactory, despite the fact that intellectual functioning is vital to adaptability. More widespread knowledge of the normative data on intellectual levels in the aged, how they change over time and more adequate understanding of the structure of intellect in normal and abnormal elderly people are urgently required.

Several earlier studies of intellectual ability over wide age ranges suggested, and most people accepted the view, that the intellectual functioning declines slowly from the third decade of life to the sixth and more abruptly thereafter. However, in spite of the above findings, intelligence, when appraised by other broader criteria than the well known intelligence tests, does not always manifest the same decline with age. For example, with increasing age, experience plays an ever increasing role in the individual's capacity to deal effectively with his environment, a criterion basic to many definitions of intelligence. General intelligence, as evaluated by pragmatic environmental criteria, appears to maintain itself unimpaired over a much greater portion of adult life, and to decline at a much slower rate than do the mental abilities assessed in some types of intelligence test. One may suggest, and indeed now show, that general intelligence is a multivariate construct. There may be differences in how we define and measure intelligence, in the rates at which it changes, or the nature of its influence on other things at different ages.

It is clear from recent research that the popular conception that after a certain age one is too old to learn has no basis in fact below 60, and much more needs to be known of the role of motivational and personality factors in the learning process. More crucial, however, is the fact that this so-called popular view has dominated supposedly scientifically respectable theories and investigations, particularly in the field of cognitive functioning and mental illness. What in fact does happen to intellectual functioning and personality after 60? Do their structures change? Are they affected by organic and functional psychiatric illness? How do the data from cross-sectional and longitudinal investigations of functioning in the elderly compare? Are normal and pathological changes in the aged similar or divergent?

The Structure and Measurement of Intellect in the Aged

Much of the confusion in the results of intellectual measurement on normal and abnormal aged individuals and groups will remain until a more satisfactory theory or analysis of the structure of intellect in the aged is available. How then can we understand cognitive functioning and change in the aged?

Several investigations in the fields of aging and senility have accounted for their findings by contrasting the results from techniques which measure the stored experiences of subjects with those from measures of learning or problem solving ability. The former are said to be more resistant to the effects of aging and brain damage than the latter. Thus, Wechsler (108, 110) distinguishes between "hold" and "don't hold" subtests on his measures of intellectual functioning, Cattell (23) suggests a distinction between fluid and crystallized ability, in which fluid ability (GF) is said to show itself best in novel or culture-free material, while crystallized ability (GC) has its highest loading in acquired, familiar, cultural activities. In the same vein, Reed and Reitan (82) have differentiated between tests that demand *immediate adaptive ability* and tests that tap *stored information*. Furthermore, research work reviewed by Payne (79) and Savage (90) indicates that this distinction between already acquired, crystallized ability or intellectual level and fluid or

FIGURE 1

The Structure and Measurement of Intellect in the Aged

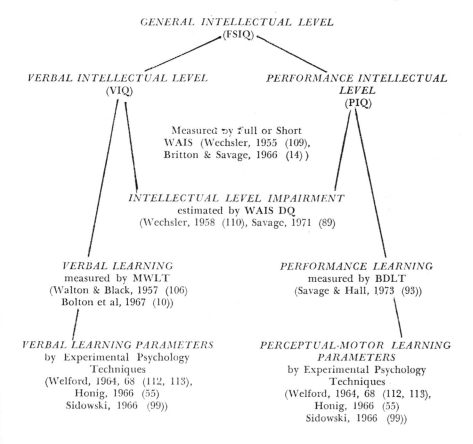

GENERAL INTELLECTUAL LEVEL
(FSIQ)

VERBAL INTELLECTUAL LEVEL
(VIQ)

PERFORMANCE INTELLECTUAL
LEVEL
(PIQ)

Measured by Full or Short
WAIS (Wechsler, 1955 (109),
Britton & Savage, 1966 (14))

INTELLECTUAL LEVEL IMPAIRMENT
estimated by WAIS DQ
(Wechsler, 1958 (110), Savage, 1971 (89)

VERBAL LEARNING
measured by MWLT
(Walton & Black, 1957 (106)
Bolton et al, 1967 (10))

PERFORMANCE LEARNING
measured by BDLT
(Savage & Hall, 1973 (93))

VERBAL LEARNING PARAMETERS
by Experimental Psychology
Techniques
(Welford, 1964, 68 (112, 113),
Honig, 1966 (55)
Sidowski, 1966 (99))

PERCEPTUAL-MOTOR LEARNING
PARAMETERS
by Experimental Psychology
Techniques
(Welford, 1964, 68 (112, 113),
Honig, 1966 (55)
Sidowski, 1966 (99))

learning ability to cope with new materials or situations is not only crucial to normal intellectual development, but has important implications for intellectual change associated with functional and/or organic pathological processes.

One can suggest from the Newcastle upon Tyne studies of the community and hospitalized aged a theory for intellectual functioning and impairment in the aged and appropriate methods of assessment. Analysis of work carried out between 1963 and 1972 by Drs. Savage, Britton, Bolton and Hall (92) gave a sound mathematical, statistical and psychological solution for understanding the structure of intellect in the aged which appears to have considerable potential. Their solution produced a structure for cognitive functioning in the aged which makes a strong distinction between *intellectual level and intellectual learning* (Figure 1). The major first factor or aspect found was one of *general intellectual level* accounting for 57.3% of the variance, but not represented in the Learning measures. The *levels of Verbal and Performance* intellectual functioning were represented by Factor 2 which accounts for 20.8% of the variance. *Intellectual learning* is seen in the third and fourth factors as *performance learning* and *verbal learning*. These learning factors account for 7.8% and 8.9% of the variance respectively. The factors or aspects of intellectual functioning highlighted by this solution are orthogonal with measures of each showing fortunately very low loadings on the other. This particular breakdown of the nature or types of intellectual functioning on the aged was gained from the analysis of the Newcastle upon Tyne information of psychometric assessment which has included over 350 normal and mentally ill aged over nine years of research.

Savage's proposed solution or explanation of the structure of intellect in the aged is extremely helpful both theoretically and practically. In effect it *breaks down intellectual functioning in the aged into level and learning components which are orthogonal or independent of one another and specifies both verbal and performance aspects of these two components.* Furthermore, the solution is consistent with the previous theoretical decisions of Cattell (23) and others who have stressed the breakdown between crystallized and fluid abilities, and is consistent with information regarding known effects of functional illness and organic lesions, accidental or natural, on cognitive functioning (79, 90, 115). It is also meaningful in terms of the longitudinal changes observed in our work, particularly the differential rate of change in verbal and performance levels in the WAIS, and in the development of learning impairment in the aged.

The importance of this theory of the structure or nature of intellect for psychometric assessment of intellectual functioning in the aged is obvious. *Intellectual level* of functioning consisting of acquired or crystallized intellectual ability is probably more resistant to the normal aging changes or processes of senility and may well be impaired less rapidly by generalized cerebral injury than fluid intelligence. What is also of practical importance is that this *level* of intellectual ability in terms of both *verbal* and *performance* may be adequately assessed in the aged by a short form of the Wechsler Adult Intelligence Scale (110) especially standardized for the aged (14). *Learning ability,* both verbal and performance, is probably affected more quickly by the normal organic changes or natural processes of aging, and such deficiencies may be expected to appear before loss of acquired intellectual level occurs. The *verbal learning* aspect of intellectual functioning can be assessed by the *Modified Word Learning Test* of Walton and Black (106) with the appropriate age norms presented by Bolton et al. (10). *Performance or motor-perceptual learning* may be measured by the *Block Design Learning Test* developed by Savage and Hall (93). Differences between Verbal and Performance levels and Verbal and Performance learning can be measured and evaluated by the norms for the aged presented by Savage et al. (92). An initial comprehensive, yet time-saving, assessment of intellectual functioning in the aged is therefore, possible.

If it is felt necessary to give the full WAIS, Wechsler's *Deterioration Quotient* can be calculated to estimate the loss in *level* of intellectual functioning (91). Despite criticisms by Payne (79) and Yates (114, 115) of the Wechsler *Deterioration Quotient* concept, it can be very helpful if correctly used and evaluated. Changes in intellectual level and learning as well as the internal subject variability of cognitive functioning can also be traced for individuals and evaluated against adequate peer group norms provided in several sources such as Savage (89, 90) and Savage et al. (92). Comparative subtest or subscale analysis of the WAIS for individuals with the appropriate statistical evaluation is occasionally useful, but rarely, and in any case only gives hypotheses which might be further investigated. It seems likely, however, that those elderly people whose levels of performance intelligence remain unimpaired should be healthier and probably better adjusted to the difficulties of old age and more likely to be normal and live in the community. Furthermore, the maintenance of a reasonable level of the ability to cope with new verbal and performance material is also associated with the continued survival in both normal and psychiatrically ill aged (92).

In summary then, the structural analysis of intellect in the aged developed from our Newcastle upon Tyne investigations suggests that applied psychology practice in the clinic or in society may be well served by a view of the structure or nature of intellect in the aged, stressing the level and learning components of cognitive processes, both having verbal and performance aspects. Fairly well standardized, reliable and valid measures to assess these functions in the aged have been presented and intellectual difficulties associated with functional, treatable psychiatric disorders such as in the affective states and with more severe degenerative senile processes indicated (89, 90, 92). Above all, however, the assessment of cognitive functioning in itself is stressed as extremely important in that it has implications for the way in which we must advise and handle people; we would hope to help them generally to cope more effectively in a variety of situations. Accurate, reliable knowledge of the intellectual functioning of an individual can help us advise that person or family on how to cope in society, at home and in numerous personal and family situations. This should help towards saving the best possible personal and social adjustment for the individual aged person and for those who surround him or her. It can also have important implications for the advice given to society on social care, on needs—personal, social and physical of the elderly in relation to the community at large: to what extent community care, hospitalization, etc., are necessary.

Work and knowledge of cognitive functioning can and, to be of practical use, should be related to extensive investigations and knowledge on social and personal adjustment and personality change in the aged for the advantage of all elderly citizens and society in general. The theory and methods of assessment of intellectual functioning presented here would also seem to have significant applications and could lead to further understanding of the development of intellectual functioning from the cradle upwards.

ADJUSTMENT IN OLD AGE

Adjustment both in terms of personal and social situations has been a major concept in psychology for many years and resulted in the development of practical measurement devices as well as elucidating theoretical problems related to aging. Much of the early work covered the age range 40-65, but more recently the assessment of personal and social adjustment has been investigated in older samples.

Since the 1940s, considerable emphasis has been placed on the development of extracting quantitative scores for "adjustment" from subjects at various age levels. Cavan, Burgess, Havighurst and Goldhamer (25) reported the use of the Adult Activity Schedule. This inventory, *Your Attitudes and Activities,* consists of some statements which are checked, others answered by "Yes" or "No," whilst others have a four or five point intensity distribution. Categories covered in the inventory include health, family, friends, leisure and recreation clubs and organizations, employment history, financial security, early life and attitudes. The inventory was sent by mail to a total of 8,441 individuals geographically distributed over the entire United States. This sample was a fairly close representation of the population of the United States aged 60 years and over with the exception that a much smaller representation of rural farm subjects was obtained than might be considered ideal. Sub-scores for the following categories were calculated: leisure activities (including organizations), religious activities, intimate contacts (friends and family), health, and security. The authors devoted considerable attention to the reliability and validity of the inventory and conclude that, although improvements could be made, both reliability and validity are high enough to warrant the every day clinical counselling or practical use of the scale.

In the sample studied, increasing age was associated with a decrease in the amount of close companionship, in less participation in many activities as shown by attendance at meetings and in fewer number of hobbies and plans for the future. There was also an increase in physical handicaps, illness and nervousness and a decrease in feelings of satisfaction with health status. Religious activities and dependence upon religion increased with age, whereas feelings of happiness, usefulness, zest and interest in life decreased. In general, the older subjects responded with lower median attitude scores indicating poorer adjustment than for the younger participants. An increased feeling of economic security, despite a lower amount of income, was reported by many of the respondents. Sex differences in adjustment were also apparent; for instance, women reported more physical handicaps, illness, nervous and neurotic symptoms, and accidents than men. Women also had more religious activity and more favorable attitudes toward religion than did men, but were less happy.

These studies, though suffering a number of methodological limitations, served to focus attention on the many variables involved in adequate social adjustment in older people and in defining what one may consider abnormal. There has also been considerable interest in interrelationships between social and personal adjustment. For example, Moberg (72) reported that those old people who had formerly been leaders in the church were better adjusted than those who had never held leadership positions, but that there was no difference between church members and non-church members in old age personal adjustment. It is generally appreciated that older people must adapt to many new life demands such as retirement, death of family and friends, changes in standards and styles of living, as well as to personal psychological and biological changes. What is also important is that those changes are largely initiated by forces beyond the individual's control. It would also seem that individual differences in social roles determine many features of adjustment in old age. Empirically there appears to be a significant correlation between the number of social roles and adjustment: indeed, activity and interpersonal contact may be prophylactic for many problems of later life (49, 50, 97). The onset of illness in late life has marked effects on personal and social adjustment (57, 68), though there is also considerable evidence that persons lacking successful adjustment in early or middle life continue to do so in old age (69, 97).

The measurement of *personal adjustment in terms of happiness* as well as social activity has also attracted considerable attention, though the reports offer conflicting results. Early studies by Morgan (73) and Landis (64) based on interview material concluded that most people of advanced age considered the happiest period of their lives to have been that between 25 and 45 years. Kuhlen (63), on the other hand, in a study of 300 adults between the ages of 20 and 80, reported that happiness ratings tended to increase up to the 20's and 30's and to decrease thereafter. The primary sources of unhappiness were bereavement and poor health. Though most of the foregoing subjects reported higher degrees of happiness at early ages, it is important to note that only 3 percent of the aged people (two-thirds being 70 or over) interviewed by Gardner (37), reported that they were unhappy. There is also considerable evidence that happiness and successful adjustment, both personal and social, in old age are intimately bound up with physical and mental health and financial security (65, 68). Happy old people were more alert and flexible than those who were unhappy, whilst the ill did not see themselves as different from normal and the hopefully ill were better adjusted than those who were less hopeful.

There are obviously many difficulties in assessing and defining "adjustment" or "successful aging," as like intelligence it is undoubtedly a multi-dimensional concept both in terms of definition and etiology. The concept requires more precise definition, and dependence upon retrospective information about happiness in previous decades of life is a hazardous method of investigation. In this respect, the work of Havighurst (46, 47, 48, 51), and his colleagues gives many useful indications of the nature and for the measurement of old age adjustment. Several of their measures recognize the *inner and outer aspects of successful aging*, in particular the *Chicago Attitude Inventory* (25, 49, 52). Scores are a combination of attitudes about activities in several areas and inner feelings of happiness independent, to some extent, of outward behavior.

This area has been extended by the work of Bernice Neugarten in 50-80 year olds in the Kansas City study. The research group began by examining measures of adjustment morale used by other investigators. After extensive interview assessments, they produced an operational definition of life satisfaction in four components: (1) zest vs. apathy; (2) resolution and fortitude; (3) goodness of fit between desired and achieved goals; (4) positive self-concept and mood tone. Each component can be rated on a five point scale (51, 76) and the ratings can be added to get a life satisfaction rating ranging from 5 to 25. *Two forms of self-report instruments* are now available from the work of this team (51): (1) *Life Satisfaction Index A*—an attitude inventory of 20 items which correlated .58 with the interview scale, N=90, mean 12.4, S.D. 4.4; (2) *Life Satisfaction Index B*—consists of six open ended and six check list items scored 0, 1 or 2 which correlates .71 with the rating scale, N=92, mean 15.1, S.D. 4.4; A and B correlate .73, total mean 27.6, S.D. 6.7.

These procedures for measuring life satisfaction all depend on inner definitions of successful aging. They can be used to study the effects of social and economic conditions on people, to assess their life satisfaction. Furthermore, the definition of successful aging as satisfaction with present and past life does not favor either of the apparently rival, though one might add not mutually exclusive, activity and disengagement theories of aging. The activity theorists believe that people should maintain the activities and attitudes of middle age as long as possible and then find substitutes for the activities which they must give up—for work when they are forced to retire, for clubs and associations, for friends and loved ones whom they lost by death. Disengagement theory is based on the observation that as people grow older they generally curtail the activities of middle age. There is no doubt that disengagement does take place with aging, but proponents of the activity theory regard this as a result of society's withdrawal from the aging person against his will and desire. It would, however, not seem unreasonable to suppose that life satisfaction may be positively related to activity for some people and to disengagement for others. A person with an active, achieving, and outward-directed life-style will be best satisfied to continue this into old age with only slight diminution. Other people with a passive, dependent, home-centered way of life will be best satisfied with disengagement. Cumming and McCaffrey (30) suggested this when they said that there may be "important non-modal groups of the die-with-your-boots-on school. We do not yet know who they are except that there is evidence that academics do not disengage, in the sense that we are using it here, to the same degree that, for example, skilled workmen or clerical workers do."

These complex interrelationships between inner satisfaction with life and outer behavior in society need careful investigation with the elderly. We can thank workers for their efforts, but wish for considerably more *evidence* on large representative samples of the aged and hope for longitudinal studies to help unravel the confusions in this area which are not only theoretically fascinating to psychologists, but of vital practical importance to a society with an increasing aged population. The effect of retirement, for example, shows interesting variations between classes, across cultures and within economic conditions. A survey has shown that in Great Britain 70 percent of men compulsorily retired at 65 would have continued working if it had been possible, though only 25 percent actually tried to find work (28). On the other hand, in America, where pensions are less generally available, Gordon (39) found men tended to retire only when ill health forced the issue. Furthermore, forced retirement will differentially affect those who have enjoyed rather than those who have tolerated or disliked their work. The evidence from Emerson (31), Thompson et al. (104), and Heron (53) suggested that there is a retirement impact which varies with occupational class. When and under what conditions one might ask does the "retirement impact" become abnormal? How do we assess this? The measurement of personal and social adjustment is obviously crucial. Changing conditions in society also mean that we must systematically review and re-evaluate our methods of assessment and theory in this area.

Some recent studies have cast doubt on the necessity of a polarized activity vs. disengagement approach to understanding life satisfaction or abnormality in old age. What are successful or unsuccessful, normal or abnormal aged types? An interview project by Buhler (18) named four groups of older people: (1) those who want to rest and relax, (2) those who wish to be active, (3) those dissatisfied with the past, but resigned, (4) those who have led meaningless lives and are now frustrated, guilty and regretful. On the other hand, Reichard, Livson and

Peterson (83), in their book *Personality and Aging,* suggested three types of "successful" agers: one active, one passive, and one mature (ego-integrated). There were two unsuccessful types: extra-punitive and self-rejective. "Life satisfaction," "activity" and "disengagement" would obviously mean different things for each of these groups. It also may mean very different things for people in different cultures or within culture subgroups. A review article by Jones (56) pointed out that there are individual life-styles (active, passive, social, asocial, etc.), environmental pressures (economic, social, familial, etc.), and, last but not least, biological deteriorations and disabilities, to be taken into account, when defining normal or abnormal, successful or unsuccessful aging. Because of the ways in which pressures and personality interact, it seems likely that we shall learn most about the aged by a thorough analysis of the components or of the structure of aged personality and adjustment by continuous longitudinal investigations.

The image of self and the measurement of *self concept* can also be useful when one is interested in understanding and helping the aged. There is considerable evidence that differences between real, imagined and ideal self in patients lead to complicated problems of personal and social adjustment. Traditionally the self concept has been stressed by many therapists and investigators such as Rogers (84) and Kelly (60); methodologically the *Q Sort Technique* (78), and the *Repertory Grid Techniques* (60) have been used to assess in this area. It is somewhat surprising that Factor Q3 on Cattell's 16 PFQ, though, in my view, very relevant to this area, has been little used in research and clinical literature in this area. I will deal with this question in the personality section later. A recent scale developed by Fitts (36) may be of some interest here. It is called *The Tennessee Self Concept Scale* and can be used for counselling and clinical purposes; it measures several aspects of the self concept and adjustment.

One is also surprised that *adaptive behavior scales or behavior rating scales* have not been used more widely with the aged. Some of these scales, for example, *The Adaptive Behavior Scale* (77), have some data on the 60 plus age group, but much more needs to be known in this area. These scales could, however, be usefully employed in clinical practice, even in their present form. A recent paper by Turner et al. (105) for instance has reported on techniques for assessing personality and their use as predictors of adaptation to institutional living in the aged in America.

PERSONALITY MEASUREMENT

The identification, description and presentation of adequate techniques for the measurement of personality characteristics in the aged have lagged behind that for cognitive assessment in the elderly. The development of more adequate personality assessment procedures by Cattell, Eysenck and others gives hope for the future, but one cannot help but be disappointed by the small amount of research in this field on old people. It is an area of investigation, for example, where latitudinal studies, because of the problems of sampling and natural selection, could give extremely misleading results. The difficulties, particularly the considerable expense of longitudinal studies, must be accepted if we are to make any real progress. Even now, few methods of measuring personality have any, let alone satisfactory, normative data for the elderly. The personality theorists have given only limited attention to changes in old age or even to adequately describing old age personality until very recently. Watson, in a review of the situation in 1954, suggested that research of personality in the elderly was in a naturalistic, exploratory stage rather than at a theoretically or experimentally based level. There has been some, but not a great deal of progress since.

Investigations using *projective techniques of personality measurement* have been reported. Indeed, the developmental changes accompanying increasing age were mentioned rather briefly by Rorschach (85), who commented that "the older individual loses the capacity for introversion and becomes more coarted or constricted." He described further influences of age as an increase in stereotype and a decrease in the freedom of association and claimed that the protocols of normal subjects 70 to 80 years of age closely resembled those of younger cases of dementia simplex.

A comparison of the similarity in test protocol as reported by the various investigators provides one method of evaluating the Rorschach for use in personality research with the aged. That is, the fact that different samples have yielded roughly comparable qualitative results indicates that whatever is being measured appears with a fairly respectable degree of consistency. One can say little, however, of the quantitative accuracy of the data in terms of evaluating personality in the aged. Furthermore, the titles of three major studies with the Rorschach Psychodiagnostic Plates, namely *Personality Patterns of Old Age, Personality Structure of the Older Age Groups,* and *Personality Characteristics of the Institutionalized Aged,* clearly illustrate how Rorschach findings are assumed to be synonymous with personality characteristics. It is significant to note that none of the studies stated as its explicit purpose the establishment of norms for older groups, although it is highly probable that this was implicit in all of them. Logically, it would seem that this should come first. The conclusions derived from the Rorschach studies of the aged, as well as the meaning implied in the titles, have also reflected a willing transposition of the assumed rationale of the Rorschach scoring categories for younger into the older age groups (21).

Implicit in all the investigations is the fact that more credit has been given to the integrity of the test than to the integrity of the subjects. That is, the assumption is made that the rationale of the test variables does not change with age, that since different profiles are found at different age levels, these must represent changes within the individual. This may well be true, but in view of the lack of conclusive evidence, it seems that one should more cautiously assume that both or either the test rationale or the individual may change with age.

The Thematic Apperception Test (74), has also been used on the aged, though very little, in an effort to describe and understand their personality. A series of studies from the Kansas City project followed up and generally substantiated the view that there are no statistically significant age differences in the analysis of ratings of flexibility, recollection, mental flexibility, ego transcendence, body transcendence, body satisfaction or sexual integration from six T.A.T. cards with 40-64 year olds.

In their study, however, Rosen and Neugarten looked at the hypothesis that four dimensions of ego functioning diminish in effectiveness with age. The *Thematic Apperception Test* was used on 144 subjects aged 40-71 years, divided by age, sex and social class: the older subjects showed fewer extra characteristics in their stories, used less conflict, less strong emotion and described less vigorous activities. Neugarten (75) concluded that personality does change significantly with age to give way to passive mastery of the situation in 60-70 year olds and that important sex differences remain at this age level. The same T.A.T. information may have very different meanings for a 40 versus a 70 year old.

Recent years have seen the introduction of *psychometric personality questionnaires* into research on old age personality measurement. This work is still in its infancy, but has immense potential though the practical and financial difficulties in this area of investigation are considerable. The *Minnesota Multiphasic Personality Inventory* (43, 45) has been used in several investigations and has highlighted the need for caution when applying tests to the aged which have not been specifically standardized on the appropriate populations. Application of this large Inventory to old people is in itself a somewhat difficult task. This no doubt accounts for the limited extent of publications in this area, though one has the impression that the MMPI enjoys extensive clinical use with all adult age groups, particularly in the U.S.A.

Hathaway and McKinley (44) reported that on *Depression and Psychasthenic Scales* the mean of the 56-65 year old male sample of 13 deviated from the mean of the general population standardization group. MMPI T scores were presented by Calden and Hokanson (20) on 15 TB patients, aged 60-69, along with those for younger age groups. They noted the significant elevation of Hs, D and Si scales score in the old age sample and stressed the need for age related normative data.

Several investigations have been interested in personality changes with age on the MMPI, but only limited normative data on samples beyond 65 years of age have been presented. The work of Aaronson (1, 2, 3) on an MMPI aging index also highlights the need for information about personality in old age. The first full scale attempt to provide normative data on the aged was by Swenson (103) who reported on the validity and basic clinical scales on the MMPI from the records of 95 subjects of both sexes, and 60+. Kornetsky (61) administered the MMPI to 43 aged males and found significant elevations on the D and Mf scales. This tendency for a rise in D scale score with advancing age had also been reported by Canter et al. (22).

British normative data on the MMPI were published from a community investigation carried out on a sample of the aged (70+) resident in Newcastle upon Tyne, by Britton and Savage (13). The full card form of the MMPI was administered to 83 subjects, representing both sexes, who were selected at random from the aged community. The questionnaire items were read to each subject during two sessions in his own home. The means and standard deviations in terms of the standard K corrected T scores for each of the validity and basic clinical scales for the investigation showed significant deviations ($p < 0.01$) on all except the Pd and Si scales from the standard MMPI normative data. The means of the K, D and Sc scales are raised by more than one and the means of Hs and Hy by more than two standard deviations. A comparison of the Swenson (103) and Kornetsky (61) and Britton and Savage (13) data showed the British sample as having higher scores than those obtained by the American subjects, but the profile pattern to be similar. Even allowing for any possible sampling bias, the results presented confirm the suggestion that the standard manual normative data for the MMPI should not be applied to aged subjects.

There are, however, other considerations to be taken into account when assessing the value of the MMPI as an instrument for assessing old age personality. For example, what is the structure of personality which it measures? The analysis of personality structure from Britton and Savage's (16) community aged sample would appear to emphasize the importance of their continued ability to adapt to physiological and environmental changes associated with advancing age. It is evident that administration of the inventory and similar personality measures has much to offer in the quest for greater understanding of personality in old age. In particular, studies involving pathological groups might be expected to show a restriction in the flexibility of personality adaptation.

However, our work in Newcastle upon Tyne leads us to the opinion that the full MMPI, *as it stands,* has little to recommend itself for use with the aged on either theoretical or practical grounds. Greater understanding of the underlying processes of personality and its changes with age is necessary before one would or could expect the diagnostic efficiency of the MMPI or new scales derived from it to be of much practical value. For example, on the basis of their factor analysis of the MMPI, Britton and Savage (15) have proposed a *screening measure for Mental Illness in the Aged.* It consists of a simple "yes-no" answer, 15 item scale, assessing general mental illness or psychopathology. A cut-off point of 6+ suggests that mental illness is present. The scale was validated against psychiatric diagnosis: 95% of those diagnosed mentally ill on clinical criteria by an independent psychiatric opinion were identified as such by the *Britton and Savage Mental Health Scale.* We would welcome more extensive information on this measure. A major advantage of the scale is that it can be easily and efficiently used by doctors, nurses, health visitors, social workers, etc. as a preliminary screening device on a large scale; for example to give an indication of the extent of the problem in an area.

The paucity of studies on the aged with Cattell's and Eysenck's well-developed measures of personality assessment is of some considerable concern to workers. Lynn (67) discussed the implications of Eysenck's theory on personality and age, and evidence on the responses of 144 normal and mentally ill aged to the *Maudsley Personality Inventory* questionnaire (33) measure of neuroticism and extraversion is provided by Bolton (9). The aged had generally slightly higher neuroticism and similar extraversion scores than the younger subjects used in the test standardization. Surprisingly the *Maudsley Personality Inventory* data showed that the E scale scores for normals, affectives, schizophrenics and organics were not significantly different from one another, nor were organics distinguishable even from normals on extraversion. On the other hand, organics did differ from the normal and schizophrenic groups on the neuroticism scale. This high organic N score confirms the work of Choppy and Eysenck (26) on younger subjects. The high N scores for the affectives are not surprising as the group was mainly aged affective depressives—reactive and endogenous. One can reasonably assume that the new *Eysenck Personality Inventory* (34) would show similar age and mental illness effects.

No normative data on Cattell's 16PF can be presented at present. Byrd (19) suggested that anxiety increased with age on Cattell's *Measure* and Sealey (94) used the 16PF on several thousand Americans aged between 16-70, but separate data for the aged are not available. It was suggested, however, that men and women become more depressed and gloomy (F), more adventurous and outgoing (H), more unconventional (M) and more tough-minded (I) with age. Sex differences emerged—the women became less dominant, (E) the men more radical. Sealey also described interesting pre- and post-forty year old patterns of change. A level of anxiety score or personality characteristic considered abnormal for under 60 or 65 year olds may not be so for those over that age in relation to peer group levels. The definition of abnormality has need of adjusting. The severe clinical abnormality may be easily identified and treated but the mildly ill or distressed need to be identified with caution. The clinical uses of *Cattell's Adult* and Eysenck's *Personality Measures* have now been shown to be extremely promising. One looks forward to their application to help resolve problems concerning the aged.

It might be interesting to add here that an attempt by Britton and Savage to administer the Cattell 16PF scale to 20 elderly people living in the community, but diagnosed "organic," showed that only six were able to complete the inventory, even though it was read to them. Present work on normal and functionally ill aged by Savage and Gaber is having more success in obtaining normative data and has identified four types of personality groups in the aged.

We await, hopefully and with interest, more data on the aged. Great care should be taken in using psychometric personality inventories with the aged, but they do have considerable potential in conjunction with cognitive and adjustment measures or information.

PSYCHOMETRIC ASSESSMENT AND APPLIED EXPERIMENTAL PSYCHOLOGY

Finally, a plea must be made to encourage practising psychologists to use information from up to date developments in general psychology in their assessments of the aged. Investigations of *perceptual and learning abilities* or in what might be broadly called the cognitive area of the normal, the mentally and the organically ill aged subjects have created a wealth of information crying out for application in the clinical setting. The *standardization* of laboratory techniques is urgently needed, and practitioners can particularly refer to the work of Heron and Chown (51), Welford (112, 113), Bromley (17), Honig (55), Sidowski (99), and Goulet (40). A very useful and brief review of information in these areas is also presented in the British Medical Council's publication on *Experimental Psychology* (101), and *Applied Experimental Psychology* (102), edited by Professor Summerfield. The applied experimental science's approach to clinical psychology has, of course, been stressed and encouraged by Eysenck (32), Shapiro (95), Zangwill (116), Savage (88) and others. The essential statistical techniques necessary to evaluate individual differences in performance, when standardized normative data are not available, are available. A good introduction to these techniques can be found in Payne and Jones (80) and in Mittler's book *The Psychological Assessment of Mental and Physical Handicaps* (71). One awaits with interest more information on the use of these techniques with the aged. The applications of development in social psychology, for example, Argyle's *Approach to Interpersonal Perception* (5) and the development of adequate methods of measuring family interrelationships in the elderly should also be encouraged.

Indeed, the *development of a practising clinical psychology more closely allied and cognizant of developments in experimental, physiological, social psychology as well as personality and psychometric theory and practice is urgently needed*. Is depth perception affected by age? If so, what of the effect on distance judgments and car driving in the aged? What changes in learning ability occur? How do changes in learning ability affect adjustment in a changing society? The Gedye's (38) approach to automated assessment of behavioral function is of interest here as work on the aged has been published. There is not, however, a single method in this area. One would like to see multi-channel, multi-purpose techniques and apparatus developed and more widely used. Using knowledge from general psychology, one would like to see the Shapiro model (96) for investigation of the individual case more extensively used with the aged.

In general, considerable progress has been made in the last twenty years in our understanding of the theoretical changes and in the availability of methods of assessing functions and their change in the aged. The application of this work generally by clinical psychologists in both medical and social service settings, however, tends to lag far behind. As I have tried to indicate in this chapter, there are a number of reasonably well developed techniques to measure various aspects of cognitive functioning, social and personal adjustment and personality in the aged. There are also quite a number of techniques which are interesting, but less well developed than the ones presented here, which should be of considerable help in the future. Further understanding and adequate use of assessment procedures with the aged do, however, demand considerably more research investment and much greater awareness of practising clinicians in medical and social fields of these techniques, their uses and abuses. I hope this chapter helps in a limited way to bring this about. One should also stress the fact that investigations, assessments, diagnoses or whatever one may wish to call them, are, and should be, an integral part of treatment, re-education, rehabilitation or handling of the patient. One cannot divorce one from the other. Operant conditioning techniques may be used to diagnose learning deficiencies or modify behavior.

REFERENCES

1. AARONSON, B. S. 1958. Age and sex influences on MMPI profile peak in an abnormal population. *J. Consult. Psychol.*, 22:203-206.
2. AARONSON, B. S. 1960. A dimension of personality change with ageing. *J. Clin. Psychol.*, 16:63-65.
3. AARONSON, B. S. 1964. Ageing, personality change and psychiatric diagnosis. *J. Geront.*, 19:144-148.
4. ANDERSON, J. E. (Ed.). 1956. *Psychological Aspects of Aging.* Washington, D.C.: Amer. Psychol. Assoc.
5. ARGYLE, M. 1972. *Approach to Interpersonal Perception.* (2nd Edit.). Harmondsworth, Middx.: Penguin Books.
6. BIRREN, J. E. (Ed.). 1959. *Handbook of Aging and the Individual.* Chicago: University of Chicago Press.
7. BIRREN, J. E. 1960. Psychological Aspects of Ageing. *Ann. Rev. Psychol.*, II:161-198.
8. BIRREN, J. E. 1964. *The Psychology of Aging.* Englewood Cliffs: Prentice Hall.
9. BOLTON, N. 1967. A psychometric investigation of the psychiatric syndromes of old age; measures of intelligence, learning, memory, extraversion and neuroticism. Unpub. Ph.D. thesis, University of Newcastle upon Tyne.
10. BOLTON, N., SAVAGE, R. D., and ROTH, M. 1967. The MWLT on an aged psychiatric population. *Brit. J. Psychiat.*, 113:1139-1140.
11. BOTWINICK, J. 1967. *Cognitive Processes in Maturity and Old Age.* New York: Springer.

12. BOTWINICK, J. 1970. Geropsychology. *Ann. Rev. Psychol.*, 21:239-272.
13. BRITTON, P. G., and SAVAGE, R. D. 1965. The MMPI and the aged—some normative data from a community sample. *Brit. J. Psychiat.*, 112:941-943.
14. BRITTON, P. G., and SAVAGE, R. D. 1966. A short form of the WAIS for use with the aged. *Brit. J. Psychiat.*, 112:417-418.
15. BRITTON, P. G., and SAVAGE, R. D. 1967. A short scale for the assessment of mental health in the community aged. *Brit. J. Psychiat.*, 113:521-523.
16. BRITTON, P. G., and SAVAGE, R. D. 1969. The factorial structure of the Minnesota Multiphasic Personality Inventory from an aged sample. *J. Genet. Psychol.*, 114: 13-17.
17. BROMLEY, D. B. 1966. Age differences in the Porteous Maze Tests. *Proc. 7th Internat. Cong. Geront.*, Vol. 6, 225-228. Wien. Med. Akad., Wien.
18. BUHLER, C. 1961. Old age and fulfillment of life with considerations of the use of time in old age. *Acta. Psychol.*, 19:126-148.
19. BYRD, E. 1959. Measured anxiety in old age. *Psychol. Rep.*, 5:439-440.
20. CALDEN, G., and HOKANSON, J. E. 1959. The influence of age in MMPI responses. *J. Clin. Psychol.*, 15:194-195.
21. CALDWELL, BETTYE, McD. 1954. The use of the Rorschach in personality research with the aged. *J. Geront.*, 9:316-323.
22. CANTER, A., DAY, E. W., IMBODEN, J. B., and CLUFF, J. E. 1962. The influence of age and health status on the MMPI scores of a normal population. *J. Clin. Psychol.*, 18:71-73.
23. CATTELL, R. B. 1963. The theory of fluid and crystallised intelligence: a critical experiment. *J. Educ. Psychol.*, 54:1-22.
24. CATTELL, R. B., EBER, H. W., and TATSUOKA, M. M. 1970. *Handbook for the Sixteen Personality Factor Questionnaire (16PF)*. Illinois: Champaign.
25. CAVAN, RUTH S., BURGESS, E. W., HAVIGHURST, R. J., and GOLDHAMER, H. 1949. *Personal Adjustment in Old Age*. Chicago: Science Research Associates.
26. CHOPPY, M., and EYSENCK, H. J. 1963. Brain damage and depressant drugs: an experimental study of interaction. In: Eysenck, H. J. (Ed.) *Experiments with Drugs*. London: Pergamon Press. Chapt. 12:313-324.
27. CHOWN, SHEILA M., and HERON, A. 1965. Psychological aspects of ageing in man. *Ann. Rev. Psychol.*, 16:417-50.
28. CLARK, F. LE GROS. 1959. *Age and the Working Lives of Men*. London: Nuffield Foundation.
29. COWDRY, E. V. (Ed.). 1942. *Problems of Ageing* (2nd Edit.). Baltimore: Williams & Wilkins.
30. CUMMING, ELAINE, and McCAFFREY, ISABEL. 1960. *Some Conditions Associated with Morale Among the Aging*. Paper presented at the Annual Meeting of the American Psychopathological Association, New York.
31. EMERSON, A. R. 1959. The first year of retirement. *Occup. Psychol.*, 33:197-208.
32. EYSENCK, H. J. 1950. Function and Training of the Clinical Psychologist. *J. Ment. Sci.*, 56:710-725.
33. EYSENCK, H. J. 1959. *The Maudsley Personality Inventory Questionnaire*. London: London University Press.
34. EYSENCK, H. J., and EYSENCK, S. B. G. 1964. *Eysenck Personality Inventory*. London: London University Press.
35. EYSENCK, H. J., and EYSENCK, S. B. G. 1969. *Personality Structure and Measurement*. London: Routledge & Kegan Paul.
36. FITTS, W. H. 1965. *The Tennessee Self Concept Scale*. Nashville: Counselor Recordings and Tests.
37. GARDNER, L. PEARL. 1948. Attitudes and activities of the middle aged and aged. *Am. Psychol.*, 3:307.

38. GEDYE, J. L., and MILLER, E. 1970. Developments in automated testing systems. In: Mittler, P. (Ed.) *The Psychological Assessment of Mental and Physical Handicaps*. London: Methuen & Co.
39. GORDON, M. S. 1960. Changing patterns of retirement. *J. Geront.*, 15:300-304.
40. GOULET, L. R. 1972. New directions for research on aging and retention. *J. Geront.*, 27:52-60.
41. GOULET, L. R., and BALTES, P. B. 1970. *Life Span Developmental Psychology*. New York: Academic Press.
42. GRANICK, S. 1950. Studies of psychopathology in later maturity—a review. *J. Geront.* 5:44-58.
43. HATHAWAY, S. R., and McKINLEY, J. C. 1951. *Minnesota Multiphasic Personality Inventory Manual*. New York: Psychological Corp.
44. HATHAWAY, S. R., and McKINLEY, J. C. 1956. Scale 2 (Depression). In: Welsh, G. S. and Dalstrom, W. G. (Eds.) *Basic Readings on the MMPI in Psychology and Medicine*. Minneapolis: University of Minnesota Press, pp. 73-80.
45. HATHAWAY, S. R., and McKINLEY, J. C. 1969. *MMPI Manual (Form R)*. New York: Psychological Corp.
46. HAVIGHURST, R. J. 1949. Old age—an American problem. *J. Geront.*, 4:298-304.
47. HAVIGHURST, R. J. 1950. Public attitudes towards various activities of old people. In Donahue, Wilma, and Tibbits, C. (Eds.) *Planning the Older Years*. Ann Arbor: University of Michigan Press. Pp. 141-148.
48. HAVIGHURST, R. J. 1953. *Human Development and Education*. New York: Longmans Green & Co.
49. HAVIGHURST, R. J. 1957. The social competence of middle aged people. *Genet. Psychol. Monogr.*, 56:297-375.
50. HAVIGHURST, R. J. 1959. Life styles of middle aged people. *Vita Humana*, 2:25-34.
51. HAVIGHURST, R. J. 1963. Successful Ageing. In: Williams, R. H., Tibbits, C., and Donahue, Wilma (Eds.) *Processes of Ageing*. (Vol. I). New York: Atherton Press.
52. HAVIGHURST, R. J., and ALBRECHT, R. 1953. *Older People*. New York: Longmans Green & Co.
53. HERON, A. 1963. Retirement attitudes among industrial workers in the sixth decade of life. *Vita Humana*, 6:152-159.
54. HERON, A., and CHOWN, S. M. 1960. *Age and Function*. London: J. & A. Churchill.
55. HONIG, W. K. 1966. *Operant Behavior: Areas of Research and Application*. New York: Appleton Century Crofts.
56. JONES, H. E. 1961. The age-relative study of personality. *Acta. Psychol.*, 19:140-142.
57. KAHN, R. L., SEAMAN, F. D., and GOLDFARB, A. J. 1958. Attitudes towards illness in the aged. *Geriatrics.*, 13:233-298.
58. KAPLAN, O. J. 1956. The aged subnormal. In: Kaplan, O. J. (Ed.) *Mental Disorders in Later Life*. (2nd Edit.). Stanford, California: Stanford University Press. Pp. 383-397.
59. KAY, D. W. K., and WALK, A. (Eds.). 1971. *Recent Developments in Psychogeriatrics*. London: Royal Medico-Psychological Association.
60. KELLY, G. A. 1955. *Psychology of Personal Constructs*. Vols. I and II. New York: Norton.
61. KORNETSKY, C. 1963. Minnesota Multiphasic Personality Inventory: results obtained from a population of aged men. In: Birren, J. E., Butler, H. N., Greenhouse, S. W., Boroloff, L., and Yarrow, M. R. (Eds.) *Human Aging: A Biological and Behavioral Study*. Bethesda, Maryland: U.S. Department of Health, Education and Welfare. Chapt. 13.

62. KUBO, Y. 1938. Mental and physical changes in old age. *J. Genet. Psychol.,* 53: 101-108.

63. KUHLEN, R. G. 1948. *Age Trends in Adjustment During Adult Years as Reflected in Happiness Ratings.* Paper read at a meeting of the American Psychological Association, Boston.

64. LANDIS, J. T. 1942. Social psychological factors of aging. *Social Forces,* 20:468-470.

65. LEBO, D. 1953. Some factors said to make for happiness in old age. *J. Clin. Psychol.,* 9:385-387.

66. LORGE, I. 1956. Gerontology (Later maturity). *Ann. Rev. Psychol.,* 7:349-364.

67. LYNN, R. 1964. Personality changes with aging. *Behav. Res. Ther.,* 1:343-349.

68. MACK, M. J. 1953. Personal adjustment of chronically ill old people under home care *Geriatrics,* 8:407-416.

69. MAYER GROSS, W., SLATER, R. E., and ROTH, M. 1969. *Clinical Psychiatry.* (3rd Edit.). London: Bailliere, Tindall & Cassell.

70. MEDAWAR, P. B. 1955. *Presidential address* to CIBA Foundation Colloquia on Ageing.

71. MITTLER, P. (Ed.). 1970. *The Psychological Assessment of Mental and Physical Handicaps.* London: Methuen & Co.

72. MOBERG, D. O. 1953. Leadership in the church and personal adjustment in old age. *Sociol. Social Res.,* 37:499-509.

73. MORGAN, M. 1937. The attitudes and adjustments of recipients of old age assistance in upstate and metropolitan New York. *Arch. Psychol.,* 30, No. 214, 131.

74. MURRAY, H. A. 1943. *Thematic Apperception Test* (3rd Revision). Cambridge, Mass.: Harvard University Press.

75. NEUGARTEN, BERNICE L. 1963. In Williams, R. H., Tibbits, C., and Donahue, Wilma (Eds.) *Processes of Aging,* Vol. I. New York: Atherton Press.

76. NEUGARTEN, BERNICE L., HAVIGHURST, R. J., and TOBIN, S. 1961. The measurement of life satisfaction. *Gerontology,* 16:134-143.

77. NIHIRA, K., FOSTER, R., LELAND, H., and SHELLHAAS, M. 1970. *Adaptive Behavior Scales.* New York: Psychological Corp.

78. NUNNALLY, J. M. 1967. *Psychometric Theory.* New York: McGraw Hill.

79. PAYNE, R. W. 1960. Cognitive abnormalities. In Eysenck, H. J. (Ed.) *Handbook of Abnormal Psychology.* London: Pitmans.

80. PAYNE, R. W., and JONES, H. G. 1966. Statistics for the investigation of individual cases. *J. Clin. Psychol.,* 13, 2:115-121.

81. POST, F. 1965. *The Clinical Psychiatry of Late Life.* Oxford: Pergamon Press.

82. REED, H. B. C., and REITAN, R. M. 1963b. Changes in psychological test performance associated with the normal ageing process. *J. Geront.,* 18:271-274.

83. REICHARD, SUSANNE, LIVSON, FLORENCE, and PETERSON, P. G. 1962. *Ageing and Personality: A Study of Eighty-Seven Older Men.* New York and London: Wiley.

84. ROGERS, C. R. 1951. *Client Centered Therapy.* Boston: Houghton, Mifflin.

85. RORSCHACH, H. 1942. *Psychodiagnostics.* New York: Grune & Stratton.

86. ROTH, M. 1955. The natural history of mental disorder in old age. *J. Ment. Sci.,* 102:281-301.

87. ROTH, M. 1971. Classification and aetiology in mental disorders of old age: some recent developments. In: Kay, D. W. K., and Walk, A. (Eds.) *Recent Developments in Psychogeriatrics.* London: Royal Medico-Psychological Association.

88. SAVAGE, R. D. (Ed.). 1966. *Readings in Clinical Psychology.* London: Pergamon Press.

89. SAVAGE, R. D. 1971. Psychometric assessment and clinical diagnosis in the aged. In: Kay, D. W. K., and Walk, A. (Eds.) *Recent Advances in Psychogeriatrics.* London: Royal Medico-Psychological Association.

90. SAVAGE, R. D. 1972. Old age. In: Eysenck, H. J. (Ed.) *Handbook of Abnormal Psychology* (2nd Edit.). London: Pitmans Medical Publication.
91. SAVAGE, R. D., and BOLTON, N. 1968. A factor-analysis of learning impairment and intellectual deterioration in the elderly. *J. Genet. Psychol.,* 113:117-182.
92. SAVAGE, R. D., BRITTON, P. G., BOLTON, N., and HALL, E. H. 1973. *Intellectual Functioning in the Aged.* London: Methuen & Co.
93. SAVAGE, R. D., and HALL, E. H. 1973. A performance learning measure for the aged. *Brit. J. Psychiat.,* 122:721-3.
94. SEALEY, A .P. E. L. 1965. Age trends in adult personality as measured by the 16 PF test. *Bull. Brit. Psychol. Soc.,* 18:59.
95. SHAPIRO, M. B. 1957. Experimental method in the psychological description of the individual psychiatric patient. *J. Int. Soc. Psychiat.,* 3:89-103.
96. SHAPIRO, M. B. 1966. Intensive investigation of the single case. *J. Gen. Psychol.,* 74:3-23.
97. SHEPARD, W. P. 1955. Does the modern pace really kill? *J. Am. Geriat. Soc.,* 3: 139-145.
98. SHOCK, N. W. 1950. Gerontology (Later maturity). *Ann. Rev. Psychol.,* 2:353-370.
99. SIDOWSKI, J. B. 1966. *Experimental Methods and Instrumentation in Psychology.* New York: McGraw Hill.
100. SLATER, E., and ROTH, M. 1969. *Clinical Psychiatry* (3rd Edit.). London: Bailliere, Tindall & Cassell.
101. SUMMERFIELD, A. (Ed.). 1964. Experimental psychology. *Brit. Med. Bull.,* 20.
102. SUMMERFIELD, A. (Ed.). 1970. Applied experimental psychology. *Brit. Med. Bull.,* 26.
103. SWENSON, W. M. 1961. Structured personality testing in the aged: an MMPI study of the geriatric population. *J. Clin. Psychol.,* 17:302-304.
104. THOMPSON, W. E., STREILS, G. F., and KOSA, J. 1960. The effect of retirement on personal adjustment: a panel analysis. *J. Geront.,* 15:165-169.
105. TURNER, B. F., TOBIN, S. S., and LIEBERMAN, M. A. 1971. Personality traits as predictors of institutional adaption among the aged. *J. Geront.,* 27:61-68.
106. WALTON, D., and BLACK, D. A. 1957. The validity of a psychological test of brain damage. *Brit. J. Med. Psychol.,* 30:270-279.
107. WATSON, R. I. 1954. The personality of the aged: a review. *J. Gerontol.,* 9:309-315.
108. WECHSLER, D. 1944. *The Measurement of Adult Intelligence.* (3rd Edit.). Baltimore: Williams & Wilkins.
109. WECHSLER, D. 1955a. *Manual for the Wechsler Adult Intelligence Scale.* New York: Psychological Corp.
110. WECHSLER, D. 1958. *The Measurement and Appraisal of Adult Intelligence.* Baltimore: Williams & Wilkins.
111. WELFORD, A. T. 1958. *Ageing and Human Skill.* London: Nuffield Foundation.
112. WELFORD, A. T. 1964. The study of ageing. In: Summerfield, A. (Ed.) *Experimental Psychology. Brit. Med. Bull.,* 20:65-69.
113. WELFORD, A. T. 1968. *Fundamentals of Skill.* London: Methuen & Co.
114. YATES, A. J. 1954. Validity of some psychological tests of brain damage. *Psychol. Bull.,* 51:359-379.
115. YATES, A. J. 1966. Psychological deficit. *Ann. Rev. Psychol.,* 17:111-114.
116. ZANGWILL, O. L. 1964. Neurological studies of human behavior. In: Summerfield, A. (Ed.) Experimental Psychology. *Brit. Med. Bull.,* 20:43-48.

20

HISTORICAL PERSPECTIVES
ON CARE

ROBERT KASTENBAUM, PH.D.

and

BARBARA ROSS, PH.D.

Department of Psychology, University of Massachusetts, Boston

INTRODUCTION

Our ideas and practices today will be the stuff of history tomorrow. Consider for a moment some of the features on the contemporary scene that might challenge the talents of a future historian:

(1) Progress in treating afflictions of the elderly is reported in specialized journals. In a typical issue of one such periodical (24), 33 different types of chemical and nutritive agents are advertised (mostly the former), representing 64 different commercial brand names. An entire page is devoted to an index or "therapeutic guide" of the advertisements alone. The commercial messages themselves appear on the front and back inside covers, on full pages punctuating the clinical and scientific reports, and, at times, share the same page with substantive articles. Also typically, the illustrations reveal an old person who is either (a) pained, isolated, anguished prior to use of the pharmaceutical agent, or (b) cheerful, sociable, or serene after the use.

(2) An unkempt man of advanced but indeterminate years shuffles along the streets of a metropolis known for its cultural and historical ambience. He approaches passers-by with a set "routine," begging coins. When the jingles in his pocket are sufficient, he

purchases the cheapest bottle of alcoholic spirits available and moves off to the sanctuary of his favorite staircase, bench, or abandoned building (51).

(3) A special committee of the United States Senate holds investigative hearings on a broad variety of topics concerning the aged: economics, housing, retirement, leisure, medical services, age-discriminatory attitudes and practices, etc. The published dialogues among senators, expert witnesses, and a variety of other citizens constitute an impressive resource of fact and opinion (30). Whatever the particular topic, one is seldom far removed from a basic theme: problems of the aged are problems of society, and must be met constructively and decisively at that level. The diligent historian will recognize, however, that the Special Committee on Aging has no legislative authority, and functions within the bounds of an austere budget.

(4) The neighbors are stunned. Mr. W., an alert, dependable, and esteemed older man, has blown a hole in his head. Everybody would like to believe his death was accidental, an error in cleaning his gun. The evidence, however, is strongly indicative of suicide (56). Why would this elderly man, a solid member of the community with many years apparently still remaining to him, take his life? Who has failed—and how?

These fragments help us to appreciate some of the critical problems in developing a history of the care that has been given to (or withheld from) old people through the centuries. Conversely, the challenge of an historical approach forces us to acknowledge tensions, diversities, and contradictions in our own time and place.

From the advertisement-saturated geriatric journal, for example, one might be tempted to conclude that the miseries of aging are to be understood principally in terms of somatic malfunction. Geriatric care is the responsibility of specialists who discharge this responsibility by prescribing chemical agents brought to their attention regularly by profit-making corporations. A history of geriatric care, therefore, should address itself primarily to the gradual achievement of chemical management in reducing symptomatology associated with advancing age; it is the history of specialists in medicine and related fields as they improve their ability to match symptoms with relief-bringing therapeutic agents. Social and psychological factors are to be acknowledged, but effective treatment hinges upon the skillful management of drug therapies.

Another kind of history might be written by the scholar who concentrates upon the panhandler, that palpable embodiment of worn-out, unproductive old age. An external therapeutic agent is once again involved.

By contrast, however, a single elixir has been found sufficient for all the ailments: a bottle of liquor, as contrasted with more than thirty types of chemical concoctions. Furthermore, the treatment is both self-prescribed and self-administered. The history of geriatric care might then begin with the discovery of alcoholic beverages as a form of insulation against the miseries, terrors, and deprivations that old age brings to some individuals (or which some individuals bring to old age).

On a broader plane, one could construct a history dedicated to the proposition that the aged have had to borrow or devise their own forms of comfort, occasionally supplemented by support from cultural institutions, misery seeking its own relief down through the centuries.

The historian who is impressed with cultural institutions will collect evidence of concern for the aged on the part of governmental and other formal authorities. He will add the *Hearings of the U.S. Senate Special Committee on Aging* (30) to the archives of "Goodwill Toward the Old," whose entries include pronouncements from some of the most ancient civilizations known to us. A history of care for the aged based upon social, political, and ideational materials would present both the problems and their recommended solutions in terms far different than the symptom-relief approach already illustrated. But the historian could find it exceedingly difficult to demonstrate the relationship between words and deeds. As Slater observes, some societies have "achieved the reputation of age-deference solely by virtue of written records containing admonitions to the young to defer to their elders—data which we might just as well interpret as revealing a lack rather than a prevalence of respect" (62, p. 234). It would require unusual perspicacity to distinguish between the good will that bespeaks good deeds actually performed, and the good will that stands instead of the deeds.

Suicide may or may not represent the keenest edge of desperation or the deepest valley of despair for an old person. It does, however, take the individual beyond the sphere of caring actions, and challenges the survivors' image of their own lives. The suicide rate among old men and women could be taken as one dramatic focus of the extent to which a culture meets the needs of its senior generation, an index of society's failure (or, if cynically inclined, of society's success in conveying its negative attitudes toward the elderly). Other major examples of human breakdown in old age could be added to establish a more general index. The history written from this viewpoint would thus concentrate upon those factors which seem to increase or decrease the index of severe anguish and vulnerability in old age: in other words, the prevalence of misery would be the first fact to establish, followed by examination of the relevant context.

These illustrations impel us to recognize that one cannot write a neutral, objective history of the topic. Selectivity—bias—is involved every step of the way. One could prepare a history to support one or another current trend, to flatter or disparage recent achievements, to conjure up a "golden age" from which we have tumbled, or project a utopian state virtually within our reach. There are significant stylistic choices to be made as well. One could unroll a comfortable succession of names and dates, and call *that* history. Or one could, at the other extreme, sweep through entire epochs on the wings of a few grand themes.

What kind of history is offered here? We seek to convey some major facts and themes that mental health specialists might find useful in formulating their own perspectives on care of the aged, but not a "psychiatric" history as such. As specialists in human complexity, readers might appreciate the opportunity to view historical events and processes without a tidy "smoothing-out" at every turn. Where discords, conflicting purposes, and ambiguities were pervasive, there we will share some of the confusion with you.

For a more extensive perspective on gerontological thought, or pursuit of specific interests, the reader should turn to original sources. Views on old age of many eras and cultures may be found in works of Aristotle (59), Cicero (54), Roger Bacon (3), Laurentius (45), Francis Bacon (2), Defoe (16), Cotton Mather (49), Luigi Cornaro (12), Sir John Floyer (21), Benjamin Rush (60), and Charcot (8), among others. Although de Beauvoir has recently spoken of the need "to break the silence" on this subject (14), the truth is that people have been speaking of the state and needs of the aged for centuries. Perhaps what is needed are more listeners.

Freeman pointed out almost four decades ago that there has been serious interest in this subject since the earliest days, and that "old age has had a notable lineage of students" (22). Spector has provided numerous references to concern about aging on the part of the Talmudic sages (63), and Griffin refers to the Bible as a source-book of history "that is . . . laden with riches of evidence that cannot reasonably be ignored by students of gerontology" (26).

CARE OF THE AGED IN ANCIENT TIMES

Reach back to the earliest pages of cultural history. Turn, for example, to the Gilgamesh epic (27, p.11), a moral adventure tale known to the

Sumerian civilization of about 3000 B.C. It is old age and death that come into focus. Can youth be enjoyed endlessly, or must every human succumb to death and, if the prime years are outlived, to the suffering and limitations of advanced age? The attempt to outwit death and ameliorate, postpone, or abolish old age seems to have continued through history to the present day; various attempts have taken forms appropriate to given epochs, and some are hardly distinguishable from one era to another. We will not be astounded, then, while exploring some of the earliest known approaches to aging and the aged, to notice occasional observations and views that appear quite contemporary in spirit.

Biblical Times

"Venerable old age is not that of long time, nor counted by the number of years, but the understanding of a man is gray hairs and a spotless life is old age" (26, p. 466). This Biblical thought rejects the proposition that chronological age is a reliable measure of a person's individual and social value. Modern technological society has made itself dependent upon the standardized calculation of age based upon years-since-birth as, for example, in mandatory retirement programs that affect millions of men and women. But current research and thought in gerontology have started to restore the Biblical conception. Functional age is now being proposed as a more appropriate way of viewing human development and aging rather than the mere empty passage of consensual time.

The Old Testament is a document that has long provided assurance for those who would like to believe that old age is a positive state of being. Righteousness is rewarded by long life and that, of course, would be no reward at all were old age entirely a negative state. The story of Job indicates that one does not attain old age by gaining power over nature: long life is a reward for humble submission to the authority of God. Again, in the *Psalms* we learn that the just "shall increase in fruitful old age . . ." (26, p. 468), and Koller cites Biblical proof of divine blessing if one achieves "three score and ten" (42, p. 7). The relationship between righteousness and long life is supported by accounts of men whose life-spans were reckoned in centuries (although Koller reminds us that the closer the lives of the patriarchs come to our own times, the more modest the longevity attributed to them (*ibid.*).

Nevertheless, the Bible does not blink the less desirable aspects of aging. Despite the reference to "good old age," there are many indications of sensitivity to incapacitation and dependence: "Cast me not off in the time

of old age, when my strength shall fail, do not forsake me" (26, p. 469).
It is striking that such a plea would have to be made explicit. Here was
a tradition-oriented society in which respect for elders might be considered to be "built in," while longevity was advertised as a divine reward
for the good life. Is it possible that enough *ambivalence* about caring
well for the aged existed even in the Biblical society to require fervent
plea? The Scriptures insist again and again upon respect for the older
generation. Sons are reminded not to become impatient with their fa-
thers; ". . . honor the person of the aged man," they are told, with the
added reminder that the sons shall also become old (*ibid.*). Ambivalence
is a theme that appears to run from historical times to our own, as there
will be other occasions to observe.

One special concern about aging deserves mention. A person does not
have to be "old" in order to be "too old" for certain activities, roles, and
satisfactions, at least in society's view. This phenomenon was known in
Biblical times as well as our own: women feared arriving at an age at
which they would be too old to marry (*ibid.*). Other "too olds" may also
have been of concern, but this is the one that comes down to us most
clearly over the years.

Defining characteristics of the dependent aged were vividly described
in *Ecclesiastes*. The descriptions given in the Scriptures are similar to those
reported at many later times in history, and are scarcely at variance with
contemporary observations. Physical characteristics associated with senescence in writings of the Biblical period are withered skin, whitened hair,
distorted vertebrae, muscular atrophy, vulnerability to chills, loss of teeth,
reduced input for vision and other senses, the "drying up" or brittleness
of bones, problems in ambulation, failing strength, and general exhaustion.

Having this dysphoric picture clearly in mind, the people of Biblical
times did not expect the aged to perform beyond their capacities (e.g.,
military service), but did seem to expect some measure of social activity and responsibility. Full maturity was a prerequisite for prudence in
government and in other ministerial functions. Later, the aging person
was expected to contribute constructively in keeping with his remaining
powers.

What type of care was proposed for the aged? Both instrumental actions
and psycho-philosophical orientations were advocated. The Bible displays
some understanding of disease, sanitation, and other factors important to
the healthful prolongation of life (22, p. 325). It was appropriate for the

aged to avail themselves of these procedures if they could. While longevity was considered a divine blessing, one was acting quite within his rights to seek human help as well. Spivak (64) believes this encouragement of longevity is related to an unusually strong attachment and respect for physicians in the Jewish culture. Be that as it may, the young and able were expected to care for the old and disabled, and the principle of parity was demonstrated by the example of Maccabaeus and the distribution of public relief, which included, "the feeble, the fatherless, and the widows, yea, and the aged also" (26).

Psychological advice is given in the *Proverbs*: ". . .a joyful mind maketh age flourishing, a sorrowful spirit drieth up the bones . . . sadness hath killed many and there is no profit in it . . . envy and anger shorten a man's days, and pensiveness will bring old age before the time" (26, p. 468). The authors of *Proverbs* seem to have pre-figured contemporary explorations of the role of emotions and life-style in the timing and manner of death (*op. cit.*). Further, it is worth noticing that those psychological characteristics deemed appropriate for a good old age appear identical with those one might recommend for a person of *any* age. In this sense, the fate of a person as he approaches and enters old age might be seen as the outcome of the personality he has become throughout his entire lifespan. Those who have not learned to live in virtue will suffer more harshly the ravages of age: old age, then, is a sort of indirect moral tale for the young.

In general, the Bible teaches that old age may bring happiness if the individual has earned respect and affection over the years through virtuous character. Reading and studying the Bible itself became a major factor in attaining to a good old age, according to Spivak (64).

Life itself, then, was the reward for the good person, and a reverence for longevity was absorbed by the young as they read the Scriptures.

The Egyptians

Religion was also a dominant framework in caring for the aged among the Egyptians of antiquity. The Gilgamesh epic, previously mentioned, came into their heritage with its hard lesson that death is inevitable; it is for the gods to decide. However, this did not mean that mortals could exercise no influence at all, especially mortals who were proving so successful in many realms of social organization.

Egyptian civilization has been characterized as possessing "intricate social organization, extensive industrial and agricultural activity, and a religious system notable for its beliefs not only in life after death but also for right living, in kindness to others, and that a good life here was the only thing that could bring happiness in the next world" (67, 68).

Protection for the aged drew its strength from a highly developed family life. The children (especially sons) were expected to care for their elderly parents (especially the father) during his life, and maintain the tomb when he journeyed to the after-life.

The Egyptians developed an outstanding medical system to safeguard the health of their citizens at all ages. History has perhaps failed to keep these achievements in balance because of the dramatic character of their efforts to preserve the human form as fit receptacle for the returning spirit. The Egyptians were deeply involved in trying to prolong and enhance life on both sides of the grave.

The art of life-prolongation was practiced in various ways. Glands were removed from young animals and eaten in hopes of retarding physical decline. Emetics and sudorifics were employed to insure longevity. The desire to postpone death and yet avoid old age was clearly manifest. A 1600 B.C. papyrus bears the confident if ambitious title, "The Book for Transforming an Old Man into a Youth of Twenty." The method involved compounding and applying a special ointment to remove all signs of age that are rooted in the flesh. Zeman tells us this is the earliest recipe written in the history of medicine for treatment of the aged (68). Obviously, it was not entirely successful, for it has not proven to be the final recipe. The Egyptians explored many modalities of treatment for the infirmities of age, including the physical (e.g., a copper compound to cure cataracts), the ritualistic, and faith-healing.

The Egyptians devoted much attention and ingenuity both to the prolongation of life and the care of the dying and the dead. Perhaps here is a precedent for a "total care system" that so far appears to have eluded contemporary societies such as the United States, a system that would provide the best available knowledge and services to the individual within a framework of genuine concern that does not abandon him at some arbitrary point in his suffering and need.

Greek and Roman Period

The Greeks viewed old age with vivid animosity. Old age was a "destructive, deadly force," an "altar of ills," the "most evil of all things." No doubt about the Greek orientation toward advanced age! Nevertheless, it was considered quite acceptable to reach old age—but not to linger there. The final period of life should have brevity, before it lacks wit; such seemed to be the Greek view. Death was often pictured as a welcome event after deterioration of body and mind became manifest (57, pp. 1-14).

A positive conception of old age is rarely expressed in Greek writings. Aristotle had nothing of a complimentary nature to say when he offered a concise account of aging and the aged in his second book of *Rhetoric*. The topic offered him an opportunity to illustrate his principle of moderation. Life begins and ends with extreme dispositions: the young overdo and are overly optimistic; the old are unsure of themselves, and tend to underdo everything. Obviously, middle life is the ideal, although bodily prime comes and goes a little earlier than mental prime (7). The old tend to fall away from the perfect balance, the moderation that characterizes human functioning at its best; the person who is past his prime finds that ". . . life on the whole is a bad business" (59, p. 325). Philosopher that he was, however, Aristotle maintained that old age was natural in that it was a part of the orderly coming-into-being, and passing-away of all things of earth. Old age and death were part of the natural life process and, thus, inevitable.

The person who "would live long and in health," must, according to Plato, "keep himself as much as he can from all violent passions. But old men more than any other must beware" (44, p. 191). For the old person who did manifest the wisdom appropriate to his experience and station in life, opportunity remained to participate responsibly in social and civic affairs. There was no arbitrary or imposed retirement age at which to disenfranchise the aged; one would become increasingly specialized or scaled-down in his activities as competency or energy diminished.

Although respect and opportunity for the aged were not unknown in Hellenic times, the prospect was bleak and anxiety-provoking for most people who approached their later years. The very gods, numerous as they were, embodied virtues associated with youth. It was in good taste to behave considerately toward the senior generation, but the press of other needs and ambitions always threatened to sweep away comfort and security.

The struggle for respect, security, and survival continued into Roman times. Cicero, in his famous essay, *De Senectute,* argued that old age *per se* was not a calamity; rather, it depended upon one's attitude. The aged too often made themselves unhappy by dwelling upon infirmities and vainly resisted the dictates of nature. Cicero attempted to rebut the most frequent complaints against old age, recommending a tranquility of mind, and gratitude for having out-lived certain conflicts, impulses, and ambitions. He focused upon the possible *assets* of advanced age (27).

A more accurate reflection of the common views held toward old age probably can be found in the advice of Horace, the Roman poet, to prospective dramatists. The aged man should be characterized as quarrelsome, miserly, lacking energy, and condemning of youth (10, p. 250). Portraying the old man in these terms remained a theatrical stereotype for centuries, and is, of course, not unknown in contemporary works, although a much enlarged repertoire of old person character types can now be observed.

Negative depictions of old age continued well beyond Horace. The sixth century poet, Maximianus, for example, lamented the various failings that accompany old age, concentrating in particular upon sexual impotence (ibid., p. 251; 66). His poetry defined old age as an insidious process of physically conditioned mental decay: the body goes, and, with it, the mind (50). He reiterated the Biblical perception that chronological and functional age are not identical; however, individuals differ appreciably in both the rate and style of their senescence.

Perhaps one of the most telling indices of the old person's situation in Roman times was the popularity of suicide. Self-destruction was an honorable solution to a number of problems. One could preserve respect in his own eyes and those of the community when the alternative to suicide appeared to be an unacceptable form of survival. Although suicide was not limited to the aged, it was a self-administered solution that many elders utilized (9). Hannibal, the powerful general of Carthage, became one of the most famous exemplars of suicide in old age. When Rome demanded his extradition from a place of voluntary banishment in 183 B.C., Hannibal chose death instead. "Before taking poison, which he habitually carried in a ring, the seventy-four-year-old hero remarked sarcastically that he wanted to deliver the Romans from the terror that an old man inspired in them" (*ibid.*, p. 24).

More important than the suicide of historic figures, however, was the prevalent sentiment in Greco-Roman times that life often is not worth the ignominy and suffering that accompany old age. The history of voluntary euthanasia (28) and suicide are thus intertwined with the history of old age.

Reflections

Even this cursory exploration of old age in ancient times prompts a few reflections.

Salient characteristics of old age were observed and appreciated many centuries ago. Furthermore, both the miseries and the potentialities of old age were acknowledged. Ambivalence was never far from the surface, whether the surface itself sparkled with the Hebraic vision of the blessed and righteous old man or with Greek dread of this "most evil of all things." The admixture of orientations toward old age probably derived in part from the admixture of old people themselves, the competent and the incompetent, the admirable and the lamentable. Another likely source of ambivalence—then as now—was the competition for available resources. Ties of affection and family solidarity bound the old and the young; yet hard choices had to be made between priorities, with the aged in frequent danger of losing out. Still another source of ambivalence was the intermediary position held by old age itself, betwixt youth and death. Old age held some appeal as an alternative to death, but few appeared interested in achieving "eternal old age." The search for "eternal youth" was already underway, among the ancient Chinese alchemists, for example, as well as among the Egyptians (27). As a decidedly imperfect alternative to early death, old age loomed as a fate both desirable and undesirable.

Care of the aged had already taken diverse forms. The individual himself was held to be at least partially responsible for his longevity, health, and happiness. Psychological factors were emphasized in all the cultures mentioned here. Admonitions regarding self-care derived in turn from values admired by the respective societies in general. Moderation and balance were among the most frequently recommended life-styles, a tradition that has had many subsquent advocates. Family responsibility for care of the aged was extolled, although its actual functioning is difficult to estimate and probably was quite variable. Professional assistance for the aged was at least prefigured in ancient times. Certainly, the more powerful old men called upon available medical knowledge to ameliorate their ailments, if not to replenish lost youth. Not all the treatments were medical in the narrow sense of the term. King David, for example, took the young virgin Abishag to bed, but did not long survive the occasion. Egyptian medicine, as we have seen, explored pathways that are still heavily trafficked today, with many a geriatric elixir having replaced the ointment of 1600 B.C.

One might reflect also upon a decided masculine bias revealed by history. Care of the aged most often could be translated to care of the old man (or the not-so-young man grasping against the sands of time). The male-favoring bias is implicit in material already presented. Many other examples could be cited. From de Ropp, for example, we learn that Romans "favored the practice of sucking blood mixed with milk from the breasts of young slave girls, a procedure revived in part by Marsilio Ficino in the fifteenth century. 'He should find a young, healthy, gay and beautiful girl and attach his mouth to her breast when the moon is becoming full and then he should eat powdered fennel with sugar.' If that failed to produce results he should suck her blood 'like a leech.' What the girl thought about all this is not recorded" (17, p. 4).

Another historical bias should also be acknowledged. Understandably, available information emphasizes the lives of the great and the near-great. The life of the "common" person comes through to us only if we make a special effect to discover him; and then, only within the limitations of surviving materials. There is nowadays a suspicion, founded to some extent upon contemporary observations, that the actual respect and support provided to the aged has been exaggerated in historical stereotypes (1, 29, 48). Current observers distinguish, for example, between authentic respect and ritualistic deference. The old person who has neither wealth, wisdom nor other special characteristics to distinguish him receives only superficial acceptance in his community. It is risky to generalize contemporary observations backward in time which historians refer to as the "presentist" approach, but it is appropriate to use caution when we are told that a particular land in ancient times deeply venerated its aged. The weight of circumstantial and/or historical evidence suggests that strong and admirable character sometimes has survived into old age and received due appreciation, but that aging itself seldom has bestowed authentic stature upon those whose individual qualities previously were undistinguished.

ANTECEDENTS OF MODERN GERIATRICS

Two of the most typical conceits perpetrated and perpetuated by historians will also blemish this presentation: (a) treating earlier epochs as anticipations of our own, and (b) regarding the medieval world as relatively monolithic and relatively dispensable. One should know better. A culture deserves consideration on its own terms. We of the moment are not the grand culmination of designs only imperfectly anticipated by our ancestors. And the "medieval mind" as in all periods was an admixture of many minds; individuality and ingenuity were not abolished during the "dark ages," nor was light entirely absent. Yet in a brief and selective history it is tempting to "arrange" the past so as to suit present need. Admission of guilt does not constitute innocence. The reader will appreciate that entire centuries, peoples, and ways of life remain silent in this presentation when their voices might well have proven instructive.

For the medieval community, as well as for those people who are classified by their biographers as "primitive," care of the aged could hardly have posed the social problem that it does today. In his review of aging in preindustrial societies, Simmons concludes that "The farther back we go into primitive and rudimentary forms of human association, the fewer old people are to be found and, quite generally, old age is attributed to these persons at an earlier chronological date than in advanced societies" (29, p. 67). Implicit here is the already familiar distinction between chronological and functional age. The "old man" (and especially the "old woman") in a relatively primitive society may be impressively aged in the functional sense ("a mass of wrinkles from foot to forehead," ibid.), but perhaps no more than fifty years of calendar age. Even with "premature" aging, by our contemporary standards, preindustrial societies suffered a mortality rate that inhibited the development of a large senior echelon. This, by the way, does not argue against the survival of a few individuals to truly advanced age. It is generally agreed that the occasional preindustrial or medieval person achieved a lifespan as great as those known today, but the odds against living out four or five decades were considerably less favorable (61).

Nevertheless, the ideas and practices that prepared the way for modern geriatrics began to emerge well before the proportion of the aged in the population showed any substantial increase. We date this movement approximately at the 13th century, a time during which the struggle was still to survive childhood and reach the early prime of life, rather than to attain and enjoy a fruitful old age. Dublin's charting of longevity from ancient to modern times estimated that only a modest increase from 18 to 22 years occurred between the Bronze Age and Biblical times, with the Britisher of the middle ages still facing the limited prospect of an average life of 33 years to live (18), an estimate that, if anything, appears to be rather generous. The old person was still the exception both in "primitive" communities and the most "advanced" cities when "geriatric activism" began to assert itself.

Longevity and "Experimental Science"

"The Cure of Old Age and the Preservation of Youth" is a title that one might expect to find on an ancient Egyptian papyrus. But Roger Bacon's essay was more than up-to-date. It offered his 13th century contemporaries a new approach for reaching and enjoying a fruitful old age. His methodical rationale included some elements that others had emphasized in the past: controlled diet, exercise, proper rest, moderation in life-style, good hygiene in general. But he also proposed a chemical medicine that would cure all diseases and prolong life. If diseases were contagious, then why not good health and youth? Some of his suggestions reverted to ancient times, such as inhaling the breath of a young virgin (3, p. 45). The novel elements, however, were of greater significance. Bacon argued that it was both possible and desirable to attain old age, even to extend the outer limits of the lifespan, and in sound body and mind. This hope, although cherished and pursued for centuries in the Orient, had largely fallen by the wayside in Europe. Secondly, his advocacy of "the secret arts" did much to stimulate the development of alchemy—and, further along the path, many of the experimental sciences that flourish today.

Pursuit of fruitful longevity through biological and chemical experiments is credited by some historians as a crucial stimulus for much that has since enriched Western culture. Gruman finds that "This prolongevitist alchemy played a role of great importance in the history of ideas as well as in the history of science and medicine. For centuries it was one of the chief vehicles for the belief that through science man may gain extraordinary powers over nature, a line of thought which was to flower richly during the Enlightenment. In regard to science, it is well known that alchemy contributed the major part of the techniques and materials for the beginnings of modern chemistry. . . . In medicine, the alchemy of long life led, through the work of John of Repescissa and Paracelsus, to the rise of iatrochemistry which, in turn, was the early antecedent for the biochemistry and chemotherapy of our own time" (27, pp. 49-50). Gruman also points out that the ridicule heaped on alchemy by vested interests in its own time and by later generations fails to appreciate the many valid hypotheses and techniques developed by its finest practitioners. The craft and dedication of the alchemist provided resources for many an emerging science.

The vicissitudes of alchemy will not be pursued here. But the notion that a long, vigorous life can and should be attained owes much to

Bacon and to the protoscientists of his time. One does wonder, however, how Bacon would regard the modern arsenal of chemicals designed to combat old age that bristle forth in so many professional and lay publications.

Humanism and "Good Old Age"

Sixteenth century humanism embraced aging and the aged along with many other concerns. Gabrielle Paleotti produced one of the major gerontological treatises of the time, *De Bono Senectutis* (52). Besides restating Biblical and other classical views, Paleotti added his own critique of treatments and remedies proposed up to his day. It is instructive to find that he could assess such procedures as occupational therapy, music, games, pleasure tours, baths, change of scene, and other recreations which are "forms of relaxation that delight the senses." Paleotti agreed that these diversions brought comfort to many individuals, but "do not reach the hidden cause of his sadness, so that when these remedies are discontinued, that intrinsic cause of sadness keeps gnawing at the mind" (52, 65). His approach seems to have been closer to modern depth psychology and existential psychiatry than to activity-oriented treatment modalities. The elderly are depressed because their remaining time is short and vigor diminishing. The old person appreciates all too accurately that he is suffering a process of decline. His own self-image gradually is invaded by the cultural stereotypes of the aged as miserly, timid, suspicious, and disagreeable. Thus, he becomes less fond and approving of himself, and more apprehensive of what the future will bring. Despair of this nature is not to be swept aside by simple jollifications or mollifications.

Luigi Cornaro, Paleotti's contemporary, brought special distinction to his *Discourse della vita sobria* (12, 13), also entitled *Sure and Certain Methods of Attaining a Long and Healthy Life with Means of Correcting a Bad Constitution*. The author reached a vigorous and fruitful old age himself after correcting his own "bad constitution." As he approached the middle years of his life, Cornaro was forced to acknowledge that his own mind and body had been dissipated by undisciplined living. He turned his life around and rebuilt his character and stamina by a determined application of the Aristotelian themes of temperance and moderation. Dietary control was especially emphasized by Cornaro. His solution to aging was relatively simple and undramatic, requiring perpetual good sense more than any other resource—complex remedies, and exotic drugs and medicines had no place in his method, although a moderate use of "new wine" was lauded. The applied side of Cornaro's thesis was in keeping with his allegiance to the humoral theory of health: when the four humors of the body are maintained in balance, all disease is avoided. His work was translated from the original Italian to Latin, English, French, German, and Dutch, all before the end of the 17th century. During the 18th and 19th centuries, fifty editions of the English version were printed (27).

Others in Shakespeare's time who held to the popular doctrine of the four humors relied more upon medical solutions to problems associated with aging (44). A representative work of this type is *A Discourse of the Preservation of the Sight; of Melancholike Diseases; of Rheumes, and of Old Age* (45), written by Laurentius, a professor of medicine at Montpellier, and later chief physician to Henry IV. In his view, all afflictions are caused by an imbalance in the humors and, almost invariably, are to be cured through diet and medicine. Regarding old age, there is a gradual change throughout life from the qualities of hot and moist to those of cold and dry. Natural heat and moisture use each other up, so the somatic climate tends increasingly toward the cold and dry. One is tempted to read into this theory intimations of Pavlov's later four-way classification of nervous system "types" in which aging involves deterioration into the "weak" type (6).

Shakespeare himself invoked a classification that is found also in Laurentius. Both divide old age into three phases of progressive decline. The four earliest stages of man described in *As You Like It* are followed by green old age, which begins at 50, "the lean and slipper'd pantaloon," and, finally, "decrepit old age," which is characterized by the oft-quoted lines,

> Is second childishness and mere oblivion,
> Sans teeth, sans eyes, sans taste, sans everything.

Laurentius, armed with autopsy data, could challenge certain medical propositions from the past, such as the Egyptian belief that the cause of old age was a diminishing of the heart. Autopsies of old men revealed their "hearts have been found as great and heavy as those of the younger sort" (44, 45). In keeping with Cornaro and others, Laurentius praised the sensible diet and especially:

> Drinke (which) is as necessarie and profitable for olde men, as it is hurtfull for children . . . it heateth all their parts . . . and reviveth

the drouping spirits of old men . . . they ought to praise God, and give him thankes for creating of so pleasant and delightsome a liquor. The wine that is chiefly to bee made choise of for old folke, must be an old, red, and good strong wine, and it should not bee much delayed (45, p. 187).

Recent studies seem again to have confirmed the value of wine for the elderly (36), and Laurentius is also in keeping with current research when he recommends that old men should take their food and drink "a little at once and oft."

Moderate exercise, social intercourse, and pure, unpolluted air—preferably warm and mild, clean, attractive clothing and good self-hygiene procedures were also emphasized by Laurentius.

Nevertheless, the King's physician had to acknowledge that old age eventually brings "nothing but paine and languishing griefe." The curvilinear theory of human development is annunciated: "All the actions both of the bodie and minde are weakened and growne feeble, the sences are dull, the memorie lost, and the judgment failing, so that then they become as they were in their infancie . . ." (44, p. 175; 45), a restatement of a theme already on record in *Ecclesiastes*.

Visions of Earthly Paradise

Hopes of a life better than the "short and brutal" existence known on earth had long centered upon visions of heavenly paradise. Greeks and Romans may have "lived for today," but the devout Christian awaited salvation and his eternal reward (or punishment). In the 17th and 18th centuries attention shifted to improvement of the human situation on earth. The re-orientation was neither simple nor sudden, but by the end of the 17th century, the scholastic tradition had essentially lost its "Battle of the Books": the "new experimental philosophy" and utilitarianism of Francis Bacon and the Royal Society had taken hold.

Francis Bacon's prospectus for a better life on earth included prophylactic measures to prolong life. Certain herbs strengthened the vital organs of the body, exercise and diet were once again emphasized, and massage and special baths recommended. More forward-looking was his advocacy of organ transplants (27, p. 81). The budding utilitarianism emphasized the practical application of information. Knowledge was to be pressed into the service of man's control over nature—a view quite at odds with tradition.

Unfortunately for the average person of the 17th century, this fresh breeze did not find general application. The poor as well as the old and the infirm seem most often to have been neglected at this dawning period of modern science. Burstein observes that the new objectivity did not appear to stand in the way of persecution (4). At the height of the witch trials, the vast majority of the accused were old women. Suspicion of and prosecution for witchcraft constituted a major hazard of female senescence for approximately two and a half centuries. Burstein speculates that old women were the "odd ones" in society during this period. The witch-character may have been associated with something inherent in the nature of the female, perhaps a superabundance of the melancholy humor. Burstein further notes that in 17th century narratives, "The typical, irritable, discontented old woman, the village scold . . . seems generally to have been careless enough of her own danger."

A minority view in the 16th and 17th century was that witches were "helpless old women caught up in an unhelpful world." Many women had out-lived family and friends during a time when society was undergoing a critical transformation: perhaps the old woman was a convenient scapegoat. Similar to currently recognized factors in cases of senile psychosis, the precipitating agency frequently appeared to be some form of loss of social integration (*ibid.*, p. 69). The loneliness, desperation, and poorly controlled behavior of some of these old women often was interpreted as a manifestation of "ill-will," perhaps of demonic origin.

The 18th century works of Sir John Floyer, including *Medicine Gerocomica or the Galenic Art of Preserving Old Men's Healths* (21), generally have been credited as the beginnings of modern geriatrics (22, p. 328). Floyer elaborated upon the Greek and Classical tradition of moderation in all realms, and took much from Bacon. Treatments included hot or cold bathing depending on the constitutional type of the individual, as well as elaborate drug therapy and other treatments. Many years later, Charcot would observe that the works of Floyer and others of this period "have a literary or a philosophical bearing; they are more or less ingenious paraphrases of the famous *De Senectute* of the Roman orator" (8, p. 19; 54).

Condorcet and the Englishman William Godwin were among the most optimistic 18th century thinkers, foreseeing decisive solutions to problems of old age (27, p. 7). In Condorcet's opinion, life expectancy should increase indefinitely with the march of progress. Environmental improvement, inheritance of acquired characteristics, and advances in medical sciences were the foundation of Condorcet's optimism.

The theme of moderation—already very familiar in this history—appears again in Condorcet's writings (15): moderation in work, a wise diet, clean air and moderate passions contribute to longevity. The intemperance and luxurious style of life cultivated by the rich were disadvantageous, as was the state of extreme poverty with its excessive problems (27, p. 87-88). In Bacon's tradition, Condorcet promoted systematic investigations of all phenomena, and was much interested in public health as part of the 18th century social and political reform movement.

Godwin explained the onset of debilitation in old age as a result of the aging person's abandonment of youthful habits. One should remain cheerful and gay, avoid morbid thoughts (for these remove elasticity from the limbs). Godwin was convinced that mind could achieve mastery over body, including the circulatory system and other functions customarily regarded as involuntary or reflexive in action. One could maintain health and achieve a long life with the increased perfection of man, and man's well justified faith in his own ability (25, p. 86).

Another exponent of prolongevity was the German physician, Christopher Hufeland. A supporter of Francis Bacon and Cornaro, his *Art of Prolonging Life* was supremely optimistic. It gave rise to a wave of enthusiasm known appropriately enough as the Hufelandist movement (22, p. 329). Hufeland debunked both alchemy and medicine and promoted a relatively basic health maintenance regime in the tradition of Cornaro. In his view, the body had a limited amount of vital power which could be used up slowly or quickly. When expended with great care under favorable circumstances, the vital power could last as long as two hundred years, the lifespan Hufeland envisioned for our species.

Hufeland extended his advice in favor of a long and healthful life to include discussions of child care, suicide, and the way to recognize and evade a mad dog. He agreed with Condorcet that the working or poor classes tended to live longer than others because of their tendency to labor out of doors, and to live simply (27, 33, p. 73). Perhaps he was influenced by a lingering sentimentality toward (idealized) pastoral life, "simple folk," and "honest poverty," a fashion among some of the cultural elite that did not long survive the onslaught of the 19th century and its crunch of industrialization.

THE DAY BEFORE YESTERDAY

Care of the aged will now be sketched for that period of time which embraces, if roughly, the nineteenth century and subsequent developments up to the recent past, "the day before yesterday," if you will.

The influence of the Enlightenment, the growth of industrialization, and concern for social order were all in evidence during the nineteenth century. The plight of many individuals increased during the dislocation, turmoil and competition wrought by the new technologies, yet organized medicine and interest in public health were also on the rise.

Medical and Genetic Views

After the French Revolution, humanitarianism became more characteristic of French medicine, based directly on observations in the clinic. In his *Diseases of Old Age* (8), Charcot insisted that special studies of old age and its pathologies must be pursued:

> We have come to recognize . . . that, if the pathology of childhood countenances clinical considerations of a special kind, and if it is indispensable that it should be known from a practical point of view, then also senile pathology presents its difficulties, which cannot be surmounted except by long experience and a profound acquaintance with its peculiar characteristics (*ibid.*, p. 17).

He added:

> It was at an epoch very near ours; in France and in this very hospital, that the pathology of old age was constructed and asserted, if I may be allowed the expression, in all its originality. Before that time one could scarcely cite a work in which the slightest indication could be found of the particular physiognomy of the diseases of old age (*ibid.*, p. 18).

Charcot was referring to the Salpêtrière Hospital, and particularly to the Hospital for the Aged (women). He stressed the importance of following patients through a long period instead of seeing them only during a single episode in their history. Thus, he and his colleagues could see "developed to its utmost limits the pathological process whose initial phase is usually the only one known" (*ibid.*).

His lecture series included discussions of special diseases of old age, as well as apparent immunities from pathology associated with old age. "In certain respect," Charcot wrote, "the organs of the aged perform their tasks with quite as much energy as those of adults." He noted individual differences, and tried to establish a type-physiology of old age, as distinctive as that of other periods of life (22, p. 332). In keeping with other perceptive observers of centuries past, Charcot was reluctant to "explain" the diseases and infirmities on the basis of age *per se*. More specific etiologies should be determined, and appropriate treatments sought.

During this period, and for some time afterward, a number of attempts were made to establish a theory of aging related to the even more general question: is life (and humankind in particular) potentially immortal? Carl Canstatt, a German (5, p. 330) was credited by Charcot with "the first dogmatic treatise" upon the diseases of old age. An earlier contemporary of Charcot, Canstatt proposed a theory in which aging and death were implied as necessary outcomes of cell death. This view was too pessimistic for some advocates of prolongevity. Fisher, for example, maintained as late as 1927 that "Modern biology finds the life cells and many tissues potentially immortal. . . . Loeb and Carrel and others have demonstrated its truth beyond reasonable doubt" (20, p. 12). According to Fisher, the ultimate hope of mankind resided in eugenics. He argued that man must keep all parts of his "machinery" as close as possible to one hundred percent efficiency. This can be accomplished only by carrying hygiene to the *nth* power as well as by eugenics or "race hygiene" (*ibid.*, p. 14). Ordinary hygiene, unaided by eugenics, would break down. Both are essential. He recognized that marriage selection was a slow process which must operate generation by generation. Eventually, however, it would be successful, he claimed, drawing support from Karl Pearson's statistics concerning the association of inheritance with longevity (55). Hygiene must be rigorously perfected in the meantime. Fisher concluded on the basis of 170 life histories of the very aged that they lived more hygienically than most people.

Support for the relevance of heredity to longevity also came from Rolleston:

> . . . long and healthy life depends to a great extent on a wise selection of parents, for heredity may counteract many sins against the laws of physiological righteousness; thus, as regards longevity, the average duration of life among a number of persons, both of whose parents reached the age of 80, was twenty years higher than in another series (58, p. 118).

By this time, incidentally, at least some of the emerging specialists in health of the aged were applying a critical perspective to earlier claims of extreme longevity. Maurice Ernest's book, *The Longer Life*, was appropriately subtitled, *A Critical Survey of Many Claims to Abnormal Longevity, of Various Theories on Duration of Life and Old Age, and of Divers Attempts at Rejuvenation* (19). He devoted three chapters to "spurious super-centenarians."

A steadfast optimist, Fisher wrote, "It may be that super-hygiene, a gland transplantation or other device or devices yet unknown will some day open up these new vistas so that man may enter and take possession. The only obstacle seems to be his highly differentiated structure. There are so many parts to get out of order, the failure of any one of which reacts to cause the failure of all—that is death" (20, p. 12). He took a rather mechanistic view which permitted him to compare human psycho-physiology with the workings of a watch. After maturity, he suggested, ". . . the body may last until some one of its million of parts suffers sufficient accidental injury to stop the whole machine, just as a watch may stop from a breaking of the main spring or a clogging with dirt." On the basis of statistical evidence available in 1927, Fisher found "absolutely no hint of any definite limit to human life."

A Fellow of the American Public Health Association, Fisher was appointed to President Franklin D. Roosevelt's Conservation Commission for the express purpose of adding human life to its study of the economic conservation of forests, minerals, and waters. He proved remarkably accurate in predicting a 15-year increase in life expectancy (*ibid.*, p. 3), based upon the effectiveness of preventive measures.

It appeared to Fisher about one-half century ago that only a relatively few people, "those of unusual initiative, ample means, or who happen to be under the care of exceptionally alert physicians, or within the jurisdiction of exceptionally competent health officers, receive the benefits of the new discoveries; but the great mass of the human race goes on as before. . . ." (*ibid.*, p. 7). One might ask if the scene has changed significantly today.

It has been possible since the early nineteenth century, if not before, to advocate either a grandly optimistic prospectus on the future of aging and longevity, or to counsel more cautious and limited hopes. A broad spectrum of positions exists today as well (11, 31, 35).

Psychiatric Developments

Emphasis has been given here to medical and genetic approaches. What was taking place in the psychiatric-psychologic realm? Perhaps one might more relevantly ask, "What was *not* taking place?"

The increasingly powerful and persuasive psychoanalytic movement surged ahead as though old age scarcely existed. In his valuable history of this topic, Cath suggests that "psychoanalytic psychotherapy of the aged was first hindered by very early statements of Freud, and then gradually stimulated by Freud's own aging pattern and by other psychoanalytic thinkers who began to treat patients in their middle years" (5a, p. 280). Freud's own early statement was given in *Sexuality and Aetiology,* when the year was 1898 and the author's age forty-two:

> The psychoanalytic method is not at present applicable to all cases. . . . With persons who are too far advanced in years it fails because, owing to the accumulation of material, so much time would be required so that the end of the cure would be reached at a period of life in which much importance is no longer attached to nervous health. And finally it is possible only if the patient is capable of a normal mental condition from the vantage-point of which he may overlook the pathological material" (23, p. 245).

These discouraging (or limit-setting) words apparently were enough to restrict the attention of the early psychoanalysts to younger clients. It is worth noting that in the decades which followed, concern about both aging and death appeared frequently in the thoughts of Freud, the Freudians, and their analysands—yet aging and death were given little formal recognition in psychoanalytic theory, with the well known exception of the death instinct.

Psychoanalysis remained virtually silent on the subject of old age during those years when a variety of medical and social programs were being introduced around the world. It is doubtful, for example, that psychoanalytic observations on aging had any influence on the retirement or public health programs emerging on both sides of the Atlantic. The then-new wave of psychiatrists were not encouraged to address their attention to the aged, and psychiatric training in geriatrics remained meager.

Gradually, a few psychoanalysts gained experience with older (but not aged) adults. It was such a novelty to take an older person into treatment that one made sure to present a paper on this exotic experience. As recently as 1940, Kaufman reported that psychoanalysis still did not have much to offer on aging and the aged (41). The situation is not quite as bleak today, but it would be difficult to assert that psychoanalysis and its immediate off-shoots have made fundamental contributions to the care of the aged, either applied or theoretical. One can identify individuals and groups who are active in this field, and acknowledge their relatively successful experiences. Nevertheless, one of the important developments in geriatric care during the past century or so is what has *failed* to develop in a whole-hearted and large-scale manner—psychiatric commitment to the understanding and treatment of the distressed older person. The psychoanalytic movement has been our example here. In general, however, mental health specialists, regardless of their particular approach, have shown much reluctance to work with the aged. Psychosocial reasons for this reluctance have been analyzed (34), yet understanding some of the factors involved does not guarantee adequate delivery of mental health services to the elderly (43).

As Cath intimates, Freud's own continued development during his last years of life spoke louder than his words. Perhaps one might say, instead, that he out-grew his own early thoughts on care of the aged by crowning his life and career with a valiant old age.

WHAT LESSONS FROM HISTORY?

There are perhaps still a few amongst us who believe that the purpose of history is to provide neat moral lessons for the present and future. This is debatable. What we call "history" is selective retrospection on people and events that existed largely for their own, not posterity's purposes. Still, it *is* tempting to look for "lessons" in history. We suggest the following, with all the appropriate trepidation:

(1) There has been a fundamental ambivalence in our orientation toward old age as a human condition. This ambivalence approaches universality. We have suggested three basic origins that are rooted in common experience: (a) the diversity of the aged themselves; (b) competition of the aged for their share of limited social and physical resources; and (c) the status of old age as an imperfect alternative both to eternal youth and early death. There is no evidence to suggest that the ambivalence has disappeared in our generation, or that it will get up and go away in the future. Perhaps the "lesson" is twofold: (a) we may as well recognize that we harbor mixed feelings toward aging and the aged, and (b) thereby minimize the harm that can be done when unacknowledged attitudes pervade our actions. We have argued elsewhere, for example, that the high suicide rate among the aged, the frequent occurrence of self-injurious behavior and non-suicidal premature deaths, and the ease with which the death of an elder is interpreted as "natural" are phenomena related to long-standing cultural ambivalence (37, 40). We have genuine affection and respect for at least some of our elders today, as in past cultures, but many of us are not ready to encourage or even tolerate a large senior echelon that demands its share of resources and decision-making. There is

an important potential role here for mental health specialists in helping us to acknowledge our ambivalence toward aging (in ourselves and in others) and avoiding at least some of the more deleterious effects.

(2) In general, the quest for longevity and renewal of youth has reflected strongly what today would be called a "male chauvinistic" bias. Although more women than men survive into advanced old age in our times, social justice and attitudes remain biased (47). Types of care provided for old men and women seem to differ, even to the very end of life (39). History suggests, then, that we cannot automatically assume that comforts and therapies will be made available on an even-handed basis for aging men and women. If we really are interested in equality, then special efforts may be necessary in various realms—perhaps starting most effectively with the attitudinal.

(3) History has provided us with two traditions regarding care of the aged. A "breakthrough" has been heralded time and again—either humankind now has the secret for defeating old age, or it is about to materialize. The Egyptian papyrus of 1600 B.C. and some contemporary geriatric writings would have equal claim as standard-bearers of this tradition. By contrast with the breakthrough tradition, with its periodic bursts of drama and promise, the theme of moderation appears to have persisted for centuries with only the details changing a bit with the times. Aristotle may be taken as perhaps the most eminent spokesman for the theory, and Cornaro as an eminent and dedicated practitioner. From one standpoint, moderation appears to be a limited and somewhat tedious approach. One is expected to keep his mode of living under control day after day; the benefits are constant rather than dramatic, and later if not sooner, one does age and die. But moderation could also be regarded as quite a radical approach. It implies that old age is not to be separated from the rest of the lifespan. And it is explicit in warning that one should not expect to reap the benefits of a fruitful longevity unless he is willing to learn and exercise an harmonious style of life. "Good old age" and "the good death" (the proper translation of *euthanasia*) flow from a "good life" and from no other source. Moderation, in its own way, is as challenging as the breakthrough tradition—perhaps more so, because it is available to all humans at all age levels, and does not hinge upon new and miraculous discoveries. The foregoing comments were not intended to dismiss the possibility that tremendous breakthroughs may be achieved in the future, or to intone that a long existence in the moderation modality is necessarily preferable to "a short life and a merry one." Perhaps what

ours and succeeding generations can contribute to history of the care of the aged will include an effective integration of technical breakthrough and wise guidance of our own lives.

(4) Environmental circumstances conducive to longevity and the enjoyment of old age have been proposed from time to time. However, history does not seem to have provided us with a strong precedent for the establishment of environmental systems especially developed for the maintenance of functioning in old age. It is possible that the current emphasis on environmental possibilities (e.g., 46, 53) will lead to achievements in care of the aged that are relatively novel in human history.

(5) History has provided some hints that have not firmly established themselves in our thought and practices. We refer here to the possibility that old age truly might be valued for itself—not social deference, trembling lip-service that seeks to deny inner fear, or acceptance of a poor substitute for continued youth. Intimations are to be found in the *Talmud*, where the deficits associated with old age are clearly enough recognized, but positive attributes as well. For some individuals, to be old is to be *zaken* (shrunk and weakened), *saba* (grey-haired), or *hashish* (unproductive, fruitless). But for others, old age is characterized by *yashish*: being substantial, mature, wise (63). There have been espousals of the wisdom of the aged, continuing to the present day, but few serious attempts to analyze old age as a phase of life with authentic values (38). It appears to be futurity's challenge not only to reduce the probability of early demise and to extend the years of optimal "youthful" functioning, but also to probe the potentialities of old age itself.

REFERENCES

1. ARENSBERG, C. M., and KIMBALL, S. T. 1968. *Family and Community in Ireland.* Cambridge, Mass.: Harvard University Press.
2. BACON, F. 1638. *History, Natural and Experimental, of Life and Death or of the Prolongation of Life.* London: Printed by I. Okes, for Humphrey Mosley.
3. BACON, R. 1683. *The Cure of Old Age and Preservation of Youth.* . . . London: Tho. Flesher at the Angel and Crown, and Edward Evets at the Green Dragon, in St. Paul's Churchyard. (Brown, Richard, tr.).
4. BURSTEIN, S. R. 1949. Aspects of the psychopathology of old age. *Brit. Med. Bull.,* 6:63-72.
5. CANSTATT, C. 1839. *Die Krankheiten des Höheren Alters und Ihre Heilung.* Erlangen, Enke. (See Charcott, *op. cit.* p. 19 and Freeman, 335).
5a. CATH, S. 1972. Psychoanalytic viewpoints on aging—an historical survey. In: Kent, D. P., Kastenbaum, R., and Sherwood, S. (Eds.) *Research, Planning and Action for the Elderly.* New York: Behavioral Publications. Pp. 279-314.
6. CAUTELA, J. R. 1972. The Pavlovian basis of old age. In: Kent, D. P., Kasten-

baum, R., and Sherwood, S. (Eds.) *Research, Planning and Action for the Elderly.* New York: Behavioral Publications. Pp. 395-407.

7. CHANDLER, A. R. 1948. Aristotle on mental aging. *J. Geront.,* 3:220-224.
8. CHARCOT, J. M., and LOOMIS, A. L. 1881. (Trans. Hunt). *Clinical Lectures.* New York: Wm. Wood.
9. CHORON, J. 1972. *Suicide.* New York: Scribners.
10. COFFMAN, G. R. 1937. Old age in Chaucer's day. *Modern Language Notes,* 52:25-26.
11. COMFORT, A. 1964. *Aging, the Biology of Senescence.* London: Routledge.
12. CORNARO, LUIGI. 1562. Discourses on the temperate life. In: Butler, W. F. (Ed.) *The Art of Living Long.* Milwaukee, 1913.
13. CORNARO, L. 1793. *Sure and Certain Methods of Attaining a Long and Healthy Life.* Tr. by Joseph Addison. First American Ed. Hall.
14. DE BEAUVOIR, S. 1972. *The Coming of Age.* New York: G. P. Putnam's Sons.
15. DE CONDORCET, ANTOINE-NICOLAS. 1793. *Sketch for a Historical Picture of the Progress of the Human Mind.* New York: Library of Ideas, 1955, tr. by June Barraclough.
16. DEFOE, D. (pseudonym, Moreton, A. J.). 1727. *The Protestant Monastery.* London: Printed for W. Meadows.
17. DE ROPP, R. 1962. *Man Against Aging.* New York: Grove Press.
18. DUBLIN, L. I. 1965. *Factbook on Man.* New York: Macmillan.
19. ERNEST, M. 1938. *The Longer Life.* London: Adam.
20. FISHER, I. 1927. Lengthening of human life in retrospect and prospect. *Am. J. Publ. Hlth.,* (January), 17, 1:9-14.
21. FLOYER, SIR J. 1724. *Medicina Gerocomica.* London: Isted.
22. FREEMAN, J. T. 1938. The history of geriatrics. *Ann. Med. Hist.* (July), 10:324-335.
23. FREUD, S. 1959. Sexuality and aetiology In: Freud, S. *Collected Papers* Vol. 1. London: Hogarth Press.
24. *Geriatrics,* March 1973.
25. GODWIN, WILLIAM. 1946. *Enquiry Concerning Political Justice, and Its Influence on Morals and Happiness.* Priestly, F. E. (Ed.), (3 Vols.). Toronto. See Gruman, *op. cit.,* p. 85.
26. GRIFFIN, J. J. 1946. The Bible and old age. *J. Geront.,* 1:464-472.
27. GRUMAN, G. 1966. A history of ideas about the prolongation of life. *Transactions of the American Philosophical Society,* 56:1-97. Philadelphia: The American Philosophical Society.
28. GRUMAN, G. J. 1973. On the history of ideas of voluntary euthanasia. *Omega,* Journal of Death and Dying, 4:87-138.
29. HARLAN, W. H. 1964. Social status of the aged in three Indian villages. *Vita Humana,* 4:239-252.
30. *Hearings* (a continuing series of publications). Washington, D.C.: United States Senate Special Committee on Aging.
31. HOLLINGSWORTH, M. J. 1967. Genetic studies on longevity. In: Platt, R., and Parkes, A. S. (Eds.) *Social and Genetic Influences on Life and Death.* London: Oliver & Boyd. Pp. 194-214.
32. HUFELAND, C. 1797. *The Art of Prolonging Life.* (2 Vols.). London: J. Bell.
33. HUFELAND, C. 1805. *Makrobiotik, oder die Kunst das Menschliche Leben zu Verlägen.* Berlin: Wittich.
34. KASTENBAUM, R. 1963. The reluctant therapist. *Geriatrics,* 18:296-301.
35. KASTENBAUM, R. 1965. Theories of human aging: The search for a conceptual framework. *J. Social Issues,* 21:13-36.
36. KASTENBAUM, R. 1972. Beer, wine, and mutual gratification in the gerontopolis. In: Kent, D. P., Kastenbaum, R., and Sherwood, S. (Eds.) *Research, Planning and Action for the Elderly.* New York: Behavioral Publications. Pp. 365-394.

37. Kastenbaum, R. 1974. Should we have mixed feelings about our ambivalences towards the aged? *J. Geriat. Psychiat.*, 74:94-107.
38. Kastenbaum, R. Time, death and ritual in old age. In: Fraser, J. T. (Ed.) *New Studies of Time*. New York: Springer Verlag, in press.
39. Kastenbaum, R., and Candy, S. 1973. The 4% fallacy: A methodological and empirical critique of extended care facility population statistics. *Aging and Human Development*, 4:15-22.
40. Kastenbaum, R., and Mishara, B. L. 1970. Premature death and self-injurious behavior in old age. *Geriatrics*, 26:70-81.
41. Kaufman, M. R. 1940. Old age and aging. Two psychoanalytic points of view. *Am. J. Orthopsychiat.*, 10:73-79.
42. Koller, M. R. 1968. *Social Gerontology*. New York: Random House.
43. Kramer, M., Taube, C. A., and Redick, R. W. 1973. Patterns of use of psychiatric facilities by the aged: Past, present and future. In: Eisdorfer, C., and Lawton, M. P. (Eds.) *The Psychology of Adult Development and Aging*. Washington, D.C.: American Psychological Association.
44. Larkey, Sandford, V. (Ed.). 1938. *A Discourse of the Preservation of the Sight.* . . . See Laurentius, *op. cit.*
45. Laurentius, M. A. 1599. *A Discourse of the Preservation of the Sight: Of Melancholike Diseases: Of Rheumes, and of Old Age*. Amen House, Warwick Square, E.C.: Humphrey Milford, Oxford University Press. 1938. (Trans. by Richard Surphlet, and published for the Shakespeare Association.)
46. Lawton, M. P., and Nahenow, L. 1973. Ecology and the aging process. In: Eisdorfer, C., and Lawton, M. P. (Eds.) *The Psychology of Adult Development and Aging*. Washington, D.C.: American Psychological Association. Pp. 619-674.
47. Lewis, M. I., and Butler, R. N. 1972. Why is women's lib ignoring old women? *Aging and Human Development*, 3:223-232.
48. Lipman, A. 1970. Prestige of the aged in Portugal: Realistic appraisal and ritualistic deference. *Aging and Human Development*, 1:127-136.
49. Mather, Cotton. 1706. *The Good Old Way*. B. Green for Benjamin Eliot. Boston.
50. Neuburger, M. 1947. The Latin poet Maximianus on the miseries of old age. *Bull. Hist. Med.*, 21:113-119.
51. Observations made by the authors in Boston, Mass.
52. Paleotti, Gabriele. 1754. *De Bono Senectutis*. Venice. (Origin, 1595.) See Stern, K., and Cassirer, T. "A Gerontological Treatise of the Renaissance." *Am. J. Psychiat.*, 102:770-773. 1946.
53. Pastalan, L., and Carson, D. H. (Eds.). 1970. *Spatial Behavior of Older People*. Ann Arbor, Mich.: University of Michigan Press.
54. (Cicero). Peabody, Andrew P., fr. *De Senectute*. Boston: 1887 (106 B.C.-43 B.C.).
55. Pearson, Karl. 1897. *The Chances of Death*, Vol. 1. London-New York: Edward Arnold.
56. Pretzel, P. W., et al. 1970. Psychological autopsy: No. 1: From the files of the Los Angeles Suicide Prevention Center. *Bull. Suicidology*, 7:27-32.
57. Richardson, B. E. 1969. *Old Age Among Ancient Greeks*. New York: Greenwood Press. Reprint (The John Hopkins Press, 1933).
58. Rolleston, H. 1929. *Aspects of Age, Life and Disease*. New York: Macmillan.
59. Ross, W. D. (Ed.). 1927. *Aristotle Selections*. Boston: Charles Scribner.
60. Rush, B. 1805. *Medical Inquiries and Observations*. Philadelphia: Conrad.
61. Simmons, L. 1960. Aging in preindustrial societies. In: Tibbitts, C. (Ed.) *Handbook of Social Gerontology*. Chicago, Ill.: University of Chicago Press, 62-91.
62. Slater, P. E. 1964. Cross-cultural views of the aged. In: Kastenbaum, R. (Ed.) *New Thoughts on Old Age*. New York: Springer. Pp. 229-236.

64. Spivak, C. D. 1927. Longevity according to Hebrew lore and tradition. *Medical Life*, 34:191-197.
65. Stern, K., and Cassirer, T. 1946. A gerontological treatise of the Renaissance. *Am. J. Psychiat.*, 102:770-773.
66. (Maximianus). Webster, Richard. The Elegies of Maximianus. Princetown: 1900. See Coffman, *op. cit.*
67. Zeman, F. D. 1942. Old age in ancient Egypt: A contribution to the history of geriatrics. *J. Mt. Sinai Hospital*, 8:1161-1165.
68. Zeman, F. D. 1944. Life's later years: studies in the medical history of old age. *J. Mt. Sinai Hospital*, 11:45-52.
63. Spector, S. Old age as viewed by the Talmudic Sages. *Aging and Human Development*, in press.

21

CARE IN HOSPITAL

ALAN D. WHANGER, M.D., D.T.M. & H. (LONDON)

Assistant Professor of Psychiatry, Duke University School of Medicine,
Chairman, Geriatric Psychiatry Group, Duke University Medical Center,
Durham, North Carolina;
Director, Geropsychiatry Service, John Umstead State Hospital,
Butner, North Carolina

and

EWALD W. BUSSE, M.D., D.SC.

J. P. Gibbons Professor and Chairman, Department of Psychiatry,
Duke University School of Medicine;
Founding Director, Duke University Center for the Study
of Aging and Human Development,
Durham, North Carolina.

INTRODUCTION

Incidence of Psychiatric Disorder

Treatment is an attempt to modify a person's physical, mental, or social state so as to reduce suffering and disability, and to enhance functioning, growth, and a sense of well-being. The elderly suffer disproportionately from many types of diseases, and perhaps especially from emotional and nervous disorders. The incidence of new cases of psychopathology of all types is over 100 times greater in the over 65 age group than in the under

450

15 age group (39). Several surveys of the elderly in communities in different areas have reported varying prevalence of mental disease among the elderly, related, of course, to the diagnostic criteria and the peculiarities of the area.

Kay, Beamish and Roth (45) reported significant organic brain syndrome in about 10% of the older people in Newcastle upon Tyne. About half of these were judged as being severe. A total prevalence of 31% of all forms of functional disorder was noted. Other studies have indicated about a 30% prevalence of diagnosable psychiatric disorder, with a likelihood of about 15% being severely disabled. In a study of community volunteers in North Carolina, Busse, Dovenmuehle and Brown reported that only 40% of these elderly were free of psychological problems (17). There has been a rapid increase in the relative and absolute numbers of those over age 65 in many countries (now about 12.5% in Britain (12), and 10% in the United States). The group over age 75 shows the most rapid rate of growth (69). Obviously, the increasing numbers of the elderly will mean increasing needs for psycho-geriatric care. Families somehow care for many of those with mental disorders at home for most of the duration of the illness (46), but most of the formal psychiatric care has been, and is still, given in institutional settings. In most psychiatric outpatient clinics, only about 2% of all the patients seen are over age 65, while a recent survey of 30 psychoanalytic psychiatrists in private practice in the United States found that none of them was treating any patients over age 60 (79). In the United States about 4% of all people over age 65 are inmates in some type of institution, with 1% being in mental hospitals. Although the elderly constitute about 25 to 40% of the total residential hospital population generally, they make up from 15 to 20% of all admissions to mental hospitals. A substantial number of these (about 50%), however, are "graduates" who have chronic mental disorders and have simply grown old in the hospital (76).

History of Mental Hospitals

Family and community responsibility for the aged was practiced among the ancient Greeks, Romans, Jews, Egyptians, and Chinese. Some early hospitals and homes for the aged were built, however, and often religious institutions would care for the sick and the elderly. The Elizabethan Poor Law of 1601 imposed a tax in order to establish almshouses to maintain the "impotent poor," which included the elderly (32). Probably the first psycho-geriatric hospital was the Salpétrière in France, which was established first for the elderly indigent in 1656, but by 1790 under Pinel was admitting an increasing number of psychiatric patients. Environmental manipulation was considered important, as was exercise and nursing care (40). It is difficult in a short space to trace adequately the complex factors which have led to the present status of the psycho-geriatric patient and the hospitals which care for him, but even some generalizations may help clarify some of the problems.

Several highly effective small and humane mental hospitals were established in Britain and the United States in the early 1800's. The founders and superintendents, such as Tuke and Rush, recommended keeping the psychiatric hospitals small enough so that all of the staff could know all of the patients and interact with them. Later the rapid increase in the numbers of the elderly, coupled with a loss of social role and prestige, resulted in a minority group status for them with the deprivation of the privileges and opportunities possessed by the majority (18). The elderly raise the fears of aging, deterioration, and death among the young. This, coupled with the difficulty of achieving a "cure" or even a substantial improvement in the multiple pathology of the aged, has led often to the lack of involvement with the aged on the part of many health professionals, which Comfort has labled gerontophobia (21). Therapeutic despair prevailed, and a custodial approach to the psychiatrically impaired elderly was adopted.

The rise of huge hospitals with thousands of inmates in the 20th century has led to almost inevitable processes of depersonalization, dehumanization, and institutionalization which have been well analyzed by many, such as Goffman (31), Barton (8), Townsend (73), and Droller (26). The mental hospital was often used for permanent and terminal care for the elderly, and the remote location of the hospital sites encouraged communities to use them as dumping grounds for their unlovely, disabled, and troublesome citizens. A still prevalent idea among many elderly sent to public mental hospitals is that this is a death sentence for them (62). In light of the chronic understaffing and underfunding that plagued public mental hospitals in many places, this fear was only too accurate. If a patient did not expire soon, he wound up being buried alive figuratively in the institution. Fortunately, the mental hospital is once again assuming the role of an active treatment center for mental illness.

Definitions

In order to discuss the care of psycho-geriatric patients in hospital, we need to understand some of the terms used in this chapter and some of the variations of facilities and programs in different countries. We will be talking primarily about industrialized Western nations, but many generalizations will be necessary, as the authors of this section will be speaking basically from their experience in the United States.

The term aging itself has many problems in that there are, of course, biological, psychological, and social aspects and variations in this process. Society has tended to make 65 years the arbiter of aging, and we will usually use this age in this chapter, although it has been stated with some justification that aging is the last five years of life, whenever it might be. Others have made the distinction between the "elderly" as the 65 to 74 age group and the "aged" as the over 75 age group, since the incidence of disease and disability is so much higher in the latter group. We shall use the terms indiscriminately. The facts that diseases are multiple in the elderly, and that often the relation between the physical and the psychological is so complex, have led to the use of several terms to describe this area of medicine; e.g., psycho-geriatrics, gerontopsychiatry, geriatric psychiatry, and geropsychiatry. Another compounding problem is that different diagnostic criteria are used in different countries, as pointed out by Kramer in noting that diagnoses of affective psychoses are far more common in the first admissions of the elderly in England than in the United States, while the reverse is true in regard to psychoses with cerebral arteriosclerosis (52). Of course, there may be real variations in the incidence of various disorders in different places, or facilities may be used for differing purposes and patients.

Recent Trends in Britain

In general the British have been considerably ahead of the Americans in the study of and the planning for mental problems of the elderly. Since the enactment of three major statutes affecting the welfare of the elderly in the 1940's there has been a variety of schemes to help provide for the comprehensive care of the elderly (12). Geriatric medical units were proposed in all district general hospitals, and a variety of long-stay geriatric beds was provided. In 1970, the Department of Health and Social Security proposed the establishment of psycho-geriatric assessment units staffed jointly by psychiatrists and geriatricians (5, 6). Assessment units will be discussed later in this chapter, but the policy obviously raises some problems, as pointed out in the publications by Howells (41) and the Tripartite Committee (75). There is concern that the existing mental hospitals will be phased out without other adequate facilities being available.

Recent Trends in the United States

Before 1950, the burden of care for the sick elderly was borne substantially by the public state mental hospitals, there being comparatively few chronic disease hospitals except for tuberculosis in the United States. The overcrowded and often abominable conditions in the public hospitals caused occasional scandal and public outcry, but as Donahue points out, there was seldom any loosening of legislative purse strings (25). By the mid-1950's several studies indicated that elderly patients were being "dumped" into the state hospitals when they supposedly could be cared for elsewhere, although Goldfarb points out that almost all of these were actually seriously psychiatrically impaired (33). Government policy, the Medicare payments for mental health care for the aged, and the establishment of community mental health programs began a rather marked movement of the elderly out of the state hospitals, with some expressing the hope of closing all of them. Many of the elderly were transferred either to old age homes or to nursing homes, but most of these were the chronic psychotics who had grown old in the hospital. Often these "alternative" institutions were even less able than the state hospitals to offer anything more than custodial care to these elderly (34). Some psycho-geriatric practice is seen now in private psychiatric hospitals, and funding policies have helped establish psychiatric units in general hospitals.

Regarding the rather complicated maze of policies, Blenkner observes that the flow of care of the aged follows the public dollar, and rather cynically describes the resultant systems and transfers as a "game of Find-the-Therapy" (9). The Committee on Aging of the Group for the Advancement of Psychiatry stated that the elderly suffer disproportionately from our "non-system of non-care" characterized by insufficient financing for both health and sickness and by fragmented delivery of services (39). One would wish that this unfortunate description applied only to the United States! The nursing homes often function as a quasi-hospital, as there are few geriatric hospitals in the United States, and even fewer psycho-geriatric facilities as such.

Goals of Chapter

In this chapter we will discuss various aspects of psycho-geriatric care in hospital as they have been tried and developed. Some of this will be idealistic and perhaps difficult to apply in some situations because of differences in facilities, personnel, and patient types. Some of the sections could be applied in other than a hospital situation only, but they will often require planning and a treatment team. We do hope, however, that this may lead to improved, more effective, and humane care for the psychiatrically impaired elderly.

Diagnostic Problems and Categories

The diagnosis of psychiatric disorder in the elderly is complicated by the frequent presence of physical disease, multiple psychiatric problems, complicating socioeconomic and family problems, and by our tendency to feel that any problem in an old person is all senility or "hardening of the arteries," which may inhibit our searching for other aspects of the disorder. Of all those living in and admitted to public psychiatric hospitals in the United States, about 54% have organic brain syndromes, 37% have functional psychoses, 2% have neuroses, and about 6% have other assorted diagnoses. However, there is considerable contrast between the newly admitted group in which the prevalence of organic brain syndrome is 77%, and the 45% in the long-term "graduate" group of patients who have grown old in the hospital (76, 80). This varies considerably from comparable admissions in Scotland, of which 49% of the acute admissions had organic brain syndrome, while the long-term patients had only 18% prevalence (69). This may be due in part to differences in diagnostic criteria, but in recent years about 52% of all psycho-geriatric patients in the United States were admitted to psychiatric wards or beds in general hospitals, and 8% were admitted to private psychiatric hospitals. Of these, about 46% had organic brain syndrome, 18% functional psychoses, and 26% neurotic disorders.

In various hospitals elderly alcoholics are admitted as psycho-geriatric patients or are included in a separate program, and they may make up 5 to 10% of admissions. Again the finding of different percentages of disease categories from the British, Scottish, and American studies for psycho-geriatric patients was noted by Burvill in Australia (14).

Factors Leading to Hospitalization

The mere presence of psychiatric disease in an elderly person does not necessarily lead either to treatment or hospitalization, as evidenced by the findings of Kay, Beamish, and Roth (45) in their community survey in Newcastle on Tyne, in which less than 20% of those with severe organic brain syndromes were being cared for in hospital or another institution, and less than 1/10th of the 31% with all functional disorders were under residential care of any type. In the extensive studies of Lowenthal and her group in San Francisco, they remarked on the "one-bed, private wards" in the homes of many severely impaired elderly where the family was caring for them. Of those actually admitted to a psycho-geriatric assessment unit, many factors predisposing the person to mental illness or disability were identified, but there were particular events which precipitated the admission in almost all cases. There were disturbances of thinking or feeling (such as delusion, depression, or incoherence) in 13%; potentially harmful behavior (such as self-neglect, wandering, or denudative behavior) in 33%; actually harmful behavior (such as heavy drinking, refusing medical care, violence, or fire setting) in 21%; physical factors (such as falls, strokes, feebleness, or malnutrition) in 10%; and environmental factors (such as depletion of funds, loss of a caretaker, or recommendation of physician) in 23% (59, 60).

Pre-hospitalization Screening Programs

In order to make the most effective use of a psycho-geriatric hospital and to best help the patient, a pre-hospitalization screening evaluation should take place. This is best done at the prospective patient's residence, as this gives an insight into the physical and social assets and liabilities of the individual, and helps the screening team see how the person relates to his family in the natural setting. We have found that a team of psychiatric nurse, social worker, and psychiatrist is most effective. On a series of 105 elderly patients who were proposed for state mental hospital admission, Wolff found after screening each that only 47% required mental hospitalization, 23% were sent to nursing care facilities, and 30% were returned to their own family, often to be followed on an outpatient basis by their family physician or a psychiatrist (85). It has been pointed out that the pre-hospitalization screening teams not only evaluate the older person as to whether he needs mental hospital care, but also may intervene or assist the patient or family to find alternate arrangements when indicated. In addition, they may provide consultative services on geriatric care to professional people and community institutions caring for the elderly (51).

We have adopted the following guidelines for appropriate and inappropriate admissions to our psycho-geriatric service. We feel that appropriate admissions would be as follows:

1. those with severe organic brain disease whose usual behavior is too disturbing to be handled at home or in another facility, such as wanderers, fire setters, physically aggressive patients, or those dangerous to themselves or others when they are actually capable of carrying out destructive behavior;
2. those with chronic brain syndromes who come for brief admission during periods of restlessness and agitation caused by stress, even at times to give temporary relief to the families and caretakers to keep them from becoming totally exhausted and disorganized;
3. those with moderate degrees of chronic brain syndrome who, after careful evaluation, are felt to be good candidates for improvement with a period of controlled environment and active treatment;
4. those with functional psychoses for whom outpatient care is not feasible, such as those with depression who need protection from self-destructive behavior, or those with chronic mental illnesses who need management and protection during prolonged periods of disruptive or disorganized behavior;
5. those with chronic psychoses who need periodic medication readjustments which cannot be conveniently or adequately handled on an outpatient basis;
6. those alcoholics and drug abusers who following detoxification need a time of inpatient care to improve their general mental and physical state; and
7. those with reversible psychiatric illness accompanied by medical illness if the general hospital has no suitable psychiatric services.

We feel that an important aspect of admitting an elderly patient to a psychiatric facility is to take some time to inform the patient of what to expect in the way of surroundings and treatment. It is best to let him enter the hospital voluntarily if he is capable of making such a decision. This short time spent in preparation for admission often reduces the trauma of hospitalization and enhances the effectiveness of the total treatment program.

We feel that the following would constitute inappropriate admission to a psychiatric hospital:

1. those who are physically sick and require urgent admission to a medical hospital;
2. those who have mild to moderate organic brain syndrome or other disorders who could live effectively in other group care facilities if they could no longer be maintained in their own homes;
3. those who are comatose or moribund; and
4. those who basically need only adequate living accommodations, or other economic, nutritional, or social support services (81).

Matching Patient and Facility

The demands for beds, the lack of criteria, and the lack of pre-admission screening have often resulted in the placement of elderly patients in the wrong, or at least less than optimal, surroundings. Perhaps the biggest problem is whether the prospective patient should be on the psycho-geriatric mental ward or the medical ward. Several have studied this problem, but the findings of Kidd are perhaps particularly revealing (48, 49). He graded elderly patients into four groups depending on the predominant problem, viz., the mental, the mental-physical, the physical-mental, and the physical. Of those placed in a psychiatric setting 24% had mainly medical problems, while 34% of those on a geriatric medical service had predominantly psychiatric problems. Those most likely to be misplaced were those over age 75, those single or widowed, and those of low socioeconomic status. The consequences of mismatching were prolonged hospitalization; increased incontinence, restlessness, disorientation, and immobility; and a markedly increased mortality rate. In addition, inappropriate admissions impaired the efficiency of the hospital staff, who were not trained or equipped to handle the particular type of problem. Various studies have shown a high incidence of mixed illness, with up to 65% of the psycho-geriatric patients having physical illness, and 63% of the geriatric patients having mental illness (54).

Assessment and Diagnosis

Ideally one would wish that an entire physical and psychiatric assessment might take place before an elderly person is moved from his home or usual surroundings. Realistically this is often difficult because of the lack of mobile screening teams, the great distances involved (some of our patients live over 200 miles from the mental hospital), and often the difficulty of getting medical evaluation. Even after fairly good pre-hospitalization screening it is often still difficult to tell what environment would be best, so a desirable service would be a psycho-geriatric assessment unit. In Britain the Department of Health recommended the establishment of units of this type (24, 47), and there has been a lively discussion since (3, 5, 6, 13, 27, 84).

Arie raised several issues, including whether psycho-geriatric means dealing only with organic mental disorders or else the psychiatry of old age, whether hospital assessment would replace the primary home assessment, and whether "joint assessment units" would not better convey the concept of psychiatrists and geriatricians working together on the same unit (7). In order to function well, such service units would need easy access to both medical and psychiatric facilities as well as good community coopera-tion and back-up resources.

On our psycho-geriatric admission and assessment ward, we obtain the following studies in addition to the psychiatric, social, and medical exam-inations: chest and skull X-rays, electrocardiogram, electroencephalogram, hemogram, fasting blood sugar, blood urea nitrogen, alkaline phosphates, SGOT, LDH, serology, urinalysis, and serum bromide (bromides are avail-able here without prescription and are still used moderately by the elderly). In cases of malnutrition, weight loss or gain, or organic brain syndrome, the following studies are helpful: serum electrolytes, T_0 and T_4, calcium and phosphorus, uric acid, glucose tolerance test, and urine culture. Obviously it is important to get adequate medical work-up and treatment where physical disease is complicating the psychiatric picture if one is to give adequate care, but we will not go into more detail about that here.

Ward Placement

Placement of the psycho-geriatric patient will depend both on what types of hospital facilities are available and on one's theoretical approach. There is debate as to whether age-segregation of patients should take place, although it seems to be generally practiced. The principal argu-ments are that on an age-mixed ward, the elderly generally tend to get less staff attention since more attention is given to the more aggressive and "more interesting" younger patients, the elderly are more exposed to phys-ical harm by young violent patients, and, on a specialized ward or service, the elderly would supposedly get more appropriate attention and be able to take a greater social role. We tend to agree with the important study of Kahana of age grouping of psycho-geriatric patients in which it was ob-served that psycho-geriatric patients did far worse on an age-homogeneous custodial ward than on an age-integrated custodial ward where the close-ness with younger people seemed to provide much stimulation and in-teraction. Age-segregated wards with an active therapeutic program were the most effective, however (43, 44).

Simply crowding many old people together on a ward may encourage the worst sorts of regression and institutional neurosis no matter how high sounding a name we may give to it. An accurate assessment of the patient's problems and capabilities must be made, and a variety of treatment locations and modalities must be available. There is a real problem with so-called transfer mortality in the elderly in which a change of environment may cause rapid disorientation and deterioration, and so some would suggest not moving a psycho-geriatric patient once he has been on a particular ward. Our feeling is that more is to be gained in the long run by a planned move to an appropriate ward, especially if the patient is apprised of the anticipated move and has a chance to visit the proposed site first.

Types of Psycho-Geriatric Wards

We feel that a psycho-geriatric service ideally should have several types of facilities available, although they all might not be at the same location. The key to adequate care is a planned program for each type of ward, and periodic reassessment so that changes in the patients' status may be noted and appropriately responded to (86). Patients will generally do best, and staff satisfaction will often be improved, if the patient has adequate stimulation and involvement so as to reduce regression, but not so much as to overwhelm a person who simply is unable to cope with a complex situation. The ward types recommended are as follows:

1. an admission ward for joint assessment and probably intensive treatment of problems that can be handled within two months or so;
2. rehabilitation wards for the chronically psychotic individuals who have grown old in the institution, and for those who need an intermediate stay in the hospital;
3. continuing care wards for those who show progressive mental deterioration and need a supportive, humane, and protective environment;
4. nursing care wards for those who are physically markedly deteriorated, and yet for behavioral or other reasons cannot be located outside of the hospital;
5. minimal care or self-care wards, rather like a half-way house, for those who are awaiting community placement or perhaps are working outside the hospital during the day;
6. ambulatory senile facilities with fencing of some type for those who are very deteriorated mentally, but not physically, and who have a tendency to wander into streets or get lost; and
7. geriatric medical or infirmary wards.

Integration of Wards

We have found that most psycho-geriatric patients do better when they have substantial contact with the opposite sex. Not only does the mixing of men and women more closely resemble the real world of society, but there is a marked stimulation to better socialization, grooming, activity, and manners for all. Some wards have men and women living on the same ward, with adequate provision for privacy, of course. In spite of the apprehensions of many of the hospital staff that this would lead to all sorts of improprieties, we have had to move only a rare individual who persisted in going into the wrong rooms or annoying the opposite sex. Certainly no pregnancies have resulted! Our wards are integrated racially as well. As the elderly in this area grew up in a rigidly segregated society, some were apprehensive about possible problems, but we have not had a single racial incident of any consequence.

Architecture and Physical Setting of Psycho-Geriatric Services

Most mental hospitals seem to have been designed with security and economy in mind rather than convenience and service. Too many resemble grim isolated dungeons, and the thought expressed by some that they should be torn down is not without some merit. Several, such as Cosin and Linden, have well-thought-out plans for psycho-geriatric wards and units. Among the features are pleasant landscaping, ground level wards, modern design, areas for gardening, sunlight, sheltered walkways, an increased number of well-located lavatories to help reduce incontinence, provision for reasonable privacy, adequate dining facilities with small tables, some private rooms for ill or disturbed patients, sitting areas which are subdivided so as to provide grouping rather than simply sitting around the walls, recreational areas indoors and out, sufficient space for workshops and various therapies, bathing areas with showers, hand rails and other safety devices in areas such as rest rooms, lockable areas to keep clothing and personal belongings near the beds, laundry and drying machines close by, facilities for hair dressing, and a lack of stairs (23, 57). A more pleasant and homelike atmosphere can be produced by such things as colorful tablecloths and bedspreads, flowers, upholstered furniture, lamps, magazines and books, personal photographs, and a television set. Carpets are attractive and reduce noise, but are quite impractical around incontinent patients.

Traditionally, mental hospitals seem to have had paint only in five shades of dull gray, which contributed mightily to the pessimistic gloom of the wards. Agate reports the successful therapeutic use of bold contrasting colors of wall paints, color coding of wards and doors, and bright floor tiles to stimulate and activate patients, to provide a more cheerful atmosphere, and to help the confused and partially blind to better orient themselves (1). Adequate levels of illumination are more important for the elderly to help distinguish color and detail, and to help in matters such as lip reading. Properly spaced night lights help to prevent falls and getting lost (64). Some think that old people want to enjoy "peace and quiet" and so try to keep noise at a minimum. As Busse points out, this deprives the elderly person of important orienting background noises and also reduces the ability to hear in some (16). Background music or the television may be quite therapeutic. The temperatures of the wards where psycho-geriatric patients are treated are important, and should be held as constant as possible between 68°F and 83°F. Air conditioning is needed in those areas where the room temperature might approach body temperature, as the elderly tolerate this extremely poorly, especially those on phenothiazines or anticholinergic drugs who may develop dehydration or fatal hyperpyrexia very quickly.

TREATMENT MODALITIES

Therapeutic Community

The treatment of psychiatric patients took a great leap forward with the development and application of the concept of the therapeutic community as put forth by Maxwell Jones (42). This has been most fully developed in the United States for the psycho-geriatric patient by Gottesman and his group at the University of Michigan (38). Basically the concepts are that the traditional mental hospital (and certain other institutions as well) expects the patient to be sick and makes few demands on him other than that he fit into a passive patient role, which unfortunately often leads to further regression and retreat. Another part of the theory is that treatment must offer patients a structured series of meaningful demands if it is to be effective.

The hospital should prepare the patient to leave the institution for the community by offering him opportunities to take normal social roles and by helping him learn to function in these roles as a worker, citizen, consumer, and friend within the protective environment of the hospital. Facets of the programs include: patients work in a workshop where contract work progressively varied for the person's abilities is done for pay; the wards are made more homelike; the patients wear their own clothes; the sexes are mixed; patients operate ward stores and facilities; patients participate in ward planning; and the staff functions more democratically and as a team. An elaborate staff training program has been developed by Coons (22). This program seems geared more to the chronically hospitalized schizophrenic patient, but considerable success with some organic patients has been reported.

Attitude Therapy

A somewhat different approach which we have partially incorporated into our psycho-geriatric program is so-called attitude therapy as developed by Folsom, in which one of five basic attitudes is assumed by the entire staff to each patient according to his problem. The approaches are called kind firmness, active friendliness, passive friendliness, matter of fact, and no demand; they provide a therapeutic approach and a consistency of attitude which can be modified as the patient changes (74).

Reality Orientation

Another technique which we have found very helpful with organically impaired psycho-geriatric patients is reality orientation as developed by Folsom (28). Basically this is a nursing assistant operated program in which a social interaction type of group is conducted to help reorient and mentally stimulate the confused patient. One phase is the formal class with about six confused patients in which the instructor in a friendly, calm way repeatedly goes over personal and current information with each, such as his name, the date, the place, the menu, the weather, and upcoming holidays and events. Correct responses are immediately rewarded verbally by such statements as "very good" or "that's right." The daily classes last for 30 minutes, and as the patient improves, more complex materials are added, such as time telling, spelling, object manipulation, and reading.

Another phase of this is the continual reality orientation on the psycho-geriatric wards where there are sign boards in prominent spots to which the patient can frequently refer with the information about place, date, weather, and activities. All of the staff continually reinforce this by calling patients by their names and by apprising them in a simple, direct, and calm way of what events are taking place or are about to take place. We find that this program provides a therapeutic structure for interaction between staff and confused psycho-geriatric patients, and that the better functioning patients often learn to use it with the less able.

Behavior Modification Therapy

Behavior modification therapies now are in considerable vogue in psychiatry and promise rather good results. They are based on the premise that many psychiatric problems and maladaptive behaviors are learned response patterns which can be altered directly by manipulating stimulus variables or by reversing the learning process. They aim at symptom relief and disturbed overt behavior, utilizing such techniques as extinction procedures, counter conditioning, desensitization, or negative reinforcement. Methods such as muscular relaxation to inhibit the effects of anxiety, the deliberate practicing of excitatory emotional reactions, inhibitions of stimuli, and operant conditioning by rewards of tokens have been used, but there is only a scant handful of reports of specific use of these techniques with psycho-geriatric patients (66).

Ankus and Quarrington report that even in the severely organically impaired geriatric patient, behavior is modifiable by a reinforcement, such as money, which is appropriate to the individual (4). Actually, many of the therapies described previously and subsequently to this have principles of behavior modification inherent in them. Most of the psycho-geriatric patients sick enough to be in hospital would probably be rather poor candidates for the usual individual behavior therapy techniques, both because of the frequent memory impairments as well as the fact that we have found it difficult to induce muscular relaxation by hypnotic suggestion in most of them. This area certainly needs further exploration, however.

Habit Training

Personal hygiene, most particularly toilet habits, is an area of major concern in psycho-geriatric patients. An enormous amount of staff time and energy can go into changing clothes and bed linens. Incontinence can be caused by many factors such as neurologic disease, bladder infection, prostatic disease, and severe confusion from senile deterioration, but it also may be an active hostile rejection of community standards because of feelings of being neglected and not given enough attention (61). Having toilets close by will help avoid many accidents when the patient has urinary urgency and cannot get far after perceiving the need to urinate. Having the doors to the toilets marked clearly by a bright color, by name, and by a silhouette of a man or woman helps many confused patients find the facility more quickly. Taking the patient to the toilet at regular intervals, such as every two hours during the day, and every three hours at night, will markedly improve the situation in some cases, but there are still those who wet themselves on the way back from the toilet. In those in whom there is a functional component to their poor personal habits, there is often improvement as the mental state improves and the elderly patient begins to enter into an active therapeutic milieu.

Recreation Therapy

Many think of recreation for the aged as being simply entertainment, such as watching the television set or a movie. Indeed it should be a time of relaxation and pleasure, but more importantly it should be the restoration or preservation of creative functions of a person, which often have been neglected or have atrophied in the psycho-geriatric patient. It should include physical activities such as rhythmical exercises, dancing, walks, sports such as fishing or bowling, and gardening, within the limits of patients' actual physical conditions, of course. Spading up part of the hospital lawn so that the psycho-geriatric patients can dig in the dirt and grow flowers and vegetables is an excellent investment in mental health. More sedentary recreation activities are important also, such as weaving, sewing, woodwork, reading, cooking, drawing, painting, games such as bingo, cards and checkers, clay and pottery work, caring for pets, and planning and having picnics and parties. A number of excellent books dealing with rehabilitation and recreation in the aged have been written recently which would provide many useful ideas for psycho-geriatric patients in hospital. The recreation therapist can provide valuable service in evaluating the capacities and progress of psycho-geriatric patients, and in providing a graduated program of therapy.

Occupational Therapy and Industrial Therapy

Rehabilitation services in mental hospitals may be subdivided in different ways, but the occupational and industrial therapists play important roles in the evaluation and total treatment of psycho-geriatric patients. They are equipped to provide detailed assessment of functional physical capacities, and to provide appropriate constructive activities which enhance self-esteem, provide outlets for aggressive feelings, and promote socialization. Special problems in psycho-geriatric patients are the short attention span, physical disabilities like tremors and arthritis, and difficulty in seeing.

Psychological Services

While psychological services are probably less often needed with psycho-geriatric patients, they can help both with diagnosis and with the assessment of mental potential and capacities. With this information more appropriate activities and goals can be established, and the baseline data are helpful in following the course of the patient and for research purposes.

Music Therapy

At least since the time that David was brought to play the lyre to refresh and heal the mentally ill King Saul, music has been regarded as having a place in psychiatric treatment. This contention is given some scientific credence by Boxberger and Cotter, who reported that the participation of psycho-geriatric patients in music activities had the following results: reduction in aggressiveness, more appropriate behavior, reduction of incontinence, less physical and verbal reaction to hallucinations, a decrease in the level of undesirable patient noise, and an improvement in personal appearance (11). These results from music alone sound out of scale to us, but certainly music is a pleasant and helpful therapeutic modality for psycho-geriatric patients, reviving old and pleasant memories, cultivating new interests, and increasing socialization. Among our patients religious songs and hymns seem to be especially meaningful, and occasionally very demented patients join in with surprisingly well-remembered verses. Rhythm bands and movement to music are helpful in expressing feelings in a group, and in getting a moderate amount of exercise as well.

Educational Therapy

For some psycho-geriatric patients an opportunity for further formal education while in the hospital may be beneficial to develop new interests, to increase self-esteem, for recreation, and to learn better to cope with the world. Some may simply develop an increased interest in reading, while others may be able to take more formal courses which might be offered at the hospital, or else by correspondence.

Physical Therapy

King David seems to have been a pioneer in psycho-geriatrics not only in music therapy, but also in physical therapy, for we read not only of the application of heat to him to revive him when he was getting old and senile, but also of finding a maiden to nurse him and lie close to him to warn him. We have not used this practice of gerocomy with our patients, but physical therapy is important in several ways for elderly psychiatric patients.

Some patients come in for emotional problems after a stroke or fracture, and the restoration of their strength and function greatly enhances their chances of satisfactory adjustment. Psycho-geriatric patients who are bedridden or restrained for a period of time for any reason rapidly lose strength and mobility unless there is an active program of preventive physical therapy. Many of the pain problems respond well to heat and massage. Symptoms of malaise, weakness, and withdrawal may respond to hydrotherapy and massage; agitation and restlessness may be treated with warm baths or packs (85). Ulcers and infected wounds which occur often in psycho-geriatric patients frequently respond well to whirlpool baths. Evaluation of physical potential and gait training can be important functions of a physical therapist. If the hospital is lacking a podiatrist, the physical therapist may be able to help with the many foot problems that hobble many psycho-geriatric patients. Old people need human touch and contact, and physical therapy may be an acceptable way to provide this in addition to more specific therapies.

Physical Aids

A large percentage of psycho-geriatric patients in hospital have visual and hearing defects which often contribute to their isolation and psychopathology. The provision of glasses will often help a person to read and to take part in crafts and activities or to lip read. Improvement in hearing, either by a hearing aid, or sometimes by cleaning the impacted wax out of the ears, will help to reduce the suspiciousness and hostility of many psycho-geriatric patients with hearing impairments, and will aid in their improvement.

Diet and Nutrition Therapy

The role of nutritional deficiencies in the psychiatric disorders of the elderly is still uncertain, and there have been widely varying reports.

Among elderly patients admitted to our hospitals, over 70% were eating doubtfully adequate or grossly inadequate diets. Of these, 50% had borderline or low levels of folic acid, and 12% had borderline or low levels of vitamin B_{12}, both of which may be associated with dementia and other psychiatric disorders (82, 83). Classical vitamin deficiencies have been relatively infrequently seen in recent years, but multiple deficiencies are the rule in the elderly when vitamin deficiencies exist. It is often difficult to tell in psycho-geriatric patients how often the observed deficiencies are the cause of the mental disorder, and how often they are the result. In most cases there is probably a vicious circle of mental illness, self-neglect, nutritional deficiency, physical illness, and further mental deterioration.

This is a fertile field for food faddists, but there is evidence from some recent Russian reports that vitamin supplements do improve central nervous system functioning and age-impaired physiologic functions to some extent in over 50% of older people (19). Our policy with hospitalized psycho-geriatric patients is to treat specific deficiencies with specific vitamins, but we do give a daily supplemental multivitamin preparation to all patients. When there is obvious malnutrition or suspicion of multiple early or borderline deficiencies, we give an initial injection of multiple B vitamins and vitamin C (after pernicious anemia is ruled out), and then give a therapeutic multiple vitamin and mineral preparation for at least 14 days. Studies by Taylor (72) indicate that it may take up to one year of therapy to reverse deficiency problems in the elderly.

Even in hospital, psycho-geriatric patients may maintain or even develop nutritional deficiencies because of altered food habits resulting in their eating mostly carbohydrates, marked loss of certain vitamins (especially vitamin C and folic acid) in institutional food preparation and service, failure to eat the food served (psycho-geriatric patients waste about 30% of what they are served (30)), and the presence of multiple factors interfering with vitamin utilization, such as decrease in digestion enzymes, altered intestinal flora, and the use of mineral oil and various antivitamin drugs like phenobarbital.

Eating is both a physiological and a social function, and attractively prepared food served in pleasant surroundings is a tonic in many ways. Some studies have indicated that the use of a glass of beer or wine daily in a pub situation on a psycho-geriatric service increases social interaction, decreases incontinence, and reduces the need for other medications (20).

Drug Therapy

The discovery and use of a variety of psychiatrically active drugs in recent years have markedly enhanced our ability to work with many disorders in the elderly. As there is little specific to their use in hospital, the reader is referred elsewhere for a full discussion of the psychopharmacology and the indications (56, 68, 71). Herein we will mention some of the aspects of drug therapy that relate particularly to hospitalized patients.

Generally we try to have a prospective patient treated first on the outside with drugs, and admit him only if there has been a complication or failure. There is wide variation in the drug tolerance and requirements of psycho-geriatric patients which can often be determined only by trial and error. We prefer to be cautious and conservative in drug use. Most severely manic patients will probably be in hospital anyway, but because of the marked toxicity and complication rate of lithium therapy in the elderly, we prefer to initiate this in hospital. There is often a marked improvement in the mania within several days on very low doses of lithium, but it may take a while to determine the proper dosage. A number of the elderly are actually hospitalized with a variety of symptoms related to drug reaction and complications, or polypharmacology which has become so complicated that it is hard to tell what is happening. In these cases, hospitalization is indicated in order to withdraw medication for re-evaluation.

Hypotension is a rather frequent complication of the phenothiazine drugs, and may manifest itself as progressive confusion, agitation, or transient ischemic attacks. Every psycho-geriatric patient examined in hospital should have his blood pressure taken supine and sitting or standing. Postural hypotension may last for 10 to 14 days when it once occurs, and may require bed rest and even corticosteroid drugs to help stabilize the vascular system. In order to reduce the incidence of this complication, we usually start a drug like thioridazine at 10 mgm once or twice daily, and increase it stepwise as needed about every three days. We have had very little cardiovascular problem with the butyrophenone drug haloperidol, and find it helpful in many psychotic states. Above 1.5 mgm daily, however, the incidence of muscular rigidity and extra pyramidal symptoms is high in the psycho-geriatric patient.

It is easy to leave a hospitalized psycho-geriatric patient on a high dose of a phenothiazine long after an acute psychosis has subsided, and hence run an increased risk of dyskinesias, Parkinsonism, or ocular complications. Periodic review and possible drug regulation or reduction are important. Motor restlessness and akathisias are fairly common side effects observed, and may lead to unfortunate increases of phenothiazine on the assumption that a psychosis is worse. We do not use anti-Parkinson agents prophylactically in psycho-geriatric patients because of the high incidence of confusion and side effects from them. Many of the psychotropic drugs are quite effective on a once or twice daily schedule, which saves nursing personnel time, enables the patient to participate in activities rather than sit around a ward waiting for medicine, and allows drug side effects such as drowsiness or dry mouth to occur more during the night. A number of chronic psycho-geriatric patients who are stabilized on a dose of phenothiazine develop either an increased sensitivity or resistance to the drug after about a six to nine month interval, and so may need periodic re-evaluation of dosage or alteration of drugs.

Many drugs such as barbiturates, tranquilizers, and antihistamines may have prolonged effects with confusion, weakness, or ataxia as a hangover in the mornings. Many outpatients will stop taking drugs with side effects on their own and never tell the doctor, but the patient in hospital may have no choice and hence run an increased risk of falling if the doctor is not alert to the problem.

Nocturnal confusion and sleep disturbance may follow a change in circumstance of a psycho-geriatric patient, such as a move to a new ward. It may take several days for the person to readjust, and we feel it is often helpful to anticipate this problem by providing a hypnotic for three or four nights routinely. In our experience chlorol hydrate is best, allowing the patient to wake up sufficiently to get to the toilet during the night, not depressing the REM sleep significantly, having little hangover or ataxia, and having a fairly low incidence of habituation.

Electroconvulsive Therapy

Age *per se* is no contraindication to electroconvulsive treatment when it is needed. Some administer it to elderly patients on an outpatient basis, but we are rather loathe to do this, feeling that the usual indications in psycho-geriatrics for ECT, such as risk of death from suicide or refusal to eat, and manic, depressive, or stuporous states which are refractory to other treatment require hospitalization anyway. While ECT is probably safer than many drugs in the elderly, there is still some increased risk and complication rate, so the use of it should be weighed carefully. Because of osteoporosis, the patient should get an adequate dose of muscle relaxant. This may interfere with the return of respiration, and the patient should be well oxygenated before and after the ECT to prevent prolonged hypoxia. Ordinarily we do not use a short acting barbiturate or anesthetic in the psycho-geriatric patient, as they increase the apnea and complication rate, and although the patient may complain more of awareness of the procedure, it is safer especially where the resuscitative facilities are not optimal.

Psycho-geriatric cases often respond very well and rapidly to ECT, some showing marked improvement after two or three treatments. We do not use a routine number of ECT but rather usually use the system of "good improvement plus two" to consolidate the gains. Following the ECT, we may use drugs such as an antidepressant for a period of time, and some type of psychotherapy and environmental manipulation. There usually seems to be little value in post-ECT confusion as such, and it usually begins to show after the third ECT. Often we give a total course of four or five ECT, and may space the last ones out to three or five day intervals to avoid the excessive confusion somewhat. There is no particular hazard to the confusion *per se,* as it usually clears in two or three weeks anyway, but it may delay the patient from participating in other helpful therapies at an earlier time.

Occasionally we use ECT in the face of some apparent organic brain syndrome when depressive phenomena are present and severe, or sometimes as a diagnostic trial when real uncertainty exists as to whether a seemingly confused patient has a masked depressive reaction instead which has not responded to other treatment. While depressions in psychogeriatrics usually respond well to antidepressant drugs and milieu therapy, some are refractory and may extend over prolonged periods. Usually we give an antidepressant drug a three-week trial on a hospitalized patient, and if little or no improvement is evident, then switch to ECT or another drug.

Group Therapies

Man is basically a social creature, and most of his important life events take place in group settings. Mental illness may result from defects in or losses of crucial group relationships, or conversely mental illness may cause deterioration or loss of those relationships. Hence, the rapidly increasing move to groups as a means and locus of psychotherapy is understandable and desirable.

A therapy group differs from others in that it is planned, has people in it identified as having some problem, disease, or concern, has at least one person who feels he has some ability to lead the group and help the others and who is the therapist, and has some type of formal or informal understanding or contract. The group should be large enough to provide variation and protection for the members, and yet small enough so that everyone has an opportunity to participate and interact. For many types of groups, from six to 12 members is a good size.

Sometimes group therapy is used for economy because there are so many patients and so few therapists to go around, a situation which often prevails in mental hospitals. This is not sufficient justification to have a group, however, as a poorly conceived group may fail, and the experience can be destructive to a patient whose defenses are unnecessarily breached or who is made to feel ridiculous or inadequate. There are differences in the needs of psycho-geriatric patients in hospitals from younger people or those outside; e.g., groups which are psychoanalytically oriented or which encourage the explosive outburst of emotion are quite inappropriate with most of the elderly.

We will discuss briefly a variety of group therapies that we and others have found helpful with psycho-geriatric patients. From his experience, Linden listed several criteria for selection of patients for groups, which include an expressed wish to join, relative alertness, ability to understand the language, fair personal hygiene, some physical mobility, evidence of fair previous adult adjustment, some range of affects, and a capacity for evoking positive responses from the nursing staff (58). These are good criteria for an insight or didactically oriented group, but are rather overstringent for other types.

In general we feel that a sexually mixed group is more realistic and active; that there should be at least two therapists, preferably a male and a female; that there should be some homogeneity as regards problems, needs, and mental capacities; and that the group should meet regularly at a specified time and place. It is difficult in a hospital to keep a closed stable group because of discharges, transfers, illness, and death, so most groups are designed as open-ended ones. This reduces the intensity of interaction and group cohesiveness, but it does perhaps provide a therapeutic forum for psycho-geriatric patients to learn to deal with the major problem of handling changes and losses effectively. Many helpful techniques and goals have been outlined by Klein, Leshan and Furman (50).

The results of group therapy with the elderly were noted by Wolff, who found within three months better verbalization and controlled feelings, better ward adjustment, increased communication and activity, better orientation, better grooming, more appropriate sex role adjustment, lessened anxiety and feelings of isolation, favorable group identification, and a sustained improvement which helped later out of hospital adjustment (85). The group leaders must be fairly active, warm, and positive.

1. *Socialization or discussion groups.* Those patients who best fit into this type of group are those who fulfill Linden's criteria. The contents of the discussion generally fall into practical problems like finances, health, food, and retirement; into relationship problems like children, grandparent roles, love and marriage; and into more abstract concepts such as religion, hope, happiness, history, and conformity. We have found it helpful to have the patients serve refreshments to each other and the therapists at the end of the meeting.

2. *Remotivation groups.* This is a technique developed to reach and motivate extremely withdrawn and apathetic hospitalized patients by using attendants with small groups of patients in a warm, accepting environment using nonthreatening material such as poetry, history, or nature study to reach healthy aspects of the patient's memory and experience in hopes of interesting and involving him in the present real world. It provides a structured framework for interaction with very regressed patients (2).

3. *Pre-discharge groups.* Those patients who are improving to the point of being able to leave the hospital, especially if they have been there for a long period, face many problems and anxieties about reentering the community. This group deals specifically with these problems, not only in talking about them, but by engaging in such group activities as visiting a boarding home, going shopping, finding their way around in such agencies as the social service department or the mental health clinic, and visiting various senior citizens organizations in the community. We feel that two or three months of this group experience greatly enhance the chances of the psycho-geriatric patient adjusting well after discharge.

4. *Conjoint and family therapy groups.* Marital difficulties and family disorder are common problems among the hospitalized elderly. Prolonged illness prior to hospitalization has often exhausted, alienated, and frightened the family, so that opportunities to work through these problems are crucial to the patient's final rehabilitation. This is usually done just with the members of the immediate family, but it can be done with several unrelated families at the same time who have similar problems.

5. *Patient government.* Opening many hospital wards and democratization by involving patients in discussion and decision-making regarding their own care have been major steps in humanizing the mental hospital. The presence of many with organic brain syndromes makes this impractical with psycho-geriatric patients, but a modification of this with a weekly joint meeting of all the ward patients and staff to discuss problems and plan programs often brings about a more healthy atmosphere.

6. *Grooming and homemaker groups.* Personal apearance and domestic skills such as cooking and ironing have often deteriorated among the older hospitalized patients. Groups to regain these skills often greatly enhance the self-esteem of the women in particular.

7. *Inspiration groups.* Some groups, such as Alcoholics Anonymous, have a religious or quasi-religious function of providing support, enhancement of values, an opportunity for testimony, and inspiration to their members. Some psycho-geriatric patients benefit greatly from them.

8. *Foster grandparent groups.* A number of our psycho-geriatric patients spend some time each week acting as foster grandparents to children in a nearby institution for the mentally retarded, playing with them, reading to them, or simply holding them. This is too demanding for some, but proves helpful to a number of the elderly in providing an appropriate role for them and allowing them to give and receive affection.

Individual Psychotherapy

The pessimism of Freud over the usefulness and possibility of individual psychotherapy with older people undoubtedly inhibited the development of interest in and techniques for psycho-geriatrics. Some, such as Meerloo, have used analytic techniques with the elderly, but these would apply more to patients able to function outside of hospitals (65). We must remember that the crucial aspect of almost any psychiatric treatment is the relationship involved, which applies equally well to the organic hospitalized patient (15). Differences in therapy with psychogeriatrics are that the therapist must be more active and positive, that transference and countertransference are complex, that ego support is given, and that therapy should be decreased but not terminated. Goldfarb and Turner developed a technique which is particularly useful with hospitalized psycho-geriatric patients, especially those with organic brain syndrome (36). The person has loss of self-esteem because of the impaired ability to cope, and is looking for a powerful parent figure. The therapist fosters the feeling that the patient has won him as a powerful ally, and allows expression of hostile and dependent feelings. At first the patient is seen frequently to establish this relationship, but subsequently only at infrequent and brief intervals.

Religious Needs and Programs

While church attendance does decrease in the elderly, this is probably due to physical factors, as most were raised in a religious environment and still maintain their beliefs. Religion provides a value system, a feeling of belonging, a ritual, and a belief in some kind of afterlife; hence it may be a very positive factor for a psycho-geriatric patient. Some are caught in religious delusions or compulsive ideas, but for most a visit from a minister or chaplain, or an opportunity to sing old hymns, or to attend the hospital chapel, is an appreciated and beneficial event.

Special Problems of Psycho-Geriatric Patients

In addition to the previously mentioned problems of adverse drug reactions and toxicity, and the process of social breakdown and institutionalism that can easily occur, there are some other problems of psycho-geriatric patients of which we should be aware. Because of inactivity and a bed being close by, many psycho-geriatric patients sleep too much during the day, and hence are awake at night. Too often this is treated by increasing drugs rather than by substituting activities.

Related both to the relative inactivity and to the use of drugs with anticholenergic effects, fecal impactions are extremely common in psycho-geriatric patients. These are manifested in a variety of ways, such as vomiting, agitation, fever, lethargy, walking or sitting bent over to one side, or increased confusion. A rectal examination should be part of the work-up of any of these problems. Other physical problems arise as well, and often the first manifestation of these may be an alteration or worsening of the mental state of the psycho-geriatric patient. He will often need a physical examination rather than an increase in tranquilizer.

HOSPITAL PATTERNS AND POSSIBILITIES

Staffing Patterns

It is rather difficult to state what an adequate or optimal staffing pattern would be on a psycho-geriatric service since this would be determined by the type of patient served and the nature of the program. Gottesman and his group studied the results of traditional type wards with usual and augmented staffs, and of therapeutic community oriented wards with usual and augmented staffs. The traditional ward with usual staff did little better than custodial wards, while that with the augmented staff showed some improvement, but at high cost. Both of the therapeutically oriented wards showed marked improvement in patient activity and behavior, but of course from a cost efficiency standpoint, the therapeutic ward without augmented staff was most effective (37).

In Scotland, it is felt that the recommendations of the British Geriatric Society for nursing staff ratios on acute assessment and rehabilitation wards of 1 nurse or attendant to 1.25 patients, and on long-stay wards of 1 nurse or attendant to 1.5 patients are suitable for psycho-geriatric wards as well (69). Of course, in many mental hospital the ratios are vastly less than this. The nursing staff-patient ratio on our admission and assessment ward is 1 to 1.8 patients, which is bare minimum, and causes disruption of the program when either staff or patients are physically ill.

Standards for other personnel have been recommended (8), but a recent United States Court ruling (Wyatt vs. Stickney) in which a state mental hospital was ordered to bring its staff up to a level to provide adequate treatment for its patients required the following personnel for every 250 patients: three psychiatrists, four medical doctors, 12 registered nurses, six licensed practical nurses, 92 attendants, 10 orderlies, six stenographers and typists, one unit administrator, one Ph.D. psychologist, three other psychologists, seven social workers, one active therapist and 10 activity aides, 10 mental health technicians, one vocational rehabilitation counselor, one volunteer services worker, and a variety of 37 other dietary, housekeeping, and maintenance personnel. How this matter will be resolved is of major interest to many of us! Physicians, and especially psychiatrists, willing to work with the aged are difficult to come by, as Arie points out (7).

Even among well motivated and trained nursing staff, working with psycho-geriatric patients can be rather exhausting. Especially if the task is made worse by a shortage of staff and an overload of patients, morale tends to fall. This needs to be countered by in-service training, good communications between all levels of staff, a sense of taking part in an active and challenging program, and some sense of equality of responsibility and opportunity which can be achieved by rotating the nursing staff among the various wards about every six months (63).

Prospective Psycho-Geriatric Bed Needs

It is difficult to summarize or clarify the prospective needs for psycho-geriatric beds in hospital both because of the uncertainties of where and how these patients might be cared for, and the wishful thinking that seems to exist on the part of governments and peoples that the problem can be legislated out of existence. The Tripartite Committee in Britain recommends a 30-bed psycho-geriatric assessment unit for each 250,000 of total population, with a psycho-geriatric unit of 120-150 beds to meet the needs of the severely demented (75). The reader is referred to some of the literature sources for further details of this crucial but muddled area (47, 53, 67). It is easy to become lost in the attempts of fill practical needs.

Costs of Psycho-Geriatric Care in Hospital

The cost of caring for psycho-geriatric patients is difficult to calculate because of the wide differences between and within countries. Public mental hospitals have been used because they were the cheapest hospital available irrespective of what the patient's problem was. Unfortunately the cost was so cheap because the care was so poor. Good care costs money; poor care costs lives and sanity! At our public mental hospital the cost has multiplied 2.5 times in the past four years, although it is still less than one quarter of what private general or psychiatric hospitalization costs.

Research Opportunities and Goals

As there is still so little known about many of the psychiatric and social disorders of the elderly, and how they may best be dealt with, there is ample opportunity for basic and clinical research on psycho-geriatric services. There are the unfortunate stigma and history of dangerous and sometimes atrocious procedures being done to psycho-geriatric patients in the name of research with no regard for their feelings or wishes, as though they were rats in a cage. There has been very understandable protest to this. When carried on in a proper way by qualified investigators under the strict supervision of a research committee and with the knowledge and consent of the patient, research not only adds to our knowledge, but it usually upgrades the quality of service by increasing the amount of observation, interaction, and the feeling of both staff and patients that they are making a contribution to society and medicine.

Education and Training Functions of Psycho-Geriatric Hospitals

Comparatively few of those working with the elderly have had any specific training in the problems and techniques particular to that age group. Many of course have learned through vast experience or direct tutelage from another. There is at present only one formal psycho-geriatric training unit in the United States for graduate psychiatrists, which is a two-year program at Duke University Medical Center. The psycho-geriatric services of the mental hospitals of course provide a wealth of practical and clinical experiences. Regular psychiatric residents also rotate through the service for one- and two-month periods in order to learn management and diagnostic techniques. Our psycho-geriatric service also serves as a community training resource for a wide variety of people, including general practitioners, medical students, student nurses, social workers, rehabilitatin workers, nursing and boarding home personnel, and the aged themselves (77, 80).

Another important training function is the in-service teaching of the staff of the hospital. We have a 240-hour course three times a year for the attendant staff to give them a theoretical and a practical introduction to psycho-geriatrics. Not only does this improve the care that the patients receive, but it raises the morale of the staff as well. A teaching program almost always elevates the standard and quality of the care at a hospital. Complaints from the patients are few, and usually the response from them is positive, as it puts the elderly in the desirable role of teaching the young.

OUTCOMES AND REHABILITATION OF PSYCHO-GERIATRIC PATIENTS

Factors Affecting Outcome

The two primary factors affecting the outcome of the hospital course of psycho-geriatric patients are the nature of the initial problem and what is done or not done about it. On a traditional custodial ward, the average psycho-geriatric patient would probably have only a 5 to 10% chance of ever getting out. Formerly, of the elderly people who reached the state psychiatric hospital, 30% were dead in two months, 50% were dead in one year, and 75% were dead in two years. This death rate was much higher than that of similar people either at home or in a boarding facility (33). Many physically ill people have been sent to a psychiatric hospital, but as mentioned previously, this results in an excessive morbidity and mortality rate. From a psychiatric standpoint, those with affective disorders are very likely to get out, those with thought disorders are fairly likely to get out, and those with organic brain syndromes or physical disease are less likely to get out. Other favorable factors are an interested family and a previous good adjustment.

There is good rationale for intensive therapy, as those who are improved to the point of being releasable by three months are much more likely to get out and back into society than those whose hospitalization is more prolonged. In an active milieu program, about 50% of new admissions can be discharged within six months. There are some situations which make placement more difficult, such as physical or psychological impediments to change, staff rigidities and resistance to change, hospital policies and resistance, and finally the fact that there is no real community alternative to the environment of the hospital (10).

Factors in Patient Mortality

There are several variables which are related to high mortality among psycho-geriatric patients. The most consistent one is urinary or fecal incontinence, and the others are marked physical dependency, such as needing help to dress or get out of bed, and a severe degree of organic brain syndrome, as determined by clinical evaluation and the mental status questionnaire (35). The type of organic brain disease determines the longevity also, as the patient with cerebral arteriosclerosis will live on the average 3.8 years after the onset of the disease, while a patient with senile dementia will likely live 5.1 years after the beginning of the disorder (78).

Rehabilitation and Discharge

The goals of hospitalization of the psycho-geriatric patient are to provide the most effective treatment possible for the patient's disorders and to rehabilitate him as much as possible. Our basic assumption is that we will try to improve the patient to the point where he can leave the hospital, although we do not subscribe to the philosophy that patients be placed "in the community," no matter how terrible that is, simply to get them out of the hospital. Many elderly can expect a reasonable remission or even cure of their emotional conditions, while for others we feel that a slowing of the rate of disability and suffering is a significant and useful goal. For some, humane comfort and support are the best that can be achieved; and for some, help in dying with a degree of dignity is a valid achievement.

When a psycho-geriatric patient has improved in hospital to the point where he can be discharged, there should be a plan already in operation for his continuing care after he has left the hospital. In order to provide adequate care, including prevention for the elderly with mental disorder, there should be a spectrum of facilities and services, of which the psychiatric hospital is only one. The other services available should include a community mental health clinic, the general practitioner, other medical facilities, home nursing services, home help services, meals services, laundry services, physical and occupational therapy, telephone checking services, provisions for transportation, social welfare services, sheltered workshops, residential facilities including nursing care, homes for the aged, facilities for the confused, hotel type rooming, foster homes, and half-way house type dwellings.

Two other extremely important facilities would be the day care center and the day hospital such as described by Cosin (23). We have a day hospital system within our psychiatric hospital wherein psycho-geriatric patients from other areas come to our service to take part in the programs during the day. Unfortunately many areas have only part of these services available, but the adequate care of the aged should impel us to develop as many of the others as possible.

An interesting arrangement is described by Lear in which a number of psycho-geriatric patients advantageously spent alternate months in hospital and in the community by arrangement, hence effectively using each hospital bed for two patients (55). Planned respite and holiday care for an ailing elderly person in hospital may help a beleaguered family maintain their own sanity and integrity, and yet keep the sick person at home most of the time.

Among psycho-geriatric patients, the general ability of self-maintenance was noted by Simon et al. to be closely related to the patient's subsequent fate, and the patient's location one and two years after hospital admission was correlated with the type of psychiatric disorder (70). The patient's motivation is a factor, in that some patients are able to adapt in a situation which would be overwhelming or repugnant to others or to the therapist.

Most psycho-geriatric patients tend to let activities and gains made in hospital fall away unless there is some continuing input and social support for them in the community. The initial adjustment to a facility outside the hospital is crucial, especially the first week, so we usually give some medication to help sleep and reduce anxiety for the patient for a few nights, have some of the hospital staff visit him soon after discharge, and indicate to both the patient and to the responsible parties at the facility that the patient may return to the hospital immediately if severe problems arise. This tends to reduce the feeling of rejection and isolation in the patient, and increases the courage of many facility operators to risk having a mental patient with them. We are on telephone consultation call as well.

Coordination of Services

Matching the psycho-geriatric patient returning to the community to the most appropriate facilities is a major task, but the even greater one is getting the patient and needed services together and coordinated. A person should be designated the coordinator for the patient, and this individual is probably best a nurse or social worker. Gaitz and his group noted a number of obstacles in the delivery of effective follow-up services and care to the patient. Among these are communication difficulties, impairment of mobility, the tendency to stop medications prematurely, traits of stubbornness and suspiciousness in the patient, poverty, resistance from the family, difficulties in following diets, rigidity and territoriality on the parts of professionals and agencies, the unwillingness of doctors to treat the aged, the tendency of some nursing homes to oversedate a patient and keep him immobilized, trouble in getting to more than one medical clinic a day, overburdening with forms and red tape, and simple lack of facilities (29). Those elderly who can speak for themselves should be encouraged to do so, but those who are impaired will often need an advocate.

SUMMARY AND CONCLUSIONS

The care of elderly psychiatric patients in hospital has been reviewed. For many years little formal psychiatric care was available to the elderly outside of public mental hospitals, and the care in them was too often custodial in nature, meager in amount, and nihilistic in outlook. In this age group, the incidence of mental illness is extremely high. Fortunately recent new approaches to psycho-geriatrics have taken place, and we are discovering again that we can do much to treat their disorders.

Hospitalization can be a hazardous move, and prior evaluation of the sick person can help in the most appropriate utilization of resources. Accurate multidisciplinary hospital assessment of both psychiatric and physical disorders is a crucial step in diagnosing the elderly person's condition, and in formulating effective treatment plans. A broad spectrum of programs and facilities should be available, both in hospital and out, in order to provide appropriate treatment of psycho-geriatric patients. Only in this way can we hope to reduce the excessive disability of this group, and help make their remaining lives more independent, hopeful, dignified, and healthy.

REFERENCES

1. AGATE, J. N. 1970. *The Practice of Geriatrics* (2nd Edit.). Springfield: Charles C Thomas.
2. AMERICAN PSYCHIATRIC ASSOCIATION. 1965. *Remotivation Kit.* Washington, D.C.: American Psychiatric Association.
3. ANDREWS, J. 1970. Psychogeriatric assessment units. *Lancet,* 1:1004.
4. ANKUS, M., and QUARRINGTON, B. 1972. Operant behavior in the memory-disordered. *J. Geront.,* 27:500-510.
5. ANONYMOUS. 1970. Mental disorder in the elderly. *Lancet,* 2:867.
6. ANONYMOUS. 1971. Psychogeriatric care. *Brit. Med. J.,* 3:202-203.
7. ARIE, T. 1971. Morale and the planning of psychogeriatric services. *Brit. Med. J.,* 3:166-170.
8. BARTON, R. 1966. *Institutional Neurosis.* (2nd Edit.). Bristol: John Wright and Sons.
9. BLENKNER, M. 1968. The place of the nursing home among community resources. *J. Geriat. Psychiat.,* 1:135-144.
10. BOK, M. 1971. Some problems in milieu treatment of the chronic older mental patient. *Gerontologist,* 11:141-147.
11. BOXBERGER, R., and COTTER, V. W. 1968. Music therapy for geriatric patients. In: Gaston, E. T. (Ed.) *Music in Therapy.* New York: Macmillan.
12. BRITISH INFORMATION SERVICES. 1969. *Care of the Elderly in Britain.* R 5858/69. London: Central Office of Information.
13. BURROWES, H. P. 1970. Psychogeriatric assessment units. *Lancet,* 1:1121.
14. BURVILL, P. W. 1971. Consecutive psychogeriatric admissions to psychiatric and geriatric hospitals. *Geriatrics,* 26:156-157.
15. BUSSE, E. W. 1956. Treatment of the nonhospitalized, emotionally disturbed, elderly person. *Geriatrics,* 11:175-179.
16. BUSSE, E. W. 1960. Problems affecting psychiatric care of the aging. *Geriatrics,* 15:673-680.
17. BUSSE, E. W., DOVENMUEHLE, R. H., and BROWN, R. G. 1960. Psychoneurotic reactions of the aged. *Geriatrics,* 15:97-105.
18. BUSSE, E. W., and PFEIFFER, E. 1969. *Behavior and Adaptation in Late Life.* Boston: Little, Brown & Company.
19. CHEBOTAREV, D. F. 1972. Biological active agents ("Geriatrics") in prevention and treatment of premature aging. In: Chebotarev, D. F. (Ed.) *The Main Problems of Soviet Gerontology.* Material for the IX International Congress of Gerontology, Kiev.
20. CHIEN, C. P. 1971. Psychiatric treatment for geriatric patients: "pub" or drug? *Am. J. Psychiat.,* 127:1070-1075.
21. COMFORT, A. 1967. On gerontophobia. *Med. Opinion Rev.* September, pp. 30-37.
22. COONS, D. H. 1971. *Developing a Therapeutic Community. A Staff Training Series.* Ann Arbor: The University of Michigan Audio-Visual Education Center.
23. COSIN, L. 1965. The role of the geriatric day hospital. Paper of British Council for Rehabilitation of the Disabled. International Seminar.

24. DEPARTMENT OF HEALTH AND SOCIAL SECURITY. 1970. *Psychogeriatric Assessment Units.* Circular H. M. (70) 11. London: H.M.S.O.
25. DONAHUE, W. 1964. Aging: a historical perspective. In: *Research Utilization in Aging.* P.H.S. Publ. No. 1211. Washington, D.C.: Public Health Service.
26. DROLLER, H. 1969. Institutionalisation. In: Lowenthal, M. F. and Zilli, A. (Eds.) *Colloquium on Health and Aging of the Population.* Bern: Buchdruckerei Pochon-Jent AG.
27. EXTON-SMITH, A. N. and ROBINSON, K. V. 1970. Psychogeriatric assessment units. *Lancet,* 1:1292.
28. FOLSOM, J. C. 1968. Reality orientation for the elderly mental patient. *J. Geriat. Psychiat.,* 1:291-307.
29. GAITZ, C. M. and HACKER, S. 1970. Obstacles in coordinating services for the care of the psychiatrically ill aged. *J. Am. Geriat Soc,* 18·172·182.
30. GERICKE, O. L., LOBB, L. G., and ALLENGER, D. E. 1961. Nutritional supplementation for elderly patients in a state mental hospital: effect on appetite and weight gain. *J. Am. Geriat. Soc.,* 9:381-387.
31. GOFFMAN, E. 1961. *Asylums.* Garden City, N.Y.: Anchor Books, Doubleday & Company.
32. GOLD, J. G. 1970. Development of care of the elderly: tracing the history of institutional facilities. *Gerontologist,* 10:262-274.
33. GOLDFARB, A. I. 1964. An exploration of research findings. In: *Research Utilization in Aging.* PHS Public. No. 1211. Washington, D.C.: Public Health Service.
34. GOLDFARB, A. I. 1969. Institutional care of the aged. In: Busse, E. W. and Pfeiffer, E. (Eds.) *Behavior and Adaptation in Late Life.* Boston: Little, Brown & Company.
35. GOLDFARB, A. I. 1971. Predictors of mortality in the institutionalized aged. In: Palmore, E. and Jeffers, F. C. (Eds.) *Prediction of Life Span.* Lexington: Heath Lexington Books.
36. GOLDFARB, A. I., and TURNER, H. 1953. Psychotherapy of aged persons. II. Utilization and effectiveness of "brief" therapy. *Am. J. Psychiat.,* 109:916-921.
37. GOTTESMAN, L. E. 1967. The response of long-hospitalized aged psychiatric patients to milieu treatment. *Gerontologist,* 7:47-48.
38. GOTTESMAN, L. E. 1969. *Some results of milieu therapy for the aging mental patient.* Paper presented at the first workshop on Comprehensive Services for the Geriatric Mental Patient, Nov. 30 - Dec. 1. Washington, D.C.: Roche Laboratories.
39. GROUP FOR THE ADVANCEMENT OF PSYCHIATRY. 1970. *Toward a Public Policy on Mental Health Care of the Elderly.* Report No. 79. New York: Group for the Advancement of Psychiatry.
40. HADER, M., and SELTZER, H. A. 1967. La Salpétrière: an early home for elderly psychiatric patients. *Gerontologist,* 7:133-135.
41. HOWELLS, J. G. (Ed.). 1971. *The Organization of Psychogeriatrics.* S. C. P. Reports.
42. JONES, M. 1953. *The Therapeutic Community.* New York: Basic Books.
43. KAHANA, B. 1970. Changes in mental status of elderly patients in age-integrated and age-segregated hospital milieus. *J. Abnorm. Psychol.,* 75, 177-178.
44. KAHANA, E. and KAHANA, B. 1970. Therapeutic potential of age integration. Effects of age-integrated hospital environments on elderly psychiatric patients. *Arch. Gen. Psychiat.,* 23:20-29.
45. KAY, D. W. K., BEAMISH, P., and ROTH, M. 1964. Old age mental disorders in Newcastle upon Tyne. *Brit. J. Psychiat.,* 110:146-158.
46. KAY, D. W. K., BERGMAN, K., FOSTER, E. M., McKECHNIE, A. A., and ROTH, M. 1970. Mental illness and hospital usage in the elderly: a random sample followed up. *Comp. Psychiat.,* 11:26-35.

47. KAY, D. W. K., ROTH, M., and HALL, M. R. P. 1966. Special problems of the aged and the organization of hospital services. *Brit. Med. J.*, 2:867-972.
48. KIDD, C. B. 1962. Criteria for admission of the elderly to geriatric and psychiatric units. *J. Ment. Sci.*, 108:68-74.
49. KIDD, C. B. 1962. Misplacement of the elderly in hospital. *Brit. Med. J.*, 2:1491-1495.
50. KLEIN, W. H., LESHAN, E. J., and FURMAN, S. S. 1965. *Promoting Mental Health of Older People Through Group Methods.* New York: Manhattan Society for Mental Health.
51. KOBRYNSKI, B. and MILLER, A. D. 1970. The role of the state hospital in the care of the elderly. *J. Am. Geriat. Soc.*, 18:210-219.
52. KRAMER, M. 1963. Some problems for international research suggested by observations on differences in first admission rate to the mental hospitals of England and Wales and of the United States. In: *Proceedings, The Third World Congress of Psychiatry, Vol. III*, pp. 153-160. Montreal: McGill University Press.
53. KRAMER, M., TAUBE, C., and STARR, S. 1968. Patterns of use of psychiatric facilities by the aged: current status, trends, and implications. In: Simon, A. and Epstein, L. (Eds.), *Aging in Modern Society.* Washington, D. C.: American Psychiatric Association.
54. LANGLEY, G. E., and SIMPSON, J. H. 1970. Misplacement of the elderly in geriatric and psychiatric hospitals. *Geront. Clin.*, 12:149-163.
55. LEAR, T. E. 1969. Sharing the care of the elderly between community and hospital. *Lancet*, 2:1349-1353.
56. LEHMANN, H. E. 1972. Psychopharmacological aspects of geriatric medicine. In: Gaitz, C. M. (Ed.) *Aging and the Brain.* New York: Plenum Press.
57. LINDEN, M. E. 1953. Architecture for psychogeriatric installations. Paper presented at the First Mental Hospital Institute.
58. LINDEN, M. E. 1953. Group psychotherapy with institutionalized senile women. II. Study in gerontologic human relations. *Int. J. Group Psychother.*, 3:150-170.
59. LOWENTHAL, M. F. 1964. *Lives in Distress.* New York: Basic Books.
60. LOWENTHAL, M. F., BERKMAN, P. L., and ASSOCIATES. 1967. *Aging and Mental Disorder in San Francisco.* San Francisco: Jossey-Bass.
61. MACMILLAN, D., and SHAW, P. 1966. Senile breakdown in standards of personal and environmental cleanliness. *Brit. Med. J.*, 11:1032-1037.
62. MARKSON, E. 1971. A hiding place to die. *Transaction*, Dec.:48-54.
63. MARTIN, M. 1962. *The Mental Ward.* Springfield, Ill.: Charles C Thomas.
64. MAXWELL, J. M. 1962. *Centers for Older People.* New York: National Council on Aging.
65. MEERLOO, J. A. M. 1961. Modes of psychotherapy in the aged. *J. Am. Geriat. Soc.*, 9:225-234.
66. MUELLER, D. J., and ATLAS, L. 1972. Resocialization of regressed elderly residents: a behavioral management approach. *J. Geront.*, 27:390-392.
67. PARNELL, R. W. 1968. Prospective geriatric bed requirements in a mental hospital. *Geront. Clin.*, 10:30-36.
68. POST, F. 1965. *The Clinical Psychiatry of Late Life.* London: Pergamon Press.
69. SCOTTISH HEALTH SERVICES COUNCIL. 1970. *Services for the Elderly with Mental Disorder.* Edinburgh: Scottish Home and Health Department.
70. SIMON, A., LOWENTHAL, M. F., and EPSTEIN, L. J. 1970. *Crisis and Intervention.* San Francisco: Jossey-Bass, Inc.
71. STOTSKY, B. A. 1968. *The Elderly Patient.* New York: Grune & Stratton.
72. TAYLOR, G. F. 1968. A clinical survey of elderly people from a nutritional stand-

point. In: Exton-Smith, A. N. and Scott, D. L. (Eds.), *Vitamins in the Elderly*. Bristol: John Wright & Sons.

73. TOWNSEND, P. 1962. *The Last Refuge*. London: Rutledge, Kegan & Paul.
74. TREATMENT TEAM. 1965. Attitude therapy and the team approach. *Mental Hospitals*, Nov.:307-323.
75. TRIPARTITE COMMITTEE. 1972. *The Mental Health Service After Unification*. London: British Medical Association.
76. U.S. DEPARTMENT OF HEALTH, EDUCATION, AND WELFARE. 1968. *Patients in Mental Institutions. 1966. Part II: State and County Mental Hospitals*. Public Health Service Publication No. 1818, Part. II. Washington, D.C.
77. VERWOERDT, A. 1971. Clinical geropsychiatry. In: Chinn, A. B. (Ed.), *Working with Older People. Vol. IV. Clinical Aspects of Aging*. U.S. Dept. of H. E. W., P.H.S. Publ. No. 1459. Washington, D.C.: Public Health Service.
78. WANG, H. S., and WHANGER, A. D. 1971. Brain impairment and longevity. In: Palmore, E., and Jeffers, F. C. (Eds.) *Prediction of Life Span*. Lexington: Heath Lexington Books.
79. WEINTRAUB, W., and ARONSON, H. 1968. A survey of patients in classical psychoanalysis: some vital statistics. *J. Nerv. Ment. Dis.*, 146:98-102.
80. WHANGER, A. D. 1971. Geriatric mental health in North Carolina. *N. C. J. Ment. Health.*, 5:43-49.
81. WHANGER, A. D. 1973. When should a mentally ill older person be sent to the hospital? In: Busse, E. W., and Pfeiffer, E. (Eds.) *Mental Illness in Later Life*. Washington, D.C.: American Psychiatric Association.
82. WHANGER, A. D., and WANG, H. S. 1974. Vitamin B_{12} deficiency in normal aged and elderly psychiatric patients. In: Palmore, E. (Ed.) *Normal Aging II*. Durham: Duke University Press.
83. WHANGER, A. D. 1973. Vitamins and vigor at 65 plus. *Postgrad. Med.*, 53:167-172.
84. WHITEHEAD, J. A. 1970. Services for old people with mental symptoms. *Lancet*, 2:1309.
85. WOLFF, K. 1970. *The Emotional Rehabilitation of the Geriatric Patient*. Springfield: Charles C Thomas.
86. WORLD HEALTH ORGANIZATION. 1972. *Psychogeriatrics*. Wld. Hlth. Org. Techn. Rep. Ser. No. 507. Geneva: WHO.

22

CARE IN THE COMMUNITY

John Cumming, M.D.

Psychiatric Consultant, Community Care Services Society,
Victoria, B.C., Canada

and

Elaine Cumming, Ph.D.

Professor and Chairman, Department of
Anthropology and Sociology, University of Victoria, B.C., Canada

INTRODUCTION

Everyone agrees that old people are happiest in familiar surroundings among family and friends. Almost everyone agrees that they should be helped to stay in their own homes as long as possible even when they are ill or disabled. Nevertheless, many old people who are taken to nursing homes, hospitals, or mental hospitals when they are ill or disturbed never return home even when they recover. Townsend (41) reports that in Britain in 1961 eight percent of persons over 75 years were in long stay institutions, while in the United States, the corresponding figure was seven percent.

In this chapter, we will first describe a specific example of what appears to be a general and widespread attempt to reduce the numbers of old people needlessly living out their lives in institutions, and we will then describe some of the community services that have been found useful in that attempt.

We will conclude our chapter with some speculations about why the

486

ideal of a full range of services for the elderly in their homes remains so far from the reality of too many old people underserved and overplaced.

In North America, the proportion of people over 65 in the population has been increasing throughout the 20th century, and this proportion is not expected to stabilize until the year 2050 at the very earliest. In the United States the population doubled during the 20th century, but at the same time the proportion of old people increased by nearly sevenfold. If Blenkner's (3) estimate that 15-20% of old people are mentally impaired is correct, there were as many old people needing some kind of psychiatric care in 1970 as there were old people altogether in 1900. In short, the problem of providing appropriate care is a big one, and can be expected to get bigger.

According to Blenkner (2), all old people develop certain "normal dependencies." Chronic illnesses, decreased mobility, and faulty memory are only the commonest of the deficits that cause older people to need help. Many old people compensate for these normal changes by making deliberate changes in their life-style; if they can no longer climb the stairs to the third floor, for example, they may proceed to find a ground floor apartment or an apartment house with an elevator, or they may turn to family or friends for help in finding it. Although the family is the mainstay of the elderly person in need of help, not all have families, and certain new American urban patterns such as the migration of young families to the suburbs leaving their elderly relatives living alone in the city center have made family help less available. Furthermore, the decreased age of marriage and the early termination of childbearing have left some very elderly people dependent on children who are themselves becoming chronically ill and in need of help (23). Because of these shifts in family and household patterns, there may be an important increase in the numbers needing protective services from public sources. Unfortunately, there are relatively few public resources available to old people in American communities. Blenkner points out that even when everyday kinds of assistance are set up, they are organized on a scale sufficient to serve only a small minority, whereas they are likely to be needed at some time by *any* elderly person. Shanas (40) and her co-workers have highlighted the lack of community services of every kind to old people in America in the course of comparing the lives of older people in the United States with their counterparts in England and Denmark.

The most important characteristic of old people in America by 1970 was that they were poor. Despite widening coverage by both social security and private pension plans, inflation and increasing life span had left the older citizen in relative poverty. From one-third to one-quarter of all of the poor were old people, a tremendous over-representation, about which little was being done. To quote Blenkner:

> American society and American social work are not comfortable about the aged in their midst, and they should not be. In comparison with the elderly living in other advanced industrial societies, the older people of the United States live in greater relative poverty and are offered social services that are deplorably underdeveloped, especially community delivered services (3).

Linked to the lack of community services was an automatic overuse of institutional care for old people, often when they did not require it.

CHANGES IN THE USE OF HOSPITALIZATION FOR THE "MENTALLY ILL" ELDERLY

Changes in Attitude Toward Hospitalization

Up until the 1960's in most of the United States, the mental hospital was used as a primary service for old people whether or not they were mentally ill. During the 1960's, however, one state government after another reversed the policies of its mental hospitals of admitting all of the old people who were referred to them. In retrospect, it is hard to understand the reasons for this change. Each jurisdiction seemed to find its own justifications as it made its policy decisions. The shift was probably determined by a number of factors: First, the number of elderly people at risk of hospitalization was increasing rapidly and few additional funds were available for either capital expenditure or for maintaining treatment programs; second, new federal government funds for nursing home care and for extended care facilities associated with general hospitals for the chronically ill became available; third, because of the virtual absence of community care, many old people who were unable to continue living alone were using nursing home beds and extended care facilities in hospitals and thus producing an artificial shortage of these places. For all of these and perhaps other reasons, overplacement became so common that restrictions on the use of mental hospital beds began to appear. This trend seems to have been nearly universal in North America.

Change in the Province of Ontario

The Canadian province of Ontario responded to the problem with a three-step program designed to cut back admissions to mental hospitals.

First, certain parts of mental hospitals were designated as "residential areas" so that "their social rather than medical function (would not be) disguised just because persons live under a hospital roof." This move was followed by the passage of the Homes for Special Care Act, 1964, which provided financial aid to approved homes for the care and maintenance of suitable patients. Hospitals themselves began to operate Residential Approved Homes (7). While patients may not have sensed any real difference when their part of the hospital was renamed as a residential area, an entirely new level of service was being developed in other parts of the program. We will consider these Ontario programs later when we discuss community care in more detail.

The reaction against the overuse of institutions seen so clearly in Ontario had counterparts in many parts of the United States.

Change in New York State

In 1967, in New York State, approximately two mental hospital beds per 1000 of general population were occupied by patients over 65 years of age, an exceptionally high figure. Elderly patients were being admitted at a rate of about 8000 per year or 40 for every 100,000 of population. The 20 large state hospitals into which these old people were going were grossly overcrowded, understaffed, and dilapidated, as well as lacking in privacy and the other amenities that anyone would wish for himself in old age.

From a common sense point of view alone these levels of mental hospitalization were too high. It was not surprising that a carefully conducted survey of all old people in institutions in one county (33) found excessive numbers of the patients to be overplaced; the proportion varied from 95% in the State Hospital to 30% in nursing homes. At the time that a change in policy was being planned, one State Hospital, located in New York City, began a trial program of screening elderly patients at admission and rejecting those who were physically ill or in social difficulties but not mentally ill (17). As this trial program presented a natural experiment, a study of the outcome of screening was mounted, using as a control an equal group of elderly patients from an adjacent district all of whom had been admitted to a hospital that accepted all patients who were referred.

The contrasting fate of these two groups of patients began to make clear the inadequacy of the services available to these old people. Of a group of 174 patients, aged over 65, who were consecutively admitted to the open-admissions hospital, 44 died within 30 days and their deaths were associated with illnesses obviously present at the point of admission. Less than half these patients could walk unaided at the time of hospitalization and nearly 20% were bedfast, including 6% who were comatose. The great majority of this group had come directly from either a general hospital or a psychiatric receiving hospital. Their admission probably reflected a widespread belief among hospital administrators and physicians that a general hospital is an "expensive" place to give service while a state hospital is "cheap," although any treatment in the same labor market probably costs very much the same whatever the setting. Markson (28), in reporting this study, suggests that the high rate of institutionalization of frail people was related not only to the lack of appropriate home nursing care, but also to an unwillingness on the part of Americans to engage themselves with the process of dying.

The high death rate experienced by elderly patients at the mental hospital under study is not unusual. Similar rates have been described in other places (22, 25). In general, old people who enter mental hospitals appear to die at higher than the corresponding age-sex specific death rates. Some authors blame the obvious inadequacies of the state hospitals for these high death rates but when the experience of the patients from the open-admissions hospital was compared with that of the group from the screening hospital, death was found to be unrelated to either screening or hospitalization. Death was, however, related to age and, as expected, sex, and to frailty at the time of screening or admission. Thus, the fact of admission to hospital appeared not to influence the patients' chances of survival.

One effect of easy hospitalization was, however, made clear by this study: At the time of follow-up, 76% of the survivors of the group admitted to the open-admissions hospital were still there while only 24% of those who were seen at the screening hospital had been admitted to that or any other mental hospital. Among both groups, the majority (61% of the screening hospital group and 75% of the open-admissions group) were judged not in need of mental hospital care but definitely in need of care at home or in a nursing home.

Results of these preliminary evaluations suggested that the patients had been caught in a vicious circle: Lack of services in the community had led to excessive admissions which in turn had led to large resident populations who did not need mental hospital care but who were very difficult to re-locate in communities where services were unavailable. This situation was obviously undesirable. On the one hand, visitors to these wards were constantly approached by patients pleading to be allowed to go home, and on the other hand hospital care was costing more than a more appropriate service in the community would have.

In the light of these studies, the Department of Mental Hygiene in 1968 instructed the directors of their state hospitals as follows:

> . . . We . . . request the Directors . . . to scrutinize more closely the condition of persons who are candidates for admission to their hospitals and to determine prior to their admission whether such persons are suitable for care and treatment. . . . Patients should not be admitted when their problems are primarily social, medical, or financial or for the convenience of some other care facility. . . . (Division of Mental Health Memorandum, 68-27, June, 1968).

As can be guessed, this move caused considerable disruption in the referring practices of the general and receiving hospitals and was followed by both professional and political protest. The new policy, although designed to redress a wrong being done to many old people, resulted in a severe strain on the scant community resources available. Because of the protest from the referring sources, a study of the fates of patients rejected by the hospitals was undertaken in 1970. Before describing this study, however, a few words must be said about a strikingly similar experience in California which had some influence on the character of the New York policy.

Change in California

In 1964, members of the Department of Mental Hygiene in California decided to study the effects of providing a community service to old people living in San Francisco who were in immediate danger of being committed to a state hospital (6). A team of a psychiatrist, an internist, and two social workers was formed for the purpose of both assessing and assisting those old people on whose behalf an application for admission to state hospital had been made. The admission of an elderly person to a California State Hospital requires court action, and the relevant court agreed not to commit the prospective patient until the team had seen him and decided that there was no alternative to mental hospital care. Members of the team, usually one of the physicians and a social worker, saw and assessed the patients, wherever possible in their own homes. This team, like a number of others, perhaps most notably MacMillan's in Nottingham (27), found many medical, social and financial problems, some of which they were able to solve with the help of existing local agencies. Mental hospital care was rarely found to be needed, although some patients were judged to require care in other institutions. Nursing home care provided a solution to most problems.

Prior to the establishment of this community service, there had been about 500 admissions a year to mental hospitals from San Francisco. In the third year of the service, there were only four such admissions. During the same period, admissions to San Francisco *County* hospital dropped from more than 700 to less than 300. This latter group of old people probably included a group who really needed mental hospital care as well as people who could not wait for the screening team, which did not work on weekends, but who might have been able to remain out of hospital if care had been available at the time of crisis.

Epstein and Simon (14) compared this group of patients a year after screening with a similar group who had been studied at a time when many more went to state mental hospitals. The two groups were found to be in roughly similar circumstances except that almost half of the patients screened by the team were in nursing homes and virtually none were in mental hospitals while about one-third of the earlier group was in mental hospital. Epstein concluded that nursing homes had to some extent replaced the mental hospital. Using a number of criteria, however, he concluded that the nursing home failed to establish itself as superior to the state hospital. Both settings were materially impoverished and lacking in social stimulation.

Addition of a Community Service in New York

In New York State, following the mandate to the Directors of State Hospitals to become more selective in their admission of old people, it soon became clear that services similar to those utilized by the California teams would have to be added. Many old people seeking hospital admission had already lost the ties to friends and families necessary to support them in the community; new services would have to be found if they were to stay out of hospital. To this end, a system of service-oriented Mobile Geriatric Teams was introduced. These teams made home visits to assess the patients, to provide medication, and to set up a routine for continued monitoring where this was necessary. Day services were provided by hospitals in which some of the teams were based and referral to other medical and social agencies in the community was used wherever possible. Although there was no way to increase the number and variety of community services available, as they fell under many other jurisdictions and no coordination seemed possible, the teams were expected to make better use of the few resources that did exist.

During the two years immediately following the new policy, admission of old people to mental hospitals in New York State dropped from about 8000 a year to about half that number. Kobrynski and Cumming reported (24) that there was also a substantial drop in geriatric mortality in the hospitals. Two state hospitals without mobile geriatric teams also showed a decline in geriatric population, admissions and mortality but to a lesser degree than the 12 hospitals that had developed teams. In spite of this success, there was considerable community opposition to the policy. While controversy tended to decrease with time, discontent persisted and finally erupted as a political dispute (5, 32). Because of continuous pressure from hospitals, doctors and politicians, and because of the desire of the state itself to be sure of the results of its own policy, a study of the patients who had been refused admission to a hospital was mounted in 1970 by the Mental Health Research Unit of the Department of Mental Hygiene (31). Four hospital districts were selected as a rough representation of a state that varies from densely urban to completely rural. In none of the hospitals was the number of old people excluded by the screening team equal to the number admitted. The ratio varied from three exclusions for every four admissions to one exclusion for every four admissions. A follow-up interview was conducted with the patient, or if this was impossible, with a relative or caretaker, at an average of six months after screening.

Overall, about 20% of the patients in each of the four groups had died. Of the remainder, about 10% were found in state hospitals and another 40% were in institutions other than state hospitals. Although a larger proportion of the New York City group was found in the community, probably because of lack of nursing home places, in the remaining three districts, the story was the familiar one of patients being both overplaced and underserved. No systematic information about the actual availability of supporting services in the community could be found by the research team, but it was obvious that the old people themselves had no knowledge of, or access to, services such as "meals on wheeels," loaning services where they might borrow wheel chairs, walkers, hospital beds and so on, friendly visiting services or telephone monitoring services. Less than 10% knew of home helpers and only a tiny handful mentioned recreational facilities.

Most of the patients described their attempts to find relief from their problems in terms of a search for medical, nursing, or institutional care.

This finding exactly mirrored Blenkner's description of the overall American situation. The field workers often found the patients in a shocking state of physical deprivation whether they were living in the community or in nursing homes. In short, as Epstein and Simon had pointed out in California, there is little gain for the patients in having had their admission to a mental hospital prevented. While some comfort could be found in the fact that almost no old people want to be in mental hospitals, the New York State policy-making group felt that is was time to face the fact that in the United States for nearly everyone over 65 who was sick and poor, all solutions were bad. Even the research group was so upset by their findings that their final reports included an editorial preface which read in part:

> Members of this research unit have in the past conducted researches into the situation of the *well* elderly, and we, like other workers, have found that most older people are fairly comfortably fitted into their social and personal environments. For the past three years, however, we have at all times had in progress some research into the problems of the *ill* elderly. Throughout that period, our field workers have battered us with stories of what they have seen in the course of carrying out their assignments: . . . deprivation, misery, squalor and despair, most of it caused by not enough money and not enough public and official concern.
>
> . . . Not only are too many people dreadfully poor . . . the halls of many of their apartment houses are strewn with garbage and some days they do not eat . . . but their own timidity stands in the way of their getting the little help to which they are entitled. It is here that official callousness is most visible.
>
> In nursing homes, with honorable exceptions, the reports are not much better. The tragedy for most old people is that they never wanted to be in them and that once in they are neglected. In some nursing, rest, and adult homes, there is physical neglect. Some (relatives of patients) told us that they suspected that the patient was not getting enough to eat. We were often told that they were never out of bed. Some patients have bedsores. The general problem is understimulation and this in turn is related to lack of program which must in the end be blamed on the fact that most nursing homes are either run for profit or by local governments in the most economical style possible. . . .
>
> . . . Our studies have led us to feel that for this small group of the poor and sick elderly, all alternatives are bad (31).

There is no reason to believe that the mobile geriatric team was not performing a useful function, but the ill elderly need a wide variety of services, many of them quite simple, if they are to be kept in the community, and these were just not there.

COMMUNITY SERVICES FOR THE ELDERLY

Nursing Homes, Intermediate Care, and Family Homes

The goal of community services should be to keep the elderly patient in his own home if he wants to be there. Sometimes, however, this is just not possible. As Kay and Roth (21) point out, demented old people put more strain on their families than most are able to bear.

The service most commonly used after community resources have been exhausted is the nursing home, and these facilities are often used in lieu of mental hospitalization. Unfortunately, as our studies in New York and Townsend's studies in Great Britain have shown, many nursing homes are inadequate environments for old people who have any mental deficits.

Nursing homes are plagued with the same problems as mental hospitals: First, a nursing home is an overplacement for many patients sent there; second, because they are defined as providing nursing care to a physically ill, largely bedfast, population, the type of care they give tends in itself to make ambulant patients bedfast. In the United States, most nursing homes are proprietory, that is, run for profit. Many, therefore, lack staff and program just as the state hospitals do. There are some exceptions to this grim picture, especially among those non-profit nursing homes run by religious organizations. The practice of running nursing homes for profit has traditionally been found acceptable in the United States. Blenkner, however, has pointed out the danger of groups having a vested interest in a single method of care, and she fears that this may at times prevent the development of better alternatives.

Because nursing home places are relatively expensive, there has been some development of "intermediate care homes" designed to provide custody and minimal supervision for those old people who are relatively healthy and mobile but who cannot live alone. Unfortunately such placements are still comparatively few, at least in the United States, and they usually suffer from the same lack of program as the nursing homes they are supposed to replace. It cannot be emphasized too much that many old people need the stimulation of active programs if they are not to deteriorate mentally.

Another type of service designed to meet the need of old people for shelter, assistance and supervision is the family care program. Family care programs are in a way direct descendents from Gheel, the town in Belgium whose citizens provided lodgings for mentally ill patients who were brought to the shrine of St. Dymphna.

In the 19th century the American reformer Dorothea Dix returned from Scotland enthusiastic about the "Scottish Method" of placing mentally ill patients in family homes. While there was one contemporary paper reported in the *American Journal of Insanity,* the movement seems to have aborted and Crutcher in 1944 refers to a "new upsurge in interest in family care" (9). She reports that programs had been developed in nine states and the Canadian province of Ontario as if this were a completely new phenomenon. Apparently the pressure for the family care that Crutcher was describing had arisen at least in part from the continuing growth in hospital populations. She reports that at that time in New York State there were about 1200 mental patients in family care, or about 2% of the hospital population. Nearly 30 years after Crutcher's report, the numbers in family care were almost identical although they included a larger proportion of old people.

When the number of patients assigned to one family is kept relatively small, and when there are activities and a system of supervision, there is every reason to believe that patients are better off than in either hospitals or nursing homes.

Resdorfer (38) describes a study of the inclusion of a geriatric group among the 130 patients in a family care program. Since a quarter of the patients had been in family care for more than five years, the program was judged to be quite successful. All patients were seen at least once a month by a doctor at which time psychotropic medications, supplied by the hospital, were renewed. Some patients were also visited between the monthly drug supervisions, and all were encouraged to attend a weekly get-together at the hospital's day center, located in the community. Many patients were found to be taking part in the lives of the homes in which they stayed, participating in such household tasks as gardening and housework. Although Resdorfer's description does not give the impression of sufficient activity, experience would suggest that the patients probably preferred it to hospital life.

Programs for Enrichment of Life in the Community

Many observers feel that elderly patients should not be moved from mental hospital to the community because they hold that hospital life is more richly textured, filled with arts and crafts, parties, films and useful work. While most of these activities are indeed available, both clinical experience and research reports of activity on geriatric wards indicate that they reach a small minority of these patients. It is our experience that when an old patient who has been in the hospital for a long time conquers his fear and consents to return to the community, he almost always wants to remain there even when he lives in what appears to be an environment lacking in stimulation.

In various New York State cities, persons who receive public assistance payments are housed in old hotels. Since they have little money, they usually have a bleak existence. Several concerned groups, such as the psychiatric department of Roosevelt Hospital, have introduced both piecework and recreational activities into these hotels. While it is hard to evaluate such programs, the sponsors reported an enthusiastic reception by the elderly residents. Response was disappointing, however, when an experimental psychiatric day center was introduced into a new group housing project for the elderly in a different city. This program was to give preventive psychiatric care rather than treatment, and its director and staff anticipated using discussion and activity groups as well as counselling with the individual elderly residents who were mainly non-married and thus at fairly high risk of eventual hospitalization. The program was terminated because of under-utilization. A third project providing medical care in a public housing unit for the elderly residents was well received and heavily patronized.

These experiences suggest that functionally specific services as well as activities that call on familiar skills and knowledge may be better received than general "counselling," but also that older people's needs are more complex than we have been assuming. Much more should be learned about both variations in the older group themselves and variations in the types of medical care and social stimulation needed to keep them in social and psychological as well as physical equilibrium. The friendly visitor (1) is probably the most ubiquitous service designed to improve the quality of daily life for old people. Unfortunately such programs often fail to reach the more seclusive and unresponsive people who need them most.

The Outpatient Psychiatric Clinic

The under-use of outpatient clinics by the elderly is a conundrum. A Group for the Advancement of Psychiatry report (20) reveals that only 2% of the patients served in outpatient mental health clinics in the United States are over 65, a figure that compares poorly with the 10% of the population who are in that age range. A study of patients who were terminated in New York State outpatient clinics between 1964 and 1967 (30) indicated that only about 1.5% of these terminations involved patients over 60 years of age. While this number increased in subsequent years as a result of very considerable pressure applied to the clinics by the funding agency, the proportion of old people never came close to the proportion of the elderly in the population.

There are a number of stereotypes about the mentally disturbed elderly patient, a common one being that the rigidities of old age preclude the possibility of effective psychotherapy. Since many clinics regard individual psychotherapy as their main therapeutic tool, it seems reasonable that old people are somehow "discouraged" from requesting outpatient clinic service. It was found, however, in the study of clinic terminations in New York that the number who received intake services only, that is were considered unsuitable for treatment, actually declined with increasing age within the elderly group. Furthermore, 70% of those over 60 remained on the clinic's rolls after the initial examination, receiving either diagnostic or treatment services, the most usual treatment being "psychotherapy and drugs." This rate of acceptance into treatment compares favorably with that achieved by those less than 60 years of age.

Further evidence of the incorrectness of the assumption that the elderly will not respond to psychotherapy can be found in the literature. Butler (4) has found that most elderly patients respond well to psychotherapy; he suggests those old patients who are too rigid for this treatment may always have been so. Goldfarb (18) and Peck (35) have defended the use of psychoanalytic approaches with elderly patients and Butler mentions a review of the literature on this subject by Rechtshaffen (37) in which the overall satisfaction of practitioners with the results of psychotherapy with the aged patient is confirmed.

There is reason to believe that psychotherapists have much to offer older patients, and that outpatient clinics do indeed produce services when they are approached. Perhaps the impression that the clinics refuse such patients comes from elderly patients not approaching the clinics. We do not know the reasons for such a failure, but it is probably over-determined. The elderly patient might think that the clinic did not welcome him, on the one hand, while on the other hand he might have serious problems in getting to the clinic. At the time of the study cited above, transportation was technically available in New York State through the public Medicare and Medicaid programs, but this fact was known to very few people and the complications in arranging for the necessary funds were considerable.

Finally, as Blenkner has pointed out, the more service contacts an elderly person has the more likely is he to be placed in an institution, and many elderly people may know or sense this. In the study from which we have been quoting, for example, while less than 20% of the patients terminated at the clinics were referrals to any other agency, when they were it was likely to be the state hospital. It is as if old people guessed that their best insurance against an unwanted service was to ask for no service at all.

The Geriatric Day Center

While the numbers of geriatric day centers and day hospitals increased in Great Britain during the 60's, presumably because they were an effective way to treat this group, they remained relatively uncommon in North America. Descriptions of British services by Farndale (15), Cosin (8), and Robertson and Pitt (39), are particularly valuable. A survey of day hospitals in the United States published in 1964 by Epps and Hanes (13), failed to find any day centers exclusively for old people. An early report of a psycho-geriatric day center was made by Goldstein, Sevriuk and Grauer in 1968 (19), who reported a service at Maimonides Day Hospital in Montreal. The Geriatric Day Service of the Fort Logan Mental Health Center in Denver, Colorado, may have been earlier but we lack a published description.

Activities at the Montreal center were similar to those of a "Golden Age Club," or social-recreational club for the elderly, except that the patients were impaired enough not to be able to participate comfortably in an ordinary recreational club. Some of the experience in Montreal is instructive; while the service was designed for about 75 patients, utilization seems to have been closer to 30, which is close to the attendance reported by a number of similar centers. There may be a reason for attendance hovering around this figure, and in situations where more than 30 places seem needed, two separately organized centers might be more successful.

Goldstein and his co-workers emphasize the advantage of a close attachment between a day care center and an inpatient hospital that can both provide some of the candidates for the center and serve as a back-up when temporarily increased care is needed.

Workers in North American geriatric centers have almost all found that they must make transportation available to the patients. The Montreal service had their own bus; in Syracuse, New York, a day center made a contract with a local taxi firm to bring their patients. The bill, in this case, was paid by Medicaid, but the cost of transportation is such a small proportion of the total cost that it raises the question of why so many American programs are frustrated for lack of support.

The staff of the Maimonides Center in Montreal found hostile, paranoid patients and those with the more severe chronic brain syndromes difficult to manage in their recreational type of day setting, and so excluded them at the point of application. At the same time, they suggested that such patients would be manageable in a center more specifically designed for them. Many of the patients who were admitted to this program were said to develop a great dependency on the center and the staff found it very difficult to reduce their attendance when it seemed clinically indicated; therefore these authors recommended that all patients be started with the minimum feasible number of sessions per week and then increased if necessary.

In contrast to the Maimonides Center, McDonald et al. (29) report that in the Syracuse Day Center much more severely impaired patients were admitted. Their efforts focused on programs specifically designed to enhance the patients' orientations to time, place and person, and to increase both awareness of the environment and the skills necessary to deal with it. The same was true of the Fort Logan Day Center. Such programs were based on the "reality orientation" techniques introduced by Folsom (16). These methods are applied in a group setting where the patient is "taught" more and more about himself and his environment. In addition, the Syracuse center had the usual crafts and recreational programs. The Fort Logan program had similar aims although the group sessions were less structured and more devoted to recent events in the lives of the patients than to more generally useable data such as dates and place names.

Both of these programs reported success in terminating patients when they were sufficiently improved to no longer need the program, and did not find the intense dependency reported by the Montreal group. We feel that the use of structured group learning tasks can be recommended both because it is often successful in reaching carefully defined clinical goals and because the patients enjoy it. The Syracuse program reported, for example, that of 139 patients served, only 14 refused to attend more than a few sessions. This is a considerably lower loss rate than is reported by many day hospitals serving a middle-aged group.

In summary, there is every indication that day centers are a relatively inexpensive yet effective way to treat the elderly psychiatric patient, and it is not easy to explain the paucity of existing facilities.

Protective Services in the Community

Perhaps the best statement of the need for protective services has been given by Blenkner. She defines protective services as those provided to old people whose "memory, orientation and judgment appear so faulty or whose perception of reality is so distorted that one questions their ability to perform effectively the simple act of day-to-day living." The significance of such deficits is clearly related to the environment in which the old person finds himself. If he has appropriate housing, a family to take responsibility for him, friends willing to assist him, and access to a variety of helping services, his incapacities will be infinitely less serious than if he lives alone in poverty and with few human contacts. Failure to cope with the problems of lessened capacity, either through self-adaptation or with the assistance of others, is one important reason for institutionalization.

Sometimes when an old person has an acute condition involving deficits of memory, orientation and judgment, or even distorted perception, it can be quelled with appropriate treatment, and he will be able to manage without assistance. Furthermore, there is evidence that retraining or rehabilitation will stabilize and even improve the mental status of some elderly people with chronic afflictions. If such stabilized patients still need assistance, however, we have to be able to mobilize environmental supports of one sort or another for them.

Basic life supports are generally available to old people in most communities if they know how to obtain them. Yet a fragmented system often results in the old person needing the assistance of a friend or the services of an advocate in order to get the financial support, housing, and medical care that he needs. For this reason and others, old people should always have ready access to legal advice. Unfortunately, as with other services, the older person often does not know how to mobilize services for which he is eligible. It might be sensible to incorporate a general referring service into a friendly visitor's role.

Besides the basics of food, shelter, and medical care, old people may need assistance within their own homes. They may need supervision for a medical regimen and sometimes actual bedside nursing care. They may be too frail to do heavy housekeeping or too handicapped to prepare all their own meals. They may need someone to shop for them, to bring them things to read, or to assist them in getting to recreation. They may need someone to help them bathe or cut their toenails. Finally, old people may want and need to be involved in some sort of friendly interaction with others in order to bring texture and satisfaction to their lives. All of these services are in themselves simple; it is the nature of the deficits of old age that many such simple services are needed if equilibrium is to be maintained.

These simple services have names that vary from place to place. The clinician should learn the services in his own area. Helping old people to get what is their due is variously known as ombudsman, walk-in center, information center for the elderly, out-reach program, and so on. The in-home services are referred to as home helps, meals-on-wheels, public health nursing, and visiting nurse services. Interactive needs are met by friendly visitors, and for those who are mobile, by community social clubs for the elderly. A daily telephone call service to old people who live alone is another simple protective service that can help prevent hospitalization. Sometimes police departments can do this.

Many old people need these services only occasionally, for instance, during a transient illness. Some need such help, either through relatives and friends or from public sources, quite regularly.

Cumming (10) studied a home care nursing service located in a public housing unit for the elderly in Syracuse, New York. She found that although the major activity of the nurses was quite naturally nursing, they also performed an invaluable function in mobilizing and coordinating other services. Arrangements for service were made with all kinds of medical and nursing services as well as druggists, podiatrists, laboratory services, and firms that supplied eyeglasses and hearing aids. These nurses also made arrangements with clergymen, social workers, lawyers and veterans' organizations, as well as friendly visitors and recreational services. Contacts were made with sheltered workshops, services for the blind and even employment agencies. Contact on behalf of the old people was made with the public assistance office, with retirement funds, with the Red Cross, with the housing authorities and with an agency that lent wheel chairs, crutches and other aids for the disabled. Finally, the staff of the service helped make arrangements with nursing homes, mental hospitals and funeral directors. The length of this list is evidence of the wide variety of assistance old people need. Blenkner estimates that about 5-7% of all old people need these and other services.

In a controlled study designed to measure the impact of such services on a group of persons defined as needing them, Blenkner (3) established that casework was provided to 82% of the patients, medical treatment to 78%, financial assistance to 75%, home help to 50%, nursing care to 47%, placement to 43%, psychiatric evaluation to 38%, legal services to 34%, and guardianship to 16%. The controls were being served by the usual social agencies in the community, and it was found that the experimental group received more of every category of service. There were very large differences in only two categories however. Among the control group only 9% as opposed to 50% among the study group received housekeeping help in the home and 8% as opposed to 38% received psychiatric evaluation.

Blenkner's careful comparison of a group of old people receiving all needed service with a group receiving only the routine service available in an American city yielded several disturbing results. First, a greater number among the special service group were placed in institutions in the first year of the study, 43% as opposed to 25%. This finding supported an earlier suggestion of Lowenthal's (26) that older persons who show the signs and symptoms of mental illness may nevertheless remain in the community "because they are capable of minimal self-maintenance and are socially submerged. Were they to . . . come to the attention of a concerned friend or relative or an official decision-maker of some sort, they might well become hospitalized."

Blenkner's second disturbing finding was that the group who received optimal service experienced a significantly higher death rate than the control group who received less service. The excess of deaths among those optimally served occurred both among those who remained in the community and those who went to institutions. In discussing this finding, Blenkner points out that she cannot even claim that those served had shorter lives but merrier ones since the study produced no evidence that they were significantly happier than the control group.

Findings such as these must, for the time being, add a note of caution to our enthusiastic sponsorship of services to old people trying to remain in their own homes. This study urgently needs reasonably exact replication, however, particularly because our own studies and those of others seem to show that under a number of service conditions only frailty is associated with death. Perhaps a study of the effect of services on populations carefully matched for physical frailty would help clear up this ambiguity. In the meantime, clinicians cannot help being impressed by the unhappiness of the many old people living in institutions or in degraded conditions in the community. Unless we can demonstrate which service raises the death rate among old people, we should not deny them services that they clearly want. At the same time, we have the obligation to attempt to both improve our services and to eliminate any harmful aspects they may have.

Quantitative Estimates are Scarce

Anyone planning a service for the elderly should know what the demand is going to be. Unfortunately, precise information is scarce and as long as old people are ignorant of the existence of some services, suspicious of services in general, and perhaps expecting that they will be denied service, demand will be lower than actual need. A few figures can be found in published descriptions. The meals-on-wheels agency of Hamilton, Canada (11) reports serving only 83 old people in a population of about 219,000, and this figure was said to include "all known cases of need." A similar report from Owen Sound (36)—a small city of 18,000 in the same geographic area—while not giving a specific figure suggests that the number served was about 20. This is obviously a much higher use rate. Perhaps in a small center the availability of the service becomes more widely known, and in a larger center some form of publicity is needed.

Home helps were used in Blenkner's study by about half of those who were in need of protective services. Reckoning from Blenkner's estimate of about 5-7% of the population needing home help, about 3% will be expected to be in need of home help on a long-term basis. Many more might occasionally need such assistance. Blenkner found in her experiment that the home helps not only trained the old people to do certain tasks for themselves, but also that the social interaction involved in the training was therapeutic in itself. If the home help were generally regarded as having such a therapeutic role, the demand for her services would automatically increase.

Because most day care units seem to stabilize at an attendance of about 30 persons it is perhaps easier to attempt to meet the need for service by stepwise increments evaluating demand at each step. This "topping off" effect casts doubt on the common assumption of no extra demand once a service reaches this capacity.

A General Guideline for Americans

Because of the lack of more specific guidance to program development for old people, a publication of the Committee on Aging of the Group for Advancement of Psychiatry (20) deserves attention. The committee is composed of respected and experienced American clinicians who have specialized in geriatric psychiatry. Their guidance should represent the best current clinical opinion. Their report recommends, among other things, that every psychiatric clinical center should have an advocate for the aged who should represent the needs of old people both within the center and to other agencies. Although the idea of a special advocate quickly loses its appeal if every "special" group is to have one, it does seem suitable that groups who are often neglected should be thus represented. The Group also felt that old people should be able to get the service they need without defining themselves as psychiatric patients and therefore they recommended psychiatric consultation services to non-professionals working with elderly patients.

The Group emphasized the need for in-service training programs for staffs of psychiatric centers, since much of the discomfort that professionals feel in dealing with older patients stems from their lack of training in appropriate techniques. They believe that all of the traditional partial care services—day hospitals, night hospitals and temporary inpatient care to relieve families, are readily adaptable for use by the elderly, and they express confidence that they will be used where they are offered. This booklet should be useful for helping lay boards and administrators to understand requests for program support. Because of the lack of empirical data upon which to base planning, for America at least, it is probably the best available opinion.

Throughout our survey of the various patterns of care recommended for the elderly in the American professional literature, we have been impressed by an overall lack of innovation and experimentation. A survey of the needs for service of the elderly, produced by the Community Project for the Aged of the Welfare Council of Metropolitan Chicago (42) published in 1952, for example, could be republished today with a few minor changes in terminology and probably be accepted as a contemporary document. Part of the reason for this seeming lack of progress may be that in spite of modest increases in services, the number of old people needing service is increasing too rapidly. This situation may not apply to countries where the population is fully aged.

A General Guideline for the British

In Great Britain, the Society of Clinical Psychiatrists has published a set of guidelines parallel to the GAP report discussed above; it is entitled "The Organization of Psychogeriatrics" (12). While the problems in the two countries seem to be essentially similar, the solutions put forward are somewhat different. Indeed, the special value of having two such documents lies in the contrasting solutions that implicitly challenge each other's assumptions about the organization of services.

The British publication sets forth the epidemiological aspects of the geriatric problem much more clearly than does the GAP report, and it provides a model for the assembling of data that could profitably be emulated in America, through the use of available data sources. Essentially, the GAP guide attributes the American failure to provide geriatric services to American attitudes, while the British authors attribute their problem to diagnostic and organizational failures. These authors propose that careful diagnostic and assessment techniques could be successfully matched with available resources, and they further suggest that responsibility for developing such services be clearly allocated to the various levels of government that should operate them. For example, their discussion of housing emphasizes that different levels of impairment require different kinds of special facilities, and that a wide variety of solutions is necessary if an optimal solution to the housing problems of the elderly is to be found. In passing, they remind us of some facts about the elderly that too often are not central in our thinking, such as that the elderly suffer from, and need help for, the same neurotic and psychosomatic problems as younger people.

The British guide emphasizes the usefulness of the short-term psychogeriatric assessment unit, both for providing intensive treatment and for the careful assessment of problems. Such a unit can then direct the patient to the most effective and economical solution of his problem.

If this small volume has a fault, it is that it might convince readers from other countries that the British have found an agreed-upon solution to all their problems and are efficiently moving toward it. To offset this feeling, one might want to review the controversy about psycho-geriatric units that appeared in the *Lancet* in the issues from April 11th, 1970 to June 13th, 1970. The manner in which this debate goes on indicates that change in psychiatric practice in Britain is, as it is in the United States, slow and painful.

Why Such Neglect of Old People

There are a number of possible reasons why services for old people do not always get past the stage of pious intent. From the clinical point of view, such services can appear as exhausting, repetitive, and in some sense, futile because the patient has so little future ahead of him. The natural tendency of the clinician to feel rewarded by marked progress is frustrated when he has to be satisfied with the very limited goal of maintaining the patient in a precarious equilibrium. The elderly patient often needs a wide variety of simple services rather than technical skills and the clinician may feel vaguely "unprofessional" providing or even arranging for such care.

From society's point of view, investment of resources in a non-productive group has to be viewed as a luxury when compared to investment in either young people who will enter the labor market, or in adults who already have useful roles in it.

In 1947, Lord Beveridge (34) went so far as to say:

> It is dangerous to be in any way lavish to old age, until adequate provision has been assured for all other vital needs, such as the prevention of disease and the adequate nutrition of the young.

Fortifying this invidious comparison between the old who have made their social contribution and others who have yet to do so is the ease with which it is possible to blame families for failing to take their responsibilities. Finally, it should be said that although the major thrust of the value system that makes modern industrial society possible is against investing much in the contentment of old people, it is as well to remember that in one way the level of our civilization will be judged by just how much we are willing to do for those who cannot contribute to the gross national product.

REFERENCES

1. BARRON, E. 1970. Friendly visitor. *Hospitals,* 44:75.
2. BLENKER, M. 1969. The normal dependencies of aging. In: Kalish, R. A. (Ed.) *The Dependence of Old People.* Ann Arbor, Mich.: Institute of Gerontology.
3. BLENKER, M., BLOOM, M., and NIELSON, M. 1971. A research and demonstration project of protective services. *Social Casework,* 52:483.
4. BUTLER, R. N. 1960. Intensive psychotherapy for the hospitalized aged. *Geriatrics,* 15:644.
5. CITY OF NEW YORK COMMISSION ON STATE-CITY RELATIONS. 1972. *State Policy and the Long Term Mentally Ill: A Shuffle to Despair.*
6. CLARK, M. L. 1967. *A Screening Program for the Aged Mentally Ill. First Workshop on Comprehensive Services for the Geriatric Mental Patient.* Bethesda, Md.: National Institute for Mental Health.
7. CONGDON, R. C. 1970. *Partial Hospitalization for Adult Psychiatric Patients in Ontario.* Toronto: Ontario Mental Health Division.
8. COSIN, L. Q. 1954. The place of the day hospital in the geriatric unit. *Practitioner,* 172:552.

9. CRUTCHER, H. B. 1944. *Foster Home Care for Mental Patients.* New York: The Commonwealth Fund.
10. CUMMING, E. 1968. *Systems of Social Regulation.* New York: Atherton.
11. CUMMINGS, M. 1970. Meals-on-wheels in Hamilton: Key is community involvement. *Canad. Hosp.,* 47:46.
12. ENOCH, M. D., and HOWELLS, J. G. 1971. *The Organization of Psychogeriatrics.* U.K.: The Society of Clinical Psychiatrists.
13. EPPS, R. L., and HANES, L. D. 1964. *Day Care of Psychiatric Patients.* Springfield: Charles C Thomas.
14. EPSTEIN, L. J., and SIMON, A. 1968. Alternative to state hospitalization for the geriatric mentally ill. *Am. J. of Psychiat.,* 124:115.
15. FARNDALE, J. 1961. *The Day Hospital Movement in Great Britain.* Oxford: Pergamon Press.
16. FOLSOM, J. C. 1968. Reality orientation for the elderly mental patient. *J. Geriat. Psychiat.,* 1:291.
17. FRIEDMAN, J. H. 1971. Misassignment of geriatric patients to a state mental hospital. *J. Am. Geriat. Soc.,* 19:172.
18. GOLDFARB, A. I. 1955. Psychotherapy of the aged. *Psychoanal. Rev.,* 42:180.
19. GOLDSTEIN, S., SEVRIUK, J., and GRAUER, H. 1968. The establishment of a psychogeriatric day hospital. *Canad. Med. Ass. J.,* 98:955.
20. GROUP FOR THE ADVANCEMENT OF PSYCHIATRY, COMMITTEE ON AGING. 1971. *The Aged and Community Mental Health: A Guide to Program Development.* New York.
21. KAY, D. W., and ROTH, M. 1961. *Physical Illness and Social Factors in the Psychiatric Disorders of Old Age. Third World Congress of Psychiatry, Proceedings.* Montreal: McGill University Press.
22. KAY, D. W., NORRIS, V., and POST, F. 1956. Prognosis in psychiatric disorders of the elderly. *J. Ment. Sci.,* 102:376.
23. KOBRYNSKI, B., and CUMMING, E. 1971. Generational changes and geriatric care. *J. Am. Geriat. Soc.,* 19:376.
24. KOBRYNSKI, B., and CUMMING, E. 1971. *The mobile geriatric team in the state of New York.* (Mimeo)
25. KRAMER, M., TAUBE, C., and STARR, S. 1968. *Patterns of Use of Psychiatric Facilities by the Aged: Current Status, Trends and Implications.* Psychiatric Research Report 23. Washington: Am. Psychiat. Ass.
26. LOWENTHAL, M., BERKMAN, P., BRISSETTE, G., ET AL. 1967. *Aging and Mental Disorder in San Francisco.* San Francisco: Jossey-Bass.
27. MACMILLAN, D. (n.d.). *Community Mental Health, The Mapperley Hospital Scheme.* Ottawa, Canada: Canada's Mental Health.
28. MARKSON, E. 1970. The geriatric house of death: Hiding the dying elder in a mental hospital. *Aging and Human Development,* 1:37.
29. MCDONALD, R. D., NEULANDER, A., HALOD, O., and HOLCOMB, N. S. 1971. Description of a non-residential psychogeriatric day care facility. *Gerontologist,* 11:322.
30. MENTAL HEALTH RESEARCH UNIT. 1968. *Some Aspects of the Treatment of Geriatric Patients in Psychiatric Facilities in New York State.* Albany: New York State Department of Mental Hygiene.
31. MENTAL HEALTH RESEARCH UNIT. 1970. *Final Report of the Interdepartmental Geriatric Study.* Albany: New York State Department of Mental Hygiene.
32. NEW YORK STATE DEPARTMENT OF MENTAL HYGIENE. 1972. *Hope Springs Eternal.* Albany.
33. NEW YORK STATE HEALTH DEPARTMENT. 1963. *A Health Survey of Older People in Monroe County.* Albany.
34. NUFFIELD FOUNDATION. 1947. *Old People: Report of the Survey Committee on the*

Problems of Aging and the Care of Old People. Oxford: Oxford University Press.

35. PECK, A. 1966. Psychotherapy of the aged. *J. Am. Geriat. Soc.,* 14:748.
36. RAGG, D. 1970. Meals-on-wheels—how it works in a small community. *Sanad. Hosp.,* 47:47.
37. RECHTSHAFFEN, A. 1959. Psychotherapy with geriatric patients: A review of the literature. *J. Geront.,* 14:73.
38. RESDORFER, E. N., PRIMANIS, G., and DOZORETZ, L. 1971. Family care as a useful alternative to the long term hospital confinement of geropsychiatric patients. *J. Am. Geriat. Soc.,* 19:150.
39. ROBERTSON, W. M. F., and PITT, B. 1965. The role of a day hospital in geriatric psychiatry. *Brit. J. Psychiat.,* III:635.
40. SHANAS, E., TOWNSEND, P., WEDDERBURN, D., ET AL. 1968. *Old People in Three Industrial Societies.* New York: Atherton.
41. TOWNSEND, P. 1968. Welfare services and the family. In: Shanas, E., Townsend, P., Wedderburn, D., et al. *Old People in Three Industrial Societies.* New York: Atherton.
42. WELFARE COUNCIL OF METROPOLITAN CHICAGO. 1952. *Community Services for Older People: The Community Project for the Aged of the Welfare Council of Metropolitan Chicago.* New York: Wilcox and Follett.

23

SERVICES IN THE U.S.S.R.

M. G. Shchirina

Research Secretary, Institute of Psychiatry,
Academy of Medical Sciences, Moscow, U.S.S.R.

Geriatric psychiatry is becoming increasingly important because people live longer and because mental disorders related to old age are increasing in many highly developed countries. Moreover, disorders previously not clearly defined are now better understood. These factors pose new theoretical and practical problems in the management of patients and organization of services. This chapter will describe how these problems have been handled in the U.S.S.R.

The Soviet health services have accumulated experience in practical and theoretical work for more than 50 years. This experience extends to the organization of mental health services. However, the constant promotion of psychiatric services inevitably creates new theoretical and practical questions in contemporary psychiatry.

MENTAL HEALTH SERVICES

In discussing some aspects of the organization of psychiatric services for the aged it is relevant to outline, concisely and schematically, the general structure of mental health services existing in the Soviet Union.

The main features of the Soviet health services are their governmental character, their emphasis on prevention, their availability and proximity to the population. These features apply also to psychiatry. However, inasmuch as the etiology of many mental disorders is yet unclear, measures of early screening, i.e. measures of secondary and tertiary prophylaxis, treatment, rehabilitation and readaptation, are of special importance.

Mental health services in the Soviet Union are provided by various agencies, each specializing in a field, under the Ministry of Health, the Ministry of Education and the Ministry of Social Welfare. Facilities related to the Ministry of Health are the following: mental hospitals, mental wards in general hospitals, psychoneurological dispensaries with day hospitals and occupational facilities, and mental health services within medical centers of large industrial plants. The Ministry of Social Welfare has within its framework such institutions as homes for invalids with chronic mental disorders, nursing homes and special homes for the mentally retarded. The Ministry of Education provides for children suffering from various forms of neuroses, speech disorders, organic brain lesions and mental retardation by supplying special sanatoria, nursery schools and schools.

Each of the above-mentioned institutions in the system of public health occupies a specially assigned place. However, the mental health services are centered and dependent upon the psychoneurological dispensary.

The dispensary services are based on a territorial principle and are accompanied by close contacts with the general medical center (polyclinic), general hospitals, industrial medical centers, physicians of universities and schools, polyclinics for children and other medical facilities in their district. Consequently, the main source of patients to the psychoneurological dispensary comes from the district physician or from the physician of an institution. Self-reference is also a source of intake of patients.

One of the main purposes of the psychiatrist working in a dispensary is an early screening of patients, and treatment takes place within the community whenever possible. In those cases when the patient for obvious reasons cannot be managed at home, he is referred to a mental hospital within the catchment area. The patient stays in the mental hospital for as long as is necessary (the mean average of hospital stay in Moscow is approximately three months). After being discharged from the mental hospital the patient returns to the same district psychiatrist who recommended him for hospital admission. Within three days a summary of his case history is sent to the dispensary, with concise information as to the clinical state and recommendations for subsequent treatment. Maintenance therapy is undertaken by the district psychiatrist who sees the patient in his office at the dispensary or, if necessary, visits him at home. All subsequent medical treatment, psychotherapy, social support or, if necessary, repeated referrals to mental hospitals or wards of general hospitals, to invalid homes, nursing houses, etc., will be through the district psychiatrist. Ideally, hospital stays are short episodes in the life of a mental patient, while outpatient treatment and social care over time are undertaken by the dispensary.

The psychiatrist/population ratio which the dispensaries cover is one psychiatrist to 30,000-40,000 of the general population. Hence, the population of the rayon (district), city, rural area or region determines the number of psychiatrists working in the psychoneurological dispensary. The task of the district psychiatrist is not only to take on the register all the patients referred, but also to identify people in need of psychiatric care from industry, institutions, universities and offices, and to participate in committees for referrals to special kindergartens, schools, sanatoria, military medical services, etc. The work of the district psychiatrists includes work with the family and acquaintance with the social conditions of the patient.

Since the patient who requires a period of hospitalization eventually returns to the district psychiatrist in the dispensary, it is possible to follow his fate and the development of his disease during a long period of time. A continuity of the inpatient and outpatient mental health services provides opportunities for a better observation of patients, a more precise diagnosis and a more rational use of treatment and social measures. Unlike the Western countries, in the Soviet Union there are no special social workers within mental services. Social work (employment, pensions, financial support, support, work with the family and in places of employment, domestic help, etc.) is entirely entrusted to the district psychiatrist and his psychiatric nurse.

The structure described is characteristic for a city psychoneurological dispensary where there are hospital and outpatient specialized services. In rural areas, where the population is decentralized, there are several ways of making the mental health service as easily available as possible. In some regions there may be a regional psychiatric hospital with an attached dispensary which undertakes the outpatient work. In the more remote regions of the country with no mental health services, the ambulatory treatment and observation are undertaken by the general physician with periodical consultations with visiting psychiatrists.

In some of the central regions of the U.S.S.R. an attempt has been made to reorganize old services into new and more rational programs. One of these programs is the so-called dispensary-hospital unit, functioning on a territorial basis and making it possible for the same psychiatrist to see the patient in the dispensary and in the hospital.

Briefly, these are the main types of organization of mental health services functioning in the Soviet Union.

GENERAL ISSUES IN SERVICES FOR THE AGED

The history of world psychiatry, and, in particular, that branch which is concerned with aged mental patients, have shown that until recent years the main form of service rendered to the elderly was custodial, with most patients suffering from physical disability and dementia. Perhaps that may explain why psycho-geriatrics started its development by describing the different forms of senile dementia and its psychotic varieties. It is known that during the past years, because of changes in the demographical processes, the growing urbanization of the population, administration of active methods of therapy in mental hospitals, etc., some psychiatric disorders have been reconsidered. Affective, delusional and hallucinatory-delusional psychoses have been the focus of special interest and study. It has become necessary to describe and classify these conditions adequately and to devise rational forms of therapy for them.

Despite great diagnostic difficulties and controversial clinical evaluation, much has been done to improve the analysis and systematization of the clinical material (4, 6, 7, 11, 12). An attempt was made to create a new clinical classification with a more comprehensive inclusion of the manifold mental disorders encountered in old age. More detailed studies were undertaken in the field of the so-called ambulatory forms of mental disorders in the aged (7, 8, 10, 12), i.e. those disorders which over a long period of time do not require hospital admission, or require infrequent hospitalization, and permit observation and treatment mostly in outpatient clinics. The questions posed by such studies are very important for the understanding and correct evaluation of the clinical conditions in this age group, and, importantly, these studies pose some new questions for public health agencies providing services to the aged mentally ill.

The field of geriatrics receives much more attention now than previously. There is a great deal of literature related to geriatric problems, although many aspects of this field are still unclear and disputable. Recent papers devoted to these problems discuss such questions as the proportion of the geriatric population admitted to mental hospitals, and the existence of outpatient and community services as a factor determining the length of hospitalization. It appears that more elderly females than males are admitted to mental hospitals. Marital status and family conditions are of paramount importance here. Clinico-epidemiological studies have demonstrated that single individuals are admitted to mental hospitals twice as often and for longer periods than individuals living with their families.

The studies of E. Ya. Sternberg (12) have shown that the ratio of females to males on the dispensary register is 2.3 to 1; this ratio is not significantly different from the ratio of sex distribution for the same age groups in the population. These figures are increased (3:1) when the geriatric population of a mental hospital was studied; in the group of schizophrenics, the proportion is 6.4:1. Rightly so, E. Brooke (2) claims that the problem of psychiatric care is mainly a geriatric problem. A. Serenko and G. Tsaregorodtsev (9) have written that the demographical prognosis for the U.S.S.R. is that in 1980 the number of people over 60 will be approximately 50 millions, and in 2000 it will reach 80 millions. All these figures are particularly important in planning psychiatric, social and welfare services for the elderly.

Many psychiatrists consider that for an adequate mental health service there should be, in addition to the existing geriatric wards in mental and general hospitals, special homes for the elderly with medical care, day hospitals, more home visits by psychiatrists, special clubs, etc. However, optimal forms of services for the aged have not yet been arrived at. At the same time most of the psychiatrists working with this group agree that it would not be correct to speak of geriatric services limited only to hospital care. We should speak of a more effective use of hospital beds, which in turn depends to a great degree upon outpatient services. For instance, Bergmann (1) and Kay (3), studying the need for geriatric help, consider that the main principle in such cases is to keep the patient as long as possible in his family, while the main efforts of health administrators should be directed towards comprehensive services for the patient at home. Where outpatient geriatric services do not exist, more pressure is put on the hospital, which in some cases is not in the position to satisfy the growing needs of the community. As a result the patient may find himself in a non-specialized institution.

As the main attention of psychiatrists working in outpatient clinics is concentrated on the younger and middle age group, the elderly receive help only if they are referred (1, 3, 5). The introduction of a wide range of therapeutic procedures into psychiatric practice has made the duration of hospital stay shorter. This, however, imposes added responsibility on the psychiatrist who undertakes aftercare in outpatient conditions.

At present the system of outpatient services for the younger patient is relatively well managed and adjusted, but the services for the elderly require some reconsideration.

PSYCHIATRIC SERVICES FOR THE AGED

The mental health services for the elderly are provided by the district psychiatrist in the framework of a psychoneurological dispensary. Those patients who, by medical indications and family conditions, may be left at home are observed and treated by the district psychiatrist. Patients with acute psychotic conditions are as a rule referred to a mental hospital in the catchment area. If the psychotic state is accompanied by severe somatic disorders, such patients are referred to psychiatric wards of general hospitals. In cases of chronic dementia the patients can be admitted to homes for the invalid elderly. A significant number of patients without severe dementia, but with a certain level of mental decline, may be referred to nursing homes for the elderly. Thus, there are relatively diverse psychiatric facilities for this type of disorder and within the framework of social welfare there are provisions for this group.

However, because of an increase of people requiring specialized geriatric aid, the time has come to think of highly qualified professionals providing these services. This inevitably produces the problem of educating special personnel, and psychiatrists in particular, working in the field of geronto-psychiatry. This can be accomplished on the one hand through post-graduate training for physicians (this form of specialization takes place, for instance, under the Professor of Psychiatry in the Central Institute for Post-Graduate Training in Moscow), and on the other hand by emphasizing the initial symptoms of mental diseases in old age during post graduate training of internists, neurologists, surgeons and other professionals. Special attention to this side of the educational program may in due time facilitate the referral of elderly patients to psychiatrists.

One of the most important current issues is the creation of specialized geriatric departments in the framework of the psychoneurological dispensary for optimal services to the aged. An analysis of the work of a district psychiatrist has demonstrated that such professionals would make possible a concentration of a certain population in the same hands, create more qualified services and timely screening of all individuals requiring observations and treatment.

Some years ago the necessity of creating a child and adolescent department within outpatient facilities became evident. Similarly today the creation of a geriatric department in a psychoneurological dispensary has become an important issue in psychiatry.

Efficient planning and improvement of medical and, particularly, geriatric assistance require the provision of scientifically based epidemiological data.

Among the research studies undertaken in the Institute of Psychiatry of the Academy of Medical Sciences an important role is being allocated to the aged aspect of mental diseases. The solution of such important questions has been related first of all to clinical studies. However, it becomes more and more obvious that many questions of clinical practice in the organization of mental health services cannot be solved exclusively on the basis of hospital patients, because such selective data cannot be considered sufficiently representative of the population in general and of such patients in particular. Consequently, the problems of promoting mental health services for the elderly may be solved only on the basis of wide epidemiological data. The continuity of inpatient and outpatient services in the Soviet Union, as well as a wide framework of extramural psychiatric services, makes it possible to study the population of patients on the register and on this basis improve the facilities.

In this connection, an overall study was undertaken of the population of elderly patients (over 60) living in two districts of Moscow (both districts are in the catchment area of one psychoneurological dispensary). The areas to be studied were the following:

1) the prevalence of mental patients in this age category;
2) the sex and age distribution;
3) the nosological forms and predilective syndromological structure;
4) the influence of social and physical factors on mental disorders.

In order to answer these questions a special epidemiological chart was devised which included more than 20 questions. The program consists of a study of the present register in one of the psychoneurological dispensaries of Moscow and of future studies of random samples of elderly patients who are observed by the neurologist, general physicians in the district polyclinic (medical center), and in the homes for disabled located in the given district.

In the middle of 1971, the number of registered patients over 60 was 12% of all patients on the register.

The first preliminary analysis of 1,000 charts (three micro-districts and part of a fourth) makes it possible to answer some general questions. It should be stressed that all the patients living in this catchment area and at the time of the program being in hospitals were also personally interviewed and included into the study.

The distribution by sex was the following:

Females	687
Males	313
TOTAL	1,000

The ratio of females to males was 2.2:1, which approximately corresponds to the sex ratio in the general population of Moscow.

The age of onset of the disease in percentages is shown in Table 1:

TABLE 1

Age of Onset of Disease

Age	1-10	11-20	21-30	31-40	41-50	51-60	61-70	71-80	81	Total
Males	4.5%	13.4%	22.0%	14.4%	16.9%	14.4%	11.8%	2.6%	—	100%
Females	3.1%	16.9%	17.3%	6.4%	20.8%	22.0%	11.9%	1.6%	—	100%

The figures show that females fall ill over the age of 40 more frequently than males.

An analysis of the admission rate to a mental hospital of this catchment area has shown that one-third of all the referrals were patients over 60 years, while the sex ratio of females to males of hospitalized patients was 2.4:1. Probably the fact that the number of lonely women is higher than men (according to the Census made in Moscow in 1970 the percentage of lonely men was 12.8%, while that of women was 73.8%) and that most likely the men were better cared for in family conditions affected this fact. Perhaps this may be one of the factors influencing the admissions to hospitals.

An analysis of the data concerning the onset of mental diseases demonstrated that males more than females are apt to fall ill before 40 years of age, while the rate is higher for women past 40. One of the possible reasons for this may be the fact that men more frequently than women fall ill in youth with schizophrenia. Furthermore, the different forms of alcoholism and brain injuries are more frequently encountered in fairly young men. Women past 40 fall ill more frequently. Perhaps this may be explained by a higher percentage of endogenous affective disorders (schizophrenia, manic-depressive psychosis, involutional melancholia) and by some social factors. Such questions as the prevalence of nosological forms, the syndromological and predilective structure, the influence of social factors on the development of the disease, hospital admission and living family conditions, etc. will be answered at the end of the program.

A mass epidemiological study of all the patients on the register will make it possible to reconsider some essential questions concerning the structure of mental disorders in the population, and some general clinical and organizational problems. These problems require a re-evaluation based on substantiated epidemiological data which consequently will promote better geriatric services.

REFERENCES

1. BERGMANN, K. 1969. The epidemiology of senile dementia. *Brit. J. Hosp. Med.*, 2: 727-732.
2. BROOKE, E. 1965. The psychogeriatric patient; some statistical considerations. In: *Psychiatric Disorders in the Aged.* Symp. of the WPA, London. 214.
3. KAY, D. W. K., BEAMISH, P., and ROTH, M. 1964. Old age mental disorders in New-castle-upon-Tyne. *Brit. J. Psychiat.*, 110:146-158.
4. KEHRER, H. E. 1959. *Die cerebrale Gafaess-Sklerose.* Stuttgart: G. Thieme Verlag. 288.
5. KRAMER, M. 1905. Classification of mental disorders. Paper presented at the Conference on Role and Methodology of Classification in Psychiatry and Psychopathology, Washington.
6. MAYER-GROSS, W., SLATER, E., and ROTH, M. 1960. *Clinical Psychiatry.* London: Cassel.
7. ROTH, M. 1965. Psychiatric aspects of old age in relation to the problem of aging. In: *Psychiatric Disorders in the Aged.* Symp. of the WPA, London, 84.
8. SAINSBURY, P., COSTAIN, W., and GRAD, J. 1965. The effects of community services on the referral and admission rates of elderly psychiatric patients. In: *Psychiatric Disorders in the Aged.* Symp. of the WPA, London, 23.
9. SERENKO, A. F., and TSAREGORODTSEV, G. I. 1972. *Sotsialnie aspekti obespecheniya pozhilikh lyudey v SSSR.* 9 Intern. Congr. of Gerontology, Kiev, July 2-7, 1972, p. 69.
10. SIMON, A. 1970. The psychiatrist and the geriatric patient. Screening of the aged mentally ill. *J. Geriat. Psychiat.*, 4:5-17.
11. SNEZHNEVSKY, A. V. 1969. Simptomatologiya i nozologiya. In: *Schizophrenia.* Klinika i Patogenes. "Meditsina," Moscow, 5-28.
12. STERNBERG, E. YA. 1970. K psikhopatologii i psikologii posdnego vosrasta. In: *Diag-nostika i klassifikatsiya psikhicheskikh zabolevaniy posdnego vosrasta.* Leningrad, 228-241.

24

CARE IN JAPAN

Ziro Kaneko, M.D.

Professor, Department of Neuropsychiatry,
Osaka University Medical School, Osaka, Japan

INTRODUCTION

The population of elderly people in Japan has increased rapidly since the Second World War and the average life span has reached the level of most developed countries in Europe. However, the medical and social welfare services for the aged are not well organized and a plan for psycho-geriatric care is now under discussion among psychiatrists. This paper will report the incidence and type of mental disorders in old age and psycho-geriatric care in Japan.

DEMOGRAPHIC AND SOCIAL BACKGROUND OF THE
ELDERLY IN JAPAN

After the Second World War, the death rate in Japan decreased owing to the advances of medical sciences and improved social conditions. Due to birth control measures, the birth rate also decreased, and the proportion of old persons in the population increased rapidly. In 1950, the average life span was 62.97 years for females and 59.57 years for males and the proportion of the general population over 65 years old was only 4.9%. However, by 1971 the average life span was 75.58 years for females and 70.17 years for males and the proportion of the population over 65 was 7.6%; it is estimated that it will reach 12% by 1990. This means that within a period of about 40 years the proportion of old people in Japan will have reached the same level as the most developed countries in Europe, a level which required more than one hundred years for them to reach.

In Japan, there are other great social changes besides the increasing proportion of aged persons. Industrialization and urbanization force the migration of young people towards urban districts, while the aged remain in the rural areas. Young married couples do not like to live with their aged parents and the nuclear family has increased in recent years. From 1954 to 1967, the average number of family members in one household decreased from 4.5 to 3.5, the proportion of extended families decreased from 44.6 to 25.07% of all Japanese families, while single member families increased from 9.6 to 19.67%, nuclear families from 46.4 to 55.4%, and the families of the aged, alone or with children under 18 years old, increased from 2.2 to 3.4%. These tendencies are more marked in urban than in rural districts. In 1967, the proportion of people over 65 years old in the whole population of Japan was 6.6%, while in the Osaka Prefecture, which includes largely urban areas, it was 4.6% and in the Shimane Prefecture, which includes largely rural areas, it was 9.7%.

The change in the family system has also been great. Before the Second World War, the Japanese family was usually a large, three-generation family, and the father's influence was very powerful. When he retired from regular work, he was respected by other family members as an experienced man and could behave freely without any specific duty. The eldest son had the responsibility to support his parents; it was regarded as a great virtue to show respect for the aged and to practice filial piety towards parents.

After the War, the large family system deteriorated rapidly; newly married couples became family units of their own and the duty of supporting the parents became the responsibility of every child instead of resting on the eldest son only. In some cases, the children do not want to support their parents and parents have to move around from one child to another.

A recent opinion survey reported that there exists a great gap of thought concerning who should support the elderly. On the one hand, 50% of old people wanted to be supported by their children. On the other hand, only 16% of the young people expressed the opinion that old persons should be supported by their children. Young people wish to live separately from their parents, while old people wish, consciously or unconsciously, to live with their children, in spite of the growing tendency of the elderly to want to live by themselves independently of their children.

However, in Japan there are many difficulties in having one's own house. There is a shortage of houses. The income of the elderly is too low to maintain a separate home. Only one-half of them gets an old age pension, and the sum of the pension is only about one-fifth of that of European countries. For these reasons, 80% of the elderly in Japan live with their children. On the contrary, only 20-40% of the elderly live with their children in European countries.

To live with one's children has the advantage that the old feel less lonely. However, it has the disadvantage that many conflicts will appear between the generations. Since the War, young people in Japan have been educated according to the principles of democracy, liberalism and individualism. In contrast, older persons were educated before the War according to the principles of feudalism, conservatism, Buddhism and Confucian ethics. Young people do not want their parents to make comments on the education and training of their children and refuse their advice. Before the War, the conflicts between mother-in-law and daughter-in-law caused neuroses in many young wives and were also the cause of many divorces. But since the War the daughter-in-law has become strong, and it is the mother-in-law who now suffers from neuroses and depression.

In 1963, the Welfare Act for the Aged was passed by the Diet in Japan and since then many institutions for the aged have been opened. However, the capacity is not nearly enough and only 1.0% of those aged over 65 years are admitted to these institutions. Community care programs have started only recently. Although medical insurance covers only half of the cost of medical care for most of the aged, the consulting rate for those aged over 65 years has trebled from 1955 to 1967.

MENTAL DISORDERS OF THE AGED IN JAPAN

The Aged in Mental Hospitals

It is very difficult to determine the accurate incidence of mental disorders in old age. Mental hospital statistics give reliable data, but aged mental patients are not all admitted to mental hospitals. Our surveys have shown that a larger part of the aged mental patients are living in their homes or in nursing homes. The rate of admission to mental hospitals depends not only on the seriousness of mental illness, but also on various social and economic factors, and especially on the number of hospital beds available. From 1954 to 1969 the number of mental hospital beds increased remarkably from 30,447 beds (3.3 per 10,000) to 226,063 beds (22.0 per 10,000). This increase of mental hospital beds means that less seriously ill patients may be easily admitted to mental hospitals.

In many advanced countries, more than 30% of the beds in mental hospitals were reported to be occupied by aged patients and the majority of them were suffering from senile dementia. In Japan, however, aged patients occupied only a small percentage of the total mental hospital beds in spite of the increasing population of aged persons.

Shinfuku (9) reported that, in 1953, 3.9% of all inpatients in mental hospitals in Japan were over 60 years old. Mizuno (7) reported that for Osaka Prefecture, in 1954, the proportion of patients over 60 years old in mental hospitals was 4.8%. In comparison, the proportion of the general population over 60 years old in 1953 was 7.7%. The small ratio of the aged among mental inpatients in Japan 15 to 20 years ago seemed to be due partially to the economic difficulties of hospitalization, but perhaps more importantly to certain Japanese cultural characteristics, such as 1) the strong family ties between the old and the young; 2) the traditional custom of respecting the old; 3) reluctance to send a family member to a mental hospital because of social shame; and 4) symptoms which seem to be managed by family members.

However, some changes are taking place in the attitude of Japanese people towards the aged with the rapidly changing structure of the Japanese family system under the influence of modern individualism. Kobayashi (5) reported that the percentage of mental inpatients over 60 years old was 7.3% in the Aichi Prefecture in 1967; Sugimoto (10) reported 6.6% in the Gifu Prefecture in 1968; Nakao (8) 12.0% in the Kyushu District in 1967; Kaneko (2) 19.0 percent over 60 years old, and 11.8% over 65 years old, in the Osaka Prefecture in 1967. In these figures the tendency towards an increasing percentage of aged patients in mental hospitals is clear and this tendency is more marked in urban areas, such as the Osaka Prefecture, than in rural areas, such as the Gifu Prefecture.

Changes in the kind of mental disorders of the aged inpatient over 60 years old from 1953 to 1967 are shown in Table 1. The most marked change is the increase in schizophrenia, which seemed to be caused by the longevity of the schizophrenic patients and not by an increase of late onset of schizophrenia or paraphrenia. General paresis has decreased following earlier penicillin treatment of syphilis. The decrease in manic-

TABLE 1

Incidence of Mental Disorders in Mental Hospitals

		60-64	65-69	70-74	75-79	80-	Total (%)
General Paresis	A*	81	16	6	0	1	104 (10.4)
	B**	53	33	15	5	1	107 (6.9)
Schizophrenia	A	30	17	8	3	0	58 (5.8)
	B	247	131	39	20	9	446 (28.7)
Manic-depressive	A	63	37	9	2	0	111 (11.1)
	B	29	20	7	5	1	62 (4.0)
Senile dementia	A	47	49	48	22	5	171 (17.2)
	B	84	105	95	82	70	436 (28.0)
Arteriosclerotic	A	144	78	50	10	1	283 (28.4)
	B	96	98	67	38	21	320 (20.5)
Others	A	159	74	22	11	2	268 (26.9)
	B	91	51	23	14	5	185 (11.8)
Total	A	524	271	143	48	9	995 (100)
	B	591	438	256	164	107	1,556 (100)

Shinfuku (1955) in Japan (rearranged by Kaneko).
** Kaneko (1967) in the Osaka Prefecture.

depressive psychosis seems to be caused by the effective outpatient treatment with antidepressants. The proportion of senile dementia and arteriosclerotic dementia has changed only slightly: 45.9% in 1953 and 48.5% in 1967, with a small relative increase in senile dementia.

Psycho-geriatric care in mental hospitals is not well organized in Japan. In 1972, there were about 230,000 mental hospital beds. However, most mental hospitals are rather small with an average of about 200 beds. The largest mental hospital has about 1000 beds. Eighty percent of beds are in private mental hospitals.

There are some geriatric units in large or moderately large mental hospitals, where the aged mental patients receive special psycho-geriatric care, drug therapy, psychotherapy, rehabilitation and recreation therapy. However, in small mental hospitals there are few distinct geriatric units and the aged mental patients receive little special psycho-geriatric care.

Besides these mental hospitals, there are beds for mental patients in general hospitals. About 200 general hospitals have departments of neuro-psychiatry and each unit has 20-40 inpatient beds. Mostly acute geriatric cases, especially those with delirium, paranoid reaction, depression and neurosis, are treated in these psychiatric units of the general hospitals.

The Elderly in Institutions for the Aged

In spite of the increase of aged people in Japan, the social welfare services for them have not been developed enough. The National Welfare Act for the Aged was passed in 1963. In 1970, there were 810 homes for the aged with 60,812 beds, 152 nursing homes for the physically and mentally disabled aged with 11,280 beds, 132 guidance centers, 6,100 untrained home helpers, 78,676 clubs for the aged (registered members 4,662,127, i.e., 43.6% of those over 60 years old). However, the integration of mental health services within a comprehensive geriatric program is not very good and there is still a serious shortage of short-term units and day care centers.

It is generally known that the incidence of mental disorders among the aged in custodial institutions is higher than in private homes. Hasegawa (1), in 1968, studied 1075 patients (292 males and 783 females) over 60 years old (average 76 years old) who were in 10 institutions (89 in low cost residential homes; 832 in homes for the aged; 154 in nursing homes) in the Tokyo Prefecture. He showed the incidence of mental disorders in different institutions to be: dementia—5.0% in low cost residential homes, 6.0% in homes for the aged, 41.0% in nursing homes; functional disorders, such as neurosis, personality deviation, depression and paranoid reaction—13% in residential homes, 11% in homes for the aged, 14% in nursing homes.

Psycho-geriatric care in these institutions is almost totally absent and even in nursing homes for the physically and mentally disabled there are only nurses (psychiatrically untrained) guided by a doctor, who visits about once a week. In the whole of Japan there is only one nursing home for the mentally disabled aged operated by psychiatrists.

The Aged in the Community

In Japan, national mental health surveys were carried out in 1954 and 1963 (6). People with mental disorders were estimated in 1954 as 14.8 per 1000 general population and in 1963 as 12.9. Of these patients the ratio of psychoses was estimated in 1954 as 5.2 per 1000 general population and in 1963 as 5.9. The comparison between these two surveys reveals that the ratio of schizophrenia and manic-depressive psychosis did not

TABLE 2

Prevalence Rate of Mental Disorders per 1000 Population
(National Mental Health Survey)

	1954	1963
Psychoses—Total	5.2	5.9
Schizophrenia	2.3	2.3
Manic-depressive	0.2	0.2
Epilepsy	1.4	1.0
Organic psychoses	1.0	2.2
Other psychoses	0.3	0.2
Mental deficiency	6.6	4.2
Others	3.0	2.8
Total	14.8	12.9

show any difference; however, the incidence of organic psychoses doubled from 1.0 to 2.2 per 1000 general population, as shown in Table 2.

The percentages of the various types of organic psychoses in 1954 and 1963 were respectively as follow: arteriosclerotic psychosis—52% and 51.6%; senile dementia—20% and 15.8%; syphilis—20% and 6.3%; brain trauma—4% and 16.8%; encephalitis—4% and 9.5%, as shown in Table 3. Senile dementia and arteriosclerotic psychosis were about 70% of these organic psychoses in both the 1954 and 1963 surveys.

The percentages of the population over 60 years in 1954 and 1963 were 8.3% and 9.3% respectively. The prevalence rate of psychoses per 1000 of the population over 60 in 1963 was 14.2 (male—14.5, female—13.9). The prevalence rate of organic psychoses was 11.8 (male—12.9,

TABLE 3

Classification of Organic Psychoses
(National Mental Health Survey)

	1954	1963
Arteriosclerosis	52	51.6
Senile dementia	20	15.8
Brain trauma	4	16.8
Encephalitis	4	9.5
Syphilis	20	6.3
Total	100%	100%

TABLE 4

Prevalence Rate of Mental Disorders of the Aged
per 1000 of Population Over 60 in 1963
(National Mental Health Survey)

	Total	Male	Female
Psychoses	14.2	14.5	13.9
Organic	11.8	12.9	10.9
Other	2.4	1.6	3.0
Mental deficiency	1.2	1.6	0.9
Others	4.5	6.7	2.6
Total	19.9	22.8	17.4

female—10.9) and other psychosis 2.4 (male—1.6, female—3.0) as shown in Table 4. From these figures it was estimated that the prevalence rate of senile dementia and arteriosclerotic psychosis per 1000 general population was approximately 1.5 and that per 1000 of the aged over 60 years old was approximately 8.0 in 1963.

As for the social background, the psychoses of the aged were found more in residential areas than in agricultural areas, and more in large cities than in rural districts. In these surveys the criterion for a diagnosis for dementia of the aged was taken to be difficulty in social adjustment because of obvious dementia. It is supposed that, in rural areas, senile demented patients adjust more easily to their environment in spite of obvious dementia.

These surveys are concerned with all kinds of mental disorders and senile psychosis is but a part of the subject. It is quite likely that the diagnostic criterion of senile psychosis was not strict enough and many senile cases were overlooked. If the surveys were aimed exclusively at aged psychotic patients, senile mental cases would probably be found with a much higher incidence.

Kaneko's (3) survey in a small town (population 8,439) in the Nara Prefecture, carried out in 1956, showed the following results. By visiting 696 people over 60 years old in their homes, Kaneko found 44 cases (6.3%) of mental disorders. The diagnoses were: 16 cases of arteriosclerotic psychosis; 15 cases of senile dementia; two cases of schizophrenia; three cases of psychoneurosis; three cases of personality disorder; two cases of mental deficiency; and three unclassified cases. The total of arteriosclerotic psychosis and senile dementia was 31 cases (4.4%) and the age distribution was: 11 between 60 and 69 (2.3% of that age group), 12 between 70 and 79 (5.9%) and eight (19.8%) over 80. When analyzed on the basis of sex, the data showed 13 (4.2%) males and 8 (4.6%) females with mental disorders. The incidence seemed higher in the middle and low social class and in the poorly educated class. When the family members of the patients were questioned as to whether the patients were ill or not, 70% of the family members replied that the patients, although demented, were not mentally ill, but were undergoing a natural course of physiological aging. Unless the patients suffered from hallucinations, delusions, excitement or violence, the family did not regard them as mentally ill, and the patients usually did not visit psychiatrists.

In 1965, Kaneko et al (4), surveyed 1869 patients over 65 years old, living in three areas of the Osaka Prefecture. They selected at random 531 cases from the 1,869, and interviews, aimed at diagnosing dementia, and intelligence tests (Osaka Intelligence Test for the Aged) were given to these cases. The age distribution of the subjects was: 305 between 65 and 74 inclusive (22% of that age in the overall survey), 196 between 75 and 84 (43%), and 30 over 85 (65%). The sex distribution was: 226 males and 306 females.

The criteria of dementia were as follows:

1. normal: no evidence of dementia clinically or with tests.
2. slightly demented or doubtful case: no obvious evidence of dementia clinically, but slight difficulty in abstract thinking and memory, decreased attention and interest. Slight impaired performance with tests.
3. moderately demented: organic dementia suspected by clinical examinations. There was definite impairment of recent memory, difficulty in doing simple additions, and often some deterioration. Impaired performance (dementia) with tests.
4. severely demented: obvious dementia clinically. Severe impairment of memory, information and orientation. Some deterioration in habits and urinary incontinence. Definite impaired performance (dementia) with tests.

The following results were obtained: normal—213 (40.1% of those studied), slightly demented or doubtful—280 (52.7%), moderately demented—35 (6.6%) and severely demented—3 (0.6%), as shown in Table 5. If moderately and severely demented cases were regarded as demented patients, the number was 38 (7.2%) and was composed of arteriosclerotic dementia (5.3%), and senile dementia (1.9%) as shown in Table 6.

TABLE 5

Incidence of Dementia in the Community
(Kaneko, 1967)

		AGE RANGE 65-69	70-74	75-79	80-84	85-89	90-	Total	
Normal	Male	41	22	17	17	2	1	100	213
	Female	44	29	21	14	3	2	113	
Borderline	Male	23	41	26	18	2	0	110	280
	Female	47	51	38	24	9	1	170	
Dementia	Male	3	3	6	2	1	0	15	38
	Female	0	1	7	6	6	3	23	
Total	Male	67	66	49	37	5	1	225	531
	Female	91	81	66	44	18	6	306	

TABLE 6

Prevalence Rate of Dementia in the Aged Over 65
(Kaneko, 1967)

		65-69	70-74	75-79	80-84	85-89	90-	Total	
Senile Dementia	Male	1.5	0	4.1	2.7	20.0	0	2.2	1.9
	Female	0	0	3.0	2.3	5.6	16.7	1.6	
Arteriosc. Dementia	Male	3.0	7.5	6.1	5.4	0	0	5.3	5.5
	Female	1.1	2.5	6.1	6.8	27.8	33.3	5.6	
Moderate Dementia	Male	4.5	3.0	12.2	2.7	20.0	0	5.8	6.6
	Female	0	1.2	9.1	13.6	33.3	50.0	7.2	
Severe Dementia	Male	0	1.5	0	2.7	0	0	0.9	0.6
	Female	0	0	1.5	0	0	0	0.3	

The incidence seemed higher in older people, in those of the lower educated class and in laborers.

The follow-up study on the same 531 subjects one year later revealed a death rate of 3% in normal aged people and 35% in those moderately and severely demented. Of 213 previously normal aged persons, 123 remained as normal, 51 showed doubtful or slight dementia, and three showed moderate dementia. However, no significant factors were found to act as the definite precipitating factor in causing dementia.

When the incidence of demented cases among the aged is to be studied, it is a problem to decide the line between "normality" and "dementia." In my opinion, dementia should be classified into at least three sub-groups: slight or borderline, moderate, and severe. It is also necessary to establish the criteria for the differential diagnosis between senile and arteriosclerotic dementia.

Community-oriented psycho-geriatric services are few and poorly developed in Japan. There are about 132 guidance centers for the aged, but no psycho-geriatric service is offered in those centers, and there are no day care centers. The number of home helpers has been increasing recently, but these helpers visit only the bed-ridden aged patients, and they are not trained for psycho-geriatric care. Recently "meals-on-wheels" and simple telephone counselling services have been organized for the aged living alone in some small cities. There are many clubs for the elderly in Japan. Hobbies and creative activities are serving to foster friendly contacts among the aged. Some clubs visit lonely and neglected old people who are unable to attend the club because of infirmity.

SUMMARY

In Japan, after the Second World War, the birth rate and death rate decreased, average life span was prolonged and the aged population increased rapidly. Industrialization and urbanization forced the migration of young people towards urban districts, while the elderly remained in rural districts.

The Japanese family system and the attitude of young people towards the elderly have changed. However, there is a shortage of houses, and the income of old people is too low to maintain separate homes. For these reasons, 80% of old people live with their children, in spite of the growing tendency of the elderly to want to live by themselves.

Epidemiological studies and mental hospital statistics have shown an increase of mental disorders of the aged, although most of the patients are taken care of by their family members in their homes. The number of aged patients in mental hospitals is gradually increasing, but not to the same extent as in European countries. This tendency is more marked in urban districts than in rural areas.

In Japan, there are many small private mental hospitals, in which special psycho-geriatric care is lacking. However, in relatively large mental hospitals there are special geriatric units and adequately planned psycho-geriatric care. Besides these mental hospitals, there are many psychiatric units in general hospitals, which treat mostly acute conditions, such as confusional states, depression and neurosis.

Community-oriented psycho-geriatric care is now slowly developing. However, there are few home helpers and visiting nurses are in short supply. Most of the psycho-geriatric patients are cared for by their family members in their homes. Confronted with a rapidly increasing aged population, the Japanese government and the psychiatrists are now planning the integration of psycho-geriatric care within a comprehensive geriatric service.

REFERENCES

1. HASEGAWA, K., ET AL. 1970. *Psychiat. Neurol. Jap.*, 72:247.
2. KANEKO, Z. 1967. Unpublished data.
3. KANEKO, Z., ET AL. 1959. *Rohnenbyo* (geriatrics), 3:131.
4. KANEKO, Z., ET AL. 1969. *Proceedings of 8 Intern. Congr. Gerontology*, Vol. 1. 284.
5. KOBAYASHI, E., ET AL. 1968 *Nagoya Med. J.*, 14:1.
6. MINISTRY OF WELFARE. 1965. Mental health survey (1963) in Japan.
7. MIZUNO, K. 1959. *Psychiat. Neurol. Jap.*, 61:11.
8. NAKAO, H., ET AL. 1967. *Psychiat. Neurol. Jap.*, 69:1060.
9. SHINFUKU, N. 1955. *Psychiat. Neurol. Jap.*, 57:167.
10. SUGIMOTO, N., ET AL. 1970. *Clinical Psychiatry*, 12:445.

25

FACING DEATH

ELISABETH K. ROSS, M.D.

*Medical Director, South Cook County, Mental Health and
Family Services, Chicago Heights, Illinois*

INTRODUCTION

Thousands of patients die every day in our hospitals. Innumerable old people may wait in a lonely room or nursing home for death to come, yet it is only recently (12) that physicians, psychiatrists, ministers, and others have started to study our role in counseling and ministering to the critically sick in institutions and at home.

This paper attempts to summarize what we have learned from interviewing over 700 terminally ill patients of all ages by asking them explicitly to be our teachers.

THE STUDY

A large teaching hospital was used for these weekly interviews. A minister, a terminally ill patient, and the writer (psychiatrist) held a dialogue behind a one-way screen window, in order to share this learning experience with students of medicine, nurses, theologians, and sociologists. Patients were chosen at random. Those who were regarded as physically able to sit in a wheelchair or be comfortable on a stretcher (for the duration of an interview lasting from 10 to 60 minutes) were introduced to the idea of our seminar on Death and Dying and asked if they wished to contribute. The majority of patients welcomed us with open arms. "I don't understand this. You are young and healthy and you actually want to talk to an old woman about her dying?" were typical expressions. Others stated, "It's nice to be needed and wanted once more," while a few questioned what they could teach "educated people."

In preliminary interviews, some of our patients immediately discussed their pain, isolation, financial concerns, or family matters related to their illness and impending death. When we asked them to "hold off" until tomorrow, the day of the seminar, they complied with our request, but were often unable to talk about it the next day. We soon learned that such spontaneity cannot be scheduled and that we had to allow our patients to ventilate and share when they were ready for it and not when it was convenient for us or for our weekly seminar. This growing awareness resulted in our frequent unplanned bedside interviews which ultimately exceeded the official sessions in the classroom. The lessons we learned from our patients not only derived from these two types of interviews, but also from home visits with preterminal patients.

In a majority of our patients the diagnosis of potentially terminal illness had been confirmed. Patients were seen between two years and two weeks prior to their actual death. More than half of these people had not been told explicitly about the exact nature of their illness, while some had actually been misinformed with the belief that it would be "best" if they were not aware of the seriousness of their illness. It was this latter group who did most poorly. Few of them trusted their physician truly, many of them expressed bitterness about "the conspiracy of silence," and some were dismayed that they had so little to say about the treatment plans. They simply could not understand why they felt progressively worse when "I am supposed to be getting better."

THE PHYSICIANS

The patients who did best were treated by a handful of physicians who were quickly identified (through the behavior of their patients). Their patients were mostly in good spirits, even when physical pain increased. They were very ready to talk about their illness, and prognosis, and quietly put their affairs in order. They often volunteered to come to our seminars on Death and Dying with the frequently expressed hope that it might help young doctors "to become as comfortable as my doctor" when it came time to face a critically ill patient.

The following common denominators found among those physicians who were "comfortable" in handling terminal patients included:

1. Personal experience in their own families with terminal illness, suffering and death. They had learned through these personal experiences to become more comfortable in dealing with death.
2. As soon as the diagnosis was confirmed, they sat with their patients and their families and informed them about the seriousness of the illness.
3. They were then able to wait until the patient was emotionally ready to "hear more," i.e., when patients asked more details or more specific questions pertaining to their illness or prognosis. All questions were answered in a language which the patient was able to understand.
4. Combined with the bad news, these physicians gave hope and conveyed to the patient that they did not plan to desert them later on (this refers implicitly to the time when the patient is beyond medical help).
5. They continued to visit them in the same manner and with the same care from the beginning of the hospitalization to the time of their death. When a patient was transferred to a nursing home or to his own home, they continued the contact by personal visits or by phone.
6. They did not avoid questions from patient or family members. Finally, and significantly:
7. They saw to it that adequate pain relief minimized the suffering and they did not hesitate to ask social services, ministers, or others for help when indicated.

The majority of our patients were not this fortunate. They were often isolated and lonely, they had to wait twice as long for a nurse to respond to a call, questions raised were often evaded. It is the patient of the difficult physician that I am describing in this paper and not the difficult patient!

Limiting myself to adult dying patients, we found that they pass through a number of stages in the process of their dying. (When a patient can no longer live at home and has to go to a nursing home, he often goes through the same stages even when he is not dying.)

STAGE OF DENIAL

The first stage is usually one of *denial* which may last from a few minutes to several months; rarely does the patient remain in this stage the rest of his life. When a patient has been properly informed and suddenly talks about his vacation next year, thus changing the topic of conversation, it seems clear that he is not yet ready to face his illness. This can be quite misleading since we found that the majority of patients in the stage of denial are quite aware of their illness but unable to talk about it because *we* need denial. The patient senses our discomfort and our wish "to get it over with" and he quickly adjusts to his environment. This is done partially to protect us and partially to avoid future desertion by us. Only one percent of our patient population remained in a true stage of denial to the end. It is of utmost importance that we respect this defense and not push the patient and force him to face something he is obviously not ready to face.

The patient's family passes through the same stage. A brief clinical example will illustrate how we can help patients when the family cannot face the situation.

An elderly man visited me in a psychiatric clinic, accompanied by two of his grown children as well as by two "in-laws." All five visitors appeared upset and extremely depressed. His wife had always been known as a hypochondriac and the family learned to ignore her complaints. As she grew older she improved somewhat, but about one year prior to their visit to my clinic she again started complaining excessively about a great variety of symptoms. No action was taken until she "passed blood." A thorough physical examination revealed widespread malignancy necessitating hospitalization. The physician and family agreed "not to tell her." The family decided to confirm that it was psychosomatic. To allay any fears and confirm that the disorder was of a psychosomatic nature, they asked me if I would see her in psychotherapy.

I told them as non-judgmentally as possible that I wished to see them rather than the cancer patient, since they obviously had a tremendous amount of guilt, grief, and unfinished business. All five members consented and participated in a total of 10 hours. During this time I became aware that this family was unable to benefit from these sessions in view of the fact that their denial was almost complete. I requested a joint session, at which the father summarized what he believed he had learned. He commented, "I have learned that we have to lie to her, that I have to play the clown, and that we all have to cheer her up." I told him that I did not wish to break down his denial and would no longer see them until they requested further help. I asked permission to make occasional housecalls on the cancer patient, a request that was not easily granted since the family was afraid I would tell her about her malignancy.

My first two visits were extremely painful for me. The old lady was constantly accompanied by at least one member of the family to prevent me from saying the "wrong thing." Mrs. W. was in great physical discomfort, whining almost constantly and provoking enormous guilt in those around her. My last visit started the same way until my tolerance was reached. I told the husband, "I am dying for a cup of coffee." He disappeared for about two minutes to heat some water. This was the only time Mrs. W. and I had ever been alone. I held her hand and simply said, "It's tough, isn't it?" With amazing strength she grabbed my hand. "I could die tomorrow, but *they* couldn't take it!" I reassured her of my awareness of the situation and my impression that the family would not face it until after her death. I also promised her that I would remain available whenever they needed help after her death. She smiled when her husband re-entered the room.

Mrs. W. died three days later. Seven months after her death, the widower still informed his old friends that his wife was "only on a vacation." Thirteen months after her death I received a wedding invitation. Mr. W. had found a delightful widow and moved overnight from the stage of denial to the stage of acceptance. I find it more humane in such cases to allow people to keep their denial, especially a man who has been married for four decades and cannot conceive of living utterly alone.

STAGE OF ANGER

When patients (or family) give up their denial, they often become extremely difficult. They complain about everything and anything, becoming highly critical of family and staff. Their anger is also displaced onto God. Unfortunately we take this anger personally and do not appreciate enough that this is progress. During this natural and temporary phase, the patient asks, "Why me?" If we can learn not to take this anger personally, but allow him to ventilate his rage, he becomes more comfortable within a very short time.

The next case history illustrates this stage. Mrs. S. was in a stage of anger and anguish when I saw him in a hallway in the hospital. I approached him with the question, "You feel like screaming?" He quickly turned around and asked very seriously if we had a screaming room in the hospital. I invited him to my office and he told me how he had never taken a day off in his life. He had raised his children and worked hard to get them through school. Then he started saving for his retirement and was finally able to buy a small place in Florida. The couple were about to move there, when his wife was diagnosed with cancer. This man also said, "Why me, why now? Don't I deserve it, what is the matter with You, God? Have I not been a good father, a good provider? Why do You do that to me?"

If we can help our patients ventilate and we do not judge them, they often bargain with God for a little extension of time to pass to the stage of depression and ultimate acceptance.

STAGE OF DEPRESSION

There are two phases of depression: the reactive, followed by a preparatory silent grief. It is important that we encourage their appearance rather than suppress the tears.

While the patient expresses his losses at first, he soon becomes silent and less willing to see visitors. He is less interested in his food or his environment and often lies in his bed, almost sulking, but non-verbal. This is when he stops mourning past losses and begins to grieve in anticipation of his future loss. Staff and family become then a greater problem because they are afraid that he is giving up, thus "dying on them." Words of "cheer up" or psychiatric consultations at this time are frowned upon by our patients. Both imply that his behavior is regarded as abnormal. It is strange that we have so much empathy in our society for a widow or a widower who loses one person, while we show so little understanding for the dying patient who is, after all, in the process of losing everybody and everything he has ever loved!

We visit these patients and say, "It takes a man to cry," implying that we admire them for the courage to face their finiteness. When we can do that, the patient passes quickly through this silent preparatory grief and begins to decathect.

STAGE OF ACCEPTANCE

The last stage is that of acceptance, when he wishes to see only a few people who are closest to him. His interest in the outside world diminishes and he often asks not to be given any further life-prolonging procedures. I am of the belief that we should respect the patient's wishes and not prolong his suffering needlessly. This is the time when a hospitalized patient should be allowed to go home to die.

Very few patients suffer at this time. In a true acceptance, the patient's hope is no longer associated with cure, treatment, or prolongation of life, but rather is expressed with phrases like, "I hope God accepts me in His garden," or "I hope my children are going to make it." A good therapist then simply reinforces the patient's hope and does not project his own needs and hopes! Needless to say, this is most difficult for physicians when they have been trained to cure, to treat, and to prolong life and have been given very few lessons in the Art of Medicine which has a most rewarding expression in the loving care of our lonely old people and our dying patients.

ACCEPTANCE AND RESIGNATION

A last case history will differentiate between acceptance and resignation. The latter is the endstage of the majority of our elderly patients in nursing homes. Acceptance is like a quiet victory, without bitterness or fear. Resignation is an anguished surrender, with such expressions as, "What's the use," "I am tired of fighting," or "Nobody cares anyway."

I recently visited an 83-year-old man who clearly stated that I could not help him in any way except, perhaps, by praying to the Lord that He should take him soon. I did not really listen carefully and simply shared his hopes with him. About a month later I visited him again and he greeted me with the words, "Dr. Ross, did you pray?" I said, "No . . ." and could not finish the sentence when he sighed, "Thank the Lord, I was so afraid He might hear you!" Mr. P. had fallen in love with a 73-year-old neighbor and was truly afraid that we had prayed too soon and the Lord might take it seriously!

This is a good example of what not to do. When he requested my prayers to help him die soon, I should have asked him, "What's your hurry?" and he probably would have been able to say, "What's the use? I sit here alone and watch television and nobody really cares if I live or die. I might as well as die." This is resignation, not acceptance. It took the old lady to make him aware how much he could enjoy life if someone would give him a feeling of being wanted, needed and loved.

TO PRODUCE RIGHT ATTITUDES

We have to learn to raise our children to accept and see the beauty in an old wrinkled face. Again we should teach them early that getting old and dying are not ugly. They are what we make of them. In the United States, 80% of the population die in an institution; almost all hospitals refuse children entrance. This is the generation that has never seen and faced death. It is also the generation that has to put lipstick on a dead man's face to make it appear as if he was only asleep! It is hard in a death-denying society to become old and die, and it is up to us to face this fact of life more realistically in order to help those who depend on us for a little bit more humanity.

The greatest tragedy in our nursing homes today is that we serve our old people without giving them a feeling of being wanted and loved. We do not appreciate enough that life is worth living only if it contains an interaction of give and take. We have to create more programs which enble us to use the many talents, assets, and wisdom of our elderly so that they may feel useful to the end. The success of our seminars on Death and Dying lay partly in the fact that we asked them to be our teachers, to give us something of their experiences so that it might enrich our lives and be passed on to others who suffer.

There are so many working parents nowadays who do not have the means to keep a housekeeper for their children. Would it not be wonderful if orphans and handicapped children, youngsters of working mothers, and retarded children were not isolated, but could be housed under one roof with our lonely old people? The youngsters would require less staff to look after them and they could bring some laughter and sunshine into the lives of the elderly. The old people could join the youngsters when they felt up to it and stay as long as they wished. They would always have a little one who would long for them and miss them if they did not show up.

No fancy nursing home or hospital, or even color television sets, would help these old and lonely people as much as the touch of a hand, an honest emotion, or the smile of a child. Life would take on new meaning until death eventually comes.

REFERENCES

1. ALDRICH, C. K. (n.d.). *The Dying Patient's Grief.* Paper, University of Chicago.
2. ANONYMOUS. 1956. Prognosis in psychiatric disorders of elderly, an attempt to define indicators of early death and early recovery. *J. Men. Sci.,* 102:129-140.
3. BURNSIDE, I .M. 1969. Grief work in the aged patient. *Nursing Forum, VIII,* No. 4: 416-427.
4. EISSLER, K. R. 1955. *The Psychiatrist and the Dying Patient.* New York: International Universities Press.
5. FEIFEL, H. 1959. *The Meaning of Death.* New York: McGraw.
6. GINSBERG, R. N. 1949. Should the elderly cancer patient be told? *Geriatrics, IV,* 101-107.
7. GLASER, B. G., and STRAUSS, A. L. 1965. *Awareness of Dying.* Chicago, Ill.: Aldine Publishing Co.

8. GLASER, B. G., and STRAUSS, A. L. 1968. *Time for Dying.* Chicago, Ill.: Aldine Publishing Co.
9. HINTON, J. M. 1967. *Dying.* Baltimore: Penguin Books.
10. JONES, E. 1951. *Dying Together, Essays in Applied Psychoanalysis.* London: International Psycho-analytic Press, V.I.
11. ROSS, E. K. 1966. The dying patient as teacher: An experiment and an experience. *The Chicago Theological Seminary Register, LVII,* No. 3, December.
12. ROSS, E. K. 1969. *On Death and Dying.* New York: Macmillan.
13. ROSS, E. K. 1970. Psychotherapy for the dying patient. *Current Psychiatric Therapies,* X.
14. ROSS, E. K. 1970. *The Dying Patient.* Brim, O. G., et al. (Eds.). Russell Sage Foundation. 156-170.
14a. ROSS, E. K. 1974. *Questions and Answers on Death and Dying.* New York: Macmillan.
15. SAUL, L. 1959. Reactions of a man to natural death. *Psychiat. Quart.,* 28.
16. SAUNDERS, C. 1959. *Care of the Dying.* London: Macmillan.
17. SCHOENBERG, B., ET AL. 1970. *Loss and Grief—Psychological Management in Medical Practice.* New York: Columbia University Press.
18. WILLIAMS, R. H., TIBBITS, C., and DONAHUE, W. (Eds.). 1963. *Process of Aging, Social and Psychological Perspectives.* I and II. New York: Atherton Press.

26

INTEGRATED SERVICES

ALVIN I. GOLDFARB, M.D.

*Associate Clinical Professor of Psychiatry, Mount Sinai School
of Medicine, City University of New York
and
Associate Attending Psychiatrist in Charge of Geriatric Services,
The Mount Sinai Hospital, New York City*

This chapter will discuss some of the features of what is referred to in Britain as an integrated psychogeriatric service, and in the United States as a comprehensive geropsychiatric health care program.

A complete psychogeriatric or geropsychiatric service must serve a large variety of psychiatric disorders in persons who range widely in age, physical health, personality, ethnic, cultural, educational, occupational and economic background. They differ also in personality, that is, their lifelong patterns of action, ways of life or life-styles. The predominant number are poor and have had lives beset by difficulties, with few early advantages and considerable deprivation. Their psychiatric disorders vary in reversibility, intensity of personal suffering and the degree of disturbance to the social environment. Also, the way in which physical and mental energy varies with mental impairment makes for different expressions of similar disorders, as do the different ways in which individuals react to their defects or limitations because of the differences in past experience and in their present circumstances and expectations of the future.

Thus, contrary to popular opinion and superficial appearances, old people do not grow more alike with aging, but rather continue to differ from each other and become more unique as they grow old. Nevertheless, it is necessary to search for and understand what common denominators in needs, or in responses to care, exist so as to make possible the delivery of useful services. The goals of services are, ideally, to decrease individuals' suffering and complaints and the complaints of the social environment about them, to ease their management and the provision of special care, to increase their social integration and sociability, and to help them toward optimal uses of their remaining resources in the most pleasurable and productive way. The many services for such care, however well and efficiently organized they may be, must be expensive in terms and concepts, as well as of programs and facilities.

DEFINITIONS AND ESTIMATIONS

If we speak of the integration of psychogeriatric services, what then is meant by this term—what is being brought together for coordinated efficient delivery? The discussion of an integrated comprehensive health care program or psychogeriatric service must include definitions of the terms and concepts, as well as of programs and facilities.

Comprehensive Health Care Services for the Aged

The following services to chronologically old persons and their communities are usually included under this rubric: population surveys to reveal the need for health services and programs of health and welfare care; evaluation-diagnostic teams or centers—both for outpatients and inpatients—for the assessment of the health problems of old persons and the family and community problems they pose; day care centers; emergency services for health, family or domestic crises; inpatient services of various kinds, including those of hotel type for residential and recreational aid to patients and families episodically or continuously; residential, nursing and infirmary units which can serve as protective or prosthetic settings for the remaining years of life of mentally and physically impaired persons, as well as hospital services for diagnosis and intensive care.

In the United States I have suggested the term geropsychiatry, however naive this may be linguistically, to refer to the practice of psychiatry with the elderly; this does not connote the combined practice of psychological and general medicine as does the term psychogeriatrics. In any case, these terms may be used interchangeably if it is understood that they refer to the psychiatry of the elderly with the addition of whatever general medical diagnostic and treatment skills should logically be a part of such medical practice. There is not yet a precise definition of geropsychiatry or psychogeriatrics. A World Health Organization Scientific Group in 1972 agreed that psychogeriatrics be understood to be "a branch of psychiatry concerned with all the mental disorders of old age, but particularly with those that first emerge as significant after the age of 65 years . . . concerned with the various forms of mental disorders of old age, their epidemiology, origin, prevention, development and treatment." While this definition is a good beginning, it does not answer many current questions.

Is the geropsychiatrist a psychiatrist with special skills, general medical diagnostic and treatment skills? Should he be a general physician with special psychiatric diagnostic and treatment skills? In many large psychiatric hospitals, geropsychiatric divisions have been placed in the charge of general physicians. Should geropsychiatric units be geographically distinct or should they be integrated with services for younger persons, although administratively separate and with special professional teams? Should psychogeriatrics include old persons who have aged in psychiatric hospitals or be limited to persons whose disorders first emerge in old age and to the mental impairments "of old age?" Should geropsychiatry be limited to the persons who are primarily and clearly mentally disabled, whether physically ill or not, exclude acutely ill, or include all persons of late life if "infirm," "frail" and in need of protective services of personal assistance best provided by psychiatrically informed personnel so as to make greatest contributions to the quality of life in old persons they preserve? Is this care of mentally-impaired old persons a welfare service with medical aspects or a medical responsibility for the person's welfare and in response to a public mental health problem?

Difficulty in defining the population, their disorders and their problems, as well as the problems they pose, is one reason for the fragmentation of services developed. Agencies and institutions have emphasized the needs for one or another aspect of care and have wittingly or unwittingly tried to specialize in its delivery.

Some of the obvious needs of old persons can be characterized as social, economic, general medical, and special medical—including those for psychiatric care because of functional or organic brain syndrome. The types of care could be listed as prosthetic, or supportive, protective of self or others, rehabilitative—including activities programs of all kinds, or intensive for acute reversible disorders. The places or programs are capable of description as home care, hospital or institutional, residential, or in terms of clubs, day care programs, and family assistance. Their criteria for the provision of care according to needs have been determined by the practical problems of care presented by individual variation in the degree of physical and mental functional capacity.

When physical functional status is relatively poor, mental functional status may be good or poor; when mental functional status is good, physical functional status may be good or poor. Poor mental functional status in a physically active person presents very special problems of protective care and simultaneously has adverse effect upon physical function; conversely, good mental functional status in poor physical function presents complex problems of prosthetic care and of optimal personal function. There are, also, multiple needs of chronologically old persons with good mental and physical functional status for the care and treatment of acute disorders of all kinds, including functional and organic mental disorders, as well as for social, economic and special personal assistance.

At present, fragmentation of services for the aged appears to be universal because "the patient goes the way the money flows." It may be that money will be the glue to bind fragmented services together. I say this because it appears to me that buck-passing—the passing of problems from one governmental level to another—has been largely based on the desire to evade the cost of the services needed. In the United States, State psychiatric hospital doors are being closed to aged persons, ostensibly to force provision of better care "at home" (in the community). The actual reasons behind such measures appear to be the great costs that would be incurred by the States if their psychiatric hospital services were enlarged and improved to solve the problems of needs of old persons for long-term, congregate protective care and prosthetic milieus.

Problems of this nature have lain behind the action of governmentally controlled public psychiatric hospitals to limit and define their services for the old for many years. In 1968, for example, the Department of Mental Hygiene of the State of New York again tried to define the problem of State responsibility. This was done by classifying old patients with acute, reversible functional psychiatric disorder as freely admissible to State hospitals, irreversibly ill persons with functional mental disorder or with chronic organic mental syndrome in which there seems likelihood of symptomatic improvement as selectively admissible, whereas persons with serious physical disability and minor mental disorder, with serious physical disease from which mental symptoms directly arise (acute organic brain syndrome), and patients who simply need physical assistance but are too poor to buy this, as inadmissible. Such solutions, by definition, unfortunately, fail to do justice to the shifting nature of disorders in the old and to the inextricable interweaving of medical, psychological, interpersonal and socio-economic factors in the determination of needs and in how they can best be answered. Most of all, such solution by classification tends to ignore the need for both inpatient care and highly complex programs of inpatient service to "make the diagnosis"—to properly evaluate and classify the patient, his family, his social situation and his outlook for improvement.

Old Age and Aging

Chronologic age here refers to persons 65 years old and over. Because persons do not age equally, many chronologically old persons are functionally youthful. By "the aged" contrasted to "the old" is meant persons in whom there has been measurable decline in physical or mental functional capacity: they are limited in their ability to perform normal, expected routine daily tasks by the adverse changes in sensory, motor, central nervous system and homeostatic functioning commonly related to "normal" aging and frequently compounded by identifiable disease.

Organic Brain Syndrome

Organic Brain Syndrome is a measurable decline in mental functional capacity. It constitutes an impairment of mentation in which there is disorientation for time, place, persons and situation, memory loss—both remote and recent—and deficiency in the recall of basic general information and in the ability to do very simple calculation. The psychiatric syndrome is one of measurable cognitive defects and is a reflection of brain damage (cell loss) or dysfunction. When the brain syndrome is irreversible because the cells for functioning are no longer present, it is called chronic. When the syndrome reflects brain dysfunction, which is reversible, it is called acute. The loss of neuronal elements—the brain damage—of the chronic syndrome can be anatomically demonstrated by pneumoencephalography, cerebral angiography or at autopsy as cerebral atrophy. The acute, reversible brain syndrome can usually be medically demonstrated to be a reflection of neuronal dysfunction on the basis of cerebral malsupport because of systemic disease, pulmonary or cardiac insufficiency, or to be otherwise related to interference with normal functioning of the brain.

Disorders of Mood, Content and Behavior, The "Functional Disorders"

Individuals can bring into their old age any of the psychiatric disorders of youth in which mood, content of thought and overt behavior are affected in the absence of that type of structural change or cerebral dysfunction which brain syndrome reflects.

Disorders of affect may be subdivided into those in which there are obvious clinical signs of biochemical or autonomic nervous system disturbance and those in which there is little or no such obvious disorder. In the first there is, along with the disturbance of affect, a physiologic move to an altered level of homeostasis signalled by change in appetite, in bowel function and sleep. The mood changes are reacted to differently, and are variously elaborated subjectively and behaviorally in persons of different backgrounds, circumstances and expectations. These disorders of mood with vegetative changes may be recurrent: either recurrently depressive, recurrently manic, or alternating (circular) in type. They are generally called psychotic, although there may be no actually gross personality change or loss of reality perception.

Affective disorders which are recurrently of depressive nature and which are not accompanied by striking alteration in physiologic function are generally called "reactive," which carries the mistaken connotation that they can be easily understood as triggered by external events; actually they appear to be complexly intrapsychically determined pathodynamic states which evolve in specially vulnerable persons, whether this be genetic, experiential, or both in its evolution. At times, the depression in mood circular disorders is so mild that the condition appears to be one of recurrent elation; more commonly the manic or hypo-manic state is considered "normal" for the person and only the depressive condition is recognized and noted as illness.

The Measure of Organic Brain Syndrome

The severity of Brain Syndrome, Chronic, can be graded by the use of the "Mental Status Questionnaire" (Table 1), as mild, moderate or

TABLE 1

Mental Status Questionnaire—"Special Ten"*

Question	Presumed Test Area
1. Where are we now?	Place
2. Where is this place (located)?	Place
3. What is today's date-day of month?	Time
4. What month is it?	Time
5. What year is it?	Time
6. How old are you?	Memory-recent or remote
7. What is your birthday?	Memory-recent or remote
8. What year were you born?	Memory-remote
9. Who is president of the U.S.?	General information-memory
10. Who was president before him?	General information-memory

* Modified from Mental Status by Kahn, Pollack and Goldfarb.
Reproduced from "The Evaluation of Geriatric Patients Following Treatment" by A. I. Goldfarb, in *Evaluation of Psychiatric Treatment,* edited by P. H. Hoch and J. Rubin. New York: Grune & Stratton, 1964, 271-308.

TABLE 2

Rating of Mental Functional Impairment by
Mental Status Questionnaire

No. of errors	Presumed Mental Status
0 - 2	Chronic brain syndrome absent or mild
3 - 8	Chronic brain syndrome moderate
9 - 10	Chronic brain syndrome severe
Nontestable	Chronic brain syndrome severe*

* In the not uncooperative person without deafness or insuperable language barrier.
Reproduced from "The Evaluation of Geriatric Patients Following Treatment" by A. I. Goldfarb, in *Evaluation of Psychiatric Treatment,* edited by P. H. Hoch and J. Rubin. New York: Grune & Stratton, 1964, 271-308.

severe (Table 2). The questionnaire consists of 10 questions which, in a condensed manner, screen for the components of the organic brain syndrome.

The deficits in orientation, memory, information and calculation, when more completely evaluated than by the short screening test alone, are generally found to be rather uniformly affected with chronic brain syndrome; when the brain syndrome is acute the defects may be less uniformly affected—they are "patchy." Also, in acute brain syndrome the defects of cognition are complicated by confabulation. This is also true when chronic brain syndrome is developing or growing worse, which can occur either episodically or stepwise. A special type of confabulation

TABLE 3

Order of Stimulation Used in Face-Hand Test*

1. Right cheek—left hand
2. Left cheek—right hand
3. Right cheek—right hand
4. Left cheek—left hand
5. Right cheek—left cheek
6. Right hand—left hand
7. Right cheek—left hand
8. Left cheek—right hand
9. Right cheek—right hand
10. Left cheek—left hand

* As modified from Bender, Fink and Green by Kahn and Pollack.
Reproduced from "The Evaluation of Geriatric Patients Following Treatment" by A. I. Gold-farb, in *Evaluation of Psychiatric Treatment*, edited by P. H. Hoch and J. Rubin. New York: Grune & Stratton, 1964, 271-308.

occurs in persons of good, well automatized, and socially adaptive patterns who, in their politeness, appear to prefer not to be troubled, troubling, or embarrassing to the social environment. Acute brain syndrome may be complicated by hallucinatory phenomena or dream-like episodes such as are commonly seen with drug intoxication or withdrawal.

The Face-Hand Test (double simultaneous-stimulation) is also helpful in screening for brain syndrome and of value in the gradation of its degree (see Table 3).

It has been fairly well established that the failure to properly report touch on the back of the hands, placed by the patient on his knees in this test, is a valid and reliable suggestion of brain damage of the senile or Alzheimer type reflected by organic brain syndrome of the chronologically old. The errors made are failure to report the touch at all—extinction, displacement of the hand touch to another part of the person's body, projection of the hand touch to a part of the examiner's body, and exsomesthesia—indicating the touch as somewhere in those "out there" or "over there." The number of errors is recorded for the test done with eyes closed and repeated with eyes open. Anxious, distressed, socially "unpoised" persons may make more errors with eyes open than with eyes closed.

Activities of Daily Life

Observation or information from family about the person's ability in the performance of several routine activities of daily life helps in grading the severity of organic brain syndrome. Routine activities may be graded from most difficult to those requiring least brain capacity as follows: ability to travel alone, to walk about outside the home without losing one's way, to shop, cook, dress and undress correctly, bathe unassisted, attend to usual toilet, feed self, find one's way around the familiar home, remain continent of bladder and bowels. Obviously, persons with psychiatrically measured brain syndrome or radiographic evidence of brain damage who are able to travel alone are less severely afflicted than persons who need help with their dressing and undressing. It is true, however, that well automatized patterns of action, early acquired, may protect persons from the early emergence of disability in many areas of functioning when brain damage is present and may even tend to invalidate specific tests. The so-called functional disorders can co-exist with developing organic brain syndrome and complicate or be complicated by it.

Some of the characteristics of old persons with mental disorders are tabulated so as to show their expected relationship to each other, to clinical and special tests, to treatment and programs (see Table 4). These data are outlined in considerable detail for the following reasons. First, while all the tests, clinical and technical, cannot be expected to be exactly concordant, wide divergence from expectation should prompt one to more intensive study and treatment—for example, a deep depression with clear sadness, suicidal ideation, and vegetative signs in conjunction with a 9+ M.S.Q. or with many incorrect Face-Hand test responses should make one doubt the reliability of the tests for organic brain syndrome and press on to a trial of anti-depressant therapy. This would mean placement in an intensive treatment care area, as opposed to a protective milieu. Second, when symptoms and signs are largely concordant, persons to the left of the line which separates the moderate from the severe organic brain syndrome may do well with treatment of their mood and behavior disorders despite the presence of brain syndrome; many of them can be helped enough to go back to their previous residences. Conversely, persons with moderately severe and severe organic brain syndrome usually need long-term protective care and rehabilitative treatment to improve adjustment to the special facility and to increase their comfort and pleasure, but not for "return back to the community."

Estimates of Needs—Population Surveys

In modern, technologically advanced societies, about 10 percent of the population is now 65 years of age or over. In developing countries, improvement in food, housing, acute infections and contagious disease control, as well as protection against chemical and biological insulting agents. will result in a similar increase from the basic three or four percent minimum to a probable 10 percent or more, and certainly in the absolute number.

Surveys must be periodic because of the changes in population with time. Otherwise, programs and institutions become inadequate and obsolete, yet tend to perpetuate themselves by attempting to redefine their purposes chiefly by excluding the patients who do not match their services. In this way, institutions developed to deal with public health problems that no longer exist insist upon providing services of little value to society and deny their responsibility for actions with respect to current health care problems. Areas differ in the percent of old persons in the population and in the varying proportions of persons in the 7th, 8th, and 9th decades of life.

Both minor and major chronic limitations of function increase linearly with age. Minor limitations affect less than 2 percent of persons in childhood and adolescence; this rises from about 5 percent in the 17- to 44-year-old groups and about 10 percent in the 45- to 64-year-olds to about 25 percent in the 65- to 74-year-olds and 30 percent in those over 75 years of age. Major long-term decrease in physical functional status, similarly, ranges from less than 1 percent early in life to about 15 percent in the 65-74 age bracket and 20 percent in those over 75. In persons over 85 years of age, this is probably over 40 percent. In the older age groups, physical functional status is greatly affected by mental impairment.

The incidence of disorders of mood and content is high in the 7th decade, since the incidence, prevalence, and severity of organic brain syndrome increase with age. Organic brain syndrome is found in 5 percent or over of persons in the 60's, rises rapidly to 15 percent or more in the 8th decade, and is probably present in about 40 percent of those 85 or older. Greater behavioral problems occur with organic brain syndrome in illiterate and educationally and occupationally deprived persons. There are also greater behavioral disorders in females with organic brain syndrome—these may possibly be related to educational and occupational status or background.

TABLE 4

The Expected Relationship of Characteristics in Chronic Organic Brain Syndrome of the Aged

CHARACTERISTIC	None to Minimal	Minimal to Mild	DEGREE OF DEFECT Mild to Moderate	Moderate to Severe	Severe
Intellectual Deficit, Clinical					
Mental Status Questionnaire					
No. of Errors	0	0 - 2	3 - 5	6 - 8	9+
Face Hand Test Errors					
Eyes Closed	0	0	0 - 2	2 - 4	4
Eyes Open	0	0	0	1 - 3	4
Activities of Daily Life (Self-sufficiency)	Good	Good	Fair	Poor	Very Poor
Mood Disturbance	0 - 4+	0 - 4+	0 - 3+	0 - 1+	0
Thinking Disorder	0 - 4+	0 - 4+	0 - 2+	0 - 1+	0
Behavior Disorder, Overt	0 - 4+	0 - 4+	1+ - 4+	2+ - 4+	2 - 4+
Incontinence					
Bladder	0	0	0 - 1+	0 - 2+	1+ - 4+
Bowel	0	0	0	0 - 2+	1+ - 4+
Electroencephalogram Amount of Slow Waves	Normal	Normal to Minimal Abnormality	Normal to Minimal Abnormality	Diffuse Abnormality	Normal or Diffuse Abnormality
Ventricular Size Echoencephalography (Angiogram, or P.E.G.)	Normal	Normal	Moderate Dilitation	Moderate to Considerable Increase	Great Enlargement
Air Over Cortex (P.E.G.)	None	None	Slight Amount	Slight to Considerable Amount	Slight to Considerable Amount
Average Brain Weight, Grams*	1300	1221	1221	1153	1025
O_2 Utilization	Normal	Normal	Normal to Slight Decrease	Decreased	Decreased
Blood Flow	Normal	Normal	Normal to Slight Decrease	Decreased	Decreased
Life Expectancy (for Age)	Normal	Normal	Normal	Usually Decreased	Decreased

* Calculated from the post mortem data of D. Rothschild by Goldfarb and Jahn.
Reproduced from "Integrated Psychiatric Services for the Aged" by A. I. Goldfarb, *Bulletin of the New York Academy of Medicine*, 2nd Series, Vol.

Estimates of need for care based on the demand for existing services do not reveal the actual incidence or prevalence of disorders in the aged. The cost of private care acts to deter persons from seeking it; and proper knowledge about the selective admission policies of nursing homes, old age homes, and public hospitals in the past and present tends to be a pre-selective factor. The multiple factors of selection based largely on outmoded admission policies and procedures obscure the use of statistics on the institutionalized or hospitalized as a reflection of needs. Extrapolation of existing data, together with observation of the financially self-protective behavior of public hospitals and institutions, suggests that the need for long-term residential protective care in the aged is two to five times that which is now provided and at present it is estimated that about 5 percent of persons 65 years of age or over in technologically advanced societies are "institutionalized."

In the past 20 years, despite the blocks to their entrance, admissions to places for inpatient care have grown chronologically older, more physically infirm, more mentally impaired, and in greater need of continuous supervision and personal care. Studies several years ago revealed that in the variety of institutions providing long-term care for the old 30 percent were bedridden, 25 percent incontinent. The majority were constantly disoriented for time, place, person, had gross memory defects both remote and recent, could not do even simple calculations, and had a dearth of general information. Depressions and paranoid thinking and behavior were commonly associated with poor physical functional status and active disease of cardiovascular-renal, pulmonary, musculoskeletal, or central nervous system. Even when disorders of affect or content of thought were not obvious either episodically or continuously, the aged with brain syndromes of even minimal degree were vulnerable to acute confusional states in which agitation, behavioral disorganization, and alterations of mood and thinking called for psychiatrically-oriented care. There has been an increase in the number of persons with needs for care because of mental impairment and its associated disturbed and disturbing behavior in those with physical impairment, disease and debility with associated depression. There is also increased need for care of chronologically old persons with relatively good physical and mental functional status who may require care for varying degrees of time because of the so-called functional psychiatric disorders.

Most of the old persons found in psychiatric hospitals have grown old there, or have been hospitalized periodically before old age. From 30 to

40 percent of the first admissions to public psychiatric hospitals were persons over 64 years old before such hospitals became restrictive and selective in their admissions of the chronically ill old. About 90 percent of persons first admitted to public psychiatric hospitals in old age had a degree of organic brain syndrome. Their high mortality rate, however, decreased their numbers rapidly so that old persons first admitted in old age comprised only about 12 to 15 percent of the resident population of public psychiatric hospitals (State Hospitals) and only 25 to 30 percent of the population of old persons in psychiatric hospitals. Pressure on "communities" to search for "alternatives to the mental hospital" has increased greatly the population of old persons in so-called community facilities, chiefly proprietary nursing homes. The failure to admit aged persons with organic brain syndrome to the psychiatric hospital is now added to the transfer of large numbers of old schizophrenic and manic-depressive patients who are regarded as improved, stabilized, or well controlled by medication.

A psychogeriatric service, whether in or outside a psychiatric hospital, then, may have as a large part of its responsibility patients with long-standing schizophrenic and mood cyclic disorders and chronic maladaptive ways of life stemming from their personalities—characteristic ways of intrapersonal and interpersonal functioning—that have led to protective custody or protection of the community. These aged-in-the-hospital persons should be distinguished from old persons with mood and thinking disorders which have first emerged as significant in that they cause personal or social distress and complaints in old age. Their outlook for improvement or recovery is different from that of those persons who have aged in the hospital because they usually have more personal resources for return to their homes as community citizens. They have had better life experience outside institutions, as reflected by their late development of need for institutional care, because they have not acquired "the barnacles" accrued from a static, depersonalizing institutional life and they probably have greater intrapsychic resources than those who "broke down" at an earlier age. On the other hand, among the reasons for the emergence of their disorder late in life may be the loss of supportive personal, social, economic or physical resources which served to help them remain adequately functional and which are now irreplaceable. Also in many, mental impairment—organic brain syndrome—complicates or is complicated by the old or new psychological and emotional problems, thus increasing the likelihood of need for long-term or permanent psychogeriatric care.

Unification of Services

The development of a single unit which would integrate the many services required for the more obviously ill, if not all of the old persons with psychiatric disorders, would mean the collection into a comprehensive health care setting of many kinds of persons who have complexly interwoven physical and mental health needs of varying types and severity. Their problems would range from relatively pure mental impairment, needing psychiatrically oriented care, to the more clearly definable, "functional" psychological or emotional disorders that are relatively uncomplicated physically or emotionally. But in old age, as previously noted, these may co-exist with moderate organic syndrome with varying degrees of physical energy and impairment.

At the present time a number of different types of long-term residences overlap in their care of mentally impaired and mentally ill old persons. This is because auspices, admission and retention policies and procedures, and modes of financing result in a mutual selection of patients and institutions not strictly based on personal needs or the facilities' ability to meet them. A large number and wide variety of persons with the same or greater needs for treatment are probably struggling for survival and care outside institutions. They may do so out of ignorance or neglect, for financial reasons or public policy, or because of personal or family fears and prejudice about inpatient care and institutionalization.

There are, therefore, institutionalized and non-institutionalized groups which overlap in their physical, mental, social, and economic characteristics. This is contrary to the popular view that there are specialized facilities which serve distinct categories of old persons which can be identified and accurately tagged as most suitable for admissions to one or another type of place for care. There has been much talk about the "misplacement" of old persons in psychiatric hospitals as contrasted to needs for general medical or nursing care. But, in the United States for example, studies have shown that over 50% of beds in "old age homes" are of the infirmary type. The "homes" were first developed and are thought by many to still meet social and retirement needs. In actuality, they care for grossly impaired and disabled persons even though admission policy and procedures pretend to screen for socially able, physically functionally, and mentally unimpaired persons.

These populations overlap with those of what are called nursing homes in the United States which—although theoretically developed to provide home-like care to persons who have great physical needs for personal and nursing services—actually serve a large number of relatively ambulatory, energetic, physically well but moderately to severely mentally impaired aged. In the past, State psychiatric hospitals had a high proportion of the more severely disturbed, relatively "young" persons of 60-70 years of age and a high proportion of very old—80 and over—persons in good physical but with poor mental functional status as compared to the other institutions. The overlap in characteristics does not signify misplacement. The distribution, rather, demonstrates that a heterogeneous group of old persons with overlapping needs tends to reach different types of facilities in different ways, for the provision of roughly similar types of care.

It is, then, services for the comprehensive health care of a wide variety of old persons that must be integrated for proper functioning of a psychogeriatric unit. This is made up of the many components of good general care—food, lodging and basic medical services, casework for person and family, activities and recreation—to which must be added the special medical care and activities, as well as social services for specific persons and problems.

Comprehensive Care and Treatment Facilities

Table 5 diagrammatically suggests some of the components of a comprehensive geropsychiatric program.

The staffing needs will include: psychiatrists, internists, surgeons, dentists, podiatrists, opthalmologists, nurses, aides, attendants, lifters, recreational therapists, occupational therapists, vocational therapists, activities therapists, physiatrists, social workers, house cleaning personnel, and many other supportive maintenance and administrative personnel. While most of these will have full time assignments in individual components, many of them, including the chief of each disciplinary type, will have overlapping functions.

The size and staffing of the various components will have been suggested by the surveys, by the actual demands for services, and by the success of their operation.

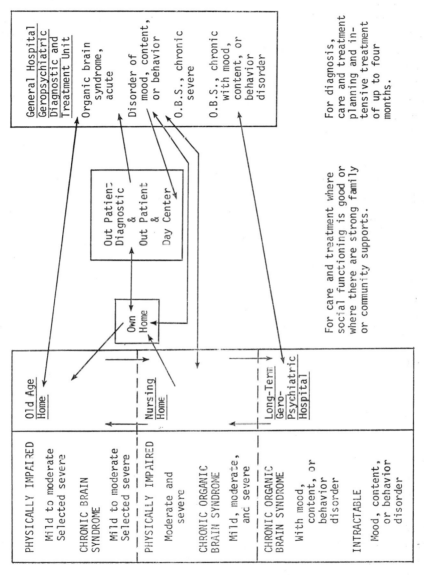

TABLE 5

Population surveys will have revealed the size of the older population and indicated the proportion of persons with brain syndrome of mild, moderate, and severe degree, as well as the proportion of persons with disorders of affect or content, with and without organic brain syndrome. The surveys will also have suggested family strengths and resources for the support of such persons in the community and provided data about community supportive resources of a similar nature, or the possibility that such services could be developed, their cost, and probable effectiveness or value. The challenges, both environmental and social, will also have been evaluated, because these can make considerable differences in the reciprocal tolerance of patient and community. From this information some estimate can be made not only of the types of care needed but of the probable size of the population to be dealt with. It is notable that in the planning of Community Mental Health Centers in the United States, such available information about the older population as the incidence and prevalence of disorders and the use and value of various programs of care has been largely, if not completely, ignored.

In Table 5 the arrow indicates the expected flow of patients from one type of care treatment area or program to another. From their own homes patients would come to the outpatient diagnostic center—or this would reach out to them—at times of crises or, in the absence of acute need, at least periodically, for advice and treatment. Those who need continued outpatient investigation or care would be followed in the combined outpatient/day center program by the same, overlapping staff members. Some of these staff persons—psychiatrists and physicians for example—would follow them into the general hospital, at least for a time, if inpatient diagnostic work or treatment was indicated. In the general hospital psychiatric unit, the "functional disorders" of mood and content would be treated and the recovered or improved patients sent home. Acute Organic Brain Syndrome, whether with or without known Chronic Brain Syndrome, would be investigated and treated, as would disorders of mood, content, or overtly disturbed behavior that can occur episodically or fluctuate in intensity with Chronic Brain Syndrome of mild to moderate severity. Such patients would then go to the outpatient and day center, or to the nursing home or long-term psychogeriatric hospital area of a protective congregate setting.

These settings would be free to call on the general hospital to readmit its patients when necessary and have a suitable arrangement for "outreach" to it or visits from its consultants for continued care of the psychiatrically ill patients, unless it has its own adequate psychiatric consultants. The dotted lines in Table 5 separating the "divisions" are meant to indicate that clear geographic separation of patients differently classified is not possible or required at all times; definition on the basis of mood, thinking or mental functional status may determine medication and the quantity and quality of nursing care or special treatment rendered, but the physical functional status may determine, in some institutions, where the bed is actually placed.

It should be noted that, while flow is reciprocally possible between nursing home and hospital, old age home, and general hospital, it is not shown to be so between own home and old age home, or own home and nursing home. This is because the decision for and choice of an old age home for the remainder of a person's life can be an individual and family decision; the choice of movement to a nursing home, on the other hand, should be made only after suitable medical investigation and treatment have also been accomplished. This is emphasized because, if an old age home has sufficient resources of hospital type in its staffing and facilities, it could receive any chronically ill person directly from his own home and perform all of the general hospital functions, in this way sparing hospital beds and perhaps assuring more adequate care for the aged. I am aware of no such units in the United States, although one geriatric center is now moving in this direction and some general hospitals appear to be preparing to deal with their own satellite nursing homes in a manner which may presage such integrated units. Had the State psychiatric hospital chosen to do so (or rather had the States chosen to do so with their psychiatric hospitals), they might have become sufficiently strong medically, surgically, psychiatrically, and residentially. By adding adequate social work, community home care, and special welfare services, they could have combined and integrated all essential components for comprehensive health care of chronologically old persons.

It was my advice in 1958 to the then Commissioner of Mental Hygiene of the State of New York that we move in that direction contrary to general trends in the United States. Despite some small efforts in that direction, there was, I think unfortunately, departure from this line of evolution. The steady pressure has been toward the removal of not only aged-in-the-hospital schizophrenics who have "become well behaved" or are "well-controlled by drugs" from State hospitals to proprietary nursing homes or make-shift hotels, but also to prevent the admission of old persons who appear likely to become lifelong "custodial" charges.

To improve the conditions of patients in nursing homes, as well as to decrease rivalry about which department should be paying for whose care, the New York State Commissions of Mental Hygiene and Social Welfare agreed in 1958 that old persons with "mild mental symptoms" referable to organic brain syndrome, who were not disturbing or harmful to others and did not require "care in a fully organized psychiatric facility," should be permitted to remain in a non-psychiatric congregate care setting if psychiatric consultation was available and utilized. Patients with prominent delusions, hallucinations, or mood disorder constituting a danger to self or others, or who needed segregated care, special protection, or restraint, were to be cared for in a psychiatric hospital.

This permitted, first, the Department of Social Welfare to continue to supervise patients openly admitted to be psychiatric problems and to finance their medical care with subterfuge from Welfare funds. Second, it made it possible for the Department of Mental Hygiene to plan for, create, organize, and maintain special units for the care of the more disturbed and disturbing old persons in so-called "community facilities" outside its own large hospitals. The first aim has been fully realized. The second has not, in actuality, but should be. Unfortunately, this concept is an invitation to abuse in that nursing homes can become the equivalent of poorly supervised and medically controlled psychiatric hospital "back wards," or areas for the exploitation of somewhat able, chronically ill patients. Conversely, the State can create pseudo-community facilities which are less well controlled and directed than its own "back wards."

As early as 1957, to avoid such fulfillments in form but not in substance and to help guarantee the proper integration of useful services, I advocated expansion and strengthening of State Mental Departments of Mental Hygiene or their equivalents to include programs for outpatient, day center, and patient and residential facilities. This was to include continuous training of personnel on all levels, an increase in staff-patient ratio for the care of old persons, architectural improvements for orientation and safety, the provision of home-like appurtenances, and greatly expanded medical care in all State programs and facilities. In addition, there were to be psychiatric assistance and consultation, given without fee by the Department of Mental Hygiene to voluntary non-profit organizations, and on a fee basis to proprietary homes, hospitals, "hotels" and agencies that care for, treat, or otherwise assist the aged.

It was recommended that there be a central office on Services for the Aged for the registration and recording of progress and movement of patients in all programs and facilities, for the coordination of programs of training and recruitment of personnel, for the maintenance of a bibliography and library, to collect and disseminate information within the department and to other agencies, to develop educational media and train personnel in special techniques, to constantly survey population for trends in morbidity, mortality, and mental health needs from the prophylactic as well as care and treatment aspects. This office would supervise and assist in nursing home, old age home, and hospital programs and screening centers and encourage and conduct research and investigate projects toward gathering information to improve services.

Among the most important improvements to be hoped for along these lines now, some 15 years later, is the expansion of training in the proper diagnosis, care, and treatment of the mentally ill aged in medical schools, hospital residences, and postgraduate schools or programs for physicians. This may lead to the development of expanded, integrated services by general hospitals, both public and voluntary non-profit, by the State hospital system, and by old age homes (the best of which are now burgeoning into geriatric centers), so that there would be a multidimensional provision by competing types of facilities of comprehensive care. In time, there may be a pooling of financing and a helpful central organization of coordinating and recording that can assist individuals in their choice of such services and in payment for them.

CONGREGATE PROTECTIVE CARE SETTINGS AND PROSTHETIC MILIEUS

General

Whatever their affiliation for additional care, the old age home, nursing home, and long-term residential facilities for older persons require special consideration. Old persons in general are opposed to the use of institutions; this is more the rule than the exception and is most obvious in the clearly mentally ill, the subtly mentally disturbed, and in the oldest and the most impaired. Thus it is that those who need protective care the most want it the least and may oppose it most vigorously, whereas those who may need it the least are less resistive to accepting the change in residence. One reason aged persons who need protective institutions also need psychiatric assistance is the intensity of their feelings that institutional use constitutes rejection by family and friends, as well as a loss of independence.

Unfortunately, the low quality of institutional care, however attractive the physical plant, tends to reinforce such beliefs and attitudes. Institutions are for the most part so poorly equipped, staffed, and organized that the resistance of families of aged persons to making use of them is more frequently related to realistic appraisal of the site of care and anger against "the system" than to guilt based not only upon giving the care of the parent over to others, but also upon "unconscious hostility," as is so often asserted.

Institutional care is usually regarded as a prelude to death by applicants and their families rather than as a new, useful experience in community living, such as it can be in the best old age homes and could be in many state hospitals which attempt to become communities in themselves as well as to remain related to the outside world. Unfortunately, most homes, especially proprietary nursing homes, do not have the potential for becoming self-contained communities and are by no means a part of the large community. Therefore, they do become points at which old persons with little or nothing to do, with senses, minds, and emotions blunted by drugs, simply wait for death.

Entrance into residence of such poor quality tends to downgrade the individual's image of himself; his disability may become greater and there may be development or exaggeration of psychological and emotional disorder. Institutional deterioration can be counteracted by the provision of "community type" activities, sheltered workshops in hospitals or homes, recreational therapy, hotel type accommodations, and the contagion of high morale in well motivated staff. These improve concept of self, improve behavior, and help decrease objections to entrance into homes as well as to continued residence in them.

Long-term protective care of physically and/or mentally impaired old persons has posed a formidable health problem for many years. The proper matching of individuals to the programs and places of care is complicated by the many parameters of need for care, its acceptability and cost, and the availability of resources. Persons with a high degree of physical functional impairment who have little or no mental functional impairment have generally been considered candidates for nursing home care, care in old age homes, or even special hospital settings. When these disorders have been complicated by depressive or paranoid mental illness, physical care has often taken precedence. Facilities for the care of functionally mentally ill and especially of severely impaired whose behavior is adversely affected by psychological or emotional problems are now large public health problems.

Contrary to general opinion, aged persons who reach points of institutional care are not the rejected, neglected discards of angry or disinterested children who could easily remain in their own or a relative's home were their kin kinder and society more amenable to the provision of home care services. Nor do old persons go to what in America are called Old Age Homes for social reasons, to nursing (domiciliary) homes for nursing care, or to state psychiatric hospitals for medical care alone. Aged persons generally reach facilities for long-term care after families have exerted much time and effort in their care and have tried a wide variety of agencies and services to find solutions to their problems and to make possible care in private residences. They reach points of care with many needs because, to use Zeman's apt phrase, "disease of old age is characterized by chronicity, multiplicity and duplicity."

Aged persons have a wide variety of physical, emotional, psychological, and social needs which co-exist in differing patterns. The ambulatory may be weak or vigorous, mentally able or with organic brain syndrome, free of serious cardiovascular or other disease or burdened by chronic cardiac failure, anemia, arthritis, glaucoma, emphysema, diabetes, or hypertension. Similarly the chronic bed-bound may vary in their systemic diseases and in their mood and the manner in which they react on interpersonal or intra-personal levels of behavior. Consequently, straightforward, simple placement of patients in institutions for the fulfillment of specific needs is a dream which can only lead to the creation of facilities which, like the Procrustean bed, would require a change in the patient if he is to fit. The ideal institution is one whose protective services, reassuring and supportive environment, general medical care, and special medical services cover a wide spectrum.

The essential services in any residential facility are, of course, food, lodging and basic medical care. Only some of the special points of importance can be touched on.

The goals of basic services, like those with special psychotherapeutic intent, are to avoid generating fear and anger, to decrease fear or anger already present, to increase the sense that one is self-sufficient and capable, to induce pleasure or at least contribute to comfort, to make easy the helpful relationship of staff to patients, and to promote social integration and sociability while permitting privacy and discouraging troubling interpersonal relations. Basic medical services, food, and lodging are paramount in achieving these goals, subject to correct delivery by staff with psychodynamic understanding.

Food

Food, of course, should be nutritive and suited to the patients' needs. Old people more often than not require special diets in that calories must not be excessive nor provided in such an unpalatable way that selection results in malnutrition. Low salt diets, low calorie balanced diets for diabetics, and other circumstances make it necessary to assure that vitamin C, thiamine and nicotinic acid as well as the necessary trace elements will be ingested. Soft diets for the toothless and debilitated and those with painful dentures may be required.

Many complaints about food—its palatability, texture, perparation, nutritive value, digestibility—are to be expected. Whether realistically justified or not, the complaints must appear to be met on a realistic level by staff while the symbolic meaning of the complaint is understood and also governs the response. Complaints about food often, if not always, are overdetermined and carry the message that the person feels he is not loved, cared for, attended to, helped to survive, as by a mother through interested parental care. Therefore, it is often the case that hearing the complaints and a promise to look into the basis and help if possible may answer the problem; when something can be done to improve the food or the way it is prepared and served, so much the better from the psychotherapeutic point of view.

Lodging

Persons in residence with severe physical functional impairment or disease may require hospital-like quarters for their comfort, safety, care, or treatment. Others may need protection without the close proximity to or frequent use of special equipment or special skilled staff. Another group may need personnel to lift them from bed to chair, to wheel them from place to place, or assist with a few or all of the routine activities of daily life, including dressing, bathing, eating, and excreting.

Living quarters should be, as much as possible, better than, or at least similar to, what the individual was used to in the past, while also meeting the needs for efficiency in management and protection. A person who is used to privacy and a room of his own should have this, where possible. When persons never have had rooms of their own and have always lived in close relationship with others, they may appreciate more space than they had in the past, but may be frightened unless a room is shared or an open door lets them view a nurse's station. This often holds true for persons who are frightened by thoughts of death and acute illness. Hospital or institutional architecture and appurtenances frighten most people but may reassure some. In general, hotel or motel like arrangements are "homier" and best accepted: rugs on the floor, pictures on walls, wallpaper instead of paint, avoidance of steel, aluminum and plastic in furniture and fittings all help to make an institution more like what the person came from; this is the important point. The old person does not actually need something from his own home to help him feel at home in a psychogeriatric unit; he needs a unit which is furnished and has warmth, which does not differ too widely from his own home or the previous residence to which he felt accustomed. At times, some personal belongings of "sentimental value" from his own home can be a comfort.

The lodgings should, of course, be neither over- nor under-heated; they should not be drafty, yet should have good air movement—static air is all too common. Marked shifts in temperature, high humidity, excessive drying are disadvantageous and unpleasant. Odor should be controlled by adequate ventilation. Refrigeration for snack food storage, bladder and bowel "training," staff attention to incontinent patients, and dietary acidification of urine (e.g., cranberry juice) in areas where incontinence is uncontrollable are of assistance. Also needed are proper assists for orientation: large numbers, color coding of rooms and walkways rails in corridors, stairways, bathrooms, near toilets and tubs; for sleeping comfort and protection there should be no side rails, but rather low beds and cushioning carpeting around beds.

Basic Medical Services

Whatever the psychological, emotional or cognitive state of an older person, meticulous medical care is usually required to avoid troublesome and dangerous somatic complications even in the relatively physically healthy. The medications prescribed for the psychiatric conditions may, at least temporarily, aggravate some of the symptoms related to the disorder. For example, phenothiazines and tricyclic drugs may add to constipation, to problems of micturation, and to dry mouth or dysphagia. Diet and an occasional need for gentle laxatives or enemata must be carefully watched. Diabetes, hypertension, and glaucoma are condi-tions very commonly present in the mentally ill old. Each is affected by depression, as well as by antidepressant medication. Also, the drugs used for hypertension may provoke or aggravate depressive reactions and may oppose the action of the antidepressants.

The frequency of respiratory infections, cardiac failure, and ischemic disorders of the heart is great in the old. Electrolyte changes are common with respiratory and renal problems as a result of the action of diuretics, with vomiting, diarrhea, and change in diabetic status. There is a close relation between these medical phenomena and cerebral support. Thus, it is possible to prevent the occurrence of acute brain syndrome by avoid-ing hypertension, hypotension, hyper- and hypoglycemia, electrolyte im-balance, and uremia; behavior can be greatly improved and maintained by proper attention to hydration, bladder and bowel function, and caloric and vitamin intake. The use of crystalline thiamine chloride, nicotinic acid, ascorbic acid, the maintenance of hemoglobin level, and good respiratory exchange are basic medical means of maintaining good cerebral function. Never to be forgotten, also, is the extreme importance of the relationship with the physician as a means of decreasing fear and release of anger in a permissive, dignity-restoring setting; the visit to the doctor or the doctor's visit to the patient can be a psychotherapeutic service of great value even if no specific medical service is performed.

Special Services

Many special medical services are needed to provide basic essential care. At the same time, they are important vehicles for psychotherapy by way of the relationship established between staff and patient. Podiatry or chiropody is generally "a must"; the feet of old people need con-siderable care for their comfort and well-being. This is especially true when diabetes is present because of the dangers of infection and gangrene. Dental care for the remaining teeth, bridgework, dentures, and gums make for comfort and improvement in eating habits. Physiatry is at least calisthenic when it is not a rehabilitative service.

Because of the relationship that can be established with patients by these services, they all have great potential for psychotherapeutic value. They can be psychonoxious if it is forgotten that failure to make use of their supportive and reassuring value can do the patient harm.

Recreational and Activity Therapies

Many kinds of recreational therapy can be of high psychotherapeutic value. Again, this is usually a matter of the relationship established with the leaders to a greater extent than it is related to the activity itself or to its socially integrative aspects. The patient first will do things—knit, cook, paint, dance, exercise—because he is encouraged to and asked to by the therapists, rather than because he "wants to." He responds to the plea of another—the recreational leader, nurse, social worker—for whom he does something which he cannot be persuaded to do for himself. He does not regard these activities as a way of relieving his "boredom" or "loneliness" even if these are complaints; rather he remains alone and isolated when social integration is possible until and unless relationships with leaders are developed and fostered. Through these relationships he may then go on to enjoy the activities themselves, but first his pleasure is through gaining the approval and the implicit or actual assistance of the reputed parent-figure. The value of activities programs for old persons who have organic brain syndrome lies chiefly in the leadership.

Staff

Good care of old persons almost invariably means a high ratio of staff to patients. This is what makes a psychogeriatric unit expensive. It is true that patients can be of help to patients and that volunteers can, under special circumstances, greatly expand and strengthen special programs. It is beyond the realm of possibility, however, that such mutual assistance or volunteerism can make sizable inroads into the cost of care or be of any great help where there is primary emphasis on economy to the sacrifice of basic personnel.

Personnel who care for aged should have training to help them understand the conditions and problems of the old. This should be continuous both because of personnel turnover and because of the need for morale-sustaining contacts with supervisors, leaders, and respected consultants.

Staff morale, in turn, is favorably influenced by vertical and horizontal staff conferences about patient problems, in which a framework for the selection and collection of information is provided and guidelines for care and management are offered and freely discussed. Such conferences are best led by psychiatrists or psychologists experienced in the care of the aged. In general, institutional staffs have too little appreciation of their importance as psychotherapists and of the importance of their non-psychiatric skills and duties as vehicles for psychotherapy; they need psychiatric consultations and conferences to educate them to these factors, to maintain morale, and for periodic reinforcement. They respond with optimism to the interest of a psychiatrist and react favorably to his policing function with respect to human transactions. Staff attitude, interest, and care of aged mentally impaired persons, the severely physically disabled, and the slowly dying or terminally ill are improved by the introduction of psychiatric assistance.

Aged institutional residents tend to respond favorably to a structured but flexible program which leads them to exploitation of their assets without unduly subjecting them to failure or confrontation of their deficits, physical or mental. In this, even skilled staff may need considerable aid so that patients may not be wrongly assessed. For example, behavioral disturbance should not be mistaken for dementia, nor mild and cooperative behavior be taken as evidence of cerebral competence. In a recent survey, staffs of unsophisticated old-age homes grossly underestimated the number of persons in their charge who had OBS; the disorder was recognized only if severe.

Staff members often need assistance in reaching decisions about the specific types of activity which can have maximal restorative or even remotivational influence. The fear that patients will lose self-sufficiency if permitted to become emotionally dependent, or that they may be vulnerable to grief at the loss of personnel by staff turnover, must be vigorously countered. Personnel on all levels need much instruction about the value of transference, rapport, "parentification," or the interest of the "significant other," found in the guise of a staff member, in promoting self-sufficiency or optimal function. The nuclear importance of a dependency relationship as a means of helping the patient toward optimal functioning and least vulnerability to personal losses is a paradox with which institutional staff must become well acquainted. They should be helped to understand that it is not the TLC (tender loving care) that helps old people to behave better, feel better, and do better, but rather their belief that they are understood, which is equated with being loved. Understanding of dependency reactions is of basic importance for all staff.

Individual personality types can be defined in terms of relative dependency striving and non-dependent behavior patterns. Dependency and non-dependency, in turn, can be defined in terms of to what degree the individual's motivating or adaptive behavior is elaborated on the basis of finding and holding relationships with and controlling persons who are regarded as partially protective and helpful, in contrast to the development of adaptive behavior in terms of mutual cooperation toward interdependence, pleasurable relationships, and constructive social and environmental control.

Cultural trends tend to favor the socialization of persons as relatively dependent. Personal experience and specific acculturation results in different experiences of early acquired or late developing defects or limitations to adjustment. When dependency is taken for granted by the person as normal, natural, and culturally acceptable, then episodic depression and physical illness, for example, may be used to justify the dependent search for aid. It will be openly exploited and the depressive or manic disorder will be openly displayed. If the individual is inclined to mask dependency, the depressive disorder may be dealt with in a guilt-ridden way. Persons who have functioned in pseudo-independent ways may be so self-critical of displaying disorder in mood as to insist on its absence, to place emphasis on the concomitant physiologic disturbances, and to refuse to accept treatment, ascribing their problems to changes outside them in a paranoid fashion instead of accepting aid for a shift in their functional state. Anti-social dependent persons may, with the mood change, become openly manipulative, coercive and angry—threatening suicide not as a means of ending the painful disorder but on the basis of reproaching, punishing, and forcefully gaining or regaining the desired protective supportive person.

An understanding of these basic concepts is essential to rational approaches to treatment of the seemingly contradictory patient behavior so often seen. If they are to feel comfortable and be most successful, staff should look on the maladaptive patterns as a patient's means of gaining aid from the delegated parent-surrogates elaborated in terms of his particular acculturation.

SUMMARY

Chronologically old persons constitute a heterogeneous group who vary in their social, economic, educational, occupational, cultural, and temperamental characteristics, as well as in health, however defined. The psychiatric disorders of the old include a wide variety which are brought along from youth and may have been recognized as of functional importance, or may first emerge as significant as a cause of personal suffering or social disturbance late in life. Other psychiatric disorders arise for the first time with aging.

In the first group are the schizophrenic reactions and disorders of mood such as recurrent depressions, mood-cyclic disorders of manic-depressive or recurrent type. Many such persons have been intermittently or continuously hospitalized for a large part of their life.

In the second group are depressions, usually recurrent, paranoid states, and the organic mental syndromes (Organic Brain Syndrome, O.B.S.). The organic syndromes of old age are psychiatric syndromes which reflect a decline in brain functional capacity. When this disturbance is known or found to be reflective of cerebral dysfunction and is potentially reversible, it is called "acute"; when the decreased mental functional status is reflective of so widespread a loss of cortical neurones that it is irreversible, it is known as "chronic." The organic brain syndromes, both acute and chronic, may complicate or be complicated by the presence of paranoid or affective features and occur in persons of widely differing "life-styles" and personality. Thus, there is obviously a wide variety of disturbed and disturbing psychiatric patterns in old persons.

These classifications are useful in terms of reaction types, personal suffering, etiology, function, social disturbance, needs for protection and support, and response to various treatment modalities. However classified, effective treatment, care, management, and prevention of complications require a wide range of services.

The ideal psychogeriatric program would cover the spectrum of needs by providing the wide range of services required with recognition of the individual differences between patients who present roughly similar reactions or whose descriptively different disorders have similar etiologic or pathodynamic factors.

Programs helpful to specific groups are often unwisely generalized. Most old people with psychological or emotional disorder, whether of early or late emergence, need comprehensive health care. A very large number must have care in a congregate protective setting—for their own comfort, well-being and social order of the family, if any, and the community from which they come. Most old persons with psychiatric problems need a prosthetic milieu because of their physical, psychological, and emotional functional limitations and the profoundly disturbing quality of their behavior.

One way of classifying aged, mentally ill patients is according to physical functional status and mental functional status—the degree of O.B.S. For example, physical functional status can be graded in terms of ambulatory capacity and measured disability and energy as "good" or "poor"; mental functional status can be described in terms of the measured degree of O.B.S., chronic with little or no O.B.S. considered as "good," and moderate through severe O.B.S. as "poor." In these terms, other things being equal, the most desirable candidates for management in nursing type facilities are those with poor physical functional status and good mental functional status—they have simple physical needs and, because of mental competence and clarity, promise to be cooperative and manageable residents. Conversely, the least likely to be manageable and acceptable by administration and nursing services are those with good physical functional status but poor mental functional status. These ambulatory, energetic persons will be wanderers, door openers, and over-active in a disorganized, troublesome way; they require close personal attention and supervision or chemical restraint with its attendant disadvantages to patient, personnel and family. The type and degree of physical impairment often leads to placement of seriously mentally ill—for example, schizophrenic—persons in long-term physical care treatment centers. At present, conversely, old persons with mental impairment are being denied admission to psychiatric facilities even when the mental disabilities related to the impairment are grossly disorganizing of behavior and even when joined by clearly "psychotic"—that is, depressive or paranoid—symptoms and behavior.

Chronologically old persons constitute a heterogeneous group whose wide-ranging psychiatric needs can best be met by proper integration of psychiatric, medical, social and other services. An integrated service should include methods of evaluating community as well as personal needs and opportunities to test models of home care, outpatient and inpatient care. Such models need not be under public auspices alone, but can be private—non-profit or even proprietary in administration. Basic financing, however, should be from public funds and there should be strong, central, coordinated and regulatory agencies.

27

TRAINING OF PSYCHO-GERIATRICIANS

Roy V. Varner, M.D.

Chief of Geriatric Services
Texas Research Institute of Mental Sciences, Houston, Texas

and

Adriaan Verwoerdt, M.D.

Professor of Psychiatry and
Director of Geropsychiatry Training Program,
Duke University Medical Center, Durham, North Carolina

INTRODUCTION

Modern psychiatry, as a medical specialty, is grounded in various basic disciplines within the fields of sociology, psychology, and medical biology. However, in the actual practice of clinical psychiatry this basic heritage can become vague and obscure at times. This kind of obscurity cannot be allowed to occur in the subspecialty of geriatric psychiatry, the psychiatry of late life, for the interaction of these three aspects of the life of the total human being becomes magnified to great proportions concomitant with and as a result of the aging process. Retirement, the death of a mate, disruption of family patterns, exaggeration of premorbid personality traits, depression, alcoholism, physical illness (both intra- and extra-cranial)—all superimposed on the natural biologic process of aging—are but a few examples of the interrelated phenomena that bear upon the emotional adjustment of the aging individual. Therefore, emotional adjustment in late life is a subject of great general psychiatric interest and, not infrequently, warrants psychiatric intervention.

THE SCOPE OF GEROPSYCHIATRY

For various reasons, geriatrics has been slow in developing in the United States as a distinct medical specialty. In Houston, Texas, a metropolitan area of nearly two million population, the telephone directory lists but one physician who identifies himself specifically as a geriatrician. Unquestionably, those physicians publicly identified as *psychogeriatricians* in the private sector of medicine generally are even fewer in number, though the need is obviously great. In actuality, *geriatrics* per se has been practiced in the main by internists and general practitioners. These specialists, as often as not, also do most of the geropsychiatry, such as it is, sometimes without recognizing the psychological aspect of their efforts. Frequently they do so with great competence, although sometimes with great indifference and misgivings. General psychiatrists also practice geropsychiatry as a part of their general caseload. Even here, however, there is some evidence that general psychiatrists do not enjoy treating the elderly and often do so with feelings of pessimism concerning outcome and doubt as to whether or not their efforts are really worthwhile. This attitude appears to have a sociocultural determinant rather than resulting from frustration over the complex challenge inherent in the diagnosis and treatment of the geropsychiatric patient.

THE DUKE UNIVERSITY CENTER FOR THE STUDY OF AGING AND HUMAN DEVELOPMENT

The Duke effort to train psychiatrists for special competency in geriatric psychiatry is the first undertaking of such a program in the United States. Geropsychiatry training directed toward other disciplines which deal with the aged and aging in many capacities has grown out of the core geropsychiatry training program at Duke. These programs are geared to the needs of those possessing M.D. and/or Ph.D. qualifications, as well as other professionals and students whose careers are directed toward aging.

Many of the non-doctorate persons in Table 1 who seek training are not interested in clinical psychiatry per se, but rather have more general

TABLE 1

Potential Psychogeriatricians

Those with, or candidates for Ph.D. degrees (widely varying backgrounds in social
  sciences, psychology, or basic biological sciences)
Physicians (with M.D. degree or equivalent, and two or three years of general psy-
  chiatry residency)
General Psychiatry Residents
Physician's Associate Trainees
Medical Students
Nursing Students
Nurses (psychiatric nurses, and those merely interested in acquiring gerontological
  knowledge and skills)
Physicians in General Practice and other specialties
Psychiatric and General Social Workers
Clergymen and -women (hospital chaplain trainees or those in public churches)
Physical Therapists
Occupational Therapists
Psychiatric Industrial Therapists
Recreational Therapists
Nursing Home and Rest Home Operators
Psychiatric Attendants or Aides

interests in aging and in dealing with the aged through their respective
careers. Most of these trainees ultimately realize, however, that the emotional happiness of the older person is the mutual goal of all, regardless
of profession. Consequently, they find it quite feasible to enter a psychiatrically oriented program which has proven to be a convenient and
feasible beginning point for anyone interested in any aspect of the
aging process.

With varying degrees of formality, it has been possible for representatives of many disciplines to get training by individually arranging professional working and training relationships within certain selected areas
of the basic clinical geropsychiatry fellowship. For example, ICSOP,
which is the Information and Counselling Services for Older Persons
of the Duke Center for Aging, has served as the "outpatient clinic" for
the fellows in geropsychiatry. This has been feasible since at least 61
percent of all referrals to this agency have been primarily psychiatric in
nature. It has served equally well as a training area for hospital chaplain
interns, social case workers, medical students, graduate nurses, occupational therapists, physical therapists, recreational therapists, and others,
all of whom wish to acquire special skills in the rendering of their
services to older age groups. Table 1 lists specific educational groups

which are receiving geropsychiatric training with varying degrees of duration and intensity through the Duke Medical Center and its affiliate, nearby John Umstead State Hospital, which has a strong geriatric orientation. Many of the Duke psychiatry and geropsychiatry faculty hold joint appointments at Duke and John Umstead Hospital.

In some instances, training occurs by "osmosis" in an on-the-job setting. For example, social workers and nurses were hired to work on the newly-formed John Umstead Hospital Geropsychiatry Unit without pre-training that could be specifically defined as geriatric. However, they soon became experts through their own work within the framework of that inpatient program which is directed by a small nucleus of professionals trained in geriatric psychiatry. Such a geropsychiatry inpatient unit has been alluded to elsewhere in this book in the chapter by Whanger and Busse.

THE ROLES OF PSYCHOGERIATRICIANS

If those in the field of Internal Medicine as a whole do not care to develop and recognize geriatrics as a discrete specialty, then the field of psychiatry may be the next most logical area for this undertaking. Indeed, a psychiatrist trained additionally in geriatric psychiatry may be in the best possible position to be the complete *geriatrician*. Due to the multifaceted nature of psychiatry as a specialty, he is probably in the best position (and may be the most able and willing) to evaluate and treat elderly individuals as total persons. His psychiatric skill will always be greater than his medical and sociological skills, and thus his primary identity will remain that of a *psycho*geriatrician. He can direct, however, the *total* treatment of the aging individual through skillful use of appropriate medical consultation and social agencies or key persons in the field of social work. Someone must take command and assume the ultimate responsibility for coordination of the total treatment of the elderly. Any of those listed in Table 1 may qualify for the title of psychogeriatrician, at least in some aspects of their professional work with the elderly. We will therefore define *psychogeriatrician* as applicable to anyone who, either in full-time or part-time vocational pursuit, offers psychologically based professional services to the aged and aging.

THE DUKE UNIVERSITY MEDICAL CENTER
GEROPSYCHIATRY TRAINING PROGRAM

The authors' training experiences, in terms of both learning and teaching, have occurred largely within the Duke program which includes the physical facilities of Duke Medical Center, main locus within the Department of Psychiatry, and the Geropsychiatry Inpatient Service of nearby affiliated John Umstead State Hospital. Some of these experiences are presented here.

Several occurrences over the past 17 years have made the Duke Medical Center an ideal training ground for not only *psycho*geriatricians, but for geriatricians and gerontologists of many varieties. Leadership in this major effort has been provided by the Department of Psychiatry and it has thus been psychiatrically oriented, though by no means psychiatrically limited or confined. The general geriatric interest and leadership of Departmental Chairman, Ewald W. Busse, earned U.S. Public Health Service grant support in 1954 for a program which would ultimately develop into the multi-disciplinary research and training organization that by the middle 1960's became known as the Duke Center for the Study of Aging and Human Development. In 1966 a formal two- or three-year training program was organized for pre- or post-Ph.D. or M.D. fellows. Today the program has two distinct components. The first component is research oriented, leading to the development of basic research and teaching skills in some aspect of the basic behavioral sciences or psychobiology of aging and human development. Through structured seminars and faculty supervised research projects, the research fellows focus upon a chosen aspect of life spectrum. Resources include the psychophysiology laboratory, ongoing research programs within the Medical Center, and the staff and facilities of the remainder of Duke Medical Center and University, including the Departments of Medical Sociology, Medicine, Physiology, Psychology, and Psychiatry. The fellows of this program come from widely varying backgrounds, including general medicine, psychiatry, social sciences, psychology, or any of the basic clinical sciences. The second component of training is more clearly that of clinical geropsychiatry and this is the heart of a current training effort in which many non-M.D. professionals can receive training and experience in less formalized arrangements with the Department of Psychiatry and its various related activities. Fellows in this program have the opportunity, while continuing with their own training, to teach other individuals who seek geriatric knowledge.

Geropsychiatry Fellows

The core training program allows individuals possessing the M.D. degree and two or three years of approved psychiatric residency training the opportunity to develop special competency in the field of clinical geropsychiatry. In the six years since the formation of this program, fellows completing training have, for the most part, gone into general psychiatric practice; at the same time they have identified themselves in some way as being particularly skillful in geropsychiatry. One of the graduates has remained on the Duke faculty and devotes nearly all of his time to clinical geriatric psychiatry practice, research and teaching. Available teaching faculty includes M.D. psychiatrists and Ph.D. gerontologists, each of whom is skilled in at least one of the basic content areas of the training program. The areas are Geropsychiatry, General Geriatrics, Psychosocial Gerontology, Psychological Gerontology, and Biological Gerontology. Knowledge is acquired in these areas through formal didactic seminar settings, individual supervisory hours, actual clinical practice (both inpatient and outpatient), case presentation, and planning conferences—all chaired by a trained geropsychiatrist or other psychogeriatrician.

The main setting for these training activities is the Duke Department of Psychiatry which offers the didactic program as well as the outpatient clinical facilities described previously. The "geriatric-psychiatric clinic," ICSOP, serves not only as a psychiatric clinic for older persons but also as a general counseling and crisis intervention clinic which offers services and referrals that may or may not include psychiatric services or referrals. The fellows spend a regular part of their time working in close collaboration with social workers, psychologists, and therapists of many other varieties in a joint undertaking of service to the elderly, mutual learning, and sharing of knowledge. Actually, ICSOP has now changed its name to OARS which is a part of the Older American's Resources and Services program. This operates under slightly different format and funding from that of ICSOP, although it remains an integral part of The Center for Aging and Human Development.

Within the OARS setting, the emphasis is now on community sociologic research, although psychiatric service and referral remain very much a part of the effort. It therefore continues to provide the psychiatric outpatient training setting for the fellows and others. The fellows attempt to understand the socioeconomic and psychological aspects of aging by interviewing and counseling the aging client and his family when possible. It is significant that OARS accepts any referral, age 50 or more, who is having any problem related to growing older. In this regard, the fellows have the opportunity to observe various emotional

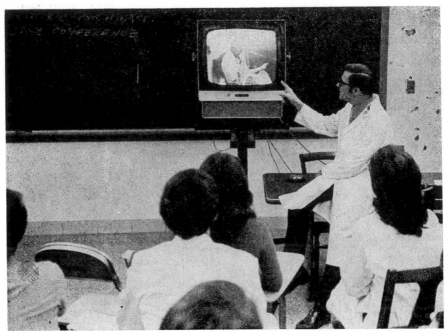

FIGURE 1. Discussion of videotape of patient interview (Duke clinical geropsychiatry seminar).

phenomena inherent in the transition from late-middle to late life. The fellows are able to present their diagnostic cases before the OARS staff, with each member contributing his own skill to the overall diagnostic assessment and referral or treatment plan as indicated. One special educational tool is the use of videotape interviewing of elderly clients by the fellows or some other staff member or trainee. The tape is played back before the conference group. The trainee's interviewing techniques and client's behavior can both be critically evaluated by a more objective method than is usually the case in this type of conference. In some instances, the fellow may feel that psychiatric hospitalization is indicated for his OARS client. Depending on financial resources of the client, the fellow may have him admitted to either the Duke or John Umstead Geropsychiatric Service. If the referral is made to John Umstead, the fellow can follow the client's progress while rotating on the inpatient service as described below.

Experience in medical-psychobiological and inpatient aspects of gero-psychiatry is obtained through rotation several days a week on the John Umstead Geropsychiatry Unit. Here the fellows function as psychiatrists under the supervision of the Unit Director, who is a trained gero-psychiatrist (see Chapter 21) by Whanger and Busse). OARS and Umstead Geropsychiatry staff members and trainees may attend each other's diagnostic and planning conferences, a practice which allows persons other than fellows to observe continuity of psychiatric care from the community to the outpatient setting, to the inpatient setting, and subsequently and hopefully back to the community once again with after-care support in the outpatient facility.

In the inpatient setting, fellows are expected to perform a comprehensive psychiatric work up on each admission to which they are assigned. Some of these will be elderly persons who have long-standing psychiatric problems compounded by the aging process. Others will be first admissions who have not shown clinically discernible psychopathology until late in life. Thus, all psychiatric diagnostic categories will be encountered. The work-up includes routine physical and medical laboratory exams as well as mental status exams and psychological testing as indicated. Specific psychobiological tests such as detailed neurological exams, cerebral blood flow studies and lumbar punctures are encouraged, if indicated. Fellows also pay particular attention to the social setting from which the patient comes and to which he will go upon discharge. In addition to the usual somatic therapies (psychotropic drugs, ECT, general medical care, and physical therapy), occupational therapy, industrial (work) therapy, and group therapy are utilized. Dietary consultation, chaplaincy services, recreational services, social services, and consultations from all medical and surgical subspecialties are available. The fellow works with and learns from a varied group of professionals. An important by-product of this arrangement is the opportunity for non-psychiatric professionals to assimilate geriatric orientation in their own practice. The fellow is also encouraged to create his own clinical research project under the supervision of or in collaboration with senior staff geropsychiatrists. (The McNiel article cited in the reference list is the result of such a project.) The management of the hospitalized geropsychiatric patient remains a fruitful area for clinical investigation. The inpatient setting allows the fellows to develop and test innovative procedures for the management of the hospitalized geropsychiatric patient.

Other Trainees

Many persons in the professions and activities represented in Table 1 have received geropsychiatric training through the Center for Aging and Human Development and its allied services and institutions through short-term structured courses, symposia, lectures, on-the-job training, voluntary attendance at scheduled conferences, and other less formalized means of learning. Often they do so on their own initiative as a result of a general interest in geriatrics which has arisen out of their own professional dealing with older persons from their respective fields of endeavor. As stated previously, psychiatric aspects per se of aging are not always what these individuals are seeking primarily, but are rather a means of increasing their knowledge in the field of aging generally. At Duke University Medical Center the psychiatric profession has assumed leadership in the fostering of *all* gerontological education, not just geropsychiatric education. Most students seem to appreciate the central importance of understanding the total picture of aging. Some have criticized portions of the Duke aging program because of its strong orientation to the Department of Psychiatry. Justification for this criticism is rather debatable, but the fact remains that no other recognized profession or discipline has thus far been willing to assume the leadership role in clinical geriatric training—certainly not one that focuses on the total person.

Psychiatric residents, medical students, and nursing students get geropsychiatric education mainly as integrated portions of their basic didactic curricula in general psychiatry seminars. The human behavior course for first-year medical students includes sections which cover specific geriatric topics. Other kinds of geriatric teaching endeavors with this group have been developing rather slowly—unfortunately, perhaps, since the need here may be the greatest. Medical students have occasionally chosen a geropsychiatric elective in the senior year, with their activities centered around the outpatient counseling service. This also has been true to some extent in the case of undergraduate student nurses, but particularly for graduate nursing students in the now defunct Gerontologic Nursing Program. Psychiatric residents have occasionally worked jointly with the fellows in the Umstead Hospital Geropsychiatric Unit. Again, this type of geriatric pursuit has been more of an elective rather than a compulsory part of basic psychiatric training.

Very little has been done, as yet, in offering continuing education courses for general practitioners and other front line professionals who deal daily with the aging and aged. One of the greatest educational needs may lie in this area since such professionals most often provide the point of contact between the elderly person in the community and available services. Decisions as to the necessity for hospital commitment are often made by busy general practitioners who frequently have little knowledge of alternate solutions to hospitalization of confused elderly persons. Frequently they possess little skill in differentiating depression from chronic brain syndrome in the elderly and, even when able to do so, often lack the time or security of skill needed to render satisfactory treatment. There have been several symposia at Duke Medical Center directed at such individuals, such as one on the subject of utilization of psychotropic drugs with the elderly. Another was directed mainly toward caseworkers and other socially oriented professionals. Elmore and Verwoerdt organized a geropsychiatry consultation program for case workers who were working with the aged within the framework of the North Carolina Department of Public Welfare. The goal of this program was to broaden the knowledge of caseworkers concerning biological, psychological, psychodynamic, and socio-cultural influences during senescence so as to increase their skill in making appropriate social placement, or in making psychiatric and/or medical referral of elderly clients. From time to time caseworkers from the local community have attended case conferences at ICSOP/OARS, usually for the purpose of sitting in on the presentation of one of their own referred problem cases.

Also, Duke social workers whose specific interest is aging offer many informal consultations to community caseworkers. Pre-Ph.D. psychologists, hospital chaplain interns, physical therapists, occupational therapists, industrial therapists, recreational therapists, and other allied professionals have attended case conferences and other group endeavors within the center for aging not only to fill personal educational needs, but also to offer consultation to full-time gerontologic workers concerning how their own professional fields may be useful in the total treatment of the aging individual. Chaplain interns have frequently held ongoing group therapy or discussion group sessions with elderly residents of a nearby retirement home. Persons from practically all medical allied professions have become aware of a special need to understand mental aspects of aging in regard to their own work.

OARS Outpatient and Umstead Hospital Geropsychiatric Inpatient Services have sponsored various day-long symposia for nursing home and boarding home operators. These have been aimed at practical problems involved in the management of behavioral and other emotional disorders among the residents of these homes. Management of medication, night-wandering, seizures, and sexual conduct have been among many subjects dealt with. In turn, we have learned much from this group concerning the problems that they face, most of which confirm a great need for the availability of psychiatric consultation to these facilities.

OTHER SPECIFIC TRAINING DESIGNS

Special mention will be made here of geropsychiatric educational efforts with Physician's Associate Trainees and Psychiatric Hospital Attendants. These two projects represent our attempt to offer structured, ongoing learning situations to individuals who usually do not possess academic degrees of any kind.

Physician's Associate Program

In the United States the training of physicians' assistants, now called associates, is gaining momentum rapidly. This is especially true at Duke Medical Center where one of the country's pioneer programs was begun several years ago in an effort to reverse the deteriorating physician-to-patient ratio that exists generally. A basic course entitled *Human Growth and Development* has been taught jointly by the Departments of Pediatrics and Psychiatry. Table 2 shows a 16-hour series of geropsychiatry lectures that initially were attached to the end of the general psychiatry portion of the lecture series in that course. Later, the geropsychiatry lecture series became more logically integrated with other subject matter of psychiatric content, so as to provide a more meaningful continuity in the behavioral study of the life cycle. Regardless of order of presentation, this block of lectures has been and can be presented as a short, self-contained course to any group of students interested in acquiring at least an introduction to geropsychiatry. The degree of complexity and detail of subject content will vary with the ability of the group. It is felt that the lecture series, as we present it to the physician's associate group, falls at a midway point of complexity between what might be presented to psychiatric aides, on one extreme, or to medical students or residents at the other. In any case, the subject matter itself can remain relatively constant for any group, but can be increased or decreased as to length of presentation, complexity, and/or detail of presentation, depending on the needs and the abilities of the particular group. The

TABLE 2

Geropsychiatry Lectures in Duke Physician's Associate Program

I. a) Introduction to Geropsychiatry and to the Duke Center for the Study of Aging and Human Development
   b) Theories of Aging
   c) Age Related Changes in Psychological Capacities
   d) Introduction to the "Brain Syndromes" of Late Life

II. a) Geriatric Medicine
   b) Geriatric Psychopharmacology
   c) Somatic Therapies

III. a) Geriatric Neurology
   b) Geriatric Nursing and Rehabilitation

IV. a) Psychodynamics of Aging—Basic Concepts
   b) Psychopathology of Aging——Depression and Psychotic Conditions

V. a) Psychotherapy Approaches with Aged Patients
   b) Family Dynamics and Conflict——Family Counseling

VI. a) Work and Retirement
   b) Sociocultural Determinants of Mental Illness in the Aging and Aged
   c) Social Attitudes Toward Mental Illness

VII. a) Ecology of Senescence and Principles of Environmental Planning
   b) Patterns of Care for the Aged and Chronically Ill

VIII. a) Community Psychiatric Service Concepts for the Aged
   b) Social and Psychiatric Services Available for Residents of the Durham, North Carolina Area
   (2 hour blocks)

lecture outline of Table 2 is thus presented as a possible didactic introduction to geropsychiatry which may be suitable for a wide variety of potential psychogeriatricians.

In-Service Training for State Hospital Attendants

Five years ago members of the Duke geropsychiatry staff organized an in-service geropsychiatry training program for attendants working in the Geriatric Unit of John Umstead State Hospital in Butner, N. C. Each class, consisting of about 10 members, receives 15 hours of lectures and seminars per week over a 12-week period. Two complete courses have been offered each year. The courses emphasize subjects primarily relevant to geriatric nursing care skills, although the course has become somewhat broadened recently following the formation of a distinct

Geropsychiatry Unit which is separate from the Nursing Care Unit. Students who are already trained psychiatric attendants are introduced to broad sociological and psychological aspects of aging in addition to the usual medical aspects. Patient evaluation and practical choices of treatment are emphasized within the overall philosophy that the geriatric patient being admitted to a mental hospital today can usually get medical treatment which will enable him to be released to a suitable outside environment. Thus, custodial themes of care for the elderly are rapidly being pushed into the background.

Both the physician's associate and the state hospital attendant courses have been well received. The physician's associate trainees expressed the feeling that the geropsychiatry lectures were most welcome as a general introduction to the problems of aging which would probably be useful to them in *any* future professional contact that they might have with elderly patients, whether the need be medical, surgical, or psychiatric. A few have even expressed interest in geropsychiatry as a subspecialty. Since the mental hospital may be one of the many areas where the physician's associate will be well received professionally, it may be that more emphasis should be placed on geropsychiatric education in basic physician's associate training of the future. The psychiatric attendants course has served to give geropsychiatry a hitherto unheard of degree of prestige within the John Umstead Hospital. There is no longer the pervasive feeling among the hospital staff that little or nothing can be done for the average geriatric mental patient other than long-term custodial care. Expansion of geropsychiatric services has now become a major priority, largely because of the dissemination of knowledge about what *can* be done for the elderly in psychiatric settings.

CONCLUSIONS

The specialty of psychiatry now has a slowly but steadily developing subspecialty of geropsychiatry. As a subspecialty, geropsychiatry finds itself in a leadership position in geriatrics generally, inclusive of medical and psychogeriatrics. The field of geropsychiatric education encompasses broad enough disciplines for the psychogeriatrician also to assume a major role of teacher generally or at least as teacher of other teachers who come from various professions related to the fields of geriatrics or gerontology. It is not clear at this time whether or not the geriatric consumer per se will buy much-needed services that carry a psycho- or psychiatric "stigma" attached to the label. We are now in the process of organizing within the city of Houston, Texas, a comprehensive out-patient counseling, treatment, and referral geropsychiatry service with some limited inpatient facility available. The service is clearly psychiatrically oriented in structure and major purpose, although we are "advertising" it mainly as a *geriatric* rather than a psychogeriatric service. We anticipate being involved in several types of training in addition to the in-service training of unit personnel. A major goal of the unit will be to offer ongoing training of students in schools of social work, nursing, public health, and medicine. Another thrust will be making available seminar-type courses for professionals and groups from the community. It remains to be seen what the final role identity of this venture will be. In any case, we all know that geropsychiatry will involve much, much more than just the practice of traditional clinical psychiatry with the elderly.

REFERENCES

1. Busse, E. W. 1965. Administration of the interdisciplinary research team. *J. Med. Educ.,* 40:832.
2. Busse, E. W. 1969. One medical school's approach to teaching problems of the aging. *J. Amer. Geriat. Soc.,* 17:299.
3. Cyrus-Lutz, C., and Gaitz, C. M. 1972. Psychiatrists' attitudes toward the aged and aging. *Gerontologist,* 12:163.
4. Eisdorfer, C. 1972. A call for training in geriatrics. *Medical World News. Geriatrics,* 72:71.
5. Elmore, J. L., and Verwoerdt, A. 1968. Geropsychiatric training for case workers. *Gerontologist,* 8:291.
6. Peak, D. T. 1970. Duke university center for the study of aging. *N. C. J. Ment. Hlth.,* 4:8.
7. Verwoerdt, A. 1969. Training in geropsychiatry. In E. W. Busse and E. Pfeiffer (Eds.) *Behavior and Adaptation in Late Life.* Boston, Mass.: Little, Brown and Company, Inc.
8. McNiel, J. N., and Verwoerdt, A. 1972. A group treatment program combined with a work project on the geriatric unit of a state hospital. *J. Am. Geriat. Soc.,* 20:259.

28

EXPRESSION OF PSYCHO-PATHOLOGY IN ART

M. Livia Osborn

Research Officer
The Institute of Family Psychiatry,
The Ipswich Hospital, Ipswich, England

INTRODUCTION

No other organism is as conscious of his destiny as man. His involvement with the past and the knowledge that his future is irrevocably limited have forced him to speculate endlessly about the nature of his life. Thus man is the continuous object of study by himself; he is under observation from many points of view: physical, philosophical, economic, moral, etc. Many words have described his ephemeral life: the precise, factual words of science; the forceful, commanding words of drama; the musical, sensitive words of poetry. But to the visual artist has been left the task of freezing his image and of documenting for the future a human caught in the act of living.

Many of these representations offer vivid and eloquent statements. The tenderness of childhood has inspired many artists: cupids, the infant Christ, suckling babes stretch endlessly through the centuries in Western art. The Greeks, the Romans, the artists of the Renaissance and many others since have delighted in adolescence: Michelangelo's David and the many young girls of Renoir are two examples. Adults, again, have been recorded in joy and in sorrow throughout time. But in comparison, the images of old people are less numerous. Yet, when they occur, they are usually powerful and uncompromising in whatever message they convey. The faces are marked by past experiences that cannot be undone; expressions of contentment, resignation, anguish and all the infinite varieties of other emotions are less subtle, as if the facial muscles were set hard, like the masks of players in ancient dramas.

Psychiatry is concerned with the most intimate aspects of man—his thinking processes and his emotions. When the mental processes are disordered because of an organic defect, chronic or acute, man is unable to function, just like a piece of broken-down machinery whose parts are faulty, worn out, or wrongly assembled. But there ends the similarity to a machine. Unlike man, a machine has no psyche. Man's vulnerability has no confines. When the psyche is sick, man is sick. Emotions are as much a part of man as flesh and blood, but their subtlety makes them difficult to grasp and record. Art, in whatever form, is an emotional expression and can help us to understand the intangible. Exultation has no better expression than Beethoven's Ninth Symphony, nor anguish more obvious depth than Michelangelo's Pietà. The appeal is to our emotion, rather than to our reason. While it is necessary and right to probe, dissect, observe, and theorize, it is also important that emotional ills should be felt for what they are. To look at some expressions of damaging emotions as preserved and stilled by artists is an exercise that those concerned with the human psyche may find humbling, but nevertheless enriching of their heritage of understanding.

The aim of this chapter is to present pictorial illustrations depicting pathological conditions of psychiatric interest in the aged. Most important, of course, are the illustrations, while the comments accompanying them are idiosyncratic contributions towards orientating the reader.

NORMALITY

"I have been young, and now am old."

Book of Common Prayer (1662), Psalter 37:25.

The above quotation states the obvious: old people were once young. Here we have normality, health. It is just as well to remember that old age in itself is not a pathological state. An individual who reaches old age has usually participated in three families: his family of origin, the family he founds and his children's family. Each group will have enriched his store of experience and contributed to his happiness and to his sorrows. Grandparents, placed as they are at the periphery of the family, need to maintain a healthy balance between an independent life of their own and involvement in the younger generations.

Familiar patterns of behavior, familiar surroundings and the feeling that they are still useful and wanted all contribute to diminish the problems faced by the aged; this was taken for granted in the past and was an easy achievement in the extended family. The small family of today has less room for the aged and society is forced to provide forms of foster care for the old, as it does for unwanted children.

In psychiatry, more than in other branches of medicine, it is often difficult to decide when emotional expression deviates from normality and becomes pathological. Old age, like other periods of life, is vulnerable to stress and sickness, but does not exclude the capacity for enjoyment, and appreciation of rewarding experiences, participation in group activities, and contributions to the welfare of others. A balanced profile of old people must take into consideration their assets as well as their liabilities. Here we have a painting showing a grandparent in a situation of normality.

Emotionally stable grandparents may have a beneficial influence on the dynamics of the family by helping in the care and upbringing of its youngest members; they are in turn helped by a feeling of participation in a process that is not limited by the time allocated to each generation.

In this painting (*Plate 1*), the old man, made ugly by age, looks wistfully and tenderly at his grandchild, who possibly resembles him at the same age. The child, on his part, seems to have complete trust in the old man, is not repelled by his ugliness, and, indeed, seeks to be as near as he can to him.

Children starting off their travels through life and old people nearing the end of the journey leading to death often seem to get on well together, as if the innocence of the first and the wisdom of the second find a common ground of understanding.

It is difficult to say why children and the aged, placed as they are at the two extremes of life, get on better with each other than those in closer age groups. It could be that the old have found many accepted attitudes wanting and have discarded false values, while the very young have not yet had the time to acquire them. Hence, their approach is more direct, the appeal to each other less encumbered and surer. Or it

PLATE 1

DOMENICO GHIRLANDAIO (1449-1494).
Portrait of an Old Man and His Grandson

could be that there is less trauma in their relationship because of the gap in age.

This particular painting, like the quotation from the Psalters, underlines the obvious: the young of today are the old of tomorrow, both are part of a continuum and co-exist side by side. To isolate old people, separating them in their daily living from other age groups, creates an artificial situation. Normality makes communications between the old and the young possible and beneficial to both.

SENILITY

"Last scene of all . . . is second childishness . . ."

Shakespeare. As You Like It, II, vii.

Shakespeare would naturally look at life as if it were a play divided into scenes, the end to be linked to the beginning. In *As You Like It* he provides a vivid description of extreme old age with its accompanying miseries. "Sans teeth, sans eye, sans taste, sans everything" is a depressing picture of decay. In senility the deterioration of all faculties makes independence impossible. Yet, despite the discomforts, many old people tenaciously cling to life and are as unwilling to die as children are to go to sleep when the day is over. Senility brings utter dependence on others and results in loss of dignity, which is the last defeat.

The painting (*Plate 2*) illustrates the story of an old man thrown in the dungeons of Rome, where he would have starved to death, but for the love of his daughter. She, forbidden to take him food, kept him alive with her own milk. It is a touching reversal of roles: the daughter had once been cared for by her father, who had nurtured and protected her in the delicate years of childhood; now, she is herself in a parenting role and literally nourishes her old, feeble father. His complete dependence and helplessness seem to obliterate the years of manhood, he has regressed to childhood. Meanwhile, life is maintained by a determined act of love. Yet, the old man's need for his daughter is perhaps no greater than her emotional need for him.

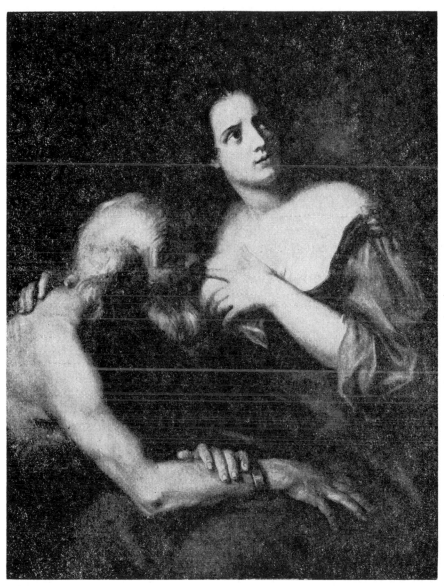

PLATE 2

BERNARDO STROZZI (1581-1644). *Roman Charity*

MOODINESS

". . . The surly advance of Decrepitude."

Winston Churchill (1874-1965). Painting as a Pastime.

". . . Senile melancholy; a state in which the old man, after a stormy and dissipated life, meditating upon the errors into which his passions have drawn him, isolates himself, becomes sad, uneasy, hard to please, avaricious, suspicious and egotistical; often unjust towards his friends, his own children and society at large."

So did Esquirol describe depression in the aged in his book *Mental Maladies* (1845). He was following a much earlier description, that of Cicero, who in his essay on old age, *De Senectude,* said that "old men are morose, troubled, fretful, and hard to please; . . . and some of them are misers too."

Titian's portrait of Pope Paul III (*Plate 3*) reminds one of the image of a malicious old man. Paul III's early life had been immoral; as a Pope he had used his power to advance family interests and elected as cardinals his two grandsons, aged 14 and 16. The infamous Inquisition originated with him, under the pressure of Cardinal Carafa, the future Pope Paul IV. So avaricious was Paul III that he would not hesitate to melt down an antique piece of jewelry for its gold content. Suspicious and superstitious, he would consult astrologers before planning important events. His portrait shows a moody old man, restless, irritable, unsatisfied, and haunted by approaching death.

ABNORMAL SEXUAL BEHAVIOR

"Though age from folly could not give me freedom."

Shakespeare. Anthony and Cleopatra, I, iii.

The moral degradation of the aged is regarded with more severity of judgment than that of younger people. The old are expected to be wise, to "know better." Moreover, indulgence by the aged in pleasures conventionally reserved for youth provokes resentment and indignation. The sexual needs of the elderly have been particularly misjudged. For

PLATE 3

TITIAN (c.1490-1576). *Pope Paul III*

instance, in old people's institutions the sexes are usually segregated and individuals who have spent all their lives in a normal community consisting of males and females find themselves in an artificial environment, where contact with the opposite sex is frowned upon or made impossible. Abnormal sexual behavior becomes a reaction to this situation.

Guido Reni provides illustrations of sexual misdemeanors in the elderly. The painting of the Biblical Lot and his daughters (*Plate 4*) is not as explicit as the painting of Susanna and the Elders (*Plate 5*).

Lot committed incest with his daughters whilst drunk; alcohol probably released his inhibitions.

The story of Susanna, because of its eroticism, has been popular with many artists, Rembrandt amongst them. Susanna was the victim of the lust of the Elders, but Reni has captured on the old faces an expression of loneliness, a plea for warmth, a hunger that is not erotic. It is perhaps a more realistic rendering of a situation expressing the sexual needs of old people (see Chapter 14 by Pfeiffer).

ISOLATION

"The arctic loneliness of age."

S. Weir Mitchell (1829-1914).

Old people tend to be lonely. Loneliness leads to the fear that they have no one who really cares for them, no one close enough to help without being asked. Their own parents have long since gone; as they advance in years, more and more of their contemporaries die; if married, they may be widowed, and their children may have left them; if unmarried, their loneliness may be even more acute. Deprived of love, of companionship, and of purpose, the old experience a loneliness that has no hope; they lose touch with reality, they become depressed and wish for the relief of death, waiting to the last for help that never comes.

The old woman painted by Cézanne is a vivid example of this "arctic loneliness."

PLATE 4

GUIDO RENI (1575-1642). *Lot and His Daughters Leaving Sodom*

PLATE 5

GUIDO RENI (1575-1642). *Susanna at the Bath*

PLATE 6

PAUL CÉZANNE (1839-1906). *La Vieille au Chapelet*

This old woman (*Plate 6*) was the painter's servant and at times she would pose for him. She had lived for many years in a convent, but at the age of seventy she suddenly felt that she could stand no longer the oppressive life within its high walls. It is strange that she should have felt the need to be free so late in life. She found a ladder and escaped over the convent wall, perhaps half knowing what she was doing and even less conscious of motivation for her actions. Cézanne found her, confused and frightened, as she wandered aimlessly in a world that must have seemed to her as anonymous as an arctic landscape. He gave her shelter and made allowances for her many shortcomings; she would, for instance, sell him rags to clean his brushes and he would discover that they were pieces of his own linen! Her portrait, unsentimental and realistic, shows her isolation: there is no communication, her thoughts, if any, remain her own. The rosary in her hands is a vestigial habit, but perhaps it still gives her comfort.

A year later, in 1900, Cézanne painted a self-portrait now in the Museum of Fine Arts, Boston. In it he appears strangely similar to the old woman; he too was isolated and embittered.

DEPRESSION

". . . A sickness of the soul without any hope."

Robert Burton (1576-1640). The Anatomy of Melancholy.

"Melancholy, watchfulness and troublesome sleep" were noted in his elderly patients by a contemporary of Robert Burton, Dr. John Hall, Shakespeare's son-in-law. Depression is still the commonest symptom in the emotionally ill at any time of life and this applies to the aged. Old people, too, suffer from traumata and vulnerabilities. For the old these include loneliness, lack of friends, retirement from work with its concomitant reduction of income and forced inactivity, family stresses, and physical disabilities.

Van Gogh, with the eyes of the artist and the sensitivity of the lonely, described senile depression undramatically, but with infinite pathos (*Plate 7*). The expression on the old man's face is left to the imagination. His small, crumpled figure is a lump of misery, unwanted and past

PLATE 7

VINCENT VAN GOGH (1853-1890). *A Man Mourning (Saint-Rémy)*

wanting—withdrawn, isolated, he defies comfort as he awaits release from an unprofitable life.

Van Gogh painted this old man while he was a patient in Saint-Rémy Asylum, when his own mood was one of deep, brooding melancholy. Thus, even more than representing a fellow man in anguish, it reflects his own grief, which eventually led to his suicide.

SUICIDE

"I'll dye, and mine own griefes release."

Thomas Campion (1567-1620). The Fourth Booke of Ayres.

Suicide, the act of self destruction, becomes inevitable when all hope is lost. When living has no significance, the prolonging of the present is too painful and the past can offer no consoling memories. Statistics show that suicide is most common in old age (see Chapter 13 by Payne).

Often, before embarking on the final act of annihilation, hints and indirect suggestions give a clue to the desperate state of mind of the depressed patient.

Although van Gogh was not chronologically old, he behaved as if his life had been very long, too long. His intense depression created a barrier, an unsurmountable wall, and for him there was no future. His allotted time was up.

Van Gogh's painting of his own empty chair (*Plate 8*) is as eloquent a statement as a suicide note and continues the theme started by the painting of the old man in the Asylum of Saint-Rémy. He had similarly painted the chair used by Gaugin, the friend who had left him. Now he painted a familiar corner of his room without himself, as it would be after he had gone. He had painted over 30 self portraits, but none of them has the poignancy of this absence. His signature, behind the chair, tolls to his memory as an inscription on a tombstone. A year after painting this picture he committed suicide. Nobody had heeded the anguished message of the unoccupied chair.

PLATE 8

VINCENT VAN GOGH (1853-1890). *Chair*

DERANGEMENT

"To Bedlam with him!"

Shakespeare. Henry VI, part 2, V, i.

Mental hospital patients include a preponderance of old people. This is not because the aged are more prone to psychosis than the young, but because the condition is usually permanent and patients grow old in institutions where they may have spent a great part of their life. Senile dementia also claims a number of victims. Art, a true mirror of life, also confirms that the emotionally ill of all ages are many.

Hieronymous Bosch, towards the end of the 15th century, provided some examples of derangement in the aged, often as symbols of a weird and fantastic world. Brueghel painted figures with the vacant expression typical of dementia. Much later Goya (1746-1828) was fascinated by the horror and degradation of the madhouse, although he seems to have been engrossed in scenes of sadistic fantasy. In the same period, the French painter Géricault (1791-1824) also produced vivid portraits on the insane, but his love for the macabre makes him an emotional witness. Leonardo, on the other hand, gives us an example which has a quality of detachment that makes it almost clinical.

These five old men *(Plate 9)* with their grotesque expressions and inappropriate garb are reminiscent of the insane painted by Hogarth in the 18th century, when the patients of Bethlem Hospital, or Bedlam, as it was then referred to, were objects of curiosity and amusement to idle visitors. Unlike Hogarth's figures, who face the onlooker, underlining the intention of the painter that they should be a social comment on the times and a reproach for indifference, Leonardo's old men are merely a statement of fact: madness exists in old age and this is what it looks like. The era of Leonardo was a civilized and humane period when the insane were not put on show and we can only speculate as to how he came to observe such a gathering.

Leonardo, with his restless genius, was interested in many fields of knowledge. We know of his interest in anatomy and of his fine anatomical drawings, but so far no study of his has been found which is directly related to mental health. Yet these heads of old men show unmistakable signs of derangement: the fatuous laughter, the delusion indicated by the wreath of old leaves (did its wearer believe himself a poet or a hero?), the strange flattened cranium of the figure on the

PLATE 9

LEONARDO DA VINCI (1452-1519). *Five Grotesque Heads*

right, the inner listening and the prolonged cry of the two figures at the back create an atmosphere of uneasiness. Moreover, the figures are all turned toward the center, forming a circle which excludes the onlooker from their private world.

LYCANTHROPY

"They shall drive thee from men, and thy dwelling shall be with the beasts of the field. . . ."

Daniel, IV, 25.

The syndrome of lycanthropy, as such, is no longer included in the nosology of psychiatry. It is, however, a relevant example of the extreme delusions that may occur in psychosis. The term derives from the Greek, literally meaning wolf-man.

Superstition and fear, born of an inability to understand a condition as baffling as insanity, led to the belief in a disease which transformed men into beasts and sent them howling through the night. Pliny, in his *Natural History*, refers to the case of Demaenetus, an Arcadian, who believed himself a beast for 10 years. Virgil wrote of Moeris, who became a wolf after ingesting some poisonous herbs. In the third century, Marcellus, a physician, described lycanthropy from a clinical point of view. The belief in werewolves persisted during the Middle Ages and lingered on into the 17th century. Medical writers called it lycanthropy and listed it in their classifications. Robert Burton, in his *Anatomy of Melancoly* (1621), attributed lycanthropy to madness and gave many examples drawn from earlier authors, including Avicenna.

The figure of the aged Nebuchadnezzar (*Plate 10*) painted by Blake illustrates lycanthropy. Nebuchadnezzar, the Biblical King of Babylon, was said to suffer from sleep disorders, deep depression, and irritability leading to outbursts of uncontrollable rage. Finally he lost interest in his own person, became unkempt and dirty, his hair became matted and his nails overgrown. In this condition it is natural that he was shunned by those around him; he would seek solitude, hiding himself in the wilderness and finally believing that he had been changed into a beast.

Blake's work is often on the borderline of reality; he experienced hallucinations and is said to have had visions of some of the subjects he painted.

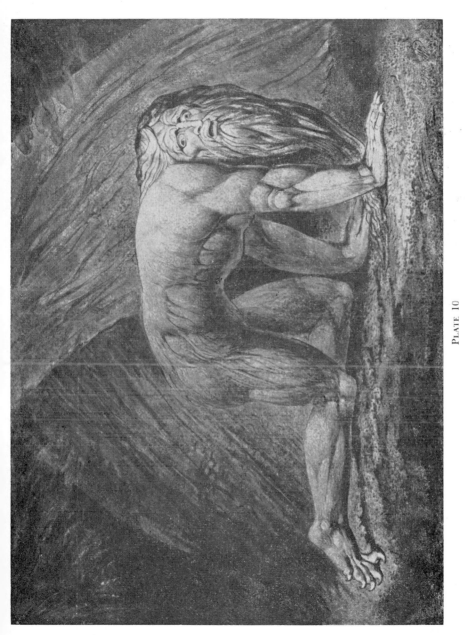

PLATE 10

BLAKE (1757-1827). *Nebuchadnezzar*

CONCLUSION

A few famous paintings have been selected as illustrations of psychopathology in the aged. They cover a small part of the field. Other conditions not depicted here have been the subject of painting, for instance, dementia in the many representations of King Lear, alcoholism in the innumerable Renaissance paintings of the aged Silenus, mania in the Sibyl of Michelangelo, etc.

Rembrandt is perhaps the outstanding and most perceptive painter of old people. Most of his portraits of aged men and women show the dignified repose and grandeur of old age, but many reveal also isolation, sadness, moodiness and withdrawal into an inner world. Another interesting painter of the old is Dürer.

The interested reader will have no difficulty in finding other examples of expression of psychopathology of the old in art.

NAMES INDEX

605

SUBJECT INDEX